Community Builders Handbook Series

DOWNTOWN DEVELOPMENT
HANDBOOK

Sponsored by the
Executive Group
of the
Urban Development/Mixed-Use Council
of
ULI–the Urban Land Institute
1980

ULI–the Urban Land Institute, Washington, D.C.

About ULI–the Urban Land Institute

ULI–the Urban Land Institute is an independent, nonprofit research and educational organization incorporated in 1936 to improve the quality and standards of land use and development.

The Institute is committed to conducting qractical research in the various fields of real estate knowledge; identifying and interpreting land use trends in relation to the changing economic, social, and civic needs of the people; and disseminating pertinent information leading to the orderly and more efficient use and development of land.

ULI receives its financial support from membership dues, sale of publications, and contributions for research and panel services.

ULI Staff for Downtown Development Handbook

Director of Publications	Frank H. Spink, Jr.
Managing Editor	Frank H. Spink, Jr.
Manuscript Editor	Barbara M. Fishel, Editech
Production Manager	Robert L. Helms
Production Assistant	Patricia E. Thach
Art Director	Carolyn de Haas

Fourth book in a new series of publications based on the
philosophy of The Community Builders Handbook
First Edition and First Printing 1947
Revised Printing 1948
Second or J. C. Nichols Memorial Edition and Second Revised
Printing 1950
Third or The Members Edition and Third Revised Printing 1954
Fourth Revised Printing 1956
Fourth or The Executive Edition and Fifth Revised Printing 1960
Sixth Printing 1965
Fifth or Anniversary Edition and Seventh Revised Printing 1968

Other books in the series:
Industrial Development Handbook, 1975
Shopping Center Development Handbook, 1977
Residential Development Handbook, 1978

Recommended bibliographic listing:
Urban Land Institute. *Downtown Development Handbook.*
Washington: Urban Land Institute, 1980.
ULI Catalog Number D–12

International Standard Book Number 0–87420–591–3
Library of Congress Card Catalog Number 80–50928

Printed in the United States of America

Authors

Ralph J. Basile, former associate,
Publications Division, Urban Land Institute

J. Thomas Black, associate director of
research for urban economics, Urban Land Institute

Douglas R. Porter, associate director of
research for growth policy, Urban Land Institute

Lyndia Lowy, summer intern, 1978
Publications Division, Urban Land Institute

with
The Urban Development/Mixed-Use Council
of the
Urban Land Institute

Acknowledgments

Every professional involved in the downtown real estate business views the private development process quite differently. These differences are compounded when a group faces the task of writing a book about the rapidly evolving field of joint public and private involvement in downtown development activities. Much like the downtown development process, the material presented in this handbook evolved after several previous manuscripts did not properly reflect a workable sequence of events resulting in downtown real estate projects. The final text does capture and detail the state-of-the-art, but no doubt it will seem less refined and sophisticated to a future reader familiar with new arrangements in the relationship between public and private entities.

The ULI handbooks are the result of the collective effort of many professionals interested in improving the quality of various aspects of land use in urbanized areas. Hal Jensen, as chairman of the Urban Redevelopment Council in 1976, provided the initial leadership and guidance in the preparation of this handbook. His efforts were continued and refined through Dick Hanson's chairmanship, beginning in 1977. Mike Clark, as chairman of the Handbook Committee of the council, was involved from the very beginning; his many hours working with the council to develop the initial approach and then as chairman of the steering committee that developed the revised approach deserve special recognition. Don Zuchelli, who became active in the development of the handbook after his appointment to the council in 1979, also deserves special mention.

The several authors melded the council's input and their own research into manuscript form. Tom Black's expertise is especially reflected in chapters 3 and 8; Doug Porter drafted chapters 5 and 6 and did the final revision, before editing, of chapter 4; Lyndia Lowy was heavily involved in the preparation of chapters 2 and 7.

Many other individuals deserve our special acknowledgment for their contributions: Mike Clark, who as vice chairman for publications as well as handbook chairman, served as a steady, reliable, and effective influence during the preparation of the numerous manuscripts leading to this text; Frank Spink, whose knowledge and experience in developing the previous volumes in the Community Builders Handbook Series were invaluable in his management of the final editing, illustration, and indexing of the manuscript after my departure from the ULI staff; Don Zuchelli, who labored many hours in the development of draft materials for chapter 4; Jerry Maier of Market Street East and W. Scott Toombs of The Gallery, who provided key material for chapter 6, particularly the history of The Gallery; Barbara Fishel, who edited with consummate skill the final manuscript into a readable document, eliminating the redundancies resulting from so many authors and blending varied writing styles into a uniform whole; and Jane Lynas, who either typed or coordinated the typing of the many drafts and redrafts.

The members of the Urban Development/Mixed-Use Council of ULI provided continuing assistance and resources in the preparation of this handbook. While the entire council deserves recognition for its contribution, Bob Siler, Steve Dragos, Peter Kory, and Keith Kelly deserve extra recognition for reviewing not one but several drafts in great detail.

To all those who helped make this handbook happen, thank you.

Ralph J. Basile

In addition to those who worked and contributed to the development of this manuscript there are many members of the Institute staff and our contract service firms whose contributions should not go unacknowledged. Ronald R. Rumbaugh, ULI's Executive Vice President, gave his continued support to this long effort and assured the resources for making it happen. Carolyn de Haas, as Art Director, spent long hours on the book's design and layout. Bob Helms, Administration Division Director, managed the production of the handbook, meeting tight deadlines through the cooperation of George Carver of our typesetting firm and Ray Barcikowski of our printing company. Paul O'Mara, Nancy Stewart, and Nadine Huff of my staff were last minute recruits for the task of indexing.

Like the job of putting the manuscript together, that of getting it published is a team effort. Thanks to all.

Frank Spink

About ULI Councils

Within the Urban Land Institute there are nine councils: Urban Development/Mixed-Use, Commercial and Retail Development, Industrial and Office Park Development, New Communities and Large-Scale Development, Residential Development, Recreational Development, Federal Policy, Development Policies and Regulations, and Development Systems and Services Councils. Each council is composed of 50 active members drawn from the ULI Membership. Council appointment is based on knowledge, experience, and a willingness to share. Developers, consultants, public officials, and academicians are included on each of the councils to provide a broad perspective and to encourage interaction among various disciplines.

Executive Group of the
Urban Development/Mixed-Use Council,
1976–1980

Chairmen:

Richard G. Hanson (1977–80)
Vice President
Gerald D. Hines Interests
Houston

Harold S. Jensen (1976–77)**
Partner
Metropolitan Structures
Chicago

Vice Chairmen:

Knox Banner (1977–78)
Chairman
Banner Associates, Ltd.
Washington, D.C.

Michael C. Clark (1976–78)
Principal
Urban Development Group
Los Angeles

James S. Dailey (1978–79)
Vice President, Real Estate Investment
  Department
AEtna Life & Casualty Company
Hartford

Stephen F. Dragos (1976–77)
Executive Vice President
Milwaukee Redevelopment Corporation
Milwaukee

Richard D. Idler (1976–77)
Land Planning Consultant
Louis T. Busch Associates
Malibu, California

Keith Kelly (1978–79)
Vice President, Development
Crown Center Redevelopment Corporation
Kansas City

James Martin (1978–80)
Executive Director
Old Philadelphia Development
  Corporation
Philadelphia

Charles F. Seymour (1977–78)
President
Jackson–Cross Company
Philadelphia

Robert W. Siler, Jr. (1977–78)
President
Hammer, Siler, George Associates
Washington, D.C.

Nell D. Surber (1979–80)
Director, Department of Development
City of Cincinnati
Cincinnati

Kenneth S. Sweet, Jr. (1976–77)
Managing Partner
K.S. Sweet Associates
King of Prussia, Pennsylania

Gerald M. Trimble (1978–80)
Executive Vice President
Centre City Development Corporation
San Diego

Donald R. Zuchelli (1978–80)
President
Zuchelli, Hunter & Associates, Inc.
Annapolis

Maurice D. Alpert
President
International City Corporation
Atlanta

Garland S. Anderson, Jr.
The Anderson Group
Houston

Edmund N. Bacon*
Vice President
Mondev International, Ltd.
Philadelphia

G. William Bahen
Vice President
Devon Estates, Ltd.
Toronto

William Bahrenberg
President
Brooks, Harvey & Company
New York

W. Anderson Barnes
Executive Director
Pennsylvania Avenue Development
  Corporation
Washington, D.C.

George B. Beardsley
Partner
Central Development Group
Denver

Brian L. Berry*
Professor of City and Regional Planning
Harvard University
West Acton, Massachusetts

Richard J. Boyle
Senior Vice President
The Chase Manhattan Bank
New York

Paul Busse
President
Economic Development Council of New York
  City, Inc.
New York

Joseph C. Canizaro
Chief Executive Officer
Joseph C. Canizaro Interests
New Orleans

Oliver T. Carr, Jr.
President
Oliver T. Carr Company
Washington, D.C.

Frank Carter
President
Carter & Associates
Atlanta

W. F. Cerne
President
Illinois Center Corporation
Chicago

Contents

Metric Conversion Table

Meters	=	feet × 0.305
Kilometers	=	miles × 1.609
Square Meters	=	square feet × 0.093
Square Kilometers	=	square miles × 2.590
Cubic Meters	=	cubic feet × 0.028
Cubic Meters	=	cubic yards × 0.765
Hectares	=	acres × 0.405

(a hectare is 10,000 square meters)

List of Illustrations

A Brief History of the Community Builders Handbook Series

The Community Builders Handbook Series came into being when the *Industrial Development Handbook* was published in 1975. This new series expands and replaces *The Community Builders Handbook*, first published in 1947.

The objective of the original handbook was to share the experience and knowledge of developers and to encourage the improvement of land use and development practices. The handbook was sponsored by the Community Builders Council (now the Residential Council), which had been formed in 1944. The first edition contained 205 pages and was sparsely illustrated, but it was a major accomplishment since, for the first time, a book was made available which described the development of residential communities and shopping centers.

The second edition, the J. C. Nichols Memorial Edition, was published in 1950. It incorporated a modest revision and updating of the original text. In 1954 the third or Members Edition, with 315 pages, significantly expanded the scope of the work. The fourth or Executive Edition of 1960 continued this expansion in response to the increasing complexity of development practices. By this time the handbook had grown to 476 pages, but it continued to focus on residential and shopping center development. The fifth or Anniversary Edition was published in 1968. The handbook had now grown to 526 pages and had been broadened once more in coverage. In addition to sections on residential and shopping center development, new material discussing a variety of special types of land development was included. Also added was a section on industrial development, drawing on the experience of ULI's Industrial Council, which had been formed in 1951. The Industrial Council had sponsored other ULI publications but was now represented for the first time in the handbook.

The Community Builders Handbook became widely recognized as a major reference source and textbook on land use and development practice based on the practical experience and accumulated knowledge of leading practitioners in the field. In 1965, as work on the 1968 edition was beginning, ULI was growing rapidly in membership and in areas of interest. The development industry was maturing and new directions for the Institute were being examined. By 1970 a decision had been made to publish future editions of *The Community Builders Handbook* in separate volumes, in order to provide the expanded and more comprehensive coverage not possible in a single text.

In 1972 the three original councils of the Institute—the Community Builders, Central City, and Industrial Councils—were reorganized into six councils in order to accommodate the new diversity in development activities and ULI's membership. Members of the Central City Council formed the nucleus of the Urban Redevelopment Council under whose aegis this volume was begun. The council structure was modified again in 1979 to expand to nine councils reflecting the expanding and diversifying nature of the Institute. The Urban Redevelopment Council was changed to the Urban Development/Mixed-Use Council. This council name change resulted in some refocusing of the council objectives and, therefore, the thrust of the handbook.

The *Downtown Development Handbook* is the fourth volume of the new series, having followed the *Industrial Development Handbook* (1975), the *Shopping Center Development Handbook* (1977), and the *Residential Development Handbook* (1978). Other volumes, each focusing on a specific land use type, will be added to the series in the future.

Frank H. Spink, Jr.
Managing Editor
Community Builders Handbook Series

Foreword

The *Downtown Development Handbook* provides a new direction for the Community Builders Handbook Series. *The Community Builders Handbook* first appeared in 1947 as a single volume which focused on suburban development. The first three books in the new Community Builders Handbook Series reinforced that tradition. The *Downtown Development Handbook* represents a significant departure from its predecessors by reflecting an inherent difference between downtown development and suburban development.

The initial three handbooks emphasized a development *product*. The *Downtown Development Handbook* concentrates on the *process* of development rather than the product. Further, it stresses the pre-development stage of the process because this is the area which has benefited so greatly from innovation during the last 5 years. The process of development in our urban areas will continue to change in the future because of the imagination and creativity generated by the public and private sectors. The discussion and evaluation of the materials in this handbook may be subject to greater change over a shorter period of time than the development processes described in the previous handbooks in the series. The new approaches to downtown development described in this book, however, have already stimulated greater momentum than earlier and more traditional approaches to urban development.

As has been the case with all of the handbooks, defining the objectives of the book and, subsequently, preparing an outline of subject matter demanded substantial contributions of time from council members. The development of this volume has involved a major commitment from the Urban Development/Mixed-Use Council for 3 years, beginning with the chairmanship of Harold S. Jensen in 1976. Unlike the other three handbooks, which had a variety of previously developed ULI literature on which to build a major publication, this handbook began with no such advantage. It drew more heavily on the knowledge and experience of the individual council members than perhaps any of its predecessors. Much of the material in the book is an assimilation and restructuring of materials contributed by individual council members who are currently implementing the "state of the art" processes described in the various chapters. Unlike any of the previous manuscripts, there was little conventional wisdom agreed upon at the outset of this handbook, which resulted in at least one major revision of the objectives of the handbook during the early stages of preparation.

The first draft of the manuscript was presented to the full council in the fall of 1977. The review of this draft led to a reorganization and restructuring of the thrust of the handbook and resulted in the decision to focus on the process rather than the product of development. A steering committee comprised of the handbook chairman, Michael C. Clark, and Peter Kory, I. Rocke Ransen, Robert W. Siler, Jr., and Donald R. Zuchelli met in the spring of 1978 to develop this new orientation. A second draft manuscript was submitted to the council in October 1978, and in November 1978, Michael C. Clark, Donald R. Zuchelli, and I met as a committee with Ralph J. Basile for several days to correlate the editorial contributions from individual council members. This meeting led to further modifications which continued through December 1979 when the manuscript was ready for typesetting.

The long road to the completion of the book could have been shortened by relying on the skills and judgment of fewer individuals; however, this handbook's strength lies in the breadth of experience, ideas, and judgment offered by the large and highly diversified group of developers, urban economists, architects, lawyers, and public officials who constitute our council. Although the council has not always concurred on every viewpoint that is presented, we believe that the variations of technique described within the process are again the source of the book's strength. We of the Urban Development/Mixed-Use Council offer this volume of the Community Builders Handbook Series in the hope that it will provide a better understanding of the process of downtown development. We also hope that it will help to achieve the goal of downtown development—the revitalization and conservation of the core of our nation's cities. As you read this handbook, the new techniques and innovations of process which it presents are being tested by developers and cities alike.

Richard G. Hanson
Chairman
Urban Development/Mixed-Use Council, 1977–1980

1.
Introduction

This handbook sets forth the steps both private and public sectors should undertake for the successful realization of a new development project in the central business district (CBD). So that the reader may fully understand the wide array of topics involved in the downtown development process, this chapter summarizes what is and what is not fully documented in the text. It describes the development process, highlighting the most important steps.

The Definition of Downtown

A downtown area, as referred to in this handbook, may or may not be the central core area of a city. The development process described in the handbook details the development activities that should take place in CBDs, but the same process can be applied to projects along urban waterfronts or in other large commercial areas of a city. A large metropolitan area may contain several business hubs, either in the city or along transportation corridors leading to suburban areas, which also provide the proper setting for development. The key to successful development is the involvement of the public sector in the development of a downtown project, no matter where "downtown" is.

The steps in the development process are essentially the same for small cities and large cities, but certain activities of the development process may be emphasized differently. In a large metropolitan area, the market may be so complex that many public/private projects could be undertaken without influencing overall market conditions. In a small city, however, the resources necessary to revitalize the downtown area may result in only a single development project.

For example, in a small city, it is highly likely that a major downtown project is less feasible because of the relative limitations of the downtown market within the region. The development would likely need to be more heavily preleased and the public sector involved highly because of low rent yields or because competing interests might have dramatic advantages of cost and access in a fringe location. It is also quite probable that the public sector's involvement would be less sophisticated and that fewer public funds would be available for the project. These differences, however, also occur between large metropolitan areas. The process itself does not change, nor does the need for cooperation between the public sector and the private sector.

Public-Sector Involvement in Downtown Projects

The downtown development process, because of the relatively weak market in many central city areas, often involves both the public and private sectors in nontraditional roles. This volume of the Community Builders Handbook Series describes the evolving state-of-the-art of cooperation between the public and private sectors in realizing downtown projects.

This handbook describes essentially the private development process, detailing public-sector involvement as appropriate. It does not advocate the public sector as developer but strongly emphasizes partnership between the public and private sectors to the benefit of the community.

Of the three stages in the development process—predevelopment, development, and postdevelopment—described in this handbook, predevelopment activities, which must take place before construction begins, are emphasized. It is at this stage that the public sector becomes most involved in defining a development project and assisting in its realization. In many central cities experiencing weak market conditions, projects simply would not materialize without public assistance during predevelopment. Thus, this handbook devotes more attention to how the public and private parties interact than to the more traditional approach where the private sector postulates development alternatives without direct involvement of the public sector.

This handbook emphasizes the appropriateness of roles for the public and private sectors in the downtown development process. Public participation in and support of private development requires political consensus. This political consensus, which is necessary if the public sector is to participate effectively as a partner, must be carefully constructed as a prelude to the process described in this handbook.

The desire or need for public involvement in a project means that the public sector must evaluate the community's sentiment concerning the city's involvement in various forms of assistance, including direct project financing. A variety of public mechanisms are available to influence the private sector's economic performance in a project—tax abatement, nominal land leases, publicly financed parking, subsidies, direct loans, for example. The use of various forms of bond financing and the use of community development funds in a commercial project in a downtown area, rather than the use of such funds to preserve residential neighborhoods, usually involve political decisions. This handbook identifies the likely sources of funds and how they might be used to make a project feasible for the private sector rather than emphasizing how the public sector should make its political decisions.

Establishing the connection between public objectives and private objectives requires special effort and skill. In some cases, neither the public sector nor private developers have the capacity to merge the parties' interests, but this handbook provides new models—for example, a third party to package the project when public and private interests both face political or economic uncertainty. This handbook clearly emphasizes public and private sectors' joint participation in determining the appropriate combination of public and private development activities and funding to revitalize a downtown area.

Types of Downtown Projects

New private development integrated with public uses has recently become a key component of urban economic development. The revitalization of downtown areas not only generates employment and tax revenues but also makes the city more attractive as a place to live and work. Accordingly, this handbook emphasizes to a greater degree the development of complex mixed use projects rather than single use development or adaptive use projects. The reader should realize, however, that the development process described in this handbook can be applied to any project undertaken in a CBD.

Citizen Involvement in Downtown Development

The role of citizens and other interest groups during the predevelopment process differs depending on the size of the community. In small cities, it is highly likely that individual citizens will have a greater role in determining the outcome of downtown development. In larger cities, it is more likely that special interest groups (single-purpose entities such as historical societies or environmental groups) will have a greater role. Even when a general political consensus has been achieved, special interest groups may pursue objectives that discourage or constrain new development. The management of public participation is an important responsibility of the public sector in downtown development efforts.

While the private sector may be willing to thread its way through the inconsistencies and pressures of different interest groups when a strong market exists, the presence of a clear political consensus and a resolution of special interests is vitally important if market conditions are marginal or uncertain. Because many of the needed arrangements and agreements in downtown development result in mixing public and private objectives and resources, the public's understanding of, agreement with, and confidence in this approach must be established. The private developer needs assurance of mutual respect and predictability before committing significant amounts of time and money to a project.

Approach to Presentation of Material

The approach taken in this volume of the Community Builders Handbook Series is dramatically different from the approach taken in the previous three handbooks of the series. The focus of the *Industrial Development Handbook*, the *Shopping Center Development Handbook*, and the *Residential Development Handbook* has been on the product of development activities, while the *Downtown Development Handbook* emphasizes the process of activities undertaken in downtown development projects. The previous handbooks focus on a specific type of development, while this handbook focuses on development that takes place in a specific location—the downtown. The previous three handbooks describe in great detail the characteristics of specific types of development; the material was organized to present complete technical details on how to produce an efficient and quality development project. This handbook focuses instead on the interaction of various parties that must occur to see the successful completion of a project in the CBD.

Another distinction between this handbook and the others in the Community Builders Handbook Series is that this handbook emphasizes less the presentation of full case studies detailing the physical characteristics of various development projects. A particular

project is mentioned only when it offers a concrete example of a point being made in the text; the description usually emphasizes the process that was necessary to structure the business deals rather than the project's physical characteristics.

The discussion in this handbook assumes that the reader is somewhat familiar with the specific tools used to define a specific type of downtown development (or product). For example, the handbook does not detail the steps necessary to complete market and financial studies or how to undertake the completion and adoption of a redevelopment plan for a blighted area in a central city. It focuses instead on the sequence of development activities that must occur before a downtown development project is constructed and on the involvement of public and private sectors in each of these activities.[1]

At the beginning of the 1980s, the future of our cities' core areas seems bright. Past efforts have proven that decay and decline can be deterred and stabilized. Recent efforts have demonstrated that carefully conceived revitalization is now not only possible but has widespread public support. Observers of the urban scene who not too many years ago were ringing the death knell now see not just the breath of life but the potential for new growth and vigor.

---

[1] Examples of many of the tools used in downtown development are presented in the appendices. A preliminary development commitment agreement, land disposition and lease agreements, financial agreements, and others are provided to elaborate upon the explanation provided in the text. To provide the reader with access to further details about a point being made or about the project itself, a list of the projects mentioned in the handbook and project contacts from the Urban Development/Mixed-Use Council is provided in appendix B.

2.
Historical Perspective and Contemporary Setting

The vitality of a city's central business district is closely related to its economic growth and the characteristics of that growth; the opportunities for investment are clearly superior in expanding cities or regions. Nevertheless, weak CBDs are found in cities of economic strength and relatively strong ones are found in stable or even declining cities.[1] Even though every CBD must be analyzed, planned, and developed on its own merits, certain basic economic and social forces, some reflecting natural market phenomena and others reflecting public policy, constrain the development potential of a CBD.

The CBD in the 20th Century

Over the last 30 years the CBD has lost some of its locational superiority for certain functions but has kept or improved others. At the beginning of the 19th century, virtually every aspect of economic and social life took place in the CBD. The CBD was the terminus of transportation lines, the site of the major industries, and the hub of commercial and professional activity. Naturally, government bodies were also located in the heart of the business district. Employees could live fairly near to their jobs, and since the major form of transportation was one's own two feet, schools, retail stores, and factories had to be close to residences.

With the development of the horse streetcar in the late 19th century and the streetcar in the early 20th century, people could move to the relative serenity of a "streetcar suburb," and the specialization of the CBD began. Businesses that required a great deal of land or specialized energy or transportation could afford to move out of the CBD and still retain easy access to both their workers and the city.[2] The extensive public transportation systems developed and run by public utilities (especially electric companies)[3] contributed to the establishment of extremely dense working populations: They could move large numbers of people quite efficiently. As the public transportation network reduced the need to live near one's employment, the CBD began to lose its residential function. However, the residential population that relied most heavily on the CBD was still able to live relatively near to it and rely on it for commerce, recreation, and government.

The Federal Housing Administration insurance program (begun in response to the depression of the

[1] *Land Use Planning Reports* (Silver Spring, Maryland: Business Publishers, Inc.), vol. 5, no. 39 (September 26, 1977), p. 306.

[2] Sam B. Warner, Jr., *Streetcar Suburbs* (Cambridge: MIT Press, 1962), pp. 15–29.

[3] For example, Salt Lake City (Utah) Light Company owned the city's trolley system.

2-1 As the downtowns of our cities declined, a variety of efforts were made to stabilize the decline. Perhaps the most frequently used concept was the downtown mall. New and attractive pedestrian spaces were created like Mid America Mall in Memphis, but the root problem of declining retail trade was rarely cured, only temporarily corrected.

2-2 San Francisco's new skyline illustrates the impact new growth has had in some cities. Managing this kind of growth has presented a new set of problems, suggesting the need for careful analysis of the cumulative effect of downtown development projects.

1930s) and the Veterans Administration housing insurance program (begun after World War II) were responsible for a boom in new suburban housing to the detriment of urban areas. This boom in suburbia occurred simultaneously with the explosion in automobile ownership, which abetted the public utilities' declining role in mass transit after the war. Massive federal support for improved roads[4] increased the population's mobility in an unprecedented way and helped to place the CBD at a distinct disadvantage. The extremely dense configuration of buildings in the CBD could not accommodate large numbers of private vehicles. The public transit system was not expanded enough to bring the new suburban residents to the CBD.[5] The interstate highway system and improved trucks freed manufacturers of their dependency on rail transportation and allowed industries to relocate wherever land was cheaply available.[6] Retail de-

[4] James J. Flink, *The Car Culture* (Cambridge: MIT Press, 1975), pp. 220–21.

[5] J. Thomas Black, *The Changing Economic Role of Central Cities* (Washington, D.C.: ULI–the Urban Land Institute, 1978).

[6] Ernest W. Burgess and Donald J. Bogue, eds., Part III, *Ethnic and Racial Groups in Urban Society* in *Contributions to Urban Sociology* (Chicago: University of Chicago Press, 1964), pp. 325–486.

velopment followed the population to the suburbs, slowly at first but then in full force.[7] Services, hotels, and entertainment followed so that by the 1960s the economic and social seeds produced by the central city were alive and growing while the old central plant was dying.

Recent years, however, have witnessed not the death of the old CBDs but their renaissance as new urban centers with their own characteristics, functions, and needs. The growing concern over energy, the slowdown in national population growth, particularly in the Northeast and Midwest, and the changing economics of the CBD have affected the potential for revitalizing the CBD. While the future outlook for the CBD varies widely from city to city, depending on size, geography, and economic mix, the CBD's economic fortunes show signs of beginning to improve.

Social Forces Affecting Development

A primary function of American cities has always been to assimilate immigrants into society. Although segregated into a particular section of a city, the immigrants came into contact with the widest variety of opportunities and were able, over a period of generations, to join the greater surrounding culture. This social role did not stop with the great waves of European immigration before World War I, continued for American blacks who migrated to Northern cities in the 1930s and 1940s, and occurs today for Hispanic residents of such cities as New York, Miami, Houston, Los Angeles, and San Diego. These minority groups are occupying a larger proportion of downtown areas than ever before, and they have generally lower personal incomes than the groups they displaced.[8]

Because many of the unskilled jobs once found in the CBD have moved out of the central city, the low-income groups most likely to hold them are faced with a reverse commute or unemployment. The change in the American economy from an industrial to a technological society has also resulted in fewer jobs that require unskilled labor. These problems were partly responsible for the social upheavals of the 1960s, which centered in the major cities and accelerated changes in their social organization. They left a generally negative image in the minds of many private investors. Other problems seriously detracted from the image of the CBD in many cities: the changes in housing occupancy from owner to renter, the declining quality that accompanies real estate speculation, the declining quality of public schools, and the amount of crime against persons and property. These

2-3 Broadway at 7th, Los Angeles, where ethnic groups have caused a reorientation of downtown retailing.

conditions, actual or perceived, intensified the flight to the suburbs and repelled potential visitors and shoppers from the CBD.

During the 1970s, however, the U.S. population has changed dramatically, with important positive implications for the CBD. Some of these changes are the result of a declining birth rate, others of changing attitudes about the city. Their most important result is the increase in the number of middle- and upper-income one- and two-person households without children.

Even in metropolitan areas with stable or declining populations, the number of households is increasing, and the demand for additional housing units continues. The large number of women in the work force has resulted in more two-person households where both people work in the central city. Empty-nesters who moved to the suburbs to obtain better education for their children but who now feel free to return to the city are also responsible for the increased demand. Younger, middle- and upper-middle-class

[7] *Urban Housing Rehabilitation in the U.S.* (Chicago: U.S. League of Savings Associations, 1977). See also National Urban Coalition, "Effects of Private Market Rehabilitation of Urban Neighborhoods," unpublished.

[8] Declan Kennedy and Margrit I. Kennedy, eds., *The Inner City in the Post-Industrial Era: A Study of Its Changing Social Fabric and Economic Function* in *The Inner City* (New York: Halsted Press, 1974).

2-4 Mercantile Wharf Building, Boston. Built to serve the shipping industry, the 120-year-old building has been adapted into 122 apartments and 13,400 square feet of commercial space within easy walking distance of downtown Boston.

childless adults who want to invest in sound housing units that need restoration or renovation or merely want to live close to the entertainment and cultural opportunities of downtown are returning to the city. Cities where this movement is particularly strong include Washington, D.C. (Adams-Morgan, Shaw, and the fringes of Capitol Hill), Baltimore (primarily Bolton Hill and, on a more limited scale, areas such as Fells Point), Atlanta (Ansley Park and Inman Park, among others), and Boston (the South End). Such factors as the relatively high cost of new housing in the suburbs, the increased awareness of the energy shortage, and the increased cost of transportation will probably help to maintain the momentum of the back-to-the-city movement.[9]

Economic Forces Affecting Development

The economic functions of the CBD have changed even more dramatically than its social functions, mainly because of basic changes in transportation systems, the decline of manufacturing as an important part of the American economy, and the rise of service industries. The function of the CBD as a business and financial center has been strengthened, which has in turn created a different retail function.

Retailing

A general shift in purchasing power from the CBD to the suburbs created the markets that support regional shopping centers at the expense of the central business district. The physical signs of decline include the deterioration of major department stores or their relocation from the CBD to suburban shopping cen-

ters, resulting in a substantial reduction in the total amount of floor space devoted to retailing in the CBD. The mammoth multilevel air-conditioned suburban malls that dominate retailing in most American metropolitan areas today have supplanted the retail function of most downtown areas. Thus, virtually everywhere sales in the CBD have declined (based on real dollars) since 1963 as a result of shifting markets and competitive changes.[10] Some retailers in the CBD have reoriented themselves to serving the lower income market of the inner city and specializing in goods and services needed by a particular ethnic group.[11]

Although retailing in smaller cities is often still vulnerable to suburban competition, the negative market factors in larger cities have run their course, and retailing has become relatively stable again. In some cities (notably Philadelphia, with its new and dramatically successful downtown Gallery), retail activity has intensified. In some areas (for example, Chicago, New York, Boston, Miami, Toronto, Los Angeles, Sioux City, Iowa, Green Bay, Wisconsin, Pasadena, California), major department stores and other downtown retailers are successfully competing with suburban centers. New stores are being built, partly to replace old or obsolete buildings, partly to create space for new retailers who replace those who moved to suburban shopping centers. These retailers are recognizing the purchasing power of young, upper-middle-class professionals.

Offices

Certain business and professional offices have traditionally been and continue to be located in the CBD. The CBD's function as the home office of national firms and the location of local firms has largely been retained. Professionals' return to the city should reinforce the retention of home offices in the CBD, as offices tend to be located near top executives' residences. In the past, firms have relocated from downtown locations to suburban sites because of the lack of space for expansion downtown or to make the office more accessible to employees commuting by car. But the suburban office park cannot provide the central location of the CBD that encourages business leaders' face-to-face meetings.

Specialist physicians who need ready access to the major medical facilities located in central cities, attorneys who need to be near their principal commer-

---

[9] Black, op. cit., pp. 22–30.

[10] Ibid., p. 22.

[11] Ibid., p. 18.

2-5 The Gallery at Market East, Philadelphia, is the most often used example of a successful approach to new downtown retailing.

cial clients, and commercial real estate agents who need access to each other and to financial and governmental centers have retained major downtown offices in most cities. Banking's traditional location in the central business district continues in most cities; in many areas commercial banking functions have indeed expanded in downtown locations.

Industry

Unlike offices, manufacturing and the distribution of goods associated with it have virtually abandoned central city locations in favor of planned industrial parks. The problem of finding sufficient low cost land, the shift to truck transportation from rail, and a declining central city labor force have made the cen-

tral city an untenable location for many industrial operations. In Louisville, Kentucky, for example, virtually all industry is located in planned industrial parks, and some 75 percent of the firms located in the parks have relocated from older industrial districts in the central city.

Manufacturing has also ceased to be a function of the CBD, except in those exceptional cases when the cost of relocating and rebuilding the plant is prohibitive, or when public pressure has induced the industry to remain downtown. The need for single-story rather than multistory buildings requires more land where it costs less—in the suburbs. The shift of skilled labor to suburban residencies also makes it desirable for most manufacturing plants to relocate in the suburbs.

2-6   The Denver Transitway/Mall illustrates the rethinking of early malls to strengthen public transit circulation within downtown.

Transportation and Environmental Concerns in the CBD

The current and growing shortage of petroleum and its derivatives clearly will affect the future form of urban areas; it may be the determining factor in future land development patterns. The energy shortage will ultimately impact the use of transportation and the forms and location of housing. It will almost inevitably lead to increased interest in the higher density sections of the city surrounding the central business district. Housing within walking distance of employment centers or convenient to public transportation will become popular, which will mean larger and higher quality consumer markets for goods and services provided in the CBD. While this impact will be felt primarily in larger cities, smaller cities will be influenced in much the same manner as greater energy shortages develop.

The land required for roads and parking lots cannot be found in an existing CBD that has been developed to a high density because of an earlier reliance on public transit, when land did not have to be devoted to parking. Transportation to and through the CBD should enhance the high density, which is its major strength.

Although new heavy rail regional mass transit systems have been introduced (the BART system in the San Francisco Bay area, Metro in Washington, D.C.) and still others are being constructed in Baltimore and Atlanta, their extremely high capital costs and numerous political problems lessen the likelihood that many more such systems will be completed. Light rail systems have potential, however, and federal program incentives are just beginning for the improvement of existing public transit facilities.[12] A great deal of opportunity lies in the modernization and expansion of existing systems, especially where transportation facilities can be enhanced by commercial development. Commuter railroad stations in Cleveland and Cincinnati are successful examples of the combination of transportation and commercial projects.

Mass transit has the additional advantage of being less detrimental to the environment than automobiles. Even though more energy-efficient automobiles are being developed under government mandate, air quality standards will be hardest to meet where cars are most concentrated. Improved public transit seems to be an obvious solution. In addition, the U.S. Department of Transportation and the Environmental Protection Agency (EPA) are examining incentives for bicycles as an efficient, healthful way to improve the transportation system. A growing number of cities are attempting to promote higher density development to reduce the need for automobiles and consequently air pollution. And denser development has the added benefit of promoting energy conservation.

Environmentalists have only begun to examine the "built environment," but it seems clear that their concerns will affect further development outside CBDs and, in some ways, CBDs themselves. Developers can usually meet environmental protection requirements more easily in the development of the central business district, where sewage and other facilities are adequate and a desire to attract private investment exists. One observer stated:

> If any force during this generation will eventually drive real estate development back into the core cities, it will probably be the environmental movement, for it is only within already developed areas that further development will be able to proceed without substantial interference in the name of environmental protection. . . . There can be no doubt that real estate developers jointly or cooperatively developing, redeveloping, or restructuring a portion of any established city with a view toward mutual profit from meeting a public need should have a much easier time than those unwise investors making further attempts to develop the remaining open spaces of the country with the attendant problems of transportation, energy conservation, and environmental protection.[13]

Functions of the CBD

Previous downtown development projects have focused on the traditional functions of the CBD. The most important ones that acted as catalysts for revitalization are government centers, cultural centers, and convention centers. In addition, some new phenomena—the establishment of historic districts, the adaptation of existing buildings, and mixed use development—are becoming more important tools for rebuilding CBDs.

Civic centers consolidating various governmental functions in a single area were among the earliest development projects in CBDs. They ranged from new, modestly sized civic office buildings to large-scale projects like the state government complex in Albany, New York. Recent federal regulations stating that new

---

[12] See Urban Land Institute with Gladstone Associates, *Joint Development: Making the Real Estate–Transit Connection* (Washington, D.C.: ULI–the Urban Land Institute, 1979).

[13] Victor Yannacone, Jr., "Limits on Development May Force Return to the Cities," *National Real Estate Investor* 19:5 (May 1977), pp. 31, 107.

2-7 Merchants Plaza, Indianapolis, illustrates the growth in new first-class downtown hotels in the 1970s. Part of a mixed use development that includes office and retail space, the entire site is on a 60-year lease from the city with renewal options. (See "Merchants Plaza," *Project Reference File*, vol. 7, no. 15.)

In the late 1960s, however, developers began to realize that the convention business could help revitalize the CBD. Cities began to build convention centers with adjoining hotels in the CBDs. As a result, major new hotels have been built in the central business districts of many cities on a scale unparalleled since the 1920s. Three large new hotels were opened in Atlanta, for example, during 3 months in 1976. Other cities where large new hotels have been constructed include New Orleans, Houston, Dallas, Minneapolis, Baltimore, Miami, Los Angeles, and San Francisco. Many of the new hotels depend heavily on convention business for support, and in cities with new convention centers in the CBD, the hotel function is probably more important now than at any previous time.

Although suburban locations have attempted to compete for some of this market by building sports complexes that can serve as meeting halls or exhibition space, these efforts have so far met with limited success unless a hotel and additional attractions are included. Anaheim, California, for example, was able to use Anaheim Stadium as a convention center (until a building expressly for conventions was built) because of the hotel space and entertainment offered by Disneyland.

The most historically significant areas of cities are almost always located in the CBDs or adjacent to them. In the past decade a number of cities have discovered that sensitive treatment of some of the architecturally interesting sections of the CBD could attract other new investment. Old Town Alexandria, Virginia, Society Hill in Philadelphia, Charleston, South Carolina, New Orleans, Annapolis, Maryland, and Salem, Massachusetts, are notable examples of historic districts attracting economic development to central business districts.

Even without the label "historic," more and more older, architecturally interesting buildings in the CBD have been recycled rather than demolished for new construction. The higher cost of new construction over rehabilitation, the greater appreciation of the architectural and functional qualities of older buildings, and the more limited advantages of new construction as tax shelters (based on the Tax Reform Act of 1976) have stimulated this recycling. Examples of successful rehabilitation into office and retail complexes include Canal Square in Washington, D.C., Ghirardelli Square in San Francisco, Faneuil Hall in Boston, Gaslight Square in Vancouver, British Columbia, and Shocko Slip in Richmond, Virginia.

A recycled building offers many retail opportunities. A growing number of new restaurants and entertainment spots have taken advantage of the

federal construction should take place in areas of high unemployment should reinforce the tendency to locate government buildings in the central city.

Cultural centers such as New York's Lincoln Center and Los Angeles' Music Center used the central city as a focus for the fine arts to renew a section of the CBD. New York City, in particular, has capitalized on its function as the theatrical center of the United States to bring new development to the CBD.

The hotel industry has changed considerably since World War II. The proliferation of the automobile and the building of interstate highways resulted in the widespread construction of motels in suburban and rural areas, and an accompanying decline in the quality and quantity of downtown hotels. Many of the older hotels in downtown areas were closed and demolished or converted to other uses during the 1960s and early 1970s.

2-8 Restoration of historic downtowns like Market Street in Corning, New York, draws attention to the conservation of our architectural heritage. A major focus for the future will be to establish a balance between this approach and the introduction of new buildings to create new space and regrowth.

unique design and space of recycled buildings. "Theme" restaurants that rely heavily on an unusual dining atmosphere that a recycled building can supply have been particularly successful.[14] Stimulated by increased expenditures for food away from home and by the larger number of visitors, they can provide great incentive for other types of development.

Certain obsolete industrial facilities have been adapted to the CBD's new needs. Perhaps the most famous example is the three-building factory complex now called Ghirardelli Square. This successful mix of offices, restaurants, and retail space not only sparked the development of an entire section of the San Francisco waterfront, but also increased recognition of the Ghirardelli chocolate company.

Taking advantage of the complex use of the CBD, new large-scale construction is beginning to move away from single use development. In fact, the emergence of large-scale mixed use developments (MXDs) is currently one of the strongest forces in the development of downtown areas. Because they require large, strategic sites, large amounts of capital, and often long leasing periods, the financial viability of some of these projects is yet to be assured. With a strong national real estate market and the required capital available, however, these projects should enhance downtown development and take advantage of multiple market opportunities. MXDs that have greatly affected the vitality of the CBD include Baystate West in Springfield, Massachusetts, Peachtree Center in Atlanta, Omni International in Miami, Eaton Centre in Toronto, Kalamazoo Center in Kalamazoo, Michigan, Embarcadero Center in San Francisco, and Westmount Square in Montreal.[15]

[14] See Urban Land Institute, *Adaptive Use: Development Economics, Process, and Profiles* (Washington, D.C.: ULI–the Urban Land Institute, 1978).

[15] See Robert E. Witherspoon, John P. Abbett, and Robert M. Gladstone, *Mixed-Use Developments: New Ways of Land Use.* (Washington, D.C.: ULI–the Urban Land Institute, 1976).

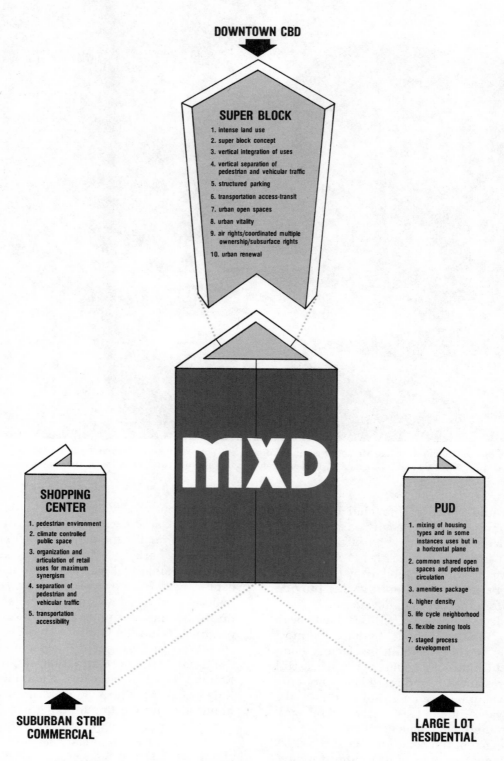

DOWNTOWN CBD

SUPER BLOCK

1. intense land use
2. super block concept
3. vertical integration of uses
4. vertical separation of pedestrian and vehicular traffic
5. structured parking
6. transportation access-transit
7. urban open spaces
8. urban vitality
9. air rights/coordinated multiple ownership/subsurface rights
10. urban renewal

MXD

SHOPPING CENTER

1. pedestrian environment
2. climate controlled public space
3. organization and articulation of retail uses for maximum synergism
4. separation of pedestrian and vehicular traffic
5. transportation accessibility

PUD

1. mixing of housing types and in some instances uses but in a horizontal plane
2. common shared open spaces and pedestrian circulation
3. amenities package
4. higher density
5. life cycle neighborhood
6. flexible zoning tools
7. staged process development

SUBURBAN STRIP COMMERCIAL

LARGE LOT RESIDENTIAL

2-9   Origins of the elements of mixed use development: the building blocks for a new concept of development.

Setting the Stage for Contemporary Development

Development opportunities in the CBD are a function of the specific dynamics of the markets in an individual city. An effective implementation strategy with private and public cooperation should recognize and capitalize on the following characteristics of a typical CBD:

- a strong financial, service, corporate headquarters, and government center that will continue as the dominant office center of the city
- a stabilized or expanding retail function, restructured to meet changing market demands generated by continued expansion of the employment base, improved quality of the inner city markets, and an expanded visitor base
- a greater dependence on convention and conference marketing to support hotels, entertainment facilities, and restaurants
- the restoration and recycling of older buildings for retail, office, and specialized residential uses
- improved transportation systems both into and within the CBD
- an increased demand for high quality housing
- an existing system of entertainment facilities, including sports centers, theaters, museums, arts centers, and urban parks.

The CBD Development Climate

Older cities in the United States face the complex problem of having to provide the largest share of services to the poorest segment of the population with a shrinking tax base. City governments are seeking new sources of income to overcome this economic squeeze, caused by the redistribution of higher income families and taxable businesses in the metropolitan area. Demand for federal and state government assistance grows, and federal general revenue sharing, with its flexibility, has become an intrinsic part of local income. Formulas prescribing how federal funds will be distributed among cities, particularly older central cities versus newer urban areas, are subject to intense debate and political pressure. Individual cities and states seek new forms of aid and press for more funds. A number of cities—New York, for example—have levied taxes on suburbanites working in the city. A very small number of cities, such as Minneapolis–St. Paul, have been able to form regional entities that share revenues or benefits or both among all the included jurisdictions. Despite these efforts, many cities face serious financial difficulties, including bankruptcy. This difficulty is forcing local government officials to examine more closely than ever the economic potential of a revitalized CBD.

Although local government officials recognize that revitalizing their cities depends on the participation of local businesses, their attitudes and regulatory posture often seem to be based on the view that the sole reason for business involvement is to make profits. Development projects are therefore surrounded by requirements for formal and inflexible competitive bidding, obstacles to worthwhile changes after an agreement has been signed, extraordinary prohibitions against conflicts of interest, and the necessity for favorable consideration of not-for-profit organizations as preferred developers.

As the CBD has lost its residential population, it has also lost the voters to whom public officials must listen. Residents prefer to have public funds spent where they live rather than where they work. Citizen groups are making more and more demands to channel all new resources into existing residential neighborhoods. Maintaining that earlier development favored downtown and commercial projects, they assert that private commercial investment in the downtown will follow after residential areas are stabilized by massive government assistance.

This approach to development has significant political implications. Cities with a bold chief executive backed by a strong legislative body have been able to involve private entrepreneurs in projects to strengthen the CBD's economic vitality.[16] Most significant to the entrepreneur is how the chief executive's attitudes are reflected in the municipal policy on taxes, labor, involvement of business leaders, and degree of government participation in development programs. Private participation is most likely when all of the following factors are present: (1) when business shares a fair distribution of local taxes but no more; (2) when the municipal administration treats labor and management evenly; (3) when local government is sufficiently self-confident to have representatives from business and community groups serve on official boards and advisory groups; and (4) when city officials are inventive and flexible in administering improvement programs and are prepared to go beyond the minimum to ensure the completion of the project.

---

[16] In Milwaukee, Philadelphia, and Cincinnati, the local government has been able to balance creative programs for revitalizing neighborhoods with positive achievements in downtown development.

The developer must remember that no matter how enthusiastic a locality may be about developing a CBD, the process must take place within the municipality's legal framework. Municipalities have certain legal powers to carry out development programs. Local governments have the right to obtain blighted property at fair market value through condemnation. The municipal government can secure the property from private owners, prepare the land or property for development, and sell or lease it to private investors. Such activities continue to be permitted in areas certified as blighted when a development plan clearly spelling out the public purpose of the development program has been adopted and when the potential for development has been clearly established. However, it has become more difficult to "clear and rebuild" than it was in the 1950s and 1960s.

Many federal and state laws and regulations have limited certain development operations. It is extremely difficult to remove or alter historic properties. It is somewhat difficult to acquire private property that is reasonably sound and for which no significant change in use is proposed. The net result of any development action should not increase, and preferably should decrease, racial concentrations. If the program is expected to produce jobs and stimulate business expansion, affirmative action programs should be incorporated into the development; indeed, federal and many state governments will not accept a plan without such programs. Strict requirements about adequate notice and time to vacate properties must be considered when planning a project so that delays do not result.

In the past 10 years, localities have significantly changed their organization of the development function. Municipal jurisdictions, no matter what the form of government, now control the various local development agencies through the regular government process responsible to the chief executive. This trend has been abetted by congressional actions like the 1974 Housing and Community Development Act, which stipulates a prime sponsor (usually the regular municipal government) that can subcontract through public and private entities. Independent authorities like urban renewal and public housing, set up at an earlier time when the philosophy was to keep such functions separate from municipal financing and removed from political pressures, are being absorbed into regular government agencies, having their operations limited, being forced to follow a policy determined solely by the municipal government, or being eliminated. Some communities have retained independent authorities to conduct activities where the regular government faces legal restrictions—property

2-10 The public sector continues to play a major role in the creation of public plazas like Carter Plaza at Charles Center.

condemnation and takings, and borrowing project funds outside the municipal debt limit. Some local governments that once relied on development agencies to coordinate the work of many city agencies have strengthened their own powers to direct development.

Despite these restrictions on rebuilding a city's CBD, a climate for development still exists. Today, however, it recognizes that a municipality must work with private developers to achieve an economically sound central city. Government may merely designate sites for development through special zoning districts, or it may be more active by acquiring a site and then selling or leasing the tract to a private developer, relocating displaced businesses and residents in the process. Government may provide indirect financial incentives, such as density bonuses for providing certain amenities, or it may directly finance parts of projects, such as off-street parking, open space plazas, or pedestrian bridges. Certain facilities may be built entirely with government funds (for example, social centers and health clinics in housing developments for the elderly). Public housing agencies may manage buildings erected by private developers, or government may even construct commercial buildings and lease them to private investors.

Another kind of partnership occurs when the municipality recognizes a civic organization not originally set up as a local development corporation as the developer in a major downtown project. This civic association may act as its own developer, using its own members and adding needed special skills, or it may arrange to bring in qualified private developers if enabling legislation has been passed and it is not restricted by constitutional limitations. These and other arrangements are more fully explored in subsequent chapters.

Objectives in Organizing for Development

All parties involved in the development of a CBD should know the project's economic, social, and political objectives. They should have an understanding—preferably a written agreement—concerning these objectives.

Both the developer and the government hope to derive economic benefits from the project. The developer and his investors hope to obtain a profit commensurate with the risk they are assuming. Normally, this objective is the private entrepreneur's principal concern. In some cases, however, developers will accept less than normal profits in exchange for prestige or a demonstration of corporate responsibility. While developers have been increasingly reluctant to spend money on frills, other considerations go into the calculation of profit and loss and reflect the private entrepreneur's actual motivation. Only the entrepreneur can weigh his specific risks based on his current and projected economic situation.

Local government also has particular economic objectives in development projects. They include improving the city's tax base, stabilizing a declining part of downtown, increasing employment, and using public dollars to stimulate private investment. The structure of the local tax system may influence the selection of a project. Cities that rely heavily on property taxes will evaluate economic objectives differently from those that receive a sizable portion of their revenues from sales tax. Cities that tax commuters will evaluate projects differently from those that tax only residents. Cities that receive a high proportion of their income from state or federal governments may evaluate objectives differently from those whose financial support is limited to their own jurisdictions.

The local government's social objectives are normally an important part of downtown development. These objectives range from employing local residents in the construction or rehabilitation project to local citizens' involvement in all phases of development. One of the difficulties in defining achievable social objectives is determining their short- and long-term costs and the political acceptability of different packages of social benefits. Now, however, some private foundation and public funds are being used with private sector resources to achieve specific social benefits. These arrangements have often strengthened a project's economic and financial reliability and ensured the necessary public support.

Meeting a project's political objectives may be the local government's highest priority. The project may have been a controversial item in a recent election. It may be one of the first projects attempted after enactment of a new local law, or it may be identified with a new initiative or a new organization. The project might have political importance beyond the region, especially if it is unusually large or innovative. In any event, these political objectives must be identified and met.

Resources Needed for Downtown Projects

Once objectives are clearly stated, it is necessary to define precisely what private and public resources are needed for the project's successful completion. In addition to the right amount of money at the right time and in the right place, numerous noneconomic resources are essential for downtown development.

Private Resources

Finding the right development team—one with sufficient experience and financial strength to complete the project satisfactorily—is perhaps the most important decision to make. The development team must contribute managerial talent, entrepreneurial skills, a quality design, and other resources suited to the project's needs. One of its most significant contributions is the expenditure necessary to make a decision about the project's feasibility. Some amount of time and money must be spent to determine whether there is a market for the project within the suggested time frame. The development team can assemble specialists in various areas to evaluate the project's desirability, undertake preliminary planning and design, and analyze the financial and market situation.

In the past it was assumed that the private entrepreneur could always supply this front-end, high-risk capital. However, as downtown development has grown more complex and risks have increased, the public sector has become increasingly involved in providing these resources to the private sector to finance front-end costs. In some cases, private entrepreneurs are given a land option at no cost or a minimum cost for the period required to complete the necessary studies. Other cooperative arrangements—interest-free loans, for example—have been made to reduce the risk to the private developer. Many cities have found that public dollars for surveys, market analyses, and design studies should be made available directly to the developer as a part of project development.[17] Increasingly, the public sector is providing these funds to the development team at no cost or under a conditional repayment plan.

---

[17] The Urban Development Corporation of New York used such arrangements extensively.

After the project is tentatively judged desirable and feasible, funds are required for more extensive planning and design. As the project is defined in increasing detail, input from civic groups is required to ensure public acceptance of the final package. The developer must involve market analysts, planners, architects, builders, and public relations experts for varying amounts of time. In some cases, financial institutions should be involved early in the project's development to ensure that sound financial policies are followed and to ease the attainment of short- and long-term financing.

Public Resources

Public resources—people as well as dollars—must focus on allowing the private sector to develop its project alternatives with public support and to proceed with the final version of a project as smoothly and efficiently as possible. The public sector must exhibit strong managerial leadership, including key decision-makers' attention to ensuring that public processes operate smoothly. The procedures that government must follow in the conduct of its business should not interfere with a development project's time constraints.

The city's budget process is often critically important because frequently public capital improvements can enhance private development. These public resources that the developer relies upon must remain available. If they will not continue to be available, the developer must know when they will be terminated. This requirement applies not only to the elective term of a mayor but also to the time and staff required to process grants, because a key to the project's success may be local, state, or federal grants or other financial support like bonds.

2-11   The provision of publicly funded parking facilities may be crucial to the economic feasibility of major downtown projects.

Scheduling Resources

A well planned schedule for providing resources is the key to successfully merging private and public responsibilities. The schedule can influence the type of development team and the total amount of money needed for the project. Unfortunately, the process requires hundreds of decisions, each one relying on previous decisions and affecting later ones. A delay in providing one critical resource has ripple effects that may affect the project's ultimate success. A realistic schedule for providing resources can speed decision making and encourage confidence between the private and public sectors.

Political Evaluation

A political evaluation of the project is essential in establishing its organization. Such evaluation goes beyond determining support from elected officials. It includes determining the amount of support from affected segments of the community and the commitment of the local business leadership. The official and informal approvals required and the people and organizations who must provide those approvals must be carefully assessed. Many of these official actions may involve zoning, possible changes of law, approval of capital projects, and other decisions that can be highly political rather than rational. In most communities certain private organizations could materially influence the speed with which the project proceeds. These groups need to be contacted to determine the public support for the project. A dramatic presentation of a project, or a forceful indication of its long-term value to the community, can reverse political opposition and develop unexpected sources of support.

The political evaluation should include a review of the history of the project being considered and similar projects proposed for that city in the past. Such a review can lead to better understanding the factors that need to be evaluated in the present project. It should also shed some light on the relative importance of various civic and business organizations and individuals who can contribute to or hamper downtown development. It often reveals which decision-makers constitute the area's real leadership and can explain the extent to which local government, the private sector, or civic and business organizations are united or divided on downtown development. Historical analysis, however, should not color the present situation to the detriment of the currently proposed project. Attitudes and the climate for development may change. The timing and extent of public involvement, the project's prospects for the future, and the public's attitudes about the project must be evaluated for the current situation.

3.
Overview of the Development Process

Real estate development is the subdivision and servicing of unimproved land or the improvement of developed real property. The process normally involves increased investment in the property with attendant increases in income and value. In most instances the return on investment provides the incentive for development. In CBDs development usually involves the removal of existing buildings and construction of new buildings in their place, construction on vacant land, or the renovation of existing buildings.

New or rehabilitated buildings commonly include commercial structures such as hotels and stores; government or other public buildings such as hospitals, courthouses, libraries, and convention centers; residential buildings; and mixed use complexes. In recent years, the most common type of downtown development—both new construction and rehabilitation—has been office buildings that incorporate retail space on the ground floor and typically include provisions for off-street parking. Because of the decentralization of retailing away from downtown over the last 30 years, most downtowns have not experienced significant development of new retail store buildings.[1] Recently, the renovation of old buildings for specialty retail shops has become a new phenomenon. Examples include the Squire-Latimer Building on Pioneer Square in Seattle, the Garage Mini-Mall in Cambridge, Massachusetts, Faneuil Hall in Boston,

Trolley Square in Salt Lake City, and Larimer Square in Denver.[2]

Large mixed use complexes combining office, retail, hotel, residential, and parking space on a single site are still relatively new, although many cities count one or two such projects. Examples include Kalamazoo Center in Kalamazoo, Michigan, Westmount Square in Montreal, Omni International in Atlanta, Watertower Place in Chicago, Broadway Plaza in Los Angeles, and Baystate West in Springfield, Massachusetts.[3]

While the character of the development process varies considerably from place to place, projects have enough common features to generalize about the development process. This chapter examines these general aspects of the development process within which development takes place; the major forces affecting development; the various approaches to development and the factors that influence them; and the major stages of the development process.

---

[1] J. Thomas Black, *The Changing Economic Role of Central Cities* (Washington, D.C.: ULI–the Urban Land Institute, 1978).

[2] See Urban Land Institute, *Adaptive Use: Development Economics, Process, and Profiles* (Washington, D.C.: ULI–the Urban Land Institute, 1978).

[3] See Robert E. Witherspoon, John P. Abbett, and Robert M. Gladstone, *Mixed-Use Developments; New Ways of Land Use.* (Washington, D.C.: ULI–the Urban Land Institute, 1976).

3-1 Larimer Square in Denver is one of the enduring examples of renovation and adaptive use of old commercial buildings into a specialty and tourist retail area.

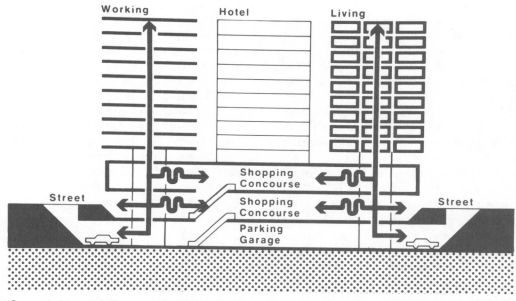

3-2 Westmount Square in Montreal illustrates the physical integration of various land use components in a mixed use development. Not shown is the underground connection to the adjacent subway station.

The Institutional Context

The term "real estate industry" most often refers to those who sell or develop property, or provide legal, financial, architectural, or other services to those who do. The real estate market combines a raw material (land), finished products (usable space), and the development process (the combination of land and space to increase their value through new improvements or a change in use).

The Real Estate Market

Real estate is a unique industry because its basic resource, land, is scarce and nonrenewable. Land is valuable whether it is improved or unimproved. Owning land is part of the American dream, and its use is therefore determined by a host of factors, not all of them economic. This cultural importance of land must be considered in definitions of the real estate industry and the real estate market.

The demand for and the supply of land are the basic components of the real estate market. Any time land or the improvements on it are bought, sold, leased, or improved, a real estate market activity occurs. The activity is generally in the form of ownership or tenancy of a residential unit, but it can also involve commercial, industrial, or agricultural properties.

Events in the real estate industry affect many other industries and markets; similarly, events in these other industries and markets affect real estate. In fact, the real estate market's dependence on the capital market is a major problem. When interest rates rise, less money is available for real estate investment. A number of such instances occurred during the 1970s.

The Capital Market

The supply of money to the real estate market comes from the same capital market that serves the other sectors of the economy. Though certain financial institutions concentrate a large percentage of their lendable funds in long-term real estate investment (savings and loan associations, for example, had 83 percent of their assets invested in mortgage-backed loans as of December 31, 1977), fluctuating interest rates can and do cause short-term shifts out of the market. The fact that real estate must compete with other potential investments for available capital is a positive constraint to ill conceived projects in the best of times and the primary cause of instability in the industry in the worst of times.

The real estate market requires a steady stream of funds at reasonable rates within some broad limits. A limited supply of funds at the market price or a high interest rate disrupts the market. Since capital is a

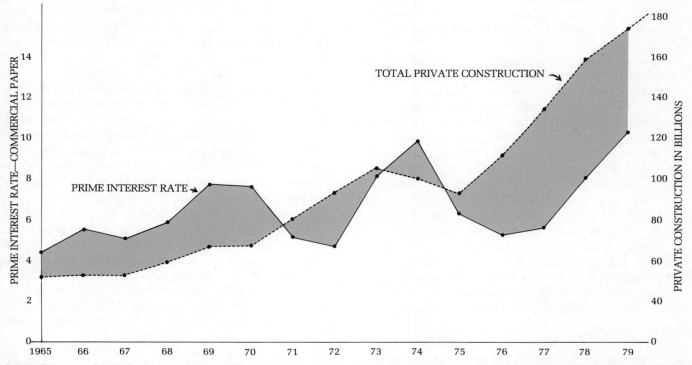

3-3   The curves depict the historical relationship between interest rates and construction activity. The slowdown in construction always follows the rise of interest rates, reflecting the use of prior commitments for funds at a favorable rate.

major component of any project, it must be available when needed or the project cannot start. It must also be available at an interest rate that allows the finished project to be sold or leased at a competitive price at the time the project is completed and marketed.

Two types of funds—equity capital and debt capital—flow through the real estate market. Equity capital involves the highest risk and has the potential for the greatest gain. It receives the residual (the profit or cash flow) after all other expenses, including a fixed return to mortgage lenders, have been paid. Equity capital almost always must be raised before debt capital is committed. Development companies, private corporate and individual investors, and, increasingly, institutional lenders like pension funds and life insurance companies frequently provide equity funds for downtown projects.

Debt capital takes two forms: construction or interim financing, and permanent or long-term financing. Almost all debt financing is secured by a mortgage. Certain lending institutions specialize in loans to real estate projects. Savings and loan associations, for example, are required by law to invest the majority of their funds in mortgage-backed loans. Most of them are permanent loans and most are on residential properties, but these institutions also make construction and land development loans. Commercial banks, on the other hand, make many construction loans to both residential and commercial properties. Life insurance companies are the most important long-term lenders for office, retail, and other commercial projects.

Cycles of boom and bust are common to the real estate industry. One of the chief reasons is fluctuating interest rates. Another is fluctuating construction costs. Yet a third, and equally important, reason is bad judgment on the part of the development industry, which manifests itself in periodic overbuilding. When short-term rates are high, all sources of capital tend to shift away from real estate into other more secure and more liquid investments. For example, in 1973, certificates of deposit at commercial banks were earning as much as 12 percent. To compete for those funds, most developers had to pay well in excess of 12 percent for real estate construction loans. Few projects could support those rates but if they chose to accept the higher rates in order to proceed, many of them experienced significant construction cost overruns, which frequently led to default and foreclosure.

The Development Industry

The development industry includes an extensive number of people. All the brokers, appraisers, developers, builders, lenders, architects, engineers, and lawyers involved in real estate constitute a very important force in the economy. Some are risk-taking entrepreneurs; others provide support services. The industry produces a variety of products: residential units, commercial space, industrial buildings, hotels, recreational facilities, to name a few. Developers engaged in CBD projects are only part of this much larger group.

The expertise, resources, and capital required to successfully complete a downtown commercial project are frequently much greater than the requirements to develop a residential project or a strip commercial center in the suburbs. Downtown developers are fewer in number and generally more sophisticated than their counterparts. The problems associated with downtown development—land acquisition, zoning, financing, and marketing—are generally so great that only a few developers consider entering this field. Developers of downtown projects tend to enter new markets cautiously, but once they are involved they tend to remain.

Many differences exist in the quality and the capacity of residential, office, retail, and industrial developers. Some enter the process with little experience and few resources; others are well schooled in the intricacies of complex projects and have qualified staffs and strong contacts with lenders. The appropriate group to undertake a specific project depends to a large extent on the project itself. For example, it is often easier for a small local firm to succeed with a project that has a major problem acquiring land than it would be for a larger, more experienced firm located in another city.

Local development companies participate in many more projects and commit much more financing than their nationally known counterparts. National and international companies are very important trend setters, however. When the Rouse Company, for example, opened innovative retail complexes in downtown Philadelphia and Boston, and when Gerald D. Hines Interests became involved in projects in Houston and a performing arts project in Louisville, Kentucky, the rest of the industry noticed.[4]

National companies have certain advantages over local firms. A national reputation for innovative and successful projects assures some companies a much better reception by local officials. Deals considered suspect when the city government and a local firm make them are often applauded if the developer is nationally known. Many projects today require sub-

---

[4] TheGalleria, a project of Gerald D. Hines Interests, Inc., was given the ULI Award of Excellence for 1979 in recognition of leadership in development and innovation.

3-4 The unique character of Faneuil Hall in Boston required new ideas for retailing. The Bull Market carts are individually leased, allowing artists, craftsmen, and small vendors an outlet for their goods within a framework of more traditional retailing.

stantial public investment for them to succeed; a commitment to a nationally known developer might have fewer political liabilities than one made to a local entrepreneur. A national reputation may also have some disadvantages, however, including a lack of knowledge of the local market and access to the local power structure. In some cases, a combination of local and national firms may be a solution.

Government

Downtown projects in stable or declining cities generally require greater public involvement than do projects in growing cities. Many developers believe that an active role by the public sector can be an advantage to development in the CBD. The amount and type of public involvement is often the key to successful revitalization. Increasingly, the public is recognizing the need to expedite development approval to avoid costly delays in project implementation.

All levels of government significantly affect real estate development in two ways: through regulation (primarily local but increasingly state and federal) and through expenditure of public dollars (local,

state, and federal) for direct and indirect subsidies (local and federal). It is fair to say that no project undertaken today is free of the influence of government, and downtown projects are most vulnerable.

Zoning regulations and others affecting development have been a way of life in cities for decades. Even Houston, the only major city in the country without a zoning ordinance, uses various other mechanisms to prescribe the type and density of development of all land within its borders. Local governments originally passed laws on land use to protect residents' health, safety, and general welfare. Mixing commercial and industrial with residential uses was thought to be detrimental to citizens' well-being and was thus precluded. Over time, attitudes have changed and now mixing land uses, particularly in downtowns, is being encouraged by government regulations and incentives.[5]

Recent time has seen a rash of new regulatory activity. Where once the primary concern was for community economies and the direct impact develop-

---

[5] Witherspoon, et al, *Mixed Use Developments*, op. sit., pp. 97–100.

3-5 Omni International Hotel is located on Norfolk's downtown waterfront. A handsome design solution, it suggests all the issues that have arisen in conjunction with waterfront revitalization—bulkheads, land fill, pier extensions, blocking views, public access.

ment would have on them, increasingly the emphasis is on protecting and enhancing the environment. For example, these new regulations are directed toward preserving wetlands and coastal zone areas or managing water and wastewater. While the wetlands and coastal zone regulations were designed to protect natural areas, they frequently apply to cities' core areas, because many cities are located in coastal areas, on rivers, on the Great Lakes, or near floodplains.[6]

Regulations affect the cost of new development in several ways. First, they frequently reduce potential revenue from the development because they may limit the intensity of site development. Second, they increase the risk to the developer because of delays and uncertainties in processing. Third, they limit the use of certain land, which reduces the supply of land that can be developed. All of these factors increase production costs and therefore increase the cost of the final product.[7]

Public expenditures on infrastructure improvements—for example, roads, water and sewer facilities, private and public transportation facilities, and pedestrian ways—directly impact development. These essential improvements determine the shape and location of private development. New expressways make land distant from cities attractive to homebuyers as well as to commercial and industrial users. Water and sewer facilities open up areas not previously available for development.

In downtowns, improved parking facilities, pleasant pedestrian spaces, improved public transportation systems, and other public investments help to

[6] See Andy Leon Harney, ed., *Reviving the Urban Waterfront* (Washington, D.C.: Partners for Livable Places, National Endowment for the Arts, and Office of Coastal Zone Management, n.d.).

[7] See Urban Land Institute, *Thirteen Perspectives on Regulatory Simplification*, ed. Annette Kolis (Washington, D.C.: ULI–the Urban Land Institute, 1979).

make downtown locations competitive with suburban locations. Without public expenditures, many major downtown development projects could not be built and could not be competitive with suburban developments. The decisions about what kinds of investment will be made to support development are usually made at the local level, but funding generally comes from state and federal governments.

The demand in many cities is not strong enough to support new projects built entirely with private resources. When the new development is clearly beneficial to the public, many cities are offering direct subsidies to the private sector. These subsidies may include land write-downs or money loaned at interest rates below the current market. Increasingly, the federal government supplies the funds through programs sponsored by the Department of Housing and Urban Development (HUD), the Department of Commerce, or other agencies. The way the funds are used varies with the program involved. For example, community development block grants are administered locally and can be applied to any project the municipality desires within broad areas of eligible and ineligible activities. HUD Section 302 loans (which offer below-market interest rates) are administered locally but must be used for specific projects. Funds from the Environmental Protection Agency not only must be used for specific projects but are also federally administered.

Indirect subsidies are determined by the way a municipality treats taxes of certain items—interest on loans, real estate deals, depreciation, or capital gains. They determine the type of project that can raise equity capital and therefore, in effect, encourage or discourage investment in real estate.

The Real Estate Development Process in Downtowns

The opportunity for real estate development exists when the difference in an existing property's value and its value in a changed state exceeds the cost of conversion. For example, a half-acre downtown site containing an older one-story retail store may have a current value of $600,000. If the market would support an office building valued at $8 million that cost $7 million for demolition of the old building and construction of the new one, the potential gain is $400,000. This potential gain provides the incentive for new development.

Numerous circumstances can create this fundamental condition necessary for development. The local government can revise its zoning ordinance to allow a type of development not previously allowed,

an expanding population and economic growth can create new demands, demand by current users of a specific site can evaporate and thereby reduce current values to the point where new development is feasible, changes in the transportation system or other public facilities may make new uses feasible, or the local government might offer a subsidy to create an artificial difference in value.

While the basic economic conditions leading to development are relatively simple, the application of these concepts to real situations is more complex. Imperfect information, the tendency of potential increased value to raise existing land values, leases and covenants, and the large number of variations that affect locational decisions, costs, development rights, and property owners' objectives can all increase the complexity of development.

The Basic Ingredients

Regardless of how real estate development projects are initiated, certain requirements are common to all projects if they are to proceed:

- either a commitment to lease or purchase the finished space at a price that will cover costs plus a return or tax benefit sufficient to attract investors, or strong evidence that the space will be rented or purchased within a reasonable time after the project is finished
- a site (which in downtown might include air rights and/or subsurface sites) on which to build the project
- the necessary public services (water, sewer, gas, electricity, roads, telephone, and transit)
- the capital required to acquire the land and to design and build the project
- the public approvals (zoning, subdivision, and building regulations, streets or highway access, sewer connections, environmental clearances, and so forth) required to permit the project to be developed.

Providing and controlling the five basic groups of resources and skills to produce a finished project is the essence of development and the developer's basic function. The individual or organization—whether public or private—that provides this function is the developer, regardless of what it is called.

The Major Actors

The Developer

The developer is the director and organizer of the development process. He conceptualizes the project, initiates activity, assumes risk, invests money, and usually expects to earn a profit. The private individual or company that played this role essentially alone in the past is now being assisted and at times replaced by public entities.

The developer may conceive of the idea for a project and convince others of its merit or respond to the needs of an office tenant or retailer requiring new facilities. In either case, he is responsible for seeing that each of the many phases in the development process is carried out expeditiously and efficiently. He assesses project feasibility; determines appropriate partners; decides when to proceed with financing, marketing, and acquiring land; and negotiates with local officials over project size, density, and provision of public services. In sum, he manages the entire operation. For CBD development, management is crucial. Like any complex production process, cost control, resource allocation, and scheduling are vital to the project's success.

As public involvement in urban development expands, the role of the private developer is being reshaped. He is spending less time initiating new projects and more time responding to public overtures. His own activities depend on the context of public and private partnerships. He will of necessity become more sophisticated as local officials learn to differentiate between different developers' qualifications. He should become an ally rather than an adversary to local officials, and his input should be sought in the early planning stages.

Local Public Agencies

The role of local governments in the development process is also changing. Local governments, instead of waiting for development to occur, are initiating development projects; Chicago, New Haven, and Philadelphia are recent examples. They have been most successful in working with local business and community leaders to focus attention on major development problems, confronting their communities with these realities, and then forcing opposing interests to agree on how best to attack and resolve their problems. If the consensus is broad enough, it becomes a mandate for action and fosters relationships with private developers that would otherwise be untenable. These partnerships between the public and private sectors tend to ensure that community objectives are met.

Until the advent of urban renewal and other federal programs in the 1950s, the local government's role in development was limited to enacting zoning laws and providing streets, roads, water, and sewerage. Massive land purchases supported by federal pro-grams created new opportunities. Because the programs' intent was to shift land use, increase density, and clear slums, many cities planned elaborate and very specific renewal projects in the mistaken belief that the private sector would assuredly develop the land according to the community's plans. Unfortunately, many projects failed because governments had ignored or misunderstood basic market forces and developers' potential contributions in formulating the project. Even with land costs written down to zero, as they were in some cities, governments' proposed projects sometimes made no economic sense because there was insufficient market demand.

Today many good examples exist of successful intervention by the public sector in the development process. Many local officials have realized the impact they can have on developers' decisions by offering a variety of incentives.

In communities with apparently strong market demand but insufficient land or inadequate infrastructure in the CBD, public funding may be necessary to get the project started. The public investment might take the form of assembling a site, writing down its cost, or providing parking. In more extreme cases, where demand for both existing and new space is insufficient, government can play a more active role. It must lead a communitywide effort to identify basic assets and then begin to build on them. In communities where the private sector sees no rationale for activity, the local government must play an even stronger role. It must adopt a comprehensive strategy to vigorously promote the central city.

Public officials' attitudes toward developers have a surprisingly significant effect on developers' willingness to engage in activity in a given city. If officials are antagonistic, do not respect the legitimacy of the developer's activity, and take a long time to approve or deny requests, the pragmatic developer will look elsewhere for opportunities. Public officials should remember that trust and goodwill are among the greatest assets they can bring to a partnership between the public and private sectors.

Equity Investors

Developers seek out organizations or individuals who wish to invest money in development projects that offer a reasonable return. The equity investor can expect three principal types of return: cash flow, tax benefits, and/or capital appreciation. In some cases, local investors may have reasons other than profit for their participation: civic interest and pride, or the protection of other property investments, for example.

Equity investment can come from many sources. For a small project the source is likely to be the de-

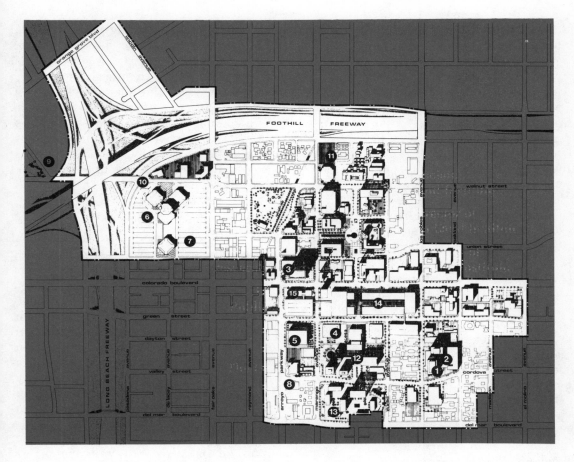

1 HILTON HOTEL
2 GROSVENOR PLAZA OFFICE TOWER
3 P.T.&T. HEADQUARTERS
4 PASADENA CENTER
5 BANKAMERICARD CENTER
6 PARSONS HEADQUARTERS
7 PARSONS EXPANSION
8 BROWN & CALDWELL
9 ORANGE GROVE VILLAGE
10 COMMERCIAL OFFICE PLAZA
11 PARK CENTER OFFICES
12 PASADENA CENTER HOTEL
13 PLAZA CORDOVA
14 RETAIL CENTER
15 FINANCIAL OFFICE COMPLEX

3-6   The redevelopment plan for Pasadena illustrates the scope of long-term public commitment required to foster private investment.

veloper's family and friends. In larger projects where land assemblage is difficult or imposes front-end costs too high for private individuals to bear, the developer might offer landowners an equity interest in the development as partial compensation for the use of their resources. Another source is investors, often unknown personally to the developer, who through a syndicate purchase part of the ownership of a project with the sole expectation of realizing a profit. Increasingly, lending institutions, which still provide debt capital but are also looking for potentially higher gain and a hedge against inflation, are a source of equity investments. It is no longer uncommon to find major life insurance companies offering equity money to developers in return for a share of the profits.

Many real estate development projects are organized as limited partnerships. This form of legal organization has two types of partners. The general partner, normally the active member of the organization, has unlimited liability. He must bear responsibility for any commitments or debts entered into by the partnership. Limited partners, on the other hand, are liable only up to a designated amount, usually the

amount of their investment. Equity investors are invariably limited partners. Though their investments are high risk, they, like debt lenders, can lose only a fixed amount.

Lenders

Lenders play a major role in development projects in two important respects. First, they are the source of debt financing; second, because they are more conservative investors, they carefully review a project's feasibility.

There are two primary arrangements for debt financing. They are related to the stages of a project. Construction loans provide capital for construction costs, as well as for some front-end costs. Permanent loans finance a completed project. Because requirements and risk vary with the stage of the development process, construction loans and permanent loans differ substantially with regard to financing terms and procedures.

Construction is characterized by uncertainty. Delays caused by weather, labor conflicts, and material shortages can all affect an activity's timing and thus project costs. Construction loans must necessarily reflect these risks. Therefore, interest rates on construction loans are higher than the rates for loans on completed projects. They are usually several percentage points above the prime interest rate.

Permanent financing is money borrowed by the developer (usually represented by a partnership or corporation) or the owner (should the project be sold) from a lending institution to cover a substantial portion of the project's total cost. The amount borrowed varies from one type of development to another, but it typically amounts to up to 75 percent of the appraised or retail market value, which is in turn equivalent to over 80 percent of the actual direct cost. On certain commercial projects, it is sometimes possible to finance out the project. In other words, the projected income stream will support a market value, and therefore a mortgage, in excess of direct costs. This process is called "mortgaging out."

Because permanent financing of a completed project involves substantially less risk than construction financing, interest rates are lower. The precise rate depends on the type of loan and on current capital market conditions. Permanent financing usually involves a mortgage, which serves as security. The mortgage entitles the lender to a first lien on a project should the owners default on loan repayments. It normally includes a fixed schedule for amortizing the loan, though it is not uncommon to make special arrangements for a flexible repayment schedule. While the term of the mortgage can vary, it generally runs from 20 to 35 years on new projects.

Lenders tend to be very conservative. They invest institutional funds with the expectation of earning a fixed return and therefore review project loan applications carefully. Almost all lenders require an economic feasibility study to be submitted for every project. Those studies for unusual or innovative projects are reviewed extensively. Developers who have track records with particular lending institutions find it less difficult to raise capital than developers without such relationships. Similarly, a conventional project is easier to fund than an innovative one.

To some extent, lenders limit the type of development project that the private sector can undertake. Without sufficient debt financing, almost all real estate development could not occur. During booms, lenders make available vast amounts of money to developers, making it possible for new or less qualified developers to enter the market.

Professionals

Professionals involved in real estate development projects include planners, economic and marketing consultants, mortgage bankers, appraisers, engineers, lawyers, building and landscape architects, public relations managers, and leasing agents. The many services they perform aid the developer, government agencies, and lending institutions. Their role is to provide technical assistance to those in decision-making positions by evaluating a project or confirming its feasibility; determining the appropriate size, scale, and design of structures and spaces; and helping the developer to avoid potential legal and financial pitfalls.

The number of professionals needed for any project depends upon the expertise of the principal actors. Larger developers have this professional capability on their own staffs. Similarly, public officials can often rely on services provided by city departments. As the complexity of a project increases, so too does the number of professionals involved.

Contractors, Permitting Officials, and Building Inspectors

A project is not ensured of success just because it has been planned, zoned, and financed. It must still be constructed. General contractors are professional

3-7   The St. Louis Civic Center area illustrates the impact of public action.

managers of construction. Their expertise lies in organizing and overseeing production. They acquire permits, purchase materials, hire laborers and subcontractors, schedule activities, and deal with setbacks like inclement weather or strikes.

Some developers use their own construction divisions for all their projects. Others subcontract either part or all of the work to outside firms. General contractors frequently are hired without submitting competitive bids. Even when bids are solicited, developers are not required to accept the lowest bid. They can and often do pay a premium to ensure quality.

Permitting officials and building inspectors include that group of public officials that oversees the public's interest in the construction process. Their judicious interpretation of building code conformance, administration of safety regulations, timely processing of utility connections, and completion of public works related to private development are vitally important to the completion of a project on schedule and within budget. Their level of competence and their integrity are important to a community seeking to encourage new development.

Citizens' Groups

Citizens' groups are playing an increasingly important role in downtown development projects. Their role has become more dominant since the early urban renewal programs, when HUD required a formal committee composed of local citizens. Today almost no project is undertaken without some citizen involvement, especially when that involvement is opposition to the project.[8] Their greatest influence derives from the National Environmental Policy Act, which provides the right to be heard on environmental matters when federal funds are involved. Time-consuming lawsuits have resulted from improper procedures. In development, the power to sue is the power to influence.

The most common type of active citizens' groups are neighborhood associations, special purpose community groups, historic preservation societies, environmental groups, and business organizations such as center city development organizations and retail merchants' associations. Their goals are varied, but many have a single purpose. Some are formed with the express intent of preventing inappropriate development. Others, business or resident neighborhood associations in particular, want greater public services in their areas to attract private investment rather than have the city concentrate its efforts in the central business district.

Another type of citizens' group affecting downtown development—and by far the most significant in terms of a city's future—is that formed to seek solutions to the city's major economic problems. Business and civic leaders in communities faced with a corporate office's moving or the departure of the CBD's sole department store sometimes bypass existing organizations to create a CBD committee to plan economic development strategy. It could subsequently be concerned with implementation. The committee's strategy is to facilitate development by seeking out developers or investors and fighting for public improvements in the CBD.

These groups can significantly affect an individual developer's activities. Zoning battles over a project have lasted for years, and even when a developer wins the court battle, he may lose the war if the market he wished to serve no longer exists. In general, however, the impact of such single-purpose organizations is limited. Nevertheless, to ensure continued economic viability, developers must try to work with these groups. Citizens' groups that cannot or will not shift their focus will remain a stumbling block to a city's future improvement.

Federal and State Governments

Federal housing, urban renewal, water and sewer grants, and highway programs have had a greater collective impact on the shape of cities in the last 30 years than all local development programs put together. Whether that impact was beneficial or destructive depends largely on the size and the location of the city. The interstate highway program, for example, increased the land area within commuting distance of CBDs, thereby accelerating residential and business flight to the suburbs. At the same time, however, it provided the South with a transportation system, made that region competitive with the northeast and north central parts of the country, and inspired a massive shift of manufacturing to the South. Federal programs will probably continue to affect development in these ways.

State policies often establish a basic framework for development and provide tools for municipal officials and businessmen seeking revitalization of CBDs. State enabling legislation often delegates responsibilities and powers for development and allows authorities to levy taxes, finance development, borrow funds, and assemble land in a specific manner. Specific innovative state legislation is discussed in chapter 7.

---

[8] See Urban Land Institute, vol. IV, *Techniques in Application*, chapter 28, "Public Participation" in *Management and Control of Growth*, ed. Frank Schnidman, Jane A. Silverman, Rufus C. Young, Jr. (Washington, D.C.: ULI–the Urban Land Institute, 1978).

DOWNTOWN DEVELOPMENT PROCESS

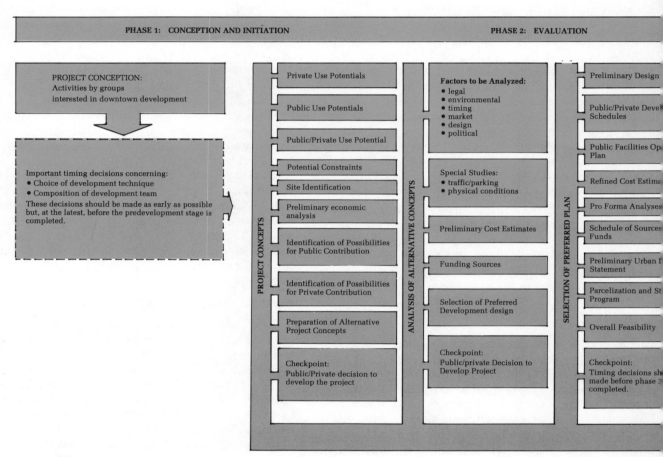

STAGE 1: PREDEVELOPMENT

PHASE 1: CONCEPTION AND INITIATION

PHASE 2: EVALUATION

PROJECT CONCEPTION:
Activities by groups
interested in downtown development

Important timing decisions concerning:
● Choice of development technique
● Composition of development team
These decisions should be made as early as possible
but, at the latest, before the predevelopment stage is
completed.

PROJECT CONCEPTS

Private Use Potentials

Public Use Potentials

Public/Private Use Potential

Potential Constraints

Site Identification

Preliminary economic
analysis

Identification of Possibilities
for Public Contribution

Identification of Possibilities
for Private Contribution

Preparation of Alternative
Project Concepts

Checkpoint:
Public/Private decision to
develop the project

ANALYSIS OF ALTERNATIVE CONCEPTS

Factors to be Analyzed:
● legal
● environmental
● timing
● market
● design
● political

Special Studies:
● traffic/parking
● physical conditions

Preliminary Cost Estimates

Funding Sources

Selection of Preferred
Development design

Checkpoint:
Public/private Decision to
Develop Project

SELECTION OF PREFERRED PLAN

Preliminary Design

Public/Private Devel
Schedules

Public Facilities Op
Plan

Refined Cost Estima

Pro Forma Analyses

Schedule of Sources
Funds

Preliminary Urban I
Statement

Parcelization and St
Program

Overall Feasibility

Checkpoint:
Timing decisions sh
made before phase 3
completed.

3-8

Stages of the Development Process

Downtown development projects proceed in three stages that include five well defined steps:

- *predevelopment*
  - project initiation and conception (those actions that lead to an idea for a project and the subsequent steps toward implementation)
  - project analysis (analysis, testing, and preliminary design)
  - final project packaging (formalizing the agreements required to proceed with site acquisition and construction of the project)
- *development*
  - project implementation (financing, leasing, design, and construction)
- *postdevelopment*
  - project management (management and maintenance of the project).

The remainder of this chapter is an overview of the predevelopment, development, and postdevelopment activities. They are discussed more fully in chapters 4, 5, and 6.

The Predevelopment Stage

Project Initiation and Conception (Phase 1)

Downtown development, like any other type of development, is usually initiated by one or a combination of the following parties:

- long-term land owners (downtown property interests)
- space users (hotel chains, retailers, corporations)
- public agencies (redevelopment authorities or planning departments)
- public or private ad hoc committees (private business and government interests)

32

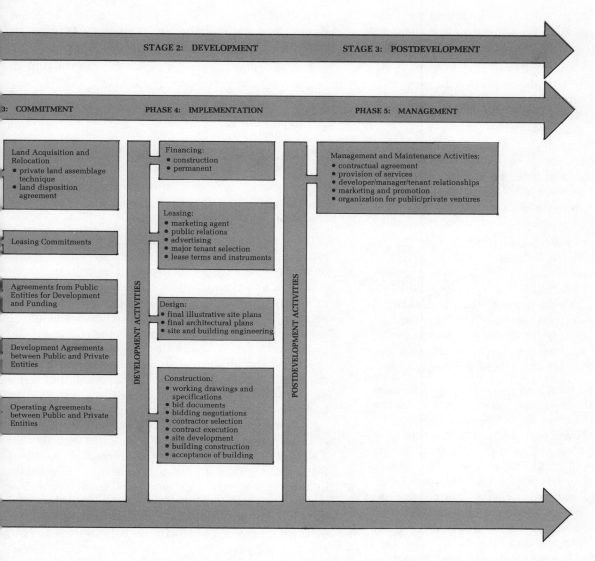

STAGE 2: DEVELOPMENT STAGE 3: POSTDEVELOPMENT

3: COMMITMENT PHASE 4: IMPLEMENTATION PHASE 5: MANAGEMENT

Land Acquisition and Relocation
• private land assemblage technique
• land disposition agreement

Leasing Commitments

Agreements from Public Entities for Development and Funding

Development Agreements between Public and Private Entities

Operating Agreements between Public and Private Entities

DEVELOPMENT ACTIVITIES

Financing:
• construction
• permanent

Leasing:
• marketing agent
• public relations
• advertising
• major tenant selection
• lease terms and instruments

Design:
• final illustrative site plans
• final architectural plans
• site and building engineering

Construction:
• working drawings and specifications
• bid documents
• bidding negotiations
• contractor selection
• contract execution
• site development
• building construction
• acceptance of building

POSTDEVELOPMENT ACTIVITIES

Management and Maintenance Activities:
• contractual agreement
• provision of services
• developer/manager/tenant relationships
• marketing and promotion
• organization for public/private ventures

- for-profit business entities (professional developers and equity investors)
- local nonprofit development corporations (private or public).

These project catalysts' motives, goals, and expected returns vary greatly. The common thread, however, is the desire to seek downtown revitalization through the formulation of one or more specific development projects.

Early in the process, the public and private parties involved should decide what type of development technique will be used and the composition of the development team. These decisions can have an important bearing on the course of development activity in the central business district.

The type of development entity depends primarily upon the strength of the downtown market. If a strong market exists for development, it is less likely that public participation will be necessary to start the project. However, if a poor market has led to a deteriorated downtown, significant public commitment to private development may be necessary.

Public involvement can range from the usual permitting and regulatory responsibilities in a strong market to direct leadership of the development stage. Between these two extremes it can comprise the private sector's programming public uses in combination with private uses under a contractual arrangement or an arrangement in which public and private groups are development partners.

One of the recent major issues with regard to downtown development is when and how the private developer should be brought into the process. Local public development agencies have frequently attempted to formulate projects without involving the potential developer of the project or consulting with experienced developers. Without this expertise, the public project too often fails to generate any response from the private sector. Increasingly, public agencies are recognizing that private developers must participate in the project initiation phase.

While the need for involving private developers is recognized, no standard models have yet been developed for such participation. A number of different approaches have been used with apparent success, however. Recently, many communities have formed quasi-public development corporations empowered with the flexibility to engage in a variety of developmental activities. By working closely with private developers, these corporations have fostered the necessary environment for development to occur.

The selection of a developer to lead project initiation has its potential problems. Developers tend to specialize in certain types of projects; they also tend to have limited capabilities in systems planning, which local governments must address in designing public standards for development. Developers are acquiring broader experience, however; increasingly, they can show a community a potential economic opportunity that the community itself had not realized.

The increasing number of projects in which local governments initiate development has led to the emergence of private consulting firms whose expertise lies in formulating and packaging projects. The firms capable of offering this assistance have strong real estate and development experience in the private sector and a working knowledge of public programs. While these firms normally work under contract to the local government agency, they may also work for a private developer who is negotiating with a local government on a project. They may direct development programming from project initiation to negotiation of terms for the business arrangement. When the consultant is working for both the public and the developer, they should jointly select the consultant and share expenses to avoid the consultant's favoring one side or the other.

In an overview such as this one, it is difficult to discuss developer selection unless the *initiator* of the development is first established. While the character of the initiator will affect the choice at some point in the process, the person or organization initiating development will seek out a professional developer to:

- enter into a joint-venture partnership with
- assume control of the project
- assist in formulating the project, possibly with an understanding that the developer will ultimately take control of the project or develop the project for a fee.

Several major criteria in selecting a developer should be used in almost any instance that might be described:

- the developer's past experience with the type of project contemplated, projects with similar demands, and projects in the local area
- the developer's financial strength, particularly his ability to raise the required equity funds
- the developer's current availability and capacity to handle the project
- the developer's reputation in the industry
- the developer's ability to assemble a competent team and produce a high level of design.

Project conception is also difficult to discuss without having a defined *initiator*. In most cases, however, the predevelopment process for project conception would be the progression from a general concept or alternative concepts for development to a specific project proposal. The exact nature and order of the activities leading to a specific project proposal depend on the known quantities in a particular case. For example, an initiator may identify a specific space need and general locational requirements but not a particular site. In that case, possible sites must be identified and evaluated. In other cases, the site may have been determined, but the uses, scale, and design of the development on that site must be determined.

Project conception would normally proceed through a logical series of considerations as outlined here and discussed in greater detail in chapter 4. Potential sites for development are the most common starting point. With a site or sites identified, economic opportunities identifying potential uses of the site are analyzed. Because much downtown development cannot be achieved without the cooperation and/or participation of both the public and private sectors, the analysis would also identify potential public and private contributions to the project. It is often difficult to determine what level of public contribution might be appropriate because this issue is frequently a political one.

If this initial analysis is favorably received, existing data and studies are reviewed during the next phase. Appropriate individuals are interviewed to ascertain tenant availability for office, retail, service, and public spaces. The following major areas are examined:

- *the potential for use by private firms:* identifying the need for office space, retail facilities, commercial space, recreation facilities, and transient or other housing facilities
- *the potential for use by the public:* identifying the need for administrative space, public facil-

ities, convention facilities, and special-use space

- *the potential for joint use*: ascertaining opportunities to combine uses of space in a development (courtyards, stairways, service areas, mechanical facilities)
- *potential constraints*: ascertaining the existence of an uncooperative public atmosphere, availability of development funds, lack of political consensus, opposition from special interest groups
- *identification of potential sites*: evaluating site alternatives in light of market demand, costs of acquisition, and other factors
- *preliminary economic analysis*: identifying potential tenants by interviews and data collection and developing a crude pro forma analysis
- *identification of possibilities for public contribution*: ascertaining the availability of public funds for front-end costs; exploring leveraging possibilities based on availability of public funds; determining other forms of public contribution such as land use control incentives, land leases, and tax assistance
- *identification of possibilities for private contribution of local equity monies (if necessary)*: ascertaining local investors' attitudes toward providing equity monies and exploring possible leveraging ratios with these private commitments in terms of federal grant applications
- *preparation of alternative project concepts*: synthesizing data into a number of possible project alternatives and discussing possibilities with potential major participants (public and private entities, potential tenants, and investors).

The initiator then presents the findings to the public body. The public entity must then decide on the merits of the package. If a clear development strategy is apparent, the public entity authorizes the initiator to prepare details of the project concept, thus moving into phase 2. If, however, a clear development strategy does not emerge at the end of phase 1, it may be necessary to proceed to selective detailed analysis, normally done during phase 2, to determine the best development strategy. Phase 2 activities include preparing a detailed market feasibility report on the top-priority project(s), the financial plan, a detailed program and design layout, an operation and management schedule, and proposed agreements between the public and private parties to ensure execution of the adopted project. At the completion of phase 2, a refined development strategy has been established.

Project Analysis (Phase 2)

After the final step in phase 1—the formulation of a development strategy—is completed, evaluation begins. It involves analyzing the alternatives and selecting the preferred option and includes the following considerations for each of the proposed alternatives:

- *general factors*
  - regulatory and legal considerations
  - environmental considerations
  - timing and sequence of development
  - political support
- *major studies*
  - market analysis
  - planning and design
  - financial, including preliminary cost estimates, refined pro forma analysis, and preliminary identification of sources of funding.

From these analyses, a preferred design and development program is identified. Further analysis of it results in:

- a final preliminary design
- development schedules
- an operating plan for public facilities to be incorporated in the project
- cost estimates
- a financial pro forma analysis
- a cost benefit analysis
- the basis for public/private negotiation toward a final project.

The objective at the end of this phase is to propose a project that meets basic physical, economic, financial, and legal requirements of the public and private participants in the project.

Before phase 3 begins, the final decisions about development technique and the composition of the development team must be made. At this point, the public and private parties should be prepared to negotiate and execute all documents necessary for the project's development.

Final Project Packaging (Phase 3)

The final phase of predevelopment includes formalizing the agreements required to proceed with site acquisition and construction. Commitments should be secured in five areas:

- *land acquisition and relocation*: acquiring land through gradual purchase or through equity participation agreements with property owners, executing a land disposition agreement

- *leasing:* securing preliminary lease agreements with prospective major tenants through letters of interest, letters of intent, or agreements to buy or lease space
- *public development and funding:* securing contractual commitments from public entities to develop and finance the project
- *development agreements between public and private entities:* executing a master agreement between the public and private parties to proceed with development
- *operating agreements between public and private entities:* executing a master agreement between the public and private parties that defines the responsibilities for operation and maintenance of public, private, and common spaces and/or facilities.

The Development Stage (Project Implementation)

The events leading to development have resulted in a single project of definable location and scale. Four tasks—financing, leasing, design, and construction—comprise the second stage of development, which sees the design become a reality.

Financing

Four types of financing must be obtained to initiate a project: predevelopment financing, long-term mortgages, equity funds for activities not covered by basic mortgages, and short-term construction loans. Financing can be either public or private.

The degree of public involvement in and public contribution to financing depends upon the strength of the local market, which is determined during predevelopment. Therefore, the amount and type of public financing has been determined before the development stage. During this stage, public activities are involved in preparing and marketing the financing instruments—usually bonds of some type (general obligation, special assessment, tax increment, revenue, etc.). Private financing arrangements and instruments are also finalized during this stage. They include life insurance companies, commercial banks, savings banks, savings and loan associations, pension and trust funds, real estate investment trusts, foreign funds, and individual or corporate investors.

Leasing

The objective of leasing is to secure final commitments from tenants. Leasing affects long-term financing arrangements of the project: Lenders are more likely to finance projects that have solid commitments from tenants. A well organized marketing program can attract numerous potential tenants. Lease negotiation is a challenging art. On one hand, the potential tenant, particularly a major one, can make difficult demands for rates and terms. On the other hand, the developer has designed a project that is attractive to potential tenants and that he hopes cannot be duplicated elsewhere except at rates and terms unacceptable to the tenant. Thus, lease negotiation, even after basic commitments have been made, can be protracted, difficult, and demanding of the developer's best skills.

Design

The design of the project is influenced by market studies, requirements of precommitted tenants, cost and site constraints, the developer's preferences, and applicable government regulations. While the concept was defined during the predevelopment stage, during development the design team creates specific plans for the project. The design team often includes many professional skills and their interaction toward a final design that achieves the development program's objectives. Ideally, the design team works directly with the principal officers of the development company.

The criteria for selecting a design team often evolve around previous experience with the developer or the possession of specialized skills, such as knowledge of local codes or ordinances. Frequently, when public and private uses are linked in the same project, two design teams can be involved—one for public components and one for private components. This situation should be avoided if at all possible, but if it must occur, then one design team should have a senior position and a way to coordinate design efforts must be established.

Construction

The final activity during the development stage is construction of the project. Construction management is a sophisticated endeavor, which includes initiating and administering contracts, overseeing bidding and negotiations, supervising contractors and subcontractors, scheduling activities, and monitoring work progress. Its objective is to complete the project according to the cost and schedule established during contract negotiations. Because large downtown projects may have many elements and phases, design and construction often overlap by the use of such techniques as design-build and accelerated or fast-track construction.

The Postdevelopment Stage
(Project Management)

After the project has been constructed, contracts must be negotiated to ensure proper management and maintenance of the project. These agreements are based on the preliminary arrangements made during predevelopment. They stipulate relationships between the developer, the manager, and the tenants.

Three management activities are necessary to operate and maintain a downtown project. First, the project manager must provide basic services to tenants—maintaining the heating and cooling plants, providing lighting, cleaning, for example—that maintain the structure's physical viability. Second, the manager must administer financial accounts and be responsible for tenant relations. These tasks include collecting rents, managing insurance and security coverage, and negotiating leases and renewals. Third, the manager is responsible for marketing and promoting the project, and public relations.

The management of a totally private project is carried out under the direct control of the owner/developer or a professional management company. The manager can provide services through its own staff or contract for services outside the organization. The objective of postdevelopment management is to ensure the long-term success of the project.

While good postdevelopment management is easy to define in concept, its application to downtown projects where there are public/private cooperative development endeavors is a relatively new and murky situation. Because such developments are all recent, little field experience of any duration can be used to define best practices. However, the development of expertise in this area may be the ultimate key to the encouragement of the joint public/private development endeavors needed to revitalize downtowns.

4.
The Predevelopment Stage

The predevelopment stage of a project begins with the initial perception of a need or opportunity for development and ends with the project packaged for development and construction. The three phases of activities—project initiation and conception, project analysis, and final project packaging—are directed to identifying opportunities for development, formulating and testing a development strategy, preparing a program for project development, and signing agreements between public and private interests. During the first phase, the location and general nature of the project are defined and the development entity organized. During the second phase, economic, financial, physical, social, political, and regulatory factors are evaluated in detail. The phase ends with a specific strategy for development and design that is satisfactory to all parties involved. During the third phase, the necessary agreements and commitments for constructing and managing the project are drafted, negotiated, and approved by the various parties.

When the predevelopment stage ends, therefore, the character of the project has been defined: The site, building size and arrangement, space users, major tenants and/or operators, public and private shares of development costs and identified financial support, and a development entity have been specified. This process generally requires 10 months to 2 years. Given the time, range, and cost of activities involved, the predevelopment stage is without doubt the most critical part of the entire development process.

Individual businessmen, developers, or investors may be the first to recognize and pursue the opportunity for development of a project in the CBD. This fairly random operation of private market forces may be assisted by public or quasi-public groups seeking to stimulate downtown revitalization, perhaps to stabilize the local economy. These groups may identify potential sites or projects or may intervene in the private market to encourage investment.[1]

---

[1] Chapter 7 discusses the various forms of public assistance for downtown development.

The primary concern during this initial phase is that a positive climate for investment exists in the CBD. Ideally it should meet the following criteria:

- private investment that has continuously responded to the market and kept downtown alive and active
- business leadership receptive to new investment
- public agencies and officials eager to encourage investment by providing a positive and predictable framework for facilitating long-term downtown development
- strong regional and downtown markets
- expanding retail, office, convention and tourist, residential, and other markets
- a generally excellent image as an area in which to live and work.

If the CBD is strong in most or all of these areas, the private sector will develop new projects as rapidly as the market will allow. Most downtowns fall considerably short of the ideal, however. They are bastions of weak or divided leadership, abnormally large numbers of older, obsolete buildings, difficult social problems, boom or bust financial cycles, limited markets, and significant restraints on downtown investment. In such areas extraordinary means will be necessary to initiate a project, perhaps by organizing the leadership, developing plans for downtown, and using public development agencies to attract and stimulate private investment.

The remainder of this chapter describes the process of initiating, planning, designing, evaluating, and programming a downtown development project. It emphasizes the means by which private and public interests can cooperate in the development of the central business district.

Phase I: Project Initiation and Conception

Phase I activities are initiated based on a perceived need for a particular downtown project. During this phase, a development entity is determined, basic economic and physical conditions analyzed, and a general design and development strategy formulated. The activities are intended to create a development organization and approach that will ensure effective management of a marketable project. The basic economic and design studies done at this time help to shape the general outline of the project and provide a foundation for the more detailed studies required during phase II.

Project Initiation

Identifying the Development Entity

One of the first tasks in initiating a project is to select or form a development entity. Many types of organizations have been active in downtown development projects, playing roles that range from promoting downtown revitalization to managing development of a specific project. Development entities capable of initiating and carrying out a project can be drawn from a number of groups or individuals. The composition of such an entity varies from city to city; it depends on the nature of public and private leadership, conditions endemic to the location, financial requirements for predevelopment planning and for the project, and legal and political constraints.

A development entity can be an association of participants from the public sector or an organization formed by private entrepreneurs. Public or quasi-public development organizations include traditional urban renewal authorities or development corporations that are empowered to participate in development projects to achieve public objectives—perhaps to stabilize a CBD's economy or to encourage development along a transit corridor.[2] Because they are public entities, public monies can be used for financing and they have the power of eminent domain to acquire land.

Major development projects in the CBD, however, usually come from private developers responding to market incentives with no extraordinary participation by the public sector. Local businesses concerned about the preservation of downtown commercial activity or investors involved in assembling capital for development ventures may form a development entity. Land owners seeking redevelopment of improved properties or businesses needing new or renovated space are frequently active participants.

A development entity can also be composed of both public and private interests. While they remain essentially separate, these interests can agree contractually to perform services, provide funds, or make commitments to build facilities. Ownership can be divided according to different elements of the structure or by the components of a mixed use project. The nature of the public/private development entity is usually determined by a combination of public and private interests. The private sector often takes the lead in stimulating public participation because it has the

---

[2] See Urban Land Institute with Gladstone Associates, *Joint Development: Making the Real Estate–Transit Connection* (Washington, D.C.: ULI–the Urban Land Institute, 1979) for an in-depth discussion of real estate developments directly tied to transit stations.

4-1 Illinois Center—1980 and planned future elements.

necessary management expertise and capital resources to initiate development.

Most downtown development projects have been initiated by one of the following types of development entities:

- long-term property owners who, as a result of their knowledge of the market and conditions affecting their own property, recognize an oppor-

tunity for development and pursue it, either individually or by joining with a professional developer

- major space users such as corporations, hotel chains, or chain stores requiring space in a given area who work through professional developers, act as their own developer, or develop space in partnership with a professional developer

4-2   Midtown Plaza, Rochester, New York, in the center of the photograph has induced substantial other development. At the left is the seven-story Seneca Building, to the right the 30-story Xerox Building, first phase of Xerox Square, and on the extreme right the base of the 28-story Lincoln Tower in Lincoln Trust Square.

- public agencies such as development authorities
- public/private ad hoc committees whose sole function is to stimulate opportunities for development
- for-profit partnerships or corporations composed of entrepreneurs or local corporations who use investor equity to develop projects
- local nonprofit, tax-exempt development corporations, either privately, publicly, or jointly funded and governed.

Property Owners

Property owners often initiate development projects because they wish to maximize the value of their properties or because they want to invest in development without selling the property and paying capital

gains taxes on it. In contributing part or all of the development site, the landowner becomes a key actor in the project.

A case in point is Chicago's Illinois Center, begun in 1969 and scheduled for completion before 1989. The impetus for the project came from the Illinois Central Railroad, the owner of the 83-acre site.[3] The railroad formed a real estate development subsidiary (Illinois Center Corporation) to enter a joint venture with a private developer (Metropolitan Structures) under the name of Illinois Center Plaza Venture (ICPV). ICPV serves as the land developer for the projects planned for the area. It purchases land from the railroad, prepares the infrastructure with city assis-

---

[3] Robert E. Witherspoon, John P. Abbett, and Robert M. Gladstone, *Mixed-Use Developments: New Ways of Land Use.* (Washington, D.C.: ULI—the Urban Land Institute, 1976), pp. 168–73.

tance, and sells the site, ready for construction, to other development groups. By acting as master developer, ICPV encourages a broad spectrum of development while retaining control over the planning and implementation of the project.

In some cases the property owner plays a more passive role, acting only in response to other initiators. The development of the new headquarters of New York's Citibank is an example. The key parcel in the assembly of land on Lexington Avenue was St. Peter's Lutheran Church, which was willing to consider a new building but only in the same location. The solution was to create a condominium in which the church and Citibank were shareholders, with Citibank paying $9 million for the church site and another $7.5 million for an adjoining parcel to provide the desired location for the new church. Through this arrangement, Citibank acquired additional allowable floor area of 200,000 square feet. Clearly, Citibank's willingness to respond to the church's objectives was the key factor in the success of this project, but Citibank also achieved significant benefits as a result.

Downtown property owners not directly involved with a development site may choose to support development to strengthen and revitalize downtown and thus increase property values. Owners of downtown properties, including banks acting as trustees for property holdings, often encourage development, hoping to capitalize on the economic benefits of specific projects. Such property owners help to furnish the leadership and positive investment climate so important to development.

Space Users

Space users—offices, hotel operators, and department store chains—initiate a large portion of development. Usually existing quarters are too small or the business requires highly specialized space. Banks and large corporations may also respond to the need for "image" in the community rather than to the need for more space. These initiators usually enter into lease agreements with developers or contract with developers to have the space constructed.

Large space users who also own substantial amounts of property clearly possess special incentives to initiate projects. Midtown Plaza in Rochester, New York, is a classic example.[4] Opened in 1962 as the first downtown shopping mall and business center in the United States, Midtown Plaza was conceived and cosponsored by two downtown retail stores—McCurdy and Company (a full-line department store) and B. Forman Company (a women's

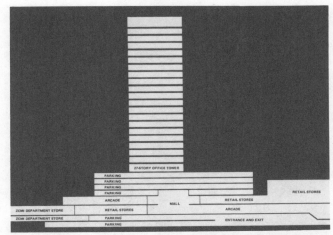

4-3 ZCMI Center cross-section illustrating the various uses within the complex.

fashion store). In cooperation with the city, which provided a municipal underground parking garage for the center, both stores were remodeled and expanded to anchor the project's 1 million square feet of retail space.

ZCMI Center in Salt Lake City is another example of a development effort sponsored by a department store. Initiated by the ZCMI department store, which had occupied its site since 1856, the $50 million project is one of the largest privately funded urban renewal developments in the United States.[5] Two million square feet of space (including 450,000 square feet occupied by the five-level ZCMI department store that anchors the complex) are under one roof. The project includes a 27-story office tower and parking for 2,000 cars.

The T. Eaton Company department store was the major initiator of the Pacific Centre in Vancouver, British Columbia.[6] The $100 million project, covering two major commercial blocks in the heart of Vancouver's business district, was developed by a private triumverate composed of the department store, Toronto Dominion Bank, and CEMP Investments, Ltd. The first phase of the project, completed in 1971, includes the 30-story Toronto Dominion Bank tower and the 500,000–square foot Eaton's department store, plus other retail space, parking, and a two-level plaza. The second phase includes a 19-story building for IBM, a 400-room hotel, and more retail and parking space. The shopping mall under the complex links the Eaton store to an existing Hudson's Bay store.

4 Ibid., p. 42.

5 Ibid., p. 9.

6 Ibid., p. 46.

4-4　Pacific Centre, Vancouver, British Columbia.

Public Agencies

Municipal governments, through their various public agencies, can actively stimulate project development through direct assistance to private developers or passively encourage development by indirectly supporting private investment. The role depends primarily on the need for public intervention in the private market. Public agencies can be relatively passive when development requires only the usual planning and management of municipal responsibilities rather than the allocation of capital funds for revitalization. This approach can succeed in a strong development market, but such strength is the exception rather than the rule for CBDs.

Public agencies can take a more active role by paying for some front-end planning and development, by providing needed public improvements like parking garages and pedestrian malls, and by facilitating development (by providing zoning incentives and smoothing the regulatory process). Public agencies thus ensure a more positive climate for investment and help to overcome investors' caution.

4-5　Faneuil Hall Marketplace, Boston, Massachusetts.

44

Many cities have been actively involved in downtown projects. Their activities range from land assembly and writing down the cost of sites to acquiring, restoring, and leasing buildings for private use. Faneuil Hall in Boston is one of the best known examples of a city's involvement in restoration. The city of Boston acquired and renovated the exteriors of three large buildings before signing a 99-year lease for the property with the Rouse Company. This direct public assistance was justified by the lack of major tenants and the market's uncertainty for development.

The San Diego Port District also participated in downtown development. The port acts as developer and landholder for revitalizing the waterfront. The Port District removed obsolete ferry slips and buildings, solicited proposals for leasing land, and selected a developer for a water-oriented area of specialty shops and restaurants with a waterfront park. It provided the city-owned land, prepared the site, and installed public improvements as an inducement to development.

The city of Richmond, Virginia, provided some funding of predevelopment activities to encourage a project package for the CBD. The city and a nonprofit corporation, Downtown Development Unlimited, contracted with a designated developer to determine prospective tenants' and local developers' interest in participating in the public/private project.

Public entities need not hesitate to take a more active role in facilitating development opportunities in the CBD. Such aggressive action can be transformed into solid business ventures when they are formulated in conjunction with qualified consultants and developers.

Public/Private Ad Hoc Committees

In many cities, downtown development groups have been organized to set goals and formulate policy. Often intended to be the first step toward public participation in revitalization, the ad hoc committee unites public and private leadership in determining a development strategy (see chapter 7). Once the strategy is determined, the committee may cease to function, may become an advisory body to review specific projects, or may evolve into a nonprofit development group. Although such a committee may prepare the way for development, it does not necessarily become directly involved in project initiation and development.

An ad hoc committee can serve several purposes in preparing the foundation for predevelopment activities. First, it may be the first united effort to recognize the need for revitalization and to involve both the public and private sectors. Second, it may function as the arena where competing private interests and disparate public groups agree about the objectives of downtown development. Third, downtown leaders can establish important personal and business relationships that can aid development.

Any leader who perceives the need for revitalization and persuades public agencies and the business community of the need can instigate the formation of a committee. The committee may grow out of a longstanding business group such as the Chamber of Commerce, or a mayor interested in downtown development might initiate it. Membership should include all economic and political forces in the downtown, suburban and regional representatives in metropolitan areas, and technical advisors from important city departments. The committee may number from 10 to 100 members, but a small, influential group is generally more effective than a large, cumbersome group. Large committees should include a steering or executive committee of 10 to 20 members who make most internal decisions.

The Central Jacksonville, Inc., task force, a public/private committee organized to stimulate development opportunities, initiated downtown revitalization in Jacksonville, Florida. The chief mandates of the task force were to determine the type of organization needed to facilitate development in the CBD and to identify specific projects that could be undertaken. The task force later evolved into a nonprofit corporation charged with negotiating public and private commitments to assist development projects.

For-Profit Development Entities

The Private Entrepreneur or Corporate Developer. The professional developer's livelihood is derived from conceiving and structuring business deals in real estate development. His primary job is to bring together the technical and financial resources needed for successful project implementation. The development entity and team that the developer organizes are his vehicle for completing the project; they blend technical expertise and detailed knowledge of local conditions with strong management capabilities. The development team may be made up of professionals from a number of organizations but must have strong central leadership.

Some developers act as individuals or have small staffs and prefer to contract for the technical capabilities required—market and financial feasibility studies, leasing, engineering, design, marketing, and property management. Other developers maintain in-house technical staffs to perform some or all of these tasks. In either case, developers maintain close contact with real estate brokers and major land own-

4-6　Nationwide Plaza, phase I.

ers who know which properties with the potential for development are or might be available. Developers also maintain close contact with sources of equity and mortgage money. With these sources of information readily available, the private developer remains the most potent force for initiating projects in downtown.

The Private Investor. Investors often choose to initiate development projects when other investment opportunities are not available or when those that are available do not meet their particular requirements. Projects available for investment may be in short supply, or they may be priced to yield inadequate returns for the investor. Investors thus initiate a project in partnership with an experienced developer or by themselves. Sometimes banks and insurance companies, which provide long-term financing of real estate development as part of their business, use their knowledge of real estate to initiate projects for their own investment account.

The Nationwide Plaza project in Columbus, Ohio, is the result of investor interest in a particular downtown area. In the 1960s Nationwide Mutual In-

surance Company was virtually the only large company remaining in the near north end of downtown Columbus. Surface parking lots and old delapidated buildings, many of them vacant, occupied most of the area. Nationwide at the same time needed greatly expanded space for its home office. After considering various alternatives, including moving to the suburbs, Nationwide decided to erect its new home office in the blighted area, using the project as the keystone for a major development of the area. The John W. Galbreath Company acted as construction and development consultant and leasing agent, and the city is relocating numerous streets and renovating other buildings in support of the Nationwide development.

The Milwaukee Redevelopment Corporation (MRC) illustrates a somewhat different approach. This limited-profit development corporation, formed by 34 corporations in the Milwaukee area, initiated the Milwaukee Retail Center and will act as the general partner in the development venture. Preliminary development studies were funded through the initial capitalization of MRC by the original shareholders. Through this mechanism, local public-spirited investors can participate directly in project development to assist downtown revitalization.

Local Nonprofit Development Corporations

Private Entities. The nonprofit development corporation is another vehicle that can involve local public and private leadership in downtown revitalization. Corporations shield both sectors from liabilities and risks that may be incurred during project initiation and development. The creation of a separate corporate entity helps to ensure access to and coordination of both public and private resources. This approach has a number of advantages:

- *independence from city government:* Private corporations are not restrained by limitations often imposed on public agencies: lengthy reviews, red tape, restrictions on travel and entertainment, and uncertain budgets.

- *expansion of public powers:* Private institutions can acquire property and finance real estate ventures using procedures and techniques for negotiating, contracting, and financing that would not be permissible for a public agency, and they are free to employ professional expertise without lengthy hiring processes.

- *privacy of negotiation:* The sale or lease of property, including public property, technical services, and construction contracts, can be negotiated without continual public scrutiny or restrictive bidding procedures.

4-7 Baystate West, Springfield, Massachusetts.

The Baystate West project in Springfield, Massachusetts, typifies the kind of project undertaken by a private nonprofit development corporation.[7] The Springfield Central Business District, Inc. (SCBD), organized by local businessmen to stimulate private investment in downtown Springfield, initiated the project in 1964–65. SCBD retained a consulting team headed by Hammer, Siler, George Associates to identify specific sites and markets in the CBD that would support viable private projects. Baystate West was conceived as a mixed use project, connecting two major department stores. SCBD financed initial land acquisition, oversaw the commitment of public improvements and tax abatement, and coordinated the agreement with Massachusetts Mutual Life Insurance Company to act as developer and to provide major equity and mortgage financing.

In San Diego, the local corporation is structured as a private membership organization open to public jurisdictions and private corporations. The corporation maintains a contract with the city to act as developer. In Philadelphia, a partnership between the city and the Chamber of Commerce resulted in the formation of the Philadelphia Industrial Development Corporation. Both parties occupy board seats and the group jointly selects additional civic and professional representatives.

---

[7] See "Baystate West," ULI *Project Reference File*, vol. 2, no. 9 (April-June 1972).

Several Duluth, Minnesota, private sector groups joined to form the Duluth Downtown Development Corporation (DDDC) in 1973 to work toward revitalizing the downtown area. Funds were solicited from property owners, businesses, financial institutions, labor unions, professionals, and other interested groups. The city and the corporation agreed that the corporation would act as the official citizens' advisory group for all public actions affecting downtown, formulate a planning and development program for the CBD, sustain business support for development projects, including provision of equity capital by local businesses, and assume functions normally undertaken by local government (identifying developers, obtaining appraisals, optioning land, and assisting with relocation).

A Michigan corporation that serves as a catalyst for downtown development is the Flint Area Conference, Inc. The corporation is a private nonprofit corporation financed partly by the Mott Foundation and partly by the General Motors Corporation. It is participating with the city in planning six central city projects, four of which, totaling nearly $200 million, are under construction.

In Jacksonville, Florida, a private nonprofit development corporation evolved from an ad hoc committee of the Chamber of Commerce, which was established to stimulate downtown development opportunities. The corporation, with the help of a predevelopment consultant, prepared development packages for selected projects by obtaining public and private commitments. The corporation was formed and staffed by the private sector for the first year (including $100,000 in nonrecoverable costs) to negotiate and carry out projects. Assisted by the corporation, the private sector provides the risk capital to participate in the development of projects and execute necessary leases. In return, the public sector is committed to pursuing federal and local development funds and to take other actions to stimulate private investment.

In Providence, Rhode Island, the Providence Foundation, a nonprofit corporation funded and supported by the city's business and civic leaders, regularly acts as a catalyst for development. The corporation identifies potential projects and coordinates government and private entities interested in the revitalization of downtown. It negotiated with local public and private leaders, federal funding agencies, and arts groups for the restoration and reuse of the Loew's State Theater in downtown.

The business community in Norfolk, Virginia, after a developer withdrew his proposal to construct Norfolk Gardens and with general inactivity in the pri-

4-8　Harbor Square, Duluth, Minnesota, is just one of several new projects in downtown Duluth.

vate sector, formed the Greater Norfolk Corporation (GNC), a local nonprofit organization dedicated to stimulating public/private reinvestment in the CBD. After evaluating project alternatives, GNC assisted with the implementation of the Freemason Harbor project, through the Norfolk Redevelopment and Housing Authority, by obtaining pledges of interim and long-term capital financing. Other projects GNC is now evaluating for implementation include the Exhibition Center for the Cousteau Society and the construction of a major mixed use project to be called Towne Point Center.

These examples depict the wide range of activities private nonprofit entities perform. Properly packaging development opportunities, however, requires direction and technical assistance from both the private sector and key public officials. Business groups can assist downtown development greatly with their monetary contributions, support, and enthusiasm, but the public/private commitments necessary to realize development opportunities must be carefully negotiated to ensure success.

Public or Quasi-Public Entities. Public corporations, in addition to the general advantages of corporate

48

status, have important powers that can be used to initiate downtown projects: the power of eminent domain, the power to sell tax-exempt revenue bonds, the right to receive revenues from the sale or lease of property, and the authority to levy property taxes, special assessments, or fees for specific public improvements. The power of eminent domain is generally granted to a public jurisdiction or authority to assemble land for development, but Missouri allows a city to delegate the power to a private corporation.[8] Eminent domain in some states can be used in areas that are not blighted or only somewhat blighted. The power to sell revenue bonds is typically given to an authority, but in some states it is given to commissions. The right to receive revenues from the sale or lease of property may be limited by law to properties in a special district (a downtown development authority, for example) or to properties zoned for a specific use (commercial, industrial, or residential).

A separate development corporation increases a city's effective management and its ability to coordinate public and private actions. Public or quasi-public corporations are often created to stimulate general downtown activity and may be empowered to support or participate in specific projects. A public corporation may become the "developer of last resort" when private investors show no interest.

The Penn's Landing Corporation in Philadelphia is a joint public/private corporation overseeing the development of a cultural, commercial, retail, and recreation project on the Delaware River. Involving several public and private agencies, corporations, and

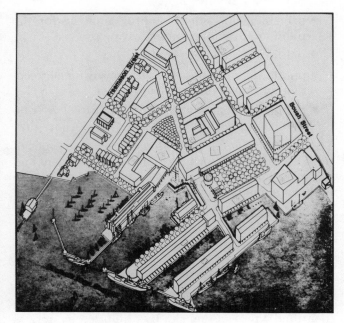

4-9   Freemason Harbor, Norfolk, Virginia—a bird's eye view.

investors, the Penn's Landing Corporation was organized by the Old Philadelphia Development Corporation (OPDC), a quasi-public development corporation. OPDC was formed in 1956 at the request of the city to coordinate private sector leadership in stimulating economic activity in Philadelphia's central city. OPDC provides the project management and direction at Penn's Landing and uses the Philadelphia Industrial Development Corporation, another nonprofit development corporation, to finance project construction and leasing.

The Centre City Development Corporation is a quasi-public nonprofit development corporation created to implement development in downtown San Diego. The corporation has contracted with the city of San Diego Redevelopment Agency to implement projects for the agency. The corporation performs all predevelopment and development activities: acquiring land in the agency's name, negotiating with developers for the agency, and entering into contracts for architectural, relocation, legal, planning, and economic services.

In 1971 the city of Pasadena began to develop conference, exhibition, and convention facilities through the creation of a public nonprofit corporation. The corporation sold lease-revenue bonds to acquire land and to construct conference facilities and parking. When additional assistance was required to attract a hotel to use the air rights over the city's parking structure, the corporation sold additional lease-revenue bonds to finance completion of public plazas and other components of the project.

The Harlem Development Corporation, a subsidiary of the New York State Urban Development Corporation, was formed to develop and oversee projects in Harlem. It uses public, semipublic, and private resources to develop this area of New York City. The corporation's goal is to stimulate business opportunities and to provide new job and training opportunities, particularly for the hard-core unemployed of Harlem. The major project now underway is the revitalization of the 125th Street commercial district through the corporation's seeking new development. Land for the project is largely publicly owned, and the corporation is seeking initial financing for much of the capital construction from public sources.

These examples illustrate the variety of roles for public and private participants in downtown development projects. In all cases, the successful implementation of a project requires each sector to retain certain key roles: political support in the public

---

[8] See pp. 171-172 for discussion of Missouri Chapter 353 provisions.

4-10 Pasadena's downtown—The conference, exhibition, and convention facilities and the hotel built on air rights are shown in the lower center. The superblock under construction is the Plaza Pasadena shopping mall.

sector and managerial and entrepreneurial skills in the private sector.

Identifying Potential Approaches to Development

From the groups interested in development an entity will be selected or formed to undertake actual planning and development of the project. The development entity must be carefully crafted to suit the particular requirements of the project in the specific conditions of its location and, as such, will differ for almost every project. In any case, a proper mix of interests and expertise is extremely important, for without it the project may fail—either during predevelopment or, worse, in operation. A government agency advertising for bids for a project in which private development interests are represented halfheartedly or not at all risks a lack of response from qualified developers, a lengthy negotiation process that may bog down after several rounds, and financial difficulties for both the city and developer once the project has been constructed.

Predevelopment activities can employ one of five basic techniques to meet the carefully defined ob-

jectives of the parties involved:

- private implementation of a project without direct public involvement
- private management of programming for the public portion of a public/private project
- public/private joint venture
- public management of programming for a project that will involve the private sector
- public implementation without direct private involvement.

The approaches reflect varying degrees and types of public and private participation in development and the spectrum of development entities that undertake predevelopment activities.

Private Implementation without Direct Public Involvement

In a strong market, private developers and investors prefer to proceed with development without soliciting public contributions or special assistance. Having identified a project that can be supported by normal market forces, the private sector has no incentive to seek public involvement beyond the usual regulatory requirements. For most developers, in fact, the added complexities, time, and financing problems are strong disincentives to public participation.

The Fidelity Mutual–Girard Bank office complex in Philadelphia exemplifies this situation. Initially, the Girard Bank, which adjoined the proposed development, had approached city government officials about using condemnation powers to assemble the high-priced property, though without a cost write-down. After assessing the complications of such an arrangement, the Girard Bank found it was easier to work out a joint arrangement with the Fidelity Mutual Life Insurance Company to proceed without government involvement. The procedure saved a great deal of time and resulted in a 37-story office complex providing both firms with attractive offices.

Thus, in private developments only the usual government involvement (plan review and regulatory control) is involved in the project, and no business deal needs to be structured between the public and private sector, because the private market is strong enough to allow the developer to proceed unassisted.

Private Management

In a project that is to combine the public and private sectors, a private development entity can be responsible for overall project development. A group of private developers and investors and a public entity sign a contract to develop specified public facilities as part of the total project. This technique has two advantages: It ensures that predevelopment and development activities are coordinated because one organization has central responsibility, and it ensures that public facilities are designed and constructed as part of the total project.

When it turns over responsibility for project direction to private parties, the public entity accepts the premise that the private group will competently evaluate, structure, and manage the project. It relies upon the private developer to package the project competently and effectively. Although the developer prepares market evaluations, cost estimates, and financing plans, the public entity should be capable of interpreting feasibility studies and financial analyses. The contract between the two entities should clearly spell out both parties' responsibilities and means of monitoring the other party.

Predevelopment for the Kentucky Center for the Arts in Louisville was completed in this manner. The state cultural complex was to be integrated with commercial uses and parking, all on land to be acquired by the commonwealth of Kentucky. After extensive discussions with potential developers, the

public sector chose Gerald D. Hines Interests to direct predevelopment activities for the entire complex. A Memorandum of Understanding between the two groups spelled out each party's commitments and designated Hines as developer consultant for the public improvements as well as the prime developer of private elements of the project. Hines agreed to reimburse the public sector a negotiated amount for services that would benefit the developer once the project was underway. Further, the public sector was under obligation to award the development management contract to Hines after predevelopment was completed.

Another such example is a development project underway in Washington, D.C. In 1974 the Dravo Corporation proposed development of the area surrounding its property in an underused, thinly populated area of warehouses and industrial property southwest of the Capitol building in Washington. After it studied the proposal, the city decided to promote development without using urban renewal funds. In 1977 the city commissioned Capitol Gateway Corporation, a subsidiary of Dravo Corporation, to prepare a development plan and feasibility studies for a 50-acre section of the development area. The city paid $200,000 for the preliminary study, which the City Council will review. If all parties agree, the Capitol Gateway Corporation will then prepare a

4-11   Fidelity Mutual–Girard Bank, Philadelphia.

4-12 Kentucky Center for the Arts, Louisville, is a combination of new and adaptive use. The new performing arts center is in the foreground, the dark buildings in the middle house visual arts in the adaptive use buildings and the office buildings to the upper left house retail space on the lower levels. A parking structure is shown in the upper right.

specific development proposal for a fee of $100,000. It subsequently will have the right of first refusal to carry out the proposal.

Public/Private Joint Venture

A development entity that directly combines, under the terms of a legally binding agreement, public and private project development is a joint venture. The joint venture partners agree on a specific formula for each one's contribution of financial resources and share of the proceeds. Formation of a joint venture does not preclude the designation of a single developer to manage predevelopment and development activities.

The new Stouffer Hotel in Dayton, Ohio, was developed jointly by public and private interests. The city of Dayton invested substantially in the construction of a convention center and 1,500-car parking garage on three of the four blocks in the Mid-Town Mart urban renewal area. The city knew from the outset that the convention center would fail without a first-quality hotel to provide sufficient rooms for large conventions and to upgrade the quality of hotel rooms available in downtown. The local government appointed a task force of business owners to obtain a hotel operator and review financing possibilities, and it appropriated funds for a market feasibility study.

After evaluating the advantages of short-term management agreements and long-term leases, the task force decided to seek an operator willing to sign a long-term lease. The city's nonprofit development corporation formed and funded one subsidiary corporation to assume the role of general partner in the venture and another subsidiary to purchase and lease back the site for the hotel. The task force took the lead in selling limited partnership units.

The active leadership of businessmen and participation by a public corporation aided this mixture of public and private objectives and interests in the development of a successful project. The final agreements between the public groups and the private hotel thus reflect the goals of all concerned. The city solicited significant involvement from the private sector early in the process and took advantage of joint efforts to package a project.

Public Management

Public management of a project that will subsequently involve the private sector is the conventional method of urban renewal. The public sector alone carries out predevelopment to the point where it offers a specific site on the market for development. Although traditional urban renewal activity is declin-ing, many downtown sites remain from past renewal projects, and a number of cities have supported locally sponsored renewal, sometimes in company with federally assisted programs such as Urban Development Action Grants.

Based on past experience, public agencies should be cautious about proceeding too far before involving the private sector. A site constrained by precise conditions for building height, location, and use may be unattractive to potential private developers. Private expertise in marketing and financing should be part of the package to ensure that the project is workable and that all possible objectives can be realized.

One variation of this development technique is a public entity's initiating a project and then selecting a private development team for advice on predevelopment. A renewal project in Iowa City, Iowa, had been dormant for some time when the city retained Zuchelli, Hunter and Associates, Inc., to repackage the project for private development. The firm revised the plans for dividing and using the 12-acre tract in downtown, and all parcels were sold after bids were solicited. An enclosed retail mall, hotel, parking, and a public plaza are currently under construction.

The Pennsylvania Avenue Development Corporation in Washington, D.C., is another example. The corporation, created by Congress to guide revitalization of Pennsylvania Avenue between the U.S. Capitol and the White House, proposes to lure private investment by making major public commitments to new development. It offered an entire city block just three blocks from the White House to private developers for a unified development project. The prospectus for the site describes the intended program and important objectives to be achieved with development. In response to the offering, a development team consisting of the Quadrangle Development Corporation, Aetna Life and Casualty, the Marriott Corporation, and the Rouse Company was selected. The project will include an 830-room hotel, office and retail space, 760 parking spaces, and preservation of the National Theatre.

In both these projects the public sector solicited significant private involvement early in the development process. With expert advice, the problems associated with old-style urban renewal were avoided and projects successfully initiated.

Public Implementation without Direct Private Involvement

The private sector is usually not involved when public entities construct buildings for their own use—convention centers, city halls, libraries, public office buildings, and fire stations, for example. The local

4-13   Iowa City, Iowa.

government hires the project architect and retains a contractor to construct the building; thus, involvement of the private sector is necessary only to design and construct the building. Funding comes directly from public monies or from a publicly secured source.

Determining the Development Approach for Public/Private Projects

When a project involving public and private interests is initiated, a development entity responsible for managing project plans and construction must be determined. Until recently the usual procedure was to formulate project objectives, employ consultants to perform economic feasibility studies, and then stage competitive bidding to select a developer to construct the project. The developer thus entered the picture after a major portion of predevelopment had been completed.

During the past decade, however, a number of more complex tools and sophisticated public/private partnerships have evolved; in some cases they include construction and property management. As a result, some entrepreneurial local governments are emerging as partners in development projects by adopting more businesslike behavior and seeking a direct share of the risks and rewards in certain development projects. This new approach means much earlier agreement between public and private sectors.

The greater willingness of the public sector to enter into more sophisticated arrangements with the private sector is partly the result of recognizing that downtown revitalization ultimately requires the attraction of new and continuing private investment. Many forms of public assistance may be needed to support the private market, but public assistance alone is not enough.

When the public sector and the private sector agree to cooperate in a development project, the strength of market activity in the downtown area largely determines the assignment of roles and the timing and method of selecting the developer. The weaker the market, the more necessary is public assistance to lure investors and public commitment to support private developers. Conversely, when the demand for development is strong and risks at a minimum, private developers are more willing to compete for projects.

The roles for the public and private sectors can overlap. It would be a mistake, however, for the city government and the developer to exchange roles. The private developer is the source of entrepreneurial and managerial skill and financing; the public sector is the principal source of political and public support for downtown development. Each participant in a productive partnership must clearly define mutually agreeable roles for a specific undertaking. When the public becomes intimately involved in the project, the need for clarity is paramount. The success of the project depends largely on how carefully the respective roles are defined and how well the actors play their parts.

The Development Team

Depending in part on the strength of the local market, a developer can be selected to participate in a public/private project at one of several times:

- at the beginning of the predevelopment stage so that he can participate in project conception and development

- after informal interviews and discussions with a number of prospects
- after a formal competition with proposals solicited by and submitted to a public body
- after competitive bidding but without the preparation of a preliminary design
- after competitive bidding and the preparation of a preliminary design.

For the first two methods, the developer is selected based on general qualifications and experience, and he is required to commit little or no money. The last three methods require his participation at his cost. For major projects these costs may be substantial, and the methods therefore are not attractive to developers unless the market is strong.

Regardless of the market, the public sector should select the development team for public/private projects early in the predevelopment stage. Early selection is especially important for a high-risk project in a poor market, because the decisions made during predevelopment affect the success of the project. For the developer, early involvement ensures coordination and proper management of a complex process and

4-14 1301 Pennsylvania Avenue, Washington, D.C., is a project developed under the aegis of the Pennsylvania Avenue Development Corporation and is a joint venture of the Quadrangle Development Corporation and Vector Realty Associates.

provides lead time to test the local market. For the public sector, it means that the initial concept and later evaluations and refinement are based on informed and experienced judgment. Even if a developer is not selected until after technical studies have been completed and the development agreement is being formulated, the public sector can be assured that decisions are based on realistic appraisals of financial feasibility. When a development team is not selected early, it should at least be available for consultation and advice.

Selecting a development team early has several advantages in terms of the project's financial feasibility:

- The developer will have ample opportunity to attract prospective tenants to the project, thus making the proposal more financially secure.

- The developer's direct control of project conception and refinement ensures a balance between creativity and financial soundness.

- The development team can plan the entire development process and more easily manage all activities.

- The developer can more easily meet the project's short- and long-term financial requirements because lenders will be assured of continued competence and accountability during the project.

- The developer can plan and coordinate construction and subcontracting.

- The development team is continually available to advise the public sector about any risks or opportunities.

- The developer can supply *reliable* projected cost estimates and operating budgets for various elements of the project.

Besides the expertise and competence that the development team brings to predevelopment, it can be a source of visionary ideas. It has an obligation, however, not to promise results that are impossible to achieve. The development team must devise creative solutions for downtown development yet interpret those solutions carefully to the community.

Public Funding of Predevelopment Activities

Involving a private developer early in the project may hinge on the public sector's willingness to underwrite some or all of the front-end expenses. For the developer, entering a partnership with a public entity usually means greater risks and longer lead times for project financing and construction. The developer normally spends as little front-end money as possible before securing short- and long-term financing, and

projects that require $100,000 or more before a developer is selected to begin a project are unlikely to attract developers' interest. Public entities, on the other hand, often become involved in long, drawn-out feasibility studies and negotiations before committing themselves to a specific approach and financial participation. To bridge this gap in operating styles, the government may choose to underwrite some of the private costs incurred during predevelopment, thus sharing the risks and rewards by its participation.

A city should consider supplying some of the initial programming costs for several important reasons. First, public funding ensures that broader community goals will be considered in the project's conception. Second, public funds entitle the local government, as a partner with private enterprise, to benefit from the data generated by predevelopment feasibility studies. Third, the local government can attract highly qualified developers to participate in a project that otherwise may be too risky.

A number of public/private arrangements stipulate that the local government will repay part of the costs incurred during predevelopment. In South Bend, Indiana, Gerald D. Hines Interests of Houston acted as development manager of a mixed use project. The city will reimburse Hines for the cost of initial feasibility studies as an initial advance against the fee of 10 percent of project costs allocated from public funds.

An arrangement made by the Pasadena [California] Redevelopment Agency is a recent variation in public sponsorship of predevelopment activity. On the recommendation of its economic consultant, the agency employed a marketing agent to seek a business that would locate its headquarters on a key parcel of land in downtown Pasadena. The fees will be credited to subsequent brokerage and/or development fees if they are earned when the development proceeds.

The Portland [Oregon] Development Commission, to stimulate long delayed construction of a hotel in the South Auditorium Renewal Project, signed an agreement with a development team (composed of the Moran Construction Company, developer/contractor; Urban Development Group, development managers and economic consultants; and Wolff, Zimmer, Gunsel and Frasca, architects and planners) to package the project. An advance of $70,000 for predevelopment costs was to be repaid to the commission if the project proceeded to construction. The development team prepared alternative designs, conducted preliminary discussions with hotel firms, and subsequently negotiated development and financing agreements between the commission, the Marriott Corporation, and financing sources.

4-15　South Auditorium Renewal Project, Portland, Oregon.

Project Conception

After the need for a project has been identified and participants organized, the parties involved must agree on the general approach, or development strategy, for the project. This initial concept defines the project's characteristics for later testing and refinement into a development program. A number of factors must be examined: the size of the building or buildings, probable capital costs, the requirement for equity financing, probable sources of financing, the role of public and private parties and their joint responsibilities, and the characteristics of other facilities in the project. Some basic studies will determine site, financial considerations, design, and other factors that shape the scope and type of project.

Identifying and Evaluating a Site

Sites for projects come from a number of sources. Those that were slated for other uses might be available, or public or private owners may promote the use of their properties.

Sites created for development by traditional urban renewal programs are often the source of land for public/private projects. In some cases these sites have been carefully designated and marketed realistically in response to specific market conditions. Often, however, the public sector has invested heavily in acquiring and preparing the sites and thus is attempting to market them for inappropriate uses to recover its costs. This situation is particularly true when site acquisition and clearance were in response to social issues that still stigmatize the site for any purpose. Owners of downtown properties may actively promote potential sites that require extensive preparation for development and may be too small or inappropriately shaped for major development. In either case the development team must be aware of the potential problems of any particular site.

To find an appropriate site, the development team must identify alternative sites and then assess them from a number of standpoints:

- general location with respect to downtown centers of activity and major transportation patterns
- cost of land acquisition, clearance, and site preparation
- potential difficulties in assembly—multiple ownerships, land with title problems, and dislocation of existing businesses and residences
- opportunities for relating development to adjacent areas where public use is already heavy—major streets, parks, pedestrian systems, and convention centers
- requirements for supporting public improvements such as access roads, malls or open spaces, or parking facilities
- unusual site conditions—either surface or subsurface—that can provide special opportunities or pose problems for development

MAP KEY

No.   Development

1   Convention Center Regional Bus/Auto Intercept (1981)
1   Hotel at Convention Center (N.D.*)
2   South Park Housing (1st Phase) and Park (1982/3)
3   Mixed Use Development (N.D.)
4   Office Building (1978)
5   Office Building (1980)
6   Office Building (1983)
7   Library Restoration (1983/4)
8   Jewelry Mart Facility (1981)
9   Old Auditorium/Office Building (1980)
10   Hill/Spring/4th/2nd Revitalization (N.D.)
11   Office Building (N.D.)
12   Office Building (N.D.)
13   MAT Associates Hotel (1981/2) (1981/2)
14   Exchange Square (1979)
15   Market-Rate Condominiums (1978–83)
16   Los Angeles World Trade Center (1974)
17   Security Pacific Plaza (1974)
18   Office Buildings (1980/82)
19   Angel's Flight Commercial (N.D.)
20   Senior Citizen Housing and Multi-Purpose Center (1980/82)
21   State Office Building (1981)
22   State Office Building (1982)
23   Auto Free Zone—Block 3 (1980)
24   GSA Parking Structure (1979)
25   Olvera Street/El Pueblo de Los Angeles (1978)
26   Union Station Regional Bus/Auto Intercept (1981)
    *N.D. = No Date

4-16   This map of the proposed downtown people mover in Los Angeles illustrates the new development opportunities presented by a major new transportation system.

- the property owner's willingness to sell or lease the property or to participate in development financially or as a tenant
- the size and shape of the site.

When public agencies evaluate sites to support downtown revitalization programs, the sites must also be evaluated in terms of the public objectives they might serve—perhaps linking existing areas of activity or infusing new activity into a declining sector of downtown. Site evaluation by public agencies, however, should be assisted by private sector expertise to judge realistically the feasibility of development. Even if a site is available and being marketed for development, it must be evaluated in terms of its meeting the goals of the project.

Site evaluation usually results in a single site's identification for further investigation. Occasionally one or two other sites will be considered viable alternatives through conceptualization, and occasionally the selected site will have options for adding or subtracting adjacent parcels, which will be evaluated as the project is analyzed and defined. Narrowing the options to a single best site reduces the need for multiple analysis and design studies.

Analyzing Economic Opportunities

The initial assessment of opportunities in the private market and potential public contributions test a project's potential uses.

Preliminary Economic Analysis

The preliminary analysis of economic opportunities does not have the scope of detailed market studies. The analysis includes interviews with knowledgeable public officials and private individuals who can identify possible tenants or uses for the project (merchants, city officials, leasing agents, and institutional officers) and a review of available data and studies to outline market opportunities.

If the development team is considering an office project, for example, the interviews will focus on gathering data about current space on the market, the lease terms of the space, the availability of vacant prime space, some identification of potential prime tenants, and the amount of support for financing and constructing a project. The team will also thoroughly analyze the regional market using available data and studies about population, income and expenditures or sales for the CBD, and primary competition.

At the same time, the development team may analyze constraints on and possibilities for development. This type of analysis detects the degree to which the project area's existing physical condition

and its relationship to the remainder of the CBD will affect market opportunities or require specialized study or treatment.

At this point the team's goal is to identify potential tenants rather than to negotiate preliminary leases. The interviews may define seven to ten possible tenants who are interested in office expansion. Although it is important to assess and encourage potential interest, no direct negotiations with potential tenants are held at this time. Out of these candidates one or two opportunities for prelease commitments, which will be negotiated during predevelopment, may be identified.

During this early examination the team considers the possible mix of the project's use and specific anchor tenants. It reviews the potential for office space, retail outlets, transient housing, recreation, entertainment, dining, and permanent housing to determine the project's potential components. In a mixed use project the components must support each other and establish a particular image for the project. A small retail development without nearby employees or residents to provide a ready market is seldom successful. Office users do not select a downtown location that provides no nearby place for out-of-town visitors to stay or for employees to shop, dine, or find entertainment. The development team attempts to achieve a marketable blend of activities that is greater than the sum of its parts.

The Settler's Landing renovation project in downtown Cleveland illustrates the need to clearly establish potential users. After 4 years and $7 million, the project was not fully leased because it was located several blocks from downtown shopping and other businesses and because the lack of other offices nearby discouraged retail and restaurant tenants. Despite those problems, the project has become a catalyst for further development. The state of Ohio is erecting a 600,000–square foot building across the street that will bring 2,000 workers per day into the area, and Standard Oil of Ohio has announced plans to locate a new headquarters building nearby. The venture may thus finally provide a return on investment.

Potential Public Contributions

At this early stage of project development, the development team must identify the potential range of local, state, or federal participation in the project—their share of physical components, financial contributions, and technical assistance.

The city of Pasadena, California, offers an example of a typical array of incentives for developers. The Pasadena Redevelopment Agency, representing the city of Pasadena, provides public assistance to private firms for the development of offices and facilities in the inner city. It offers reduced prices for land, constructs parking facilities and pedestrian walkways, provides offsite public improvements, represents the development in City Hall, prepares environmental impact statements, requests zoning changes and variances, obtains building permits and waivers of some fees, and reduces processing time.

A public/private project can often satisfy the demand for certain public facilities. In that case the public facility can create some market or financial leverage for private investment that would not be realized if the public facility were built on a separate site. And private users can share the open spaces, parking, and other amenities of a public facility. The key to combined space use is the ability it affords the developer of a mixed use project to avoid duplicating facilities and to minimize the requirements for open space that cannot be amortized by privately incurred debt. Thus, the impressive foyer, lobby, entryway, and parking garage the city needs can be shared with private users to amortize or set aside these aspects of the public/private development that cannot be amortized.

Some of the potential public uses a development team should explore include office space, sports complexes, convention facilities, meeting and exhibition space, performing arts centers, libraries, museums, and educational facilities. Quasi-public uses like private clubs, YMCAs, and public utilities are possibilities. A review of public office space gathered throughout the area may indicate a need to combine offices that are in dispersed locations or inadequate buildings. The city's capital improvements program may include proposed public facilities, and public officials may identify others during interviews.

The Greenville Commons project in Greenville, South Carolina, illustrates coordinated public facilities' stimulation of private development. In return for public sector participation (a partnership consisting of the Greenville Community Corporation and the Greenville Hyatt Corporation), private interests agreed to construct a 350-room hotel, a major office building, and retail space. The city agreed to construct at public cost a public parking garage to accommodate 550 vehicles and an enclosed, 45,000–square foot public civic center containing a banquet room, exhibition space, meeting rooms, a kitchen, and other enclosed space for the private sector's use. The city also agreed to fund and construct an enclosed and landscaped public atrium to integrate public and private uses.[9]

The city's contribution, costing approximately $7.5 million, recognized the substantial increase in taxes that would accrue to the city, the generation of sub-

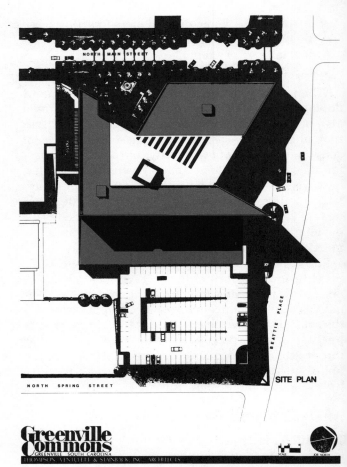

4-17 Greenville Commons—The parking structure for the complex is at the bottom of the plan with the convention center adjacent. An atrium connects the hotel and retail space (the triangle) to the IBM Building (the parallelogram).

stantial tourist and convention income, and the alleviation of blighted conditions in the downtown area. It also was the result of the willingness of the Greenville business community to commit and place at risk more than $4 million in equity to sponsor the construction of the hotel and office space.

Another example of the public sector's stimulating private development is the Rainbow Center Mall and Winter Garden in Niagara Falls, New York. Recognizing that an urban renewal project with seasonal appeal would not interest developers, the city provided a year-round glass-enclosed mall and a two-level pedestrian walkway, thereby broadening the project's market appeal and stimulating developers' interest.

The proposed street and park improvements along Pennsylvania Avenue in Washington, D.C., are also intended to attract and coincide with private invest-

[9] See appendix N for complete case study and appendix F for documents related to Greenville Commons.

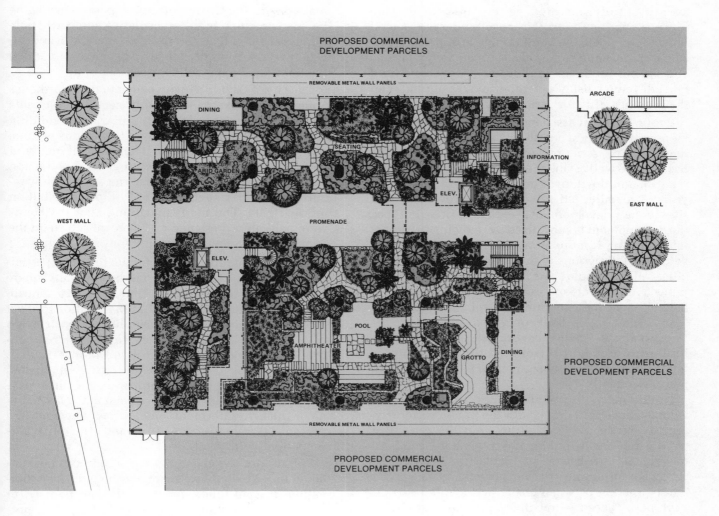

PROPOSED COMMERCIAL
DEVELOPMENT PARCELS

REMOVABLE METAL WALL PANELS

DINING

SEATING

ARID GARDEN

ARCADE

INFORMATION

ELEV.

WEST MALL

PROMENADE

EAST MALL

ELEV.

POOL

AMPHITHEATER

GROTTO

DINING

PROPOSED COMMERCIAL
DEVELOPMENT PARCELS

REMOVABLE METAL WALL PANELS

PROPOSED COMMERCIAL
DEVELOPMENT PARCELS

ment. The Pennsylvania Avenue Development Corporation will spend over $70 million to create four new parks and plazas and to transform the present sidewalks into tree-lined esplanades with brick paving, new signs, and street furniture.

In addition to identifying physical components, which the preceding examples tend to emphasize, the development team should also explore the prospects for the public sector's financial participation in a project. Three techniques can be employed to direct public monies into development projects: (1) local funding that does not require a referendum (new bonds, surplus monies, or indebtedness financing, for example); (2) monies gained through the bonding capacity of local government authorized in a referendum; and (3) state and federal funds under established programs.[10] The development team must analyze the city's current financial status to identify

4-18   The Winter Garden, a key element along the spine of Rainbow Center Mall in Niagara Falls, New York, is designed with side walls that can be removed as new commercial development is undertaken.

---

[10] See chapter 7, pp. 159-170 for detailed discussion of public financing assistance.

surplus funds, accrued general funds, unused revenue-sharing funds, the capacity to issue general obligation bonds, the bond ratings to support the issuance of revenue bonds, and the availability of state and federal funds for improvements. Essentially, it must develop a list of potential sources of funds and their applicability for various purposes.

Public financial assistance is becoming more common, particularly when the local market for private development is depressed. Some public financing has become well established during traditional urban renewal and downtown revitalization of the past 20 years. Typically, federal programs provide cleared sites for new development at reduced prices. In effect, the development is subsidized by reducing the cost of land, making it more attractive and feasible for development. Programs of this type still exist in many cities, either as holdovers from old federally assisted projects, as projects sponsored solely by the city, or as federally assisted community development projects. Many other cities have provided specific public improvements—pedestrian bridges, parking garages, underground connections to other downtown buildings or public transit, plazas, parks, or covered pedestrian malls.

Traditionally, the public sector and private developers have split costs, with the public sector paying for offsite public facilities and the developer paying for onsite public improvements. Such arrangements are becoming increasingly outmoded, partly because projects cover several blocks, making the distinction between onsite and offsite less relevant, partly because downtown projects may require public improvements as integrated components, and partly because public agencies have found more flexible ways to use public funds. Conversely, it is also true that private developers often agree to provide public improvements, sometimes as a condition for approval.

A significant concept of current development theory is that public expenditures should be directly tied to a commitment of much larger private investment; that is, the public expenditure should "leverage" private investment. In fact, the leverage ratio (private to public funds) is one of the aspects expressly considered in HUD's evaluation of projects under its Urban Development Action Grant program; projects with higher ratios of private to public investment are viewed more favorably, other things being equal. By requiring that public funds be leveraged, public agencies ensure that public investment generates known and immediate or short-term benefits and that public investment aids projects that require relatively small amounts of public assistance to make them attractive private investments. Leveraging tends to preclude highly speculative and costly public investments that do not result in significant private investment, as has too often been the case under the traditional approach to urban renewal.

The city of Dayton's involvement in the Courthouse Square project exemplifies public sector investments and incentives. The city built a plaza, the building substructures, and the below-grade portions of three new buildings for $3 million. It financed all front-end money for this construction with general obligation bonds and passed the costs on to the developer by requiring lease payments and a $1 million contribution for air rights. The funds remaining after the bonds were paid off represented a 12 percent return on the $1 million of assessed valuation for the air rights.

Another example of direct public financial participation in a much larger project is the Fountain Square South project in Cincinnati, Ohio. The city contributed over $18 million of the $84 million project through site assembly and demolition, construction of a parking garage and service deck, street improvements, and construction of second-level bridges connecting the complex to the city's established walkway system. The developer made three payments to the city—a land lease payment, a tax increment financing payment, and a direct payment of a percentage of net profits—to finance the city's participation in the project.

Public and private monies sometimes can be combined to enable otherwise impossible public participation. Private funds, for example, can be used to provide the matching share of funds for public programs. Under HUD's urban renewal program, private investment in parking garages was often used to meet the requirement for matching funds, and various sources of public development capital available to economically distressed areas can be packaged with private funds.

A combination of public and private monies can also overcome the public sector's problem of sustaining an adequate cash flow to meet debt service payments and operating and maintenance expenses. If both parties contribute, the public sector can pay debt service and the developer operating and maintenance expenses.

Another form of financial participation for the public sector is equity partnership in a project, which means that the public sector provides funds on its ownership position in the private development portions of the project. The public sector's financial participation would then be rewarded, perhaps with a percentage of net cash flow in the project. Keyser Marston Associates, Inc., and attorney Joseph Coomes assisted the city of Fairfield, California, in negotiating an agreement with Ernest W. Hahn, Inc., that includes such a net cash flow participation (above a stipulated minimum net cash flow to the developer).[11]

Public contributions can take a variety of forms of incentives to the developer.

- Density bonuses may allow more residential units or more commercial square footage than existing codes allow to give the private developer a competitive advantage over adjacent locations.

- Long-term leasing of ground owned by the public sector at low rates may avoid the problem of absorbing high costs for land and site assembly in the center city.

- Outright grants or long-term government-insured financing at below-market rates can improve the project's financial feasibility.

- The public sector can agree to rent space in the project at a guaranteed rate, thereby attracting other tenants.

- The abatement of real estate taxes or a reduction in the assessment can reduce annual real estate tax expenses and improve the project's financial feasibility.

- Transferring development rights and air rights from restricted or historical preservation areas adjacent to or within the project can allow building at higher densities and higher floor area ratios on the buildable portions of the site.

- Federal or local income tax incentives—for example, deducting all interest and associated

_____

[11] See appendix C for the agreement.

4-19   Courthouse Square, Dayton, Ohio.

fees during construction and accelerating depreciation rates—help to make the project financially viable.

- Public agencies can provide technical studies and plans that help to initiate and guide development projects.

As its final step in assessing the public contribution to a project, the development team must evaluate the public sector's positive commitment to downtown development. The city's track record on previous projects is the best clue—the extent to which potential public assistance has been documented by public plans and proposals, and positive action toward relieving regulatory obstacles to development. Civic leaders' commitment to cooperating with private developers assures the developer that public support promised will be delivered and that public response to resolve unforeseen problems will be positive.

Potential Private Contributions

While public funds can be instrumental in improving the investment atmosphere, particularly if the downtown economic market is weak, some private money may be needed to close the gap between the amount a developer normally finances and the total amount needed for the project. Many civic-minded local citizens or companies often invest personal or corporate funds in the equity requirements of a new downtown project. These funds are more than civic contributions or tax writeoffs: They are investments in the community's health. Local equity investors are willing to contribute funds if the principal can be recovered over a few years and to forgo or defer a return on the amount pledged. Because the project will generate new ad valorem taxes and business taxes, it will relieve property owners of an increased tax burden. The new project may also attract other development, which will in turn further increase the tax base.

4-20   A major commitment of funds to initial planning by the Mott Foundation, further funding by Mott through the Flint Neighborhood Improvement and Preservation Project, and an Urban Development Action Grant attracted the private investment required for the Riverfront Center, which will include offices, a hotel, shopping, a convention center, and community meeting spaces.

This kind of local contribution may be necessary only in a weak market or for a pioneer project. The catalytic effect of the initial equity investment has been demonstrated many times; that initial investment often has a snowball effect to secure additional financing.

The key to the success of such fund raising is strong local leadership. Perhaps a dominant business has enough power to attract similar contributions from other local businesses. If the private corporate structure is fragmented, however, it may be necessary to ask a respected local individual to be the initial investor. These commitments, whether from individuals or companies, will be instrumental in leveraging other funds. Combined with funds contributed by the developer and the public sector, they can be the successful formula for downtown development.

Both public and private parties must make firm commitments, or development could be disastrously aborted. Later attempts to develop a public/private project will be tainted by the bad example, and the downtown, as well as the entire community, will continue to decline.

Initiating Design

The design of a project begins with its first conception and continues throughout development. During predevelopment, design activities range from initial site evaluation to the preparation of preliminary plans detailed enough for financial analysis of the project. The first phase of predevelopment concentrates on determining the development's feasibility and suitability for the site and on defining its relationship to adjoining development or public spaces.

The initial design analysis begins with the known—the site—and explores the unknown—the size and combination of potential activities—to determine the possible ways that development can be contained and placed on the site. During this earliest phase, the development team can also evaluate alternative sites. At this point, design analysis addresses the major design parameters rather than details and the response to specific constraints of the site.

Site and Area Analysis

Site analysis determines the basic qualities of the site that will affect its potential for development and its relationship to the surrounding area. The analysis usually includes the designer's personal observation of the site to familiarize himself with the general location, the relationship at street level with surrounding buildings, exceptional views from the site, the relationships between pedestrian and open spaces, access to the site and area by highway or railroad, and

distinctive natural or man-made features. The developer interviews key officials to gather additional data that can be used to design alternative approaches to the development. He also reviews existing plans and data pertaining to the site—utility services, easements, covenants, deed restrictions, and subsurface conditions.

Frequently the designer documents his observations on a base drawing or map of the project area. These graphic presentations help to understand the composite picture of the proposed development.

Design Schematics

After the site and area analysis, the design group formulates several approaches to design in the form of alternative site development schematics. Based on initial findings of the economic and site analyses, these alternative schematics take into consideration land use, density, building type, relationship between activities, land assembly, open space and pedestrian networks, and vehicular circulation and parking. The design group and the client usually review and revise the schematics in work sessions during which numerous suggestions and observations are translated onto tissue overlays. The designer prepares overlays in rough sketches, usually with vague details and relationships between uses on the site.

One of the prime purposes of this initial effort is to gauge the project's marketability—its capability to be developed over time for interrelated uses that will attract both tenants and patrons for the proposed uses. The goal is to produce an initial proposal that expresses the project's physical character and major components. The team examines the degree to which site, parking, and access requirements, pedestrian circulation, and functional links affect each proposed use. It interprets results of initial marketability studies that define rough space quantities to obtain fairly specific building envelopes that can be assigned to components of the proposed site. This initial architectural interpretation should not be carried so far into the design process, however, that it becomes insensitive to the financial advantages of staged development that might be identified later.

Typically, schematics and graphic materials are prepared at a scale of $1'' = 100'$, with the scale depending primarily on the size of the area being studied. They usually include a calculation of land area, by use, and of approximate amount of space that is represented in the schematic. This "space yield" is stated in dwelling units or square footage of floor area, by use. The initial design schematics should be prepared in sufficient detail to show the three-dimensional characteristics of the proposed development.

The initial schematics, the alternative programs for the site, and their major implications (in terms of accessibility, circulation, open spaces, and relationships to other areas) furnish the basic material to formulate a development strategy. This initial design has several direct benefits that start moving the project toward implementation:

- It tests the site's capacity to accommodate alternative proposals for development and reveals the limits that may be imposed by parking, open space, and building space standards.

- If site limitations unreasonably confine development or densities, the designer can investigate methods of expanding the site.

- When the development team considers the relationship between the site and adjoining uses, it may discover new opportunities for development.

- The size and shape of the site may suggest particular advantages or disadvantages for certain activities, requiring a review of marketability.

- The initial definition of pedestrian and vehicular access and circulation, and open spaces may reveal the need for greater development to support the costs of such facilities or a change in the activities to require fewer facilities.

Formulating a Development Strategy

After initial economic and design studies have outlined several approaches to development, the development team must formulate a preliminary conception of the project or projects worth investigating further. Subsequent analyses will test and refine the overall concept of the potential project.

The development strategy may take a number of approaches. A single project may quickly take shape and require further detailing and evaluation only to refine the major concept. The major approach to a project may have several possible variations to investigate further (possible tradeoffs in use, site size, or participation by public and private interests). Two or three alternative approaches to development may warrant more or less equal attention.

It is to the developer's benefit to limit the number of options for further study. Doing so not only reduces the magnitude of future analyses and expenditures but also simplifies relationships among the interested parties. Large projects, however, are complex and important enough to require careful study before the developer settles on a single approach to the project. At the end of project conception, questions about the project's feasibility and desirability may require further work before they can be adequately answered.

The development strategy should contain the following elements:
- a clear expression of the project's principal function (e.g., a convention center/hotel, a retail mall with offices in the downtown core)
- a development program that lists the components of the project, their approximate square footage, probable responsibility (public or private), possible staging, and potential major tenants
- schematic designs that identify the boundaries of the site and indicate specific links to adjoining development
- a definition of the nature and amount of public participation in the project
- a first estimate of income and expenses, debt service, and equity return for each participating party and the probable sources of funding for each use element
- a general plan and schedule for proceeding with the project, including target dates for completion of detailed planning and design, construction, and occupancy, the nature of the development group, and important decisions to be made.

This information is a preliminary, general statement rather than a highly detailed description. It is not necessarily a formal proposal; in fact, much of it may not even be committed to paper. For this development strategy to be credible, however, the developer may also include the results of certain analyses in more detail to support the strategy's feasibility—a very quick or a more refined pro forma financial analysis for a complex project to test its financial feasibility or special investigations of potentially troublesome legal, site, or other problems. At any rate, its outline should be clear enough to provide the basis for phase II of predevelopment activities. At this point, the developer's aim is to have a list of options that can eventually be narrowed down to a specified project and development program.

A more detailed statement of development strategy may be necessary if public participation is important to the success of the project. To obtain even preliminary approval from the public sector requires a documented presentation to public officials. If the developer wishes to become the official developer of public portions of the project or to receive predevelopment funding from public sources, he may have to provide even more material to describe the potential project. A more detailed presentation may also be necessary to a potential major tenant or investor. Formal presentations for various purposes should be kept deliberately rough to keep later evaluation and refinement flexible.

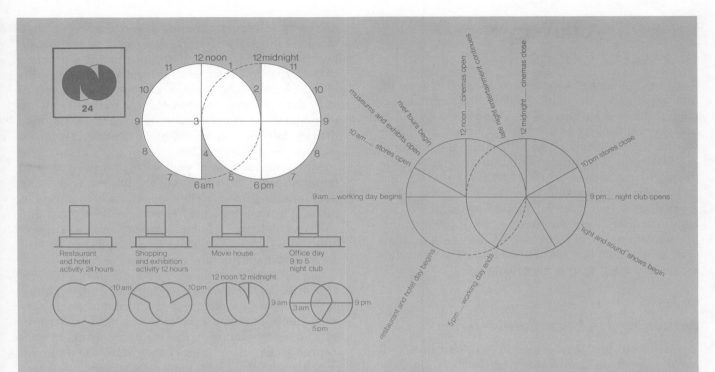

24

12 noon   12 midnight

museums and exhibits open
river tours begin
12 noon.....cinemas open
late night entertainment continues
12 midnight.....cinemas close
10 am......stores open
10 pm stores close
9 am.....working day begins
9 pm.....night club opens
restaurant and hotel day begins
5 pm.....working day ends
"light and sound" shows begin

Restaurant
and hotel
activity 24 hours

Shopping
and exhibition
activity 12 hours

Movie house

Office day
9 to 5
night club

10 am
10 pm
12 noon 12 midnight
9 am
9 pm
3 am
5 pm

4-21   A 24-hour design cycle is a major objective of downtown projects.

Phase II: Analysis of Project Concept

The development strategies now are subjected to intensive analysis, evaluation, detailing, and refinement to arrive at a project plan. This section describes the general factors to be analyzed and the major studies to be conducted, and discusses the nature of the final plan and implementation program. While three major analyses—market, planning and design, and financial (discussed below)—are conducted in great depth, four general factors—regulatory and legal considerations, environmental considerations, timing, and political factors—also receive special attention. The conclusions of these four general studies are needed for the three major studies.

General Factors

Regulatory and Legal Considerations

Federal, state, and local laws and policies can have a major impact on a downtown project. While they must be applied to the specific development proposed to see whether they will influence the project's feasibility, federal or state tax laws may encourage or discourage certain types of development, and economic development programs may provide special market opportunities. Local zoning requirements and local building codes may have peculiarities that affect the design concept. State and local laws and policies regarding the use of air rights, public land or building leasing, and operation and management of public spaces may preclude certain alternatives' being available for consideration. Antidiscrimination and equal opportunity policies affect planning, construction, and operation of the project. Constraints on the use of the site—uncertain land titles, easements, deed restrictions, and covenants—may delay the project or constrain desirable use of the land. During this phase of predevelopment, the developer must be quite certain of the impact these factors will have on the project.

Environmental Considerations

Both onsite and offsite environmental concerns may affect the project's cost, timing, and even feasibility. Physical conditions at the site may dictate a number of environmental studies. Soil and subsoil conditions will have an impact on the size and proportions of the project. Archeological artifacts may be discovered in old sections of the CBD.

The project's effects on the general environment must be studied. Air pollution from automobiles driven by employees, shoppers, and visitors may be a factor, especially if traffic causes congestion on poorly designed streets. If air pollution is a problem in the city where the project is located, the provisions of the Clean Air Act of 1970 and the amendments of 1977 may govern the size and type of development. Rainfall runoff from commercial areas could produce flows greater than storm drainage capacity, requiring expensive improvements.

An environmental impact statement (EIS) may be required for a federally assisted project with more than local impact or in states specifically requiring it. Preparing the report may entail special studies and could result in extended and expensive delays; therefore, the need for an EIS should be determined early to allow sufficient time for studies and reviews.

Energy requirements may also affect the project. The efficiency of energy use, the availability of alternative sources of energy, and the cost of energy requirements must be carefully analyzed. Orienting buildings to reduce energy requirements could substantially cut project costs but may also constrain the arrangement of uses. A consolidated energy system for both public and private components of a project may cut costs but also require coordination of public and private construction and operation. Even the location of the energy supply in a project affects costs.

Timing and Sequence

Each project must be timed and phased to reflect market demands, financing requirements, and design constraints. Construction and occupancy of large projects, or those with public participation, may be carried out in phases over several years. The project must be timed to find financing at desirable rates and to reach completion when the market will absorb more space, and the sequence of project construction must be planned to avoid overbuilding or outpacing market demands at each step.

Private financing will be made available in phases tied to market absorption. Public entities participating in the project may require several fiscal years to raise necessary funds. These considerations may dictate a design that can be implemented in phases. In turn, the design may constrain the ways the project can be separated into phases suitable for marketing and financing.

Timing of development may also have to be related to the anticipated development schedule for other new, competitive projects. No developer wants head-to-head competition with another new development and therefore would prefer a schedule that allows project completion either before or after occupancy of competitive projects.

4-22   Colonial American National Bank Building, Roanoke, Virginia.

The time it takes the local government to process development applications may also affect the project's timing; a slow permitting process adds measurably to indirect administrative costs. Some jurisdictions are now willing to commit themselves to specific time periods, after which an application is automatically approved. For example, in the contract for land sale between the Roanoke Redevelopment and Housing Authority and the partnership formed by Gerald D. Hines Interests and Colonial American National Bank, both parties were assigned firm dates for completion of certain activities. The developer had 120 days to submit construction plans for approval, and the public agency had to approve or reject the plans within 90 days or they would be considered legally valid.

Political Factors

Projects in which a private developer is strongly associated with the public sector depend on securing and maintaining firm community support, especially to withstand shifts in governmental policies and personnel. Garnering early political support is a must if the project is to be approved. This exercise may prove unsettling to the developer accustomed to marketing his project as a potentially profitable business venture. Instead, he must convince the public as a whole and specific civic groups that the project will be an asset to the community.

In initial project conception, the development team sounds out the strength of public support for general participation and for a specific role. During the second phase of predevelopment, the development team attempts to establish a positive attitude in the community toward the project, which will translate into broad political support. It also seeks to strengthen its relationships with important public officials and with technical personnel who must approve the project.

During this phase, the developer probes the political and legal position of the public sector to reveal any weaknesses that could threaten the development process or undermine public commitments. If it finds a problem, the developer works with the public sector to solve it, even to the point of formulating new approaches to public involvement or encouraging new municipal or state legislation.

Major Studies

Detailed analyses of market demands, intensive planning and design studies, and analyses of financing requirements are undertaken to evaluate and refine the development strategy. They are usually prepared by consultants with knowledge in those areas.

Market Analysis

At this point the development team must study general market conditions and the demand for specific types of activities the project could fulfill. Analyses of regional population trends and characteristics, employment projections, distribution patterns, and data about disposable income supply clues to the general market. Specific market studies determine the demand for a highly specialized use such as a convention center or the magnitude of demand for retail, office, and hotel space. Such studies estimate and project retail sales by type of goods, the demand for office space and housing, and vacancy rates.

The method of evaluating potential markets for specific uses varies greatly among developers; no single method can be advocated. A number of common factors should be examined in testing the market for additional retail development, however.

- the annual growth rate of retail sales in the region and any shifts in retail activity resulting from the construction of suburban shopping centers
- the relationship of the regional growth rate of retail sales and population (sales increasing faster than population indicates rising levels of disposable income)
- the downtown area's historic share of regional retail sales, relative to overall shifts in population within the metropolitan area
- shifts in retail activity within the downtown area and their impact on the economy of downtown

- trends in the type of retail activity in the downtown area—specialty retail outlets, personal services, or competition with regional and community shopping centers
- total current and projected employment downtown, its geographic location, and the disposable income of downtown employees
- the impact of publicly sponsored development (beautification, demolition, street furniture) in stabilizing the erosion of retail sales or supporting further expansion
- the existing mix of commercial activity in the downtown area—retail versus business versus personal services
- expansion and modernization plans and possible new major tenants in the downtown such as department stores

Based on the estimates and projections of sales and expenditures, the developer can estimate square footage that will fulfill the demand and allocate space to shopper goods (department, clothing, furniture, and variety stores) and convenience goods (drugs, food, beverages).[12]

The market for downtown office space can be analyzed by surveying existing conditions and identifying circumstances likely to alter the demand for office space. Surveys of existing office space should include a number of factors for each office building in the CBD: total leasable square footage, amount of square footage occupied by primary and secondary tenants, amount of vacant space, rent and lease terms of existing or future tenants, and information about plans for future building renovation. A survey of firms likely to consider expansion or relocation (banks, corporations, manufacturers, and government agencies) and their current lease terms will indicate future demand for space. The analysis should also include the downtown's historic share of regional office demand and current and projected trends in business functions.

The market for downtown hotel space can be evaluated by surveying the age of existing hotels, the total number of rooms, the annual occupancy rate, the yearly number of rooms sold, the average room rate, the annual gross income, and the meeting room capacity. Total air and rail passengers can be used to gauge trends in hotel demand. Trends in nonagricultural employment indicate the number of business

[12] See Virginia A. Criste and Warren W. Wilson, "Downtown Retail Centers," *Market Research for Shopping Centers*, ed. Ruben A. Roca (New York: International Council of Shopping Centers, 1980), pp. 55–74.

4-23   Baystate West—Marriott Hotel

travelers likely to require hotel accommodations. Part of the analysis is to estimate current demand and project future demand. Since the demand for hotel space and the convention business are closely related, the analysis should focus on the ability of new public or private convention facilities to attract conferences and conventions, commercial business travelers, and tourists at rates that will sustain a new hotel in the central business district. However, there may also be a demand for smaller "carriage trade" or "businessmen" hotels.

The results of these investigations forecast the quantities of institutional and speculative space that the market might support in excess of prelease commitments from major tenants. These estimates should reflect any trends and changes in space use like an increase in space for meeting rooms, customer services, and reception areas or a decrease in storage capacity with the advent of electronic memory/ storage equipment.

The market analysis will define the range of possibilities for attracting activities and tenants to a downtown project. Often the results are qualified, that is, with ranges of potential demand depending on defined conditions, either of the market or of the project. The analysis may conclude, for example, that a project of a certain magnitude or including certain components may attract a larger share of the regional market than projects without such amenities. Or it may conclude that other planned projects would positively or negatively affect the marketability. The Baystate West project in Springfield, Massachusetts, was originally planned as a retail and office complex. Because a special market study indicated strong support for a first-class hotel, a 270-room facility was added to the development program.

An assessment of the market, to be most useful, must acknowledge such possibilities and evaluate their potential influence. A useful analysis provides technical data the developer can use to decide the nature and specific components of the project. It will also add credence to the proposal in negotiations with public and private participants in development.

Planning and Design Studies

Phase II involves two kinds of planning and design work: to refine the design concept and to undertake specialized studies of important elements. Both tasks build on the initial schematic, analysis, and development strategy of phase I. While the strategy establishes design relationships and variations in the main approach or alternatives to that approach, phase II details, tests, and refines the concept and its alternatives to arrive at a preliminary design plan.

Since this design work takes place more or less concurrently with the detailed market analysis, the interim results of the market analysis should be fed back periodically into the design process and vice versa. If one option is to expand the project to incorporate more office space, the detailed design analysis will have to determine the physical implications of land and building space and costs while the market analysis tests the downtown's capacity to absorb the extra space. If an alternative calls for incorporating major amounts of residential space, the development team must assess the physical, legal, and financial aspects at the same time it evaluates the marketability of such space.

Because the project is still being financed with front-end money, the second phase of design activity should be neither highly detailed nor costly. The principal design effort in this phase should be to provide enough analysis of options and alternatives upon which to base a reasoned decision. The questions raised during the first phase must be answered by some additional data and a somewhat more detailed analysis but only to the extent necessary for the preparation of a preliminary design for the project. The preliminary design is not a polished design or set of detailed drawings; it is an interim statement of design decisions based on market and other factors.

Preliminary designs are more specific than phase I schematics in that they describe the size, shape, and relationship of structures on the site. They are sufficiently detailed to clearly identify programmed uses, open spaces, pedestrian ways, vehicular access, parking, and building configuration. The drawings usually include line or block drawings for all principal levels, schematic sections, elevations, and possibly a perspective or isometric view or study model to indicate the three-dimensional character of the complex in its environs. These plans and graphic materials are best prepared at a minimum scale of 1 inch to 100 feet for the overall study area and 1 inch to 40 feet for

specific structures within the area. Plans at this level of detail can be measured with reasonable accuracy to determine the "fit" between program objectives and "yield" of particular design solutions.

Specialized planning and design studies conducted during this phase may include investigations of any potential problem areas identified by the initial site analysis or design work. Such factors as traffic accessibility, availability and cost of parking space, streetscape relationships, unusual subsurface conditions, or special climatic characteristics can be critical to the decisions made on the preliminary design.

Traffic and parking studies are often conducted at this time. The importance of transportation studies cannot be stressed too strongly for a central city project. Unlike suburban locations, where roads provide the only access of any importance, an established CBD is served by a number of transportation systems—automobile, bus, train, and possibly subway. And the more public transportation service provided, the more important pedestrian access becomes. For most projects in a downtown area, the handling of pedestrian circulation to and from parking garages and other transportation terminals is a key element in the design.

Project designers must be able to identify major access routes, available parking, and main pedestrian routes to link the project with the downtown circulation system. Special traffic and parking studies can identify the components of the system and project and evaluate alternatives within the project. The key is to strike a balance between the activities in the project and their demands for access and parking. Certain mixes of office, residential, shopping, and entertainment space might use parking space most efficiently because their peak requirements for access and parking differ. Existing offsite parking may be available to absorb the overflow.

Special design studies may be necessary to determine the relationships that should be established with the area surrounding the project. Integrating the project with the entire downtown can improve its marketability and help to revitalize the CBD. Design studies at this time may point to the need for concurrent public programs to renovate nearby pedestrian areas or buildings.

Peachtree Center in Atlanta, Georgia, illustrates such integration. The new Regency Hyatt House on one side of Peachtree Street was combined with development of the opposite side of the street to revitalize the area. In contrast, the walled fortress created by some mixed use developments has reduced projects' internal and external effectiveness. To many professionals, Omni International, also in Atlanta, is

4-24 Peachtree Center (foreground) includes the Regency Hyatt, the first of the new atrium hotels designed by John Portman, and the tall cylinder of the Peachtree Plaza. In the background is Omni International.

just such an enclosed, protected environment that has little relationship to the rest of downtown.

Other specialized studies may examine subsurface or climatic conditions peculiar to the site or area that may affect the project's financial feasibility. The presence of rock formations, high water tables, and other underground conditions may increase costs for foundation work or underground parking. Climatic conditions may dictate covered pedestrian spaces and paths or affect the costs for heating and cooling. Alternative building arrangements or parking provisions may be necessary before the final design can be determined.

Financial Studies

The project now is sufficiently well defined to prepare a preliminary estimate of costs, refine the pro forma analysis, and identify funding sources. Although earlier rough calculations have been made, decisions can now be based on better and more detailed data. Design and market studies have begun to narrow the alternatives and to provide more certain data on components and activities. Project cost estimates, equity and mortgage requirements, and public capital requirements can now be calculated with some degree of certainty to aid in determining the final project plan.

Preliminary Cost Estimates

Unit costs for each component of the project are the bases for cost estimates. For example, the cost of a hotel is calculated by estimating the cost of construction, furnishings, fixtures, and equipment per room. These cost estimates should be prepared by qualified cost estimators, who are often available on the developer's construction management staff, from a general contractor employed for this purpose, or from the staff of larger architectural-engineering firms. Cost estimates should be calculated within 10 percent of the final cost figures even at the most preliminary stages of analysis. There is a great tendency to adjust cost figures based on new or more refined information without challenging the original estimate. The effects are undesirable—either lending a sense of economic feasibility where it does not exist or constraining any change in the project that may increase costs.

Preliminary cost estimates for the entire project and its alternatives are usually presented in a separate memorandum. They are not made public at this time because project programming is still undecided and because premature exposure may hamper the successful structuring of a development program. State law may require public review of cost figures if the public sector will participate in the project. In this case, the alternative cost estimate should be carefully presented as one aspect of many that should be considered in determining a final project plan. The tradeoffs between the costs of marketing the project and its financial effectiveness should be clearly portrayed.

Refined Pro Forma Analysis

Any earlier rough pro forma analyses should be refined at this point. The detailed pro forma analysis must be done when a preferred design and development program has been selected.

Preliminary Identification of Funding Sources

After preliminary cost estimates are prepared, the developer can consider funding sources for the project and its alternatives. Potential major tenants who can contribute to the basic financing structure and who will attract other tenants can be identified from the initial list prepared in phase I, which has been continually expanded and refined. For the private com-

Stouffer Dayton Plaza—Financial Arrangements

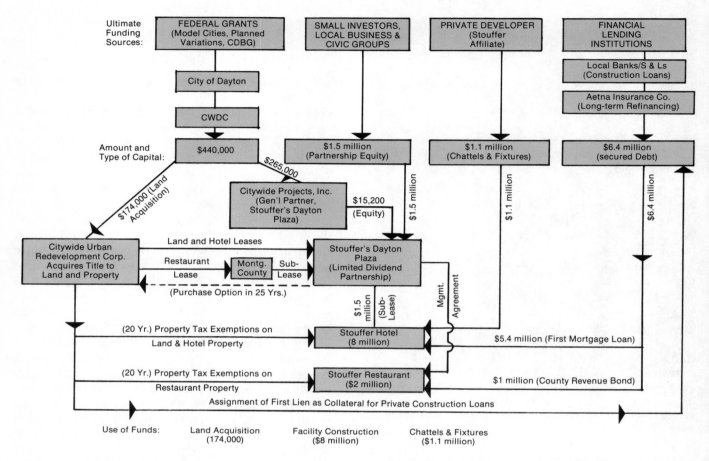

4-25   Downtown projects require complex funding arrangements as this diagram for Stouffer's Dayton Plaza illustrates.

ponents of a project, the developer should define certain conditions for each alternative:

- *for projects containing a significant amount of retail space:* one or more major tenants—generally, creditworthy retail anchors whose base rentals will substantially contribute toward fully amortizing the permanent loan for the project—before financing

- *for large office projects:* one or more anchor tenants and preleasing of a significant portion of space before financing, identification of other tenants, determination of special requirements (display areas, meeting and conference rooms), attainable rent levels, and the time it will take to fully lease the project

- *for hotel space:* a precommitted operating/management agreement or lease (generally by an established, financially sound hotel management company) before financing.

It is usually not possible at this time to obtain a firm commitment from a major or anchor tenant, but the developer must be certain that such space users can be attracted to the project or its alternatives. It would not be productive to consider an alternative calling for a major retail anchor if market studies cannot identify a potential candidate. It is more likely, however, that each alternative will affect the *probability* of attracting such a tenant; this probability then adds to the pros and cons considered for each alternative. Some alternatives are simply not possible without a specific anchor tenant. For example, in the absence of a firm commitment from a department store, an alternative requiring this use could not be pursued. Other options must be available in a complex mixed use project where the loss of a major tenant may require a complete redesign.

Private sources of equity for each alternative are also evaluated at this time. The private parties may wish to syndicate a for-profit group or offer a limited partnership. The developer may contribute equity. The major tenants may be equity participants as well. Such preliminary financial decisions must be reached for each critical financial element, even at this preliminary point of project financing.

The developer must also identify potential public financing for each alternative, either as direct contributions of facilities or a component of overall development financing. For each source of public financial participation, the developer must assess potential political problems. For instance, funds supplied from community development block grants could invite disruptions from neighborhood groups. The developer must evaluate the advantages and disadvantages of the alternatives.

Financing requirements can change significantly as economic conditions, the money market, government policy, and the investment objectives of individuals and institutions change. They vary depending on the capabilities and financial qualifications of the developer, the local market, and other circumstances. For example, projects financed on a speculative basis may have special requirements imposed in the mortgage terms—perhaps a base floor loan with specified leasing targets as a condition for full funding.

Preferred Design and Development Program

The development team at this point in predevelopment has determined the following information for each of the alternatives defined in the development strategy:

- site requirements, cost, and potential difficulties in acquiring property
- a preliminary design portraying the project in two- and three-dimensional form
- the potential advantages or disadvantages of the project in terms of regulatory, environmental, timing, and political issues
- an assessment of the project's market, including the size and characteristics of the demand
- a development program listing all components, other space allocations, and the general character
- cost estimates for constructing and equipping the project described in the development program
- a refined financial pro forma analysis
- a preliminary definition of public and private financing sources and potential problems concerning them.

With this information in hand, the development team must agree on a preferred project. In the process of weighing the pros and cons for each alternative, the team may form a composite project from two or more alternatives. To the extent that a preferred project contains a risk that one part may not succeed, the development team should structure a contingency approach. This approach is often necessary for a large, complex project that includes major public facilities or requires construction over many years. Thus, a project incorporating a 20-story office tower in an uncertain market may require an option for a smaller tower that will meet future market conditions, with the necessary reduction in parking space or increase in space for other activities. The developer should define such potential adjustments to the project for later use as necessary.

When the market is strong and capable public partners are involved, the decision on a preferred plan may come easily. More often, however, it comes with difficulty after carefully studying the implications of each alternative. The private development team is likely to push for a rapid decision, a clear definition of the development program, and a firm commitment for public participation. The public entity, however, often wishes to scrutinize each alternative in detail, postpone a firm decision in favor of qualified or conditional commitments, and ask for firm commitments for private financing that are unobtainable at this point. It may require commitments from key anchor tenants or operators before it will promise financial support. Making the final decision thus becomes difficult and time-consuming. The object, however, is to agree on a single project and to define that project in terms of its scope, financial feasibility, timing, and management. The final product may include several elements: the final preliminary design, development schedules, an operating plan, cost estimates, a financial pro forma analysis, the financing program, and a cost/benefit analysis. It culminates in the preparation for negotiation between private and public parties.

Final Preliminary Design

During this stage, the sketches and plans for the alternatives are refined into a final plan for the selected project development program. The primary purposes of this process are to ascertain that the development program (which may have been altered from any previously defined program) can be realized on the selected site and to define any consequent adjustments to the program. Typically, this plan is more specific in terms of size, shape, and relationship of

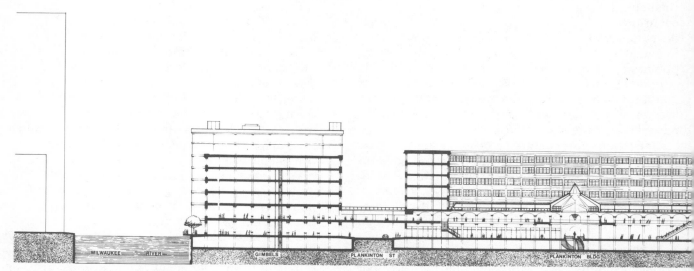

4-26   This cross-section of the Milwaukee Retail Center, with its continuous pedestrian route, suggests the problems regarding management and maintenance of common public/private areas that require early consideration during predevelopment.

structures on the site, but it still stops short of detailed floor plans or building elevations. Some drawings may also be made at this time for the development team to present during negotiations for final project packaging.

Development Schedules

After the concerned parties have approved the final preliminary design, the development team prepares a detailed schedule for execution of the project. The schedule should identify, by time periods, the specific development activities both public and private parties are required to execute. It should include an explanation of the significance of each activity in successfully completing the project. And it should provide a basis for the final financing program for the public and private parties.

To prepare useful pro forma and cash flow analyses for specific portions of the project, the development schedule must be sufficiently detailed to assign explicit responsibilities to each party. The timing of each phase affects the capital budget and borrowing obligations of public and private parties. The city must have substantial lead time to prepare a bond prospectus and to enter the municipal bond market to secure funds for capital projects; the amount of lead time available will suggest the most appropriate type

of municipal financing. It may be necessary to redesign a project because constraints on public indebtedness require a simpler project. Some elements originally planned for initial construction may be postponed to enhance sound overall financing.

Likewise, the financing consequences of certain elements that would normally be private uses can impose an inordinate risk on the private developer. It is often necessary to reduce high risks and increase low yields by publicly funding parts of development components (for example, exhibition space, meeting rooms, or the lobby in a hotel/convention complex). Marginally cost-effective private uses like eating, drinking, and entertainment establishments can also be rescheduled to later stages of development after enough high-yield components like office and retail establishments are in operation.

Operating Plan for Public Facilities

One of the biggest deficiencies in public/private ventures is failing to recognize the need for postdevelopment operation and maintenance. Often the public sector does not recognize the continuing cost of providing a high level of maintenance after a facility is built. The development team must thus identify operating expenditures that will be required for all public uses.

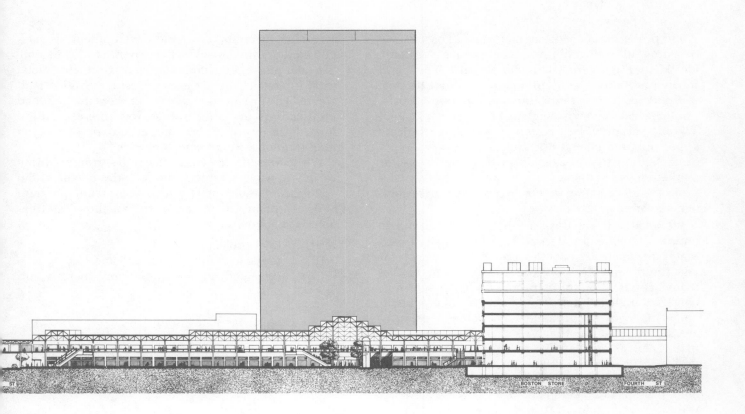

Operating funds are the most difficult funds for local governments to provide consistently (even though increased tax revenue from the private portions of the project should justify continuing public expenditures to maintain public areas and facilities). One solution to this problem is for the municipality to hire the private developer to maintain public areas in a joint development. Such an agreement is more economical because two management entities will not be necessary for the same site and because it avoids uneven levels of maintenance or later disagreements. Most developers prefer maintenance by the private sector of a joint project. The likelihood of such an arrangement should be decided even though a specific agreement is not negotiated at this stage.

Cost Estimates

Based on the latest preliminary design, development schedule, and refined cost estimates, the development team must recalculate project costs for all components of the preferred project and for the whole project. The public capital program, which may require bonding, and public operating costs for public components are included. The completed cost estimate summarizes all private costs and public costs for the project.

Financial Pro Forma Analysis

The financial pro forma analysis and the cash flow analysis (following section) constitute the two most important tools for evaluating the financial merits of a project. The pro forma analysis combines estimates of all capital and operating costs and revenues to paint a financial picture of the entire project in operation. Its object is to indicate the probability of a successful project by indicating expected income, operating expenses, and net operating income.

The analysis is a process for determining a project's financial feasibility. From a first cut it evolves through several refinements to an adopted pro forma analysis and budget for design and cost control. It is refined further after preliminary cost estimates until it is ultimately adopted and backed up by contracts. Preliminary pro forma analyses can be used to determine optimal financing conditions and to negotiate public contributions that will make the project financially possible.

The pro forma analysis is best accomplished after cost estimates have been prepared and after basic assignments of responsibilities for construction and operation have been agreed upon. Most developers, however, insist on various degrees of pro forma analysis much earlier to evaluate alternatives, using broad assumptions if necessary.

The pro forma analysis has many uses. The exercise of listing all costs and revenues provides a realistic checklist of financing factors for all participants and forces preliminary assumptions (e.g., interest rates, profit percentages, rental income, operating costs, public/private cost sharing) to be explicitly stated. The analysis provides a bottom line that may indicate either program changes or greater public participation. And finally, the analysis furnishes a useful marketing tool to display the financial viability of the project and its components to potential investors, tenants, or operators.[13]

Included in the analysis are estimates of costs, revenues, and financing terms. The detailed cost estimates for construction of the project include costs for site improvements, building construction, professional services, administration and management, construction loan interest and financing charges, and an estimate of supportable land value. Operating costs are based on the type of management and maintenance required for each component of the project. Specialists estimate the costs using national and local costs, recognizing that complex development projects often entail operating costs (pedestrian walkways and enclosed atriums, for example) that are not found in typical buildings. Similarly, revenues for each component are based on national and local trends. The financing terms and conditions that will be required by the long-term mortgagee and any points or fees required by lenders according to conditions of the money market must be anticipated.

The estimator's judgments about these costs and revenues are the basic assumptions for the analysis. These assumptions must be recorded as part of the analysis because they are often critical to a project's feasibility. In fact, these assumptions about financing terms, sharing of costs for site improvement, operating responsibilities, and even tenant improvements may be subject to negotiation between the parties; therefore, the failure to be precise in their recordation can lead to later misunderstandings.

The pro forma analysis can be calculated to obtain a variety of bottom lines. The most direct tabulation is a sum equaling the private developer's profit. However, when public participation includes writing down land costs for the project site, the pro forma analysis can be worked using an assumed profit level to obtain the residual land values and/or site improvement costs that the project can support. This calculation provides the rationale for negotiating a site subsidy from the public sector.

Often public interests consider proceeds from the sale of land as a measure of the public value created by the project, when in fact the long-term tax value and secondary benefits of private development are usually more significant. In fact, postponing such income to a later phase of development may stimulate crucial early interest in the project and result in higher land values. The pro forma analysis can show the financial implications of using public, low-interest capital funding in return for private participants' assuming long-term operating responsibilities.

While a pro forma analysis can be structured in a variety of ways, a typical one includes a general description of the project and development program and a summary of project costs, revenues, and expenses as follows:

(i)   total project costs
(ii)   projected annual gross income
(iii)   projected annual operating expenses and taxes
(iv)   net income before debt service
(v)   mortgage loan amount
(vi)   annual mortgage payment (debt service)
(vii) cash equity investment
(viii) net cash flow
(ix)   cash-on-cash return (before income tax considerations).

Total project costs (i) include direct costs (for land and construction) and indirect costs (for professional services, tenant allowances, direct administration of marketing, miscellaneous administration, land, and interest and financing charges).

Construction costs include both site improvements and direct building costs. Site improvements include grading and excavation, paving, storm drainage, sanitary sewer, water service, lighting, signs, and landscaping. Direct building costs cover foundations, floors on grade, the superstructure (above-grade structures), roofing, exterior walls, partitions, wall finishes, floor finishes, ceiling finishes, communications systems, fixed equipment, HVAC (heating, ventilation, and air conditioning), sprinklers, plumbing, electrical works, and special project features (fountains, sculptures, etc.). The contractor's fee is often included in direct costs, but it and/or the construction management fee can be included in indirect costs.

---

[13] For a more thorough discussion of pro forma financial analysis and discounted cash flow analysis, see David Sirota, *Essentials of Real Estate Investment* (Chicago: Real Estate Education Company, 1978); Lincoln W. North, *Real Estate Investment Analysis and Valuation* (Winnipeg: Saults and Pollard, 1976); John L. Hysom, *Financial Feasibility Analysis in The Real Estate Handbook* (Homewood, Illinois: Dow Jones–Irwin, 1980); and Urban Land Institute, *Optimizing Development Profits in Large Scale Real Estate Projects,* Technical Bulletin 67 (Washington, D.C.: ULI–the Urban Land Institute, 1972).

Indirect costs must be added to land, site improvements, and direct construction costs to arrive at the total project cost. They are a significant portion of overall project costs.

Professional services include fees for architects, engineers, consultants who prepare drawings for tenant improvements, landscape architects, and interior designers. A small contingency is often provided for professional services.

The developer's overhead attributable to the project—amounts to be expended for accountants, the project director, the construction manager, leasing brokers and agents, legal services, advertising and promotion, other leasing fees, lease-up expenses, taxes, and insurance—is included in indirect costs.

Contingency reserves are critically important; they cover changes and costs not specifically anticipated but normally occurring during the development process. A contingency amount is generally established for indirect costs, which is in addition to a contingency included in the contractor's direct cost and an overall contingency fund.

Interest and financing expenses associated with construction loans and other interim financing are additional indirect costs. They include charges for interest during construction, appraisals, legal fees, construction loan fees (or points), permanent loan fees, mortgage banker fees, inspection fees, settlement costs, escrow fees, and a contingency for other interest and financing charges (including, if appropriate, an interest reserve to carry the project until it is leased to the point where the project will carry itself).

To determine the net present value of the project (for loan financing) and the expected rate of return on equity to be invested in the project, future revenues, expenses, and net cash flows must be forecast. In complex projects involving investment over a period of years and substantial variance in revenues and expenses from year to year, it may be necessary to prepare a year-by-year projection of cash outlays and income and then compute a net present value or rate of return by discounting future annual cash flows. More typically, it is assumed that revenues and expenses will stabilize after the first or second year of operation, and, therefore, calculations of net present value and rate of return are based on this forecast of stabilized revenue and expense, which is then assumed to remain constant over the life of the project.

Annual gross income (ii) is projected by forecasting the rents and other income obtainable from the project and adjusting that figure for vacancy and collection losses. Annual operating expenses and property taxes are then estimated. Annual operating expenses (iii) include janitorial services, security, utilities, maintenance charges for common areas, insurance, general maintenance (building, site, elevators, parking lot), any management fees, and any leasing fees after initial lease-up.

Net income before debt service (iv) is then determined by subtracting total annual operating expenses and property taxes (iii) from annual gross income (ii). To determine the value of the project for mortgage financing purposes, the net annual income is capitalized.

The mortgage loan amount (v) is then determined by applying the current loan-to-value ratio for the type of project being analyzed. (Lenders typically will lend up to 75 percent of a project's value.) Given the loan amount, term, and interest rate supportable, one can calculate the loan constant and resultant annual mortgage payment required (vi) and the amount of cash equity investment required for the project. Cash equity required (vii) is determined by subtracting the loan amount (v) from total project costs (i). The annual mortgage payment (vi) is calculated by applying current loan terms (period of loan, interest rate, and resultant loan constant) to the amount of the loan. Loan amortization tables are commonly available or the following formula can be used.

$$\text{loan payment} = \text{loan amount} \times \frac{\text{interest rate}}{1 - (1 + \text{interest rate})^n}$$

where n equals the number of years over which the loan is to be amortized.

To determine net cash flow (viii) from the project, the annual mortgage payment (vi) is subtracted from net income before debt service (iv). If the project involves other claims against project income (for example, subordinated ground leases or additional payments to the lender above normal debt service as a result of lender participation), these payments are also subtracted from net income before debt service. The remainder is the project net cash flow (viii) available to the equity investor(s) as the annual cash return on investment. The cash-on-cash return (ix) can then be calculated by dividing the net cash flow (viii) by the amount of cash equity investment (vii).

Financing Program and Cash Flow Analysis

The next, somewhat concurrent step in determining the feasibility and desirability of the preferred development project is the establishment of a financing program that identifies all requirements for private and public funding in each phase of development and operation. The program reflects the assumptions and findings of the pro forma analysis and development schedule. The principal purpose of the financing program in projects involving public/private partnerships is to reach a full understanding between the public and private participants about each party's financial obligations.

Part of the financing program deals with the provision and maintenance of common areas. The understanding worked out in the preparation of the operating plan for the public facility is reflected in the way the financial program treats funding for these areas.

A cash flow analysis is based on the initial formulation of the financial program to evaluate its feasibility. The cash flow analysis defines cash requirements at any point during the life of the project. Its primary purpose is to test the project's capability to generate a sufficient return to make it a viable investment compared to other investment opportunities. The focus on investment over time is its essential difference from the pro forma analysis.[14]

The cash flow analysis can also be considered a refinement of the pro forma analysis, representing a more comprehensive financial evaluation. It does not account for other reasons that a project may be desirable—civic betterment or corporate image—but it does provide potential equity and long-term investors with an assurance that the project will stand on its own financial feet. It also provides a way to identify the need for greater front-end or long-term public participation.

The technique of cash flow analysis most used in the real estate industry today is the discounted cash flow internal rate of return method. Basically, deficits—e.g., initial capital investment, carrying costs in excess of income, and net incomes—are discounted back to a specific point—e.g., initiation of the project—and calculated as a single rate of return for the entire project. For a full return to be calculated, it is customary to assume a sale (or refinance) point—e.g., 6th, 10th, 15th year—to reflect (and discount back to the present) the profit (or loss) from appreciation and debt reduction upon sale. Increasingly these analyses are computerized, particularly for complex multiuse projects. Computerization is particularly useful in testing sensitivities to such variables as absorption, appreciation rate, alternate methods of financing, and impact of financial participation by the public sector.

Cost/Benefit Analysis

A cost/benefit analysis is the public's technique for evaluating the "profit" to the community from public investments. It attempts to quantify public costs (in some cases these costs cannot be measured in dollars) and compare them to benefits (which again may not be quantifiable). Meaningful cost/benefit analyses for public/private development ventures can be very difficult to devise. For example, the construction of a new hotel may be seen as a source of totally new taxes, but the transient tax income generated by a new hotel does not represent totally new income because many of the guests expected to use the new hotel are already served by existing hotels. To the extent that the new hotel will capture market growth rather than absorb an existing market, the hotel will generate new revenues. This situation is also true of other forms of development such as restaurants, office buildings, and retail stores.

The cost/benefit analysis must also consider the staging of the project. Often public costs are concentrated in the first phase of a project, which also has the greatest risk and lowest return on investment. Such public costs are difficult to allocate to specific private components of the development because they often arise from public facilities that will serve all phases of the development and because there is no absolute assurance that later phases of private development will materialize. If public benefits depend too much on the second or third phases of development, it may be difficult to establish the public feasibility of the project in strictly financial terms. A thorough cost/benefit analysis should also include a complete discussion of costs and benefits that cannot be quantified for subjective evaluations, e.g., an improved working and living environment.[15]

The cost/benefit analysis is often the final accounting of project feasibility. This analysis identifies the impact of the project on the municipality and its citizens, including its effects on the municipality's operating and capital budgets and direct, indirect, and induced benefits. Direct benefits include the jobs provided by construction of the project and by businesses that will locate there, and the tax revenues the project will generate. Indirect effects include the stimulation to existing local businesses from new business or visitors and shoppers attracted by the new businesses. Induced effects arise from wages spent by the new employees.

Another view of the project's benefits is the effect of not proceeding with the proposed development. With a continued decline in the physical and economic condition of the CBD, the city's overall financial health is adversely affected. Conversely, if the proposed project stimulates downtown economic expan-

[14] Ibid.

[15] See Peter G. Sassone and William A. Schaffer, *Cost-Benefit Analysis: A Handbook* (New York: Academic Press, 1978) and Michael J. Frost, *How to Use Cost Benefit Analysis in Project Appraisal* (New York: John Wiley & Sons, 1975) for insight into cost-benefit methodology.

sion, the city's financial situation is positively affected. Thus, the project's benefits may be greater than those measured by the project alone.

For example, a hotel project might generate 250 short-term construction jobs and 350 permanent jobs. It would pay city property taxes and special taxes (occupancy taxes imposed by the city or state, for example). These are the direct benefits. Its indirect benefits include purchases of food supplies, laundry and other goods, and services for the hotel, worth several million dollars annually. The project's induced effects are the expenditures of hotel employees for locally produced goods and services, which create additional jobs and income for the citizens as a whole.

While it is fairly easy to quantify and predict direct and indirect benefits, the induced benefits are usually more difficult to quantify because the rate at which income is recaptured differs for each community. Induced benefits, however, may have the most important effect on the economic health of the community.

Preparation for Negotiation

Preparing the final preliminary design, schedule, operating plan, and financial plan establishes the project's physical and financial feasibility. The preparation for negotiations between public and private participants includes certain concluding activities: a final design; a staging, parcelization, and disposition program; and a detailed financing program.

The final design expresses the results of the various feasibility analyses of the preferred project. Drawings that can be used to describe the proposed project in public meetings are prepared. They include:

- diagrammatic single-line floor plans, which indicate horizontal space use within the building(s)
- section drawings, which represent vertical space use within the building(s)
- a perspective rendering and/or elevation drawings of the site, which is the artist's conception of the appearance of the project and its relationship to the surrounding area
- a site plan, which shows suggested landscaping, traffic flow, and building location and size
- possibly a conceptual model.

Design plan graphics are usually prepared at a scale of 1 inch to 40 feet, or a similar scale that shows considerable detail. Drawings are of sufficient quality to use in reports and presentations to potential lenders or tenants. The designer may also prepare technical or analytical drawings to illustrate staging, parcelization, and property disposition. Together, these draw-

4-27 Conceptual graphics like this artist's sketch for Plaza Pasadena or a model are prepared at this stage of the design process.

ings illustrate the preferred development concept in more detail than at any previous time.

The parcelization plan describes the sections of the project that can be developed separately. It identifies parcels that will be developed by individual development entities and defines the parts of the development schedule for each stage of construction. For complex projects, the plan may have to be three-dimensional, depicting vertical as well as horizontal parcelization. The parcelization plan must be detailed enough that the site survey team can use it; it is also a reference for standards and controls embodied in deed covenants.

In formulating the financing program, the public and private participants must determine allocations for capital funding and for initial cash outlays. The private developer will wish to defer costs as much as possible to minimize front-end cash requirements. The public participant, on the other hand, may be willing to provide more initial cash financing in lieu of long-term operating and maintenance costs, which may be assigned to the private participant.

Phase III: Packaging the Final Project

All of the designs, analyses, and plans from the earlier phases of predevelopment must now be translated into binding agreements that commit each party to management and financial obligations. The commitments may deal with land disposition, conditional leasing, commitments for public funds, and the final development agreement between all parties.[16]

The negotiations that take place at this time presuppose an intimate knowledge of the evaluation that has gone before and a willingness to deal with economic realities. Some amount of trust on the part of the development team, the public officials, and citizens must be present. Any of the parties involved in the negotiations may employ consultants experienced in complicated real estate transactions, either to conduct negotiations or to advise negotiators.

Site Acquisition and Disposition

Method of Site Assembly

Acquiring the site on which the downtown development will take place is one of the most critical phases of predevelopment, particularly for large mixed use developments in built-up business districts. Most developers will not sign land acquisition agreements or general development agreements until they have secured sufficient lease commitments to receive permanent financing on the project. If the developer cannot secure tenants, the projects likely will not materialize. Land can be acquired at three times: (1) before project initiation, (2) during predevelopment, with the public sector often bearing the risk before the development agreements are executed, or (3) during design, which takes place in the development stage.

Many times, a suitable site must be assembled from diverse parcels with different owners and buildings that must be vacated and demolished. Parcels of land often have several owners, sometimes in highly fragmented estates with remote heirs. Some property may only be purchased subject to restrictions or lease obligations. Cutting through this pattern of land holdings can be a difficult, time-consuming task that requires the developer to be a diplomat.

Either party can assemble land for a public/private project, depending on local circumstances. Both approaches have advantages. The appropriate means of site acquisition should be determined only after all options have been considered and the costs, time constraints, need for public subsidy, feasibility of purchase from individual owners, and modifications in site boundaries have been carefully weighed.

If the project site is not publicly owned by this stage of predevelopment, the land purchase normally is consummated after the agreements with the developer are executed. It is generally not in the public interest to acquire land until the development agreement is executed. As predevelopment proceeds, however, the public sector might gain sufficient confidence to allow acquisition of land before the agreement is executed. For example, in the Greenville [South Carolina] Commons project, the local government because confident enough that the project would proceed that the municipality began acquiring land before the agreements were executed.[17] In other localities, where agreements must be negotiated and executed before land acquisition, land is assembled concurrently with the design of the project during the development stage.

Private developers can acquire land for downtown development using one of three approaches. If prices are escalating rapidly because of speculation, the developer can assemble the required parcels as rapidly and quietly as possible. If few parcels are involved, if the developer can deal with the owners relatively directly, and if all owners agree to sell, this approach is the quickest. When many parcels are involved, the developer should acquire key parcels first. Local developers or brokers are often familiar with specific owners' attitudes and objectives and can be very helpful in determining a strategy for acquisition.

The second approach is the opposite: Real estate investors gradually purchase properties as they are made available. For the outside developer, this method is clearly unsatisfactory, although he may find a local investor who has assembled a site and is willing to sell it or associate himself with the project. For a developer undertaking several projects, however, it may be possible to proceed with one site while waiting for another site to be assembled this way.

The third approach is to assemble a site from property owners who are interested in equity participation in the project. This approach is possible even if only some of the owners are interested. Participation is normally based on the proportional share of the property value to the total contribution required.

The private developer can secure land by a contract of lease or sale or by an option agreement. In a contract the buyer and seller agree to terms and conditions for sale or lease, whereas in an option agreement the prospective buyer has the right, for a consideration and within a specified time period, to lease or purchase the property at a prearranged price.

---

[16] See appendix D for an example of a preliminary development commitment agreement that would form the basis of all final binding agreements.

[17] See appendix N for a case study of Greenville Commons.

4-28 This model of Greenville Commons, Greenville, South Carolina, illustrates the value of models in depicting the relationship between major elements of a multiuse downtown project.

Contracts are more common but require significantly greater expenditures of nonrecoverable capital. Because the purchase or lease is made early, however, it may be a lower total cost. The option agreement, on the other hand, obtains control of the property at a fraction of the purchase price. The property owner agrees to sell or lease the land, but the completion of the agreement is deferred to a specified time. The purchaser has the option not to complete the transaction, but if he does not, he will lose the amount invested so far.

Land Acquisition and Disposition Agreements

In many public/private downtown projects, a site that one party has acquired must be transferred to the other party. Typically, public land will be sold or leased to a developer, but in some instances, private participants may own part or all of a site that a public agency will acquire or lease for the project. The site may have been acquired before or during predevelopment and may have been cleared and pre-

pared for development with certain improvements. Or the site may be identified for acquisition after a development agreement has been signed.

In any event, acquisition or disposition agreements involve transferring land rights or air rights between participants. An agreement to acquire and then dispose of the property may be necessary unless one party already holds the site.[18] Disposition agreements normally contain the following elements:

- the scope of development
- a legal description of the property and a site map
- the purchase price, subject to all the terms, covenants, and conditions of the land sales contract
- the form of property conveyance, including type of deed, time and place for delivery of deed, apportionment of current taxes, and provisions for recordation of the deed
- the amount required for a deposit as security for the performance of obligations, the form it is to

[18] See appendix E for an example of a land disposition agreement.

83

take (cash, certified check, or irrevocable letter of credit), and the terms for its application to the purchase price, retention by the city, or return to the contracting entity

- a schedule of performance for both parties, including a stipulated time for beginning and completing improvements and submitting construction plans
- the maximum time allowable for approving construction plans, deadlines for the city's action on changes in construction plans, and the time allowable for submitting evidence of equity capital and mortgage financing
- restrictions upon the use of the property, including the period of duration
- rights and remedies available to the contracting parties.

The agreement also may provide for grants of easements to the property, allowing the right of entry for utility service and access to the property. Leases covering ground or air rights could also provide for covenants and agreements to use the top deck of the city structure as the lower floor of the private building or to join any pipes, fittings, valves, or other related fixtures to the city-installed fire protection system.

Agreements transferring rights from a public to a private party may be categorized according to the method of payment. Many techniques have been used singly or in combination: deferred land payment, residual land value and land writedown, public participation in cash flow (which might include ground leases), land contracts with contingencies, and air rights with computed or noncomputed value.

Deferred Land Payment

In this method, the public entity holding the land agrees to transfer it to the developer in installments, based on previously approved stages of development. In effect, the public entity acts as a land bank, disbursing development sites as needed. It agrees to forgo immediate benefits in return for greater value—and higher tax receipts—over the long run or as an incentive to develop property.

Normally, land values for the private uses in the intended project are negotiated before the development stage begins so that parcels that will be developed over a period of time can be acquired at the predetermined cost. The benefit of this technique is that the developer does not have to pay for sites until they are scheduled for development. It reduces the requirement for front-end cash and decreases debt service on capital expenditures.

Residual Land Value and Land Value Writedown

The term "residual value," in its simplest form, refers to the difference between the value of a project, calculated by capitalizing the net income, and the capital cost of producing or replacing it. Although it may be used to determine the value of the project excluding land, it is most commonly used to determine the value of a site. This type of agreement establishes a price for land consistent with the type of development proposed. Land value thus reflects specific public objectives for the project rather than simply its market value.

Analyzing the residual value of the land can establish the proper value to be used for the "writedown" (the reduction of price to a level the proposed development can support). Most traditional urban renewal projects used land writedown to attract developers to renewal sites. For example, the value of an office development that cost $13 million to construct on land purchased for $4 million may differ from the $17 million total cost. If net income equals $2 million and the capitalization rate is 12 percent (the present value of future income), the project has a value of $16.7 million ($2 million divided by 0.12), which indicates a land writedown requirement of $300,000. Residual land value is determined by subtracting the cost of replacing the project (calculated as the income of the project, in present dollars) from the capitalized value of the project. The remainder, or residual, represents the maximum value of the land itself.

Some assumptions are necessary when residual value is used to appraise land. The first is that a developer will be relatively conservative about estimating his income, because that income must support the cost of the land. The second is that the value of the project is based on the "highest and best use" of the site, the highest degree of development permitted by the zoning regulations.

Public Participation in Cash Flow

This agreement calls for the public land holder to waive payments for land and site improvements in return for participation in the proceeds of development and operation. In effect, the public entity contributes land and improvements to the project, thereby establishing an equity position and benefiting from cash flow just as any other equity participant. The developer therefore is not required to invest large amounts of front-end capital, and the public entity will be directly involved in the long-term operation of the project.

Two examples illustrate the use of this technique. In the Greenville Commons project in Greenville,

South Carolina, the city government agreed to construct and equip the public portions of the complex and lease them to the private development entity. The city's investment would be repaid in two ways. A minimum annual amount of $35,000 would be paid in monthly installments for the first 20 years of operation to cover use of the public atrium, civic center, and parking garage. This payment is subordinated to the first mortgage in the private components of the project but not to any other obligations. In addition to this minimum fixed payment, the developer would pay the city $55,000 per year for 20 years ($1.1 million total) from the project's available cash flow. If available cash flow in any year is less than $110,000, the available cash flow would be divided equally between the city and the developer, with the amount due accumulating as an unpaid balance to be paid after the 20-year period.[19]

Under the land disposition agreement between the Norfolk Redevelopment and Housing Authority and Freemason Harbor Associates, the Authority will lease parcels from time to time to the Associates for development. The term of the lease will be from 40 to 60 years, depending on the developer's or lender's current requirements. The rental for the project will be computed each year according to the residual land value for that parcel and period. Each year the net operating income will be capitalized at 14 percent to determine total project value. The parties agreed that 17 percent of the total value would be ascribed to land and that the maximum payment would be 8 percent of that land value. Rental will be payable from the next year's cash flow (net operating income less total debt service), up to 40 percent of the net cash flow. In addition, if net cash flow to the project exceeds 10 percent of the value of improvements (83 percent of total project value) after rent has been allocated, the Authority will be entitled to 50 percent of that profit.

Land Contracts with Contingencies

The use of land contracts containing contingencies protecting the parties is another method used to negotiate land agreements between public and private entities. For example, in the Los Angeles Bunker Hill project, the contingency contract recognizes the risk to the developer of pioneering development in a new sector by selling the land at a below-market price. If the capitalized value of the project exceeds cost by a certain level, however, the developer must make an additional payment to the Redevelopment Agency. The contract allows the developer to take control of the land in two phases, but an escalation factor is built into the land price for the second phase.

Because a contingency contract does not firmly commit both parties to a specific course of action, it is difficult to determine the leverage of private monies using the undetermined public figures. Determining the project's capital worth is also difficult. Hence, the potential return on real estate investment cannot be predicted easily.

---

[19] See appendix F for this agreement.

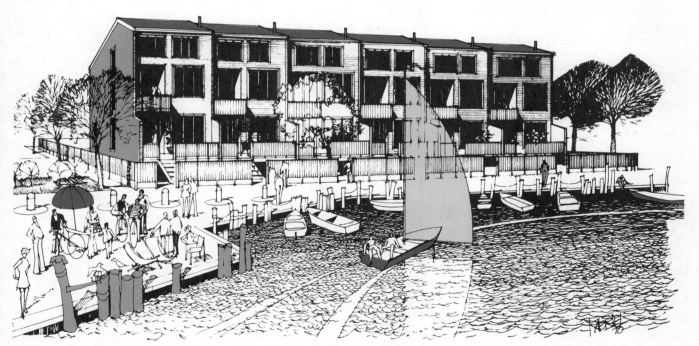

4-29 Townhouses under construction at Freemason Harbor, Norfolk, Virginia.

Air Rights

Public entities can use air rights over public land or facilities to induce developers to consider projects where the risk without assistance is too great in proportion to potential return. Because the ground-level public use is charged with the value of the land, the developer's initial cost is reduced. For example, a private development built over a public facility such as a parking garage or a highway can be initiated by merely transferring the rights to develop in that space to the private party for a specified consideration. The value assigned to the use of the air space could be computed at a high value or, as an incentive to development, proffered at virtually no cost to the developer.

A good example of such a project is the Hartford Civic Center. The Hartford Redevelopment Authority owned the land parcels for both the hotel and coliseum/commercial development. Aetna Life and Casualty Insurance Company and the city of Hartford prepared plans for a combined project integrating private retail and office space with a public coliseum, exhibition space, and a parking garage. Aetna has the right to lease air rights over the city parking garage and exhibition halls for 50 years, with an option to renew for another 40 years. The agreement includes a leasehold over the elevators leading to the private space, easements for structural support elements, and access over city property.[20]

Another example is Fountain Square South in Cincinnati. The city is assembling and clearing the site and providing garage and service decks. It will retain ownership of the land and lease air rights for private development of a hotel, office building, and retail space to the developer for $200,000 per year for 65 years. A form of tax increment financing will permit the developer to pay the taxes on the increased value of the development directly to the city for 30 years. In addition to the lease payment and the tax increment payment, the developer will pay directly to the city a percentage of the net profits on the project. These three payments plus the revenue from the publicly operated parking garage will finance the city's $18 million participation in the project.

Preliminary Commitments for Tenants and Private Financing

Before signing an agreement with the public entity, the private developer will seek tentative commitments from the major tenants and lenders whom he has identified earlier as interested in the project. Neither tenants nor lenders are likely to give binding commitments at this time, because design work and public commitments have not reached the point that definite space allocations and costs are available. The developer will nevertheless solicit tentative commitments to ensure both public and private participants that the project is receiving significant support in the market and from lending institutions.

Securing leasing commitments is important to the development process as a whole and to persuade lenders that the project is viable. One of the key requirements for obtaining financing is an indication of interest by potential tenants, especially tenants like department stores or hotels who will occupy a major part of the space or who can be expected to attract other tenants. Most developers' objective is to obtain leasing agreements or understandings for 40 to 60 percent of the space in the project by the time construction starts. The developer may also seek these tenants' equity participation in the project; their financial interests will require long negotiation before agreements are reached.

For a project incorporating one or more office buildings, the development team seeks prime tenants among banks or other financial institutions, corporate headquarters or regional offices, or major accounting and law firms. In a project emphasizing retail sales, one or more department stores or major specialty stores will be the anchor. Department stores that are part of national or regional chains usually have employees who identify potential sites for new stores or negotiate basic terms for space in a project. Most larger hotel and motel chains have development officers who can evaluate potential sites and projects.

A potential tenant's willingness to commit itself firmly to a project is greater as the project moves closer to actual construction. Because tenants are usually reluctant to make firm commitments during predevelopment, developers obtain letters of intent or letters of interest. Neither a letter of intent nor a letter of interest represents any firm legal obligation on the part of the potential tenant, but they are significant to potential lenders because they indicate specific interest in a project. Their primary function, in fact, is to indicate the demand for space in a proposed project for the lender. A letter of intent, committing the tenant to join the project on mutually satisfactory terms and with certain conditions met, is particularly useful.

Normally, a bona fide letter of intent that states the terms and conditions of the subsequent lease is the minimum commitment acceptable to a developer. Other times the developer will accept the execution of a lease document contingent upon obtaining and

---

[20] See appendix G for an example of the complexity of such a leasehold agreement where public and private facilities are intertwined.

executing the disposition and other development agreements with public entities and upon securing acceptable long-term financing. A letter of interest is much more general and usually represents a less advanced stage of interest, but it may carry as much weight as a letter of intent if the company expressing the interest is a large organization with a national reputation. In both cases, the letters state that a company is interested in occupying a project only if the terms and conditions of a lease can be successfully negotiated.

Letters of intent or letters of interest generally include statements that preclude a specific legal commitment.

This letter is not intended to constitute a binding agreement to consummate the transaction outlined herein nor an agreement to enter into contract. The parties propose to proceed promptly and in good faith to conclude these arrangements with respect to the proposed development, but any legal obligations between the parties shall be only those set forth in the executed contract and lease. In the event for any expense of the developer or for any charges or claims whatsoever arising out of this letter of intent or the proposed financing or otherwise; and similarly the developer shall not be in any way obligated to us.[21]

A letter of intent states that a company will enter into specific negotiations about the express terms of a lease for space in a particular project. Ordinarily, a letter of interest states only that a company *may* enter into such negotiations.

The development team may desire similar statements of intent or interest from potential lenders. Although this procedure is not normal for private real estate transactions, the public participant may sometimes ask for an assurance of interest from investors. A letter of interest from a lending institution will be even more general than one from a potential tenant.

Development and Funding Agreements with the Public Sector

A typical public/private downtown project requires agreement between at least two parties—the city and the development team—and may also involve other parties such as a development authority. When more than one public entity participates in the project, a cooperative agreement between them is a necessary prelude to an agreement with the private entity. For instance, the city may sign a cooperative agreement with a development authority setting forth its justification for carrying out the project, authorizing the development agency to acquire and clear land if

necessary, allocating funds for the agency's activities, establishing a schedule for development, committing itself to the construction of certain public improvements, and agreeing to contract with a specified private party as development manager. The city may also sign a contract for the sale of land with the development agency, or a lease for ground or air rights with the developer, or a general development agreement with the developers. The development authority, in turn, may agree to sell the developer the land needed to construct the project, to provide parking and other public improvements, or to carry out general development activities in connection with the project. In some cases the development agency may contract with certain private entities (a hotel operator, for example) separately from the principal developer.

An example is the cooperative agreement between the city of Richmond and the Redevelopment and Housing Authority for the Project One development. The city authorized the release of funds to the authority for acquiring properties and relocating residents, while the authority agreed to deed portions of the site to the city for public use and to negotiate agreements with the private developers for the sale of land at a lower value. Another cooperative agreement with the local parking authority assigns responsibilities for owning and operating parking facilities for the project.

Normally, the public agency stipulates the format that the documents should have, and the development team starts preparing drafts of all the pertinent documents. When the documents are drafted and overall project feasibility determined, the coventure partners negotiate unresolved issues, changes are included in subsequent drafts of the documents, and the documents are prepared for formal authorization and execution. The agreement could be in the form of a general development agreement that refers to subsequent specific agreements or individual collections of agreements that in total form a general development agreement.

Every development agreement is tailored to fit the particular project or set of participants. In general, however, the agreement states the intent of the parties to undertake and complete the project, which is described in appended drawings and statements, sets forth each party's responsibilities, and spells out the financial requirements and commitments for each party. It includes safeguards for ensuring appropriate timing and availability of funds and conditions for each party to allow for project changes because of inescapable changes in conditions.[22]

[21] John W. Reilly, *The Language of Real Estate* (Chicago: Real Estate Education Company, 1977), p. 255.

[22] See appendix H for an example of a financial agreement.

4-30 Project One, Richmond, Virginia, includes a proposed retail mall, hotel, office building, convention center, and parking.

Some projects are initiated using an interim contractual agreement or memorandum of understanding to proceed with design and construction before more detailed agreements can be worked out and approved. This procedure was used in Hartford. The city manager issued a letter of intent, which Aetna accepted, that outlined the purpose of the project but supplied no details on the form or size of private facilities. In the Project One development in Richmond, the development began operating under a memorandum of understanding negotiated with the assistance of Zuchelli, Hunter and Associates, Inc., that designated the developer for the $88 million project before predevelopment began. At this point the developer may deposit a refundable letter of credit or certified check as a good faith deposit. This action establishes the developer's bona fide intent to carry out the preliminary findings according to the conditions agreed upon.

A letter of credit represents a legal obligation to lend a certain amount of money on demand, under specified conditions. Such a device was used in the Loring Park Redevelopment Project in Minneapolis to guarantee construction lenders that the Downtown Development Corporation, a for-profit group composed of 23 corporate and financial institutions, would back up the developer in case of emergency. The corporation took interest in the project after an initial agreement, reached by the developer and a major commercial lender, for construction and long-term mortgage financing failed because of the interest rate. The corporation decided to back up the developer's equity, or risk money, position to guarantee on demand any monies owed in interest, taxes, or assessments if the developer's plans went awry. Thus, the mechanism met the needs of both the construction lender and the developer. The letter of credit was backed up through subscriptions by members of the corporation to nonvoting stock. The arrangement shielded corporate members from direct legal responsibility for the construction debt by obligating only the corporation itself.

4-31   Glendale Galleria, Glendale, California.

In the Glendale, California, Galleria project, the private development team presented the public redevelopment authority with a $500,000 letter of credit containing provisions for the agency to draw additional funds until the agency's revenue bonds were sold. With the credit advance, the redevelopment agency immediately began negotiating the purchase of the 160 individually owned parcels that comprised the 28-acre site for the downtown shopping mall. The advance to cover the early costs eventually grew to $5 million. The letter of credit was presented immediately after both parties signed a disposition and development agreement.

The execution of agreements between the public and private entities signifies the end of predevelopment activities. Many of the activities initiated during predevelopment—design, leasing, and financing—are refined and completed during the next stage, development.

5.
The Development Stage

By the time the development stage begins, several important preliminary steps have been completed. All public and private groups associated with the project have agreed on the project's major objectives and elements. A developer has been selected and his role and that of the public entity have been determined. The public sector has committed specific amounts of assistance. Preliminary plans and designs have been completed for a specific site. A development program has been designed, financial studies completed, financing responsibilities agreed upon, and a general construction schedule established.

The analyses and negotiations carried on during predevelopment are now focused on a single project's location, components, scale, potential tenants, financial requirements, and construction. The general framework created during predevelopment will be continually refined to secure financing, obtain detailed designs, and organize the several phases of construction.

During development the timing of financial support and the activities of the professionals and contractors who design and build the project must be coordinated to produce the project that meets the objectives formulated during predevelopment. The private developer's relationship with the public sector becomes more complex. The public components of the project—streets, parking facilities, utilities, walkways, etc.—will have to meet the municipality's standards and regulations, involving permitting and inspection officials and perhaps municipal designers. If the project developer is responsible for managing public improvements, public officials must approve all phases of the project. Schedules must be closely coordinated.

The partnership between public and private sectors demands new working methods and greater sensitivity to public objectives from the developer. The developer must accommodate the municipality's interest in all details of construction. The public sector must thoroughly understand development methods and the importance of meeting schedules. The working relationships defined during predevelopment are now put into practice. Even the best of relationships will develop flaws and misunderstandings that will require modifying agreements and negotiating problems to reach a solution within the principles of the joint development agreement.

This chapter discusses the principal actors and their complex relationships for the four broad areas of the development stage—financing, leasing, design, and construction.

5-1　Westmount Square, Montreal, a first generation MXD, was developed without public participation. The experiences gained in this type of project, which includes a mix of uses and in this case an underground connection to the Montreal Metro, have become the prototypes for more complex public/private ventures.

Financing Construction Activities

Financing for downtown developments has recently changed substantially. The gradual disappearance of federal urban renewal funds has encouraged the emergence of a wide range of new financing arrangements between local public and private groups and the private developer. These changes have affected the entire range of project financing, from seed money to long-term loans, and reflected the closer relationship between the parties. This part describes several elements of the financing process: (1) the types of financing required, (2) negotiations for public and private contributions, (3) sources of private financing, and (4) preparations for the loan package.

Financing Requirements

A downtown development project requires financing for many direct and indirect costs. The direct costs include land and the actual construction of the development; they comprise all funds paid to contractors, including their fees. The indirect costs include:

- fees for various feasibility studies
- legal fees
- design fees for the architect and engineer (A&E)
- interest on loans during construction of the project
- fees or other charges for permits and inspections
- salaries and overhead for the developer's staff
- profit for the developer
- contingency and reserve funds

- reserves for unleased space
- sales and leasing commissions
- expenses for relocating tenants
- costs of finishing leased space.

To meet these costs the private developer must obtain at least four types of financing: (1) funds for predevelopment activities, (2) short-term loans to finance construction before the permanent or long-term mortgage becomes effective, (3) long-term mortgage loans to provide the basic funds, and (4) equity financing for the share of the cost and initial funding not covered by the mortgage. Commitments for all four are necessary before construction can begin.

The developer involved in a complex public/private project needs much more front-end money. His staff must spend much more time identifying the most viable concept and negotiating specific agreements for the project. A project involving both the public and private sectors demands careful assessment of its characteristics and thus more plans, designs, and feasibility studies than privately sponsored projects.

Larger projects are increasingly using partial or total public funding for predevelopment and some portions of development. To ensure both the city and the developer of professional studies useful in defining a feasible joint project, it has become the practice for the public partner to fund these preliminary studies. The results of the studies become public property, and the information in them facilitates subsequent negotiations between the parties. For example, in South Bend, Indiana, the city is reimbursing the developer for all costs of predevelopment services, including consultants' fees for feasibility studies and all incurred A&E fees for a proposed project.

Short-term construction loans provide working capital during project development. They are usually advanced in installments based on the lender's evaluation of progress or on completion of predetermined stages of the project. Because interest rates on construction loans are higher than for long-term mortgage loans, developers often stage construction in short phases so that components of the project can be converted to long-term financing as soon as possible. It also minimizes interest payments during construction. The term of the construction loan is established to allow completion of the project before the loan is repaid, to provide time for the developer to convert the construction loan into a permanent loan, or to refinance the mortgage if necessary.

First mortgages provide the primary financing for almost all projects. Typically, first mortgages provide up to 75 percent of the appraised value of the project, to be repaid with interest in installments over periods of 25 to 35 years or more. The property and improvements are pledged as collateral or security for the mortgage loan. Specific terms of mortgages vary according to current economic conditions, requirements of state laws, practices of individual lenders, and the type of project being financed. Because a mortgage is based on the appraised value of the project, the amount of the mortgage loan is not related to the direct costs of construction. Instead, it is based on the income stream generated by the project and its appraised value. In some cases, the 75 percent mortgage also covers part of the indirect costs as well.

Long-term equity financing provides the difference between the cost of the project and the mortgage loan. Methods of acquiring equity funds depend almost entirely on the developer, who will shape the venture to fit his particular financial objectives. The developer may rely on his own financial resources, or he may form a partnership or joint venture with one or more associates or corporations interested in investing or speculating in real estate. A general partnership may be expanded to include limited partners who do not share in the liability or in the management of the partnership but who wish to invest in real estate. Syndicates of investors who employ an agent to obtain investment opportunities may be involved in equity financing. Institutional lenders, real estate corporations, and real estate investment trusts (REITs) offer other sources of equity financing. Another mechanism is sale and leaseback; the developer sells the entire project to an investment group or institutional lender with provisions for a long-term leaseback (usually 20 to 30 years) with possible extensions. Land can also be sold and leased back through a long-term ground lease (51 to 99 years) to reduce the total equity required.

The methods used to obtain equity financing will be determined by the strength of major tenants, the financial objectives of the developer, and the nature of the particular project. Often development entities have different equity partnerships or corporate joint ventures for specific components of a particular project, as well as for the overall project. The specific financial relationships usually evolve over time as relationships with major lenders and major tenants are defined. For larger projects, the corporate form of participation may be favored for its protection from personal liability, although partnerships are more advantageous for tax purposes. Corporations can act as general partners in a partnership, and the developer may choose this form for protection.

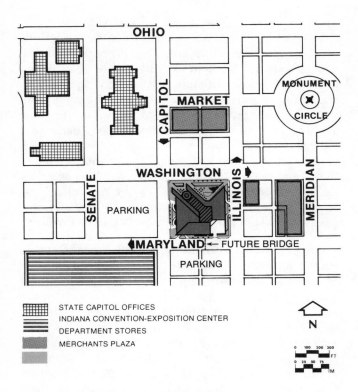

OHIO

CAPITOL
MARKET

MONUMENT
CIRCLE

WASHINGTON

SENATE
PARKING
ILLINOIS
MERIDIAN

MARYLAND ← FUTURE BRIDGE

PARKING

STATE CAPITOL OFFICES
INDIANA CONVENTION-EXPOSITION CENTER
DEPARTMENT STORES
MERCHANTS PLAZA

N

0   100 200 300
                FT
0 25 50 75
                M

5-2   Merchants Plaza in Indianapolis was developed under a ground lease.

Committing to the Mix of Public/Private Funding

If the project to be financed is sufficiently well planned, substantiated, authorized, and coordinated, private funds can be committed to it solely on the basis of market-rate investment criteria. In other words, the element of risk must be clearly identified, the potential for profit as determined by careful market analysis must be equally well defined, and the tradeoff between risks and rewards must warrant the expenditure of capital by investors who could choose alternate opportunities for investment.

Under ideal conditions, access to capital markets can be expected. Individuals and institutions skilled in real estate investment will consider a sound project almost without regard to geography. If the market for the project is strong, the public sector is a bystander providing only the normal modifications to public utilities or bordering streets. Many developers are interested in and capable of undertaking relatively short-term, single-purpose projects. Financial in-

stitutions have had long experience with them, the time frame for project development corresponds to their investment criteria, and lenders have little difficulty with the size of debt and equity investment. Even so, financing is complex. Lease negotiations may be long and arduous, financial arrangements may involve private joint venture and participation mortgages, and special interim financing may be required for the construction period. The amount of time and money involved may be substantial. The process, however, is the special province of the private developer, who finds these complexities more familiar than those of an integrated public/private "mixed" development project.

This normal process of project development is also quite familiar to the public sector. The participation required of the public sector is minimal. The city's role is to provide public approval of applications in conformance with zoning or variances to zoning, assess fees, check plans, issue building permits, process environmental impact reports, inspect construction, approve utility hookups, and issue certificates of completion. Any public improvements are those normally provided to any project or are the subject of special public action during the approval process.

In many downtown revitalization projects, however, these normal relationships become intertwined with one of the public/private joint development strategies described in chapter 4. This situation occurs when substantial public assistance is required to finance the project because the private risk is greater—because of the long-term nature of the project or because the market is relatively untried. The entire process is characterized by a much higher degree of uncertainty and greater risk. As such, the project is not one that could be undertaken through normal private market procedures.

To attract professional developers and lenders to such projects, the public sector may have to finance some of the project, either directly by supplying cash or improvements, or indirectly by underwriting private financing. The motivation for public involvement in higher risk projects is to spread the risks and costs of development, and to alter the circumstances for private investment through public support.

The degree of public involvement is determined well before this point in the development process. No developer would negotiate with key tenants, finance preliminary design, and then attempt to negotiate public participation. At this point, the public entity would be involved in preparing bond prospectuses and issuing bond obligations. During the development stage, the developer deals with finalizing private short-term and permanent financing.

5-3 San Bernardino Mall, San Bernardino, California, illustrates the complexities of public/private developments. Although the design is fairly traditional, the city owns and built the pedestrian mall separately, then sold the building pads to a developer to build the stores.

Sources of Private Financing

Private conventional financing supplies the major part of the capital for most downtown development projects. While the project may be partially funded by substantial public funds, private capital spells the success of most projects. The potential investor evaluating a public/private downtown project will be aware of several features that indicate a high-risk project:

- Downtown ventures are more complicated financially than other projects.

- The necessity for public sector involvement suggests that private development only is not feasible.

- The long-term project predominantly tailored to meet specific public objectives may sacrifice the profitability of the total project to meet those objectives.

Therefore, expertly prepared and supported cost estimates and financing plans are extremely important.

To overcome this reluctance, the well organized developer should take several steps to reassure potential investors. One such step is to line up substantial financing by local institutions. The selling point for local financial groups may be a desire for a good image recognized by the community at large or the need for additional space for its own offices. Such participation by local investors is often a major attraction for other investors.

Another way to increase potential investors' confidence is to stage development in several short phases rather than in a continuous long-term project. As the time from project inception to construction completion lengthens, the risks of general economic changes grow. The financial risks of long-term projects, which have to withstand changes in national or local economic trends, political and social conditions, and participating organizations and personnel, are simply too great for most investors to sustain. Staging development in a series of 2- to 3-year subprojects increases the possibility of meeting time and cost targets, thus ensuring an adequate return on investment. The longer the term of the commitment, the more difficult it is for private institutions to agree to make money available at some future date.

Finally, strong lease commitments are powerful inducements to sources of equity and mortgage money. A long-term lease with terms that are fair to both lessor and lessee goes farther than any market study in answering questions about the project's marketability. Evaluating the lease involves considering the lessee's reputation and credit standing and whether the terms and provisions are equitable for both lessor and lessee. Very long-term leases at below-market rates, which do not include the lessee's participation in increased costs and no protection for the owner against inflation in the form of additional rentals, are severe handicaps to development rather than stimulants of it.

The restrictions federal, state, or municipal agencies place on public or quasi-public financing complicate obtaining the necessary long-term commitments. Federal programs, in particular, are subject to changes, delays, the availability of funds Congress has allocated, limitations on the number of projects that can be funded at a given time, and red tape and bureaucratic procedures.

The entity a developer forms to finance a project is determined as much by the developer's objectives as by the sources of financing available. A development company may decide to form a partnership to build a project and then benefit from continued ownership after the project is completed, or a developer may become the general partner and sell limited partnership shares to outside investors. Such an arrangement can distribute benefits in a number of ways to meet different objectives of different investors. They can provide that the development company, as general partner, has effective control of project management by owning 50 percent or more of the project. The developer may choose this type of ownership as a means of attracting equity to the project without losing control of project management. Limited partners are attracted to the arrangement by one or more investment potentials of appreciation in the value of the property, long-term cash flow, and substantial depreciation to use in sheltering other income from taxes even though they cannot participate actively in project management. The developer's previous business experience, reputation, and financial success should be important considerations for prospective limited partners.

Syndication is another method of attracting investors. It may involve a public stock offering requiring registration with the Securities and Exchange Commission. Although this method is complex and lengthy, it may become more desirable for larger projects with greater and more complex financial requirements. Regardless of the developer's business structure or the amount of public funding, the major sources of private long-term debt financing are life insurance companies, commercial banks, savings and loan associations and savings banks, pension funds, REITs, and foreign funds. These same sources can in some instances take an equity position in the project (see discussion below).

Life Insurance Companies

Overall, life insurance companies account for about one-fifth of all mortgage debt. They account for the majority of mortgage loans to other than single-family dwellings and are the major source of funds for large projects, primarily because of their ability to make much larger loans than other sources.

Mortgages are an important investment for life insurance companies because of their attractive yields, the flow of amortization payments, the opportunity to spread investments over geographical areas, and the flexibility they offer. The availability of funds for any single investment opportunity is determined by overall market conditions, the availability of alternative investments, and the yield of real estate investments compared to the alternatives.

Because life insurance companies will lend money for many types of commercial, industrial, and residential properties, they are the prime source of permanent financing for major downtown developments. Several factors influence an insurance company's evaluation of a project and thus its willingness to invest:

- location
- market
- tenant interest (measured by leasing commitments)
- economic appraisal of the project
- quality and reputation of the developer and general contractor
- project design
- rate, term, size, and coverage ratios of the loan required.

The size of the mortgage loan is based on a maximum of 75 percent of the appraised value of the completed project. Value is primarily a function of a project's net income-producing ability. The project's cost

5-4 Western Electric Company is a major tenant of Gateway, Newark, New Jersey. The commitment of a major tenant or the participation of a major company as an owner/occupant can be crucial to acquiring acceptable overall financing for a large-scale mixed use project.

Gil Amiaga

is a factor, but it is secondary to income valuation. Once the lender is satisfied with his analysis of the seven criteria listed above, the critical factors then become the validation of estimated income and expenses. Projected income is best supported by leasing commitments. Projected expenses are best supported by the developer's record on previous projects and by carefully developed and documented calculations.

Life insurance companies are also a prime source of equity funds for major projects, primarily because prime real estate will most probably appreciate over time. Major institutions view equity investments as opportunities to balance portfolios with an investment that can increase yields through both cash flow and substantial capital gains. Major insurance companies have holdings in directly owned real estate in excess of $10.5 billion today; Prudential and Equitable combined hold $4.6 billion.

Traditionally life insurance companies have purchased existing properties or entered a joint venture with an established developer. Joint ventures usually provide the insurance company with a share of ownership of a project in return for the required equity capital. Life insurance companies today are more conservative in their approach to joint ventures and may require more than "sweat equity"—that is, the developer's talent, skill, and experience—as the developer's contribution. The large companies are concentrating on the acquisition of existing projects, entering joint ventures with proven partners on prime projects, or committing to the purchase of an interest in a proposed project after completion or after certain performance criteria are met. Insurance companies have also formed their own real estate development subsidiaries to invest funds for project ownership and equity participation.[1]

Commercial Banks

Commercial banks are the largest source of construction or interim financing available to the real estate developer today. Because of the organization and nature of a bank's deposits, it is primarily interested in short- to intermediate-term lending, usually not exceeding 5 years. The ability and interest of a commercial bank in lending funds for a real estate project are determined by the answers to several questions: What is the borrower's financial condition? What type of loan is required? Has a bona fide permanent commitment been made on the project? What are the terms of the loan? What is the appraised value of the project? Is the project local? What are the borrower's total financial needs? How much money does the bank have available for investment? What is the impact of the project on the community?

[1] An example of a joint venture between a developer and a life insurance company is Burlington Square, a joint venture of Mondev International and Fidelity Mutual Life.

5-5   New Market in the Penn's Landing area of Philadelphia is a combination of new construction and adaptive use. It is a joint venture of Kravco, Inc., Van Arkel & Moss Properties, Inc., and Fidelity Mutual Insurance Company.

The answers to these questions indicate the similarities and differences in the approach of life insurance companies and commercial banks to a real estate loan. Usually the two institutions form a complementary relationship and provide a complete financing package. Life insurance companies lend money based on a finished operating property, which justifies their reliance on the income approach to valuation. Banks, however, are attracted to short-term, construction mortgage loans because they are a reasonably secure investment when backed by a permanent mortgage takeout commitment. The bank fills the financial gap during the construction period, assuming the greater risk, at a higher interest rate but for a shorter term, of successful construction and performance required to secure the permanent loan.

The bank's analysis of the project is slightly different from the insurance company's. It will have a special interest in funding a development project in its own business area because a successful project can attract other business to the bank. This potential market impact is quite important to the construction lender; it becomes even more critical when a construction loan is made before permanent financing has been secured.

When the developer has unusually strong financial resources and the project design, leasing commitments, location, and economic valuation are extremely attractive, a bank may offer a 2-year construction loan with the option for 1-year extensions. The total loan term rarely exceeds 5 years. The rate is normally floating but tied to the prime rate; the spread between the actual loan rate and the prime rate is a function of the project's financial analysis and the borrower's credit rating. With this type of loan, the developer can establish an operating record before committing himself to permanent financing. He can also time the permanent financing to take advantage of a favorable money market.

Savings and Loan Associations and Savings Banks

Savings and loan associations and mutual savings banks analyze potential loans in many of the same ways that life insurance companies and commercial banks do. Underwriting procedures, rates, and other conditions of the loan are similar, except that the term may not exceed 30 years. One other difference is that in many cases, savings and loan associations underwrite both construction and permanent financing in one loan.

Three key factors for most savings and loan associations are the location of the project, the market, and the developer's reputation. Like banks, savings and loan associations are interested in real estate projects in their own market area and in the project's overall benefits to the community. They normally invest in commercial loans only in areas with which they are most familiar.

The typical loan from a savings and loan association is relatively small; most savings and loan associations lack the resources to make the substantial loans required for large development projects. The most common solution to this problem is underwriting by several savings institutions or a combination of savings institutions and life insurance companies.[2]

Pension Funds

Pension funds are the newest source of major development investors. Investment by pension funds is growing rapidly. While only 2 percent of their assets are presently invested in real estate, this amount represents over $400 million, and it is increasing steadily. On the whole, they are more diverse and less regulated than other financial institutions. Usually pension funds invest in real estate that has started to produce income and has a proven history of income and expenses. However, commingled funds managed by banks and insurance companies have been investing more aggressively in real estate and are starting to enter joint ventures or developing property on their own. Pension funds may provide a large source of equity capital in the future.

Pension funds have underwritten mortgage loans for several years. Major union pension funds can provide substantial funds for mortgage loans, and downtown development projects are attractive investments. They use similar criteria to evaluate the investment as insurance companies. The major difference is that pension funds do not have the same legal constraints to their investment activity and therefore can be much more flexible in how they approach a new investment opportunity as compared to the rest of their investment portfolios.

Real Estate Investment Trusts

Real estate investments trusts are financial intermediaries that specialize in real estate investment. They can be divided into five major categories: (1) construction and development or short-term mortgage trusts, (2) long-term mortgage trusts, (3)

---

[2] The Gallery, a Rouse Company downtown retail complex in Philadelphia, is a typical example of a development project for which the permanent financing was provided by a consortium of financial institutions and insurance companies.

equity or property-owning trusts, (4) hybrid—both mortgage and ownership—trusts, and (5) specialty trusts. In many ways REITs are similar to mutual funds, except that they invest in real estate rather than stocks and bonds. At least 75 percent of a REIT's assets must be in real estate holdings, and at least 75 percent of its income must be derived from these investments. REITs do not pay federal income tax so long as 90 percent of all net taxable income is paid to shareholders.

Some REITs invest nationwide so as to spread their risks geographically. Others focus solely on one or two market areas, preferably near their home offices. Although REIT assets are distributed throughout the United States and a few other countries like Canada and Mexico, they are most heavily concentrated in states that grew the most in population and employment in the late 1960s and early 1970s. Although California, Georgia, Florida, and Texas had only 22 percent of the population in 1977, they had 43 percent of all REIT assets.

REITs were not important sources of financial support for major developments until the late 1960s. Beginning in 1968, changes in the tax laws and tight money allowed REITs to take advantage of the lack of funds available and to make development loans at more favorable rates than banks and other lending institutions. Two REITs began to specialize in making mortgage loans rather than owning income-producing property, and their records were so good that some major investment banking firms were willing to market shares of similar trusts. This mark of confidence allowed REITs to double their assets each year until 1972. In retrospect it is apparent that the expansion of REITs was propelled by overly optimistic expectations about the ability of the economy to absorb the large number of real estate projects being built at the time. The economic recession of 1973 was easily the worst real estate recession since the 1930s and caused a period of major retrenchment for REITs. Total assets that had reached $21.6 billion in the second quarter of 1974 fell to $13.5 billion by July 1978.

By 1976, many of the surviving REITs had shaken off the worst of the adverse effects of the recession. Those trusts whose assets had been concentrated in property ownership had done better than those specializing in construction and development loans, so many of the trusts shifted toward equity ownership. Although the REIT market is better than it has been in some time, the balance sheet for the industry as a whole continues to be dominated by the 40 percent of the trusts whose assets have been shrinking. These trusts have been forced to exchange assets for cancellation of debt with creditor banks because of

the high proportion of nonearning assets in their portfolios. Continuing exchanges imply that the asset base of these trusts will continue to decline. Because the dollar value of these exchanges has exceeded the increase in investments by the healthy trusts, it is likely that total industry assets will continue to shrink over the next few years. However, the largest trusts are actively seeking new properties, so it is likely that the healthy trusts will once again be an important source of funds for large developments.

Foreign Funds

Foreign financial institutions, pension funds, and wealthy individuals are now competing for shares of investment in prime income-producing properties in the United States. For these investors, the major incentive is the relative stability of the U.S. economy and currency compared with conditions at home. The money comes mostly from Canada, West Germany, England, and The Netherlands. Other foreign investors are active only in particular regions; investors from Japan and Hong Kong, for example, are active primarily on the West Coast. Typical deals are large, ranging from $10 million to $30 million. Some foreign companies hold portfolios of U.S. real estate with market values over $300 million.

Foreign investors prefer office and shopping center properties rather than hotel, motel, and specialty properties. The competition for prime commercial properties is very keen, so some foreign investors are willing to pay a higher price and therefore accept a lower yield than most American investors in exchange for the security of American investments. If the value of a property is likely to appreciate substantially, some foreign investors will accept a yield about 1 percent less than domestic investors.

Because good existing properties are difficult to find, foreign investors are frequently willing to enter joint ventures with a proven American developer on a high quality property. An example of this situation that also illustrates the hazards of foreign investors in developing projects is Canal Place in New Orleans, Louisiana.

Canal Place, when completed, will be an integrated complex that will ultimately contain 1.75 million square feet of office space, 750,000 square feet of multilevel retail space, a 500-room luxury hotel, 800 dwelling units, and accommodations for 5,000 cars. Planned by the developers as a means to reunite the city with the Mississippi River, the site will include a great deal of open pedestrian area as well. In October 1976 the American developer joined with Lanac Corporation, N.V., which represented Bank Omran, a subsidiary of the Pahlavi Foundation of Tehran, to

5-6 Canal Place, New Orleans, is being developed in several phases. The initial financing by foreign investors subsequently had to be replaced.

form a development partnership, Canal Place Venture. As a consequence of the upheaval in Iran, the Bank Omran is no longer involved in the project, which required restructuring the development group. Thus, while foreign funds enabled the project to move forward, their loss because of circumstances beyond the developer's control could have disastrous effects on a well conceived project.

Securing Financial Commitments

Before construction contracts can be awarded, the developer must reach final agreements to secure financial support. During the predevelopment stage, the developer has explored possibilities for public and private sources of financing and has identified the most suitable or likely sources. He has also reached agreements with the public sector that commit public funds to the project. He has established his own financial participation in the project, which in turn depends partly on the interests of proposed major tenants. As the design of the project moves closer to completion, the developer will finalize financial terms and arrangements with potential lenders, hav-

ing defined the amount of money required for interim construction loans and equity and mortgage funds.

The structure of private financing is different for each project, because it depends on the developer's objectives, the types and financial strength of the major tenants involved, the amount of public participation, the strength of the local financial market, and the size and scope of the project. The complexities that can result from this mix of factors are exemplified in the private financing for the Courthouse Square project in Dayton, Ohio, developed by the John W. Galbreath Company. The developer, through a corporate subsidiary, formed a partnership with public and private investors, including the Mead Corporation, to obtain lease rights to one office building from a special-purpose, limited-profit corporation (for more information on the legislation, see chapter 7). In turn, the partnership subleased the office building to the Mead Corporation. A consortium of local banks, pension funds, insurance companies, the leasing partnership, the special-purpose corporation, and the Mead Corporation underwrote construction and mortgage financing. The developers were obligated to pay front-end, equity, construction, and mortgage financing expenses, and to commit themselves to a long-term leasing arrangement.

The commitment to private financing comes when design development drawings are complete. Before that time, lenders can be encouraging but noncommittal. With drawings in hand, the developer can prepare his loan package, making sure that it provides all the essential information required to persuade the

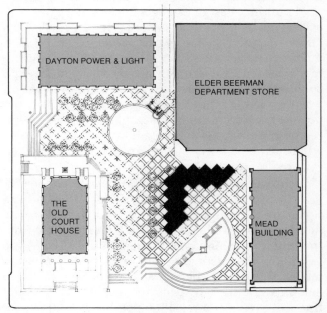

5-7 Site plan, Courthouse Square, Dayton, Ohio.

lender of the project's feasibility. The package includes at least the following items:

- market and planning studies that define the project's attraction to potential tenants
- pro forma and cash flow analyses that define the project's financial feasibility
- development cost estimates prepared by the designers and/or the construction managers
- design development drawings and general specifications that describe the development's physical character
- copies of written agreements and commitments from public authorities that define their interest in and financial support for the project
- statements showing the developer's financial condition
- copies of letters of intent or agreements with prime tenants
- any other documents that provide evidence of the project's potential financial viability.

Leasing

One of the developer's primary concerns that affects the project's viability is securing tenants to occupy the space programmed for the project. During predevelopment, the developer has contacted major potential tenants and secured commitments for large blocks of space, perhaps as much as 75 percent of the floor space. Firming up lease commitments before final building design can be a great asset to the project's success. It is much easier to design space for a known tenant than it is for a hypothetical tenant with unknown needs. This process therefore begins during predevelopment and continues through and beyond completion of construction. The greater the start on leasing, the more predictable all other aspects of the process become, the more favorable the financing that can be arranged, the more accurate the cost estimates will be, and the fewer the design changes that will be required.

Securing leases with adequate rent early in the process is critical to the developer's cash-flow projections and to the project's entire financial basis. The developer wants to move as quickly as possible from the initial financing commitment established by his lenders to the maximum loan level, which depends on leasing a high percentage of the space. Large amounts of unleased space will necessitate unusual financing costs and raise the possibility of financial failure. The financing structure of most buildings is predicated on paying off interim construction loans

to execute long-term mortgage loans, which in turn depends on successful leasing to generate cash for loan amortization payments. This structure will be strained and finally broken by a lower-than-expected cash flow resulting from a lower-than-expected percentage of space leased when construction is completed and the takeout mortgage executed.

The lender will expect a certain amount of space to be leased before he commits himself to long-term financing. The amount of leased space usually regarded as acceptable is 40 to 60 percent for 75 percent financing, although the lender may request a higher percentage for a special-purpose building. The break-even point for many buildings may be an occupancy of 80 to 90 percent; each percentage point over that amount represents a return on equity. The rule of thumb is that leases should be signed for at least half of the building before the building is ready for occupancy and long-term loans are executed.

The developer has several options to take care of leasing. He may appoint one of his staff as leasing manager whose primary responsibility is to secure tenants for uncommitted space. Many larger developers have experienced in-house staff members responsible for marketing new buildings. In some cases, the developer may choose to retain a local firm of commercial brokers that specializes in leasing office and retail space and already has connections in the market area. Smaller developers or developers whose projects have only a small portion of floor space to be leased use this method. When the project is nearly completed, the developer might also form or employ a building management firm to finish leasing the building and carry out other management activities for the finished project. There is no "best" leasing program. Each arrangement will be tailored to the needs of the project. However, because the financial success of the project hinges on income from tenants, leasing must always be a major and effectively executed activity in the development process.

Marketing to Prospective Tenants

Securing leases for retail and office space in downtown projects requires a well organized program of merchandising. It involves identifying prospective space users, persuading prospects to consider space in the project, demonstrating the type and adaptability of available space, establishing the value of the space for the prospect, and negotiating and closing lease arrangements.

Potential tenants can be found in a number of places. Organizations and firms that are affiliated with financial institutions or other businesses already involved with the project are a good first source.

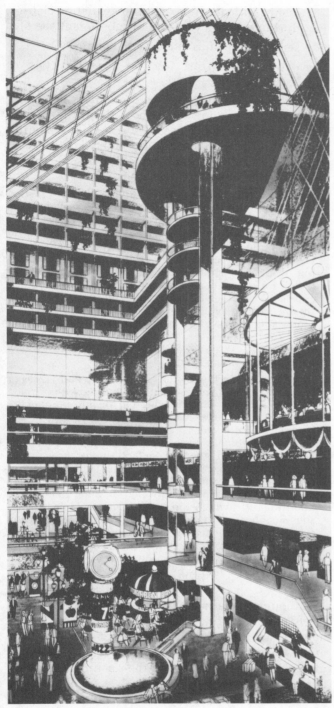

5-8 Identification with and connecting to a dramatic design amenity is an important marketing tool, as suggested by the interior sketch of the Grande Galleria at Canal Place, New Orleans.

Every major business firm has links to other firms: contractual relationships with law and accounting firms, seats on boards of directors, accounts in financial institutions, and subsidiary companies. Such firms can likely attract other tenants, many of whom can be identified in the early stages of leasing.

One of the reasons for initial determination of prime tenants, aside from the amount of space they will absorb, is the likelihood of using those space demands to attract other potential tenants. For retail space, the commitment of a major anchor tenant such as a department store will likely attract other retail shops already connected with other branches of that store. A large corporation's agreeing to lease space for its corporate or regional headquarters could attract other tenants who might feel that proximity will be to their advantage.

A second possibility for tenants is to define the advantages of the project's location. Buildings near the courthouse will interest lawyers; other locations may favor financial institutions, brokerage houses, or branch offices of national companies. Within the building, specific users may suggest categories of potential tenants. A good law library or a notable law firm may attract lawyers, for example. Identifying these possibilities will suggest potential business for retail space, because employees of the firms are the obvious first source of customers. Thus, a building full of attorneys may suggest a high quality clothing store and a restaurant, while offices with large clerical staffs may favor moderately priced apparel and a cafeteria.

Leasing and design will affect each other. The desires of major tenants and the results of market studies will in part determine the layout of floors and the functioning of the heating, ventilation, and air-conditioning system. The leasing manager can then tell whether he should market whole floors or partial floors, which will set the direction of the marketing approach.

Although interested tenants may initiate some inquiries, the leasing manager must usually actively promote contacts and arrange meetings to gain prospective tenants' interest. An astute publicity campaign can heighten interest in the project. It would publicize groundbreaking and other events and distribute attractive brochures to promote the project and provide basic information about facilities and floor plans.

The leasing manager can use several arguments to persuade prospective tenants that the project will meet their requirements for space in the most cost-effective way:

- the prestige of the location, nearby businesses and stores, major tenants of the building, and special attractions of the project
- the value of the space, with a comparison of rent for the project and other locations, and additional advantages like attractive open space or parking within the building

- the efficiency of the location, as demonstrated by savings in time and effort because of the project's proximity to related businesses
- the economy of the space, emphasizing the building's adaptability to efficient use and changing conditions.

The leasing manager must also be prepared to discuss special conditions of the lease and to negotiate special situations such as subleasing, escalation of operating expenses, and expansion options. Once the parties have agreed on the amount of the rent and the improvements to be provided by the lessor, a draft "work letter" specifies exactly what interior construction (partitions, electrical wiring, flooring material) the lessor will provide and which items the lessee will pay for, either in direct payments or by amortizing rental charges.

Lease Conditions and Requirements

Although a lease is a legal instrument, no particular form or wording is required by statute to create a valid lease. (In most states, however, a lease for more than 1 year must be in writing.) No universally applicable leasing document applies to all types of projects, all tenants, or all jurisdictions, but most leases restrict use and occupancy of the leased premises to a particular activity, such as retail or office.

Because it helps to shape the project's financial success, the lease should be drafted by a lawyer well versed in real estate law. In most leases, the rental payment covers only the use of space and common areas and facilities. The retail tenant is usually responsible for finishing and furnishing his space, including interior partitions and special telephone and utility wiring and connections. The lessor usually furnishes these improvements for office tenants to a defined level, with the lessee having the option to upgrade any part to meet his specifications. To attract a desirable tenant, the developer may agree to install some or all of such excess improvements, either as an inducement or with an increase in rent over time to amortize the improvements. The lessor may permit his architectural services to be used for the design of this work, if required. Such special terms are negotiated and written into the lease agreement.

Most lease agreements contain a number of common provisions. Besides naming the lessor (landlord) and the lessee (tenant), most leases also stipulate:

- the leased premises (leasehold)
- the term, or time period, of possession
- the use to be made of the leasehold
- the consideration (the base rental and any ad-

justments to the base rental, or escalation clauses, during the base year and in subsequent years)
- services to be furnished by the lessor
- other provisions for the specific type of leasehold.

The description of the leased premises must adequately differentiate this property from the lessor's other properties. The lease should specify the building address, its legal description, and the net rentable area. For a single floor rented to one tenant, the net rentable area is usually measured:

. . . from the inside surface of the outer glass or finished column walls of the building to the inside surface of the opposite wall, excluding only the areas ("service areas") within the outside walls used for elevator mechanical rooms, building stairs, fire towers, elevator shafts, flues, vents, stacks, pipe shafts and vertical ducts, but including all columns within the leased area and any such areas which are for the specific use of the particular tenant such as special stairs or elevators, plus an allocation of the square footage of the building's elevator mechanical rooms and ground and basement lobbies.[3]

If the tenant rents only part of a floor, net rentable area is usually measured:

. . . from within the inside surface of the outer glass or finished column walls enclosing the tenant-occupied portion of the floor and measured to the mid-point of the walls separating areas leased by or held for lease to other tenants or from areas devoted to corridors, elevator foyers, rest rooms, mechanical rooms, janitor closets, vending areas and other similar facilities for the use of all tenants on the particular floor (hereinafter sometimes called "common areas"), but including a proportionate part of the common areas located on such floor based upon the ratio which the tenant's net rentable area on such floor bears to the aggregate net rentable area on such floor plus an allocation of the square footage of the building's elevator mechanical rooms and ground and basement lobbies. No deductions from net rentable area are made for columns or projections necessary to the building.[4]

Although the term and consideration are not absolutely necessary to establish a valid lease, they are almost always included in a lease agreement. The terms of the lease must be clearly stated to reduce possible disagreement, particularly if the document is tested in court. In most states, leases with terms of 3 or more years can be recorded, which gives notice of the terms that affect the use of the property and protects interests of all parties.

The clause that covers the consideration usually gives a base rental as an annual sum due and any adjustments to it, and calls for payment in 12 equal installments to be paid on a particular day of each

---

[3] Typical lease instrument, supplied by Gerald D. Hines Interests, Houston, Texas. See appendix I.

[4] Ibid.

month. Terms for prorating the rent are also included if the lease becomes effective in the middle of a month. The provision also stipulates that any late payments will be subject to a certain percentage rate of interest per year from the date due until paid.

The adjustment clauses in the lease agreement contain the various escalation clauses intended to supplement base rents during periods of inflation. The adjustments to the base rental can be calculated according to a number of factors, including changes in ad valorem taxes, operating expenses, and the cost of utilities.

Frequently, ad valorem taxes are prorated to leases so that as taxes rise, costs are adjusted at some agreed upon frequency. For example, if the actual ad valorem tax at the time the contract is executed is greater than the projected figures stated during negotiation, the base rental will be adjusted by the amount of difference times the number of square feet of net rentable area contained in the leased premises.

The adjustment factor for operating expenses might be calculated based upon changes in the local minimum wage for janitorial personnel or some other basis, but in no case is the base rental reduced below a certain amount per year per square foot of net rentable area. The escalation clause for utilities provides for rent adjustments according to published changes in the rate schedules and fuel price adjustments for the costs of gas, electricity, and water.

If in subsequent years the base rent must be adjusted under these various clauses, the lessor usually provides a statement of the current year's basic costs and a comparison with the prior year's basic costs within a stated period of time after the close of the calendar year. Within a stated period of time, the lessee must pay his proportional share of the increase as additional rent. If costs for the current year are less than those for the previous year, the lessor refunds any overcharges.

The statement of services to be provided to tenants usually includes which utilities will be provided and the terms for providing utilities by season and for special instances such as availability or levels of heat or cooling on weekends or holidays. For example, air conditioning and janitorial services may be provided on weekends only if additional rent is charged. The lease may also stipulate that the lessor will furnish sufficient electrical power for typewriters, voice writers, calculating machines, and other common office machines, but that the lessee must pay additional charges for power for electronic data processing equipment or special lighting.

A typical lease agreement usually describes in detail the rights and obligations of both the lessor and the lessee. The lessor is obligated specifically and by implication to provide private and peaceful possession of the premises by the lessee, except (as is usually the case) when the lessor shows the property just before the end of the lease or enters it to make repairs or comply with governmental requirements. It describes charges for the maintenance of common areas, restrictions on the appearance and condition of the premises, including the posting of signs and advertising, and, if applicable, dues for membership in merchants' associations and participation in promotional activities. The lease could also cover items like improvements to be made by the lessor, provision of parking, repairs by lessor and lessee, right of assignment to sublease by the lessee, alterations, additions, or improvements made by the lessee, and insurance.

Types of Leases

The most common ways to classify leases are by the method that rent is set and by the period for which the lease is written. Lease agreements classified by the method of setting the rent can take several forms:

- fixed, or flat, or straight leases
- percentage leases
- net and net-net leases
- index, or escalated leases
- graduated, or step-up leases
- reappraisal leases.

Leases classified by the term include:
- definite tenancy
- periodic tenancy
- tenancy at will
- tenancy at sufferance.

The type of lease depends on the project, the business involved, and current economic conditions. Percentage leases, for example, apply to retail businesses with sales on the premises. Net leases shift burdens of rising taxes and other costs to the lessee. Escalated leases are intended to overcome the effects of inflation and higher costs. Graduated leases are used to encourage new enterprise. A definite tenancy lease is used for major tenants because they desire a long-term leasehold, which is the basis for obtaining favorable financing. Periodic tenancy (month to month) might be used to generate income from vacant space until the right long-term tenant is found. In practice, many lease agreements include combinations of several of these concepts.

Classification by Method of Setting Rent

Fixed Leases

The traditional and least complicated method of establishing the amount of the rent is a fixed sum determined at the outset of the lease, paid periodically throughout the term of the lease. Once used almost exclusively, this type of lease is now used mostly for short-term leases of up to 3 years. Although lessees prefer a fixed, predictable rent, lessors are reluctant to establish fixed rents during periods of rapid inflation.

Percentage Leases

Percentage leases are presently the most commonly used type for retail commercial leasing. The lessee pays a minimum rental plus a percentage of his gross sales from goods and services sold on the premises. The base rent, which normally is set to cover operating expenses and debt service, may range from 40 to 80 percent of the fair market rental. Percentages may range from 1 or 2 percent for major stores up to 75 percent for highly volatile commercial operations like parking lots. Generally, percentages for smaller retail stores are about 3 to 10 percent.

The percentage lease is useful because it can be adapted to changing market situations. On the one hand, the base rent ensures a predictable return for the lessor while reducing the fixed rental for the lessee. On the other hand, the percentage of gross sales provides both lessor and lessee with an equitable rental based on how well the business does. This relationship reflects the fact that many of the individual stores' customers are attracted by the vitality and amenities of the project.

In a downtown project where the market is uncertain and the uncertainty is to be resolved by the nature of the project, the lessor, by offering a lower base rent, can attract tenants who would rather pay a low rent and a percentage of sales because they believe that location involves the risk of insufficient business to support a higher but stable fixed rent. In turn, the lessor's rental income depends somewhat on the lessee's abilities and resources. The lessor will not make money unless the tenants make money, so he assures lessees that his resources will be used to ensure the overall success of the project. This process of negotiating and conveying a percentage lease thus involves both parties in a close business relationship that has many of the aspects of a limited partnership.

Other types of percentage clauses may be added to the basic lease. The minimum rate may be based on specified levels of sales. Large chain stores in an untested market often prefer the "percentage against a minimum," which bases rent entirely on sales. A "maximum rental" clause sets a ceiling on rent and may be used with any lease that has escalators to assure a lessee that rent will not exceed a certain amount. Lessors avoid it, however, because it offers inadequate protection against inflation.

Net Leases

Net leases, often used for larger office buildings, industrial buildings, and other major properties, substantially reduce the lessor's risks related to income. A net lease requires the tenant to pay directly all operating costs, including maintenance of common areas, real estate taxes, and insurance, in addition to the base rent. The developer or owner passes to the tenant virtually all of the costs associated with the building and risks only the tenant's continuing ability to meet payments.

The terms "double net lease" and "triple net lease" are defined in a number of ways. Many net leases are only partially net as, for example, when the lessee pays only taxes and insurance. Terminology varies in different parts of the country. (For example, a triple net lease is also known as a net-net-net lease.) Partially net leases should clearly state the expenses both the lessor and the lessee will pay.

Index Leases

Recent persistent inflation has encouraged the use of index leases, which contain escalation clauses for rental adjustments. The fixed rental payment is increased periodically (usually annually) by amounts that are tied either to increases in direct costs like insurance, taxes, and utilities, or to indexes of cost of living or wholesale prices.

One of the most common forms of index leases is a fixed rental with a provision for the lessee to share in future increases in real estate taxes. This arrangement protects the lessor's profit from one of the most significant cost inflators, while providing the lessee with a well defined standard and relatively small additional cost. Tax escalation clauses are normally based on taxes paid in the initial year of the lease, with the lessee paying his share of any subsequent increase. The language of the lease should clearly define the lessee's share, how subsequent improvements will be treated, and what procedures should be followed to contest increases in tax assessments.

Another form of direct-cost lease, which has become common in recent years, sets a fixed rental plus a share of increased operating expenses, such as utilities, repairs, and maintenance costs. This type of lease, common in office and retail developments where substantial services are required, is formulated in much the same manner as the tax-escalator lease. The lease must clearly define what costs are included in operating expenses.

Graduated Leases

Graduated leases call for stepped increases in rental amounts throughout the term of the lease. They are used primarily when new businesses are being established that are expected to grow. The lessor risks early returns from rentals against the potential for growth.

Reappraisal Leases

Seldom used today, reappraisal leases establish rentals as a percentage of property value at specific intervals of 3 to 5 years. It is a difficult lease to administer because of inherent problems in determining periodic property values and consequent pressures for litigation.

Classification by Term of Lease

Definite Tenancy

A definite tenancy specifies duration of the lease in months or years. The term of the lease is based on the lessee's desirability and potential long-term performance and the developer's strategy for growth of the project. The lessee's concern is that the lease term establish a stable location for as long as possible and allow his investment in equipment, fixtures, and interior construction to be amortized. His wish for a long-term lease must be balanced against the developer's need to retain some flexibility to respond to changing economic conditions or to desirable modifications of the mix of tenants. Major retail tenants such as department stores commonly have lease terms of 20 or 30 years, other major tenants of 10 to 15 years. Smaller retail tenants normally obtain leases for 7 to 10 years, office tenants for 5 to 10 years.

At the end of the lease period, the lessee and lessor may execute another lease to extend the term. In fact, the original lease may include a renewal clause that the lessee can exercise automatically. This clause may include provisions for agreeing upon modifications to other terms of the lease (such as rent) or the basis for negotiating various specifics of the renewal. A lessee continuing in possession of the premises after the stated lease term is a holdover and can be dispossessed on notice from the lessor. However, the lessor's acceptance of rent from a holdover tenant is usually construed as a renewal of the lease for 1 year regardless of the original term, unless the initial lease specifies a shorter holdover period.

Periodic Tenancy

A periodic tenancy is one in which a tenant continues to use the premises with no lease agreement. Month-to-month tenancies are most common, but year-to-year tenancies also are offered. The lessor gives notice of termination 15 days or 1 month in advance, governed by laws that vary from state to state.

Tenancy at Will

A tenancy at will is a general agreement to lease with termination at the will of either party, either by implication at the end of a specific time or by express agreement. Laws in some states require prior notice from the lessor; in other states the tenant is required to give notice.

Tenancy at Sufferance

Tenancy at sufferance occurs when a lessee continues to occupy the premises without permission. Such a lessee must leave without prior notice when the lessor desires.

In practice, most lease agreements in major downtown projects are definite tenancies with options to renew for certain periods under specific conditions. Options generally favor the tenant by setting a rental ceiling and allowing the tenant the choice of renewing or not. Lessors therefore may insist on options for periodic tenancy with the right to terminate at the end of the period. For retail stores, the lessor may require some level of sales performance as the basis for extending the lease.

Design in the Development Process

Once the developer has secured government approvals, detailed planning, design, and engineering begin within the guidelines provided by the approved general concept. Detailed design, which follows those guidelines, is undertaken in two phases: final preliminary drawings, and working drawings. Nearly all large commercial projects are designed by architectural firms the developer retains for the specific project. Engineering firms work on the development's structural, sanitary, and energy requirements. The design and engineering plans are prepared as part of the full preliminary and detailed specifications. Because they are so interrelated with the acceptability of

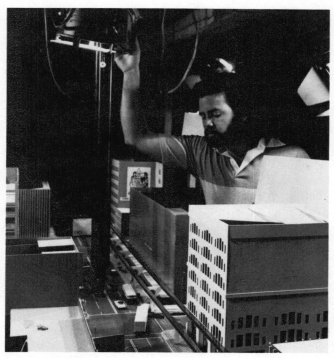

a design, building management plans and legal documentation for the project continue to be further detailed from those initiated during predevelopment.

Initial design ideas proposed during predevelopment address three principal concerns: the "fit" of the proposed development on the selected site; opportunities and requirements for elements like pedestrian spaces, street access, and compatibility with adjoining buildings; and cost levels for the project. These schematics guide detailed design. During the development stage of the development process, much more information is available for design. Major tenants' needs and desires are known, the management and legal structure are being developed, and the market has been more precisely identified. As a result, initial design ideas may be significantly altered based on this greater knowledge.

The completion of schematic or preliminary drawings represents a critical point for confirming costs. They can be confirmed by the developer's construction division or by an outside contractor. After those costs are confirmed, commitments for major tenants, project management, and financing are usually made before the working drawings are developed. The working drawings comprise a mass of detailed drawings and specifications requiring input

5-9   The VISIT system developed by the Rice Center in Houston illustrates the type of sophisticated design analysis that is required for effective integration of downtown projects into an existing environment. Using a video camera and crude models, it is possible to look inside a project for three-dimensional analysis.

5-10   Illustrative sketches like this one of the proposed Westlake Park project in Seattle showing the direct link to an existing monorail may be the most effective way to depict the value of direct access to transit.

from a number of specialized professionals. This section details the role and services of the design group, the important steps in the design process, and the design products.

The Role of the Designer

Either an A&E firm or an architect affiliated with various engineers forms the core of the design team, with specialists added to the group as appropriate for the project. This design group, under contract to the developer or his designated agent, provides the essential plans and specifications necessary for development. The A&E's most important contribution is his design skill, which stamps the product with a visible identity.

An architect usually manages the design team. Engineers specializing in mechanical, structural, and electrical systems are also members. Depending on the project, the group may include other professionals such as landscape architects, interior designers, lighting specialists, acoustical engineers, environmental specialists, foundation engineers, and specialists in specific building types like parking garages or restaurants.

The traditional services offered by full-range A&E firms include creating schematic plans and final designs for buildings and open spaces; preparing special studies such as subsurface investigations and environmental assessments; analyzing structural, electrical, and mechanical problems; translating designs into contract documents, working drawings, and detailed specifications; assisting in bidding, negotiations, and selecting contractors; assisting during construction to interpret and modify drawings and specifications when necessary; and monitoring work done by construction contractors. In providing these services, the A&E sometimes also assists in construction management by acting as a liaison between construction contractors and the developer.

The A&E's role has changed in recent years as building projects have become larger and more complicated. Many larger development companies have organized in-house groups that provide management control before and during construction, thus diluting the role of the A&E in such matters as cost estimating and control, selecting and monitoring contractors, subcontractors, and construction supervisors, and overall quality control. Furthermore, some large institutions and organizations that once employed A&Es as the principal overseers of their construction projects now use construction managers for coordination, scheduling, and administrative services during construction. On the other hand, a number of architects and A&E firms have become developers in their own right, expanding their services to include the entire design development process. The designer's responsibilities can therefore be tailored to meet the needs of the owner or developer as well as the complexity of the project itself.

In the Kentucky Center for the Arts, for example, the development company, acting as construction manager for the entire complex, coordinated the work of architects selected for the various project components by managing contractor bidding and negotiation and by monitoring construction activities, including contractors' adherence to schedules and budgets. In several projects developed by Mondev International, Ltd., the architect worked with the developer's staff from the earliest feasibility studies through project development.

The complex Crown Center project in Kansas City, Missouri, exemplifies the advantages of bringing in the design team early in the predevelopment process. The Crown Center development team hired one architect to prepare a land use plan and another, "master" architect to review the total land use concept, establish building massing, and select materials. (All parties understood from the beginning that the master architect might not be the design architect for all portions of the project.) At about the same time that architect was selected, the developer chose a separate management company to manage the project and to estimate and control costs and, shortly thereafter, a general contractor with whom he negotiated a guaranteed maximum contract for the first phase of the project and for the major mechanical and electrical subcontractors. When the architect completed schematics for the first phase of the total master plan, the owner, the designer, the project manager, and the contractor could jointly prepare and evaluate cost estimates for the project.

The developer accepted the architect's proposals for the initial phase of the project (an office structure, the 2,300-car garage beneath it, and a retail complex); the master architect then participated in the search for the architect to design the hotel for the complex. The design for the hotel was more complicated than for the office buildings, involving a connection to the retail structure. Once the two architects, working in conjunction, approved the hotel design, final cost estimates could be prepared and working drawings begun. As the architects were preparing working drawings, the contractors could contribute knowledge about techniques and materials to enable the architects to design the most economical building. The hotel operator recommended design changes that would improve the hotel's operation. The close coordination between designers, operators, and constructors, with the developer retaining final authority to make decisions, is the ideal arrangement to move a large project expeditiously and cost effectively through design and construction.

At the same time, the developer chose a design team for the residential portions of the first phase. This group and the master architect consulted frequently to create a compatible design for the office and residential portions of the project. Even when a separate development entity erected a building on land purchased from Crown Center, as was the case for the Mutual Benefit/IBM building, the designs were compatible. The architect for that building worked with the master architect to continue the project's overall scheme.[5]

Selection of the Design Team

Selecting a design team may be simple or complex. If a developer has worked with urban design and A&E firms on several similar projects, has been satisfied with their work, and can choose whichever firm he wants, his choice is somewhat easier. Other projects, however, such as those with public use components, may require competitive bidding, a local firm familiar with specific codes and procedures, or a special design.

A design group that worked on the project during predevelopment may not continue to provide service during development for several reasons. Planning skills required for predevelopment emphasize conceptualization rather than detailed design. The designers involved in predevelopment may have been chosen before the developer was selected and could be incompatible with the developer's organization or approach to the project. In most cases, however, it is most efficient to have the original design consultants continue to work on the project until it is completed.

A public/private project may make selection even more complicated. The project's visibility, because of its public nature, will arouse the interest of public officials and civic leaders. They may pressure the developer to select a well known architect because of the prestige or to employ an array of design specialists in

5 See "Crown Center and Crown Center Shops," ULI *Project Reference File*, vol. 4, no. 17 and 18 (October-December, 1974).

5-11 Models are a most effective way to present a large-scale downtown project, as shown by this model of Lafayette Square in Boston.

landscaping, lighting, or other design elements. These pressures may necessitate public competition or another highly visible process of selection that involves public officials. Public participation should not become public control, however, and the developer should avoid the public sector's dictating the selection of design professionals. The private developer is a member of the development team because of his experience in such matters.

When the project involves the design of public facilities and separate designers for different parts, the developer must establish some mechanism to resolve design disagreements and ensure compatible designs. For large projects, he can name a principal designer to be responsible for the overall design and its coordination. In the Courthouse Square project in Dayton, Ohio, for example, the developer employed an architectural firm to act as both principal architect for the private parts of the development and coordinating architect for the public parts. In a Cincinnati project, the architects for a privately developed air-rights structure coordinated their work with a different team of architects who designed the public platform.

In the Greenville Commons project in Greenville, South Carolina, the coventure included representatives from the Hyatt Corporation and the city. The two-member team established an overall budget for A&E services and each party's share of professional fees, negotiated the public and private components of the project with the project architect, and monitored the design process. The principal architect handled negotiations for subcontractors (for engineering, landscaping, interior design, and other special services) within the overall budget allocation.[6]

If the developer is unable to unilaterally select an architect, he may follow these general procedures adopted by local, state, and federal governments for public projects to select an A&E firm:

- invite several A&E firms to submit information on their qualifications, experience, and capabilities to perform the type of work being considered (known as a request for qualifications)
- after preliminary evaluation, discuss these submissions with representatives of the firms that appear to be most highly qualified

---

[6] See appendix N for a case study of Greenville Commons.

5-12   At Crown Center, different architects designed the Mutual Benefit Life Building on the left and the residential building under construction on the right, after consultation with the master architect for the entire project.

- rank the top two or three firms to evaluate competence, understanding of the project, and ability to carry out the project within time and budget constraints
- meet with the highest ranked firm to ascertain its specific capabilities to perform the work and to negotiate fees.

The set of instructions in the request for qualifications provided by the Kentucky Cultural Complex Committee (KCCC) for the proposed Kentucky Center for the Arts in downtown Louisville exemplifies the type of information such a request elicits. The request called for each architect's offering to be submitted in two parts: (1) a single portfolio of the firm's relevant design work and background information (including project title, location, construction cost, year of completion, and consultants and associates on each project); and (2) a written response to the following seven items:

1. a summary of the firm's background and capabilities, including information on the firm's history, areas of specialization or particular expertise, awards and other special recognition, and current staffing
2. a statement of the firm's philosophy of design and approach to design problem-solving, as evidenced by past projects and as applicable to the Kentucky Center for the Arts
3. a statement of the firm's proven techniques for managing architectural and engineering design and production, including interdisciplinary coordination, client involvement, and project cost control
4. the proposed organizational chart for the project with the names and responsibilities of key individuals
5. resumes of those key individuals
6. a list of at least five projects (completed or under construction) for which the firm had primary design responsibilities, including year of completion, project cost, consultants, client, client contact for reference, and a brief written description of the project
7. a list of all the firm's projects currently being designed or having construction documents prepared, including estimated construction cost, percent completion of services (through construction documents), and client.

This request for such detailed information is aimed at defining the designer's abilities to provide expert professional services in a timely manner and at a reasonable cost. Many architects believe that ability to perform, not cost of services, should be the primary consideration, and they may not compete on the basis of fees unless required by statute. A range for the fee can be negotiated during discussions with the two or three leading firms; the discussions will reflect both the developer's and the designer's understanding of the project's specific requirements. The initial ranking of the top two or three A&E firms need not be on the basis of fees; it should be made on the basis of the quality of design, and the final determination of the fee should be considered only after the firm has been selected.[7]

For large and complex projects, design may be competitive.[8] While this procedure makes the project highly visible across the nation and may result in a noteworthy design, it also requires considerable time, effort, and money. The process can result in a greater expense for design because the cost of the competition can be greater than fees negotiated with a single firm for preliminary design. Equally important, it may create false expectations about the developer's ability to pay for an innovative design unless cost estimates and guidelines are clearly established in the competition. Even with that precaution, there is no assurance that the winning design can be executed within budget. Experience has suggested the opposite is true. Because designers in competition strive for creativity, originality, and innovation, they frequently propose designs that have never been tried and therefore are not subject to conventional cost estimate analysis.

The basis for A&E fees has changed greatly since 1972. Before that year, architects used a standard schedule of fees that was based on a percentage of construction cost, with a sliding scale that depended on the project's size and complexity. Since a court case in 1972, architects have revised their procedures and now negotiate their fees based on their estimate of the time and effort required to accomplish the work.[9] The most common methods of reimbursement are direct cost plus fee, per diem rate, direct cost times a multiplier, and lump sum. The method most suitable for a particular project depends on the developer's ability to specify the detailed scope of services needed or the parties' ability to agree on the amount of flexibility available if the scope of the project changes.

---

[7] See appendix J for an example of a Request for Qualifications.

[8] The American Institute of Architects has developed "Guidelines for Architectural Design Competitions," a 13-page booklet that sets forth the rules and procedures under which such a competition would be conducted within the ethics of the profession. It is available free from AIA.

[9] For more information, see American Institute of Architects, *Compensation Guidelines for Architectural and Engineering Services*, 2nd ed. (Washington, D.C.: AIA, 1978) and *Your Architect's Compensation* (Washington, D.C.: AIA, n.d.). Both publications describe various methods for estimating fees.

If the scope of work is not well defined, the cost-plus-fee method is commonly used. The designer proceeds on specific work items as they are mutually agreed upon and is reimbursed for his direct costs plus a fee to compensate for overhead and profit. This type of compensation is also used when the services of a consultant are desired or when unusual design efforts are required. Per diem rates are used for special consultant services.

When the work to be performed is well defined, especially for commercial projects, compensation is based on the direct cost for personnel expense times a multiplier to cover overhead. This method allows the designer to proceed without committing the developer to a fixed fee; it also allows the design to proceed in stages as the project requires. A maximum limit may also be established subject only to a clear change in the scope of the work. For the few projects in which design services can be clearly defined, a lump sum fee may be appropriate.

The services to be provided by the designer (or design group) and the compensation method agreed upon are incorporated into a written contract with the developer. In turn, the manager of the design group (usually the architect) executes written agreements with his subcontractors or partners in the joint venture. In both cases, agreements may provide for services that are not specifically included in the current contract but may be required later.

The Design Process

The design period begins during predevelopment programming and continues into the development stage. Like most complex decision-making processes, design proceeds through a series of tentative solutions in response to the project's critical building and site requirements. These decisions are compared with the developer's other requirements to achieve a well integrated building design. Although no project is designed in quite the same series of steps as another, any design process has three major phases: preliminary design, design development, and final design. Preliminary design and design development together account for about 60 percent of the total design effort.

Preliminary Design

During this phase, the A&E explores alternatives for building systems and designs to arrive at site and floor plans, and selects basic materials and building systems. The design's fundamental shape and massing are determined at this time so that design criteria and general performance specifications for the project can be established. Preliminary cost estimates and

unusual contract or material requirements are also defined. Depending on the complexity of the project and the allocation of design time, this phase typically requires from 4 to 6 weeks. It is most often accomplished during predevelopment and will be re-evaluated and possibly revised extensively during design development.

The "Agreement to Lease and to Construct Improvements" for the Fountain Square South project in downtown Cincinnati exemplifies the type of information supplied in schematic or preliminary design plans. The contract stipulates that the schematic designs shall include the following information:

1. circulation plans (orthographic or isometric), showing:
   - the approximate outline and use of proposed enclosed, sheltered, and open spaces
   - truck docks and method of accommodating truck maneuvering space
   - the method of accommodating movement of materials within the development
   - the method of accommodating access, circulation, and storage of automobiles
   - the method of accommodating pedestrian circulation, including access to public transit
   - points of vertical circulation and type proposed (elevators, escalators, stairs, ramps, etc.)
2. a simple mass model showing buildings and open areas proposed in their relationship to:
   - existing buildings and open spaces expected to remain within one-half block of the property
   - buildings and open areas planned by the developer
   - anticipated buildings and open areas planned by other developers within one-half block of the property, if known
3. an outline of the developer's intentions in terms of:
   - type and extent of proposed building uses.
   - basic construction materials and mechanical systems
   - future building expansion
   - policy regarding design, size, and placement of signs
   - policy regarding public use of open spaces
4. nature of schematic materials required to establish the physical parameters of a cooperative working relationship as early as possible in the planning process.

Design Development

This phase, which usually requires from 1 to 3 months of design time, emphasizes the technical details of how to construct the project: designing the basic structural and mechanical systems; preparing drawings of elevations, sections, and typical exterior walls; analyzing construction details to resolve uncertainties; preparing outline specifications; selecting materials; identifying special conditions; and preparing renderings to aid the developer in his negotiations with financial institutions and public officials.[10] The final element of this phase is the confirmation of cost estimates, which should involve the developer and contractor or construction manager.

Final Design

Final design usually requires 2 to 3 months for completion. During that time final drawings, specifications, and contract documents are prepared. They are the basis for construction contractors' bids, contract award, and actual construction, and must therefore be quite detailed. Also during final design, the parties confirm budgeted costs and provide a preliminary construction schedule.

Cost Checkpoint and Design Coordination

At intervals during design, the A&E and the developers or owners review work in progress. They formally review and approve the preliminary design and work completed during design development before beginning final design. Other reviews are held at the desire of either the developer or designer as key decision points are reached. Reviews and responses are fully documented to provide a record of progress, changes made, and reasons for them.

At three points during the process cost figures related to design work are generated. The first point occurs during predevelopment when the preliminary design is sufficiently completed so that preliminary cost estimates can be prepared. At this point, initial cost figures are calculated and cost responsibilities divided between public and private parties. These figures can be used for later negotiations. The developer and representatives from the public sector review these initial cost figures and decide to proceed with, modify, or abandon the project.

The second point occurs during the development stage after preliminary design is completed. The developer secures estimates of costs from the construction manager or contractor to determine whether the project is within the established budget. These costs are often used to negotiate leases, to prepare reports aimed at obtaining financing, and to decide whether or not to commit the parties to construction.

The final point occurs when approximately 85 percent of the budget for the A&E fee has been expended. Costs are reviewed to confirm previous representations to the lenders and to assure the developer and other interested parties that design has proceeded as projected.

This outline of the design process only hints at the amount of work and time required. Design judgments affect project costs, construction methods, and timing and, therefore, require constant confirmation by the owner, developer, or contractor. Consultants must supply their input; the construction management staff must approve the decisions. The need to conform to local codes and regulations requires countless hours reviewing design and negotiating decisions with public officials. The feedback from these interactions can expand "normal" design by many months.

When more than one design group is involved, design of one component requires coordination with design of the others. A coordinating architect usually decides how one component will mesh with another. As he is fully aware of design problems that may be encountered on the various components, he can provide a fulcrum for design decisions.

For example, in the Courthouse Square project in Dayton, Ohio, the principal coordinating architect determined the massing and spacing of buildings for most of the project. The department store involved in the project, however, employed its own architect to design the store within the predetermined mass of the building established by the coordinating architect. The architects' informal coordination ensured that structural components were compatible.

When more than one designer is involved in a project without a coordinating architect, the developer must coordinate the designs. Although this arrangement can work successfully when developers and architects have worked together before, it can pose problems when designers have entirely different approaches to the project. It should be discouraged unless extenuating circumstances apply—perhaps when a public entity commissions a separate designer for its part of the project or when some buildings are being rehabilitated as part of the overall project. An experienced developer, however, is careful to select or suggest designers who have complementary abilities and attitudes.

---

[10] See appendix K for an example of an agreement to lease and construct outlining the mass of detail that is addressed during final design.

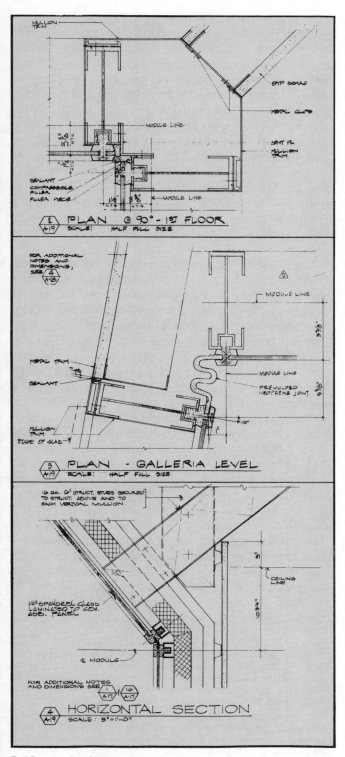

5-13 As the design process moves toward completion, a large project may produce hundreds of sheets of detailed drawings.

Products of the Design Process

The preparation of contract documents is the last step of the design process. Contract documents provide the basic data for contractor bidding or negotiation, contractual relationships, and actual construction. They are provided to potential contractors for their use in evaluating a project proposal. The documents include working drawings, specifications, general and supplementary conditions, and proposed agreements between the developer and contractors. Each of them must be sufficiently detailed to provide the best legal foundation for contracts as well as a step-by-step guide to construction.

Working drawings must include detailed drawings of all architectural, structural, mechanical, and electrical systems, site development, and special engineering required for the project. A single office building may require dozens of pages of drawings; a major project may require several hundred drawings, including overall building systems and highly detailed drawings of specific parts. Notes on the drawings describe materials, quantities, and locations.

The technical specifications for the project are the written complement of the drawings, describing the type and quality of materials, the scope and manner of construction, instructions for finishes, and other aspects of building components illustrated in the working drawings. Specifications are addressed primarily to the general contractor for the project and are organized according to the building trades that will be involved in the project.

Five types of specifications are common.

- *Descriptive specifications* specify the types of materials to be used—their major characteristics, the size and number of parts, the relationships of moving parts, the procedure for assembly, for example. The designer assumes responsibility for the adequate performance of the product once the contractor has constructed it according to the description.

- *Performance specifications* define the results to be obtained from the work to be done. The architect or engineer specifies the function or appearance of the product and allows the contractor to determine the particular product that will meet those specifications. The responsibility for ensuring that work meets specifications rests with the contractor or, often, the manufacturer of the product.

- *Trade name specifications* specify the manufacturer and model of the product. The designer takes responsibility for naming a specific product that will meet the requirements of the design but risks stifling competition and increasing costs.

- *Reference specifications* refer to standards established by recognized authorities like the National Bureau of Standards or Underwriters Laboratories. Their use ensures that products meet recognized standards.

- *Base-bid specifications* name one or more manufacturers or fabricators for a product; their prices must be used in the contractor's proposal. If the contractor proposes alternate products, their prices are shown as higher or lower than the specified price. This type of specification is often used to ensure quality control.[11]

General and supplementary contractual conditions are also part of the contract documents. They include a definition of responsibilities and relationships for the parties to the contract, requirements for insurance and bonding, procedures for settling disagreements, and schedules and methods of payment. They may also include other conditions peculiar to the particular project or developer—provisions for temporary structures, onsite utilities, and construction management.[12]

If appropriate, bidding requirements are included as part of the contract documents. They usually include an advertisement for bids (especially if the project is publicly financed), an invitation to bid (used primarily for private projects), instructions to bidders, and the proposal form for bidding. Instructions to bidders define requirements for preparing and submitting bids, the date, time, and place of bid opening, provisions for withdrawal or rejection of bids, comments or additions to the specifications, and arrangements for site visits.

Construction Management and Operations

The construction process required for complex downtown development projects encompasses an array of expertise, intricate contractual arrangements, complicated delivery and completion schedules, and management of hundreds, perhaps thousands, of entrepreneurs, journeymen, laborers, professionals, and other workers. The line of decision-making runs from the developer's offices through a maze of managers, contractors, and subcontractors to the workmen actually pouring the concrete, shaping the ductwork, or affixing the sign with the building name. This section describes basic construction organizations and procedures, techniques of construction management, and types of contractual arrangements.

Organization of the Construction Process

The major actors directly involved in the construction process include the developer or owner, the architect-engineer, the construction manager, the construction contractor and/or subcontractors, and the material suppliers. Each of these groups has a particular perspective on the project. The owner or developer is concerned with obtaining a high quality marketable building at the minimum price within the shortest feasible time period. He pays constant attention to the balance sheet and to the fluctuating money and real estate markets. The A&E's principal concerns are ascertaining that the building is constructed as specified in the construction drawings and specifications. He also acts as the agent of the owner or developer to ensure that required changes are within the cost, quality, and time constraints established by the developer.

The construction manager, who may be the general contractor, is the prime link between the developer and the subcontractors and material suppliers. He supervises the various construction contractors and subcontractors. The contractors' and subcontractors' concern is to complete specified portions of a building or building system. The material suppliers' concern is to provide all of the physical parts of the building as specified by the designers and ordered by the contractors.

These groups share management functions in various ways, depending on the type and complexity of the project and the organization of the developer and A&E. The developer, owner, project manager, job superintendent, general contractor, and construction supervisor for the architect are the people most responsible for completion of the building, but traditionally, management of a development project is the primary responsibility of a general contractor. He administers the construction, often with oversight from a representative of the A&E firm that designed the project. The general contractor is obligated to supervise all construction, initiate and administer all contracts with subcontractors and suppliers, and de-

---

[11] The Construction Specifications Institute and the Associated General Contractors have developed standard forms for technical specifications. Many architects have developed their own methods of writing specifications, employing specialists and sometimes computers to perform the task.

[12] Experienced designers and developers often prepare a set of general conditions suited to their own needs to serve as the basis for contract documents, but the American Institute of Architects has developed a standard form called "General Conditions of the Contract for Construction." It can be applied to most projects by adding to or modifying conditions as necessary.

5-14   Buildings under construction attract attention and sidewalk superintendents.

liver the building at the time and under the terms agreed to. The A&E ensures that the contractor fulfills the terms of the contract and guides the contractor in interpreting the documents.

Increasingly, however, these traditional responsibilities are being divided in other ways. Developers now sometimes assign a construction manager from their organization to replace or supplement both the general contractor and the A&E. Developers also may choose to contract separately with a construction manager to oversee construction. In other cases, package or "turnkey" building companies design, manage, and construct a building for a client.

The transferral of some of the management duties of the general contractor and A&E to a distinct construction management organization, whether by contract or within a development company, has been a feature of many recent large, complex projects. The management organization may assume some of the general contractor's responsibilities, such as negotiating or administering subcontracts, or may maintain principal management control over the job. The developer retains direct control over the conduct and quality of the work, phasing the construction work as required by the nature of the project without having to make day-to-day decisions.[13]

The developer's assumption of construction responsibility recognizes the need for his continuing presence in complex projects. The developer cannot rely on drawings and documents to transmit a perfect understanding of the project to the contractor. Placing responsibility with the developer also means responsibility for accepting risks and liability for errors. The scale and cost of a large project, however, often make it difficult to obtain competitive, realistic bids for a single contract. Very few contractors are large enough to undertake such projects and are forced to measure risks and responsibilities for many years in the future. Thus, a series of contracts with continuity of construction management ensured by the owner's participation as manager can be a cost-effective alternative and provide more flexibility for the developer.

The concept of construction management is partly the result of the special requirements of longer term,

[13] A sample contract for construction management services is contained in "The GSA System for Construction Management," prepared by the Public Buildings Service of GSA, 1975 revised edition.

complex building projects such as those in CBDs and partly a response to the need for accelerating construction. Phasing a project over several years with some components under construction while others are being designed demands firm managerial focus on the process to ensure continuity. Mixing public and private interests requires a supervisory mechanism that can combine diverse requirements.[14]

Construction Management Tasks

The construction manager must be familiar with the types of construction that will be used in the project, local conditions, and the qualifications of the primary subcontractors, or he may actually increase project costs. In general, construction managers are responsible for contractor bidding and negotiations, contract and subcontract administration, scheduling, field supervision, and community and labor relations. A construction manager employed by the developer or as a consultant may also be involved in design, chiefly in cost estimating, cost control, and project scheduling. The construction manager may also advise the developer about the contents of the contract documents and review subcontractors' qualifications. In these capacities the manager supplants or supplements the services of the A&E.

The following list summarizes construction managers' possible activities. Responsibilities are divided among the developer, the A&E, and the general contractor or construction manager, depending on the scope of the project and the capabilities of each organization.

- predevelopment stage
  - develop, monitor, and update program budget as required
  - develop, monitor, and update project schedules as required
  - evaluate construction materials, components, and subsystems for potential implications on cost and timing
  - recommend early purchase and delivery of construction items as appropriate
  - evaluate design in progress for implications on cost and timing
  - advise designer on site conditions, construction techniques, and possible shortages of materials
  - review contract packaging, phasing, and documentation
  - prepare a bidding schedule or procedure for negotiation
  - conduct bidding or negotiations
  - assist in preparation of contract documents

- development stage
  - develop procedures for job meetings, progress reports, and payment schedules
  - supervise project, including operation of site office, maintenance of job records, and inspection and approval of work in progress
  - assist in securing permits and approvals
  - develop, monitor, and update detailed project schedules for all participants
  - develop, monitor, and update detailed cost estimates and current and future cash flow requirements
  - monitor contractors to ensure their adherence to requirements for bonding, guarantees, job safety programs, equal opportunity programs, and other contract-related items
  - maintain responsibility for storing items purchased by the owner until they are turned over to contractors
  - coordinate procedures for obtaining and approving shop drawings
  - establish procedures for change orders, recommend changes, review requests for changes, and negotiate changes with contractors
  - establish procedures for processing claims and disputes
  - determine that work is ready for final inspection
  - coordinate some or all of the items covered by the general conditions such as watchmen, fencing, the field office, temporary toilets, first aid, temporary utilities, trucking, cleaning, and signs[15]

Contractor Bidding and Negotiations

Managing bidding and negotiation is one of the most important steps toward construction. This process, in which contractors are named and contracts awarded, is instrumental in determining the quality, pace, and cost of development.

The developer decides whether to invite bids or to negotiate terms with selected contractors, based on several considerations:

- the developer's knowledge of and experience with contractors

---

[14] In the Kentucky Center for the Arts, which involves both public and private elements, the developer acted as general manager, with overall responsibility for packaging, designing, and constructing the project. A general contractor was responsible for field supervision, but the developer negotiated and awarded all subcontracts. Thus, the developer had direct control of the construction process.

[15] American Institute of Architects, *Project Delivery Approaches* (Washington, D.C.: AIA, 1975), pp. 10–16.

- the developer's ability to control the project so it is constructed within budget
- the developer's established working relationship with specific contractors
- the amount of time available before construction must begin
- the general availability of contractors in the area
- the type of contractor required for the particular project
- any legal prohibitions preventing the awarding of contracts on a negotiated basis.

Barring legal impediments, a negotiated contract should be considered for public/private mixed use projects. Open bidding is required on most public construction projects where the public sector awards the contracts. Large developers of private projects, on the other hand, tend to select contractors for negotiation or conduct informal bidding with selected contractors. In a public/private development, open bidding for public components and invitational or closed bidding for private components can create serious problems, particularly when the overall project has joint-use areas. One solution to this problem that allows invitational or negotiated bidding is the creation of a public development corporation, which has greater freedom in the conduct of its business.

Most contractors have had considerable experience responding to invitations to bid so they are able to draw upon completed work to formulate their proposals. In preparing a bid, the contractor considers the labor, skills, and materials required for the work, determines which trades should supplement the contractor's staff, and obtains bids from selected subcontractors and price quotations from suppliers. He submits the bid, including his estimate of costs, in the form specified by the contract documents at the time and place given in the invitation to bid.

Although for most public projects bidding is open to any qualified firm, in purely private projects developers can select potential bidders based on their experience, past working relationships, proximity to the project, and availability for new contracts. Once identified, prospective bidders can be invited to meet with the construction manager, view models and drawings, and discuss the timing and general budget for the project. At this early meeting, the developer can determine bidders' availability and interest, and the parties can organize their schedules to accommodate the dates for bid invitations, prebid conferences, and bid submittal. From these potential bidders, the developer usually selects five or six bidders to receive an invitation to bid for each prime contract.

About midway in the bidding period, usually 4 to 6 weeks after contract documents have been issued to bidders, the parties attend a prebid conference at which the developer evaluates bidders' interest, briefs bidders, subcontractors, and suppliers on the project schedule, and interprets contract documents if there are questions. After bidders submit their bids, the developer with the A&E or construction manager evaluates the responses, clarifies various points, selects contractors, and awards the contracts.

Certain developers favor direct negotiations with selected contractors rather than the bidding process. In this case, the developer selects a prospective contractor on the basis of prior work and experience and asks him to submit a proposal for construction. Frequently the developer identifies the contractor early enough so the two parties can consult during design, particularly on scheduling, cost estimating, cost control, construction methods, and materials. This early participation can reduce costs by establishing a realistic schedule and a maximum price earlier in the development stage, which the developer can use to secure financing.

Contract and Subcontract Administration

Several types of contracts are available. A lump-sum contract establishes a single cost for all services and materials to be supplied; a unit-price contract fixes the cost for unit quantities of work or materials when quantities cannot be ascertained at the beginning of the job. If plans and specifications are not complete enough to allow preparation of a detailed price quotation, a cost-plus-fee contract is written. It covers the actual costs of the contract plus an agreed amount above defined costs, which is stated either as a percentage of costs or as a lump sum. A maximum price usually limits total costs. The design-construction contract is usually written for turnkey or package building projects. Many contracts now feature options on both services and fees to make contracts for large buildings more flexible.

The A&E or construction manager's administration of contracts involves monitoring the progress of the work to confirm its completion and recording changes and extra work. The administrator ensures that work complies with contract documents, issues certificates that the work has been done properly, and authorizes payments. The A&E or construction manager approves drawings of construction details (shop drawings) and materials samples when the contract calls for their submittal. He is also responsible for contractors' relationships with subcontractors and material suppliers, all of whom have written agreements.

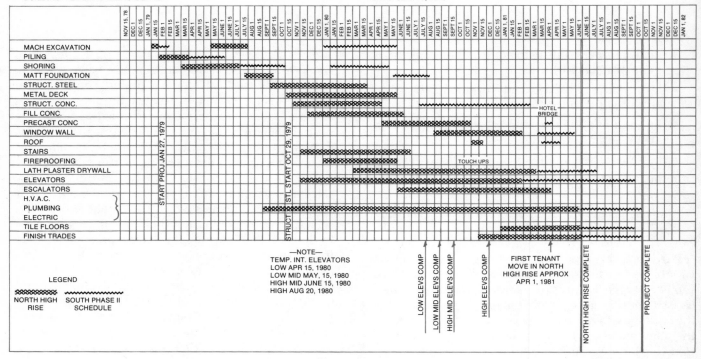

5-15 This bar chart of the construction schedule for a single high-rise structure within a much larger project illustrates how various activities can occur simultaneously or consecutively.

Scheduling

Scheduling begins early in predevelopment and continues throughout construction. Overall schedules establish general target dates for completion and occupancy of major components of the project, and detailed schedules show dates for procurement and delivery of materials and labor. Schedules are a key part of managing a project; they serve as the basis for measuring progress, approving requests for payment, evaluating the potential effects of delays or changes, and maintaining an accurate account of costs and cash flow.

Normally, the construction manager formulates a master schedule for the entire project and individual schedules for each contract. The master schedule evolves during design and is based on preliminary design and engineering forecasts. Final building plans refine the schedule and complete details. The master schedule then becomes one of the key documents that control contracting and construction. It sets dates for initiation, completion, and occupancy of major components of the project; start-up and completion dates for each of the principal construction activities (site excavation, foundation work, etc.); and the specific times for acquiring, installing, and testing equipment.

Detailed schedules are related to the complexity of the project. They include varying degrees of generality and can cover several time periods—total construction, or 1-year and 90-day control schedules. The

bases for detailed schedules are separate schedules submitted by and negotiated with each contractor and subcontractor for the work he is to do. Individual contracts usually prescribe the type of schedule to be submitted; they are then negotiated to fit within the overall schedule.

The detailed schedules assist the construction manager to administer contracts and supervise the job. To be most useful, detailed schedules should contain at least the following items:

- start-up and completion dates for each activity and/or contractor
- cost breakdown of items of work in the contract for payment purposes
- dates for procurement, fabrication, delivery, and installation of materials and equipment
- requirements for construction relationships between contractors
- dates for submitting and approving shop drawings and materials samples
- sequence and dates of official public inspections and approvals
- dates for completion and occupancy of each section of the project.

For relatively simple projects, the schedules can be shown as bar charts that list each activity, show the time it occupies during the project period, and symbolically indicate special relationships and details.

120

More complex projects require the critical path method (CPM), which shows the sequence of each task, notes about required times and float time (extra time available during one task while awaiting completion of other tasks), and perhaps financial data. The "critical path" is the sequence of steps that requires the most time to complete. CPM and similar methods let the construction manager evaluate the potential effects of changes or delays and provide a convenient accounting device for judging progress of the contracts. Such schedules also provide early warning about potential costly delays in the project. For some larger projects involving intricate contractual relationships, the schedules are computerized to speed calculations and revise timing as necessary.

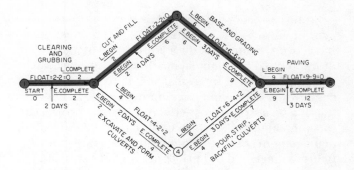

5-16 The network for the critical path method of scheduling comprises arrows representing steps or tasks and numbered nodes representing completion of those tasks. The colored line marks the "critical path," the sequence of steps taking longest to complete. (Source: Frederick S. Merritt, *Building Construction Handbook*, New York: McGraw Hill Book Company, 1975.)

Field Supervision

In many public building projects, a general contractor provides construction management and supervision services. Many large private development organizations name project and construction managers from within their own organizations. These positions also have their counterparts in each of the contracting firms doing the work, with a project manager and a field superintendent assigned to each job.

Field supervision of individual contractors involves a wide range of duties. The construction manager is responsible for:

- managing the flow of materials and equipment to the site and their location on the site
- maintaining relationships between contractors, with the A&E, and with inspectors
- reporting daily on progress and consulting on schedule changes
- detecting variations from the contract documents and initiating change orders or back-charges
- identifying and solving problems.

Community and Labor Relations

The manager's ability to achieve his objectives related to cost, time, and quality will depend substantially on maintaining good relations with community and labor groups. The manager will need to:

- use local contractors and subcontractors
- hire local labor
- satisfy local public interest groups about the project's objectives
- acquire the necessary approvals from public agencies
- maintain successful labor relations.

Because many downtown projects are built near residential areas housing the poor and in areas where other projects involving the local government are underway, it may be advisable or necessary to use local contractors and local labor. Using local contractors or subcontractors is one way to ensure employment of local labor, but local labor may also be hired through local equal opportunity and nondiscrimination programs or by recruiting labor at the job site. In many projects involving the public sector, contractors are required to use local or minority contractors. These agreements may necessitate contractors' assisting subcontractors with inadequate capital, subdividing work into smaller contracts, entering into joint ventures with subcontractors, or awarding small pilot contracts to subcontractors managed by another subcontractor. These agreements require that the contractor actively seek such relationships, identify possible subcontractors, and maintain good liaison with local groups interested in labor and business development.

Maintaining a smooth relationship with labor is one of the construction manager's most difficult and complex tasks, chiefly because of the cyclical nature of the industry and the multitude of craft unions working on a job. Strikes or jurisdictional disputes can delay construction for weeks or months. Fierce competition in the local labor market may require incentives such as overtime pay or reimbursement for travel and living costs for skilled out-of-town labor. The construction manager must balance public desires to use local or small or minority contractors with the necessity for hiring contractors and subcontractors with good records of labor stability.

Some projects where private developers have sought to achieve community and business goals have been hampered by a multitude of public requirements. The financial health of any project can be adversely affected by unreasonable requirements for community economic development rather than contracting on a strictly cost-effective basis. A project can incur greater costs when contracts are subdivided; management costs are higher, schedules are more difficult to meet, and bid prices are higher because each contract has provisions for overhead and profit. The community must be made aware that public costs added to development projects are inevitably passed to the private users of the development, possibly to the detriment of the project's marketability.

Civic groups' interest in the project often is stimulated by construction. Through lobbying, court action, public hearings, and political influence, they can impede the project's construction and marketing. Therefore, one of the construction manager's most important responsibilities is to maintain good public relations with such groups, from predevelopment until the project is completed.

One of construction managers' continuing concerns is acquiring the necessary approvals from public agencies. The personnel of contractors who have worked in the area are already familiar with the requirements and staff of regulatory agencies. Construction managers must also maintain constant personal contact with inspectors and other agency staff members so that they are informed of the project's progress. An expeditor or coordinator with the public agency most involved in the project can help in dealing with public officials, particularly when a problem of jurisdiction among public agencies arises.

Methods of Construction

A project can be constructed in one of three ways: design-award-build, accelerated construction, or design-build. Most private and public development projects follow the design-award-build approach, in which a typical project follows certain steps:

- architectural commission
- program analysis
- schematic design
- preliminary design and outline specifications
- final design and contract documents
- advertising for bids
- bid opening
- contract award
- construction
- inspections, approvals, occupancy.

The major phases are linear, with designs completed before contracts are awarded or construction begins. Contracts are awarded during a single time period and on the basis of prices fixed at that time.

If everything goes well, a $10–15 million project may require 2½ to 3½ years before completion. Some problems are inherent in such a lengthy process for both designer and builder. The amount of time involved in completing each step before another step begins escalates project costs. Interest costs for interim construction loans are incurred for a longer time until a takeout mortgage at lower interest can be executed. Once designs are completed and contract documents prepared, the developer has little flexibility in responding to problems of pricing or materials availability, because the necessity for comprehensive and complete construction documents freezes design at an early stage. In addition, a large project has considerable impact on the marketplace: If the entire project is completed at the same time, the market may, at least for a while, become overbuilt, depressing rents that could be charged if new space were delivered to the market more gradually.

To overcome one of these problems, that of the cost of construction loan funds, many developers overlap design and construction periods to shorten the time required to complete the project and to save construction costs by obtaining early bids, smaller packages, and shorter-term financing. This method, known as accelerated, fast track, or phased, emphasizes concurrent contracts and a sophisticated level of construction management. Each major building system is designed, contracted, and constructed on separate but coordinated time frames.

In any building project, some decisions made early in the design phase can lead directly to construction contracts. Determining the basic building siting, for example, allows a contract for rough site work to be awarded. Decisions on basic structural elements permit foundation and structural contracts to be let. And early decisions on materials or equipment requiring a long lead time allow advance orders to be placed.

Accelerated construction is most useful in projects with one or more of the following characteristics present:

- a particular construction problem that requires extra time, such as complicated subsurface work or unusual requirements for fabrication
- industrialized building systems that encourage early contract award to gain time in fabrication and erection
- a large or long-term project for which some components must be completed before other compo-

nents, where a contract for the entire project would be too large, or where some components would be completed too far in the future to make reasonable estimates of cost.

Accelerated construction need not be used for all phases of a development project. It may be used for the early stages of development, with more traditional contracting used for the later stages. Successful accelerated construction is carefully controlled throughout. Early cost estimates must be accurate to maintain the projected budget, and design must progress concurrently with construction to coordinate individual contracts.

Accelerated construction has certain drawbacks. It increases demands on designers, the lack of assurance that bids will conform to early cost estimates, and the reluctance of some lenders to commit financing before all design work is completed. For large, multiphase projects, however, phased construction provides maximum management and cost control.

The third type of construction method that integrates design and construction is the design-build method. It is used less often for major public and commercial facilities than for industrial and commercial projects whose requirements are fairly explicit. The owner/developer contracts for both design and construction services with one entity. The parties determine a price from a statement of performance and standards required for the project and commit themselves to it before detailed design and actual construction. This approach provides certain benefits to the developer:

- One firm is responsible for design and construction, minimizing problems with coordination and thereby shortening the construction period.
- Establishing a firm price early resolves uncertain project costs and assists in obtaining financing commitments.
- The freedom to select products, building systems, and construction techniques allows a more flexible response to changing market conditions.

The firm responsible for design and construction is chosen through a negotiated contract or through a competitive selection based on proposals. The basis for award may be the lowest cost or the highest quality product that falls within a fixed cost range established in the request for proposals.

6.
The Postdevelopment Stage

The completed development project must be managed and maintained to realize the full potential of its market. In a large, complex project combining public and private interests, management and maintenance will necessarily require careful forethought and special arrangements if the project is to contribute successfully to a revitalized downtown. Each project's particular requirements and the nature of its legal, financial, and other constraints provide guidelines for a specific agreement between public and private interests. This agreement will normally be fashioned during predevelopment, but during the postdevelopment stage the developer, manager, and tenants refine—and perhaps find it necessary to modify—each party's responsibilities.

Although management and maintenance agreements vary considerably and are evolving quickly as experience is gained, they share certain common requirements. They must clearly define which party will be responsible for management and maintenance for what portion of the project, and who will pay which costs on what basis. The general trend is to consolidate most management and maintenance under one entity with other participants paying for their share of services.

Management and Maintenance Activities

Types of Activities

Management activities for a downtown project—whether it is a single office building or a complex incorporating offices, hotels, retail stores, and parking—can be grouped into three areas:

1. providing basic operating services and maintaining the structure's physical viability
2. administering the financial accounts and tenant relations
3. marketing the project and promoting community relations.

The building management is usually responsible for the following operating services:

- maintaining the heating, cooling, lighting, electrical, gas, and telephone systems
- providing building security
- maintaining elevators and escalators
- washing windows and floors

125

- disposing of trash
- maintaining landscaped and parking areas
- cleaning sidewalks and removing snow
- controlling pests
- painting and decorating common areas and tenant spaces
- making repairs and minor modifications
- providing any special services for tenants.

These services must be provided dependably on a daily basis; the management can provide them from its own staff or through contracts with outside firms. Maintaining the structure's physical viability requires periodic inspections to detect the need for building renovation or replacement of equipment. The manager is responsible for maintaining common areas and initiating periodic improvements that will ensure the building's continued use. As building management services are expanded from a single office building to a complex of buildings with varying construction and tenancy, the complexity of building management grows.

The project's financial viability depends on the sound management of income and expenses, rent collections, tenant relationships, and marketing for replacement tenants. The manager's chief responsibilities are to provide services in the most cost-effective manner, to attract and retain tenants with the most desirable leases, and to maintain detailed accounts of all financial transactions. These responsibilities are especially significant in a large complex where tenants' lease terms, rents, and sharing of responsibilities may vary substantially. Generally, management is responsible for:

- administering insurance coverage on employee bonds, plate glass damage, and personal injury
- paying taxes
- billing and collecting rents and paying expenses
- negotiating lease renewals and replacements, and leasing vacant space
- periodically analyzing market conditions and tenant mix
- contracting for special services
- managing the in-house staff providing services
- responding to tenants' special requests and needs
- providing business and financial assistance to selected tenants under special circumstances.

Promoting the project, the third area of management responsibility, is concerned with marketing the development and with maintaining good community relations. The groundwork will again have been provided as early as the predevelopment stage, when promotion is designed to win public acceptance, ease construction, and attract tenants. During the post-development stage, however, several related marketing activities become important:

- promoting the project as an attractive shopping and business area
- organizing and providing support for any merchants or tenants associations
- promoting community events in common areas of the project
- maintaining contact with public agencies like the police, fire, and building inspection departments
- promoting the project through community contacts in schools, churches, and public meetings
- maintaining contacts in the business community to support marketing and financial concerns.

Management Organization and Procedures

Project management can take two forms. The owner/developer of the property might control management directly, or a professional manager or management company might be contracted to provide management services for a fee. The largest projects, however, are generally managed by the owner/developer's professionally trained employees. Owners of most projects containing over 500,000 square feet of gross leasable area usually participate directly in the project's management.[1] Their role varies from general overseer to day-to-day operations manager. The reason for their involvement is the size of the investment and the tendency for large projects to remain under the ownership of the original developer for a long time.

Owners or developers directly involved in management control might be represented by a corporate subsidiary or by a limited partnership in which the general partners actually oversee management. When two or more entities own or control the project, a subsidiary management corporation is often formed.

Compensation for a management firm is usually based on the project's monthly rental income. Fees range from 2 to 6 percent of total rental income; they are based on the responsibilities assigned to the man-

---

[1] Horace Carpenter, Jr., *Shopping Center Management: Principles and Practices* (New York: International Council of Shopping Centers, 1974).

6-1 Postdevelopment management is a most important element of project success. It can be as simple as the management of a single office building or as complex as that required for Illinois Center, the 83-acre project shown above, which began in 1969 and is scheduled for completion in about 1989.

ager, the size of the project, and its condition. Normally the owner pays directly for goods or services, while the manager is reimbursed for wages and salaries for all personnel providing services. Wages and salaries for the manager's office staff and principals of the firm are considered to be reimbursed through the management fee. Managers often receive separate reimbursement for negotiating leases and for supervising major repairs or renovation.

Contracts with management firms are usually renewed annually, commonly with no changes unless ownership of the property changes or the quality of management is considered to be declining. The standard contract includes the following major items:

- exclusive management agreement
- terms of renewal and termination
- rent and lease negotiations
- monthly statements to owners
- separation of owner's and manager's funds
- bonding of employees
- manager's authority for repairs and remodeling, employee management, and management of service contracts

- limitation of liability by owner
- payment to manager for services rendered.[2]

Regardless of who manages the project, the manager usually employs both in-house staff and contractors to supply services. The in-house staff usually includes office and operations personnel. The operations personnel usually include a chief engineer, who is responsible for the physical plant and the building heating, plumbing, and electrical systems; a building superintendent, who is responsible for cleaning, renovation, and providing services to tenants; and a night superintendent. Other services—security, cleaning, renovation design, and construction—can be provided by the in-house staff, but increasingly managers are contracting with special companies to perform these services. Elevator and escalator maintenance and window cleaning are almost always contracted out.

---

[2] Suggested by the Institute of Real Estate Management. A standard management agreement form is available from the Institute of Real Estate Management, 155 East Superior Street, Chicago, Illinois 60611 (form no. 7–12, *Management Agreement*).

127

Developer/Manager/Tenant Relationship

The manager is also responsible for establishing and continuing successful relationships between the owner/developer and the tenants of the project. Day-to-day management requires administering the lease agreements between the owner and tenants and leading the effort to secure public patronage so important to the prosperity of both owner and tenants.

The manager, as the owner's employee or contractor, should place the owner's concerns first in dealings with tenants, other employers, or contractors. His objectives in serving the owner are to obtain the maximum gross income while reducing operating, maintenance, and financing costs; and to extend the property's productive life and enhance its capital value by ensuring adequate maintenance and repair and by adapting the property to changes in the market environment.

The way the manager meets these objectives depends on the number and nature of the project's tenants. Since the manager is often responsible for administering leases with the tenants, he must be very familiar with the terms of the leases and the understandings between the parties.[3] He will also be required to deal with situations not specified in the lease. In these dealings with tenants, the manager is the owner's key to the success of the project.

Lease Administration and Renewal

As the agent of the owner/developer, the manager is responsible for carrying out the terms of the lease for the owner and for ensuring that tenants meet their obligations. His responsibilities include:

- collecting and accounting for rents and other monies due
- ensuring the proper physical condition of the building when tenants move in and when they move out
- enforcing the provisions of the lease pertaining to tenants' use of space
- revising, renewing, or replacing leases.

One of the manager's most important tasks is to compute rents accurately and collect them promptly. The lease agreement spells out the basis on which rent will be computed; it may be a percentage of gross sales, with or without some or all utilities or taxes included. If rent is based to any extent on tenant sales, the manager must make certain the figures the tenant supplies are accurate, perhaps obtaining them from an annual report prepared by an outside auditor.

Many recent such leases have provided for quarterly or monthly estimated payments, with the account reconciled at the end of the year. Sometimes a manager must have the tenant's estimate audited several times a year if they vary too much from actuality. The manager is also responsible for calculating periodic increases in rent if the lease stipulates them. In his calculations he may have to consider special provisions that put a ceiling on the tenant's share of maintenance expenses for common areas, real estate taxes, or improvements. He may also have to figure in utility and other charges.

Once the manager submits the bill to the tenant, he must ensure that it is paid on time. Failure to pay promptly may signal the tenant's financial weakness, a poor accounting system, or a deliberate postponement to help with cash flow. Any of these reasons could mean future problems for the manager and ultimately the owner.

Ensuring the project's proper physical condition is one of the manager's continuing responsibilities. Both the owner and the tenants rely on the manager to keep common areas neat, the shell of the building in good condition, and all equipment in good working order. The manager is also responsible, however, for ensuring that tenants comply with their obligations to preserve the property. Ensuring their compliance is largely a matter of regular observation of the premises to detect small problems before they become large ones.[4] The manager's scrupulous observations and firm, courteous, and corrective action best serve both tenants and owner.

Interpreting and enforcing lease provisions regarding tenants' use of space also requires the manager's constant attention. Leases often prohibit a change of ownership or subletting without the lessor's consent and, in the case of retail tenants, forbid tenants from locating another store within a certain distance. Enforcing these provisions can entail many questions of definition and potentially lead to unhappy tenant relations. Early detection of possible problems and prompt action to solve them are essential to prevent their becoming aggravated.

Revising, renewing, or replacing lease agreements is another of management's ongoing responsibilities. Over time the lease terms may need new provisions to react to changes in marketing or to counteract inflation. When the lease comes up for renewal, the manager will have to negotiate new and revised provisions with the tenant and arrive at a mutually satisfactory understanding. If the parties cannot

---

[3] See chapter 5, pp. 102-108 for a detailed discussion of leasing.

[4] Carpenter, op. cit.

6-2 The Commons at Courthouse Center, Columbus, Indiana, functions as a civic space for the whole community. A great variety of public events, including dances, exhibits, and concerts, are staged.

agree, the manager must weigh carefully the results of renewing the lease according to the tenant's wishes or losing a tenant.

When he reviews lease terms, the manager must compare the income received from tenants with expenses incurred for services. Since his performance as a manager will ultimately be measured by net income, the manager needs to constantly monitor income and expenses in other projects in the area.[5]

The manager may decide to replace a particular tenant when his lease expires because maintaining the space costs more than the income received or because the tenant is otherwise unsuitable for the project. He can make this decision only if he continually monitors finances and assesses the market for potential replacement tenants. In making the decision, the manager must weigh the costs of temporary vacancy and changeover against the chance to upgrade the tenancy of the project, which may benefit all tenants.

Promotion and Community Relations

Promoting a project helps attract trade to retail stores, it increases the marketability of the entire project, and, as the number of projects increases, it helps to maintain a vigorous competitive position for the development. Overseeing a promotional program that establishes the project's identity as an interesting, convenient, even exciting place to work and shop is one of management's necessary responsibilities.

[5] To aid him, comparable income-expense data for projects across the nation can be found in *Downtown and Suburban Office Building Experience Exchange Report*, Building Owners and Managers Association International, 1221 Massachusetts Avenue, N.W., Washington, D.C. 20005 (annual); *Dollars and Cents of Shopping Centers*, ULI–the Urban Land Institute (triennial report—most recent edition 1978); *Income/Expense Analysis: Apartments*, Institute of Real Estate Management, Chicago (annual).

In large projects, the management office staff is often responsible for promotion. The management can also elect to hire an advertising agency, usually for cost plus fee (10–15 percent). In either case, promotion includes the following activities:

- supporting the activities of the tenants or merchants association by keeping records, participating in its meetings, and carrying out its directives
- planning and budgeting promotional activities, including advertising campaigns and the schedule of promotional activities
- implementing the program by executing contracts for media space and time, and providing associated materials
- working with management and tenants to coordinate and publicize community-related events.

In downtown projects these activities must be coordinated with similar events that other downtown business may have planned. Downtown merchants associations, chambers of commerce, or similar groups are increasingly emphasizing promotion campaigns for the entire CBD. Cooperation from the project's management improves community relations in general and helps to strengthen the attractiveness of the entire downtown.

Security

One sensitive issue the manager must deal with is to what extent the development should become a gathering place for community groups that may create problems—picket lines, political rallies, panhandlers, demonstrations, noisy youth, vagrants, and street people. The manager must be able to weigh peoples' right to free assembly against his tenants' right to conduct their businesses in peace. He must know what the legal implications are of permitting or prohibiting the use of common areas. The benefits of expanding community activity within the project must be balanced against the disadvantages—to visitors, merchants, and employees alike—of creating potential security problems. Every manager must develop ways to deal with these situations before they become serious community issues.

Besides controlling the use of common areas in the project, the manager must provide security for tenants, shoppers, and visitors. Security for tenants means protection against intruders after business hours and prompt response to emergencies. For shoppers and visitors, it means protection against crime and violence, medical assistance when needed, and supplying information.

In some projects, security of tenant spaces may be the responsibility of the tenants, who contract with

6-3   Hartford Civic Center

protection services for alarm systems and other protection devices. A merchants association may also be responsible for providing security for tenant and common spaces, although the management is usually responsible for implementing the security plan.

Management can hire its own security staff or contract the services of a security agency. Because security is often the most visible service provided by management, personnel must be carefully selected and trained. Management and its security personnel should develop close relationships with regular city police and fire services so that they will quickly provide assistance when needed.

Managing the Public/Private Project

Activities and Procedures

As the project becomes more complex, so too do the manager's responsibilities. Management and maintenance of a downtown project that combines both public and private interests requires special considerations. Many new concerns complicate management's job. The quality of maintenance often varies between public and private areas; public maintenance tends to be less certain, slower to respond to needs, and less able to obtain adequate funds. It is difficult to assign costs for heating and cooling systems and operations and maintenance because it is difficult to separate public and private use. Management may be required to maintain public access to common areas at all hours, regardless of regular hours for private businesses. Maintenance personnel used by private firms are often unionized and paid higher wages than city employees, which may lead to conflicts.

These issues are most critical in the portions of the project where public and private control intersect—adjoining spaces or in walkways, corridors, pedestrian bridges, plazas, and other common areas that link public and private spaces. A project such as the proposed Milwaukee Retail Center, for example, that links two department stores and several other retail and office buildings with city parking structures and a proposed federal office building provides unique management problems.

Management Organization for Public/Private Projects

Management requirements for public/private projects are still evolving. Management organization can take several forms, from dividing responsibilities accord-

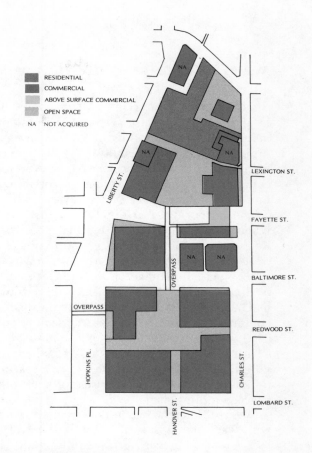

6-4 Charles Center site plan.

ing to ownership, with responsibility for common areas apportioned similarly, to total control by one interest subject to overall direction from the other.[6]

The more common method is to divide responsibilities according to ownership of specific parts of the project. The city of Hartford (Connecticut) operates and maintains the parking garage and exhibition halls that it owns in the Hartford Civic Center, while Aetna Life and Casualty Company is responsible for operating and maintaining the hotel and retail areas of the structure. Each party maintains the common areas on land or air rights it owns and pays half the maintenance costs. At the Charles Center in Baltimore, the city is responsible for maintaining all public parking and plaza areas, and private interests are responsible for their own building complexes within the development.[7]

---

[6] See appendix L for an example of an agreement to sublease, operate, and maintain a parking facility.

[7] See Robert E. Witherspoon, John P. Abbett, and Robert M. Gladstone, *Mixed-Use Developments: New Ways of Land Use.* (Washington, D.C.: ULI–the Urban Land Institute, 1976), pp. 141–47, for further discussion of the Charles Center project.

Charles Center—Inner Harbor Management, Inc.—Management History

Charles Center–Inner Harbor Management, Inc., is a private nonprofit corporation formed to manage Baltimore's downtown development project. It makes available to the city government the skills and experience required for large commercial developments that are not normally found among civil service employees.

The corporation originated in June 1959, when the Commission of the Baltimore Urban Renewal and Housing Agency appointed a recently retired, top-level department store executive as general manager of the pioneering $145 million Charles Center project. The executive had been one of the major figures in the business community's drive to reverse the decline of the CBD. When he became general manager of Charles Center, he executed a personal contract with the city that provided for $1 per year plus reimbursement of his expenses for staff, office space, supplies, etc.

One year later, he was joined by a Baltimorean who was then Assistant Commissioner of the U.S. Urban Renewal Administration, and who became deputy general manager of Charles Center on October 1, 1960. The Charles Center management office was operated on the basis of personal contracts with the two principals, who were responsible for the Charles Center project during its crucial years of development, 1960–65.

In 1965, with the Charles Center project on its way to completion, the city government asked them to undertake planning and implementation of the next phase of downtown development: a 20-year program of renewal for the area surrounding the inner harbor and encompassing 240 acres adjacent to the CBD. To undertake the Inner Harbor project, they formed the non-profit corporation known as Charles Center–Inner Harbor Management, Inc.

On September 1, 1965, the corporation and the Mayor and City Council executed a contract for the corporation to manage the planning and execution of the Charles Center and Inner Harbor projects under the direction of the city's Urban Renewal and Housing Commission—now replaced by the Commissioner of Housing and Community Development. Under the direction of the Commissioner, the corporation performs or coordinates all activities that a city renewal agency would normally perform in a project.

Unlike a city agency, which is permanent, Charles Center–Inner Harbor Management, Inc., provides a special service to the city on a contractual basis. The city has advanced a revolving fund from which the corporation pays its expenses and which is reimbursed by the city monthly.

The city government—acting through the Mayor and the Commissioner of Housing and Community Development—establishes the policies under which the corporation conducts its activities. The corporation provides a mechanism through which the business community can become involved with the execution of projects, and the corporation's unique arrangement with the city enables it to occupy a third-party role when appropriate. This feature of Baltimore's downtown development program is not present in any other city. It has been indispensable to the corporation's success in attracting developers and enabling them to achieve the city's objectives.

Charles Center, Baltimore's 330-acre urban renewal project in the very heart of the CBD, is now nearly complete. A public investment of approximately $35 million created a setting that attracted a private investment of approximately $145 million. The public share includes landscaped plazas with fountains and sculpture, overhead pedestrian walkway systems, and an 1,800-seat theater. The private development has resulted in the construction of 15 major structures, including 1,750,000 square feet of commercial office space, 400 apartment units, 335,000 square feet of retail or related commercial uses, 4,000 parking spaces, and a 700-room hotel. The success of the Charles Center project has spurred additional private development and renovation that have created more buildings containing another 1,500,000 square feet of office space adjacent to the project area.

In some cases, the public entity, usually the city, controls the maintenance of public facilities even where they are linked to or within the private development. The most common examples of this type of arrangement are pedestrian malls and bridges for which the city has sponsored construction to revitalize downtown and has accepted maintenance as a related responsibility. The skyway system in Cincinnati, the mall portion of the Central City Mall shopping center in San Bernardino, California, and the Winter Garden and pedestrian mall in Niagara Falls, New York, were built with public funds and are

6-6   Winter Garden, Niagara Falls, New York, is the central element in the revitalization of downtown Niagara Falls. Commercial space will be tied in on either end.

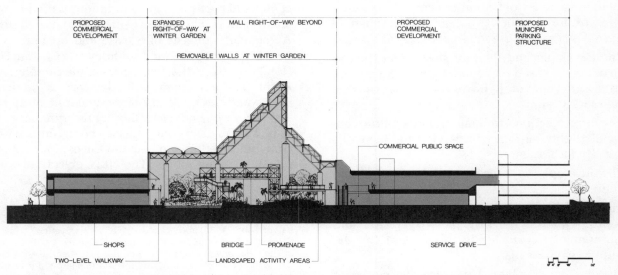

6-7   Cross section showing Winter Garden, Niagara Falls, in relationship to future development.

maintained with public funds.[8] At Nicollet Mall in Minneapolis, the city pays maintenance costs equal to what it would spend on a regular street, and benefited property owners make up the difference.

While management and maintenance are provided most efficiently when there is a clear relationship between ownership and management responsibilities, in many projects the separation is not apparent, and assignment of management responsibility becomes correspondingly less certain. One solution to the problem is that used at Kalamazoo Center in Kalamazoo, Michigan.[9] This convention center was designed as a mixed use development by the city of Kalamazoo and the Inland Steel Development Corporation. Inland Steel built the hotel, retail space, office space, other revenue-producing spaces, and a portion of the enclosed central mall, including one escalator. The city owns the convention center and meeting rooms, and a portion of the central mall, including the other escalator.

City employees manage, maintain, and set up the meeting rooms. The city administrative staff and the hotel staff jointly book meeting rooms, creating the need for an extraordinary amount of coordination. The city has set a standard fee for the meeting rooms, and the hotel charges whatever it can for the space. Occasionally the city rents the spaces at a discount to community groups. The hotel caters all events and charges the users directly.

The city and the developer share some of the cost of operating and maintaining the mall; other costs are borne by one or the other. For example:

- The developer and the city have a joint agreement for security of the entire center; they retain one firm for all security services. Their share of the fee is based on the square footage each owns.

- The developer and the city share cleaning services, again based on square footage. Retail tenants and the hotel, however, share the developer's cost.

- The developer pays for major repairs for the center (skylights, entrance doors, etc.) and then bills the city for its share.

- The developer pays for all mall decorations and plants.

- The central space has two separate heating and cooling plants; the city pays operation and maintenance costs for its plant, and the developer pays for his.

- The city and developer have separate service for trash pick-up and disposal.

6-8   Ground level plan of Kalamazoo Center showing public/private common circulation areas.

- Because the city maintains its own union crew for setting up meeting rooms and the developer's maintenance staff is nonunion, some friction has resulted because of the difference in wages. The city and the operator of the hotel are therefore discussing a joint management agreement that would allow the developer and/or the hotel operator to manage and maintain the convention and meeting room spaces.

Another example of shared responsibility is the Monterey Conference Center and Doubletree Inn Hotel in Monterey, California. The hotel is located partly on air rights over a portion of the conference center and partly on land contiguous with the conference center. The agreement, called the Ballroom Agreement, consists of a lease and operations contract between the city of Monterey and Custom House Hotel Company, the developers of the Doubletree Inn Hotel. The agreement provides for the conference center and the hotel to share a major meeting room. The hotel's objectives in signing the agreement were to be able to market hotel space contiguous with the conference center and to avoid the capital cost of duplicate meeting rooms. The city's objectives were to

[8]   See "Central City Mall," ULI *Project Reference File*, vol. 3, no. 9 (April-June 1973) and "Cincinnati Skywalk System" ULI *Project Reference File*, vol. 9, no. 20 (October-December 1979). In the case of the Cincinnati skywalk system, the responsibility for maintenance has been transferred from the city to benefited private owners through special agreements.

[9]   See Witherspoon, et al, *Mixed-Use Developments*, op. cit., pp. 106–12.

have the shared ballroom available for large conferences and to avoid paying for the room when it was not being used. The agreement also allowed the hotel to spend $200,000 to finish the space in accordance with its design specifications.

Easements provide for mutual exits to meet fire and building code requirements. A service tunnel and pedestrian easements provide for public passage through certain common areas of the hotel at all times. The developer and the city share maintenance costs for certain areas that adjoin both the conference center and the hotel. Both the city's selected caterer and the hotel can provide food service in the shared meeting room. In other meeting and ballrooms in the conference center, however, only the city's caterer can operate.

Because of the experience gained in projects where responsibilities are split, more recent examples tend to assign responsibility for management and maintenance to a single operating entity, usually with a group representing both sides making policy and overseeing the operation. Management of public spaces may be assigned to the public entity or to the management entity; management of some or all of the common areas may be assumed by the entity; certain services may be furnished separately by the public or private parties; financial obligations may be assigned to the new entity or divided among each or some of the parties. Such arrangements are the result of several factors.

- A single management entity is a more efficient way to use staff and to coordinate planning and administration.

- A single entity centralizes responsibility and minimizes the potential conflicts that arise when two or more organizations try to do the same job.

- The developer concerned with maintaining a high-quality project usually wishes to exercise continued control over the level of maintenance and repair in all parts of the project that adjoin the private portions.

- The public entity may be reluctant to commit itself to long-term operation and maintenance that is of a higher standard than it normally provides in other public areas. In addition, it may not wish to become entangled in the special management problems that often are present in complex downtown projects.

One form of such an agreement is to have the developer or owner of the project supply management services for all common areas as well as the private space. A management policy group composed of several public officials and representatives of the major private interest oversees the arrangement. The Milwaukee Retail Center, for example, will be managed by the Rouse Company under contract to a nonprofit management corporation made up of major public and private interests. City representatives will include aldermen and appropriate city department

6-9   Monterey Conference Center and Doubletree Inn Hotel, Monterey, California.

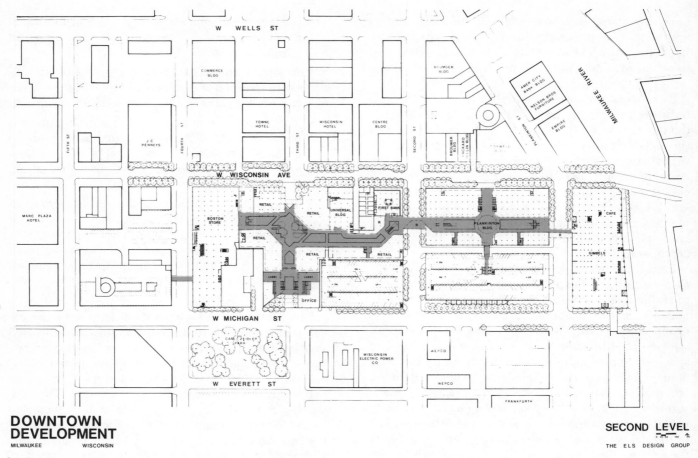

6-10 Plan of Milwaukee Retail Center, Milwaukee, Wisconsin.

heads; private interests will include representatives of the two department stores, the Milwaukee Redevelopment Corporation, and other building owners. The Rouse Company will be responsible for overall management of the center, routine maintenance, promotional activities, and supervising operation of the parking garages.[10]

The use of such an intermediary group to provide a public presence while permitting control by private management appears to be a growing trend; it parallels the increasing use of developers as construction managers for entire projects. Several cities that have experimented with public control or a division of management responsibilities have subsequently contracted with private firms to provide management services. Cincinnati's skyway system of pedestrian bridges and concourses was initially maintained by the city. However, the expense of maintenance and providing the quality of service desired by affected properties prompted the city to give up maintenance. Under a legal ruling that such pedestrian ways qualify as sidewalks, which in Cincinnati must be main-

tained by abutting property owners, the city is gradually turning over maintenance responsibilities to the private businesses adjoining the bridges and walkways. In fact, when new bridges and walkways are built, the affected property owners agree to maintain them.

In Courthouse Square in Dayton, Ohio, the private investors and the city have agreed to a joint operating and maintenance arrangement. The three private participants—the Mead Corporation, Dayton Power and Light Company, and Elder-Beerman Department Stores, Inc.—share responsibilities for common areas and for substructures constructed and owned by the city. The city therefore, although it holds title to the land and substructures, has no responsibility for maintaining any part of the project except Courthouse Plaza, the original part of the project that the city has always maintained.

---

[10] This arrangement is similar in many respects to the management organization for the Gallery in Philadelphia, which is described at the end of this chapter. See also appendix M.

The intermediary group also provides an excellent forum for resolving management's policy problems. The question of how to deal with undesirable gatherings—social and political demonstrations, groups of noisy teenagers, for example—might be resolved best by a public/private policy-making body.

The Management and Maintenance Agreement

Responsibilities for joint management and maintenance of a public/private development are contained in a formal contract. This agreement contains the basic understandings necessary to ensure smooth and efficient operation. It is a logical next step to agreements on sharing predevelopment and development costs and responsibilities.

Function and Contents of an Agreement

The major purpose of an agreement is to clearly assign responsibilities for operation, maintenance, and costs to the various interests in the project. To do so, the agreement must:

- clearly identify the owners of various parts of the project who are parties to the agreement
- specify the precise parts of the project the agreement covers
- describe the management mechanism to be used, that is, separate management by the parties involved or joint management by a newly created entity
- define membership, procedures for meetings, and rights of all parties if a new entity is created

6-11   Courthouse Square, Dayton, Ohio

- specify financial responsibilities for management for each party to the agreement and define revenue sources each party may use.

The agreement must also specifically cover "who decides," "who does," and "who pays" for all aspects of the project's management and maintenance:

- housekeeping (cleaning, repairs, etc.)
- maintenance, repair, and replacement of fixtures and equipment
- maintenance, repair, and renovation of the building or project
- tenant services (heating and cooling, security, elevator maintenance, etc.)
- lease administration, renewal, and negotiation
- fire and liability insurance, which can be complicated when both public and private sectors are involved
- a provision for a management office, if the agreement is for unified management
- understandings as to major staffing and contracting authority
- a definition of accounting, auditing, and billing procedures
- management's relationships with a merchants or tenants association.

The Separate Management Entity

Although no typical structure can be recommended, some underlying characteristics of a professional agreement that creates a separate management entity determine its suitability. Does it:

- provide for centralized management of common areas?
- establish uniform standards for maintenance, operation, and use, regardless of ownership?
- provide mutual protection for all owners against deterioration of their surroundings?
- provide equitable sharing of financing by the major beneficiaries of the operation?
- provide insulation from policy or organizational changes in public agencies that will be parties to the agreement?
- ensure a permanent organization?
- provide public accountability for public funds?

Organization of a Prototype Management Entity

A new corporation could be established to provide all services required for operating the public or common-use areas of the project, with the authority to contract for or otherwise provide services to owners or operators of adjoining parts of the project. The corporation's long-term structure would be established by the bylaws, the necessary flexibility would be provided by delegating duties to a single manager, and control would be ensured by the budget, the policy requirements, and the bylaws.

The corporation would be nonprofit and would not issue stock. Each participant would be entitled to votes proportionate to the value of money and/or service it contributes to the corporation. Nonvoting members could be appointed to maintain proper coordination with government or private groups.[11]

Daily operations and maintenance would be delegated to an executive committee and a general manager. The general manager could be one of the members of the corporation (for example, the principal developer) or a separate management firm. The general manager would carry out daily maintenance in accordance with the policies determined by the corporation and the approved budget. He would recommend changes in the policies or budget, keep accounts for the maintenance entity's income and expenses, hire and discharge maintenance personnel and contractors, keep the members informed of the general operation, and notify members of extraordinary events.

Principal Functions of the Organization

The corporation, through its general manager, would be responsible for major operating functions: maintenance, utilities, climate control, standards for use, design approval, security, and financial administration.

Maintenance

The corporation would be responsible for all maintenance services in the common areas, including cleaning, repairing and replacing worn facilities, removing trash, washing windows, removing snow at outside entrances, and any other activities needed to keep the facility maintained to a defined standard. It might also be available under contract to provide similar or specialized services in noncommon areas

---

[11] For example, the Milwaukee Retail Center is proposing to establish a Board of Directors with members including the Milwaukee Redevelopment Corporation (the sponsor of the project), Rouse Milwaukee, Inc. (the developer), First Bank, the Mayor of Milwaukee, the Commissioner of the Department of City Development, and one member chosen by the private property owners and two major stores involved in the project. The membership would vote on budgets, review fiscal or policy changes requested by the general manager or executive committee, coordinate matters between the management entity and each member's organization, and perform the general duties of directors.

of the project. The corporation should be free to fulfill these responsibilities by the most efficient means available: direct hire, subcontracting to an independent maintenance firm, purchasing management services from the developer, or any other appropriate method.

Utilities

The corporation would furnish all utilities, including lights, electrical power, natural gas, and water. They would be provided by whatever method the corporation deems most appropriate.

The requirement to maintain separate accounting and billing for the common areas means that metered wiring, plumbing, and other utilities would also be designed and constructed separately. The feasibility of this arrangement should be determined before the corporation is formed. If separate systems are not feasible, tenants can be charged for utilities based on the square footage they occupy or some other fair method.

Heating, Ventilation, and Air Conditioning

The corporation would maintain and operate the heating, ventilation, and air-conditioning systems of the common areas. It should be free to manage the systems in the optimum manner. The need for separate cost accounting and control over these systems probably requires that they also be physically independent from the privately controlled facilities in the complex. The feasibility of establishing separate systems should be determined by engineering studies; if separate systems are not feasible, charges should be based on tenants' pro rata share of benefits.

Standards for Use

The corporation would establish standards for the use of the area under its authority and maintain control over activities carried out within it. It would ensure that the general public, tenants, merchants, workers, and customers are afforded free access to the areas during normal business hours and would regulate access after hours. This function includes issuing permits to merchants, other tenants, the developer, the city, civic organizations, or anyone else who wants to use the area for sales, shows, special displays, other promotional activities, and special events deemed appropriate based on the nature of the space and the purpose for which it was designed into the project. The corporation might collect fees to defray the costs of maintenance and utilities for such special events.

Design Approval

Approving design changes that affect the physical appearance, safety, convenience, or efficient use of the common areas would also be a responsibility of the corporation after the project is completed. It would also control signs, permanent advertisements, and decorations.

Security

The corporation would be responsible for protecting the physical security of persons and property in the common areas. It would provide security personnel during and after the normal hours of operation, coordinating measures with security personnel who operate in adjoining public and private spaces. The corporation would negotiate operating agreements for patrols with the city police department. It might also hire private security guards. The corporation must continuously coordinate and maintain security arrangements with both public and private security forces.

Financial Administration

The corporation would be authorized to collect and manage fees from the various parties of the management corporation for the services it provides in common areas. An assessment and fee formulas may be stipulated in land disposition or land leasing agreements between public and private participants in the development, but a mechanism would be provided to modify the formulas when changed circumstances result in inequities. Because common areas will also be used by the public, the corporation would retain the ability to receive and manage funds from the city or other public bodies.

Negotiating the Management and Maintenance Agreement

Two important considerations are involved in negotiating a management and maintenance agreement:

- Such an agreement means shared responsibilities and operating and capital construction costs for the public and private sectors.
- The management and maintenance agreement must be part of the package of agreements worked out during the predevelopment stage.

The management and maintenance agreement is the final element in the series of shared responsibilities that begins with the project's conception. Public and private interests joining forces for a complex development project should be as concerned with the project's operation as with its construction. Sharing responsibilities for the project's construction and financing will be reflected in the management agreements for the completed project. The costs of

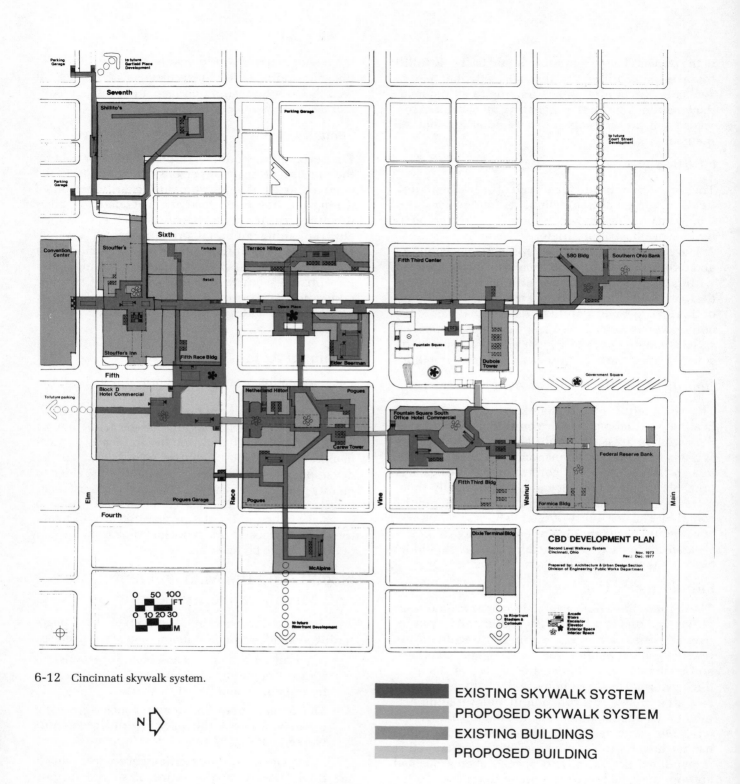

6-12   Cincinnati skywalk system.

N

EXISTING SKYWALK SYSTEM
PROPOSED SKYWALK SYSTEM
EXISTING BUILDINGS
PROPOSED BUILDING

management should be included in the formula for sharing project costs, and to do so they must be considered during predevelopment.

Negotiations for a management and maintenance agreement encompass several phases:

- recognizing that management is a necessary part of the development agreement package
- establishing the public or private nature of each of the project's major components
- determining public and private objectives for the areas common to both
- estimating the benefits and costs of managing the project by alternative means
- agreeing on a specific management structure for meeting the objectives
- defining costs for management
- agreeing on the sharing of operations and management costs.

The negotiations must balance the interests of all parties involved. Because agreeing on a specific agreement may be a lengthy process, it may be necessary to fashion an interim, more general, agreement that simply designates the management structure and duties but leaves room for further negotiations on the mix of participants and sharing of costs.

Private developers will insist on a basic understanding about responsibilities and costs for management and maintenance. Initial estimates of costs will assist in determining the expenses to be negotiated. Other factors shaping the agreement are the developer's interest in participating in the operation of the project and the public entity's objectives and experience in similar projects.

Past projects have shown that inexperienced public agencies assume that efficient management will somehow happen. In general, public officials are more concerned with initial capital costs than with future operating costs. Even cities with experience in public/private projects usually attempt to minimize the public role in management, except when a specific public service can be performed on publicly owned space—for example, a public parking garage.

The Cincinnati skywalk system is an example of a project that was developed jointly by the public and private sectors. The early elements of the system were publicly maintained, but experience has caused the city to turn over maintenance responsibilities to adjoining property owners. For new projects like the Stouffer Hotel skywalk, the city supplied capital costs, provided that the private owner assumed responsibility for maintenance. Cash in the initial stage of development is much more attractive to the developer than the city's promise to provide maintenance. The Cincinnati Department of Development exemplified the premise that most cities do not have money to spend annually for maintenance but can often expend one-time funds for capital construction. Identifying such possible tradeoffs is a major step in the negotiations.

6-13 Cincinnati skywalk system—a totally enclosed walkway.

The Gallery in Philadelphia—An Example

Project Initiation

The Gallery, part of the Market East project in downtown Philadelphia, is a recent example of how a management and maintenance agreement was negotiated and the tradeoffs that were considered. The Market East project was conceived as an indoor pedestrian mall that would link various modes of public transit and provide new retail and office space. It was to include a truck service street, three subway stations, a new Reading Railroad commuter station, and parking structures with connecting skywalks. The Department of Housing and Urban Development agreed to fund $18 million of site improvements for public spaces. The project had been in planning for over 15 years, and an immense amount of data had been gathered to project the amount of public space that would be required to accommodate the projected volumes of people riding mass transit. The Gallery, opened in 1977, is the first phase of this project. During its development, many of the issues concerning operation and maintenance of common areas had to be resolved in a way that would work for this first phase and also be applicable to future phases.

A typical suburban mall has approximately 1 square foot of common area for every 3 square feet of gross leasable area. Even the earliest planning for the Gallery indicated that the ratio should be 1:1. Because the mall was to be enclosed, the pedestrian walkway as well as all the air-conditioning, lighting, and other building systems were integrated into the project's total physical system. The mall's planned use by mass transit riders necessitated full-time operation and thus higher operating costs. Thus, operating costs comprised a large portion of total project costs.

Two of the public sector's goals directly affected operating costs. The first goal—removing truck traffic from city streets and reducing traffic congestion—resulted in substantial operating and security costs. The mall was designed with a truck tunnel underneath to serve Gimbel's department store, retail shops in the project, 8 million square feet of office space, and 1 million square feet of retail space adjacent to the Gallery. Thus, costs for mechanical ventilation and lighting were far in excess of normal.

The second goal was to provide a major public plaza at the northwest corner of Ninth and Market Streets. City planners felt that the plaza would relieve the area's dense urban feeling. The projected operating costs for the plaza were substantial because they included cleaning, planting, landscaping, and lighting.

These elements required costs in excess of the normal costs of operating common areas in suburban malls. To complicate matters, the project site was a designated urban renewal area, and it was difficult to predict the cost of maintaining public areas at the same level of quality that suburban customers have come to expect in competitive suburban malls. If a downtown mall were to compete effectively, maintenance would have to be of this high quality. It was clear that the cost of maintenance would be in excess of what the developer could afford to pay and remain competitive.

Maintenance was the subject of considerable discussion during initial negotiations. Resolving the problem centered on negotiating a fixed contribution

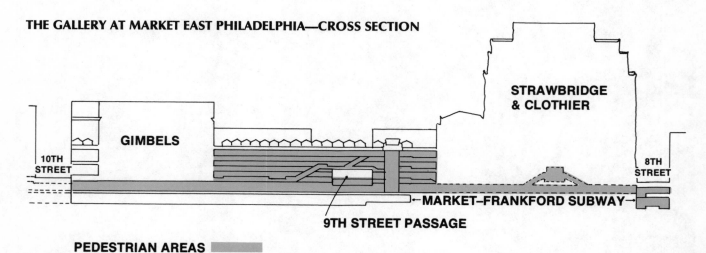

THE GALLERY AT MARKET EAST PHILADELPHIA—CROSS SECTION

6-14   East-west section of the Gallery at Market East, Philadelphia. This diagram shows the four levels of the mall with the subway connection on the lowest level. Gallery II, a continuation of the Market East project, is underway to the west on the other side of 10th Street.

6-15 The public plaza at Ninth and Market Streets is also the main entrance to The Gallery.

from both parties, but detailed maintenance cost estimates were not available. The developer also wanted the responsibility for maintenance to be controlled daily by the private sector and the costs allocated according to public and private use.

Determining which entity should manage the common areas involved a number of factors: the development strategy, ownership interests, operational requirements, and space control or accountability. Five types of potential management arrangements were considered, with the lead entity being the city of Philadelphia, the Redevelopment Authority, the project developer, a special nonprofit corporation, or a special "mall assessment" district.

The mall assessment district, which would have created a special-purpose tax assessment district, was immediately rejected because its formation would have required special enabling legislation from the commonwealth of Pennsylvania. All parties felt that the alternative offered no apparent advantage over a nonprofit corporation, for which a number of precedents existed. The other four management alternatives were compared in terms of project development, ownership of common areas, and operations and con-

trol before the special nonprofit corporation was chosen as the best method of management for the Gallery.

Project Development

The development of common spaces focused on two locations: the area now occupied by the Gallery and four additional blocks slated for future development to the west of that site. Normally only one entity is involved in the responsibility for construction of common spaces. The assignment of responsibilities is usually related closely to the rights of mall ownership and ultimately to management responsibility. Typically, a single developer assumes responsibility for the costs of construction, maintenance, and operation of common areas adjacent to retail areas.

The Market East project was atypical, however. Major public infrastructures were involved: the underground truck tunnel, subway stations, the commuter rail station, significant utility relocations, and the complex heating, ventilation, and air-conditioning system. Because of the variety of anticipated development approaches and the need for varying physical and financial arrangements for individual parts of the Market East project, a manage-

143

ment entity had to be designed with maximum flexibility. Accordingly, the parties made several early decisions:

- to keep design among projects uniform, including the critical area of finishes

- to consider maintenance and security of the completed project from the earliest phases of predevelopment

- to maximize federal funding

- to minimize capital costs by having all major construction conducted by various project developers

- to simplify legal, administrative, and code requirements.

Ownership of Common Areas

Because the Market East project has unique characteristics, ownership of the common areas did not necessarily determine the method of their management. The public sector felt it should have a strong voice in making decisions because of the various sources of public assistance for development and the public responsibilities for public areas. The private sector, represented by the Rouse Company as the developer of the first phase (the Gallery), wanted to be assured of a certain level of maintenance and an equitable distribution of public and private costs.

Public ownership by the city, the Redevelopment Authority, or a quasi-public corporation would ensure that mall activities would be managed in the public interest and that maintenance and security would be provided as a regular municipal function. Private ownership would maximize tax revenues from the project and would ensure a high quality of maintenance.

Analyzing the alternatives for maintenance and management and thus the form of management involved several factors. If the city of Philadelphia owned the space, a single agency, such as the city's Department of Public Property, could provide uniform management. The developer raised many questions, however, about a city department's ability to respond to the business needs of major commercial tenants:

- Does the city have both the desire and the financial resources to undertake long-term management of the common areas?

- Can the city maintain and enhance the common area's appearance and character to attract shoppers and tenants?

- Can the city respond to the profit incentive of others when it is itself not profit oriented?

6-16   The skylighted mall from the top level—The Gallery.

- Are the standards that apply to the maintenance of city buildings and facilities adequate to maintain common areas adjacent to privately leased commercial space?

- In light of the city's salary structure, would the cost of the city's providing services be far in excess of the cost of services provided by the private sector?

Answering these questions led to the conclusion that the city should not be responsible for maintaining the project's common areas. Similarly, the parties decided that the Redevelopment Authority should not be responsible for maintaining common areas of the completed project because the Authority does not have the major continuing maintenance capabilities the city does in its Department of Public Property.

In the interim, however, the Authority was to be responsible for maintenance and security of the common areas. Because the Authority wished to expedite construction, Gimbel's and the Rouse Company agreed to those terms even though the parties in-

Structure of Development and Management
The Gallery: Philadelphia

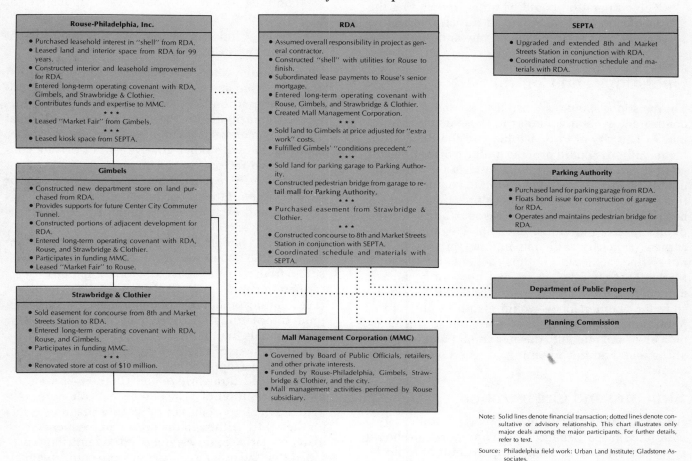

Rouse-Philadelphia, Inc.
- Purchased leasehold interest in "shell" from RDA.
- Leased land and interior space from RDA for 99 years.
- Constructed interior and leasehold improvements for RDA.
- Entered long-term operating covenant with RDA, Gimbels, and Strawbridge & Clothier.
- Contributes funds and expertise to MMC.
    * * *
- Leased "Market Fair" from Gimbels.
    * * *
- Leased kiosk space from SEPTA.

Gimbels
- Constructed new department store on land purchased from RDA.
- Provides supports for future Center City Commuter Tunnel.
- Constructed portions of adjacent development for RDA.
- Entered long-term operating covenant with RDA, Rouse, and Strawbridge & Clothier.
- Participates in funding MMC.
- Leased "Market Fair" to Rouse.

Strawbridge & Clothier
- Sold easement for concourse from 8th and Market Streets Station to RDA.
- Entered long-term operating covenant with RDA, Rouse, and Gimbels.
- Participates in funding MMC.
    * * *
- Renovated store at cost of $10 million.

RDA
- Assumed overall responsibility in project as general contractor.
- Constructed "shell" with utilities for Rouse to finish.
- Subordinated lease payments to Rouse's senior mortgage.
- Entered long-term operating covenant with Rouse, Gimbels, and Strawbridge & Clothier.
- Created Mall Management Corporation.
    * * *
- Sold land to Gimbels at price adjusted for "extra work" costs.
- Fulfilled Gimbels' "conditions precedent."
    * * *
- Sold land for parking garage to Parking Authority.
- Constructed pedestrian bridge from garage to retail mall for Parking Authority.
    * * *
- Purchased easement from Strawbridge & Clothier.
    * * *
- Constructed concourse to 8th and Market Streets Station in conjunction with SEPTA.
- Coordinated schedule and materials with SEPTA.

Mall Management Corporation (MMC)
- Governed by Board of Public Officials, retailers, and other private interests.
- Funded by Rouse-Philadelphia, Gimbels, Strawbridge & Clothier, and the city.
- Mall management activities performed by Rouse subsidiary.

SEPTA
- Upgraded and extended 8th and Market Streets Station in conjunction with RDA.
- Coordinated construction schedule and materials with RDA.

Parking Authority
- Purchased land for parking garage from RDA.
- Floats bond issue for construction of garage for RDA.
- Operates and maintains pedestrian bridge for RDA.

Department of Public Property

Planning Commission

Note: Solid lines denote financial transaction; dotted lines denote consultative or advisory relationship. This chart illustrates only major deals among the major participants. For further details, refer to text.

Source: Philadelphia field work: Urban Land Institute; Gladstone Associates.

tended to form a separate management entity. Time constraints simply did not allow the question of mall maintenance to be resolved before contracts were signed and construction of public and private facilities began. The management entity was not formally established and its obligations delineated until 18 months after the Gallery opened in August 1977.

Other considerations affected the negotiations. If individual developers were to maintain their own parts of the larger Market East project, uniform service would have been difficult to maintain throughout the project. If each developer were to be responsible for maintenance in his own area, contracts delineating standards and responsibilities would have to be devised and an independent authority created to ensure compliance with the standards. More importantly, private developers could not legally manage the public facilities like the subway and rail stations because of insurance and liability requirements.

A special nonprofit corporation to manage and maintain common areas would minimize these objections. Such a corporation would have several advantages:

- It would establish a single, central administrative office for the Gallery that had the ability to expand as the Market East project grew. Thus, uniform standards throughout the project would be ensured.

- Through disposition agreements and other instruments, it would have the ability to collect fees equitably from the various parties.

- The corporation would be a relatively small body, limited to the Market East project, and therefore more accessible than a large city department.

- The corporation would be a permanent organization responsible for the common areas, the subway stations, and the rail station long after the

Redevelopment Authority had left.

- The corporation could be organized so that the membership of the board of directors could be evenly split between the private and public sectors, effectively giving both sides veto powers.

Operations and Control

The questions about responsibility for operations and control are generally similar to those about maintenance. The city of Philadelphia and the Redevelopment Authority could provide uniform operation and control and protect the public interest but might be unable to devote special attention to complex operational problems. Individual developers would again be unable to legally assume responsibility for the public spaces. Individual developers would be concerned primarily with maximizing private profits rather than achieving optimal benefits for the total Market East complex. A special nonprofit management corporation, however—the same entity responsible for maintenance—would also best protect the public interest, coordinate all activities for the common area, and attend to the operational requirements of the mall and the adjoining commercial establishments.

Structure and Organization

After considering all the questions and the alternative solutions, the parties agreed that a corporation should be established whose sole responsibility would be maintenance of the common areas. The entity was named the Mall Maintenance Corporation (MMC); it assumed management responsibilities through its agent, Rouse Maintenance, Inc. Ownership of the common area was placed in the Redevelopment Authority so that the numerous private developers that would ultimately be involved in Market East would be relieved of liability and the necessity to acquire insurance for public spaces. Each private contributor to the MMC consented to the public sector's ownership of the common areas and the MMC's assuming maintenance of the project. Consent was based on several conditions, however:

- The Authority would retain ultimate responsibility for the proper performance of maintenance.
- The Authority would ensure that the MMC had adequate financial resources to meet the expected costs of the proposed budget.
- All contributions from other sources for maintenance would also be assigned to MMC.
- The developer would have primary responsibility for daily maintenance.

- The developer's consent to the agreement would continue as long as Rouse was responsible for operations.
- The developer must approve the management entity and its bylaws.

Structurally, MMC is a nonprofit corporation that does not issue stock. Each participant is entitled to vote in proportion to the value of money and/or services it contributes to the corporation. Additional nonvoting members can be added to maintain proper coordination with other government or private concerns. The directors vote on budgets, review fiscal or policy changes requested by the general manager or executive committee, coordinate activities of the corporation and each member's organization, and perform other general duties.

A detailed budget projecting the annual cost of operation at $625,000 was formulated. The budget resulted from a year of analyzing the comparative costs of operating other malls. It also reflected the results of investigating other types of operations, like Philadelphia International Airport, and arrangements for truck tunnels in other parts of the city.

In the course of establishing an operating budget, the developer approached the department stores—Gimbel's and Strawbridge and Clothier—for an annual contribution of $100,000 each. Both stores recognized the importance of providing adequate funds for the MMC. Although the proposed payments were extraordinarily high, each agreed to contribute provided that the other department store contributed an equal amount and provided that Rouse was retained as developer. The department stores' contributions were finally determined to be the greater of $100,000 or 16 percent of the total cost of maintenance ($100,000 ÷ $625,000 = 16%). Both stores made equal monthly payments.

The developer's payment was based on:

- forty cents per square foot of the leasable retail area (as defined in the lease) for maintenance and operation of the public area, including the provision of heated and/or cooled air plus
- three cents per square foot of leasable area per year for maintenance and operation of the service corridors, service and passenger elevators, and truck dock plus
- fifty cents per square foot of leasable area per year towards a reserve fund for replacements.

In addition to its monetary contribution, the Rouse Company agreed to provide office space in the retail area, office equipment, mall manager services, assistant manager services, and other related services or equipment necessary for the proper performance of the MMC. These services have an estimated annual value of $70,000 (if the corporation had to purchase them). The Rouse Company's regular contribution is $81,000, or 13 percent of the total cost ($81,000 ÷ $625,000 = 13%). The developer also serves as general manager/treasurer of the MMC.

The city and the Redevelopment Authority's contributions to the MMC are based on that portion of the total cost not paid for by Gimbel's, Strawbridge and Clothier, and the Rouse Company. The annual public contribution is $344,000, or 55 percent of the total contribution ($344,000 ÷ $625,000 = 55%).[12]

The MMC's specific duties are as follows:

1. to maintain the mall and plaza in a clean and neat condition and to keep them clear of debris, ice, and snow

2. to light the mall and plaza so as to provide reasonable security and to keep exterior lighting fixtures in good operating condition

3. to provide sufficient landscaping services to keep the mall and plaza and adjoining outdoor areas in attractive condition

4. to empty all trash containers in the shopping mall and plaza regularly

5. to clean all drains in the common areas and the store premises regularly

6. to inspect all paved and terrazzo surfaces in the shopping mall and the plaza regularly

7. to clean and inspect all stairways in the mall and plaza areas regularly

8. to clean all glass, plate glass, and glass enclosures, not including space frame panels or the roof, in the mall and plaza areas frequently and regularly

9. to maintain all benches and signs in a clean and attractive condition

10. to inspect, adjust, and maintain all escalators

11. to provide no sound amplification system au-

dible in the mall and plaza areas except one providing soft background music

12. to ensure that no vendors are permitted in the mall and plaza area

13. to provide adequate equipment and personnel to supervise these functions

14. to provide adequate security forces for the mall

15. to keep the truck tunnel clean, free of ice, snow, and debris, adequately ventilated, and in good repair.

The contract also stipulates that the developer and tenants use a system of engineering controls to ensure that the heating and cooling of one area does not draw heated and cooled air from the other.

Summary

The success of a project during postdevelopment is clearly the result of all the previous effort expended during the predevelopment and development stages. It is also the result of superior maintenance and management provided by an effective organization designed for that purpose. Downtown projects with public and private participants present complex problems in the design and execution of this management organization. While much of the discussion in this book is about new concepts and development approaches that are continually being refined, nowhere is the rapid change and limited experience more apparent than in this last stage of the development process. Because no examples have been in operation long enough to have been truly tested by time and circumstances, it is more important to understand the issues involved—the need for strong central control to maintain quality, the balance required between the public interest and private needs, and the need for flexibility so that as time passes the structure and the details of the management process can be modified on the basis of experience.

---

[12] See appendix M for complete language of the agreement.

7.
Public Assistance for CBDs

Public incentives for downtown development reduce the developer's risk or otherwise positively affect the developer's cash flow, leverage, or taxes. They can be applied at any point in the development process—planning, land assembly, financing, construction, marketing, or property management—and can take many forms: direct assistance to developers (e.g., public acquisition of property by eminent domain and subsequent disposition to a private developer with land-cost-write-downs), public improvements (e.g., a transit station stop or pedestrian mall), or measures that cut red tape and construction time.

The range of development incentives is probably far greater than has been generally documented. In most conventional renewal projects, land-cost-write-downs, provision of public infrastructure, tax abatement, and tax increment financing have been the major tools. This picture is now changing as states and localities experiment with new programs to promote city rebuilding and urban economic development.[1] HUD's Urban Development Action Grant program and the Urban Mass Transportation Administration's transit station area joint development program are other areas where experience is being gained.

Local governments considering public assistance to private developers should ascertain that the public benefits justify the costs. Active public assistance need not mean massive outlays of funds. Incentives can be analyzed for their cost effectiveness to ensure that the incentive most effective in attracting private investment is also least costly to the public sector.

Responsive Public Planning

Comprehensive plans for downtown range from general statements to detailed specifications. They are usually categorized as one of four types:

- The *policies plan* sets forth broad community objectives like controlled growth and rehabilitation of residential neighborhoods and establishes a set of policies that foster these objectives.

- The *generalized land use plan* outlines permitted land uses, preferred locations for new private development, and needed public improvements and neighborhood facilities.

- The *urban renewal plan* specifies plans for the acquisition or rehabilitation of certain parcels, building demolition, land clearance, and eventual disposition for one or more projects.

- The *capital improvement program,* while not a conventional plan, outlines public investment programs to which the city will commit itself (usually for 5 years) and the public resources that can be used to fund development.

---

[1] See Gladstone Associates, *Redevelopment, Rehabilitation and Conservation: A Compendium and Annotated Bibliography* (prepared for U.S. Department of Housing and Urban Development, October 1975). This survey and assessment of development incentives covers (1) development ranging from "conventional renewal" to innovative state programs such as tax increment financing and promising partnerships between local public and private sectors; (2) rehabilitation (e.g., financing aids, property tax incentives, and urban homesteading); and (3) conservation (e.g., code enforcement and historic preservation programs).

7-1 Nicollet Mall, Minneapolis, Minnesota, is but one of many public improvement and action programs initiated by the city of Minneapolis to encourage downtown investment. An element of the skyway system is also shown.

Some plans, particularly for CBDs, require unusual development—underground parking, elevated walkways, or extensive plaza and landscaped areas. These extraordinary requirements and other restrictions (zoning, street layout, utilities, setback, site access, and coverage) can frustrate private investment. Too often, development plans are not flexible enough to adjust to these special situations or changing market conditions, resulting in their constraining rather than encouraging development.

The ideal downtown development plan should be open-ended so that it can be reevaluated to reflect changing requirements. Modifications may be difficult to accomplish, especially when the adopted plan has strong public and political support, but if plans cannot be adjusted, local governments may find private developers uninterested. If existing development standards discourage potential developers, local governments should be prepared to seriously consider changes to their development plans.

Local Public Assistance

Much of the support for downtown development must come in the form of locally initiated strategies and programs. In general (as discussed later), the states' role has been to enact enabling legislation that permits local initiatives, and the federal government's role has been to fund programs that support the initiatives.

Organizations for Development

Development organizations can be structured in various ways (city agencies, local public agencies, quasi-public entities, and private development corporations and private development organizations created to foster a public purpose), all of them designed to encourage private investment.

- *City agencies* (for example, a department of community development) have direct access to city funds and the ability to make grants but are subject to civil service constraints, political pressures, and certain state or local laws that may limit their ability to engage directly in real estate development.
- *Local public agencies* (LPAs) are urban renewal authorities. Typically endowed with the power of eminent domain and the authority to issue bonds and develop blighted areas, they may lack political accountability and the ability to operate outside of areas designated as "blighted."
- *Quasi-public entities* are legally constituted private nonprofit corporations, distinct from

municipal corporations. They typically enjoy administrative autonomy combined with some degree of political accountability, have access to important development powers typically limited to municipalities, and have some tax advantages, but they usually lack the degree of political accountability that city agencies have.
- *Private development corporations* are typically limited dividend corporations established by private interests registered under special state enabling legislation (for example, Missouri's Chapter 353 or Ohio's Impacted Cities Act). They can be endowed with delegated powers of eminent domain and may be granted tax abatement and/or long-term leases of municipally owned land or property. They lack political accountability, similar to quasi-public entities.
- *Private development organizations* (like the typical downtown business association) act as a catalyst in initiating projects. They have the ability to mobilize public and private resources but have limited capabilities to implement long-term financing and rarely are politically accountable.

A specific city department or office should be the lead agency to analyze policy alternatives, propose policy, and coordinate budget requirements and development activities with other city programs. The city agency should coordinate broad policy decisions (project and budget approvals) with community representatives to ensure that their concerns are reflected in the city's policy.

General planning and policy-making for traditional urban development were assigned to a planning commission and the city executive branch, while specific planning and implementation were assigned to a separate redevelopment authority. Redevelopment authorities, usually governed by a board appointed by the mayor, were restricted both in the types of activities they could undertake and the area in which they could operate (usually designated as "blighted"). While this type of organization remains the most prevalent style today, other forms have been adopted.

A special national program demonstrating the effectiveness of using public/private partnerships was established in Louisville, Kentucky. Zuchelli, Hunter and Associates, Inc., was the consultant responsible for establishing a local/federal partnership agreement in which the city of Louisville, Jefferson County, the commonwealth of Kentucky, and key private sector parties initiated a coventure agreement with the federal government to oversee the implementation of a master action program geared to fostering economic development in Louisville's urban core.

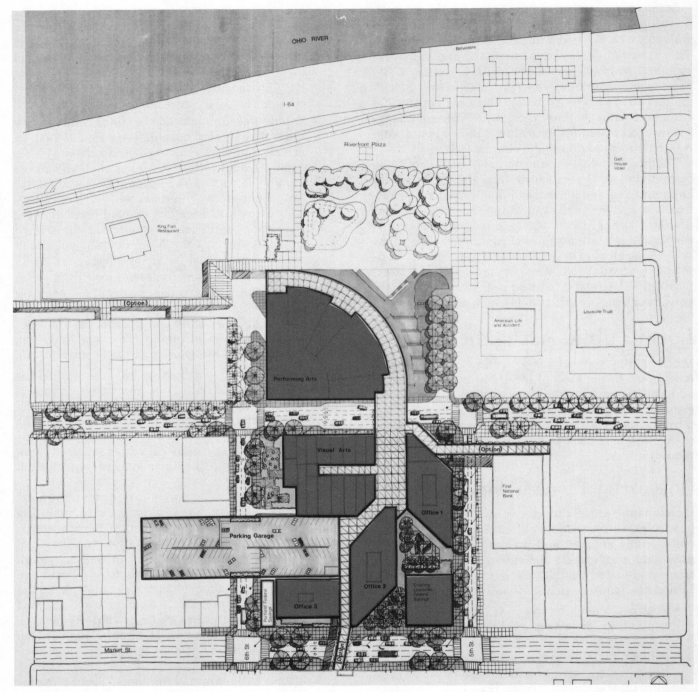

7-2 Louisville, Kentucky. The Kentucky Center for the Arts is the most recent element of an ongoing program of downtown revitalization that began in 1966. The Belvedere and the riverfront plaza, which have a 1,600-car garage underneath, are the major elements of public commitment that set the stage for other public and private development.

The city, the county, the commonwealth, and the private sector negotiated an agreement formalizing each local party's responsibilities and obligations to fund economic development activities in the city. With all local interests firmly committed to providing resources to the revitalization, the parties approached the federal government to join the coventure to reduce the obstacles of effective federal stimulus of public/private development. Under the terms of the coventure agreement, formally announced on October 9, 1979, by the Federal Southeast Regional Council, the partnership allowed the President to appoint a person who would represent various federal agencies and be responsible for coordinating all federal resources. The assignment of federal agency personnel to work with the program staff in Louisville in packaging applications for federal funds enhanced local skills and provided opportunities for federal staff to become knowledgeable of the local development process.

As a further incentive to such partnerships, a term in the agreement reduced processing time in response to applications for federal funds. The terms established a maximum of 60 days from receipt of the application to encourage important private investment.

One of the most important elements of the coventure agreement was the negotiation of a firm commitment by the federal government to the 3-year program. This commitment will be a powerful incentive to local public and private interests to participate and will minimize the effect of changes in federal policy and personnel.

Strictly public agencies are seldom sufficiently effective in urban development because legislation or local politics constrains their actions. They are rarely permitted to invest public funds in private development and must often follow time-consuming processes that limit their capability to respond quickly to development opportunities. To overcome these limitations, many communities have established quasi-public/private development corporations. Since these corporations are not public agencies, they are not restricted by politics or the same legal constraints that public agencies are.

Quasi-public economic development corporations are usually governed by a board of directors whose members are from the public and private sectors. They are usually staffed by full-time professionals paid by public and private funding. They operate as nonprofit entities, generally under contract to the city, but may also enter into profit-making ventures with private developers. Any resulting profits are then channeled into the organization's capital revolving fund for future development activities. Such organizations can also profit from their special legal

status as private bodies because they are not considered municipal corporations under most state constitutions. They provide an alternative to city governments that would otherwise be prohibited from entering directly into certain types of development projects.

The purpose of development organizations—whether a city agency or a quasi-public entity—is to alter downtown market conditions to promote development. The public sector can alter the market by increasing the demand for the developed space, assisting in site assembly, providing innovative land use controls, investing public funds in downtown, providing special taxation policy, providing project improvements and public facilities, and sharing costs.

Public Actions to Induce Demand

A key to the success of downtown development projects is the leasing or selling of space at a price high enough to cover development costs and ensure a profit for the investors and the developer. Demand is the primary variable in determining whether or not private development will occur. In some urban areas and for some types of development, the public sector helps to create and foster the demand for space in the project. Even with high demand by the private sector, income from the development may not cover the high costs of land assembly, relocation, demolition, and public improvements.

Local officials can stimulate demand for a private development in a number of ways. One way is to communicate to potential lessees the advantages of a downtown location through a regular and carefully directed public affairs program that "sells downtown." Tax incentives for developers are another effective tool. By reducing taxes, the local government can increase the attraction of a downtown project. Favorably pricing public services like water and sewerage can also reduce the cost of doing business for private firms, increasing the demand for space in the jurisdiction offering favorable rates.

The public sector itself can be a major source of new demand for space. A public lease commitment for space in the new development makes it considerably easier for the developer to obtain financing. Even if the government commits itself to lease only a minor portion of a proposed project, its triple-A rating as a lessee makes it easier for the developer to obtain other lease commitments. By carefully structuring the terms for rent escalation and renewal options and through special arrangements, a municipality can minimize the cost of space at the same time it encourages private development.

The public sector's decision to lease space should be based on an analysis of the direct costs of the alternatives. Subsidizing private real estate development should not be the main motive for public leasing. But if leasing is the most cost-effective alternative, the municipality can use its leverage as a major grade-A tenant to make possible a real estate venture that might otherwise not have materialized. The overall impact can be substantially greater than if the public space were in a single-purpose government complex.

Assisting in Site Assembly

In a city where most of the land has already been subdivided and developed, the acquisition of a suitable site can be a major problem. Because most of the land has been divided into relatively small parcels owned by separate parties, the problem of acquisition increases with the size of the site required. Assemblage is typically hindered by the relatively high property values resulting from existing improvements, owners who are unwilling to sell regardless of price or who hold out for the maximum price possible, clouded titles, and the time and legal costs required to negotiate for a number of parcels. The public sector can alleviate these problems for the private developer in a number of ways. The techniques that might be used, separately or in combination, are quick take by eminent domain, land banking, ground leases, transfer of air rights and development rights, private use of eminent domain, land swaps, and relocation assistance.

Quick Take by Eminent Domain

Eminent domain is the power to take private land for public use, compensating the owner based on the land's current use. It is the major tool that redevelopment authorities possess to create parcels of land for new development. Quick take is a mechanism that allows immediate public possession. Final disposition of the action is accomplished after the taking either by negotiation or by court-determined compensation.

An example of this technique is the amendment to California law, which became effective in 1976, providing that a redevelopment agency has the right of immediate possession. This provision reduces considerably the time required to assemble and develop the land. The redevelopment agency can thus negotiate an agreement with a developer and commit itself to a delivery date for the site before the assembly of land. Some cities have assigned a limited version of the power of eminent domain to their local development corporations, allowing them to seize land that has been abandoned or on which taxes are owed and then sell it to a commercial or industrial user for development.

Land Banking

Land banking allows a city agency or local development corporation to acquire and assemble land suitable for development and hold it until a suitable user is identified. The city can reserve land when it becomes available, assembling large parcels of land. The banked land can effectively lure new development to the downtown area and retain companies that need more land.

An economic development corporation in San Diego banks land for commercial and industrial development. The corporation secures properly zoned city-owned land with a first option to purchase or lease it at approximately one-half of fair market value. When a developer shows interest, the corporation exercises its option to purchase or lease the land and then immediately sells or leases it to the private developer. Net proceeds from the sale, or 50 percent of the lease payments for the first 5 years, are placed in a trust fund for future land transactions. Interest on the money held in trust funds defrays some of the corporation's overhead expenses.

The industrial and commercial land bank and revolving fund operated by the Philadelphia Industrial Development Corporation (PIDC) encourages private investment by selling city-owned industrial or commercial property at below-market prices. The practice reduces the amount of financing a company needs for expansion or relocation. PIDC also acquires additional properties for development and funds site improvements on existing properties. The proceeds of land sales are returned to the fund so that the city can buy more land when it is available. The revolving fund is an important part of the land banking arrangement because it enables PIDC to market center city land at prices competitive with other city and suburban sites (which are more plentiful), and it enables PIDC to pay the costs of preparing the sites for development.

The city of Columbus (Ohio) entered into a form of negotiated purchase with the development corporation for the Capitol South project. The Capitol South Development Corporation, after completing negotiations with a property owner (with a representative of the City Attorney's office present), would request the city to acquire the parcel, while committing itself to lease it from the city until developers were secured. The City Council would authorize the financing of the acquisition through the sale of short-term notes. When the city acquired the land, the development corporation's rental payment to the city was equal to the annual interest rate on the notes times the purchase price paid by the city. When Capitol South exercises its exclusive option to purchase the land, it

7-3   Artist's rendering of first private office building to be located in Capitol South, Columbus, Ohio.

pays the city the actual acquisition cost of the property plus other incidental costs—appraisal, title search fees, court costs, overhead, carrying charges, and so forth.

Ground Leases

Long-term ground leases are increasingly used in publicly assisted development because they are so flexible. The lease can provide for a minimum base payment plus a percentage of income generated by the project or by some other graduated arrangement. Thus, if the project does well, the city shares in the income and can recover some or all of its costs. Ground leases, moreover, can be subordinated; that is, the city can execute a mortgage of its land as security for the development loan made to the lessee.

For the developer, such long-term leases can greatly improve the net return on investment through improved financing terms, reductions in equity outlays, and tax advantages. With a subordination clause in the lease, the advantages are even greater. The disadvantage is that cash flow is reduced when the land is leased rather than purchased.

A properly structured ground lease can have the same effect as a loan, decreasing the required equity investment (by eliminating the purchase price of the land) or the developer's risk exposure. The decrease in turn tends to increase the developer's return on investment. Because the leased land becomes subject to the lien of the mortgage taken out by the developer, the lender usually lends more money and charges less in interest than for a loan made on leased property without a subordination clause. The lessor charges a slightly higher rent if the lease is subordinated because subordination entails a greater risk on his part.

With subordination the developer can deduct the full amount of the lease payment from his income taxes. Had the land been purchased and financed, only the interest payments would be deductible. Of course, the lessee can still depreciate the improvements.

The relationship of the lease to the mortgage must be considered in the decision to lend money for development. If any agreements of sale or lease are signed before the developer applies for a loan, a copy of the lease should be included in the application. Such a situation is most likely to happen when some rehabilitation of existing space is included as part of the project. The package should also include an analysis of the lease prepared by the mortgage banker. If, for example, a building is to be constructed for the occupancy of a specific tenant, the lender may request that a signed lease be recorded before the mortgage is granted to ensure that the lease is not disturbed if foreclosure occurs. If, however, the investor plans to take possession of a property in the event of foreclosure, the lease must be recorded after the mortgage, allowing the foreclosure to negate the leases.

Long-term subordinated ground leases also benefit the city. Default on a lease could mean that the city loses its land, but the default provision in the lease can be worded so that only rent payments are lost until income increases or some other event takes place. Land does revert to the city eventually.

Leasing increases a developer's leverage at little cost to the city; in fact, the rent is additional direct income. Subordinated leases provide even greater leverage at even less cost to the city if the project succeeds. Although subordinated leases are highly cost-effective, municipalities have seldom used them to attract real estate investment, perhaps because of restrictive state legislation or because of local governments' unfamiliarity with them.

By leasing its land or other property to private developers, the city can specify in the lease how the property is to be developed and operated and thus exercise greater control than if it were sold outright. Leasing can also stimulate real estate development by structuring payment terms adapted to the project's requirements for cash flow.

Toronto used such leasing to facilitate development of excess land condemned for the rapid transit system, especially around transit stops. The leases tailor time and rent escalation clauses to help the developer meet the requirements of lending institutions. They specify when the developer will begin and complete the proposed project (subject to renegotiation), that the Toronto Transit Commission must approve elements of the project that directly affect the subway, and that the lease can be terminated if the developer cannot obtain the necessary public approval.[2]

7-4 Atrium of Merchants Plaza, Indianapolis. The 367-acre site for this MXD was consolidated by eminent domain and then leased to the developer for $360,000 per year until 2034, with two 15-year renewal options.

Air Rights Transfer

An air rights transfer is similar to a lease arrangement because it provides usable sites for development while the city retains control and use of the land below the development. It can also be an incentive for development: The city can develop ground space to complement the private use, or it can offer attractive lease payments and property taxes on the space and improvements. Lease payments and property taxes on the air space and improvements can be calculated to provide incentives for the developer at the same time they provide the city government with a share of the profits—effectively the same as a return on capital invested in the land.[3]

[2] See Urban Land Institute with Gladstone Associates, *Joint Development: Making the Real Estate–Transit Connection* (Washington, D.C.: ULI–the Urban Land Institute, 1979), pp. 151–79.

[3] See Real Estate Research Corporation, *Air Rights and Highways* (Washington, D.C.: ULI–the Urban Land Institute, 1969).

Hartford provides an example of air rights transfer. In Hartford, Aetna Life and Casualty Company leased the air rights over the city's convention and parking facilities for 50 years; it has three 10-year renewal options. When the lease expires, all improvements constructed by Aetna will revert to the city.

Development Rights Transfer

Transferring development rights not only encourages development within a given location but also relieves development pressures on other sites, notably where historic structures are located.[4] New York City has used this technique actively, particularly for the South Street Seaport project. The Special South Street Seaport District, a special zoning district, established the development rights transfer. The city wished to preserve several blocks of 19th century buildings, the last vestiges of lower Manhattan's heyday as a seaport, that were slated for demolition to permit high density development. The city purchased the properties, paying the owners a sum equal to their equity and compensating the banks that held mortgages on the properties by giving them title to the unbuilt development rights. The banks are then permitted to sell the development rights to developers of designated "receiving" sites elsewhere in New York City. The development rights thus transferred can be used to increase a building's total floor area and to increase its lot coverage beyond what the zoning ordinance would normally allow.

Private Use of Eminent Domain

Several states have enacted laws that allow localities to grant the power of eminent domain to private developers, who develop properties in accordance with locally approved plans. This delegated power of eminent domain is commonly used to resolve land assembly problems like the lack of large parcels and the high cost of purchasing and preparing land for development. Many states, however, limit their use to blighted areas. The power is further limited in that the developer must comply with certain limitations on earnings and interest payments.

Land Exchange

Land exchanges or land swaps can be used to reorganize land ownerships. The trade between public and private parties is based on values set by an independent appraiser so that each party has a consolidated and usable land parcel.

The city of Dallas, which is legally barred from offering any direct incentives to the private sector and does not have traditional urban renewal powers, used a land swap to encourage development of its railroad

7-5 The Pasadena Athletic Club was relocated to allow clearance of a key parcel for the development of Plaza Pasadena.

station project. The city and a local businessman both held significant amounts of land in the area of the railroad station, but the parcels were too fragmented to allow development by either party. Based on an independent appraisal, the city and the private party traded lots of equal value so that each held a consolidated and usable land parcel and development could proceed.

The Pasadena Redevelopment Agency arranged a similar land exchange to facilitate a downtown retail development. The Pasadena Athletic Club was located in a 50-year-old, 8-story building containing 85,000 square feet of space in athletic, commercial, restaurant, office, and residential use. The building was located within the site specified for development of a 600,000–square foot urban retail complex containing three department stores. The developer of Plaza Pasadena and the department stores could not develop the retail complex and its underground parking with the athletic club remaining.

To facilitate proceedings, the agency allowed the owner to exercise owner participation rights in another location in the development project. The agency acquired the building and leased it back to the owner for 15 months. During that period the agency sold a 2-acre parcel of land to the owner approximately 6 blocks from its original site. The owner of the athletic club was allowed to design and construct a new facility of 50,000 square feet that included athletic facilities, some retail space, and apartments.

The agency retained control of the design to ensure its compatibility with the project. When the new ath-

---

[4] See John J. Costonis, Vol. III, *Development Rights Transfer: Description and Perspectives for a Critique in Management and Control of Growth* (Washington, D.C.: ULI–the Urban Land Institute, 1975), pp. 92–98, and Frank Schnidman, Vol. IV, *Techniques in Application,* "TDR: A Tool for More Equitable Land Management" in *Management and Control of Growth* (Washington, D.C.: ULI–the Urban Land Institute, 1978), pp. 52–57.

7-6   Plaza Pasadena—artist's rendering.

letic facilities were completed, the agency took possession of the old athletic club and demolished the building, which allowed construction of the underground parking facilities to begin.

Relocation Assistance

Even though a public agency may not directly aid site acquisition, it may help a private developer assemble a site by helping to relocate space users in the property slated for development. Relocation assistance can take the form of loans and grants to pay moving expenses or aid in finding or developing a new site for those who must move. Both parties benefit: The relocated activity has a chance to leave obsolete facilities and an inadequate location, and the community gains economic benefits from new businesses.

Relocation assistance is one of the most difficult problems to overcome in downtown development. One recent approach to the solution in California is facilitating the transaction. In 1972 the California Community Redevelopment Law was amended so that state relocation assistance would be comparable to the federal law for all public land acquisition (including street widening, building conservation programs, and revitalization projects). Some new development projects in California have been created within communities to accept relocated businesses for the primary purpose of keeping the business and job base within the city.

Innovative Land Use Controls

Municipalities can also encourage private development with innovative land use controls. Flexible regulations and new zoning measures can create market opportunities in depressed areas. The special zoning districts in New York City, for example, were designed to encourage specific kinds of development.

Certain provisions of the Special Greenwich Street Development District in lower Manhattan permitted the maximum floor area of a development to be increased in exchange for the provision of improved pedestrian circulation, greater public open space, better shopping, and coordinated development. The Bankers Trust Building, the first office building constructed under these special zoning provisions, includes a combination of mandatory and elective improvements: an elevated plaza linked by a bridge to the World Trade Center, and shopping arcades at street level and at the level of the elevated plaza. The developers also contributed money to a special city fund that pays for improvements to subway stations within the district. In exchange for the improvements, the permitted floor area ratio (FAR) of the development was almost doubled, from FAR 10.0 to FAR 18.0, and the percentage of the lot covered by the buildings was increased by one-third.

Two other special zoning districts are located in midtown Manhattan: the Special Fifth Avenue District, which is specific to Fifth Avenue, and the Commercial/Residential District, which can be used in various areas of Manhattan. The Special Fifth Avenue District was a response to the disappearance of quality retail shops at street level along the avenue and their replacement with banks and ticket offices. The District had several objectives: to support 24-hour activity, to encourage retail activity at ground level along the avenue and covered pedestrian spaces in the interior, to eliminate the need for parking in the area and curb cuts fronting Fifth Avenue, to include residential units in midtown Manhattan, and to strengthen the vitality of the street wall along the avenue.

To meet these objectives, the zoning district permits boutiques, restaurants, and galleries at ground level and excludes ticket offices. Retail use is mandated along the avenue, but requirements for coverage, height, and setback are flexible. The developer receives a bonus of additional floor area for including pedestrian arcades and residential units.

The developer of Olympic Towers, the first building constructed under the Special Fifth Avenue District zoning regulations, increased the allowable floor area by providing covered pedestrian space. Floor area increased 14 square feet for each square foot of covered pedestrian space. The skylighted 30-foot-high pedestrian arcade at midblock connects 51st Street to 52nd Street and is open to the public. Since the building was completed in 1975, retail space fronting Fifth Avenue has been fully leased, but the developer experienced difficulty leasing retail space inside the arcade.

Commercial/residential zoning allows vertical mixed use on a single zoning lot to encourage 24-hour activity in the Manhattan CBD. Separated land uses are replaced by multiple uses in one building. The new concept promotes residential use in high density commercial areas rather than penalizing it through restrictions on floor area ratio.

In a commercial/residential zoning district, up to two-thirds of a building may be residential. Two kinds of amenities are mandatory for all buildings in a commercial/residential zoning district: recreational facilities for residential tenants and pedestrian space on the ground level for commercial tenants. Covered pedestrian spaces and through-block arcades are encouraged because of the large number of pedestrians and the complex circulation pattern resulting from two separate uses for building lobbies. In return, height and setback regulations are more flexible.

The Galleria in midtown Manhattan east of Park Avenue was the first mixed use building developed under a Commercial/Residential District. Its 57 stories contain 100,000 square feet of office space, 8,000

7-7 Olympic Towers. Innovative zoning provided a public midblock pedestrian connection.

square feet of retail space, and 260 luxury condominium apartments. The building includes a nine-story through-block skylighted galleria connecting 57th Street to 58th Street, which is defined in the zoning as a covered pedestrian space. The galleria has the mandatory retail space at its periphery. Office and condominium spaces have been successfully marketed since the building was completed in 1974, but renting the retail space has been less successful. The owner hopes that the addition of a cafe will draw pedestrians to the galleria and its shops, which are not readily visible from the street.

As these examples show, the objective of innovative or special land use controls is to encourage the form and character of development by providing incentives that are tied to public objectives. For these approaches to be effective, they must be tailored to the particular circumstances. An incentive in one city may become a disincentive elsewhere if applied to other circumstances. Because all incentives must be inherently economic, the particular application must be carefully tested to determine its value. For example, allowing a height increase may not be an incentive if subsoil conditions would increase costs for the foundation.

Public Financing Assistance

A major part of local public assistance to downtown development is funding. The infusion of public funds can tip the balance between feasibility and infeasibility, and public financing can be used to leverage loans, grants, or equity funds from other sources, particularly from state or federal governments. The underlying objective of direct public assistance is to spur private investment. To this end, the type and character of public financing assistance and the timing of its availability (before, during, or after private development) must be carefully planned.

159

7-8 The Galleria in Midtown Manhattan—a mixed use development combining condominium, office, and retail space, and a nine-story galleria connecting 57th Street to 58th Street.

The market for both equity and loan capital for real estate development is fairly well organized and operates nationwide. Therefore, most large projects compete for funds with other similar projects throughout the nation and with other investment instruments such as stocks and bonds. In a highly competitive capital market, a project that may benefit the community may not be able to attract the necessary financing from the private market at supportable interest rates. Direct loans from the public sector at below-market interest rates are a solution to this situation. The public sector can borrow money at a lower interest rate because the interest it pays is tax exempt. The interest it earns on money it lends is also tax exempt and can therefore be at a lower rate. Thus, many projects that would not be feasible with private financing only are feasible with a public loan at lower rates.

Direct loans can fill a gap when no private funds or insufficient funds are available for a particular portion of a project's financing needs. Local governments' major benefit from this kind of participation, beyond the benefit of encouraging new development, is that it enables the local government to exercise some control it would not ordinarily have.

The city may wish to offer a below-market direct loan even if a project does not require it financially when the city's interests are at stake.

Developers find direct loans attractive for two reasons. The lower interest rate means the developer's cost is lower. If the loan is in the form of a second mortgage, private lenders may be more willing to finance the remainder of the project because the risk is less. Should the project fail, first mortgage lenders are repaid before second mortgage lenders. Despite these advantages, most state constitutions prohibit the use of public funds for direct loans, investments, or grants for business development. Many states have resolved this problem by enabling legislation allowing the creation of economic development corporations or other such special vehicles that serve as a conduit for city grants, loans, and contracts to private entities.

The public sector can also influence the availability of financing for private development projects by stipulating that certain types of loans be made in return for deposits of government funds in private financial institutions. This technique is gaining in popularity as cities realize the concessions that banks are willing to make to receive large government deposits. While not a direct loan program, it can have somewhat the same effect in that it creates a supply of loan funds that otherwise would not exist.

If funds are not available for direct loans, cities can also achieve somewhat the same results by guaranteeing loans, thereby shifting some of the lender's risk to the local government. If a public agency agrees to guarantee repayment of a loan from a private lender, the chance of the developer's obtaining private funds improves significantly, again because the risks to the lender are reduced. Similarly, if the local government agrees to lease or purchase the project at a percentage of projected market value in the event the projected return does not materialize, the project becomes more attractive to equity and mortgage investors.

Subsidizing the interest rate on a loan is another technique that increases the loan's attractiveness to lenders. This subsidy is normally implemented through loan pools established with local funds matched to federal assistance. Most commonly, pooling is designed to leverage other loan, grant, or equity funds, particularly from federal and state governments. The local funds in the pool can be a mix of public and private funds, including various sources of nonlocal development capital available to economically depressed urban municipalities. These nonlocal development funds include community development block grants, Economic Development Administration (EDA) programs (public works, economic planning, technical assistance, and Title IX grants, which are designed to assist cities affected by the closing of federal facilities), and grants available under the Comprehensive Employment Training Act. Public sources of business development funds include EDA business development loans, programs sponsored by the Small Business Administration (business loans, loan guarantees, local development company loans), and grants from the Office of Minority Business Enterprises.

An integral part of the revitalization of Greenville, South Carolina, was the development of a loan pool to provide incentives to businesses, tenants, property owners, and individuals to reinvest in existing properties. The pool's objective was to improve the appearance and viability of the downtown area while stimulating long-term reinvestment. Launched with community development block grant monies and funded by local commercial banks and savings and loan institutions, it provided low- to medium-term loans at favorable interest rates.

The program lends money for rehabilitation, working capital, and real estate acquisition. Rehabilitation loans can be used for both internal and external renovation. Signs, awnings, painting, electrical rewiring, structural modifications, and partitions qualify for such loans. The participating financial institutions offer loans at 0.5 percent per year over the prime rate at the time funds are advanced. This interest rate remains in effect for the length of the participation in the program up to a maximum of 7 to 9 years.

The amount of money available has no upper or lower limits. Instead, loan terms remain at the discretion of the participating bank or savings and loan institution. The city, through its community development department, subsidizes the interest rate to an effective rate to the borrower of 4 percent under the bank rate.

Greenville's loan program also makes funds available for expansion of inventory, new business fixtures and equipment, purchases, operating expenses, and carrying of accounts receivable. For working capital loans, interest rates for the bank are 0.5 percent per year over the prime rate with a maximum interest rate of 7 percent per year. The amount of money loaned to an individual borrower and the terms for repayment are left to the lending institution's discretion, with some limit on the maximum term.

Assistance through Taxation Policy

Taxation policies can positively affect development. They include property tax incentives, tax abatement incentives, special taxation districts, and tax increment financing.

7-9   Greenville Commons model, Greenville, South Carolina.

Property Tax Incentives

Property tax incentives aid real estate development in two ways: First, they eliminate uncertainties about taxes for the developer, and, second, they improve the developer's cash flow by reducing taxes, particularly during the early months of a project when income and expenses are unbalanced. Evidence on how effective property tax incentives are for stimulating real estate investment is inconclusive. Unless concessions are carefully tailored to specific real estate objectives and offered selectively, they can become subsidies for construction that would have occurred in any case. Conversely, they can make possible marginal development that should not occur.

Broadly applied tax rate differentials between major cities generally are ineffectual in influencing decisions to relocate a company's regional offices. But local differences can play a major role once the general area has been chosen. High tax rates in central cities that are surrounded by suburban communities offering relatively low property tax rates can discourage development in the CBD. Tax incentives, however, are not necessarily the best way to encourage development. The local government must weigh the benefits and consequences to select the most effective type of incentive at lowest public cost. The analysis should determine whether the tax incentive is critical in securing development and whether benefits exceed the taxes the city would have received. In many states, however, differential tax rates for various portions of a city or for certain land use categories would violate the state constitution.

Two other forms of restructuring property taxes—graded property taxing and land value taxation—are rarely used in the United States.[5] If existing applications in Colorado and Pennsylvania prove workable, however, other states could adopt them. They are based on the value of the land rather than the im-

---

[5] See R. W. Archer, *Site Value Taxation in Central Business District Redevelopment: Sidney, Australia* (Washington, D.C.: ULI–the Urban Land Institute, 1972).

Downtown Decision-Making Process
Cincinnati CBD Case Study

Major renewal efforts often arise out of disastrous events. Such an event occurred in Cincinnati during 1961, when assessed valuations of properties in the CBD were reduced wholesale by 12½ percent. While the CBD tax base represented 47 percent of the total city tax base in 1910, 26 percent in 1931, and 17 percent in 1955, the figure suddenly dropped to 11 percent after the devaluations. Downtown Cincinnati was in serious trouble.

In April 1962, the City Council held three public hearings where business, civic, and social groups could discuss the problem and what would happen if the area deteriorated further, what could be done to remedy the situation, how much the remedy would cost, and how it could be financed. The proposed program was to consist of four major undertakings:

- a CBD core program projected at $7.6 million in local councilmanic general obligation bonds plus $32 million in federal Title I funds
- a central riverfront project estimated at $6.6 million in local referendum general obligation bonds plus $17 million in federal Title I funds
- a $13 million convention center financed with $10 million in local referendum general obligation bonds plus $3 million in federal Title I funds
- a new stadium estimated at $15 million, to be financed partly through revenue bonds, plus some $9 million in site work, parking, railroad relocation, and so forth.

In the fall of 1962, voters approved the $16.6 million in referendum bond moneys ($6.6 million for the riverfront project plus $10 million for the convention center). HUD (HHFA at the time) reserved $52 million for the CBD core, the central riverfront, and convention center projects, and talks were underway to establish the most effective financing vehicle for the stadium. The stadium was eventually financed through a combination of county revenue bonds, parking system bonds, a city lease commitment for the stadium, and sublease commitments from the Cincinnati Reds and a newly acquired National Football League franchise.

During the same period of time, the city sought proposals from developers to undertake the concurrent development of six blocks interspersed in the core of the CBD plus a major site along the riverfront.

By the end of 1962, Cincinnati had full public funding for its entire downtown program, a developer for all of the sites scheduled to be cleared, and the concurrence of a substantial portion of the electorate, the political establishment, and the business leadership. One key element was missing however: There was no consensus on a plan. While words, ideas, plans, data, and studies abounded, the issues were not clear and for lack of their resolution, there was no consensus on policy. The city was thus forced to begin the business of making decisions that would represent a consensus, although not necessarily unanimity, and that would allow the proposed development to be implemented.

The decision process used to achieve this end is now known as the "Cincinnati process." It was not carefully predesigned but evolved out of day-to-day necessity. It had no single author but enough concerned and near-desperate backers of development to enable the subordination of strong wills to the desire for consensus.

The process began with the City Council's appointment of a working review committee, whose purpose was to make recommendations for decisions. The committee was perceived as a value judgment group. Its purpose was to judge proposals, with the presumption that the proposals were technically sound and feasible. The Planning Commission and then the City Council were to ratify the recommendations before they in fact became decisions. The committee would be dissolved after all decisions were ratified.

The composition of the committee was a key factor in its success. It consisted of members from both the public and the private sectors. Public representatives included a majority of the City Council (five out of nine councilmen), a majority of the Planning Commission, including its Chairman, the City Manager, and the Director of Planning. Private sector representatives included three business leaders (all members of the Downtown Development Committee), the chairman of a major bank, two key industrialists, and two representatives of the developer. The chairman of the working review committee was a highly respected, recently retired businessman, Mark Upson.

Meetings were open to the public and the press, which discouraged petty politics, bickering, and self-serving orations. The five councilmen and the members of the Planning Commission could vote without necessarily being held to the vote later in council and commission meetings. No substitutes for its members were allowed, which aided the committee's credibility.

A technical team consisting of three consulting firms—Hammer, Siler and George, Alan M. Voorhees and Associates, and Rogers, Taliaferro, Kostritsky & Lamb—prepared proposals for the committee's consideration. This team, which was selected by the working review committee, was headed by Archibald Rogers, its principal spokesman before the committee. Besides the talent it represented in the fields of economics, transportation, and urban planning, the team's members had not yet been involved in Cincinnati's proposed development and could bring objectivity to the task. The team was to add technical judgment to the committee's value judgments.

Yet a third part of the process was its day-to-day administration. This effort was the responsibility of the city's Urban Development Department, specifically its Downtown Coordinator (a position created for this purpose). Administration consisted of three basic elements: acting as executive secretary for the working review committee, acting as contract officer for the technical team by processing its proposals through city administrative channels to ensure their administrative, legal, and financial feasibility before they were presented to the committee, and guiding the committee's recommendations for decisions through legislative ratification.

The committee's meetings occurred in pairs, alternating between a "presentation meeting" and, usually within a week or two, a "decisions meeting." Presentation meetings allowed extensive discussion of the proposals, while decisions meetings tended to be brisk tallies of votes against a checklist of recommendatis for decisions. The period between the meetings was devoted to extensive informal meetings where proposals were tested in terms of their responsiveness to the broad range of potentially conflicting political, business, and special interests involved.

The proposals were presented incrementally in accordance with a "ladder of decisions," which began with fundamental objectives, ranged through basic strategies for transportation, land use, and functions of downtown, and culminated in detailed proposals for the urban design of each street and block within the core of the CBD. Each proposal was presented in the form of a statement of decision (later reflected in the decisions checklist) backed up with a rationale and technical documentation discussing the implications of the proposal. Almost all proposals had alternatives; where possible, a "decision tree" technique was used to show where the alternatives would lead.

In all, over 250 decisions were presented and acted upon at eight pairs of meetings over 14 months. They were grouped into four basic phases. Each group of recommendations for decisions was then formalized into a city ordinance, and each ordinance was enacted into law by the City Council. In this fashion, each group of decisions became a firm given, serving as a solid basis for the next and more detailed level of planning and deliberation by the committee. At the end of the process, all decisions and groups of decisions were consolidated into a single ordinance, which the City Council enacted after a major public hearing. Cincinnati had its consensus, its plan for downtown, represented by an urban design plan, the documented report, a brochure and working model of downtown, and minutes of all committee meetings.

As this decision-making process was occurring, work was proceeding with finalizing federal loan and grant applications, and as funds became available, the city initiated property acquisition, relocation, and clearance. The result was that the plan was implemented, in effect, as it was prepared.

Today, over 90 percent of the decisions have been translated into brick and mortar. The plan has been implemented with few changes to the original decisions. The stadium and convention center are in full operation, and over 2,000,000 square feet of new office space, some 250,000 square feet of new retail space, 500 new hotel rooms, and over 5,000 parking spaces have been added. Downtown has been made more accessible with an extensive system of public/private skywalks lacing the core and interconnecting all parking facilities and department stores and a substantial amount of office space. And the downtowns been made more comfortable with an unusual system of street furniture, lighting, sidewalk plants, and decorative paving.

Downtown Cincinnati has been transformed. It is now poised for a second generation of development, which is still occurring within the tight framework established by the original plan.

A massive transformation such as this one does not usually occur easily or smoothly. Successful as the Cincinnati development is, the program was peppered by court battles, false starts, delays, strikes, legal problems, defaults, and a plethora of controversial issues. Nor is the product by any means perfect. Some of the architecture is clearly mediocre and much could have been done better. Downtown housing has not materialized and one site still stands vacant. On balance, however, the objectives have been accomplished, and many successes have become the pride of Cincinnati.

Columbus Dispatch Photo—Tom Sines

provements on it. Graded property taxing taxes land at relatively higher rates than the improvements.

Land value taxation taxes the value of the land excluding any improvements; it is therefore based exclusively on the parcel's location and its highest reuse value. It reduces the operating costs of new improvements and increases the costs of holding idle land or underused property. Thus, the method encourages existing owners who cannot afford a higher level of taxation resulting from this approach to sell to developers interested in using the land for its full economic potential and, according to its proponents, stimulates intensive land development and property rehabilitation.

Tax Abatement Incentives

Tax abatement incentives are addressed to specific types of developments, projects, or areas rather than to changes in the overall taxation system. Tax abatement—in the form of tax stabilization, a tax freeze, or a tax exemption for a limited time—means that the city encourages privately financed improvements in specified areas by not collecting the real estate taxes on those improvements for a number of years or by freezing the assessment at the predevelopment level. The developer gains by not having to pay real estate taxes for a time, and the city gains from the economic growth that development encourages. Whether tax abatement should be used depends on the development, its location and financing, and how the incentive is structured.

Because commercial projects tend to generate substantially more tax revenues than they require in servicing costs, cities can negotiate with developers to reduce the surplus as an incentive for development to occur. This incentive is possible if a project will have a multiplier effect on local economic activity by generating increased tax revenues from other sources. The increased tax revenues from new adjacent development can be used to retire the debt on the public portion of the development.

Ohio cities have made most effective use of tax abatement. Because of the incentive, a new hotel in Dayton was able to lower room rates to be competitive. Without lower room rates, the project would not have been feasible, and the city would not have received the income from meetings and conventions, restaurants, shopping, and entertainment that a new hotel brings.

In Cincinnati the local government invested heavily in public improvements along the riverfront as a commitment to a proposal from a local private developer to construct a 26-story, 225-unit luxury apartment tower. The developer requested tax abate-

ment for the project to eliminate some maintenance expense during the initial leasing period and to keep rents as low as possible until the demand for the apartments was clear. The assistance was especially important because the project was the first of its kind in the downtown area and because rents were projected to be much higher than for the general Cincinnati market.

The city resisted unconditional tax abatement because it would have been politically unacceptable and because the city wished to share in the project's profits. The two parties agreed that 15 percent of the project's gross income—or $219,000 on the initial projected rents—was a reasonable profit for the developer. The city agreed to allow 100 percent tax abatement for the first 5 years, after which the developer would pay the County Treasurer the amount of net profits over $219,000. When the payments reach the amount of projected taxes, the developer's profit may exceed $219,000.

A second project in Cincinnati also gained significantly from the city's willingness to grant a tax abatement. The Crowninshield Corporation of Boston, Massachusetts, proposed converting two 19th century city-owned structures into 200 middle-income one- and two-bedroom apartments. The corporation proposed parking for 200 cars in the first two floors of one building (originally a garage) and 8,000 square feet of retail space in the other (originally an office building). The city agreed to sell Crowninshield the two buildings for $350,000 and grant the project 100 percent tax abatement for 20 years. Because the debt on the garage exceeded $1 million and it was politically unacceptable to grant unconditional tax abatement, the city had to receive some revenue from the project. The developer therefore pays $6,000 yearly directly to the city plus an amount equal to 35 percent of the project's increase in net profits, computed yearly after the first year.

Special Taxation Districts

Special taxation districts, or special benefit assessments, have been used only recently as an economic tool to spur downtown development. Typically, the city levies a charge on the property in a specified single- or multipurpose district—perhaps a downtown area, a commercial strip, or an historic preservation area. Funds are used to provide special services and public improvements in areas targeted for development or financing for project planning or operating costs.

Depending on the specific state enabling legislation, special taxation districts can be used to levy either regular ad valorem property tax assessments or special benefit taxes based on the value of the land excluding improvements. Regular ad valorem property taxes depend on market value and are based on the entire floor footage of a building as well as unpredictable market changes (for example, revenues received from the property). Such taxes tend to be relatively high for high-rise downtown offices and stores and, combined with the unpredictability of assessments based on market value, tend to discourage downtown development.

Special benefit taxes levied through special taxation districts, in contrast, are assessed using a negotiated formula based on the predictable factors of the property's front footage or square footage. Revenues may be included in the formula as well, and the formula can provide a sliding scale for payments. This type of tax can stimulate new investment because it has the net effect of providing new enterprises with front-end public financing.

Tax revenues are used to retire bonds issued by the city (or the district itself) to pay for the improvements and services in the district. Depending on the specific state legislation, the bonds can be included in or excluded from the city's debt and tax levy ceilings. The bonds are repaid directly from the tax revenues collected or from the city's general fund, which is later reimbursed by the special tax revenues.

A city can choose what kind of development it wants to encourage in a specific area by selecting the factors in the formula. Allocations based on front footage benefit large multilevel buildings; those based on square footage benefit small businesses. From the viewpoint of the general public and the city government, special benefit assessments allow the cost of providing public services in development areas to be passed on to the parts of the private sector that benefit most directly from the improvements. One drawback of the method is the difficulty associated with allocating additional tax liability among the various private parties.

A Pennsylvania law enabling cities and towns to create business improvement districts in any urban commercial area is one of the more flexible statutes for special taxation districts. Cities can use the special levies to finance utility and other public improvements, landscaping, demolition, acquisition, remodeling blighted structures, and fees for professional services and planning studies. Pennsylvania cities have the option of assessing ad valorem or special benefit taxes.

Nebraska cities can create an unlimited number of business improvement and parking districts in their commercial areas, within which they can collect special benefit assessments based on front footage,

square footage, or other special values. The special district assessments may be distributed over a maximum of 20 years. Municipal bond financing for the business improvement districts is limited by the city's debt limit, but the city may finance improvements in the district from general revenues and then use the special benefit tax revenues to repay the general fund.

New Jersey cities can designate special benefit assessment districts to finance pedestrian malls. An example is the Trenton Commons Commission, which used HUD financing for physical improvements to a 3-block pedestrian mall and levied beneficial assessments based on front footage to finance operation and maintenance costs.

Tax Increment Financing[6]

Tax increment financing for development projects became popular in the late 1960s as federal funds for urban projects became scarce. This flexible, low-cost mechanism uses projected increases in property tax revenues in a development area over a specific period to back bonds that are used to finance project costs in the area. Only the tax base—not the tax rate or the tax revenue—is frozen during the years when a tax increment program is in effect. All tax increments realized during that time by all taxing entities with jurisdiction in the development area are turned over to the local development agency to be used to retire the tax increment bonds. The decisions about whether and how to use tax increment financing are made entirely by local officials.

The tax increment district is usually a deteriorating area of the city where redevelopment or new private development requires some kind of municipal incentive to take place. With the adoption of a redevelopment plan for the area, the area to be included in the tax increment district is established and the tax base determined.

The tax base is the assessed valuation of each property in the tax increment district or development project area at the time of the last equalized tax roll. Each taxing jurisdiction continues to receive its percentage of the taxes collected based on the level of

6 This section is based primarily on Richard G. Mitchell, "Tax Increment Financing for Redevelopment," *Journal of Housing* (May 1977):226–29; Arthur Abba Goldberg, "Tax Increment Financing: Redevelopment Alternative for American Cities," *Housing and Development Reporter* (July 1974):211–22; Gerald M. Trimble, "Regrowth in Pasadena," *Urban Land* (January 1977); Gerald M. Trimble, "Tax Increment Financing for Redevelopment: California Experience Is Good," *Journal of Housing* (October 1974): 458–63; Ralph Andersen and Associates, "Redevelopment and Tax Increment Financing" (January 1966); and Ralph Andersen and Associates, "Redevelopment and Tax Increment Financing—Housing Supplement" (August 1977).

assessed valuation at the time the plan was adopted, but any increased taxes (the increment) resulting from increased property value or new construction are allocated to pay for improvements in the project area. The formula used to determine the amount of the tax increment is

$$I = r(n - i)$$

where

I = the tax increment

r = the tax rate

n = the new assessed valuation produced by development

i = the assessed valuation at the time the plan was adopted.

Thus, during the time the land has been cleared but no new development has taken place, the tax increment is negative. When new development reaches a certain point, the assessed valuation is the same as at the time of the freeze. All development after that point produces positive additions to the assessed value. This projected increment is used to guarantee repayment of indebtedness.

Tax increment financing can be used for long-term debt service or direct capital costs. Typically, it covers land acquisition and site preparation, relocation expenses, public improvements, public facilities, administration costs, and consultant costs. After project-related indebtedness is paid off, the increased tax increment then reverts to general revenues.

Tax increment financing places the burden on the private development to produce tax revenues. If bonds are sold, they are generally the obligation of the redevelopment agency, a separate legal entity. Further, the debt service on the project does not increase property taxes citywide.

Usually, revenues resulting from tax increment financing are assigned to the redevelopment agency responsible for the project area. The funds may be applied against already existing indebtedness, but improvements may be funded by using the increment each year as it is collected and allocated to the appropriate agency or by using tax anticipation notes or longer term tax increment bonds before taxes are actually collected. Issuing notes or bonds makes a greater sum available for front-end expenses and therefore can help accelerate development. Like ordinary municipal bonds, tax increment bonds are tax exempt and require evidence of financial feasibility to be marketable.

The redevelopment agency typically purchases land for development and then sells the prepared site to the developer. When tax increment financing is envisioned, it is in the community's interest to have the land in public ownership for as short a time as possible. Some research indicates that land speculation often occurs shortly before a development plan for an area is announced, artificially raising the assessed values of some properties in the tax allocation district. This amount, however, is never enough to offset the amount of taxes lost in the project's earliest phases, when the title is being transferred to the municipality and being cleared.

Property should remain on the tax rolls until public action is needed to acquire, prepare, and sell the site for development. Because land assembly is tied directly to a project, the redevelopment agency should make site assembly the last item in the predevelopment process. Most of the agency's effort goes into locating a developer and securing an agreement from him to buy the site and develop it in a specified manner within a given time. With this agreement in hand before the redevelopment agency purchases any property, the agency can compute its costs and the approximate amount of tax increment the project will produce, and then estimate when the increment should become available. It can thereby determine whether the proposed project will be financially feasible before committing public funds to it. In California this approach, called "back-to-back escrows," has been used to couple land acquisition as closely as possible with disposition.

Phased development is also important when tax increment financing is used. If one part of the project produces incremental funds relatively quickly, those funds can be used for additional work in the project. Phased development not only accelerates progress but also shortens the time when tax increments are needed for the project. Debt can thus be retired more quickly and the increment returned to the general revenue fund.

The revenues generated by tax increment financing could exceed the public investment in the project. In that event any outstanding bonds can be retired early. The redevelopment agency also has the option, however, to return the funds to the various taxing jurisdictions in the project area as they need increased services. For example, if a housing project financed by tax increments increases the general demand for educational services, then the redevelopment agency could assign funds to the school district to provide the additional services required.

As of 1978, 20 states had enacted enabling legislation that allows development projects to be funded from tax increments.[7] The oldest and most often used

---

[7] The 20 states are Alaska, California, Colorado, Connecticut, Illinois, Iowa, Kentucky, Massachusetts, Minnesota, Montana, Nevada, New Mexico, North Dakota, Ohio, Oregon, Texas, Utah, Washington, Wisconsin, and Wyoming.

is in California. Since 1952 over 100 California cities and counties have relied on tax increments as a principal source of funding for community development.

Known in California as tax allocation financing, the technique has been used for residential, commercial, and industrial development. To speed up the development process, California redevelopment agencies issue revenue bonds that are secured by the projected increase in tax revenues in the development area. Though more expensive than general obligation bonds because of the greater risk associated with their use, tax allocation bonds can be issued relatively quickly because they do not require a referendum and are outside of the city's debt limitation. Tax allocation bonds thus make financing available for public/private development.

In California the increased cost of tax allocation bonds is offset by designating taxes on personal as well as real property to the tax increment fund. For partnerships and proprietorships, the personal property tax is levied on all movable equipment used for business purposes. Possessory interest tax, when levied on a leasehold interest with underlying fee held by a public entity, flows to the redevelopment agency. California has also used lease revenue bond financing in conjunction with tax increment financ-

ing to pay for the development of public facilities. The bonds are guaranteed by long-term lease agreements and are repaid by lease revenues received by the public or private operator of the public building.

Proposition 13, or the Jarvis/Gann Initiative, significantly reduced property tax revenues in California. The impact on cities with outstanding bonds varies. Because nearly all bond issues require debt service coverage of 1.25-to-1 plus substantial reserve funds, the immediate impact was less severe than anticipated.

Proposition 13 has a bright side too, however. The California legislature, after the passage of Proposition 13, established a $30 million fund from surplus state funds that local agencies can borrow against to meet debt service in lean years. Proposition 13 has thus stimulated private real estate development because it has reduced one major fixed cost. Many developers and property owners are passing the savings from Proposition 13 on to the redevelopment agency or the city. The new development spurred by Proposition 13 will create new tax revenues and will assist local agencies to meet debt service requirements and sell additional bonds. Proposition 13 has not precluded the sale of tax allocation bonds, but fewer issues are being marketed and those that are are being marketed where tax revenues are sufficient to amortize the issue.

Plaza Pasadena is an example of a downtown retail complex financed by tax allocation bonds. When completed, the development will have 600,000 square feet of department stores, small shops, restaurants, and other retail establishments, a two-level subterranean garage on a 10.9-acre main site, and two adjacent garages on 2.4 acres. The Pasadena Redevelopment Agency sold $58 million of tax allocation bonds to refinance existing bonds and to fund land assembly and construction of parking garages. Such a center could have been constructed much more easily and much less expensively on the periphery of downtown. The City Council decided instead to locate the center strategically adjacent to the civic center and the convention center and on the city's major ceremonial street, Colorado Boulevard, because of the tremendous positive effect it would have on surrounding development. The center could not have been undertaken in this location without tax increment financing and public participation to lower costs.

Ohio has allowed tax increment financing for a number of years, but municipalities have relied almost exclusively on tax abatement instead. According to the Ohio statute, owners of projects financed by tax increments are required to make semiannual payments in lieu of taxes on improvements equal to the amount of real property taxes that would other-

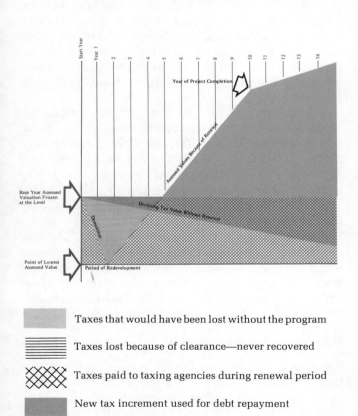

Taxes that would have been lost without the program

Taxes lost because of clearance—never recovered

Taxes paid to taxing agencies during renewal period

New tax increment used for debt repayment

7-11   Tax increment financing—a graphic explanation.

wise have been paid. The payments are deposited in a special urban renewal debt retirement fund that is used to repay the tax increment bonds.

The Central Trust Center in Cincinnati, Ohio, used tax increment financing for its successful development. Cincinnati's largest bank holding company, the Central Bancorporation, joined with Gerald D. Hines Interests to identify sites and to determine the feasibility of a major office project with the Central Trust Company as the anchor tenant. Central Bancorporation selected a parcel in downtown; the city owned two-thirds of it, and the rest was privately owned. The corporation chose the parcel with the understanding that the city would assemble the entire block at an economically feasible price, complete certain improvements to the surrounding area, and deliver the site and approve the plans expeditiously. The revenues the project generated to the city were used to fulfill the city's financial contributions to the project.

The city acquired the privately owned portions of the parcel without using its power of eminent domain. The average cost of land to the joint venture was set at $13.75 per square foot. The original parcel designated for urban renewal was valued at $10 per square foot under the federal program, the remainder at $40 per square foot. The parties elected tax increment bond financing as a means to write down the land price to an average of $13.75 per square foot for the whole parcel. Tax increment bond financing had no meaningful precedent in Ohio and the city had not previously considered it, but both parties proceeded with the expectation that the technique would work. A problem arose when the city could not market the tax increment bonds at acceptable rates until the Central Bancorporation guaranteed them. Some of the improvements to the surrounding area were financed by a grant from the U.S. Department of Transportation, some were financed with city funds, and others were to be financed by subsequent tax increments secured by the property.

Minnesota uses two approaches to tax increment financing. Housing and development authorities can issue general obligation bonds to stimulate development in blighted areas. Although these bonds require a referendum, they are not subject to a city's debt limitation because they are for public improvements. They are repaid from the tax increment collected over a specified period. The second option, the development district, does not require the area to be blighted but is subject to a variety of other state requirements. Minneapolis has successfully used the development district in Loring Park, where property value is expected to increase more than 800 percent in a decade, generating enough revenues to pay for the entire

public investment and retire the tax increment bonds early as well.

The major disadvantage of tax increment financing is its potential for abuse. Unless time limits are imposed, the tax base can be frozen indefinitely so that the city never recaptures the full tax revenues of the developed area. Similarly, unless the size of tax increment districts is limited, a city may be faced with a shortage of funds while a substantial portion of its tax base is frozen. Setting arbitrary boundaries for development districts to siphon off tax increments for other purposes and financing public facilities that could be financed by other methods are two other abuses. The tax increment should be used only to generate developments that will produce new taxes.

Probably the most extreme abuse occurs in small cities that include all or most of the city in a tax increment district to capture all new tax revenues to repay debt for improvements in a much smaller area. The development will require increased public services that the local government may be able to provide only by increasing taxes outside the development area. Thus, those who receive minimal benefits from the development subsidize it.

The second major disadvantage is the risk involved. Because tax increment financing rests on projected development, the incremental tax revenues generated by development may not meet expectations, forcing the local development agency to find other sources of funds to avoid defaulting on its bonds. Even so, the risk to the bond buyer is offset somewhat because interest from the bonds is exempt from state and federal taxes.

Tax increment financing is a useful technique for funding development in downtown areas. Carefully and imaginatively used, it can give local governments access to the large amounts of capital necessary to stimulate private development in specific locations. It enables a development project to virtually finance itself from the increased tax revenues resulting from the development. It gives the city increased borrowing power through its development agency because the debt is not subject to the city's debt limitations. Tax increment financing, however, works only as well as the project it supports. Sound planning, a feasible, marketable project, and skillful management are necessary to make this financing tool useful.

Public Improvements

To attract private investment in specific neighborhoods or designated districts, the local government can provide a range of improvements either adjacent to or on the project site. They can include major citywide capital improvements (transit systems,

7-12 Birmingham Green, Birmingham, Alabama, is an example of a major streetscape public improvement program designed to encourage reinvestment.

highway and street alignment, transit stops, storm and sanitary sewers, utilities), major public facilities (schools, parking, a civic center, government office buildings, hospitals, neighborhood centers), or public amenities (outdoor recreational facilities, pedestrian malls, open spaces, plazas, landscaping). A city's investment in public facilities can generate demand for specific kinds of private investment. For example, convention centers, transportation terminals or transit stations, public office buildings, and public recreation facilities can spur the development of hotels, restaurants, and shops. Other projects are designed to give the downtown equality with—if not a competitive edge over—other locations.

Parking facilities are among the most common public services a local government can provide to stimulate development in the CBD. The lack of sufficient parking spaces can push a project to the more spacious suburbs. The city can usually assemble the necessary land more easily than the private developer, and it can usually borrow the necessary

funds at lower rates than a private developer. Frequently, a parking facility is insufficient without a pedestrian walkway and bridge system to make the parking accessible to the development.

A somewhat unusual public service cities can provide to attract development is cheap energy. Cities that can take advantage of new technology to provide lower cost energy may find private investors seeking them out. Trenton, New Jersey, for example, is including an integrated community energy system in its downtown renewal plan. The new plant, which will be part of a complex consisting of three office buildings and a parking garage, will serve eighteen existing buildings and nine new developments. Cost savings from the new plant are expected to be a significant incentive to private downtown investment.

A crime prevention program is another unusual attraction for downtown development. The 50-block Union Avenue commercial strip in Portland, Oregon, was a declining area selected as a demonstration project by the National Institute of Law Enforcement and

169

Criminal Justice and the Westinghouse National Issues Center. The city installed additional lighting, dial-less emergency telephones, and bus shelters, and provided increased police patrols. Police security surveys and a public awareness campaign discouraged people from carrying cash on the streets. Within 3 years sales increased, the number of existing businesses desiring to relocate dropped 60 percent, the first major new investment (a $225,000 BMW dealership) occurred, and some existing businesses underwent major renovation.

Cost Sharing

With the new form and scale of downtown development projects, it has become difficult to define public improvements and private responsibilities. For example, when several blocks are combined to create a superblock, the intervening public streets are vacated, but the new plan for the area still requires a pedestrian and vehicular circulation system. Under these circumstances, the public and private sectors have established widely varying programs for sharing costs. Only a difference in form exists between a dollar-for-dollar sharing and the use of tax abatement to share costs. The importance lies in the legitimacy of the concept that cost sharing for public/private facilities is a necessary part of a creative approach to the design and development of downtown projects. There are many examples of cost sharing throughout this book.

While cost sharing for actual improvements is a relatively common practice, costs for the studies leading to the definition and design of downtown development projects can also be shared when both public and private sectors are involved. If the planning and feasibility studies undertaken during predevelopment are done solely by the public sector, it is likely that solutions will not reflect the private sector's needs and private development will therefore be discouraged. On the other hand, these studies should rightfully be done at public cost and expecting the private developer to undertake them at his own expense also discourages private investment. Therefore, sharing the cost for these studies, which means both parties' involvement in their conduct, is more likely to result in a feasible development program. Likewise, sharing development management costs is another opportunity for both public and private interests to become involved.

Many times the willingness of local government to undertake some front-end development costs—perhaps some of the planning, engineering, architectural, and appraisal costs—will create an atmosphere for further negotiations. The local government could pay a developer to evaluate and package the project. When past efforts have not produced results, the city could pay a developer for advice during predevelopment and for construction management of the public portions of the project. These fees might cover only the developer's out-of-pocket expenses rather than the developer's expenses incurred in all the preliminary studies. If the project proceeds, the developer could repay the city directly or credit them to the project to diminish public expenses. If the project does not proceed, the city still has the benefit of the information in the studies.

When the proposed development has some unusual parts in which only a few developers are expert, the city could pay a developer to define the concept of the proposed project and thus better define the project's chances of success before being locked into an unwise commitment. For the Kentucky Center for the Arts, a private developer agreed to reimburse the commonwealth of Kentucky $42,000 for certain services performed during predevelopment for the commercial components of the project. The provision for reimbursement did not legally commit the commonwealth to award the contracts for management of the public components of the project or development of the private components to that same developer.

State Enabling Legislation for Public Assistance in CBDs

Several states have passed legislation specifically designed to assist cities in their efforts toward downtown revitalization. One major objective has been to stretch the limits of the taking power of eminent domain beyond the traditional limits of blight, which are constrained by constitutional interpretation. This end has been achieved by legislative definitions of blight that go beyond previously agreed upon limits. The other objective has been to develop ways to pass this right in varying degrees from the municipality to another body typically not elected or to the private sector. This other body, which might be generically described as a public/private development corporation, therefore has some unique public powers—eminent domain and taxation—combined with some private corporation characteristics not usually available to the public—confidential negotiation, ability to hold and manage both public and private funds, and freedom from political pressures, among others.

In Michigan, the Downtown Development Authority Act [8] authorizes the acquisition of buildings and

---

[8] Act 197, Public Acts of Michigan of 1975.

multiple-family dwellings for public or private use that will contribute to the economic development of CBDs as well as the acquisition of a broad variety of public facilities and utilities. The downtown development authority itself is not endowed with the power of eminent domain, but the incorporating municipality may condemn property for the authority's use and transfer it to the authority. Relocation assistance must be provided when residential property is taken. A special ad valorem tax and tax increment financing support the authority's activities, and these nonprofit public corporations have the power to issue revenue bonds and retire incurred debt.

In Ohio, state legislation enabling condemnation for economic reuse eliminates most requirements for determining physical blight. Chapter 1728 of the Ohio Revised Code allows "impacted cities" to develop "blighted areas."[9] For purposes of the act the "impacted city" becomes a municipal corporation that takes authoritative measures to deal with urban slums. The key provision of the state legislation allows the impacted city to condemn and develop an area merely because its potential reuse is better.

The Capitol South project in Columbus, Ohio, a complex containing office, retail, hotel, parking, and residential space, is being developed pursuant to Chapter 1728. The Capitol South Community Urban Redevelopment Corporation was chartered as a non-profit public corporation under the provisions of Chapter 1728. The local government declared the project area substandard and underutilized within the scope of the definition of a blighted area. The financial agreement between the city and the corporation provides that the corporation is obligated to develop or have developed the entire area in accordance with an approved land use and development plan. The corporation, in addition to possessing all the usual powers of development—acquiring land, planning, developing, constructing, altering, maintaining, and operating the project—has two key powers not traditionally accorded development agencies. It may ask the city of Columbus to use its power of eminent domain to acquire parcels in the project area when negotiated purchase fails, and it may exempt the improvements from real estate taxes for up to 20 years for commercial improvements and 30 years for 1-, 2-, or 3-family residential units.

Approximately 85 percent of the Capitol South project area is under the corporation's control. Seven condemnations have been instituted and all have been settled out of court. With the presence of some 55 property owners in the area, the authority to invoke the city's power of eminent domain undoubtedly played a major role in assembling the significant amounts of land that were required.

Chapter 353 of the Revised Missouri Statutes allows an innovative approach to development. The city can grant the right of eminent domain to the developer to acquire property within the project's boundaries, and tax abatement can be used for 25 years.[10] Although the development corporation's profit is limited to 8 percent of the total development cost, profit is computed after taking into account operating expenses, including debt service. The developer also has the right to carry forward to future years or backward to previous years any losses or excess profits in computing the permissible profit. Initially, the interest rate the developer could pay was restricted. In the original law, this figure was established at 6 percent. In 1969 and 1970, the law was amended to allow for interest rates of up to 10 percent, and subsequently, after experience had demonstrated that the requirement was unrealistic, the law has been amended to take out the limit on interest.

To qualify for Section 353 treatment, a developer must show that the site he proposes to develop is

---

[9] See Appendix H(3) for the complete language of Chapter 1728

[10] The specific provision of the statute in Section 353.110 is as follows:

Real property exempt from taxation—limitation—1. The real property of the urban redevelopment corporations acquired pursuant to this chapter shall not be subject to assessment or payment of general *ad valorem* taxes imposed by the cities affected by this law, or by the state or any political subdivision thereof, for a period of ten years after the date upon which such corporations become owners of such real property, except to such extent and in such amount as may be imposed upon such real property during said period measured solely by the amount of the assessed valuation of the land, exclusive of improvements, acquired pursuant to this chapter and owned by such urban redevelopment corporation, as was determined by the assessor of the county in which such real property is located, or if not located within a county, then by the assessor of such city, for taxes due and payable thereon during the calendar year preceding the calendar year during which the corporation acquired title to such real property, and the amounts of such tax assessments shall not be increased during said ten-year period so long as the real property is owned by an urban redevelopment corporation and used in accordance with a development plan authorized by the legislative authority of such cities. . . . For the next ensuing period of fifteen years *ad valorem* taxes upon such real property shall be measured by the assessed valuation thereof as determined by such assessor or assessors upon the basis of not to exceed fifty percent of the true value of such real property, including any improvements thereon, nor shall such valuations be increased above fifty percent of the true value of such real property from year to year during said period of fifteen years, so long as the real property is owned by an urban redevelopment corporation and used in accordance with an authorized development plan. After said period totalling twenty-five years, such real property shall be subject to assessment and payment of all *ad valorem* taxes. . . .

The formula for computing real estate taxes for the eleventh through the twenty-fifth year is as follows:
(a) construction costs of improvements
(b) land at 125% of improvements
(c) abatement value equals 50% of (a) plus (b)
(d) the assessed valuation is 30% of abatement value (c)
(e) the tax is determined by applying the rate of $100 of assessed valuation against (d)

physically or economically blighted. He must establish specific project boundaries and prepare fairly detailed plans and specifications for the proposed improvements. The plans must show which streets will be vacated or kept and what lands will be devoted to public use. The police and fire departments must approve the plans, and the general plan must conform to the city code. The developer must demonstrate his financial capability to carry out the project.

One of Section 353's incentives is the real estate tax abatement on improvements during the initial period of development. It should be noted that while the tax abatement begins when the development corporation takes the real estate, it does not become a real benefit until the buildings or improvements constructed on it are open for business.

Numerous projects have been developed under Section 353 in both St. Louis and Kansas City. Crown Center, by far the largest project in Missouri, illustrates the impact of this legislation.[11] Crown Center is an 85-acre project in midtown Kansas City. The development organization is the Crown Center Redevelopment Corporation, formed by Hallmark Cards, Inc., as the development entity. The site of Crown Center had 240 separate parcels comprising 25 city blocks, including Hallmark's general offices, manufacturing, and distribution facilities on a 12.7-acre site.

The original Crown Center Redevelopment Corporation plan was filed with the city of Kansas City on January 5, 1967; approval was granted on March 31, 1967. After the plan was approved, it was amended six times. Most of these amendments were changes in the scope and design of the project. At the time it sought approval for the plan, the development team indicated that it expected to change both the size and concept of the project but that it did not expect to change the original land use concept. Generally, that concept has remained unchanged.

The focus of the Crown Center project is the Crown Center Hotel and Crown Center Shops. Because both of these elements were pioneering efforts in this location, the tax abatement allowed the developer a competitive edge. If at any time the Crown Center Redevelopment Corporation wishes to be relieved of the duties and restrictions of a development corporation, it may do so and immediately begin paying full real estate taxes. It may assign development rights and tax abatement privileges to another development corporation, which might purchase land from the original development corporation. Such a situation occurred at Crown Center when a joint venture of Mutual Benefit Life Insurance Company, IBM, and a developer purchased two blocks from Crown Center and constructed the first of two office towers and related parking on the site.

Federal Programs

Since the 1940s, various federal programs have been created to aid in the revitalization of cities. To define the current programs as those that will remain important and useful would not be supportable based on the major shifts in focus or levels of funding that have occurred. However, a number of current federal programs do provide assistance for downtown developments. The most important is the Urban Development Action Grant (UDAG) program, but Economic Development Administration funds and community development block grants also provide significant funding.

Urban Development Action Grants

UDAGs are authorized under Section 119 of Title 2 of the Housing and Community Development Act of 1977 and are administered by the Department of Housing and Urban Development. Their purpose is to supply the incentive for private investment. Communities must meet strictly defined criteria of distress to receive the funds and must use them to help

---

[11] See "Crown Center and Crown Center Shops," ULI *Project Reference File*, vol. 4, no. 17 and 18 (October-December 1974).

7-13   St. Paul Town Square—a UDAG project.

stem or reverse negative economic trends. For UDAG grant applications to be approved, the private sector must be committed to the project, and construction must realistically be possible within 4 years.

The grant should compensate for a small shortfall of local funds; the federal funds should in turn encourage a large amount of private investment. Because supplementary grants or provisions for project cost overruns are not allowed, accurate cost estimates are extremely important. While only one UDAG per project is allowed, cities may apply for grants for several projects.

Program Elements

While UDAG funds can be used in a number of ways, certain kinds of activities are specifically prohibited:

- Metropolitan cities may not use UDAG funds to plan a project or develop a UDAG application.
- Small cities (population under 50,000) may be reimbursed for the costs of planning a project and preparing its application, but only up to 3 percent of the approved amount of the grant.
- No city may use UDAG funds to pay for public services.
- No assistance will be provided to relocate an industry from one metropolitan area to another, unless the move will not adversely affect the unemployment or economic base of the area losing the industry.

Residential, commercial, and industrial projects are eligible for UDAG assistance. In determining a project's eligibility, HUD considers:

- the importance of the project in stimulating private investment
- the amount of long-term employment that would be generated for low- and moderate-income people
- the potential economic impact of the project on the community
- the effect of the project on the downtown economy.

New housing may be eligible if, in addition to these factors, the proposed project is consistent with the community's plans for development and housing.

Successful proposals share a number of traits. Funds for residential projects have usually been subsidies to write down the cost of land or for loan financing in the form of loan interest subsidies to individuals using the property or directly to the developers. Some traditional urban renewal programs have also been financed with UDAG funds. The

financing has covered relocation costs, land purchases, and new construction.

UDAG funds for industrial projects have most commonly been awarded for utility expansion, road construction, land purchases, or financing subsidies, which were used to underwrite land costs or to lend money to owners to improve existing plants. Funds for commercial projects have been awarded for construction of parking structures, general improvement of streets and utilities, and business financing subsidies.

Competitive grants are awarded four times each year. Cities are divided into "metropolitan" cities and "small" cities.[12] A metropolitan city for the purpose of UDAG funding is the same as a metropolitan city or urban county under the Community Development Block Grant program. Over 300 metropolitan cities and 1,800 small cities are eligible for UDAGs. A project could be located so that it could be considered a metropolitan city (urban county) or a small city.

The basis of the competition for awards is the relative amount of distress in the city, as measured by weighted factors, and the relative amount of private funds available if federal funds are awarded. Leveraging ratios for the first two rounds of awards to metropolitan cities averaged 5:1; ratios for the first round of awards to small cities measured 10:1. That is, the amount of private funds was 5 and 10 times, respectively, the amount of federal funds. However, many of the projects funded under these rounds were industrial, involving large private investments. Thus, the leveraging ratios were probably higher than can be expected for future awards to commercial and residential proposals.

Any applicant for an Urban Development Action Grant must pass three separate tests: (1) economic and physical distress, (2) performance, and (3) project feasibility. The tests for metropolitan cities are different from those for small cities; the tests for small cities take into account special conditions relating to city size.

Before submitting an application, communities must request a determination of eligibility from the HUD area office. The HUD area office supplies the necessary data to calculate eligibility and determines whether the applicant has met performance and project feasibility tests. A copy of the request for eligibility is sent to the appropriate A-95 clearinghouse (usually a regional planning commission) when the request is sent to HUD. If the A-95 review determines that the proposed plan is inconsistent

---

[12] A *metropolitan city* has a population of 50,000 or more in a central city of an SMSA, an urban county, or a town, township, or municipality not in an SMSA. A *small city* has a population of 2,500–25,000 or 25,000–50,000 (see p. 175).

with environmental regulations or civil rights laws, the applicant can then show how the problems will be resolved before it submits the final application.

At the same time, a city must have held at least one public hearing on the needs of the community that will be affected by the proposed project and at least one hearing on the actual project under consideration. Citizens must be made aware of the funds available for development and possible alternative uses for them. Low-income people, members of minority groups, and residents of the area most likely to be affected by the proposed project should have an opportunity to participate in the hearings. The application should include a certified document stating that the city has followed a written plan to involve citizens. The city must also certify that it will comply with federal regulations on the environment, labor standards, flood insurance, equal opportunity for training and employment, contracts for residents of the area, property acquisition and relocation assistance, access by physically handicapped individuals, and access to books and records.

HUD evaluates the application based on certain criteria to measure the community's economic and physical distress. The key criteria are weighted as follows:

- housing—0.5
- poverty level—0.3
- population growth—0.2.

Other criteria are weighted equally.

Performance Tests

Applicants for UDAGs must have provided housing in accordance with equal housing and employment opportunity laws for low- and moderate-income people and for members of minority groups. HUD reviews local activities that show the community's efforts to provide housing: removing impediments in local ordinances and in land use requirements for the development of assisted housing, forming a local housing authority, if necessary, to carry out a Housing Assistance Plan, and providing sites for assisted housing. HUD will also look for the existence of an approved Housing Assistance Plan.

If a city previously participated in a Community Development Block Grant program as part of an urban county and then withdraws, HUD considers the applicant's performance in accordance with the Housing Assistance Plan. If the city never had a HUD-approved Housing Assistance Plan, it must pass other tests that demonstrate its effort to supply low- and moderate-income housing:

- *geographic dispersal:* At least some government-assisted housing should be located outside areas where minorities and/or low-income families are concentrated.
- *areawide affirmative marketing:* The applicant should encourage fair housing practices in the private housing market.
- *relocation:* The relocation of residents because of other federally assisted programs should have resulted in expanded housing opportunities for low- and moderate-income people outside areas where minorities and/or low-income families are concentrated.
- *participation in a housing opportunity plan:* The applicant should be a participant in a housing opportunity plan if it is in the jurisdiction of such a plan.
- *employment:* The applicant should make efforts to hire, train, and promote minorities, females, and low-income people.

Project Feasibility Tests

Each application is evaluated for six major project feasibility tests:

- impact of the project on low- and moderate-income people
- private participation
- additional financial assistance
- impact of revitalization
- unique opportunity
- ability to complete project.

Project Impact

A proposed project is evaluated on the extent to which it can reduce the problems of low- and moderate-income people. It should provide employment, training for employment, or the opportunity to establish minority-owned businesses. An assistance plan in conjunction with an existing program such as the Comprehensive Employment and Training Act of 1973 (CETA) is adequate.

Low- and moderate-income people should be provided an opportunity to live in any housing that is part of a project. Projects in which minorities hold an equity interest are given priority.

If the project requires relocation of households or businesses, the applicant must assist households to move outside areas of low-income or minority concentration. Businesses should be given the opportunity to return to the area after the project is completed.

Distress Criteria

Each city must meet three of the applicable tests unless exceptions are made according to the formulas below.

Distress Criteria	Metropolitan City		Small City	
	Population 50,000 or more, central city of an SMSA, an urban county	Population 50,000 or more in a town, township, or municipality not in an SMSA	Population 25,000–50,000	Population 2,500–25,000
Per Capita Income: Net increase 1969–1974, based on U.S. Census data	$1,424 or less. If below the median for metropolitan cities, check against poverty level	Criteria same for both kinds of metropolitan cities.	$1,433 or less	$1,433 or less
Population Growth: 1960–1975, based on 1960 and 1975 respective boundaries	15.52% or less		-0.31 or less percentage rate of change in population	-0.31 or less percentage rate of change in population
Housing: Year-round units built before 1940, according to latest available U.S. Census data	34.15% or more		34.15% or more. If 68.30% or more, city need only meet the poverty test.	34.15% or more. If 68.30% or more, city need only meet the poverty test.
Employment Growth: 1967–1972 in manufacturing and retail, based on U.S. Census data	7.08% or less		7.10% or less	Not applicable
Unemployment in 1976, based on August 1977 Bureau of Labor Statistics figures	7.69% or more		Not applicable	Not applicable
Poverty Level: Percentage of population living at or below the poverty level	11.24%, based on 1970 U.S. Census data. If equal to or greater than 1½ times the median and income is below the median, a Unique Distress Factor may be used instead of one of the other distress criteria. If poverty level is less than ½ the median for metropolitan cities, the city must pass an additional distress criteria test.		11.24%, based on 1970 U.S. Census data and 1975 population estimates. If 2 times or greater, worth 2 distress criteria. If poverty level is less than ½ median for metropolitan cities, the city must pass an additional distress test.	Equal to or greater than ½ the median of metropolitan cities. If 2 times or greater than the median for U.S. cities, worth 2 distress criteria.
Additional Criteria	Criteria for a Unique Distress Factor: • It is a fiscal, physical, or economic condition that severely affects the vitality of the community. • It has a basis for comparison with other communities in the state. • The data used to substantiate the factor pertain to the period 1970–1977. • The data used pertain to the community as a whole. • The factor represents a condition other than those for which the city has been credited. For example, a city that has already met the *unemployment* distress test cannot use other unemployment factors as a "unique distress factor." • The factor must not be the result of federal, state, or local court actions (such as the cost of complying with a court order), laws, or regulations.		No additional criteria applicable	Must prove capacity to carry out a UDAG program

The project will be reviewed to determine the effect of these moves on low- and moderate-income people, minorities presently employed, and the area vacated by the facility.

Private Participation

The private participants must have made a binding commitment to the project in the form of a letter of intent as a prerequisite for consideration. Most applications that have been rejected have failed to provide adequate evidence of such a commitment.

A city may request bids from more than one developer, but it is not necessary if the local government is trying to retain an existing industry. A company's agreeing to remain in a locality is an acceptable commitment if the company also agrees to expand or modernize its facilities.

The firmness of the commitment by a private sector actor is one of the more competitive factors in the awarding of a UDAG. The regulations for administration of the program state that HUD must consider "whether the private commitment is more firm than for other projects being considered" for funding.

Letters of intent from private participants should contain some basic information:

- *the identity of the participants:* All private parties participating in the deal, the level of their participation, and their financial commitment should be described. The authority of the person signing the letter should be included.

- *the investment:* The nature of the private investment—construction of a new facility or rehabilitation of an existing one—should be specifically described.

- *the investment package:* The identity of investors and any contingencies or special terms applicable to the investment should be described.

- *legally binding commitments:* A letter of intent should clearly state that an authorized individual will sign a legally binding commitment to the project if the application is approved. The person who will make that commitment must sign the letter of intent.

Every lending institution that will supply part of the private investment should submit a slightly different letter of intent. It should include the amount of the loan, the type of loan (interim financing, construction financing, etc.), and terms and conditions of the loan, including interest rate, contingencies, and purpose. The loan's relationship to the UDAG program is also important. The lending institution should state its willingness to sign a legally binding commitment if the project is funded. The applicant should be able to recapture its financial participation in the project through loan or lease repayments or through a share of the profits.

Additional Financial Assistance

Projects with financial assistance from local, state, or other federal programs "will be given more favorable consideration." This criterion further illustrates the desire to leverage UDAG funds.

Impact of Revitalization

HUD regulations state that projects causing minimal displacement and disruption of occupants and jobs will be considered more favorably. The effects of the proposed project on a community's fiscal, physical, and economic health will also be considered. Fiscal benefits will be measured by the proposed improvement in the city's tax base. Physical effects will be measured by the degree of improvement in the community's housing or public, commercial, or industrial facilities, and the extent to which other facilities will be provided or already exist to support the project. Economic benefits will be measured by the resulting long-term employment opportunity for local residents.

Unique Opportunity

The extent to which the project represents a special or unique opportunity to achieve economic revitalization will be considered.

Ability to Complete Project

Projects are more likely to be funded if a majority of the predevelopment work has already been completed. A project is less feasible if substantial additional planning is involved or if legal or environmental constraints will impede development.

Awarding UDAG Funds

UDAG funds are awarded quarterly. If an application is not funded in the first quarter in which it is considered, it is usually reconsidered in the following quarter. An application not approved after the second quarter usually is not considered further. An award may be given only conditional approval subject to complete local environmental review or to a change in one aspect of the project. HUD must notify applicants in writing of the action taken on each proposal, including the conditions that might cause a rejected proposal to be reconsidered. Cities generally are not given their funds until the private sector's commitment is ensured.[13]

---

[13] Appendix N includes two UDAG case studies—the Town Square project in St. Paul, Minnesota, and the Greenville Commons project in Greenville, South Carolina.

7-15   The Centrum, Capitol South, Columbus, Ohio, is a year-round multipurpose activity center funded by the EDA Title I program.

Economic Development Administration Funds

The primary purpose of the Economic Development Administration (EDA) is to enhance the national economy by assisting communities and areas experiencing economic distress. As such it is responsible for administration of certain programs under the Public Works and Economic Development Act of 1965 (P.L. 89–136). Two sections of the act—Title I and Title IX—provide capital funding to projects in downtown areas.[14]

Designation of Areas Eligible for EDA Assistance

A host of entities may be eligible for EDA assistance: states, redevelopment areas, economic development districts, cities or other political subdivisions of a state, private or public nonprofit organizations representing any development area or part of it. The legislation specifies the criteria:

- substantial and persistent unemployment as indicated by a rate of unemployment during the most recent calendar year averaging 6 percent or more, or at least 50 percent above the national

average for 3 of the 4 preceding calendar years, or at least 75 percent above the national average for 2 of the 3 preceding calendar years, or at least 100

---

[14] The provisions of Title I and Title IX will undergo major revisions if pending bills S. 914 and H.R. 2063 (as of February 1980) are resolved by the conference committee. More than likely, Title IX will be changed to an adjustment program, and the assistance elements of this Title will be merged into Title I. Three major new features are under consideration:

- *Guarantees* for up to 90 percent of fixed assets or working capital loans. Objective: To reduce the risk of loss on a loan made by a private lender and enable the lender to charge lower interest and set a longer term than he might otherwise; and to create additional liquidity for local lenders by establishing a secondary market for EDA-guaranteed loans.
- *Interest subsidies* on guaranteed and nonguaranteed loans for fixed assets and working capital, to allow interest rates to be reduced by up to 7 percentage points (to a rate no lower than 3 percent annually). Objective: To provide reasonably priced working capital or expansion capital to existing firms in distressed areas, or to offer an incentive to firms to locate in such areas.
- *Grants* to local public entities to defray up to 15 percent of the capital costs of an eligible private sector project. Objective: To provide an additional subsidy, particularly in the most distressed areas, geared to reducing the capital costs of a firm.

A major area in dispute is eligibility. Current legislation qualifies 85 percent of the U.S. population. Eligibility in the bills under consideration varies from 68 percent in the Senate bill to 90 percent in the House bill.

percent above the national average for 1 of the 2 preceding calendar years

- an unusual and abrupt rise in unemployment, possibly the result of loss or curtailment of a single, major source of employment
- a median family income no more than 50 percent of the national median
- special impact areas such as a large concentration of low-income people or a rural area with substantial outmigration
- per capita unemployment areas that experienced a significant decline in per capita employment during the most recent 10-year period. (For 1960–70, significant decline is defined as a decline of more than 1.2 percentage points, coupled with a net outmigration.)

Title I of the Act

Title I of the act establishes a program to fund infrastructure and public improvements. Cities, states, quasi-public entities, or private or public nonprofit organizations may apply for funds, but the project must be located within a designated redevelopment area or economic development district.

A number of projects are eligible for funds: providing utilities, access, and site preparation to make land suitable for commercial use; improving public facilities at airports and harbors; renovating buildings in the inner city; building or improving publicly owned recreational facilities to promote tourism; and improving the appearance and efficiency of public facilities in run-down, congested commercial areas. Ineligible projects include projects that would unfairly compete with a privately owned public utility, projects that would help an industry where production capacity currently exceeds demand, and projects that would result in relocating rather than creating jobs.

Eligible projects may be funded up to 50 percent of total eligible project costs. The rest of the cost must be provided by the state or city or from nongovernmental funds. The local matching share cannot include general revenue sharing funds but can include community development block grants.

Many components of the project are eligible for funding:

- preliminary expenses, including services directly related to development that are incurred before the application is submitted
- land, easements, rights-of-way, and site acquisition if title to the land remains in public ownership or for public use

- construction costs comparable to local work secured through open competitive bidding
- machinery and equipment
- architect and engineer fees, inspection, test borings, and testing materials
- legal and administrative expenses, including the opinion of bond counsel and audits
- capitalized interest paid during the construction period if privately provided
- all expenses related to securing project funding
- previously acquired assets, including the value of land and facilities acquired by the recipient before EDA assistance if they are used as an in-kind contribution toward the local matching share.

The applicant must also describe the project's expected impact on long-term employment opportunities and the opportunity for further economic growth in the area. After approval the recipient must comply substantially with the terms and conditions of the grant and must provide construction surveillance, contract administration, and maintenance and operation of the facility.

Title IX of the Act

Title IX of the act authorizes EDA to assist recipients to avert a sudden decline in an area's economic activity. Two basic situations may make the community (or the smallest entity capable of dealing effectively with the economic change) eligible for funding: (1) situations that result or threaten to result in a permanent loss of jobs (the closing of a military base, enforcement of environmental requirements, rapid changes in technology affecting businesses, depletion of natural resources, or the closing of a major private employer); and (2) situations that precipitate sudden changes in an area's economy (sudden growth or natural disasters).

Two types of grants are available under Title IX—development grants and implementation grants. Development grants are designed to assist eligible applicants with an economic problem but that have not been able to devise a strategy to counter the situation. They are used primarily to identify needs and goals, establish priorities, and analyze alternatives. The recipient may use the funds only for direct expenditures.

Implementation grants are designed to assist applicants who have developed a strategy to combat the economic problem. They may be used for public facilities, public services, business development, planning, unemployment compensation, rent supplements, mortgage payment assistance, training, research, technical assistance, relocation of individuals, or any other appropriate use. Funds may be used for direct expenditures or may be in the form of grants, loans, or loan guarantees. Private, for-profit entities are ineligible.

Community Development Block Grants

The Community Development Block Grant (CDBG) program, administered by the Department of Housing and Urban Development, is a special revenue sharing program that, in 1974, replaced a number of categori-

7-16 City Centre Mart, Middletown, Ohio, created an enclosed, climate-controlled mall in the street right-of-way. A HUD Neighborhood Development Grant funded $12 million of the project.

cal HUD assistance programs.[15] Under CDBG, economic development, although not well defined in the 1974 act, became an eligible HUD grant activity. For a variety of reasons, CDBG-funded activities have been directed mainly toward housing problems and the physical problems of low-income neighborhoods more than toward problems related to industrial and commercial development.

Amendments enacted in 1977 substantially expanded the list of eligible economic development activities. Made explicitly eligible for community development assistance were activities carried out by public or private nonprofit entities. They include acquisition of real property; acquisition, construction, reconstruction, rehabilitation, or installation of public facilities, site improvements, and utilities, and of commercial or industrial real property improvements; and planning. The 1977 legislation also authorized grants to neighborhood-based nonprofit organizations, local development corporations, and Small Business Investment Companies for the purpose of neighborhood revitalization or community economic development projects.

The primary purpose of CDBG programs is the development of viable urban communities by providing decent housing and a suitable living environment and expanding economic opportunities, principally for persons of low and moderate income. To achieve this objective, federal assistance is provided for the support of community development activities directed toward:

- elimination of slums and blight
- elimination of conditions that are detrimental to health, safety, and public welfare
- conservation and expansion of the nation's housing stock, principally for the benefit of low- and moderate-income persons
- expansion and improvement of community services that are essential for sound community development
- a more rational use of land and other natural resources
- reduction of the isolation of income groups within communities and geographical areas and the promotion of increased neighborhood diversity and vitality through the spatial deconcentration of housing opportunities for persons of lower income and the revitalization of deteriorating or deteriorated neighborhoods to attract persons of higher income
- restoration and preservation of properties of special value for historic, architectural, or esthetic reasons

- alleviation of physical and economic distress through the stimulation of private investment and community revitalization in areas with population outmigration or a stagnating or declining tax base.

The 1977 legislation added the last objective on this list. However, the support of marketable economic development projects still needs to be reconciled with community development's principal intent of assisting low- and moderate-income persons directly. Using CDBG as an economic development tool will require considering a good portion of its outlays as investments that can leverage long-term private sector economic investment to create jobs and improve the tax base.

Economic development activities eligible for funding under CDBG are those that would promote the objective of alleviating physical and economic distress through the stimulation of private investment and community revitalization. Economic development activities that can be funded by CDBG include:

- acquisition of real property
- acquisition, construction, reconstruction, or installation of public works, facilities, and site or other improvements
- clearance, demolition, renewal, and rehabilitation of buildings and improvements—including financing of public or private acquisition for rehabilitation and the rehabilitation of privately owned properties
- disposition of any real property acquired
- activities necessary to develop a comprehensive community development plan
- activities carried out by public or private nonprofit entities, including acquisition, reconstruction, and rehabilitation of commercial or industrial real property improvements
- grants to neighborhood-based nonprofit organizations, local development corporations, or profit or nonprofit Small Business Investment Companies (organized under sec. 301(d) of the Small Business Investment Act of 1958) to carry out a neighborhood revitalization or community economic development project.

---

[15] Material in this section is taken from U.S. Department of Housing and Urban Development and U.S. Department of Commerce, "Local Economic Development Tools and Techniques" (Washington, D.C.: U.S. Government Printing Office), a guidebook for local government authored under contract by J. Thomas Black, Fran Rothstein, Allan Borut, Libby Howland, and Robert Byrne of the ULI Research Division.

A number of these eligible activities should help local officials immeasurably in implementing comprehensive economic development strategies for their cities. To support eligible economic development activities, the applicant's grant must provide HUD with a description of the activities and of their relationship to the applicant's overall economic development strategy. In authorizing activities, HUD will take into account:

- the amount of long-term employment to be generated that is accessible to low- and moderate-income persons
- the necessity of the activity to stimulate private investment
- degree of impact on the economic conditions of the area
- availability of other federal funds.

A firm private commitment to participate in the proposed project is required. Projects must also be able to be carried out in a specified time period, which will usually not exceed 4 years.

Business capitalization can be financed through grants to neighborhood nonprofit organizations and local development corporations. Eligible activities by private nonprofit entities, local development corporations, or Small Business Investment Companies include:

- activities otherwise eligible for CDBG assistance
- grants, loan guarantees, and technical assistance to small businesses (noneligible community development activities)
- capitalization of a Small Business Investment Company or a local development corporation (a noneligible community development activity)
- other activities appropriate for community economic development or neighborhood revitalization.

CDBG-funded economic development activities that principally benefit lower income persons may be freely undertaken. But those that do not principally benefit them cannot be undertaken by cities that do not meet the distress criteria under UDAG regulations. Distressed cities can spend up to 25 percent of their grant amounts for economic development activities that do not principally benefit lower income persons, but these sums must be spent on projects that will provide new or rehabilitated housing and related improvements to attract higher income persons or on projects aimed at improving the city's tax base and employment characteristics.

8.
Future Trends in Downtown Development

The preceding chapters have discussed the process that local governments and private developers must pursue to effectively and efficiently develop central business districts and revitalize urban economies. Implicit in the discussion and in the development itself is the idea that cities and particularly their downtowns *should* play a vital role in our national and regional economies. A question not addressed is whether or not CBDs can or will play a vital role in the future in view of the fundamental technological, demographic, political, and economic forces that have led to continuing suburbanization and exurbanization of firms and population in recent years. Also not addressed is what the future of central cities will mean in terms of the types of economic activities that will remain, expand, and develop or in terms of the types of physical environment and community systems required to accommodate and foster that role.

Effective public strategies for development and successful private investment in the cities will certainly hinge on a realistic assessment of where these dominant forces are taking the cities. This chapter paints a broad, general picture of where present trends and conditions appear to be leading the cities and what they mean in terms of development opportunities. Such generalizations will obscure the diverse character of central cities and their equally diverse futures; still, most central cities appear to be undergoing similar transformations.

The Major Issues

The long-term economic future of the cities and the concomitant opportunities for development are by no means clear. The picture is clouded by a large number of uncertainties, including energy supplies and prices, future technological changes, regional shifts in the economy, the performance of the national economy, shifts in the industrial mix, and future public policy. In the next 10 to 15 years, however, the picture is somewhat less clouded. During that time frame, it seems unlikely that technological, energy, or economic changes will be severe enough to change the fundamental pattern.

Two major issues appear to affect the near-term future of central cities:

- whether or not the regional economic shifts away from the northeast and north central regions, and particularly the large metropolitan areas in those regions, will result in general economic decline there

- whether or not, given the continuation of the general decentralization of businesses and population within metropolitan areas, CBDs will retain locational advantages for certain activities sufficient to generate opportunities for economic expansion and development.

The Future of the Large Metropolitan Economies

The economic future of CBDs is tied inextricably to the future of the metropolitan and regional economies they serve. If the economy of the metropolitan area is expanding, the CBD at least has the potential for economic expansion, whereas if the entire metropolitan economy is declining, there can be little hope for economic expansion in the CBD.

Until recently the cities' economic future was not questioned. To the contrary, they were universally expanding and absorbing the bulk of increases in investments and jobs. In the late 1960s and 1970s, however, the large metropolitan areas, primarily those in the midwestern and northeastern regions of the country, began to show signs of economic weaknesses. From 1970 to 1975, half of the standard metropolitan statistical areas (SMSAs) with populations of 1,000,000 in 1970 lost population.[1] Many observers thus forecast economic decline for the larger metropolitan areas, which would preclude any opportunities for significant new development in the CBD. Basic economic indicators such as employment and personal income indicate, however, that the large areas are still growing economically—most at substantial rates—although Sunbelt metropolitan areas are expanding more rapidly than Frostbelt areas.

For the 35 largest SMSAs, all except New York experienced real increases in total personal income from 1969 to 1975. Not surprisingly, the Houston SMSA experienced the largest gain ($4.6 billion in 1975 dollars), but others also experienced sizable gains; 22 of the 35 added over $900 million in real personal income and the group as a whole experienced an average real gain of $1.2 billion. The Chicago SMSA outdistanced all of the Sunbelt's large metropolitan areas except Houston in personal income. Even the Boston SMSA, one of the slowest growing, experienced a real gain in total personal income of over $1 billion. Thirteen of the 16 Sunbelt metropolitan areas exceeded the national average growth rate, while all 19 of the Frostbelt metropolitan areas lagged behind the national growth rates.

In most of the large metropolitan areas, the increases in personal income have been related to growth in employment. Of the 35 largest metropolitan areas, all but one (again, New York) have gained jobs since 1970. The New York SMSA lost approximately 360,000 jobs. The 35 largest SMSAs as a group accounted for one-third of the total increase in employment in the United States in the 1970s. The average increase from 1976 to 1977 was 42,000 jobs, with the range extending from a 360,000-job loss in the New York metropolitan area to a 258,000-job gain in the Houston area. Most of the older, large metropolitan areas gained significantly: Chicago gained 58,000 jobs, Cincinnati 29,000, Cleveland 25,000, Pittsburgh 40,000, Minneapolis 82,000, Milwaukee 28,000, Baltimore 34,000, Los Angeles 219,000, Columbus 24,000, Hartford 21,000, and Detroit 46,000.

Consistent with other trends, the higher rates of growth in employment were in the Sunbelt metropolitan areas. Houston again was the leader, with an increase of 31 percent from 1972 to 1976. Phoenix, Dallas, San Diego, Nashville, San Antonio, and Portland (Oregon) each gained from 12 to 17 percent.

On the whole, the larger metropolitan areas are continuing to expand their employment base, although the New York SMSA is a significant exception with its major loss in employment. Sixteen of the 19 northeast and north central metropolitan areas are continuing to gain jobs, while all 16 in the south and west are gaining.

Thus, contrary to the gloomy picture many are painting, central cities in general, including those in the large metropolitan areas, can look forward to being part of a growing local economy and expanding business and investment. The critical questions facing CBDs, then, are whether and how they will share in that economic growth.

The Economic Potential of Central Cities

The long-term trends in the location of economic activity within metropolitan areas since World War II, as even the casual observer knows, have been decentralization and deconcentration of activity away from CBDs in favor of suburban areas and, more recently, nonmetropolitan areas.[2] A combination of factors explains the shift: changes in transportation and manufacturing technology, which have made outlying locations with intercity highway links more attractive to industry; the rural ethic, which plays up the pastoral rural village as the ideal lifestyle and plays down the urban lifestyle; high densities and congestion in the cities; the in-migration of low-income rural blacks and whites to the inner city, creating problems of blight and crime; federal policies and programs favoring suburban growth; the aging of the physical plant

---

[1] Except where otherwise indicated, the data cited in this chapter are from J. Thomas Black, *The Changing Economic Role of Central Cities* (Washington, D.C.: ULI–the Urban Land Institute, 1978).

[2] See Glenn V. Fuguitt, Paul R. Voss, and J. C. Doherty, *Growth and Change in Rural America*, Management and Control of Growth Series (Washington, D.C.: ULI–the Urban Land Institute, 1979).

Change in Employment in 35 Large SMSAs, 1972–1976 (1,000s of jobs)

	1972	1976	Change	Percent Change
Atlanta	712.9	767.3	54.5	7.6
Baltimore	819.5	853.9	34.4	4.2
Boston	1,282.2	1,261.9	−20.3	−1.6
Buffalo	485.3	489.5	4.2	0.9
Chicago	2,945.3	3,003.4	58.1	2.0
Cincinnati	512.0	540.7	28.7	5.6
Cleveland	838.0	862.9	24.9	3.0
Columbus	431.6	455.4	23.8	5.5
Dallas	974.1	1,118.4	144.3	14.8
Denver	561.3	612.5	51.2	9.1
Detroit	1,582.2	1,628.4	46.2	2.9
Hartford	319.7	340.7	21.0	6.6
Houston (Highest Gain)	838.8	1,094.4	258.6	30.9
Indianapolis	435.1	463.7	28.6	6.6
Kansas City	526.3	549.9	23.6	4.5
Los Angeles	2,888.1	3,106.8	218.7	7.6
Miami	563.8	585.6	21.8	3.9
Milwaukee	579.0	607.2	28.2	4.9
Minneapolis–St. Paul	825.0	907.1	82.1	10.0
Nashville	277.7	315.8	38.1	13.7
Newark	857.0	857.0	0.0	0.0
New Orleans	395.6	435.5	39.9	10.1
New York (Highest Loss)	3,950.3	3,591.2	−359.1	−9.1
Philadelphia	1,802.3	1,798.1	−4.2	−0.2
Phoenix	384.3	449.7	65.4	17.0
Pittsburgh	858.1	898.4	40.3	4.7
Portland	409.6	459.9	50.3	12.3
Rochester	371.2	387.0	15.8	4.3
San Antonio	291.6	328.8	37.2	12.8
San Diego	423.6	493.6	70.0	16.5
San Francisco	1,250.1	1,362.3	112.2	9.0
Seattle	506.4	587.9	81.5	16.1
St. Louis	903.4	905.8	2.4	0.3
Tampa–St. Petersburg	379.1	420.4	41.3	10.9
Washington, D.C.	1,258.6	1,363.7	105.1	8.4

Source: U.S. Bureau of Labor Statistics, *Employment and Earnings,* September 1977.

8-1   Change in employment in 35 large SMSAs—1972–1976.

of the city; the development of freeways that provide good access between suburbs and city; the vertical and horizontal integration of modern business enterprises, which has made them more independent; and the automation and computerization of routine functions, which has made the quality of labor more important for most firms than the quantity of labor.

While overall the decentralization of employment and population continues in most cities, signs of a strong resurgence in office, retail, and residential activities are occurring in the core areas of most cities.

This resurgence is associated with a number of factors: the national shift in employment toward management, administrative, financial, and governmental activity and the economies of agglomeration associated with this activity; the large number of households composed of highly educated young people who do not share their parents' antiurban values; the huge increase in childless households who are not affected by school problems; and the public investment that has enhanced cities in general and their core areas in particular.

**DOWNTOWN
DEVELOPMENT**

MILWAUKEE   WISCONSIN

THE ELS DESIGN GROUP

8-2   The Milwaukee Retail Center will have a two-block-long skylighted arcade creating a new downtown retail main street.

Whatever the future economic growth of CBDs, it clearly will not be in manufacturing. A recent examination of job shifts from 1970 to 1975 in 10 metropolitan areas (Atlanta, Baltimore, Boston, Denver, New Orleans, New York, Philadelphia, St. Louis, San Francisco, and Washington, D.C.) found that the loss of manufacturing from central cities has accelerated and has even infected most suburban rings. From 1970 to 1975, the 10 areas showed a net loss of 312,000 manufacturing jobs from their central cities and a net loss of 67,000 manufacturing jobs from their suburban rings. Of the 10 areas, only the Denver central city gained in manufacturing jobs, and only four areas (Washington, D.C., Atlanta, Denver, and New Orleans) gained in the suburbs. On average, the cities lost one out of every five manufacturing jobs existing in 1970, while the suburbs lost one out of 30. Clearly, the international and national shifts in manufacturing activity are now taking a heavy toll in jobs from

the older central cities and have reversed the postwar growth trend in the suburbs of most larger metropolitan areas. There appears to be no reason to expect any reversal in the near future.[3]

More importantly, it appears that the trend in the 1960s toward an expansion in service activity in central cities was reversed in the first half of the 1970s. In the 10 cities examined, six—New York, St. Louis, Baltimore, Boston, New Orleans, and Philadelphia—lost some service jobs since 1970. New York suffered the greatest loss (125,000 service jobs), while St. Louis suffered the largest relative loss (15 percent, or roughly one out of every six service jobs there in 1970).

On the other hand, service sector employment in the suburban rings of this group of cities generally

---

[3] See Urban Land Institute, *Industrial Development Handbook* (Washington, D.C.: ULI–the Urban Land Institute, 1975), pp. 226–31.

grew substantially. Nine of the 10 suburban rings gained service jobs, for a total net gain of roughly 600,000 jobs compared to a net loss of 60,000 in the central cities.

The post-1970 trends thus indicate that central cities that have not become regional or national service nodes (as have Atlanta, Denver, San Francisco, and Washington) and thus depend primarily on local consumer and business service activity have suffered an erosion of that activity to their surrounding suburbs. It further indicates that in contrast to earlier periods, most central cities cannot rely on service sector growth to replenish the losses in manufacturing. Even Atlanta, which gained a substantial number of service jobs, was not able to offset its losses in manufacturing. In contrast, five of the six suburban rings that lost manufacturing jobs realized substantial net gains in employment as a result of the large increases in service jobs.

The poor performance of central cities in attracting and maintaining service activity is particularly striking when one compares their experience to that of the nation as a whole, which experienced an 18.7 percent increase in service employment from 1970 to 1975. Of the four cities with expanding service sectors, only one, San Francisco, expanded service employment at a faster rate than the nation. It is clear that central cities generally do not have the locational advantages for *most* service activities that they were once thought to have.

Consequently, overall performance of most of these 10 central cities relative to their metropolitan areas has declined. In 1970, these central cities accounted for 49 percent, or roughly half, their metropolitan area's employment on an average. By 1975, the average central city share was down to 43.1 percent, with nine of the 10 losing in relative share of employment. Only San Francisco managed to increase its share, but even then only a slight gain of less than 1 percent.

While the overall economy of most central cities is continuing to shrink because of the decentralization of the manufacturing and retailing functions and, more recently, the service function, most cities are experiencing a significant expansion of office activity in their downtown areas. A recent study of CBD office space found that almost all the large central cities had experienced sizable gains in downtown office space since 1970. Data on 20 central cities indicate an average increase of 43 percent.[4]

With the recent expansion in office activity, downtowns have remained the dominant concentration of office activity in metropolitan areas. On an average, the large central cities contain approxi-

---

[4] ULI—the Urban Land Institute, "Central City Investment Survey," 1979 (unpublished).

Change in Service Employment[1] in Selected Cities, 1970–1975

City	1970	1975	Amount	Percent
Atlanta	155.4	165.6	+ 10.2	+ 6.6
Baltimore	147.5	138.9	− 8.6	− 6.1
Boston	354.0	348.2	− 5.7	− 1.6
Denver	109.0	120.7	+ 11.7	+10.8
New Orleans	109.5	108.1	− 1.4	− 1.3
New York[2]	2,089.3	1,963.8	−125.0	− 6.0
Philadelphia[2]	478.1	476.4	− 1.7	− 0.4
St. Louis	140.3	118.5	− 21.8	−15.6
San Francisco	215.9	269.6	+ 53.7	+24.9
Washington, D.C.	199.7	206.5	+ 6.8	+ 3.4
U.S. Total Change				+18.7

[1] Includes employment in transportation, public utilities, finance, insurance, real estate, health, business, education, and other services. New York, Boston and Philadelphia figures include government employees also.

[2] For 1972 to 1976 period.

Source: Boston figures furnished by the Research Department, Boston Redevelopment Authority, and New York figures are from U.S. Bureau of Labor Statistics, *Employment and Earnings*. The remainder are from U.S. Bureau of Census, *County Business Patterns, 1970* and *1975*.

8-3   Change in service employment in selected cities—1970–1975.

8-4 Denver's office development boom.

Office Space Expansion in CBDs of Selected Cities, 1970–1975

City	millions of square feet		Increase	
	1970	1975	Amount	Percentage
Atlanta	17	21	4	24
Baltimore	8	10	2	25
Boston	34	45	11	32
Chicago	63	84	21	33
Cincinnati	12	13	1	8
Cleveland	11	15	4	36
Dallas	21	24	3	14
Denver	8	11	3	38
Detroit	18	22	4	22
Los Angeles	33	42	9	27
Milwaukee	9	11	2	22
Minneapolis	10	13	3	30
Newark	14	14	0	0
New York	240	290	50	21
New Orleans	6	10	4	67
Philadelphia	34	43	9	26
Pittsburgh	22	26	4	18
St. Louis	17	20	3	18
San Francisco	26	37	11	42
Washington, D.C.	54	71	17	31
Average Percent Increase				27

Source: Regional Plan Association, New York

8-5 Office space expansion in CBDs of selected cities—1970–1975.

mately 40 percent of the metropolitan office market. New York, Washington, D.C., and Dallas have heavier than average concentrations of downtown office activity, while Los Angeles, Detroit, and Cleveland have below average concentrations.

A few studies have analyzed the reasons for the expansion of downtown office functions in the face of general deconcentration and dispersal of economic activity. The most important reason appears to be that central corporate offices, financial institutions, and the more specialized business and consumer services, all of which have been expanding generally, continue to value central locations because of the benefits of face-to-face contact among professionals and managers and the economies in the agglomeration of different high-grade, specialized services and other business and financial activities. Another reason is that the difference in the cost of space and in taxes between central core locations and suburban locations is less critical to office functions in general, because they amount to a very small proportion, generally less than 10 percent, of operating costs.

Some have questioned the strength of the forces keeping and expanding offices in downtowns, pointing to (1) the corporate movements from New York City and to a lesser extent from other cities, (2) the development of large office complexes in the suburbs, which may at some time reach the volume necessary to support the specialized services now concentrated in downtowns, and (3) trends toward the relaxation of branching restrictions on banks and other financial institutions that have forced them to stay in the city. Recent studies of office expansion in New York City indicate, however, that while some corporate headquarters have been relocated to suburban areas, they still rely on firms in the city for banking, legal services, accounting, advertising, and marketing, and that expansion in these corporate service activities more than offsets losses from the move of headquarters. Moreover, while the office market in downtowns was depressed following the 1974–75 recession and the overbuilding of downtown office space in the early 1970s, recent data on office construction in central cities indicate a continuation of the office expansion of earlier years. Thus, there appears to be no reason to suspect that the past forces tending to concentrate office activity in the CBD have abated or will abate in the near future.

Indeed, if anything, past office expansion in CBDs, public investment in new facilities such as convention centers, parking structures, freeways, transit systems, sports arenas, cultural facilities, and the like, and improvements in streets, plazas, and other public areas have vastly improved the physical environment

of downtowns to the point that physical blight seldom deters downtown investment. Rather, the downtown physical environment is an attraction in many areas with its dramatic new towers, well landscaped and well designed public spaces, and outstanding views from high-rise offices. If problems of congestion can be avoided and means can be found to meet the internal circulation needs of downtowns, CBDs can expect to continue to capture a substantial share of the national increase in office activity.

The expansion of office activity and the other advantages that cities have traditionally offered—cultural facilities, interesting architecture, historic places, and pedestrian-oriented physical environs—have created, and can be expected to continue to enhance, conditions ripe with opportunities to attract middle- and upper-income households to city neighborhoods and to increase retailing.

The potential market for middle- and upper-income housing in central cities is being clearly and forcefully demonstrated in those cities that have experienced the most rapid and the strongest transition to high-grade service and administrative functions—Washington, D.C., Atlanta, and San Francisco—and the extensive resettlement of older areas by middle- and high-income households in those three cities indicates what can occur in most central cities as a result of the expansion of high-status jobs in downtown areas. The young and highly educated professionals who form the work force for the expanding jobs in downtown offices have shown a strong proclivity for residing in the city. In Washington, all of the residential areas within a 2-mile radius of the downtown office area are under strong pressure for

8-6 Newberry Plaza, Chicago, is an example of high-rise residential space for upper income people.

8-7 Society Hill in Philadelphia and the Victorian Crescent in San Francisco are two examples of the renovation and restoration of close-in residential areas of historical significance and architectural character.

housing from this group. Areas that were almost exclusively low-income and experiencing abandonment and declining housing prices in 1965 are now undergoing renovation and rapid price escalation. In these areas, houses that were traded for $12,000 to $20,000 in 1970 were selling unrenovated in 1979 for $50,000 to $90,000. The close-in Atlanta neighborhoods are all experiencing resettlement by the higher income, more highly educated households that work in downtown. San Francisco is experiencing the same phenomenon in the extensive Victorian Crescent, which wraps around its downtown.

Few attempts have been made to measure the extent or nature of the trend, which has occurred for the most part since the 1970 census; however, a survey of central city planning agencies, building officials, and real estate broker associations in 1975 indicated that approximately 75 percent of central cities over 250,000 in population were experiencing significant private-market housing renovation in formerly deteriorating areas.[5] More recently (1977), recent inmigrants to older neighborhoods in Washington and Atlanta have been studied.[6] The study of the Virginia Highlands neighborhood in Atlanta found that new migrants are generally young (median age 26.8 years),

married, extremely well educated, employed in high-status professional occupations, with high incomes. They chose the Virginia Highlands neighborhood because of its proximity to downtown, the low cost of housing, and their preference for old houses and city living. The recent movers into the Capitol Hill area of Washington, D.C., had similar characteristics. More than 75 percent possessed graduate degrees, the median age group was 30 to 34 years, and more than three out of four households earned over $25,000 in income. They moved to Capitol Hill to be close to work, because they felt their investment in a Capitol Hill house would appreciate substantially, because of the favorable price of housing there relative to other locations, and because of the historical and architectural character of the area.

One can already see what office and middle- to upper-income residential expansion can mean to the future of retailing in the cities even though many cities are continuing to suffer deterioration in the

---

[5] J. Thomas Black, "Private-Market Housing Renovation," *Urban Land* (November 1975).

[6] Donald S. Bradley, "Back to the City?" *Atlanta Economic Review* 28:2 (March-April 1978): 15–20.

overall totals of retail sales. In Philadelphia, the new Gallery shopping mall is doing extremely well by serving downtown office workers and the relatively affluent residents who have moved into the neighborhoods surrounding downtown, as well as many outlying residents who still find it desirable to journey downtown to shop. In Los Angeles, the Broadway Plaza, a relatively new mixed use project with a department store and mall shops is doing well in its location on the west side of downtown Los Angeles near the major concentration of new office buildings. Also in Los Angeles, Bullock's is now planning to relocate into a new mixed use project near the Broadway Plaza. In San Francisco, major amounts of new retail activity have been added in the CBD, with a great deal of the space on ground floors of new office buildings or one- to two-story shopping malls at the base of office complexes. Similar retail expansions have occurred in Washington, D.C., Boston, Chicago, and Atlanta. There is every reason to believe that continuing office expansion and the increasing numbers of middle- and upper-income households moving into areas surrounding CBDs will generate even far greater potential for retail expansion than has occurred to date.

Moreover, the pioneering efforts of the early 1970s have discovered a new market for downtown retailing—the recreational shopper. With increasing affluence and leisure time for consumers and increasing homogeneity in the conventional shopping centers, consumers are seeking unusual shopping places offering exotic, highly specialized, or at least unconventional goods in a pleasant, unconventional environment—interesting and entertaining places to visit even if one plans to buy nothing. Ghirardelli Square in San Francisco is the original model for such places

although it was and is oriented toward the tremendous tourist market of San Francisco. Faneuil Hall in Boston demonstrates better the market for local residents for this type of retail activity. Developed by the city and the Rouse Company, the center has drawn area residents from homes and offices in large numbers to visit the historic marketplace with its renovated buildings and small specialty and craft shops and restaurants. While the current and future magnitude of the market for such retail activities is difficult to assess, there clearly is much greater potential now than is being realized. It is reasonable to expect that the market potential will grow with national economic growth and as other conditions in CBDs improve.

On the whole then, the future economic potential for central cities is somewhat mixed. Clearly the forces of decentralization leading to a more complex and sprawling urban structure with multiple activity centers will dominate the next decade of growth. The overall growth rate will be higher in the Sunbelt cities as the economy continues to adjust to differences in the cost of labor and the cost of living. Still, while many central cities may face general shrinkage of their overall economies and populations, the expansion of downtown office, residential, and retail activities will provide the basis for new investment and development opportunities in the cities.

Future Types of Opportunities for Development

Given the nature of the economic changes taking place and the pioneering efforts of the 1970s, the forms of future downtown development can be forecast with some confidence. Most private projects will consist of:

- new office towers, often incorporating retail space in the ground floor
- mixed use projects (MXDs) combining office, retail, hotel, and residential use in the same complex
- enclosed shopping malls modeled after the Gallery project in Philadelphia
- specialty or recreational shopping complexes in both old and new structures
- new hotels in proximity to convention centers, and hotel renovations
- office and/or retail projects tied directly to transit stations (joint-development projects)
- luxury high-rise housing and townhouse projects.

8-8   Broadway Plaza in Los Angeles is a MXD with a 500-room hotel, 733,000 square feet of office space, a 250,000–square foot department store, and 200,000 square feet of other retail space.

8-9　Faneuil Hall, Boston.

The most popular of these various types of projects is likely to be the new office tower, simply because the demand for office space is most certain, because they can be developed on small sites (making land assembly easier), and because they are easier to finance and manage. However, the rapid escalation of construction costs and the increased demand for office space have led developers to renovate many of the pre-World War II buildings in CBDs. With continuing inflation and office expansion, now coupled with the tax benefits for renovation enacted in 1976 and 1978, more opportunities for the renovation of older buildings suitable for office use are likely.

While opportunities will exist for major MXDs in the 1980s, it is likely that they will be less grandiose and more closely integrated with other activities in the CBD than in the past for several reasons. First, the general improvement in the downtown environment has lessened the need for such developments to create their own, insular environment. Second, many of the more grandiose and insular projects have not proven successful and thus are not likely to be replicated. Third, the market in CBDs has become attractive enough that many of the uses typically included in MXDs can be developed independently without the increased costs and risks associated with large MXDs. Still, the mutually reinforcing aspects of office, hotel, and retail space in a closely linked format will make MXDs desirable and feasible in many situations.

Possibly the most exciting development opportunities of the 1980s will lie in the new retail potential of CBDs through the development of downtown shopping malls and specialty centers. The Gallery project in Philadelphia has demonstrated the potential for general merchandise shopping malls that take advantage of the office employee and downtown residential market, and plans for similar projects are underway in other cities. It now appears that major department store chains have realized the potential for downtown retail activity, although in many cases they must relocate their downtown stores and/or integrate their stores into a modern mall-type facility with good parking and pedestrian and transit access.

Specialty retail center projects are likely to take many forms, ranging from the conversion of old warehouses or factories to new construction such as that planned by the Rouse Company for the Inner Harbor area of Baltimore. Generally, they will be located within walking distance of downtown offices and hotels with good access to the regional transportation network. They will be designed for small shops and restaurants and will stress unusual architectural or historical qualities.

Expanding office activities downtown coupled with general increases in meetings and conventions will create new opportunities for hotels. Many will be developed in conjunction with private office buildings and public convention centers to take advantage of the functional dependencies between the uses. The demand for new hotels will also create opportunities for renovating the grand old hotels remaining in many cities that are well located to serve surrounding offices.

Those cities planning or constructing new transit systems or expanding existing systems will have special opportunities to combine private development with public development of the transit stations. The federal government, the primary funder of transit system construction, is pushing the concept of joint development because of the obvious benefits gained from the integration of high-density private uses with the transit system. From the private investor's point of view, the advantages of access and the large volume of traffic generated by transit stations make such joint-development projects very attractive. With the growth of CBDs and the resulting congestion that will make the use of the automobile more difficult, public transit can be expected to play an increasing role in personal transportation for trips from home to downtown and for circulation within downtowns.

Probably the greatest untapped development potential is market-rate (unsubsidized) housing, which, because of development costs, means middle- to upper-income housing. Those cities that have experienced the greatest expansion of downtown office activity have seen considerable investment in new housing and in the renovation of older buildings for middle- and upper-income residences. On a wider scale, limited investment in select areas of historical interest or in choice locations has occurred. Given the

8-10   Lafayette Place in Boston will be a second-generation MXD.

8-11   The blending of new construction with existing, renovated, or restored buildings will be an important design approach in the 1980s, as illustrated by this photo of old and new side by side in Salem, Massachusetts.

improvement in the downtown environment, increasing white-collar professional and technical jobs in CBDs, and the obvious preference for a substantial percentage of metropolitan residents to live close to their jobs or in an urban environment, it appears likely that the current limited demand for new and renovated housing in the city will increase. As long as current housing price inflation and tax laws persist, the majority of this demand will be for owner-occupied units, either condominium apartments or townhouses, with good access to downtown by foot or public transportation.

Future Public and Private Interaction in Downtown Development

The future of public/private interaction in downtown development appears somewhat mixed. Downtowns' expanding economic functions are creating much stronger markets for development, but at the same time the public sector is expanding both its capacity and willingness to assist in development and many private developers are realizing that private facilities can operate more efficiently if they are integrated with public facilities. This combination of forces seems likely to result in more of both kinds of projects: those that are essentially private undertakings with the traditional public involvement in zoning and building permit approvals and those where the public sector participates more actively in some aspect of the project.

Public participation in downtown development is changing rather quickly for a number of reasons. First, the flow of federal dollars to local governments to support private investment is increasing. Second, the increase in concern about the economic future of central cities has led to favorable local, state, and federal support for urban economic development programs. Third, the public sector is becoming increasingly sophisticated. The excessive costs and frequent failures of the approach to urban renewal in the 1960s led to a recognition that the public sector had to be more flexible and more efficient. In turn, public agencies have begun to better understand private development and the tools and techniques for assistance, and have begun to apply these tools and techniques more sensitively. The increased sophistication and sensitivity of public development agencies is resulting in private developers' greater willingness to enter into projects with public agencies.

A number of recent innovations in public/private interaction are likely to be practiced more widely in the future:

- the assistance of professional firms that specialize in packaging public/private projects

- the use of quasi-public development corporations that act as agents of the city government but are not restricted by the typical legal, bureaucratic, or political limitations on public bodies

- consultation between public development agencies and potential developers early in project formulation to ensure that the project will conform to the requirements of private investors and developers

- the use of percentage leases, flexible interest rate loans, and other devices to allow the public sector a greater share of rewards as well as risks

- public underwriting of initial predevelopment feasibility studies and other related activities

- tailoring public involvement to fit the project's particular market and risk characteristics.

8-12   A professional service firm repackaged a dormant renewal project in Iowa City and successfully attracted private development.

Professional Packagers

The expanded use of professional service firms that operate as intermediaries between public development agencies and private investors and developers is likely. Their role will be to formulate a project that meets public objectives and attracts private investors and developers. Generally, their client will be the public development agency, although they may also work for private developers who are negotiating with public agencies for some public involvement in a project. For the public sector, they offer an understanding of the private development process and the current guidelines governing private investment and development. For the private developer, they offer an understanding of public sector programs and funding possibilities and their possible application to a particular project.

Quasi-Public Development Corporations

Quasi-public development corporations organized for public purposes have proven highly successful in several cities. Freed from the restrictions of government bureaucracy, such organizations can act quickly, be flexible, and conduct their business privately. As local governments recognize the advantages of flexibility and expeditious actions, more similar organizations are likely.

Early Developer Involvement

A theme of the preceding chapters is that public development agencies should consult with potential developers in the initial stages of project formulation. This approach is gaining wider acceptance. The methods of involving the developer early in the process are likely to vary considerably, depending on market conditions, complexity of the project, and the legal and political constraints on the local public agency. In particularly risky and complex projects where developers' interest is weak, public agencies are likely to seek out a single developer who would be given an option to develop the project. In the absence of developers' interest, the public agency is likely to contract with a professional packager who can represent private interests in the early stages and assist in interesting developers early in the planning process.

Public Profit-Sharing

Historically, public agencies have assumed part of the costs and investment risks for urban development projects without participating in the returns on that investment beyond the normal tax revenues the project generates. This situation will continue to be true for most public/private ventures, but as public agencies become more sophisticated and assume a role more like that of an equity partner, they will seek a greater return on their investment. If the public shares in the costs and risks of the project and the project is successful, the public should share in the rewards. As downtown economies expand and prospects for projects shift from being clearly infeasible to uncertain without public subsidy, more public agencies will want to share in the rewards.

To be acceptable to private investors, the public's share of the return will in most cases come after private investors have earned a return sufficient to attract their investment in the first place. The profit-sharing objective is likely to lead to leasing public sites for low base rates plus a percentage of income once certain maximum levels are exceeded—or provisions similar to lease terms for shopping centers. It also will lead to a shift from outright grants to private developers to loans with the repayment schedule and interest rate depending on project performance—or provisions for participation similar to those conventional mortgage lenders frequently use.

Public Underwriting of Initial Feasibility Studies

One of the major obstacles to urban development is the difficulty in convincing developers to invest time and money in an initial assessment of project feasibility in weak or uncertain markets. Most developers view the probability of a reward from this investment as very low and therefore choose not to make it. Several cities have recognized this problem and have funded all or part of the costs of conducting this type of analysis. The technique has successfully attracted developers to assess the potential for a project and, in several instances, has led to the successful negotiation of a project. With both local and federal governments tending toward requirements for commitments from the private sector before committing substantial public expenditures for land acquisition and public improvements, it seems likely that the number of cities offering to underwrite all or part of initial feasibility investigations will increase.

Tailoring Public Assistance

One of the likely changes in public/private relationships is the growing recognition that different market and development conditions call for different kinds of public assistance. In the past, public development agencies have used fairly standard formulas for public assistance—land acquisition and writedown, tax abatement, and public improvements—regardless of the particular problem restricting private development. Increasingly, the public sector is recognizing that the same development objectives can often be achieved by a public construction loan, private land assembly backed by the threat of holdout condemnation, below-market loans funded by tax exempt bonds, or public funding of front-end costs. In this way, public assistance is focused on the particular problem frustrating private investment and development.

On the whole, the future of public/private interaction is optimistic. The public sector's increasing understanding of private development and its emphasis on economic development and fiscal conservatism are leading to a more businesslike and sensitive approach to public support and intervention. Coupled with the economic expansion in CBDs, it is leading to greater interest from private investors and developers in working with the public sector to formulate and develop projects.

APPENDICES
AND
INDEX

APPENDIX A

Selected References and Information Services

Books

Administration and Management Research Association of New York City, Inc. *Economic Development: Central Business District Study*. Washington, D.C.: U.S. Department of Commerce, 1978; Springfield, Va.: National Technical Information Service.

Administration and Management Research Association of New York City, Inc. *Transit Station Area Joint Development*. Washington, D.C.: U.S. Government Printing Office, 1976.

Alexander, Laurence A., ed. *Downtown District Action Guide*. New York: Downtown Research and Development Center, 1979.

Alexander, Laurence A. *Financing Downtown Action*. New York: Downtown Research and Development Center, 1975.

American Bankers Association. *Bankers and Community Involvement*. Washington, D.C.: American Bankers Association, 1978.

Berk, Emanuel. *Downtown Improvement Manual*. Chicago: American Society of Planning Officials, 1976.

Black, J. Thomas. *The Changing Economic Role of Central Cities*. Washington, D.C.: ULI–the Urban Land Institute, 1978.

Carpenter, Horace, Jr. *Shopping Center Management: Principles and Practices*. New York: International Council of Shopping Centers, 1974.

Chamber of Commerce of the United States. *Downtown Redevelopment*. Washington, D.C.: Chamber of Commerce of the United States, 1974.

Chung, Hyung C. *Harbor and Waterfront Development Planning*. Springfield, Va.: National Technical Information Service, 1977 (PB 270 685/1WU).

Downtown Research and Development Center. *The Downtown Shopping Center*. New York: Downtown Research and Development Center, 1975.

Frost, Michael, Jr. *How to Use Cost Benefit Analysis in Project Appraisal*. New York: John Wiley, 1975.

Harney, Andy, ed. *Reviving the Urban Waterfront*. Washington, D.C.: Partners for Livable Places, National Endowment for the Arts, and Office of Coastal Zone Management, n.d.

Iowa Office for Planning and Programming, Division of Municipal Affairs. *Downtown Improvement Manual for Iowa Cities*. Des Moines: Office for Planning and Programming, Division of Municipal Affairs, 1978.

Libassi, Peter, and Hausner, Victor. *Revitalizing Central City Investment*. Columbus, Ohio: Academy for Contemporary Problems, 1977.

Moore, Arthur Cotton, and others. *Bright Breathing Edges of City Life: Planning for Amenity Benefits of Urban Water Resources*. Springfield, Va.: National Technical Information Service, 1971 (PB 202–880).

National Council for Urban Economic Development. *Coordinated Urban Economic Development: A Case Study Analysis*. Washington, D.C.: National Council for Urban Economic Development, 1978.

National League of Cities, U.S. Conference of Mayors, Skidmore, Owings and Merrill, and Development Research Associates. *Transit Station Joint Development*. Washington, D.C.: U.S. Department of Transportation, 1974; Springfield, Va.: National Technical Information Service.

North, Lincoln W. *Real Estate Investment Analysis and Valuation*. Winnepeg: Sault and Pollard, 1976.

Parking Consultants Council and the National Parking Association. *The Dimensions of Parking*. Washington, D.C.: ULI–the Urban Land Institute and National Parking Association, 1979.

Planning Services Group and the Massachusetts Department of Community Affairs, Office of Local Assistance. *Revitalizing Small Town Central Business Districts*. Boston: Massachusetts Department of Community Affairs, Office of Local Assistance, 1976.

Redstone, Louis G. *The New Downtowns: Rebuilding Business Districts*. New York: McGraw Hill, 1976.

Roca, Ruben A., ed. *Market Research for Shopping Centers*. New York: International Council of Shopping Centers, 1980.

Sassone, Peter G., and Schaffer, William A. *Cost-Benefit Analysis: A Handbook*. New York: Academic Press, 1978.

Sirota, David. *Essentials of Real Estate Investment*. Chicago: Real Estate Education Company, 1978.

U.S. Department of Housing and Urban Development and U.S. Department of Commerce. *Local Economic Development Tools and Techniques*. Washington, D.C.: U.S. Government Printing Office, 1979.

Urban Land Institute. *Adaptive Use: Development Economics, Process, and Principles*. Washington, D.C.: ULI–the Urban Land Institute, 1978.

Urban Land Institute. *Dollars & Cents of Shopping Centers*. Washington, D.C.: ULI–the Urban Land Institute, 1978 (most recent ed. of triennial report).

Urban Land Institute. *Industrial Development Handbook*. Washington, D.C.: ULI–the Urban Land Institute, 1975.

Urban Land Institute. *Management and Control of Growth: Issues, Techniques, Problems, and Trends*. Vol. I, II, III. Washington, D.C.: ULI–the Urban Land Institute, 1975.

Urban Land Institute. *Management and Control of Growth: Issues, Techniques, Problems, and Trends. Techniques in Application*, Vol. IV. Washington, D.C.: ULI–the Urban Land Institute, 1978.

Urban Land Institute. *Optimizing Development Profits in Large Scale Real Estate Projects*. Technical Bulletin 67. Washington, D.C.: ULI–the Urban Land Institute, 1972.

Urban Land Institute. *Residential Development Handbook*. Washington, D.C.: ULI–the Urban Land Institute, 1978.

Urban Land Institute. *Shopping Center Development Handbook*. Washington, D.C.: ULI–the Urban Land Institute, 1977.

Urban Land Institute with Gladstone Associates. *Joint Development: Making the Real Estate–Transit Connection*. Washington, D.C.: ULI–the Urban Land Institute, 1979.

Warner, Raynor, and others. *Business and Preservation*. New York: Inform, 1978.

Witherspoon, Robert E., Abbett, Jon P., and Gladstone, Robert M. *Mixed-Use Developments: New Ways of Land Use*. Washington, D.C.: ULI–the Urban Land Institute, 1976.

Periodicals

Center City Report (monthly). International Downtown Executives Association, 915 15th St., N.W., Suite 900, Washington, D.C. 20005.

Challenge (monthly). U.S. Department of Housing and Urban Development. Available from the Superintendent of Documents, U.S. Government Printing Office, Washington, D.C. 20402.

City Economic Development (monthly). National League of Cities, 1620 I St., N.W., Washington, D.C. 20006.

Downtown and Suburban Office Building Experience Exchange (annual). Building Owners and Managers Association International, 1221 Massachusetts Ave., N.W., Washington, D.C. 20005.

Downtown Idea Exchange (bimonthly). Downtown Research and Development Center, 270 Madison Ave., New York, N.Y. 10016.

Housing and Development Reporter (looseleaf). Bureau of National Affairs, 1231 25th St., N.W., Washington, D.C. 20037.

National Civic Review (monthly). National Municipal League, Carl H. Pforzheimer Building, 47 E. 68th St., New York, N.Y. 10021.

Nation's Cities Weekly (weekly). National League of Cities, 1620 I St., N.W., Washington, D.C. 20006.

Planning (monthly). American Planning Association, 1313 E. 60th St., Chicago, Ill. 60637.

Project Reference File (quarterly—20 projects per year). Urban Land Institute, 1200 18th St., N.W., Washington, D.C. 20036.

U.S. Bureau of the Census Reports:
Census of Retail Trade, 1972. Vol. 3, Major Retail Center Statistics. Issued in years ending in 2 and 7.

Current Retail Trade Reports:
Advance Monthly Retail Sales.
Monthly Department Store Sales in Selected Areas.
Monthly Retail Trade: Sales and Accounts Receivable.

Urban and Community Economic Development (monthly). American Bankers Association, 1120 Connecticut Ave., N.W., Washington, D.C. 20036.

Urban Innovation Abroad (monthly). Council for International Urban Liaison, 818 18th St., N.W., Washington, D.C. 20006.

Urban Land (monthly). Urban Land Institute, 1200 18th St., N.W., Washington, D.C. 20036.

Organizations

American Planning Association
1313 East 60th Street
Chicago, Illinois 60637

Downtown Research and Development Center
270 Madison Avenue, Suite 1505
New York, New York 10016

International Downtown Executives Association
915 15th Street, N.W., Suite 900
Washington, D.C. 20005

National Council for Urban Economic Development
1730 K Street, N.W.
Washington, D.C. 20006

National League of Cities
1620 I Street, N.W.
Washington, D.C. 20006

Urban Land Institute
1200 18th Street, N.W.
Washington, D.C. 20036

APPENDIX B

Projects Used as Examples with Council Contacts*

Project Name	Location	Urban Development/ Mixed-Use Council Contact
Baystate West	Springfield, Massachusetts	Robert W. Siler, Jr.
Bunker Hill Project	Los Angeles, California	Eugene B. Jacobs
Burlington Square	Burlington, Vermont	I. Rocke Ransen
Canal Place	New Orleans, Louisiana	Joseph C. Canizaro
Capitol Gateway	Washington, D.C.	Melvin A. Mister
Capitol South	Columbus, Ohio	Joseph G. Madonna
Center City Mall	San Bernardino, California	Eugene B. Jacobs
Central Trust Center	Cincinnati, Ohio	Nell D. Surber
Charles Center	Baltimore, Maryland	Martin L. Millspaugh
Citibank	New York, New York	Albert A. Walsh
Colonial American Bank	Roanoke, Virginia	Donald R. Zuchelli
Courthouse Square	Dayton, Ohio	Joseph G. Madonna
Crown Center	Kansas City, Missouri	Keith Kelly
Fidelity Mutual/ Girard Bank	Philadelphia, Pennsylvania	William L. Rafsky
Fountain Square South	Cincinnati, Ohio	Nell D. Surber
The Gallery	Philadelphia, Pennsylvania	James Martin
Glendale Galleria	Glendale, California	Michael C. Clark
Greenville Commons	Greenville, South Carolina	Donald R. Zuchelli
Hartford Civic Center	Hartford, Connecticut	James S. Dailey
Illinois Center	Chicago, Illinois	Harold S. Jensen
Iowa City Project	Iowa City, Iowa	Donald R. Zuchelli
Kalamazoo Center	Kalamazoo, Michigan	Robert Witherspoon
Kentucky Center for the Arts	Louisville, Kentucky	Donald R. Zuchelli
Loring Park	Minneapolis, Minnesota	Nicholas V. Trkla
Manhattan Galleria	New York, New York	Raquel Ramati
Midtown Plaza	Rochester, New York	Beda Zwicker
Milwaukee Retail Center	Milwaukee, Wisconsin	Stephen F. Dragos
Monterey Conference Center	Monterey, California	A. Jerry Keyser
Nationwide Plaza	Columbus, Ohio	Joseph G. Madonna
New Market	Philadelphia, Pennsylvania	James Martin
Pacific Centre	Vancouver, British Columbia	Beda Zwicker
Pennsylvania Avenue Development	Washington, D.C.	W. Anderson Barnes
Plaza Pasadena	Pasadena, California	Gerald M. Trimble
Project One	Richmond, Virginia	Donald R. Zuchelli
Rainbow Center Mall/ Winter Garden	Niagara, New York	Beda Zwicker
South Auditorium Renewal Project	Portland, Oregon	Michael C. Clark
South Bend Project	South Bend, Indiana	Richard E. Hanson

* See the council member list on page v for further information on addresses. Also see the index for page references for each of the projects.

APPENDIX C

Example of Participation in Cash Flow
Fairfield, California
METHOD OF FINANCING

I. PARTICIPANT'S PURCHASE PRICE FOR SALE PARCEL AND OTHER CONSIDERATION

A. *Size of Sale Parcel.* The Sale Parcel is approximately 26.02 acres, including one-half of the area of the extension of Second Street and of the relocated Tooby Drive. The exact square footage of the Sale Parcel shall be determined by a survey prepared by the Agency and approved by the Participant prior to conveyance of the Sale Parcel by the Agency to the Participant.

B. *Purchase Price.* The purchase price to be paid by the Participant to the Agency for the Sale Parcel shall be the cash sum of $.95 per square foot of land in the Sale Parcel.

C. *Contribution.* In addition to and at the same time as the Participant pays the Agency the purchase price for the Sale Parcel, the Participant shall pay the Agency as its contribution toward the Travis Boulevard interchange work, the cash sum of $1.10 per square foot of land in the Sale Parcel. This contribution shall be in addition to the required participation of the Participant Parcel and the Sale Parcel in the assessment district referred to in Section IV of this Attachment. . . . The Agency shall not be restricted in its use of the amount contributed by the Participant under this Section I.C. and may use said funds for any purpose related to the Project.

D. *Payment of Percentage of Cash Flow.*

1. For purposes of this Section I.D. . . . .:

(a) "cash flow" means:

(i) the gross cash receipts generated by the Participant from the Site from any source whatsoever including, but not limited to, rent; overage or percentage rents; payments received for common area, property taxes and special assessments; payments for utilities; insurance proceeds in excess of costs of restoration; net proceeds from condemnation; and miscellaneous receipts; less

(ii) all customary and reasonable business expenditures of the Site made by the Participant (including reasonable management costs payable to shopping center management, provided that if Ernest W. Hahn, Inc., or any subsidiary thereof is the manager of the shopping center, then any management fee shall not exceed the management fee charged by such manager for managing other comparable regional shopping centers in the Northern California area; and less

(iii) interest, amortization and other charges pursuant to any construction loan or any permanent or other loans (including interest and repayment of principal for any loans or advances of any partner to the Participant, provided that the total of all such construction, permanent and other loans does not exceed the Total Cost of the Project, as hereinafter defined), the proceeds of which are used for the sole purpose of financing costs of land, costs of construction and customary and reasonable expenses related to the construction and operation of the shopping center (including lease payments on land and for improvements pursuant to a sale and lease-back financing); and less

(iv) provisions for the customary and reasonable working capital requirements of the Participant, and a customary and reasonable reserve for capital replacements, repairs, maintenance, management, promotion, security, utilities, real estate taxes and insurance; but excluding, for the purposes of determining cash flow, depreciation and other non-cash items.

It is the intention of the parties hereto that the maximum amount of cash should be distributed and considered "cash flow" on a cash basis accounting format which is consistent with prudent shopping center management practice;

(b) "gross leasable area" shall have the same meaning as the term "Floor Area" as defined in the REA approved by the Agency;

(c) "open for business" means the earlier of: (i) the REA date for opening of the shopping center or (ii) the opening for business of at least one department store and at least fifty percent (50%) of the gross leasable area of mall stores in the shopping center, whichever first occurs;

(d) "Site" means the Participant Parcel, Sale Parcel and Penney Parcel as defined in Section 104 of this Agreement;

(e) "shopping center" means the shopping center on the Site, exclusive of the Penney Parcel but including, without limitation, the department stores, mall stores, freestanding or ancillary businesses, and all other enterprises and businesses of any kind whatsoever conducted on the Participant Parcel and the Sale Parcel from time to time;

(f) "Total Cost of the Project" means the total cost to the Participant of constructing, reconstructing and developing the shopping center, according to plans and specifications approved by the Agency, and shall include: the purchase price of the Participant Parcel (which amount has been stipulated to in separate letter between the Agency and the Participant) and the Sale Parcel, less the purchase price paid by any department store for land, air rights, parking or store; the construction or reconstruction of the Participant's improvements on the Participant Parcel and the Sale Parcel, including necessary improvements related thereto by the Participant to the Site; architectural, engineering and design fees; salary and expenses of the project manager that are charged to the project; construction interest; loan fees and points; assessment district payments during construction; permanent loan fees and points; consulting and professional fees; property taxes and insurance during construction; tenant allowances and leasing commissions.

2. As additional consideration for its development opportunity under this Agreement, and in consideration for the undertakings of the City pursuant to the Redevelopment Plan and this Agreement and the provision of municipal services to the shopping center, the Participant agrees to pay (and the Agency hereby agrees and consents to such payment) to the City an annual amount equal to ten percent (10%) of the Participant's cash flow from the shopping center between the amounts of $250,000 and $500,000 annually, plus fifteen percent (15%) of the Participant's cash flow from the shopping center in excess of $500,000 annually (as illustrated in Example 1), subject to the following:

(a) The determination of the Participant's annual cash flow shall be based on the fiscal year of the Participant, which is a calendar year, with the City's percentage to be applied to the proportionate amount of cash flow for the first partial fiscal year that the shopping center is open for business, prorated on a daily basis (as illustrated in Example 2). The Participant shall not change its fiscal year thereafter without making an appropriate adjustment with the City to continue without interruption the City's rights to a percentage of the Participant's cash flow as herein set forth.

(b) The payments due the City hereunder shall commence the first fiscal year or partial fiscal year that the shopping center is open for business and shall continue until the expiration date of the REA (provided that the REA may not be voluntarily terminated without the consent of the City).

(c) The annual payments, if any, due to the City shall

be made by the Participant hereunder in two installments: the first on October 15 based on the Participant's results of operations for the then partial current fiscal year through September 30, and the second on March 1, based on the Participant's results of operations for the immediately preceding full fiscal year for which the payments are made.

(d) Within one hundred twenty (120) days after the end of each fiscal year or partial fiscal year for which payments to the City are due hereunder, the Participant shall provide the City with an audited statement (audited and certified by an independent firm of certified public accountants) of the results of operations of Participant from the shopping center, which shall include a balance sheet and statement of all receipts and expenses for said completed fiscal year, a profit and loss statement, and a cash flow statement. The City and the Participant shall promptly adjust the amount owing to the City for said fiscal year on the basis of such audited statement. Any payments due the City which are not paid when due shall bear interest at the rate of ten percent (10%) per annum on the unpaid balance thereof until paid. Such information as the Participant deems confidential to its operations shall be kept confidential by the City, provided, however, that the City may make public disclosure of a summary of such information using gross amounts summarizing operations of the shopping center and not disclosing results of operations of individual stores. To the extent that any such confidential information supplied to the City cannot lawfully be maintained by the City in confidence, then such information shall be made available on a confidential basis to the City through an inspection of the books, records, accounts and audits of the Participant by representatives or agents of the City.

(e) The examples below illustrate the preceding provisions.

3. Proceeds of any permanent financing of the shopping center in excess of the Total Cost of the Project shall be deemed cash flow.

4. The following provisions shall apply in the event of a sale, transfer or refinancing of the shopping center or any parcel thereof or interest therein by the Participant:

(a) If the Participant shall sell, assign, transfer or otherwise convey the shopping center or any portion thereof, the Participant shall, as respects the shopping center or portions thereof so conveyed, be released from the obligations of this Agreement arising after such sale, assignment, transfer or conveyance, provided:

(i) It gives notice to the City of its sale, transfer or conveyance promptly after the filing for record of the instrument effecting the same; and

(ii) Participant delivers to the City an instrument signed by its grantee or assignee that acknowledges such grantee's or assignee's assumption of the obligations imposed on Participant by this Agreement and assumed by such grantee or assignee, which instrument must be in a form and content reasonably satisfactory to the City.

Any such sale, assignment, transfer or conveyance

Example 1
(Section I. D. 2)

Participant's Annual Cash Flow	Payment Due City
$250,000	0
500,000	$25,000 (10% of $250,000)
750,000	$62,500 (10% of 250,000 plus 15% of 250,000)
1,000,000	100,000 (10% of 250,000 plus 15% of 500,000)

Example 2
(Section I. D. 2(a))

Days Open for Business in First Partial Year	Calculation of Payment Due City
200	10% of cash flow between $136,990 and $273,970, plus 15% of cash flow in excess of $273,970

shall not affect the right of the City to participate in the cash flow hereunder (including the calculation of such cash flow which shall continue to be determined in accordance with this Attachment . . . and without regard to or modification by any financing or other term or condition pertaining to such sale, assignment or transfer) from the ownership and operation of the entire shopping center.

(b) In the event the Participant desires to sell a parcel or building in the shopping center which was previously subject to a lease with Participant (other than a sale and lease-back for financing), the Participant shall promptly notify the City of such proposed sale and the terms thereof and the City shall share in the net proceeds available to the Participant from such sale in the same proportion that the City's entitlement to payments from cash flow bears to the total cash flow from the shopping center (as illustrated in Example 3); provided that if the parcel or building was generating only minimum or base rentals at the time of such sale, then cash flow shall be calculated for purposes of this provision by excluding overage rents from the shopping center (as illustrated in Example 4). If the sale occurs during the first partial fiscal year of the Participant after the shopping center is open for business, the total cash flow and the City's proportionate share thereof shall be projected and calculated for such partial fiscal year. If the sale occurs during the first full fiscal year of the Participant after the shopping center is open for business or within the last six months of any fiscal year thereafter, the total cash flow and the City's proportionate share thereof shall be projected and calculated to an annual amount for such fiscal year. If the sale occurs following the first full fiscal year of the Participant after the shopping center is open for business and within the first six months of any subsequent fiscal year, the total cash flow and the City's proportionate share thereof shall be the total cash flow and the City's proportionate share thereof from the full fiscal year immediately preceding the sale.

(c) In the event the Participant desires to sell a parcel or building in the shopping center which was not previously subject to a lease with Participant (other than a sale and lease-back for financing), the Participant shall promptly notify the City of such proposed sale and the terms thereof and the City shall share in the net proceeds available to the Participant from such sale, to the extent that such proceeds are not reinvested by the Participant in the construction, reconstruction or improvement of the shopping center, in the same proportion that the City's entitlement to payments from cash flow bears to the total cash flow from the shopping center, calculated in the same manner as set forth in the immediate preceding subsection (b) (as illustrated in Example 5).

(d) Proceeds from any refinancing of a permanent loan including sale or lease-back or any other permanent financing method shall be deemed cash flow to the Participant under this Section I.D. except to the extent such proceeds are expended by the Participant on the construction, reconstruction or improvement of the shopping center or to payment of interest or principal or prepayment charges on loans or advances made by any permanent lender or by any partner to the Participant for such purposes.

(e) The following examples illustrate the preceding provisions:

Example 3
(Section I. D. 4(b)—overage rents)

Net Proceeds from Sale of Leased Parcel	Annual Cash Flow of Participant	Payment to City from Cash Flow	City Share in Proceeds of Sale
$10,000,000	$1,000,000	$100,000	$1,000,000

Example 4
(Section I. D. 4(b)—minimum rents)

Net Proceeds from Sale of Leased Parcel	Annual Cash Flow of Participant Less Overage Rents	Payment to City from Cash Flow Less Overage Rents	City Share in Proceeds of Sale
$10,000,000	$800,000	$70,000	$875,000

Example 5
(Section I. D. 4(c))

Net Proceeds from Sale of Parcel Not Leased Less Reinvestment of Proceeds	Annual Cash Flow of Participant	Payment to City from Cash Flow	City Share in Proceeds of Sale
$10,000,000 −6,000,000 ——————— $ 4,000,000 net	$1,000,000	$100,000	$400,000

(f) In the event of a sale pursuant to the provisions of subparagraphs (b) or (c) above, the purchaser or grantee shall not be deemed a successor to the Participant for purposes of this Section I.D. . . ., and the City shall have no interest thereunder in any income of the purchaser or grantee with respect to the property or parcel so sold.

5. For purposes of verifying payments due the City hereunder, representatives of the City shall have reasonable rights, upon written request, to inspect the books and records of the Participant and independently audit the results of Participant's operations. The Participant shall keep all books and records for not less than five (5) years from the end of the fiscal year to which they pertain. If, as a result of an independent audit of the Participant's books by an independent certified public accountant hired by the City, an additional amount is due the City for any fiscal year which exceeds by two percent (2%) or $1,000, whichever is greater, the amount actually paid to the City for such fiscal year, the reasonable cost of such audit shall be paid by the Participant.

6. The Participant, Agency and City shall execute and record a memorandum of this Section I.D. in form and content satisfactory to the City, to make the obligations of the Participant hereunder obligations which run with the land and enforceable against the partners of and the successors and assigns of the Participant so long as any such party owns or has an interest in the shopping center.

7. Payments due the City hereunder shall be due without any right of offset or retention for any reason whatsoever.

8. Participant, its members and successors and assigns thereto shall not contest, directly or indirectly, the validity of payments to the City or Agency hereunder. In the event for any reason it should be determined that the City is restricted by law from receiving payments from the Participant under this Section I.D., then Participant agrees to make such payments to the Agency, City hereby assigns its rights to such payments to the Agency and Participant hereby acknowledges and agrees to be bound by such assignment. The validity or invalidity of this Section I.D. shall not affect the validity or enforceability of any other provision of this Agreement.

APPENDIX D

**Preliminary Development Commitment Agreement
for the
Development of the Downtown Hotel/
Convention Center/Retail Complex in Pueblo, Colorado,
between
the City of Pueblo, Colorado,
and**

_____

This Preliminary Development Commitment Agreement, made this _____ day of _____, 19 _____, by and between the City of Pueblo, Colorado (hereinafter referred to as "City"), and _____ (hereinafter referred to as "Developer").

WITNESSETH THAT:

WHEREAS, the City, a municipal corporation of the State of Colorado, wishes to implement a program for the purpose of rebuilding and revitalizing the core area pursuant to state and local laws; and

WHEREAS, the City has retained development consultation services from the firm of Zuchelli, Hunter & Associates, Inc. (ZHA), of Annapolis, Maryland, and has authorized them to act in cooperation with the Developer to determine the size, reuse characteristics, and the potential relationships of publicly provided facilities to complement the construction of privately owned facilities as part of an integrated project to be redeveloped in Pueblo, Colorado, and to assist the City's needs to define financial implications for public involvement in the aforementioned project elements; and

WHEREAS, ZHA, in concert with the Developer, has indicated that the designated site area, defined as the blocks bordered by 1st Street, Santa Fe Avenue, Union Avenue, Richmond Avenue and Mechanic Street, or any contiguous parcel(s) that might be subsequently designated, is appropriate for the development of a combination of public and private buildings; namely, a "mixed-use" redevelopment project consisting in part of the following uses and approximate sizes: a hotel of 300 rooms; retail facilities of 60,000 square feet gross leaseable area; exhibition and meeting space of between 30,000 and 40,000 square feet gross floor area; and a variety of public site improvements (parking garage, plazas or malls, etc.); and

WHEREAS, the parties hereto deem it to their mutual benefit to cooperate and coordinate the development to maximize its attraction and beauty as an asset mutually beneficial to each party hereto; and

WHEREAS, each party hereto deems it to be to its mutual benefit to outline and establish this Preliminary Development Commitment Agreement as a guideline for all subsequent cooperation and interaction between said parties; and

WHEREAS, each party hereto recognizes and deems it to its mutual benefit, subject to further determinations of feasibility, to commit the maximum coordination for public and private financing of the project in order to maximize the commitment to high standards of quality, use and utility; and

WHEREAS, to accomplish the purpose herein described, the City has determined that the public interest can best be served by the execution of this Preliminary Development Commitment Agreement with the Developer in which the Developer: warrants the contribution of in-kind consultation and packaging services in conjunction with the filing of federal grant applications related to the project; warrants to program and construct the privately owned components of the Preferred Development Program in concert with the publicly owned components of said Program, which shall be designed and constructed under applicable state and local law; and

WHEREAS, in recognition that both the City and the Developer shall incur project-related costs prior to the site being secured by the public sector (October 30, 1980), the City and the Developer agree that in the event either party defaults on the terms of this Agreement prior to November 1, 1980, the party not in default shall be fully reimbursed for all reasonable and documented project-related costs up to a maximum of Twenty Thousand Dollars ($20,000). The party not in default may, solely at its discretion waive the payment of such funds, concur in an extension date to facilitate public ownership of the project site, and continue to operate under the terms of this Agreement; and

WHEREAS, the City shall continue its association with Zuchelli, Hunter & Associates, Inc., of Annapolis, Maryland, during the provision of architectural and engineering services in the construction of said components; and

WHEREAS, this Preliminary Development Commitment Agreement is to be followed by more definitive agreements specifically defining the roles and responsibilities of all involved parties in the development of this Project,

NOW, THEREFORE, for and in consideration of the mutual promises herein contained, the receipt and sufficiency of which is hereby acknowledged, the parties heretofore mutually agree as follows:

Section 1. Public Sector Commitments

A. The City hereby acknowledges that the public capital funds necessary to construct the Convention/Conference Center and the project infrastructure (parking, utilities, roads, etc.) are not now locally available, therefore necessitating the City's application for state and/or federal funding assistance to carry out its construction obligations. As a priority commitment the City is now prepared to apply for funds available under the Urban Development Action Grant Program and programs of the United States Economic Development Administration. The remaining public funds shall be provided from federal Community Development monies and appropriate local sources on a timely basis. Depending upon the timely execution of preliminary development commitments, the City shall obligate itself and its consultants to make appropriate applications for the aforementioned federal grants no later than April 30, 1980.

B. The City shall commit its resources and efforts in a timely manner to the completion and adoption of an Urban Redevelopment Plan as required under applicable Colorado law. This plan is to be completed and adopted no later than April 30, 1980. The Redevelopment Plan shall reflect the findings of the redevelopment programming efforts undertaken to date and shall include at least the following additional items: the development of a land acquisition and financing strategy oriented toward the acquisition of any land necessary to effectuate the formal Redevelopment Plan and Program; a detailed description of land acquisition procedures; a detailed description of relocation requirements; and a description of the general procedures to be used for property demolition and land disposition.

C. The City shall devise a budget by identified sources for immediate site acquisition as contained in the execution schedule to be outlined in the Redevelopment Plan.... For purposes of this Agreement, land acquisition parcels shall be defined as follows: all land necessary to create a site sufficient to accommodate the hotel facility, the retail facility, the convention/conference center, the parking structure and related landscaped open space and access areas. Collectively, these areas total approximately 448,450 square feet or 10.3 acres and shall include land allocated to the following uses: hotel facility—34,575 square feet or 0.79 acres; retail facility—43,000 square feet or 0.99 acres; convention/conference center—38,400 square feet or 0.88 acres; parking structure—103,950 square feet or 2.39 acres; access to the parking structure—15,600 square feet or 0.36 acres; related landscaped areas—212,925 square feet or 4.89 acres. It is understood by the parties to this Agreement that the City shall adopt a tentative budget for land acquisition (including obtaining the funds described therein) subject to the exact amount stipulated by land acquisition appraisals no later than April 30, 1980.

D. The City or its designated agency shall undertake land acquisition appraisals for those identified parcels during the time period commencing no later than April 30, 1980, and ending no later than June 30, 1980. The City or its designated agency shall initiate the acquisition of these previously identified parcels during the time period commencing no later than June 30, 1980, and ending no later than October 30, 1980. The City or its designated agency shall undertake land acquisition procedures which shall include negotiations concerning the methods and value of land acquisition and the procedures to be followed in the event that condemnation is required. If it is necessary to alter the originally defined land acquisition schedule, the City or its designated agency must offer, and the Developer must accept, no later than July 30, 1980, the revised land acquisition schedule. If the Developer deems the revised schedule detrimental to the feasible development of the project, he may, at his option, declare the conditions imposed under this Preliminary Development Commitment Agreement null and void.

E. The City or its designated agency shall undertake procedures to relocate existing tenants and demolish existing structures in the previously identified acquisition parcels. The relocation and demolition process on these identified parcels shall be undertaken during the time period commencing no later than July 30, 1980, and ending no later than September 30, 1981.

F. The City shall ensure that the enactment of appropriate zoning, street access and the issuance of all necessary permits, licenses, and approvals of any kind which shall be required with respect to the Developer's construction shall be available on proper application, payment of requisite fees, and other compliance with applicable laws, rules and regulations.

G. The City shall make available to the Developer a site, together with the provision of City sewer service adequate to service the proposed development, within the previously described acquisition area, for development of a hotel facility and a retail facility (see Section 1, Item C) including directly related landscaped open space and access areas. The sewer hookups to the project shall be provided at no charge to the Developer. The City shall also cause the provision of water, natural gas and electrical services to the site adequate to service the proposed development. The Developer agrees to pay for utility hookup charges required by these quasi-public utility companies. These sites shall be made available to the Developer by either of the following two means at the Developer's option:

1. _Fee_

The City or its designated agency shall dispose of the hotel facility site and the retail facility site to the Developer at a negotiated fee, based upon reuse appraisals conducted under permissible law to determine fair market value for sale to the Developer. If the Developer wishes to purchase the site, the City agrees to provide a land writedown on the cost of land acquisition to the private sector. The City hereby commits to conduct these appraisals during a period commencing no later than April 30, 1980, and ending no later than June 30, 1980.

2. _Lease_

The City or its designated agency hereby pledges itself to consider, in lieu of Item 1 (G.1) above, leasing the previously identified hotel facility site and retail facility site to the Developer according to such terms and conditions as can be mutually agreed upon by the parties.

These dispositions, within the previously identified acquisition area, disposed of either through title fee simple or a lease, shall be determined no later than April 30, 1980, through the execution of a Land Disposition Agreement or a Parcel Lease Agreement.

H. The City agrees that the capital cost of the Convention/Conference Center shall be publicly financed. The Convention/Conference Center shall be designed and constructed concurrently with the hotel facility under the terms of a subordinated lease agreement with the City to be subsequently negotiated. The following design/financial specifications shall serve as a pro forma statement of the quality level associated with the development of the Convention/Conference Center, with said specifications subject to modification by the City, with the concurrence of the Developer, or his assigned designated hotel operator, from a time period commencing upon execution of this Agreement and subsequent execution of more definitive agreements no later than April 30, 1980:

**MAXIMUM PROGRAM OF SPACES
CONVENTION/CONFERENCE CENTER**

Exhibit Area/Banquet Hall	16,000 NSF
Meeting Rooms	8,000
• 6 rooms @ 500 SF	
• 4 rooms @ 1,000 SF	
Storage	2,000
Receiving	1,500
Lobby Space (and Prefunction Areas)	3,000
Office	1,800
Coat Room	250
Toilet Rooms	1,200
Undesignated Space	250
Net Area (85%)	34,000 NSF
Gross Area (100%)	40,000 GSF

The City shall publicly finance the capital costs of the program of spaces itemized above in a range of 30,000 to 40,000 gross square feet at an average per-square-foot cost of Ninety-Five Dollars ($95.00). The maximum total development cost of the Convention/Conference Center shall be approximately Four Million Two Hundred Thousand Dollars ($4,200,000) which shall include the following approximate allocation of capital expenditures:

• Construction cost estimate (including site improvements, landscaping and contingencies)	$2,549,400
• Professional services (including architect, engineer and contingencies)	252,000
• Construction management fees (including contingencies)	210,000
• Furniture, fixtures and equipment	888,700
• Estimated land costs	299,900
TOTAL	$4,200,000

The City further agrees to provide the initial furniture, fixtures and equipment for the Convention/Conference Center, to replace structural and mechanical defects which occur during the lease and to be responsible for payment of hazard insurance on the structure and its contents. In return, the City requires the Developer, or his designated hotel operator, to enter into an exclusive marketing and management agreement, the terms of which are delineated in Section 2, Item G of this Agreement. Since the convention center is publicly owned the City shall not require the Developer to pay property taxes or debt service charges on the convention/conference space.

I. The City agrees to offer second mortgage financing to the Developer for private costs associated with development of the private components of the project. This second mortgage instrument, which would be financed through funds received under the Urban Development Action Grant Program of the United States Department of Housing and Urban Development, shall be subordinated to the cash flow required to satisfy any first mortgage instrument and all operating expenses of the private facilities. An amount of the cash then available, which shall be subsequently negotiated between the Developer and the City, shall then be directed to pay for the debt service on the second mortgage, prior to any return on equity. If circumstances in any given year during the duration of the second mortgage prove insufficient in terms of cash flow to meet the full debt payment on the second mortgage instrument, the Developer then shall pay the available portion of the proceeds to the City, and shall defer the balance to the 21st year of the hotel operations. The accumulation of these deferred charges would be on a non-interest basis and shall become due in the 21st year, in an amount to be subsequently negotiated between the Developer and the City.

J. The City agrees to assist the Developer in securing municipal development bond financing for the private costs associated with development of the private components of the project (see Section 2, Item F for the terms of participation).

K. The City shall develop, or cause to be developed, a minimum of 500 parking spaces as an integral part of the

project, adjacent or contiguous to the proposed project area, and available to the Developer. However, nothing herein contained shall prevent charges for use of such facilities. Any charges for use of such facilities shall be based upon reasonably necessary rates to cover operating fees, management fees, operational expenses and debt services, and such other necessary and incidental expenses, including payment in lieu of taxes as may become necessary or desirable for the City of Pueblo. The City shall guarantee an adequate number of parking spaces and shall make provisions for potential future changes in supply. These parking spaces are to be available no later than September 30, 1983.

Section 2. Private Sector Commitments

A. The Developer agrees to either purchase the required portions of the site in fee simple from the City at a written-down cost or lease the required portions of the site under lease terms and conditions that are commensurate with fair market value. This land disposition shall be manifested through a Land Disposition Agreement to be conditionally executed no later than April 30, 1980.

B. The Developer agrees that the design of the private sector components of the project is of paramount importance to the City and for that reason will allow the appropriate public agencies designated by the City to exercise the approval rights (including the selection of the architect) over the design plans of the private sector components of the complex. In selecting project architects, the Developer shall submit not less than three (3) acceptable architectural firms. The City shall then select from those submitted by the Developer and designate one to serve as the project architect. It is understood by the parties hereto that the preferred architect selected by the City shall then negotiate a contract for services for the planned hotel and retail facilities with the Developer.

C. The Developer agrees that the joint public/private objective manifested through the coordinated design process can best be realized by the designation of the same construction management entity for the public and private components of the project. In selecting a construction manager, the Developer shall submit not less than three (3) acceptable firms. The City shall then select one from those submitted and designate one to serve as the construction manager for the public components, with the expressed understanding that the selected construction manager shall negotiate a contract for services with the developer of the private components.

D. The Developer shall secure the appropriate financing mechanism for the private components during the time period commencing no later than April 30, 1980, and terminating no later than January 31, 1981, within the requirements of the Redevelopment Plan and the potential contractual commitments arising between the City as grant recipient and the appropriate public funding agency involved.

E. The Developer agrees to construct a hotel facility at the location designated in the Land Disposition Agreement and consistent with the publicly adopted Redevelopment Plan. The Developer also agrees to cause the development of a retail facility on the site, either through agreeing to construct the facility or exercising assignability to a successor organization mutually acceptable with the City. The following design/financial specifications shall serve only as a pro forma statement of the quality level associated with development of the hotel facility, with said specifications subject to modification by the Developer, with concurrence by the City, from the time period commencing upon execution of this Agreement and subsequent execution of more definitive agreements no later than April 30, 1980:

1. *Hotel Facility*

The minimum required standards, architectural requirements and physical development guidelines for the hotel component of this project . . . represent the acceptable minimum required by Sheraton Inn's, Inc., and are in no way meant to limit the quality level of a proposed project from being designed in a manner superior to those standards.

The total development costs of the hotel facility shall be approximately Fifteen Million Nine Hundred Thousand Dollars ($15,900,000) which shall include the following approximate allocation of capital expenditures:

• Construction cost estimate (including site improvements, landscaping and contingencies)	$10,843,800
• Professional services (including architects, engineer, legal, project administration and contingencies)	636,000
• Furniture, fixtures and equipment (FF&E)	2,241,900
• Start-up costs (including pre-opening expenses, operating losses [years one	492,900

and two], other costs and contingencies)

• Working capital (including construction and permanent loan fees and construction loan interest)	1,224,300
• Estimated land costs	461,100
TOTAL	$15,900,000

2. *Retail Facility*

The following design/financial specifications shall serve as a pro forma statement on the quality level associated with the development of the retail facility, with said specifications subject to modification by the Developer, or a subsequently assigned successor organization, with concurrence by the City, upon execution of this Agreement and subsequent execution of more definitive agreements no later than April 30, 1980. The Developer shall cause the development of 60,000 gross square feet of retail space to be leased to a minimum of eighteen (18) tenants and/or shopowners offering a wide variety of specialty and convenience merchandise. This retail space shall be designed in such a way as to complement existing retail space along Main Street in the downtown area and to provide continuity in pedestrian travel between the parking structure and the central business district. The total development costs of the retail facility shall be approximately Three Million Six Hundred Thousand Dollars ($3,600,000) which shall include the following approximate allocation of capital expenditures:

• Construction cost estimates (including site improvements, landscaping and contingencies)	$2,401,200
• Professional services (including architects, engineer, legal, project administration and contingencies)	255,600
• Start-up costs (including pre-opening expenses, tenant inducements, operating losses [years one and two], leasing fees and contingencies)	306,000
• Working capital (including construction and permanent loan fees and construction loan interest)	367,200
• Estimated land costs	270,000
TOTAL	$3,600,000

Construction of the private components shall be initiated no later than September 30, 1981, and completed no later than September 30, 1983.

F. The Developer agrees to pay a fee to the City, up to Twenty Thousand Dollars ($20,000), to cover the costs associated with the issuance of municipal development bonds if they are used to finance the private portions of the project. This fee shall cover costs incurred by the City associated with retaining appropriate private sector assistance to aid the City in ascertaining the feasibility of such a bond issuance. It is anticipated that the City shall retain the services of a bond counsel, a market analyst, a financial analyst and other appropriate professionals in this regard. The Developer agrees to pay this fee in full prior to the City securing the professional assistance required.

G. The Developer, or his designated hotel operator, agrees to enter into an exclusive marketing and management agreement with the City whereby the hotel operator shall receive all catering and operating revenues and assume all catering and operating costs associated with use of the Convention/Conference Center. The Developer, or his designated hotel operator, also further agrees to make all needed capital expenditures for replacement of furniture, fixtures and equipment in the Convention/Conference Center.

Section 3. Cooperative Commitments

The parties to this Preliminary Development Commitment Agreement agree to enter into more definitive agreements which shall supersede this Agreement. These agreements shall include but shall not be limited to a General Development Agreement, a Land Disposition Agreement or a Parcel Lease Agreement, a Subordinated Lease Agreement, a Parking Lease Agreement. These agreements shall be negotiated and conditionally executed no later than April 30, 1980, with subsequent execution upon the federal grant commitments being received by the City.

Section 4. Miscellaneous

This Preliminary Development Commitment Agreement entered into on the date here first written above, shall bind the parties hereto for a period not to exceed nine (9) months. It is initially agreed by the parties hereto that this Preliminary Development Commitment Agreement may be given such extension or extensions to reasonably effectuate the purpose hereof where a delay is caused for unforeseen reasons or other complications beyond the control of either party hereto. Neither party shall unreasonably withhold such extension.

IN WITNESS WHEREOF, the parties hereto have hereunto caused their hand and seal to be affixed the day and year above first written.

The City of Pueblo, Colorado

By: _____   By: _____

Title: _____   Title: _____

Date: _____   Date: _____

EXHIBIT 1

	Predevelopment Programming /	Design and Financing /	Construction /	
	1980	1981	1982	1983
	J F M A M J J A S O N D	J F M A M J J A S O N D	J F M A M J J A S O N D	J F M A M J J A S

Public Adoption of Redevelopment Plan ———— April 30

Adoption of Budget/Secure Public Funds ———— April 30

Preparation/Submission of Grant Application* ———— April 30

Land Acquisition Appraisals (2 Mo.) ——June 30

Secure Site for Developer ——————— October 30

Acquisition, Relocation & Demolition (15 Mo.) ——————————————— September 30

Hotel Site Appraisals —— June 30

Execution of Final Agreements ———— April 30
- Land Disposition Agreement
- General Development Agreement
- Subordinated Lease Agreement
- Parcel Lease Agreement (if necessary)

Developer Financing Secured (9 Mo.) ——————— January 31

Design of Public and Private Project Components (17 Mo.) ——————————————— September 30

Construction (24 Mo.) ——————————— (To September 30, 1983) ———————

*If the private sector development and financing commitments necessary for federal funding under the UDAG program cannot be obtained by this date, the next deadline for submittal is 90 days later (July 31, 1980). If delayed, the remaining activities will commence later than scheduled above.

APPENDIX E

Land Disposition Agreement
Contract for Sale of
Land for Private Redevelopment
Downtown Revitalization Project
Greenville, South Carolina

THIS AGREEMENT, . . . made on or as of the _____ day of _____, 19 ____, by and between the City of Greenville, South Carolina, a Municipality (hereinafter called "City"), and the Greenville Community Corporation, a corporation organized under the laws of South Carolina (hereinafter called "GCC"),

WITNESSETH:

WHEREAS, in furtherance of the objectives of the laws of the State of South Carolina, the City of Greenville, South Carolina, has undertaken a program for the clearance and revitalization of slum and blighted areas in the Central Business District of the City, and in this connection is engaged in carrying out a redevelopment project known as The Downtown Revitalization Project (hereinafter called "Project") in an area (hereinafter called "Project Area") located in the Central Business District, and

WHEREAS, as of the date of the Agreement, there has been prepared a Redevelopment Plan for the Project approved by the City Council on June 21, 1977, in resolution No. 77–12(R), and

WHEREAS, a copy of the Redevelopment Plan is on file with the City Clerk for the City of Greenville and on the date of the finalization of the Agreement, land controls and restrictions for parcels referenced in Schedule A attached and herein incorporated by reference into this Agreement, have been recorded among the land records for the place in which the Project Area is situated, namely, the Register of Mesne Conveyance of Greenville County in Book _____ at Page ____, and

WHEREAS, to achieve the objectives of the Redevelopment Plan and particularly to make Project Area land available for redevelopment by private enterprise and in accordance with the uses specified in the Redevelopment Plan and this Agreement, the City has undertaken to provide and has provided a substantial degree of aid and assistance through various funding sources, and

WHEREAS, the City has offered to sell and the GCC is willing to purchase certain real property located in the Project Area, and more particularly described in Schedule A annexed hereto and made part hereof (which property as so described is hereinafter called "Property") and to redevelop the property for and in accordance with the uses specified in the Redevelopment Plan and in accordance with this Agreement, and

WHEREAS, the City believes that the redevelopment of the property pursuant to the Agreement, and the fulfillment generally of this Agreement, are in the vital and best interest of the City and the health, safety, morals and welfare of its residents and in accord with the public purposes and provisions of applicable Federal, State and local laws and requirements under which the Project has been undertaken and is being assisted,

NOW, THEREFORE, in consideration of the promises and mutual obligations of the parties hereto, each of them does hereby covenant and agree with the other as follows:

Section 1. Sale: Purchase Price.

Subject to all the terms, covenants and conditions of the Agreement, the City will sell the property to the GCC for, and the GCC will purchase the property from the City and pay therefor, the amount of Seven Hundred Ninety Thousand Dollars ($790,000), in accordance with Schedule A to be paid in cash, or by certified check simultaneously with the delivery of the deed conveying each parcel of property referenced in Schedule A to GCC.

Section 2. Conveyance of Property.

(a) *Form of Deed.* The City shall convey to the GCC title to the property by warranty deeds (hereinafter collectively called "deeds"). Such conveyance and title shall, in addition to the condition subsequent provided for in Section 704 hereof, and to all other conditions, covenants and restrictions set forth or referred to elsewhere in the Agreement, be subject to:

[Insert land controls and restrictions, exceptions found in title policy and any other reservations, encumbrances or exceptions.]

(b) *Time and Place for Delivery of Deed.* The City shall deliver the deed and possession of the property to the GCC in accordance with Schedule A, or on such earlier date as the parties may mutually agree in writing. Conveyance shall be made at the principal office of the City, and the GCC shall accept such conveyance and pay the purchase price to the City at such time and place.

(c) *Apportionment of Current Taxes.* The portion of the current taxes, if any, on the property which are a lien at the date of delivery of the deed to the GCC allocable to buildings and other improvements which have been demolished or removed from the property by the City shall be borne by the City, and the portion of such current taxes allocable to the land shall be apportioned between the City and the GCC as of the date of the delivery of the deed. If the amount of the current taxes on the property is not ascertainable on such date, the apportionment between the City and the GCC shall be on the basis of the amount of the most recent ascertainable taxes on the property, but such apportionment shall be subject to final adjustment within thirty (30) days after the date the actual amounts of such current taxes is ascertained.

(d) *Recordation of Deed.* The GCC shall promptly file the deed for recordation among the land records at the place in which the property is situated. The City shall assume the cost of documentary stamps and recording fees.

Section 3. Good Faith Deposit.

(a) *Amount.* The GCC has, prior to or simultaneously with the execution of this Agreement by the City delivered to the City a good faith deposit of cash or a certified check satisfactory to the City in the amount of One Hundred Thousand Dollars ($100,000), hereinafter called "Deposit," as security for the performance of the obligations of the GCC to be performed prior to the return of the deposit to the GCC, or its retention by the City prior to conveyance, as the case may be, in accordance with this Agreement.

The Deposit shall be deposited in an account of the City in a bank or trust company selected by it.

(b) *Interest.* The City shall be under no obligation to pay or earn interest on the deposit, but if interest is payable thereon, such interest when received by the City shall be promptly paid to the GCC.

(c) *Application to Purchase Price.* In the event the GCC is otherwise entitled to return of the deposit pursuant to Paragraph (e) of this Section, upon written request of the GCC, the amount of the deposit shall be applied on account of the purchase price at the time payment of the purchase price is made in accordance with Schedule A.

(d) *Retention by the City.* Upon termination of the Agreement as provided in Section 703 hereof, the deposit as listed in Schedule A or the proceeds of the deposit, if not theretofore returned to the GCC pursuant to Paragraph (e) of this Section, including all interest payable on such deposit or the proceeds thereof after such termination, such shall be retained by the City.

(e) *Return to GCC.* Upon termination of the Agreement, as provided in Section 702 hereof, the deposit shall be returned to the GCC by the City as provided in Section 702 hereof. The City shall return a portion of the deposit to the GCC upon tender of the purchase price for the parcels in accordance with Schedule A and upon receipt by the City of the following:

(1) A copy of the commitment or commitments obtained by the GCC for the mortgage loan or loans to assist in financing the construction of the improvements (as defined in Section 301 hereof), certified by the GCC to be a true and correct copy or copies thereof;

(2) Evidence satisfactory to the City that the interim mortgage loan or loans to assist in financing the construction of the improvements have been initially closed;

(3) A copy of the contract between the GCC and the General Contractor or Contractors for the construction of the improvements, certified by the GCC to be a true and correct copy thereof; and

(4) A copy of the contract bond provided by the General Contractor or Contractors in connection with the aforesaid construction contract or contracts which bond or bonds shall be in a penal sum equal to and not less than ten percent (10%) of the contract price under said construction contract, certified by the GCC to be a true and correct copy thereof.

Section 4. Time for Commencement and Completion of Improvements.

The construction of the improvements referred to in Section 301 hereof shall be commenced in accordance with Part III of this Agreement.

Section 5. Time for Certain Other Actions.

(a) *Time for Submission of Construction Plans.*

(1) Phase I. (As referenced in Part III of this Agreement) The time within which the GCC shall submit its "Construction Plans" (as defined in Section 301 hereof) to the City in any event, pursuant to Section 301 hereof, shall be not later than ninety (90) days from the date of the Agreement.

(2) Phase II. (As referenced in Part III of this Agreement) The time within which the GCC shall submit its "Construction Plans" (as defined in Section 301 hereof) to the City in any event, pursuant to Section 301 hereof, shall be not later than eight (8) months from the date of the Agreement.

(3) Phase III. (As referenced in Part III of this Agreement) The time within which the GCC shall submit its "Construction Plans" (as defined in Section 301 hereof) to the City in any event, pursuant to Section 301 hereof, shall be not later than one (1) year from the date of the Agreement.

(b) *Time for Submission of Corrected Construction Plans.* Except as provided in Paragraph (c) of this Section 5, the time in which the GCC shall submit any new or corrected construction plans as provided for in Section 301 hereof, shall be not later than thirty (30) days after the date the GCC receives written notice from the City of the City's rejection of the construction plans referred to in the latest such notice.

(c) *Maximum Time for Approved Construction Plans.* In any event, the time within which the GCC shall submit construction plans which conform to the requirements of Section 301 hereof, and are approved by the City, shall not be later than sixty (60) days after the date the GCC receives written notice from the City of the City's first rejection of the original construction plans submitted by the GCC.

(d) *Time for City Action on Change in Construction Plans.* The time within which the City may reject any change in the construction plans, as provided in Section 302 hereof, shall be fifteen (15) days after the date of the City's receipt of notice of such change.

(e) *Time for Submission of Evidence of Equity Capital and Mortgage Financing.* The time within which the GCC shall submit to the City, in any event, the evidence as to equity capital and any commitment necessary for mortgage financing as provided in Section 303 hereof, shall not be later than thirty (30) days after the date of the written notice to the GCC of approval of the construction plans by the City, or, if the construction plans shall be deemed to have been approved as provided in Section 301 hereof, after the expiration of thirty (30) days following the date of receipt by the City of the construction plans so deemed approved.

Section 6. Period of Duration of Covenant on Use.

The covenant pertaining to the use of the property, as set forth in Section 401 hereof, shall remain in effect from the date of the deed until December 31, 1999, the period specified or referred to in the Redevelopment Plan, or until such date thereafter to which it may be extended by a proper amendment of the Redevelopment Plan, on which date, as the case may be, such covenant shall terminate.

Section 7. Notices and Demands.

A notice, demand or other communication under Agreement by either party to the other shall be sufficiently given or delivered if it is dispatched by registered or certified mail, postage prepaid, return receipt requested, or delivered personally, and

(a) in the case of the GCC, is addressed to or delivered personally to the GCC at: _____ ; and

(b) in the case of the City, is addressed to or delivered

personally to the City at: P.O. Box 2207, Greenville, South Carolina, 29602; or at such other addresses with respect to said parties as that party may, from time to time, designate in writing and forward to the others as provided in this

Extracts from
"Terms and Conditions
Part II
of
Contract for
Sale of Land for Private Redevelopment
by and between
the City of Greenville
and
Greenville Community Corporation"

ARTICLE I. PREPARATION OF PROPERTY FOR REDEVELOPMENT

SEC. 101. Work to Be Performed by City. The city shall, prior to conveyance of the Property and without expense to the GCC, prepare the Property for redevelopment by the GCC in accordance with the Redevelopment Plan and the Agreement. Such preparation of the Property shall consist of the following (unless the City and the GCC hereafter agree in writing that any of such preparation shall not be done, or that it shall be done subsequent to the conveyance of the Property):

(a) *Demolition and Removal.* The demolition and removal to the surface elevation of the adjoining ground of all existing buildings, other structures and improvements on the Property, including the removal of all bricks, lumber, pipes, equipment and other material, and all debris and rubbish resulting from such demolition, except such material and debris as may be used for any filling required by this Section.

(b) *Reduction of Walls.* The reduction of all walls, including foundation walls, to the surface elevation of the adjoining ground.

(c) *Breaking Up Basement Floors.* The breaking up of all basement or cellar floors sufficiently to permit proper drainage.

(d) *Removal of Paving.* The removal by the City or by the appropriate public body of all paving (including catch basins, curbs, gutters, drives, and sidewalks) within or on the Property.

(e) *Removal of Public Utility Lines.* The removal or abandonment by the City or by the appropriate public body or public utility company of all public utility lines, installations, facilities, and related equipment within or on the Property.

(f) *Filling and Grading.* Such filling, grading, and leveling of the land (but not including topsoil or landscaping) as will permit proper drainage and place the Property in a safe, clean, sanitary, and nonhazardous condition.

(g) *Filling Materials.* The filling of all basements or other excavations exposed as a result of the work performed by the City pursuant to this Section, with noncombustible materials to a level twelve (12) inches below the surface of the adjoining ground on all sides thereof.

SEC. 102. Expenses, Income, and Salvage. All expenses, including current taxes, if any, relating to buildings or other structures demolished in accordance with Section 101 hereof shall be borne by, and all income or salvage received as a result of the demolition of such buildings or structures shall belong to, the City.

SEC. 103. City's Responsibilities for Certain Other Actions. The City without expense to the GCC or assessment or claim against the Property and prior to completion of the Improvements (or at such earlier time or times as the GCC and the City may agree in writing), shall, in accordance with the Redevelopment Plan, provide or secure or cause to be provided or secured, the following:

(a) *Vacation of Streets, Etc.* The closing and vacation of all existing streets, alleys, and other public rights-of-way within or abutting on the Property.

(b) *Replatting, Resubdivision, or Rezoning.* The replatting, resubdivision, or rezoning of the Property, if necessary for the conveyance thereof to the GCC.

(c) *Improvements of Existing Streets.* The improvement (by the City or by the appropriate public body) by resurfacing, rebuilding, or new construction, in accordance with the technical specifications, standards, and practices of the City, of the existing streets, alleys, or other public rights-of-way (including catch basins, curbs and gutters, drive and curb cuts, and drives between the property line of the Property and the public rights-of-way) abutting on the Property.

(d) *Construction and Dedication of New Streets.* The construction (by the Agency or by the appropriate public body), in accordance with the technical specifications, standards, and practices of the City, and the dedication of all new streets, alleys, and other public rights-of-way (including catch basins, curbs, and gutters) abutting on the Property.

(e) *Installation of Sidewalks.* The installation (by the City or by the appropriate public body), in accordance with the technical specifications, standards, and practices of the City, of public sidewalks along the frontage of the public streets abutting on the Property or within the rights-of-way lines of such public streets, together with sodding or seeding of any such public area between such sidewalks and the curb lines of such public streets.

(f) *Street Lighting, Signs, and Fire Hydrants.* The installation (by the City or by the appropriate public body), in accordance with the technical specifications, standards, and practices by the City, of street lighting, signs, and fire hydrants in connection with all new streets abutting on the Property and to be constructed pursuant to this Section.

(g) *Installation of Public Utilities.* The installation or relocation (by the City or by the appropriate public body or public utility company) of such sewers, drains, water and gas distribution lines, electric, telephone, and telegraph lines, and all other public utility lines, installations, and facilities as are necessary to be installed or relocated on or in connection with the Property by reason of the redevelopment contemplated by the Redevelopment Plan and the development of the Property: *Provided,* That the City shall not be responsible for, nor bear any portion of the cost of, installing the necessary utility connections within the boundaries of the Property between the Improvements to be constructed on the Property by the GCC and the water, sanitary sewer, and storm drain mains or other public utility lines owned by the City or by any public utility company within or without such boundaries, or electric, gas, telephone, or other public utility lines owned by any public utility company within or without such boundaries, and the GCC shall secure any permits required for any such installation without cost or expense to the City.

(h) *Soil Borings.* Soil borings shall be conducted by a qualified engineer using a standard 50-foot grid system or as is otherwise mutually agreed upon by the City and GCC.

SEC. 104. Waiver of Claims and Joining in Petitions by GCC. The GCC hereby waives (as the purchaser of the Property under the Agreement and as the owner after the

conveyance of the Property provided for in the Agreement) any and all claims to awards of damages, if any, to compensate for the closing, vacation, or change of grade of any street, alley, or other public right-of-way within or fronting or abutting on, or adjacent to, the Property which, pursuant to subdivision (a) of Section 103 hereof, is to be closed or vacated, or the grade of which is to be changed, and shall upon the request of the City subscribe to, and join with, the Agency in any petition or proceeding required for such vacation, dedication, change of grade, and, to the extent necessary, rezoning, and execute any waiver or other document in respect thereof.

ARTICLE III. CONSTRUCTION PLANS; CONSTRUCTION OF IMPROVEMENTS; CERTIFICATE OF COMPLETION

SEC. 301. Plans for Construction of Improvements. Plans and specifications with respect to the redevelopment of the Property and the construction of improvements thereon shall be in conformity with the Redevelopment Plan, the Agreement, and all applicable State and local laws and regulations. As promptly as possible after the date of the Agreement, and, in any event, no later than the time specified therefor in Paragraph (a), Section 5 of Part I hereof, the GCC shall submit to the City for approval by the City, plans, drawings, specifications, and related documents, and the proposed construction schedule (which plans, drawings, specifications, related documents, and progress schedule, together with any and all changes therein that may thereafter be made and submitted to the City as herein provided, are, except as otherwise clearly indicated by the context, hereinafter collectively called "Construction Plans") with respect to the improvements to be constructed by the GCC on the Property, in sufficient completeness and detail to show that such improvements and construction thereof will be in accordance with the provisions of the Redevelopment Plan and the Agreement. The City shall, if the Construction Plans originally submitted conform to the provisions of the Redevelopment Plan and the Agreement, approve in writing such Construction Plans and no further filing by the GCC or approval by the City thereof shall be required except with respect to any material change. Such Construction Plans shall, in any event, be deemed approved unless rejection thereof in writing by the City in whole or in part, setting forth in detail the reasons therefor, shall be made within thirty (30) days after the date of their receipt by the City. If the City so rejects the Construction Plans in whole or in part as not being in conformity with the Redevelopment Plan or the Agreement, the GCC shall submit new or corrected Construction Plans which are in conformity with the Redevelopment Plan and the Agreement, within the time specified therefor in Paragraph (b), Section 5 of Part I hereof, after written notification to the GCC of the rejection. The provisions of this Section relating to approval, rejection, and resubmission of corrected Construction Plans hereinabove provided with respect to the original Construction Plans shall continue to apply until the Construction Plans have been approved by the City: *Provided,* That in any event the GCC shall submit Construction Plans which are in conformity with the requirements of the Redevelopment Plan and the Agreement, as determined by the City no later than the time specified therefor in Paragraph (c), Section 5 of Part I hereof. All work with respect to the improvements to be constructed or provided by the GCC on the Property shall be in conformity with the Construction Plans as approved by the City. The term "Improvements," as used in this Agreement, shall be deemed to have reference to the improvements as provided and specified in the Construction Plans as so approved.

SEC. 302. Changes in Construction Plans. If the GCC desires to make any change in the Construction Plans after their approval by the City, the GCC shall submit the proposed change to the City for its approval. If the Construction Plans, as modified by the proposed change, conform to the requirements of Section 301 hereof with respect to such previously approved Construction Plans, the City shall approve the proposed change and notify the GCC in writing of its approval. Such change in the Construction Plans shall, in any event, be deemed approved by the City unless rejection thereof, in whole or in part, by written notice thereof by the City to the GCC setting forth in detail the reasons therefor, shall be made within the period specified therefor in Paragraph (d), Section 5 of Part I hereof.

SEC. 303. Evidence of Equity Capital and Mortgage Financing. As promptly as possible after approval by the City of the Construction Plans, and, in any event, no later than the time specified therefor in Paragraph (e), Section 5 of Part I hereof, the GCC shall submit to the City evidence satisfactory to the City that the GCC has the equity capital and commitments for mortgage financing necessary for the construction of the Improvements.

ARTICLE IV. RESTRICTIONS UPON USE OF PROPERTY

SEC. 401. Restrictions on Use. The GCC agrees for itself, and its successors and assigns, and every successor in interest to the Property, or any part thereof, and the Deed shall contain covenants on the part of the GCC for itself, and such successors and assigns, that the GCC and such successors and assigns, shall:

(a) Devote the Property to, and only to and in accordance with, the uses specified in the Redevelopment Plan; and

(b) Not discriminate upon the basis of race, color, creed, or national origin in the sale, lease, or rental or in the use or occupancy of the Property or any improvements erected or to be erected thereon, or any part thereof.

ARTICLE VII. REMEDIES

SEC. 701. In General. Except as otherwise provided in the Agreement, in the event of any default in or breach of the Agreement, or any of its terms or conditions, by either party hereto, or any successor to such party, such party (or successor) shall, upon written notice from the other, proceed immediately to cure or remedy such default or breach, and, in any event, within sixty (60) days after receipt of such notice. In case such action is not taken or not diligently pursued, or the default or breach shall not be cured or remedied within a reasonable time, the aggrieved party may institute such proceedings as may be necessary or desirable in its opinion to cure and remedy such default or breach, including, but not limited to, proceedings to compel specific performance by the party in default or breach of its obligations.

SEC. 702. Termination by GCC Prior to Conveyance. In the event that

(a) the City does not tender conveyance of the Property, or possession thereof, in the manner and condition, and by the date, provided in the Agreement, and any such failure shall not be cured within thirty (30) days after the date of written demand by the Redeveloper; or

(b) the GCC shall, after preparation of Construction Plans satisfactory to the City, furnish evidence satisfactory to the City that it has been unable, after and despite diligent effort for a period of sixty (60) days after approval by the City of the Construction Plans, to obtain mortgage financing for the construction of the Improvements on a basis and on terms that would generally be considered satisfactory by builders or contractors for improvements of the nature and type provided in such Construction Plans, and the GCC shall, after having submitted such evidence and if so requested by the City continue to make diligent efforts to obtain such financing for a period of sixty (60) days after such request, but without success;

Then the Agreement shall, at the option of the GCC, be terminated by written notice thereof to the City with respect to the particular parcel referenced in Schedule A that is affected by one or both of the above conditions, and, except with respect to the return of deposit as provided in Paragraph (e), Section 3 of Part I hereof, neither the City nor the GCC shall have any further rights against or liability to the other under the Agreement.

SEC. 703. Termination by City Prior to Conveyance. In the event that

(a) prior to conveyance of the Property to the Redeveloper and in violation of the Agreement

(i) the GCC (or any successor in interest) assigns or attempts to assign the Agreement or any rights therein, or in the Property, or

(ii) there is any change in the ownership or distribution of the stock of the GCC or with respect to the identity of the parties in control of the GCC or the degree thereof; or

(b) the GCC does not submit Construction Plans, as required by the Agreement, or (except as excused under subdivision (b) of Section 702 hereof) evidence that it has the necessary equity capital and mortgage financing, in satisfactory form and in the manner and by the dates respectively provided in the Agreement therefor; or

(c) the GCC does not pay the Purchase Price and take title to the Property upon tender of conveyance by the City pursuant to the Agreement, and if any default or failure referred to in subdivisions (b) and (c) of this Section 703 shall not be cured within thirty (30) days after the date of written demand by the City;

Then the Agreement, and any rights of the GCC, or any assignee or transferee, in the Agreement, or arising therefrom with respect to the City or the Property, shall, at the option of the City be terminated by the City in which event, as provided in Paragraph (d), Section 3 of Part I hereof, the Deposit shall be retained by the City as liquidated damages and as its property without any deduction, offset, or recoupment whatsoever, and neither the GCC (or assignee or transferee) nor the City shall have any further rights against or liability to the other under the Agreement with respect to the particular parcel(s).

SEC. 704. Revesting Title in City upon Happening of Event Subsequent to Conveyance to GCC. In the event that subsequent to conveyance of the Property or any part thereof to the GCC and prior to completion of the Improvements as certified by the City

(a) the GCC (or successor in interest) shall default in or violate its obligations with respect to the construction of the Improvements (including the nature and the dates for the beginning and completion thereof), or shall abandon or substantially suspend construction work, and any such default, violation, abandonment, or suspension shall not be cured, ended, or remedied within three (3) months (six (6) months, if the default is with respect to the date for completion of the Improvements) after written demand by the City so to do; or

(b) the GCC (or successor in interest) shall fail to pay real estate taxes or assessments on the Property or any part thereof when due, or shall place thereon any encumbrance or lien unauthorized by the Agreement, or shall suffer any levy or attachment to be made, or any materialmen's or

mechanics' lien, or any other unauthorized encumbrance or lien to attach, and such taxes or assessments shall not have been paid, or the encumbrance or lien removed or discharged or provision satisfactory to the City made for such payment, removal, or discharge, within ninety (90) days after written demand by the City so to do; or

(c) there is, in violation of the Agreement, any transfer of the Property or any part thereof, or any change in the ownership or distribution of the stock of the GCC or with respect to the identity of the parties in control of the GCC or the degree thereof, and such violation shall not be cured within sixty (60) days after written demand by the City to the GCC;

Then the City shall have the right to reenter and take possession of the Property and to terminate (and revest in the City) the estate conveyed by the Deed to the GCC it being the intent of this provision, together with other provisions of the Agreement, that the conveyance of the Property to the GCC shall be made upon, and that the Deed shall contain, a condition subsequent to the effect that in the event of any default, failure, violation, or other action or inaction by the GCC specified in subdivisions (a), (b), and (c) of this Section 704, failure on the part of the GCC to remedy, end, or abrogate such default, failure, violation, or other action or inaction, within the period and in the manner stated in such subdivisions, the City at its option may declare a termination in favor of the City of the title, and of all the rights and interests in and to the Property conveyed by the Deed to the GCC and that such title and all rights and interests of the GCC and any assigns or successors in interest to and in the Property, shall revert to the City: *Provided,* That such condition subsequent and any revesting of title as a result thereof in the City

(1) shall always be subject to and limited by, and shall not defeat, render invalid, or limit in any way, (i) the lien of any mortgage authorized by the Agreement, and (ii) any rights or interests provided in the Agreement for the protection of the holders of such mortgages; and

(2) shall not apply to individual parts or parcels of the Property (or, in the case of parts or parcels leased, the leasehold interest) on which the Improvements to be constructed thereon have been completed in accordance with the Agreement and for which a certificate of completion is issued therefor as provided in Section 307 hereof.

In addition to, and without in any way limiting the City's right to reentry as provided for in the preceding sentence, the City shall have the right to retain the Deposit, as provided in Paragraph (d), Section 3 of Part I hereof, without any deduction, offset, or recoupment whatsoever, in the event of a default, violation, or failure of the GCC as specified in the preceding sentence.

It is further provided that, in the event of a default, violation, or failure of the GCC as specified in this Section; and in addition to the City's right of reentry and retainer of the deposit as provided in Paragraph (d), Section 3 of Part I hereof; the GCC shall pay liquidated damages to the City in the following manner:

(1) For a default, violation, or failure of the GCC as specified in this section related to the development of Phase I, as delineated in Part III of this Agreement, the liquidated damages shall be _____.

(2) For a default, violation, or failure of the GCC as specified in this section related to the development of Phase II, as delineated in Part III of this Agreement, the liquidated damages shall be _____.

SEC. 704.1 Default by the City

(1) For a default, violation, or failure of the City as specified in this section related to the development of Phase I, as delineated in Part III of this Agreement, the liquidated damages shall be _____.

(2) For a default, violation, or failure of the City as specified in this section related to the development of Phase II, as delineated in Part III of this Agreement, the liquidated damages shall be _____.

APPENDIX F

Subordinated Lease Agreement
Civic Center Lease

THIS LEASE, made and entered into in Greenville, South Carolina, this _____ day of _____, 1978, by and between THE CITY OF GREENVILLE, a municipal corporation chartered under the laws of the State of South Carolina (hereinafter referred to as "Lessor"); and GREENVILLE COMMUNITY CORPORATION, a corporation organized and existing under the laws of the State of South Carolina (hereinafter referred to as "Lessee");

WITNESSETH:

WHEREAS, Lessor is, or will become, the owner of certain real property located on Main Street in Greenville, South Carolina, . . . ; and

WHEREAS, said parcel of property is or will become a portion of a larger development to be constructed and operated in conjunction with a number of parties, said project to consist of a civic center, a hotel, retail space, an office building, a common "atrium" servicing all portions of the development, and additional common areas serving the public and the facilities within the development; and

WHEREAS, Lessor has made plans to construct upon the property . . . as an integral part of said larger project, a civic center, and has agreed to lease said civic center to the Lessee; and

WHEREAS, Lessee has made plans and has agreed to lease such civic center from the Lessor and to operate it for the benefit of the public and the users of the other facilities included within said project, all upon terms and conditions hereinafter set forth;

NOW, THEREFORE, in consideration of the rental payments hereinafter described and other forms of consideration, as well as the mutual covenants and promises set forth herein; the parties hereto agree as follows:

Lessor does hereby demise and lease unto the Lessee, and the Lessee does hereby lease and take from the Lessor, the real estate . . . , together with and including all buildings and other improvements thereon or to be constructed thereon, in accordance with the terms set forth below.

1. **CONSTRUCTION OF IMPROVEMENTS.** Lessor shall construct upon the leased premises a civic center, consisting of meeting rooms, banquet facilities, a kitchen, together with appropriate kitchen equipment, and certain other related improvements, all of which are to be constructed in accordance with architectural plans and specifications prepared or to be prepared by architects selected by Lessor and approved by Lessee. All obligations of Lessee hereunder are subject to its approval of such plans and specifications, and to Lessor's compliance with such plans and specifications in the actual construction of said improvements, which approval on the part of Lessee shall in no event be unreasonably withheld.

2. **LEASE TERM.** The term of this Lease shall begin on that date when the architects referred to above shall have given final approval to construction of said improvements and shall have determined that the civic center is completely ready for operation as such, provided all necessary occupancy permits shall also have been issued by appropriate governmental authorities. The term of the Lease shall be a period of thirty (30) years.

3. **RENTAL PAYMENTS.**

(a) Lessee shall pay to Lessor, subject to terms and conditions hereinafter set forth, an annual "Minimum Rental" of $50,000. Said rental obligation is payable only out of "Available Cash Flow" from the overall operation of various elements of the aforesaid project to be owned and/or operated by Lessee or its assignees. For purposes of determining "Available Cash Flow", operational income from all of the following facilities shall be taken into consideration: hotel, office building, and leased retail space. All of these facilities shall be built on land owned or leased by Lessee, and shall be operated by one or more companies pursuant to one or more leases, subleases, and operational agreements entered into by the Lessee. These facilities, improvements, and operations are hereinafter together referred to as "The Project".

"Available Cash Flow" from the Project shall be determined on an annual basis, and any and all rentals payable to Lessor hereunder shall be due on April 1 of the following year. "Available Cash Flow" shall consist of the gross operational income from The Project for a calendar year, less (i) all sums required for the operation of all facets of The Project, including personnel expenses, utilities, insurance, maintenance, security, supplies, and other expenses reasonably and fairly attributable to the operation of such facilities; and (ii) payment of interest and principal installments on any loans secured by first mortgages on any portion of The Project. The "Available Cash Flow" after payment (or making necessary reserves for payment) of all such amounts shall then be divided equally, up to $100,000, between the Minimum Rental payment to the Lessor hereunder, and the payment of certain accrued and current interest which will be due on notes from the entity or entities operating The Project to Camel Company, a partnership consisting of Lessee and other parties, which partnership is or shall own the land on which The Project is constructed, and which shall have loaned moneys to the entities operating The Project for use in the construction thereof.

(b) Lessor shall also pay to Lessee, as "Additional Rental", from "Available Cash Flow" above $100,000 per year, amounts equal to the following:

(i) 10% of gross revenues from the sale of food and non-alcoholic beverages within the civic center during the year; and

(ii) 12% of the gross revenues from the sale of alcoholic beverages within the civic center during the year. The Additional Rentals shall be payable only out of the balance of "Available Cash Flow" for any year remaining after the $100,000 allocation described above, and after payment by such operational entities of all accrued and current interest on any notes due from such operational entities to the Camel Company. For purposes of this provision, "gross revenues" shall consist of total revenues received from all such sales, less rebates and overcharges, complimentary meals served to speakers, etc., sales taxes collected from customers, uncollectible items or bad debts, refunds to customers, credit card charges paid to credit card companies, and similar allowances and set-offs. Lessor shall have reasonable access to the books and records of such operational entities and of Lessee for purposes of verifying the amounts of Additional Rentals, if any, to be paid under these provisions in any year. Not later than sixty (60) days after the end of each fiscal year, Lessee shall submit or cause to be submitted accurate and complete statements of all accounts of the operating entities, as may be necessary or appropriate in order to determine the amount of Additional Rentals and the balance of "Available Cash Flow", if any, from which such payments may be made.

4. **USE OF PREMISES.** Lessee may use the premises for any lawful commercial purpose. It is the expectation of the parties herewith that Lessee shall rent, lease, or license space within the leased premises for meetings and social occasions, to customers of and guests in the aforesaid hotel as well as to members of the public and various types of organizations and agencies. Lessee and its assignee(s) under this Lease shall also provide food and beverage service on the premises to such uses and customers. Lessee shall have exclusive control over, and exclusive right to establish, rentals, charges, and prices to be collected for use of such space and for food and beverage sales and service within the premises. In setting and applying such prices and rates, Lessee shall not discriminate between individuals or groups, provided that any differences in rates or prices based upon certain valid and pertinent factors shall not constitute discrimination, and that among such factors shall be (i) date of advance reservations, (ii) size of group, (iii) extent and frequency of use of civic center and/or hotel by the customer, and (iv) expectation of excessive demand within the Greenville area during certain periods of the year, based on previous experience of the hotel and civic center operator as well as the operators of comparable facilities (such as the textile exhibitions).

5. **FIXTURES AND FURNISHINGS.** Lessor shall provide and install, as an intrinsic element of the leased premises delivered to Lessee at the beginning of the lease term, a complete commercial kitchen adequate for the preparation of meals and beverages for large groups of people, in accordance with the aforesaid plans and specifications to be provided by architects. Lessor shall likewise purchase and provide all furnishings necessary and appropriate for the kitchen and all food and beverage serving areas, such as cookware, silverware, china, serving dishes, tables, chairs, tablecloths, and related items. This obligation shall also include the provision of chairs, tables, rostrums, public address systems, and other furniture and furnishings as may be appropriate for meetings, small conventions, seminars, and similar activities within the civic center. After providing said items initially, Lessor shall have no further responsibility for repairing or replacing any such items of personal property. Lessee shall utilize such personal property in its operation of the civic center, and shall replace and repair them at its own expense thereafter. Since all such items shall have a useful life shorter than the term of this Lease, Lessee shall not be expected to return any such items of personal property to Lessor upon the expiration of the Lease term and any such items of personal property which may be purchased by and brought onto the premises by Lessee during the term shall be the sole property of Lessee, and may be removed from the premises by Lessee upon the termination of this Lease.

Lessee shall conduct its business in accordance with applicable laws, statutes, ordinances, and regulations, provided no alleged illegal or unlawful uses of the premises shall constitute breaches of this Lease unless and until such illegality shall have been adjudicated to exist, and then only if such adjudication can be made the basis for substantially curtailing the use of the premises. Lessee shall keep the interior of the leased premises in reasonably good repair and shall not intentionally nor carelessly permit waste to be committed upon or destruction to be inflicted upon improvements constructed or to be constructed by the Lessor. Throughout the term of this Lease, Lessee shall carry and pay for comprehensive public liability insurance in a policy or policies acceptable to Lessor which shall protect both Lessor and Lessee with limits of not less than $500,000 for a single claim, $1,000,000 for multiple claims arising from a single accident or occurrence. Lessee shall also carry and pay for fire and extended insurance coverage in amounts suitable to Lessor, though Lessor shall in no event require such limits to be more than the insurable value of the premises.

6. **ACCESS TO CIVIC CENTER.** Lessor has made plans and has agreed to construct at its sole expense a common entrance/lobby area, or "atrium", to provide access from Main Street in Greenville, South Carolina, to the civic center, the hotel, and various other portions of The Project. Lessee is hereby granted the right to use, in common with Lessor, as a means of ingress and egress for its customers, officers, employees, invitees, and visitors, all portions of the aforesaid atrium, including all space originally constructed in the atrium and any space which may be added at any time in the future. It is understood and agreed that the atrium will be open to a public street at all hours and on all days, and that Lessor will construct no barriers or other facilities to prevent access to the civic center by such customers and other parties at any time when the Lessee may choose to grant such access to such parties. Lessor shall cause the plans and specifications for the atrium to be prepared prior to the beginning of this Lease term, and Lessee's approval of such plans and specifications shall constitute an additional condition precedent to its obligations hereunder, provided such approval shall not be unreasonably withheld.

7. **ASSIGNMENT AND SUBLEASING.** Lessee shall have the right to assign or to sublet all or any portion of its rights under this Lease as to all or any portion of the leased premises, to any part at any time; provided, such assignment or sublease shall not have the effect of relieving Lessee from its obligation to make rental payments under the terms and conditions set forth herein.

8. **SIGNS AND ADVERTISING.** Subject to Lessor's approval, which approval shall not be unreasonably withheld, Lessee and its assignees and sublessees shall have the right to erect upon the leased premises reasonable signs and advertising relating to the business authorized by this Lease. Lessee shall also have, subject to Lessor approval as stated above, the right to install signs at various locations within the "atrium" and other portions of The Project owned or operated by Lessor, for the purpose of directing its customers to the civic center itself and to

specific portions of the civic center, and to advertise the existence and location of the civic center itself. Lessee agrees that all such signs shall be consistent with the architectural design and decor of the "atrium" and any other portions of The Project on which they shall be located.

9. UTILITIES. The improvements to be contracted by Lessor on the leased premises shall include a complete self-contained heating and air-conditioning system appropriate for the civic center. Once said system or systems have been completed and certified to be ready for operation by appropriate inspectors, Lessee shall be obligated to pay all utility costs and charges for the leased premises, including electricity, water, sewerage service, and natural gas.

10. REPAIRS AND MAINTENANCE. Lessee shall be responsible for regular and ordinary maintenance of all improvements built on or placed upon the leased premises, and shall provide and pay for all janitorial services, security services, supplies, and similar ordinary maintenance charges. Lessee shall also maintain in good repair the floors, stairwells, interior walls, ceiling coverings, and similar portions of the buildings themselves on the leased premises. Lessor shall be responsible for repairs to and replacement of the exterior walls, roof, and structural members of any buildings constructed on the premises. Lessor shall also be responsible for major repairs to and replacement of the heating and air-conditioning system, except any repairs necessitated by the willful or careless acts of Lessee or any or its assignees, sublessees, or any customers, employees, or invitees of any of such parties.

11. TAXES. Since the Lessor is a municipal corporation, it is not anticipated that any ad valorem taxes shall be levied upon the leased premises as described herein at any time during the term of this Lease. However, in the event any such ad valorem taxes shall be so levied by any party against the real property . . . or any personal property purchased and provided by the Lessor under this Lease, the amount thereof shall be paid by the Lessee and the same shall be deducted from any rent required to be paid by the Lessee to the Lessor at any time in the future. Lessee shall have the right to actively oppose the imposition of any such taxes, and Lessor and Lessee will cooperate in all respects in pursuing such opposition. Lessee shall be responsible for and shall promptly pay any taxes assessed against any personal property which Lessee purchases and places upon the leased premises.

12. CONDEMNATION. If, during the term of this Lease, the leased premises or any portion thereof shall be taken, appropriated or condemned by reason of eminent domain, Lessor shall be entitled to the award or proceeds for the value of its fee simple interest in the property. . . . Lessee shall be entitled to the award or proceeds for the value of its leasehold estate. There shall be such abatement of rent and other adjustments made as may be just and equitable under the circumstances.

13. MECHANIC'S LIENS. During the term of this Lease, there shall be no mechanic's liens upon the leased premises and the buildings and improvements located thereon, arising through the act of Lessee or any person claiming under, by or through the Lessee, and no person shall ever be or become entitled to any lien, directly or indirectly derived through or under Lessee, or through or under any act or omission of the Lessee, superior in rank or dignity to that of this Lease reserved to the Lessor upon the leased premises, or upon any insurance policies or insurance moneys received for or on account of any materials or things whatsoever; and nothing in this Lease shall be construed in such a way as to contradict this provision. The mere fact of the filing of a mechanic's lien or materialman's lien, however, shall not of itself operate as a for-

feiture or termination of this Lease, provided the Lessee, within thirty (30) days after notice of the recording of such lien in the appropriate recording office of Greenville County, South Carolina, causes the same to be cancelled, released, or extinguished, or causes the premises to be released therefrom by the posting of a bond or other method prescribed by law. All persons with whom the Lessee may deal are hereby put on notice that the Lessee has no power to subject Lessor's interest to any claim for mechanic's or materialman's liens or any other liens, and all persons dealing with Lessee must look solely to the credit of the Lessee and the Lessee's assets, and not to the Lessor or Lessor's assets for such claims.

14. DEFAULT. It is understood and agreed that this is a "non-recourse" Lease; and that Lessor may look only to those portions of the "Available Cash Flow" from The Project allocated to rentals payable hereunder, and to personal property of the Lessee located on the leased premises, for collection of any amounts declared or adjudged to be due to the Lessor hereunder in the event of default by the Lessee under any of the provisions of this Lease.

Any failure by the Lessee to make a rental payment due to the Lessor, after demand for such payment has been made and not satisfied for a period of sixty (60) days, shall constitute a default hereunder; provided, if a dispute exists between Lessor and Lessee as to the actual amount of Minimum Rental or Additional Rental due to the Lessor, non-payment of the disputed amount by Lessee shall not constitute a default until such matters shall have been finally adjudicated by appropriate court or courts of law or any appropriate arbitrators, inspectors, or auditors agreed upon by the parties hereto. Alleged violations of this Lease on the part of Lessee other than payment of rent shall constitute defaults hereunder only after Lessee shall have failed to cure such defaults for a period of sixty (60) days after a demand for such cure shall have been made in writing by the Lessor.

In the event of any such uncured default, and upon the expiration of the requisite time periods and events as stated above, the leased premises and any remaining personal property placed thereon by Lessor shall immediately become the property of Lessor, together with accrued and unpaid rentals and charges. Lessor may then re-enter and take possession of the premises and determine this Lease to be terminated; provided no such re-entries shall affect the rights of any sublessee who attorns to the Lessor pursuant to provisions hereinafter set forth.

In the event Lessor fails to comply with any of its obligations hereunder, and such failure by the Lessor threatens the continued uninterrupted operation of any portion of the leased premises, Lessee shall have the right to remedy such default from its own funds, using its reasonable discretion in selecting contractors, purchasing materials, and taking other steps as may be necessary to cure such default. Lessor shall then be liable to the Lessee for the full cost of such actions, and in the event Lessor fails to pay such amounts when notified, all such amounts may be deducted by Lessee from any future rental payments due to the Lessor. This right on the part of Lessee shall be applicable only in the event Lessor fails to remedy any such default after reasonable written notice and demand shall have been made by Lessee.

15. LESSEE'S MORTGAGE. It is contemplated by the parties that the Lessee's interests herein will be assigned to one or more first mortgage lenders in connection with the financing of The Project. No default by the Lessee or any other party under the terms of any such construction and/or permanent mortgage shall in and of itself constitute a default by Lessee under the terms of this Lease; and provided such mortgagee (or any purchaser or assignee claiming under such mortgagee, including purchasers at

foreclosure sales) shall comply with Lessee's obligations hereunder, including payment of rents as prescribed hereunder, this Lease shall continue in full force and effect with such mortgagee or other person claiming under such mortgagee or other person claiming under such mortgagee being considered and deemed as the successor to the Lessee named herein.

In the event Lessor shall be notified by Lessee or any mortgagee of the Assignment of Lessee's Interest in this Lease to such mortgagee, thereafter if Lessor determines that Lessee is in default in any payments due under this Lease or any other covenant or condition hereof, Lessor shall give notice thereof to the Lessee and to any such mortgagee; and such mortgagee shall have the same rights to cure such defaults as are given to the Lessee by any provision hereof. The fact that such cure shall be effected by a mortgagee rather than the Lessee shall not constitute a default or an event giving rise to termination of this Lease.

16. ATTORNMENT. No termination of this Lease shall affect the interests of any sublessee of the Lessee, provided such sublessee in writing attorns to the Lessor and agrees to pay the rents required by such sublessee's lease, and to perform all of the terms, covenants, and conditions of such sublessee's sublease as well as all terms, covenants, and conditions of this Lease applicable to that portion of the premises embraced by the sublessee's sublease. Thereafter, such sublessee shall become the tenant of the Lessor. Upon request, any sublessee shall be entitled to receive from the Lessor an instrument in writing providing that upon such attornment his occupation, possession, and use of the leased premises (or applicable portion thereof) shall not be disturbed by the Lessor.

Termination or transfer of the Lessor's interest in the leased premises shall not affect the interests of the Lessee therein or in this Lease, provided that the Lessee attorns in writing to Lessor's successor in interest and agrees to pay the rent required hereunder to such successor Lessor, and to perform all of the terms, covenants, and conditions of this Lease, thereby becoming the tenant of Lessor's successor in interest. Upon request, Lessee shall be entitled to receive from Lessor's successor in interest an instrument in writing providing that upon such attornment, Lessee's occupation, possession, and use of the leased premises shall not be disturbed by Lessor's successor in interest.

17. QUIET ENJOYMENT. Lessor hereby warrants that it, and no other person, corporation, or other entity, has the right to lease the premises leased to the Lessee hereunder. The Lessee shall have continual peaceful and quiet use and possession of the leased premises without hindrance on the part of the Lessor, and the Lessor shall warrant and defend such peaceful and quiet use and possession against the claims of all persons claiming by, through, or under the Lessor.

18. SUCCESSORS. This Lease, and all rights and obligations of both parties hereto, shall be binding upon and shall inure to the respective successors and assigns to such parties.

IN WITNESS WHEREOF, the parties, through their respective duly authorized officer, have hereunto set their hands as of the day and year first above written, to quintuplicate original copies thereof.

WITNESSES: Lessor:
THE CITY OF
GREENVILLE

_____   By:_____

       Lessee:
GREENVILLE
COMMUNITY
CORPORATION

_____   By:_____

APPENDIX G

Agreement
and
Grants of Easements

THIS INSTRUMENT, executed by and between the REDEVELOPMENT AGENCY OF THE CITY OF _____, a public body, corporate and politic (said corporation, its successors and assigns, being herein referred to as "Agency"), and _____, a Joint Venture (said Joint Venture, its successors and assigns, being herein referred to as "Developer"), together with the schedules . . . , is herein referred to as "This Agreement."

RECITALS:

A. Pursuant to and under those certain agreements referred to below, Developer has the continuing right to acquire from Agency all of the parcels of real property in the City of _____, County of _____, State of _____, collectively hereinafter referred to as the "Commercial Parcel," . . . and by Grant Deed bearing even date hereof, all of said parcels have been conveyed to Developer by Agency with the exception of Parcels U-1 and U-6 (which remain subject to acquisition by Developer) and Parcel U-5 (which has been acquired by Developer from a third party). The parcels of real property collectively hereinafter referred to in this Agreement as the "Garage Parcel" . . . have been and will be reserved by Agency. The Commercial Parcel consists of parcels of real property constituting airspace lying above the Garage Parcel, and the real property lying below the Garage Parcel, and certain other real property lying adjacent to the Garage Parcel. The aforedescribed Commercial Parcel and Garage Parcel, and the hereinafter referenced Easement Parcels, are shown and designated on the Parcel Map recorded on _____, in Book _____ of Parcel Maps, Map No. _____, records of _____ County, and a full and complete copy thereof is attached hereto as Schedule _____ through _____ . . . .

The aforementioned conveyance, and this Agreement, are entered into and executed pursuant to the provisions of that certain Contract for Sale of Land for Private Redevelopment entered into between Agency and Developer, as of the _____ day of _____, recorded on _____, in Book _____ of Official Records, page _____, County Records as amended by Supplement to Agreement for Sale of Land for Private Redevelopment, dated _____, recorded on _____, in Book _____ of Official Records, Page _____, County Records, and pursuant to the provisions of that certain Agreement for Sale dated the _____ day of _____, recorded on _____, in Book _____ of Official Records, Page _____, _____ County Records.

B. The initial structures will include up to two levels of offices and trade shops and other structures and facilities to be constructed within that portion of the Commercial Parcel lying above the Garage Parcel, up to three levels of offices and trade shops and other structures and facilities to be constructed within Parcel A-2, and a two-level public parking garage now constructed within the Garage Parcel. The concrete slabs, together with the horizontal beams supporting them (which slabs and beams are hereinafter called the top deck of garage), shall constitute the floor of the lower level of the structures to be constructed within the portion of the Commercial Parcel which lies above the Garage Parcel. They are entirely within the Garage Parcel. They will constitute a portion of the roof of the garage, and will be owned by Agency (regardless of encroachment as in paragraph 4 hereof provided).

C. The structures to be constructed within the portion of the Commercial Parcel which lies over the Garage Parcel will be supported by the top deck of the garage, and through the walls of, and through columns within, the garage in the Garage Parcel. The parties hereto agree that the walls of the garage and the aforesaid columns will be owned by Agency (regardless of encroachment as in paragraph 4 hereof provided).

D. Within the Easement Parcels GS-1, GS-2, GS-3, GS-4, S-1, S-2, S-3, S-4, stairways will, among other things, provide access from the garage to the first level of Commercial Parcel and from the first level of Commercial Parcel to the garage through the portions of the Commercial Parcel lying above the Garage Parcel and through the Garage Parcel. The portions of each of said stairways lying within said Easement Parcels GS-1, GS-2, GS-3 and GS-4 shall be owned by Agency. The portions of said stairways lying within Easement Parcels S-1, S-2, S-3 and S-4 shall be owned by Developer. Said stairways in both Garage Parcel and Commercial Parcel are hereinafter referred to as the "Access Stairways."

E. Within Easement Parcels E-1, E-2, M-1 and M-2, passenger elevators are to be installed by Agency. Said elevators will, among other things, provide access from the garage to the Commercial Parcel and from the Commercial Parcel to the garage. Easement Parcels E-1 and E-2 are owned by Agency, and Easement Parcels M-1 and M-2 are owned by Developer. Each of said elevators and all related equipment shall be owned by Agency. Said elevators are hereinafter referred to as the "Common Passenger Elevators."

F. Within Easement Parcels Y-1 and Y-2, service elevators are to be installed by Developer. Said elevators will, among other things, provide transportation for freight, merchandise and other materials through the garage to and within the Commercial Parcel, and from the Commercial Parcel through the garage. Each of said elevators and all related equipment shall be owned by Developer. Said elevators are hereinafter referred to as the "Service Elevators."

G. Within Easement Parcel Y-1, an Elevator Equipment Room has been built by the Agency for the purpose of housing electrical and mechanical equipment relative to the operation of the Service Elevators. Within the Garage Parcel adjacent to Easement Parcels E-1 and E-2 in the lower level of the garage, Elevator Equipment Rooms also have been built by the Agency for the purpose of housing electrical and mechanical equipment relative to the operation of the common passenger elevators.

H. Within Easement Parcel EL-1, a Transformer Vault "A" and Switch Gear and Pump Rooms will be hereafter built by Developer for the purpose of housing electrical and mechanical equipment for use in connection with the Commercial Parcel.

I. Within Easement Parcel AV-1, an enclosed ventilation shaft is to be constructed by Developer from the garage to the roof of the Commercial Parcel for the purpose of providing ventilation for the garage.

J. Parcel A-4 has been conveyed to Developer from Agency reserving to the Agency an easement and right-of-way across the surface thereof for public pedestrian and vehicular use, with the right to dedicate or convey said easement and right-of-way to the City.

K. Parcel R-3 is that area occupied by the garage which encroaches into the public right-of-way of _____ Street.

L. The parties hereto desire in this Agreement to enter into certain agreements and to grant each other certain easements to facilitate the use and enjoyment by each party of the aforementioned parcels of real property and airspace and of the structures to be constructed therein, and to make certain covenants and agreements concerning said parcels and the respective use, enjoyment and operation thereof. Reference herein to the "Maintenance Agreement" is to that Maintenance and Operation Agreement referred to in paragraph 13 hereof.

EASEMENTS, COVENANTS AND AGREEMENTS:

The parties hereto, in consideration of their mutual obligations hereunder, do hereby grant the following perpetual easements and enter into the following covenants and agreements.

1. (A) Agency hereby grants to Developer, and Developer and Agency hereby covenant and agree that Developer shall have, the perpetual right and easement appurtenant to the Commercial Parcel (i) to use the top deck of the garage as the floor of the lower level of the offices and shops and other structures and improvements in the Commercial Parcel; (ii) (a) to join to, to obtain substantial loadbearing support from, to tile, paint or otherwise surface, to remove the surfacing from, and to resurface said floor, (b) to support wiring, utilities and fixtures of all sorts, (c) to run pipes, lines, wires, mains, ducts, conduits, vents and related equipment and facilities through said floor and (d) to maintain and repair the surface of said floor; and (iii) as to that portion of the floor lying below the upper surface of top deck, to construct, reconstruct or repair said portion of the floor and to maintain, repair, replace and use any floor so constructed or reconstructed for the purposes and as set forth in clauses (i) and (ii) above, if said floor or any part thereof should ever be so far damaged or destroyed as to fail, or should for any other reason fail, or be in danger of failing, to serve the functions as above set forth, and should not be repaired or reconstructed by Agency within 90 days (or such shorter period as may be reasonable in event of emergency) after written notice to Agency specifying the nature of the requisite repair or reconstruction.

(B) Developer and Agency hereby covenant and agree (i) that upon completion of construction of the offices and shops and other structures and improvements within the Commercial Parcel there will exist a building wall supporting and enclosing said structures, and said wall will be owned by Developer and a portion thereof will be located within Parcel U-2 and along and contiguous to the property line between Parcels U-1 and U-2 upon and above the Garage Parcel; (ii) that Agency shall have, and Developer hereby grants to Agency as an appurtenance to Parcel U-1, the perpetual right and easement to use said portion of said building wall (a) as a party wall for any structure hereafter constructed upon Parcel U-1, with the full right to use such party wall for the insertion of beams or otherwise upon the construction of any structure upon Parcel U-1 and said party wall may constitute the south wall of any such structure; (b) to join to, to paint or otherwise refinish, to support wiring, utilities and fixtures of all sorts, to run pipes, lines, wires, mains, ducts, conduits, vents and related equipment and facilities through said party wall; (c) to maintain and repair said party wall if said party wall or any part thereof should ever be so damaged or destroyed as to fail, or should for any other reason fail, or be in danger of failing, to serve the functions as above set forth, and should not be repaired or reconstructed by Developer within 90 days (or such shorter period as may be reasonable in event of emergency) after written notice to Developer specifying the nature of the requisite repair or reconstruction; (iii) provided, however, (a) that the use of such party wall pursuant to subsection (ii), above, of this paragraph 1 (B), shall not injure the adjoining structure or building and shall not impair or diminish the structural characteristics of said wall or the benefits and support to which the adjoining structure or building within Parcel U-2 is entitled, nor create any substantial interference with use of such adjoining structure or building; (b) said party wall easement is subject to the condition that the same shall terminate and become ineffective in the event that Developer, while owning Parcel U-2, acquires title to and develops Parcel U-1.

(C) Developer and Agency hereby covenant and agree that Developer shall have, and Agency hereby grants to Developer, the perpetual right and easement appurtenant to the Commercial Parcel to join and connect to the north-south bulk main for the fire protection system located within the Garage Parcel any pipes, fittings, valves and related fixtures necessary to connect and integrate the fire protection system of the improvements constructed within the Commercial Parcel to said bulk main and fire protection system installed in the Garage Parcel, and also to maintain and repair all such pipes, fittings, valves, fixtures and connections, all subject, however, to the condition that Developer and Agency shall first make and enter into a written agreement, satisfactory in form to the Agency, for the maintenance, operation, repair, inspection and replacement of said bulk main and for sharing the cost of the original installation thereof. In the event that the rights granted by this easement have not been exercised prior to the completion of construction of the Developer's improvements within Commercial Parcels U-2, U-4 and A-2, the Agency and the Developer covenant and agree to execute an appropriate document extinguishing said easement.

(D) Developer and Agency hereby covenant and agree that Developer shall have, and Agency hereby grants to Developer, a perpetual right and easement appurtenant to the Commercial Parcel to use the air ventilation system and venting now located within the Garage Parcel in the south wall of the garage for the purpose of ventilating, and exhausting air from, the truck service area that will hereafter be constructed within Parcel A-2 of the Commercial Parcel.

(E) Developer and Agency hereby covenant and agree that the Garage Parcel shall be used for public parking of automobiles and other conveyances for the transportation of people, together with any and all uses incidental or accessory to said purpose, and Agency hereby grants to Developer the perpetual right and easement to the aforesaid use of the Garage Parcel and ingress and egress therefrom in common with and upon the same conditions as members of the public generally. Provided, however, that in the event automobiles or other conveyances requiring the use of the Garage Parcel for such parking are at any time no longer used as a major means of such transportation, then the Garage Parcel may be used for any other lawful purpose, except commercial and office uses.

2. In addition to the rights and easements provided in paragraph 1 (B) hereof, Developer hereby grants to Agency the following perpetual easements, and the parties hereto covenant and agree as follows:

(a) Non-exclusive easements appurtenant to the Garage Parcel (i) for the installation within Commercial Parcel of pipes, lines, wires, mains, conduits, ducts, vents and related equipment and facilities, including blowers, fans and motors for the transmission of air, gas, water and other utilities and of expansion joints (during the construction of the garage structure, and of the structures to be erected in the Commercial Parcel, in the locations for the installation thereof as may be agreed upon by the parties hereto, such agreement being conclusively presumed to have been made upon the expiration of 60 days after completion of construction of each such facility unless written objection thereto is given the other party and recorded in the Office of the Recorder of the County of ________ ________, State of ________, prior to the expiration of said 60-day period); and (ii) for the inspection, maintenance, repair, alteration, reconstruction, replacement and use thereof, provided that such installation, inspection, maintenance, repair, alteration, reconstruction, replacement or use shall not substantially interfere with the use and employment of Developer's improvements within the Commercial Parcel.

(b) Non-exclusive easements appurtenant to the Garage Parcel, for ingress and egress by the owner of the dominant tenement, from the dominant tenement to adjacent public areas or adjacent pedestrian access Easement Parcels as hereinafter provided, and from said areas or Parcels to the dominant tenement, in, over and upon the Access Stairways; and in addition, with respect to said Access Stairways owned by Developer, to construct, reconstruct or repair said Access Stairways and to maintain, repair, replace and use any portion thereof so constructed or reconstructed for the purposes and as set forth above if said Access Stairways owned by the Developer or any part thereof should ever be so far damaged or destroyed as to fail, or should for any other reason fail, or be in danger of failing, to serve the functions above set forth, and should not be repaired or reconstructed by Developer within 90 days (or such shorter period as may be reasonable in event of emergency) after written notice to Developer specifying the nature of the requisite repair or reconstruction. The parties covenant and agree that the aforesaid easements and rights shall be subject to and be exercised in accordance with provisions of the Maintenance Agreement applicable thereto.

(c) Non-exclusive easements appurtenant to the Garage Parcel, for ingress and egress by the owner of the dominant tenement, from the dominant tenement to the ________ Street Mall or adjacent pedestrian access Easement Parcels, and from the ________ ________ Street Mall and said Parcels to the dominant tenement, in, over and upon Easement Parcels F and H. The parties covenant and agree that the aforesaid rights and easements shall be subject to and be exercised in accordance with provisions of the Maintenance Agreement applicable thereto.

(d) An easement appurtenant to Garage Parcel for placing, replacing and maintaining an enclosed ventilation shaft from the garage to the roof of Developer's improvements hereafter constructed within the Commercial Parcel and for ventilation and the free passage of fresh air through said shaft, in and through Easement Parcel AV-1.

(e) An easement appurtenant to the Garage Parcel to place, construct, reconstruct, replace, maintain or repair in, within and upon that portion of the Commercial Parcel below the lower limits of the Garage Parcel (i) the pilings, pile caps and all related structural members required for the support of the garage structure constructed within the Garage Parcel; and for the support of structures and improvements to be constructed within the Commercial Parcel; (ii) the mains, pipe lines and related facilities for drainage and sewer, pumping facilities, elevator pits, sewage disposal units and all related equipment and structures in connection therewith.

(f) An easement appurtenant to the Garage Parcel for the free and unimpeded flow of outside air over, through and across those portions of Parcel A-2 of the Commercial Parcel upon which there hereafter will be constructed and created a truck service area, to and into the venting and ventilation system now constructed in connection with the venting located and incorporated into the south wall of the garage erected within the Garage Parcel.

(g) An easement appurtenant to the Garage Parcel to place and maintain the pilings, pile caps, footings and foundations, and all related structural members, now in place along the common boundary between Garage Parcel and Parcel A-2 and the common boundary between Parcel A-2 and Parcel R-2, and now supporting that portion of the garage structure constructed on Parcel R-2 and along the southerly boundary of Garage Parcel, and extending downward therefrom, for the support of said garage structure, together with the right to repair, maintain, replace or reconstruct said pilings, pile caps, footings, foundations and other related structural members; provided, however, (i) that such repair, maintenance, replacement or reconstruction shall not substantially interfere with the use and enjoyment of Developer's improvements within the Commercial Parcel, and (ii) that this easement shall not prevent Developer from locating and constructing structures and improvements together with all supporting elements within Parcel A-2 over and around said pilings, pile caps, footings and foundations in such a manner that will not place any load whatever upon Agency's existing footings without the consent of the Agency. The Agency and Developer agree that the piles, pile caps, footings, foundations and structural members of Developer now in place along the northerly boundary of Parcel A-2 do not violate the foregoing provisions.

(h) Non-exclusive easements appurtenant to the Garage Parcel, in, over and upon Easement Parcels FL-1, FL-2 and FL-3, for emergency, service and repair vehicle access to and from public streets and Parcel U-3 (Mall area), for secondary pedestrian travel by the public and the owner of the dominant tenement, for the installation and maintenance upon the easterly wall of the ________ ________ Street Underpass of appropriate signs, lights and railings, and for the exhaustion of air from the garage through grates and other apparatus as now in place.

(i) A non-exclusive easement appurtenant to the Garage Parcel for vehicular and pedestrian ingress and egress by the owner of the dominant tenement to the Garage Parcel from the public streets, and from the public streets to the dominant tenement, and for pedestrian travel and for the erection and maintenance of appropriate light standards and traffic signs, in, over and upon that portion of Parcel U-6 lying above the upper limits of the Garage Parcel.

3. In addition to those rights and easements provided in paragraphs 1 (A), (C), (D) and (E) hereof, Agency hereby grants to Developer the following perpetual easements, and the parties hereto covenant and agree as follows:

(a) Easements of support appurtenant to Commercial Parcel in, over and upon Garage Parcel as follows:

(i) Easements and rights of support on, over, upon and through the Garage Parcel extending downward and throughout said Garage Parcel from the upper limits of the Garage Parcel, upon and along the top deck, walls, columns, pile caps, piles, foundation and other structural members of the garage structure for the support and stability of the structure or structures of the Developer to be hereafter constructed within the Commercial Parcel.

The parties agree that Agency has erected support walls, columns and other structural members (with related columns) within the Garage Parcel, with footings, pile caps and pilings extending below the lower level of the Garage Parcel not more than 60 feet. Without limiting any provision of this sub-section (i) of this sub-paragraph (a), the parties agree that the aforementioned columns, footings, pilings, pile caps, support walls and structural members as now constructed constitute substantial supports (with respect to live loads and dead loads) for the aforementioned structures to be erected by Developer within the Commercial Parcel.

(ii) Easements and rights through the Garage Parcel so as to utilize the top deck of the garage for structural connections and anchorage of the new structure or structures to be erected within the Commercial Parcel to the existing garage structure and for the use of the top deck of the garage as the floor system of the new structure or structures and for the placement of utilities and any appurtenances pertaining thereto.

(iii) Easements to construct, reconstruct or repair the aforementioned top deck, columns, footings, pilings, pile caps, support walls and structural members of the garage, and to maintain, repair, replace and use any such structural elements so constructed or reconstructed (or as strengthened or reconstructed pursuant to subsection (iv) hereof), for the purposes and as set forth in this section, if any of aforesaid structural elements or any part thereof should ever be so far damaged or destroyed as to fail, or should for any other reason fail, or be in danger of failing, to provide support as above set forth, and should not be repaired or reconstructed by Agency within 90 days (or such shorter period as may be reasonable in event of emergency) after written notice to Agency specifying the nature of the requisite repair or reconstruction.

(iv) Easements to strengthen or reconstruct, at Developer's sole cost and expense, the aforementioned structural elements in such manner as to provide additional support, if Developer should desire to erect structures within the Commercial Parcel or any portion thereof requiring greater load-bearing support than is herein required to be borne by the above described structural elements; provided that the said present structural elements shall not be increased in size to such an extent as substantially to interfere with the operation of the garage; and provided, further, that Developer shall reimburse the owner of the Garage Parcel for any reasonable costs or expense incurred by such owner because of any substantial interference with the use, enjoyment or operation of the garage caused by the exercise of the rights to strengthen or reconstruct as herein provided.

(b) Non-exclusive easements appurtenant to Commercial Parcel in, over and upon Garage Parcel (i) for the installation within Garage Parcel of pipes, lines, wires, mains, conduits, ducts, vents and related equipment and facilities, including blowers, fans and motors for the transmission of air, gas, water and other utilities and of expansion joints (during the course of the construction of the garage structure, and of the structures to be erected in the Commercial Parcel, in the locations for the installation thereof as may be agreed upon by the parties hereto, such agreement being conclusively presumed to have been made upon the expiration of 60 days after the completion of construction of each such facility, unless written objection thereto is given the other party and recorded in the Office of the Recorder of the County of ________ ________, State of ________, ________, prior to the expiration of said 60 day period), and (ii) for the inspection, maintenance, repair, alteration, reconstruction, replacement and use thereof, provided that such inspection, maintenance, repair, alteration, reconstruction, replacement or use shall not substantially interfere with the use and enjoyment of the garage constructed within the Garage Parcel.

(c) Temporary easements, rights and rights of way, as required from time to time, appurtenant to Commercial Parcel in, over and upon the Garage Parcel and that portion of Parcel U-3 lying above the Garage Parcel, and any portion of Commercial Parcel still owned by Agency, for use by the owner of the dominant tenement, during the course of construction of the structures to be constructed within Commercial Parcel, in such manner and to such extent as may be necessary in connection with the construction by Developer of structures and improvements within the Commercial Parcel, provided that utilization of such temporary easements and rights shall not interfere with the normal use, enjoyment and operation of the garage except as necessary during said construction. The exercise of said temporary easements and rights shall terminate and cease, from time to time, upon completion of the construction of Developer's improvements in the Commercial Parcel for which the exercise of said easements and rights is required.

(d) Exclusive easements appurtenant to Commercial Parcel (i) for the use by the owner of the dominant tenement of an elevator equipment room within Easement Parcel Y-1, (ii) for the construction and installation in Easement Parcels Y-1 and Y-2, and for the inspection, maintenance, repair, alteration, reconstruction and replacement, and use in each said parcel, of service elevators (2) and of elevator equipment, electrical, mechanical and telephonic equipment, other related equipment, and motors, machinery and other equipment serving the aforesaid elevators, (iii) for the furnishing, maintenance and repair of the said equipment room, and (iv) for vertical transportation of service personnel, freight, merchandise and other materials by said service elevators.

(e) Non-exclusive easements appurtenant to the Commercial Parcel (i) for use by the owner of the dominant tenement of the elevator equipment rooms within the

Garage Parcel adjacent to Easement Parcels E-1 and E-2 in the lower level of the garage, and for the use of two passenger elevators (Common Passenger Elevators) and related equipment in each of Easement Parcels E-1 and E-2 and in each of Easement Parcels M-1 and M-2, for vertical transportation of the owner of the dominant tenement to the Garage Parcel from the Commercial Parcel, and to the Commercial Parcel from the Garage Parcel; and, in addition, to construct, reconstruct or repair said Common Passenger Elevators and elevator equipment rooms and related equipment, and to maintain, repair, replace and use any portion thereof so constructed or reconstructed for the purposes and as set forth above if either of said elevators or any part thereof should ever be so far damaged or destroyed as to fail, or should for any other reason fail, or be in danger of failing, to serve the functions above set forth, and should not be repaired or reconstructed by Agency within 90 days (or such shorter period as may be reasonable in event of emergency) after written notice to Agency specifying the nature of the requisite repair or reconstruction. The parties covenant and agree that the aforesaid easements and rights shall be subject to and exercised in accordance with provisions of the Maintenance Agreement applicable thereto.

(f) Non-exclusive easements appurtenant to the Commercial Parcel, for ingress and egress by the owner of the dominant tenement, from the dominant tenement to the garage, and from said garage to the dominant tenement, in, over and upon the Access Stairways; and in addition, with respect to said Access Stairways owned by Agency, to construct, reconstruct or repair said Access Stairways, and to maintain, repair, replace and use any portion thereof so constructed or reconstructed for the purposes and as set forth above if said Access Stairways owned by the Agency or any part thereof should ever be so far damaged or destroyed as to fail, or should for any other reason fail, or be in danger of failing, to serve the functions above set forth, and should not be repaired or reconstructed by Agency within 90 days (or such shorter period as may be reasonable in event of emergency) after written notice to Agency specifying the nature of the requisite repair or reconstruction. The parties covenant and agree that the aforesaid easements and rights shall be subject to and be exercised in accordance with provisions of the Maintenance Agreement applicable thereto.

(g) Exclusive easements appurtenant to the Commercial Parcel (i) for the use by the owner of the dominant tenement for ingress and egress to and from adjacent public streets and adjacent pedestrian access Easement Parcels and for a walkway in, over and across Easement Parcels W-1 and W-2, and (ii) for attachment to, and support from, the garage structure for walkways and stairways within said Easement Parcels W-1 and W-2, provided, however, that the lower limits of Easement Parcel W-1 shall be at least seven (7) feet above the inclined plane of the existing garage ramp in Parcel R-1.

(h) Non-exclusive easements appurtenant to the Commercial Parcel, in, over and upon Easement Parcels R-2, FL-1, FL-2 and FL-3, for emergency, delivery, service, maintenance and repair vehicle access to the Commercial Parcel from public streets and Parcel U-3 (Mall area), and from said public streets and Parcel U-3 (Mall area) to the Commercial Parcel, and for secondary pedestrian travel by the owner of the dominant tenement from the Commercial Parcel to the public streets and Parcel U-3 (Mall area) and from said streets and Parcel U-3 (Mall area) to the Commercial Parcel.

(i) Exclusive easements appurtenant to the Commercial Parcel for air curtains, troughs and related equipment extending through the slab constituting the concrete slab ceiling of the garage constructed within the Garage Parcel, but the same shall not extend lower than the bottom of the beams supporting said concrete slab ceiling. Said air curtain facilities shall be located in, on and across Easement Parcels AC-1, AC-2, AC-3 and AC-4.

(j) An exclusive easement appurtenant to the Commercial Parcel in and upon Easement Parcel EL-1 for the purposes of constructing, reconstructing, inspecting, altering, maintaining, storing, repairing and replacing, a Transformer Vault "A" and Switch Gear and Pump Rooms, and using therein the electrical and mechanical equipment, including, but not limited to, pipes, lines, wires, mains, conduits, blowers, fans, motors, machinery and other related equipment necessary or desirable to furnish electrical power to the Commercial Parcel.

(k) Exclusive easements appurtenant to the Commercial Parcel to place, replace and maintain overhanging canopies into Easement Parcels P, R, T and V, together with the right to inspect, repair and alter said overhanging canopies.

(l) Non-exclusive easements appurtenant to the Commercial Parcel for the use by the owner of the dominant tenement for pedestrian ingress and egress and for use as a walkway to and from public streets and other Mall areas and to and from the Commercial Parcel in, over and across Parcel U-3 (Mall area) excepting therefrom any portion of said Parcel U-3 (Mall area) lying within or below the top deck of the garage.

(m) An exclusive easement and right appurtenant to the Commercial Parcel to install, construct, reconstruct, repair and maintain a pedestrian bridge permitting access over Parcel U-3 (Mall area) between the second level of any building or structure hereafter constructed within Parcel U-2 and the second level of any building or structure hereafter constructed within Parcel U-4, together with easements and rights to (i) occupy said Parcel U-3 (Mall area) for said purpose, (ii) locate and install, construct, reconstruct, repair and maintain in Parcel U-3 (Mall area) necessary columns and supporting structures for said bridge and to use said Parcel U-3 (Mall area) for structural connections and anchorage, and (iii) obtain support from and through the Garage Parcel and garage, based on the garage as now constructed, for said bridge and supporting structures; provided, however, that the exercise of the easements and rights granted by this subparagraph (m) shall be conditioned upon and subject to the approval by Agency of plans for said structures to the same extent as required for Developer's improvements within Commercial Parcel under the Declaration of Restrictions recorded and applicable to the Commercial Parcel. The Agency's approval of said bridge plans may be made subject to the condition that the Developer shall pay any cost or expense to the Agency for any alterations to the mall or garage structures required by the exercise of the above easements.

(n) Non-exclusive easements and rights appurtenant to Commercial Parcel for the use of Parcel R-1 by owner of the dominant tenement for pedestrian and vehicular ingress and egress between the public streets and the truck loading area to be constructed within Parcel A-2.

(o) Non-exclusive easements and rights appurtenant to the Commercial Parcel for connecting to and the use by the owner of the dominant tenement of the mains and pipe lines for sanitary sewer, the sanitary sewer pumping facilities, the sewage disposal units and all the related equipment, facilities and structures in connection therewith, located within the Garage Parcel. This easement does not include the right to connect to or use any of the storm sewers or drains, or any of their related facilities, now constructed within or beneath the Garage Parcel, except as provided in the Maintenance Agreement.

(p) Easements and rights appurtenant to the Commercial Parcel (i) to place, replace and maintain an overhanging canopy into Easement Parcel N, together with the right to inspect, repair and alter said overhanging canopy, and (ii) for the use of the owner of the dominant tenement for reasonable pedestrian ingress and egress and for walkways between the Commercial Parcel and public streets and pedestrian access areas in Easement Parcels FL-1 and FL-2, in, over and across Parcels U-1 and U-6; provided, however, that the easements and rights provided in this sub-paragraph (p) are subject to the condition that the same shall terminate and become ineffective in the event the Agency conveys title or transfers possession to Parcel U-1 for development and construction of commercial improvements commences on said parcel.

(q) A non-exclusive easement and right appurtenant to the Commercial Parcel to place, construct, inspect, reconstruct, replace, maintain and repair Developer's structures and improvements or any part thereof, in, within and upon that portion of tte Garage Parcel lying outside the garage structure and adjacent to ____________ ____________ Street and ____________ Street, provided that such placement, construction, inspection, reconstruction, replacement, maintenance or repair shall not substantially interfere with the use and enjoyment of the garage by Agency; and, further, an exclusive easement and right to place, construct, inspect, reconstruct, replace, maintain and repair a vehicular ramp within the above-described portion of the garage to provide vehicular access from the surface of ____________ Street to the Developer's truck service area within Parcel U-2.

(r) In addition to the easements and rights heretofore granted, and with respect to Easement Parcels FL-1, FL-2, FL-3, R-1, R-2, W-1, W-2 and U-3 (but with respect to Parcel U-3 only until such time as the Mall area of said Parcel is dedicated or conveyed as a public pedestrian right-of-way), easements and rights appurtenant to Commercial Parcel to construct, reconstruct or repair that portion of the Garage Parcel or garage lying in, within or under said Easement Parcels or serving the easements therein granted the dominant tenement, and to maintain, repair, replace and use any portion thereof so constructed or reconstructed for the purposes and as set forth above if either of said portions of Garage Parcel or garage or any part thereof should ever be so far damaged or destroyed as to fail, or should for any other reason fail, or be in danger of failing, to serve the functions above set forth, and should not be repaired or reconstructed by Agency within 90 days (or such shorter period as may be reasonable in event of emergency) after written notice to Agency specifying the nature of the requisite repair or reconstruction.

4. The parties grant each to the other easements for encroachment upon the property or airspace of the other to the extent necessary to permit full use and enjoyment of their respective structures and properties (including property interest) upon completion of construction or reconstruction of the structures to be built upon the Garage Parcel and the Commercial Parcel by Agency or Developer in accordance with the intent expressed in this Agreement, insofar as such necessity arises from or out of deviations of the construction or reconstruction from the plans therefor; provided that such easements shall not permit any encroachments which would substantially interfere with the use and enjoyment of the servient tenement or tenements, including the use and enjoyment of rights and easements hereinabove provided. The parties further grant each to the other easements for encroachment upon the property or airspace of the other, to the extent necessary to permit full use and enjoyment of their respective properties (including property interests) subsequent to any such construction or reconstruction, in accordance with the intent expressed in this Agreement, insofar as such necessity arises from or by reason of vertical or lateral displacement of any of said structures; provided that such easements shall not permit any encroachments which would substantially interfere with the use and enjoyment of the servient tenement or tenements, including the use and enjoyment of rights and easements hereinabove provided.

5. (a) Except as the parties may otherwise provide and agree in the Maintenance Agreement, each party hereto covenants and agrees that it will at all times maintain in good condition and repair and at its sole cost and expense the party walls, support walls, floor slabs, columns, footings, pilings, pile caps, stairways, elevators, entranceways, doorways, and related fixtures and equipment, and any other structures and related fixtures and equipment which are to be owned by it and which are subject to any of the easements granted by it in this Agreement; and in the event of any alteration, removal or replacement of any such structure by said party that it will, at all times during such alteration, removal or replacement, and at all times thereafter, provide, as the case may be, walls, slabs, beams, footings, pilings, pile caps, stairways, entranceways, doorways or other structures serving substantially the same functions and to substantially the same extent with respect to the dominant tenement, as the structures altered, removed or replaced served before such alteration, removal or replacement; and any structures so provided or erected shall be subject to the same easements and the same covenants as the structures first to be erected were subject before such alteration, removal or replacement. Without limiting any other remedies available to the parties for breach of any of the covenants or agreements entered into between them, the parties covenant and agree that if either one of them fails to perform its obligations or any of them under this sub-paragraph (a) of paragraph 5, and if, pursuant to the easements and rights granted in clause (iii) of paragraph 1 (A), in section (b) of paragraph 2, or sub-section (iii) of section (a) and sections (e), (f) and (r) of paragraph 3, the other party shall construct, reconstruct, replace, repair or maintain the structure or structures to be maintained or repaired by the defaulting party pursuant to this paragraph 5 (a), then the defaulting party shall reimburse the other party for the costs of such construction, reconstruction, replacement, repair or maintenance.

(b) Each party hereto covenants and agrees with respect to each easement granted to it in this Agreement that if it should disturb or remove, or cause or permit to be disturbed or removed, any improvements (of whatever nature, whether real or personal), to the tenement or tenements servient to such easement, then it shall, with all reasonable diligence and promptness, restore such improvements to a condition as good as that existing immediately prior to such disturbance or removal.

(c) Each party hereto covenants and agrees that in the event of any casualty, including, without limitation, any fire, explosion or earthquake, and proceeds of any applicable casualty insurance maintained by it will be applied first to replacement, reconstruction or repair of the structures which are to be owned by it and which are subject to any of the easements granted in this Agreement, to whatever extent necessary to restore such structures to a condition as good as that existing prior to such casualty.

(d) Each party hereto covenants and agrees that the other party hereto, in addition to all other rights retained by it in the various Easement Parcels with respect to which it has granted easements herein, shall have the right to, and each to the other hereby grants an easement to, enter upon such Easement Parcels and perform such repair, maintenance, reconstruction or replacement as is necessary to prevent the property of said other party described in this Agreement within which is located the particular Easement Parcel or Parcels, from becoming or remaining unsafe for its intended use or uses or to prevent the operation, use and enjoyment of the said property from being interfered with by acts of government based upon or arising out of claims by any governmental authority that such repair, maintenance, reconstruction or replacement is necessary, and correspondingly, the parties hereto hereby covenant and agree that each of said parties shall have the right to, and each to the other hereby grants an easement, to enter upon that property or airspace of the other that is subject to an easement granted herein to the party so entering, and to perform such repair, maintenance, reconstruction or replacement as is necessary to prevent the said property or airspace which is entered from becoming or remaining so unsafe as to interfere with the operation, use and enjoyment of the easement affecting said property or airspace or to prevent the operation, use and enjoyment of the said easement from being interfered with by acts of government based upon or arising out of claims by any governmental authority that such repair, maintenance, reconstruction or replacement is necessary.

6. Except in those instances in this Agreement and Grants of Easements, and in the Maintenance and Operation Agreement whereby the parties hereto, or either of them, expressly assume or undertake liability or responsibility for damage or loss to the property and improvements of the other resulting or arising, directly or indirectly, from a cause *force majeure* or Act of God, the parties do not intend by said documents, or either of them, to change, alter, diminish or increase in any manner any of the rights or liabilities of either party toward the other as the same may then be established by law for any such damage or loss to the property or improvements of the other resulting or arising, directly or indirectly, from a cause *force majeure* or Act of God.

7. All covenants and agreements entered into by Agency in this Agreement shall remain binding upon Agency personally so long as it is either owner or lessee of Garage Parcel, or any portion thereof, but then only with respect to said portion owned or leased. All covenants and agreements entered into by Developer in this Agreement shall remain binding on Developer personally so long as it is either owner or lessee of the Commercial Parcel or any portion thereof, but then only with respect to said portion

owned or leased. Nothing in this paragraph shall be construed to limit any obligation which would be incurred by any party (including any successor or assign) under this Agreement but for the operation of this paragraph.

8. Each and every covenant and each and every agreement made herein by either party hereto is made by such party for its successors and assigns (which term shall include successors and assigns of any interest, equitable or otherwise), and to and for the benefit of the other party, its successors and assigns, and the performance thereof shall be for the benefit of said other party's property described in this Agreement, and the burdens and benefits of such covenants and agreements shall run with the respective properties of said parties; provided, however, that, wherever herein covenants relate to particular easements herein granted, such covenants shall run with the dominant, or, as the case may be, the servient, tenement or tenements of such easements. Wherever herein covenants are to run with or easements are appurtenant to the Commercial Parcel, if said Commercial Parcel is subsequently divided into one or more separate portions by sale or lease, such covenants shall nevertheless run with and such easements shall nevertheless be appurtenant to each and every said portion of said Commercial Parcel.

9. Each grant of an easement or right hereunder shall inure to the benefit of the owner or owners of the dominant tenement or tenements and their successors, and assigns, and may be used and enjoyed by the owner or owners of the dominant tenement or tenements and their successors and assigns, and their lessees and sub-lessees, and contractors, employees, tenants, licensees, and business visitors and invitees.

10. The names given to the various parcels herein are for identification only and shall not be construed to limit or enlarge the purposes for which such parcels may be used.

11. Each notice required or desired to be given pursuant to this Agreement shall be in writing and shall be deemed to have been served when the same has been deposited in the United States mail, certified or registered mail, return receipt requested, addressed as follows:

Redevelopment Agency of the City of _____

_____

_____

or to such other person or address as may be designated in writing and servedby one party on the other party.

12. The terms and provisions hereof are subject to the Agreement, dated _____, as amended by Supplement dated _____, the Agreement for Sale dated _____, and (except as otherwise provided therein) the deed to the De-

veloper referred to in recital A above. No merger or extinguishment of either the first or second Agreement above mentioned, or any of the provisions thereof, shall be caused, created or accomplished by the execution of this Agreement, and the same shall remain in full force and effect until all of the terms, covenants and conditions contained therein have been complied with or fully performed.

13. Contemporaneously with the execution of this Agreement, or as soon thereafter as is reasonably possible, the Agency and the Developer shall make and execute that certain Maintenance and Operation Agreement. . . . Said Maintenance and Operation Agreement shall be binding upon and for the benefit of each party and its successors and assigns as fully and with the same effect as the easements, covenants and agreements contained in this Agreement. The purpose of said Maintenance and Operation Agreement is to establish and set forth the covenants, agreements, rights and liabilities of said Agency and Developer with respect to the maintenance, operation, repair and replacement of certain of the stairways, elevators, bulk mains, storm drains, truck service areas, malls, walkways, driveways, sewage system and other structures, and the facilities, machinery and equipment related and appurtenant thereto, that are now in place and constructed, or will hereafter be constructed and placed, in said airspace and in said real property. It may be amended from time to time as the parties may agree.

14. Whenever an easement or right herein granted is extinguished pursuant to the provisions of this Agreement or by merger of title, the parties hereto agree, upon the request of either party, to mutually execute such documents as may be necessary to confirm or accomplish said extinguishment. Whenever an easement or right herein granted but not herein precisely located is exercised and becomes precisely located, and the assertion of said easement or right has not been challenged by the recording of a written objection as provided herein in paragraphs 2(a) and 3(b), the parties hereto agree, upon the request of either party, to mutually execute such documents as may be necessary to confirm the precise location and exercise of said easement or right.

IN WITNESS WHEREOF, the parties hereto have executed this Agreement as of the _____ day of _____, 19___.

Approved as to form

_____

Agency Counsel

REDEVELOPMENT AGENCY OF THE CITY OF _____

_____

"AGENCY"

APPENDIX H

Capitol South Documents

APPENDIX H(1)

Financial Agreement
between
City of Columbus
and

Capitol South Community Urban Redevelopment Corporation

This Financial Agreement made this _____ day of _____, _____, by and between the City of Columbus, Ohio (the "City"), an Ohio municipal corporation, and Capitol South Community Urban Redevelopment Corporation (the "Company"), an Ohio non-profit public purpose corporation with its principal place of business located at 101 East Town Street, Columbus, Ohio 43215,

WITNESSETH:

WHEREAS, the Company has made and submitted its Application for Financial Agreement and for Approval of Redevelopment Project (including this Financial Agreement as a separate part thereof) (the "Application") to the City Council of the City (the "City Council") and the Mayor of the City requesting approval for a project to re-develop a blighted area located within the City pursuant to Chapter 1728 of the Revised Code of Ohio (the "Project"); and

WHEREAS, the Project consists of the undertaking and execution by the Company of the redevelopment of a blighted area (the "Property") described in Exhibit "A," which is included herewith and incorporated herein; and

WHEREAS, the Project will be located in a blighted area as that term is defined by Section 1728.01(E) of the Revised Code of Ohio; and

WHEREAS, the City is an impacted city as that term is defined by Section 1728.01(C) of the Revised Code of Ohio; and

WHEREAS, the City has not designated any community improvement corporation as the agency of the City, or confirmed any plan prepared by a community improvement corporation under the provisions of Chapter 719 of the Revised Code of Ohio; and

WHEREAS, the City Council is the governing body and legislative authority of the City; and

WHEREAS, the Company is a community urban redevelopment corporation qualified under Chapter 1728 of the Revised Code of Ohio to acquire, construct, operate and maintain the Project; and

WHEREAS, the City and the Company wish to make this Financial Agreement in order to evidence the terms and conditions pursuant to which the Company will undertake and execute the redevelopment of the Property and in order to evidence the mutual agreements and undertakings between the City and the Company;

NOW, THEREFORE, in consideration of the premises and the mutual covenants and agreements contained in this Financial Agreement, it is mutually agreed between the City and the Company as follows:

1. Description of the Project. The Project is to consist of a multi-use complex which may include office facilities, retail stores, hotel facilities, residential dwellings, service facilities, public areas, streets and parking structures. The general architectural and site concepts for the Project are described in Exhibit "B," which is included herewith and incorporated herein. The Company plans to undertake the Project in several phases as conditions permit. Each phase is to serve to enhance an orderly progress toward completion of the entire Project. However, upon the completion of each phase, the functioning of the partially completed Project is not to be dependent upon any further redevelopment of the Property.

2. Land Acquisition by City. The City shall use its best efforts (including, if necessary, its power of eminent domain) to acquire the fee simple title (or such lesser title as the Company may request) to such parcel or parcels of the Property as the Company may, from time to time and at any time during the existence of this Financial Agreement, agree to lease from the City for redevelopment as a part of the Project. The title to each such parcel acquired by the City shall be free and clear from all defects, liens, mortgages, encumbrances, easements, restrictions, reservations, conditions, agreements and encroachments except (a) taxes and assessments due and payable after the date of such acquisition, (b) zoning laws and regulations and other laws and ordinances affecting the use of the parcel, (c) public streets, roads and highways, and (d) such exceptions to title as Lessee may be willing to waive in writing.

3. Conditions Precedent to Land Acquisition by City. The City's obligation to acquire any particular parcel of the Property shall be contingent upon the prior fulfillment of the following conditions:

A. The delivery by the Company to the City of a written commitment by the Company to lease the parcel from the City for redevelopment as a part of the Project in accordance with the provisions of this Financial Agreement;

B. The Company's not being in default under this Financial Agreement or under any of the Lease Agreements made in accordance with the provisions of this Financial Agreement; and

EXHIBIT A-1

Capitol South Property Map

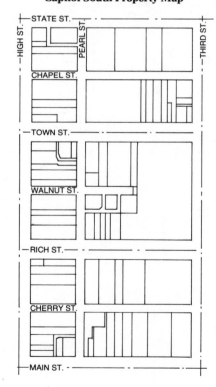

C. The sum of (a) the principal amount of outstanding notes previously issued by the City in accordance with the provisions of this Financial Agreement plus (b) the principal amount of notes which would be issued by the City in accordance with the provisions of this Financial Agreement in order to acquire the parcel, not being in excess of Eighteen Million Dollars ($18,000,000.00).

4. Use of Notes. For the purpose of obtaining the funds needed to purchase the parcels of the Property to be acquired by the City hereunder, the City Council shall cause the City to issue general obligations notes having a term of not more than five (5) years and paying the lowest rate of interest then obtainable.

5. Leasing of Land to Company. Following the City's acquisition of each parcel of the Property in accordance with the provisions of this Financial Agreement, the City shall promptly lease such parcel in accordance with the provisions of Section 1728.03 of the Revised Code of Ohio to the Company by a lease (the "Lease Agreement") in substantially the same form as Exhibit "C," which is included herewith and incorporated herein. The purchase option price in the Lease Agreement shall be the price paid for such parcel by the City plus the City's expenses of acquiring the parcel (a) including court costs, appraisers' fees and the City's legal and other expenses involved in purchase negotiations, but (b) excluding the City's legal and other expenses in any condemnation proceedings. In the event that the City has, at the request of the Company, acquired less than the fee simple title to such a parcel, the provisions of the Lease Agreement shall be appropriately adjusted.

6. Improvements Exempt from Taxation. All improvements in the Project constructed or acquired by the Company shall be exempt from taxation for the maximum period provided by Section 1728.10 of the Revised Code of Ohio. In order to use this redevelopment incentive most effectively, the Company shall, in determining the provisions of any lease, sublease or other agreement for the use of the Property, obtain from the potential lessee, sublessee or other user sufficient information so as to satisfy the Company that the financial and other provisions of the proposed lease, sublease or other agreement are economically justified. During the time when any improvements in the Project (except residential dwellings) are exempt from taxation under the provisions of this Financial Agreement, any of the Company's funds which the Company determines are not needed by it for the redevelopment and operation of the Project shall be transferred to the City to be used by the City in cooperation with the Company for improvement of public facilities within or immediately adjacent to the Property.

7. Payments in Lieu of Taxes. Pursuant to the provisions of Section 1728.111 of the Revised Code of Ohio, so long as the improvements in the Project constructed or acquired by the Company are exempt from taxation, the Company shall make payment to the Franklin County Treasurer, on or before the final date for payment of real estate taxes in Franklin County for each half year, of a semi-annual service charge in lieu of taxes on such improvements, which charge, together with the taxes on the land, in any year after first occupancy of the Project, shall be equal to the total taxes assessed on all real property in the area then constituting the Project in the calendar year immediately preceding the initial acquisition of such area or any part thereof by the City or by the Company, whichever shall have occurred first. No such charge shall be paid by the Company for any period prior to the first occupancy of such improvements in the Project.

8. Redevelopment in Accordance with Community Development Plan. Although the City has no specific master plan, general plan or official map, the Project conforms to the provisions of the City's existing Downtown Area Development Plan. In accordance with the provisions of Section 1728.07(C) of the Revised Code, whenever the Company, its successors and assigns, shall use, develop or redevelop a portion of the Property, the Company, its successors and assigns, shall do so in accordance with, and for the period of, any applicable community development plan (as defined in Section 1728.01(D) of the Revised Code). which plan (a) shall permit the continuance of existing uses, (b) shall conform to either the general architectural and site concepts described in Exhibit "B" or such other architectural and site concepts agreed upon by the City, the Company and any of the Company's successors and assigns, using, developing or redeveloping such portion of the Property, and (c) shall extend either for the period of this Financial Agreement or such other period agreed upon by the City, the Company and any of the Company's successors and assigns using, developing or redeveloping such portion of the Property; and the Company shall so bind its successors and assigns by appropriate agreements and covenants running with the land enforceable by the City.

9. Elimination and Prevention of Blight. The Company's undertakings and activities for the elimination and for the prevention of the development or spread of blight extend to the total redevelopment of the acquired Property by constructing and operating the Project.

10. Relocation. Any relocation assistance which may be required by law to persons displaced by the Project shall be provided by the Company, and the City shall be bound by the provisions of Section 1728.07(E) of the Revised Code of Ohio. Such relocation assistance shall be provided in accordance with the relocation plan described in the Application, which relocation plan is determined to be feasible and is approved by the City.

11. Submission of Auditor's Report. The Company shall submit annually, within ninety (90) days after the close of its fiscal year, its auditor's reports to the Mayor and the City Council, which reports shall be certified by a firm of independent certified public accountants of national reputation licensed to practice in the State of Ohio as being in accordance with generally accepted accounting principles, consistently applied.

12. Examination of Property and Records. The Company shall, upon request, permit inspection of property, equipment, buildings and other facilities of the Company, and also permit examination and audit of its books, contracts, records, documents and papers by authorized representatives of the City.

13. Arbitration. In the event of any dispute between the parties, the matters in controversy shall be resolved by arbitration to the extent permitted by law. Such dispute shall be submitted to arbitration by a panel of three disinterested arbitrators. The panel shall be composed of one arbitrator appointed by the City, one appointed by the Company, and the third, who shall be an attorney admitted to practice in the State of Ohio, shall be appointed by the mutual agreement of the two arbitrators chosen by the City and the Company. If the two arbitrators chosen by the City and the Company are unable to agree upon the choice of the third arbitrator, the third arbitrator shall be appointed by the presiding Judge of the Court of Common Pleas of Franklin County, Ohio. The panel shall sit in Columbus, Ohio, and its procedures shall be governed by the Ohio Arbitration Act contained in Chapter 2711 of the Revised Code of Ohio. Any decision made by a majority of the arbitrators shall be final, binding and conclusive on the parties for all purposes, and judgment may be entered thereon by any court having jurisdiction thereof. The cost of arbitration shall be borne equally by the parties.

14. Company's Right of Termination. Operation under this Financial Agreement is terminable by the Company in the manner provided by Chapter 1728 of the Revised Code of Ohio.

15. Company Bound until Termination. The Company shall, at all times prior to the expiration or other termination of this Financial Agreement, remain bound by Chapter 1728 of the Revised Code of Ohio.

16. Wages Paid to Laborers and Mechanics. All wages paid to laborers and mechanics for work on the Project shall be paid at the prevailing rates of laborers and mechanics for the class of work called for by the Project, which wages shall be determined in accordance with the requirements of Chapter 4115 of the Revised Code of Ohio for determination of prevailing wage rates; provided, however, that the requirements of this section shall not apply where the federal government or any of its agencies furnishes by law or grant all or any part of the funds used in connection with the Project and prescribes predetermined minimum wages to be paid to such laborers and mechanics.

17. Modification of Agreement. Modifications of this Financial Agreement may from time to time be made by agreement between the City and the Company.

18. Continuation of Tax Abatement upon Transfer. In the event that the Project is sold or otherwise transferred to another community urban redevelopment corporation which, with the consent of the City, assumes all the contractual obligations of the Company under this Financial Agreement, the tax exemption of the improvements as provided by Section 1728.10 of the Revised Code of Ohio shall continue and inure to the transferee corporation.

19. Security for Completion of Project. As security for the completion of the Project and for the disposition of the Project property including the buildings in the event of a default in construction or abandonment of the work, the Company shall obtain standard performance completion bonds from each contractor on the Project and shall name the City as an insured as its interests may appear; and such security is hereby approved by the City.

20. Completion of Financial Agreement. All of the terms, conditions and covenants herein contained shall be fully performed within twenty (20) years from the date of completion of the Project.

21. Assistance by City. The City may, with the prior written approval of the Company, undertake and carry out any work, which a municipal corporation may legally undertake, in order to assist in the completion of the Project.

22. Plans for Management of Project. The Company represents and covenants that it proposes to manage or operate the Project primarily by leasing or subleasing portions of the Project for varying lengths of time to public or private persons. Such leases, subleases or other contractual arrangements shall include provisions assuring that the redevelopment is constructed, managed and operated in a manner which would benefit the public purpose of the Company. The Company shall continually monitor the performance of each such lessee or sublessee in an effort to obtain full compliance with the provisions of the lease or sublease.

23. Plans for Financing of Project. Information regarding the Company's plan for financing the Project (including the estimated total Project cost, the amortization rate on the total Project cost, the source of funds, the interest rates to be paid on the construction financing, the source and amount of paid in capital, the terms of mortgage amortization for repayment of principal on any mortgage, and the rental schedules and lease terms to be used in the Project) is contained in Exhibit "D," which is included herewith and incorporated herein.

24. Commitment of Federal or State Funds. In the event that any funds for the planning, design, acquisition, construction or operation of any portion of the Project can be obtained from any federal or state agencies by the City but not by the Company, the City, in cooperation with the Company, shall use its best efforts to acquire such funds and shall, to the maximum extent possible, transfer the funds to the Company for the appropriate purpose or, if such transfer is not possible, use the funds directly for the appropriate purpose.

25. Zoning, Restrictions and Variances. In the event that the Property shall, from time to time or at any time, be subject to any zoning law, regulation, restrictive covenant or other restriction which prohibits or in any material way interferes with the performance by the Company of its obligations under this Financial Agreement or with the reasonable redevelopment by the Company of the Property in accordance with the uses outlined in this Financial Agreement, the Company shall at its expense and in the normal manner first seek whatever variance is required in order to eliminate such prohibition or material interference; but if such variance shall not be granted to the Company in a timely manner, and if the Company shall subsequently give notice to the City of the Company's request for the elimination of such zoning law, regulation, restrictive covenant or other restriction, then if the City fails to eliminate the same within ninety (90) days after the Company's giving of such notice, such failure shall constitute a violation of this Financial Agreement.

26. Securing of Variances and Approvals. The City shall cooperate with and, where possible, join with the Company in executing and prosecuting to completion, at the Company's cost and expense, such applications for such orders, zoning variances, regulations and approvals of or by any governmental or regulatory authorities as may, in the opinion of the Company, be necessary or desirable in connection with the exercise by the Company of its rights under this Financial Agreement.

27. Adjacent Zoning and Land Use. The City shall continually monitor the applications for any changes in the zoning classification of all properties in the area surrounding the Project. The City shall use its best efforts to insure that the ultimate land uses established in the surrounding area are compatible with and complement the Project and the public purposes being served by the improvements to be constructed or acquired by the Company.

28. Development of Other Surrounding Public Areas. In the areas adjacent to and in the vicinity of the Project, the City shall use its best efforts in order to improve the streets, bridges, tunnels, walkways, sidewalks, control systems and graphics for vehicular and pedestrian traffic. All of these improvements shall be undertaken by the City in cooperation with the Company and in such a manner as to facilitate the use of the Project and its relationship to the surrounding area.

29. Vacation of Secondary Streets. Upon receipt of a written request from the Company, the City shall, to the extent permitted by law, take such actions as are necessary and appropriate to vacate and transfer to the Company (at no cost to the Company) any part of Pearl Street, Chapel Street, Walnut Street or Cherry Street (or any other secondary street or alley) which borders or passes through the Property and which divides land owned or leased by the Company; provided, however, that such vacation shall neither impair the public health, peace and safety, nor cause the normal activities necessary to service such lands to be conducted from major thoroughfares bordering on or crossing through the Project.

30. Availability of Water and Sewer. Prior to or contemporaneously with the completion of the initial phase of the Project, the City shall provide at prevailing rates all water and sewer services in sufficient capacity to serve the respective needs of the Project. The City shall not be obligated to insure the availability of other utility services. Within the area of the Project as it may be constituted from time to time, the Company shall have the obligation of providing at its own expense the needed water and sewer lines having sufficient capacity to accept the services provided by the City, and the Company shall have the further obligation of relocating, replacing or providing the needed gas, electric and telephone services at its own expense.

31. Equal Employment Opportunity Provisions. The Company shall comply with all federal, state and local laws designed to insure nondiscriminatory employment opportunities. The Company shall include or cause to be included in all of the construction contracts for the Project the following provisions requiring the affirmative action of employers in this regard:

During the performance of this contract, the contractor agrees as follows:

(1) The contractor will not discriminate against any employee or applicant for employment because of race, color, religion, sex or national origin. The contractor will take affirmative action to ensure that applicants are employed, and that employees are treated during employment, without regard to their race, color, religion, sex or national origin. Such action shall include, but not be limited to the following: employment, upgrading, demotion or transfer; recruitment or recruitment advertising; layoff or termination; rates of pay or other forms of compensation; and selection for training, including apprenticeship. The contractor agrees to post in conspicuous places, available to employees and applicants for employment, notices to be provided by the contracting officer setting forth the provisions of this nondiscrimination clause.

(2) The contractor will, in all solicitations or advertisements for employees placed by or on behalf of the contractor, state that all qualified applicants will receive consideration for employment without regard to race, color, religion, sex or national origin.

(3) The contractor will send to each labor union or representative of workers with which he has a collective

EXHIBIT A-2

Description of the Property

The Property consists of the blighted area situated in the State of Ohio, County of Franklin and City of Columbus bounded by High Street, State Street, Third Street and Main Street excluding, however, all legal streets and public rights-of-way except those portions of such streets and rights-of-way which may be vacated from time to time.

EXHIBIT B-1

Capitol South Site Plan

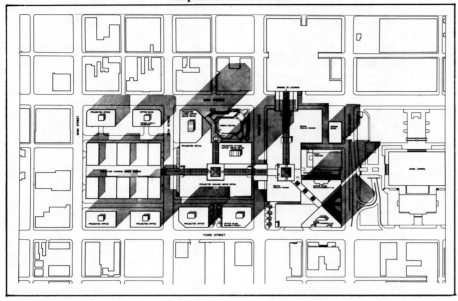

bargaining agreement or other contract or understanding, a notice, to be provided by the agency contractor officer, advising the labor union or workers' representative of the contractor's commitments under Section 202 of Executive Order No. 11246 of September 24, 1965, and shall post copies of the notice in conspicuous places available to employees and applicants for employment.

(4) The contractor will comply with all provisions of Executive Order No. 11246 of September 24, 1965, and of the rules, regulations and relevant orders of the Secretary of Labor.

(5) The contractor will furnish all information and reports required by Executive Order No. 11246 of September 24, 1965, and by the rules, regulations and orders of the Secretary of Labor, or pursuant thereto, and will permit access to his books, records and accounts by the contracting agency and the Secretary of Labor for purposes of investigation to ascertain compliance with such rules, regulations and orders.

(6) In the event of the contractor's noncompliance with the nondiscrimination clauses of this contract or with any of such rules, regulations or orders, this contract may be cancelled, terminated or suspended in whole or in part and the contractor may be declared ineligible for further Government contracts in accordance with procedures authorized in Executive Order No. 11246 of September 24, 1965, and such other sanctions may be imposed and remedies invoked as provided in Executive Order No. 11246 of September 24, 1965, or by rule, regulation or order of the Secretary of Labor, or as otherwise provided by law.

(7) The contractor will include the provisions of Paragraphs (1) through (7) in every subcontract or purchase order unless exempted by rules, regulations or orders of the Secretary of Labor issued pursuant to Section 204 of Executive Order No. 11246 of September 24, 1965, so that such provisions will be binding upon each subcontractor or vendor. The contractor will take such action with respect to any subcontract or purchase order as the contracting agency may direct as a means of enforcing such provisions including sanctions for noncompliance: Provided, however, That in the event the contractor becomes involved in, or is threatened with, litigation with a subcontractor or vendor as a result of such direction by the contracting agency, the contractor may request the United States to enter into such litigation to protect the interests of the United States.

32. Termination Procedures. In the event that either party hereto believes that the other party is violating any provision of this Financial Agreement, the first party may notify the second party of the alleged violation, and the second party shall then have sixty (60) days after the receipt of such notice in which to either (1) remedy such alleged violation to the satisfaction of the first party or (2) submit the dispute to arbitration in the manner provided herein. In the event that the second party shall not submit the dispute to arbitration in a timely manner, the alleged violation shall be conclusively presumed to exist, and the first party may at any time during the continuation of the violation terminate this Financial Agreement by giving notice of such termination to the second party. In the event that the second party shall submit the dispute to arbitration in a timely manner, and in the further event that the panel of arbitrators shall decide that the alleged violation exists, the second party shall then have sixty (60) days after receipt of the decision of the panel of arbitrators in which to remedy the violation or to initiate action which will within a reasonable period remedy the violation; and if the second party shall fail to take such action in a timely manner, the first party may at any time during the continuation of the violation terminate this Financial Agreement by giving notice of such termination to the second party. In either event, such termination shall be effective upon receipt of such notice by the second party. However, if, as the result of casualty damage, war, insurrection, natural forces, strikes, material shortages or other events substantially beyond the second party's control, the second party is prevented from remedying any alleged or actual violation within the sixty-day period provided herein, such period shall be extended for sixty (60) days after the termination of the adverse effect of such event.

33. Procedures for Service of Notice. All notices and other communications required or permitted to be given or delivered under this Financial Agreement by the City or the Company, which notices or communications shall be in writing, shall be mailed, postage prepaid, addressed as follows:

(A) If to the City, to:
Mayor of the City of Columbus
City Hall
Columbus, Ohio 43215
with a copy to:
City Attorney of Columbus
City Hall
Columbus, Ohio 43215

(B) If to the Company, to
Capitol South Community Urban
Redevelopment Corporation
101 East Town Street
Columbus, Ohio 43215
with a copy to:
Vorys, Sater, Seymour and Pease
52 East Gay Street
Columbus, Ohio 43215.

The City or the Company may, by notice received by the other, from time to time and at any time designate a different address for the giving of notices or other communications to the party designating such new address. Any notice or communication required or permitted to be given in accordance with this Financial Agreement shall be deemed to have been given when the same shall have been placed in the mail, postage prepaid, addressed in accordance with the foregoing provisions.

34. Successors and Assigns. This Financial Agreement shall inure to the benefit of and be binding upon the respective successors and assigns (including successive, as well as immediate, successors and assignees) of the City and of the Company.

35. Governing Law and Forum. This Financial Agreement shall be governed by and construed in accordance with the laws of the State of Ohio.

36. Remedies Cumulative. All rights and remedies of the City and of the Company enumerated in this Financial Agreement shall be cumulative and, except as specifically contemplated otherwise by this Financial Agreement, none shall exclude any other right or remedy allowed at law or in equity, and said rights or remedies may be exercised and enforced concurrently. No waiver by the City or by the Company of any covenant or condition or of the breach of any covenant or condition of this Financial Agreement to be kept or performed by the other party shall constitute a waiver by the waiving party of any subsequent breach of such covenant or condition or authorize the breach or non-observance on any other occasion of the same or any other covenant or condition of this Financial Agreement.

37. Duplicate Originals. This Financial Agreement may be executed in one or more counterparts, each of which shall be deemed to be a duplicate original, but all of which, taken together, shall constitute a single instrument.

38. Headings. The headings contained in this Financial Agreement are included only for convenience of reference and do not define, limit, explain or modify this Financial Agreement or its interpretation, construction or meaning and are in no way to be construed as a part of this Financial Agreement.

39. Provisions Separable. If any provision of this Financial Agreement or the application of any such provision to any person or any circumstances shall be determined to be invalid or unenforceable, then such determination shall not affect any other provisions of this Financial Agreement or the application of such provision to any other person or circumstance, all of which other provisions shall remain in full force and effect; and if any provision of this Financial Agreement is capable of two constructions, one of which would render the provision void and the other of which would render the provision valid, then such provision shall have the meaning which renders it valid.

40. Entire Agreement. This Financial Agreement constitutes the entire agreement between the City and the Company in respect of the subject matter hereof, and this Financial Agreement supersedes all prior and contemporaneous agreements between the City and the Company in connection with the subject matter of this Financial Agreement. No officer, employee or other servant or agent of the City or of the Company is authorized to make any representation, warranty or other promise not contained in this Financial Agreement. No change, termination or attempted waiver of any of the provisions of this Financial Agreement shall be binding upon the City or the Company unless in writing and signed by the party affected.

CITY OF COLUMBUS, OHIO

By _____
    Mayor

CAPITOL SOUTH COMMUNITY
URBAN REDEVELOPMENT CORPORATION

By _____
    Executive Director

Approved as to form by

_____
City Attorney

EXHIBIT B-2

Capitol South Concept Rendering

> (Not Shown)

EXHIBIT C

Lease Agreement
between
City of Columbus
and
Capitol South Community Urban Redevelopment Corporation

This Lease Agreement made and entered into at Columbus, Ohio, this _____ day of _____, _____, by and between the City of Columbus, Ohio, a municipal corporation duly organized and existing under and by virtue of the Constitution of the State of Ohio (the "Lessor"), and Capitol South Community Urban Redevelopment Corporation, a non-profit public purpose corporation organized and existing under the laws of the State of Ohio (the "Lessee");

WITNESSETH:

That for and in consideration of the premises and of the covenants herein contained, the parties hereto make the following agreement, intending to be legally bound thereby:

ARTICLE ONE
Demised Premises

1.01. *Leasing of Premises.* Lessor does hereby demise and let unto Lessee, and Lessee does hereby lease and hire from Lessor, all of the real property situated in the City of Columbus, Franklin County, Ohio, described in the Legal Description Annex which is included herewith and incorporated herein, together with any and all improvements which are now situated on said real property and the appurtenances thereunto belonging (the "Demised Premises").

1.02. *Ownership of Buildings and Improvements.* The Demised Premises shall not include any buildings or other improvements which may hereafter be placed thereon by Lessee, which buildings and improvements shall be the sole property of Lessee during the Lease Term; but, except as otherwise provided in this Lease Agreement, all buildings and improvements existing on the Demised Premises at the termination of the Lease Term shall become the property of Lessor free and clear of any and all claims by Lessee.

1.03. *Ownership of Fixtures and Personal Property.* The Demised Premises shall not include any fixtures, trade fixtures, furniture, furnishings, equipment or other property installed or maintained on the Demised Premises by Lessee. Prior to or within thirty (30) days after the termination of the Lease Term, Lessee may from time to time and at any time remove any of such property from the Demised Premises.

ARTICLE TWO
Lease Term and Form

2.01. *Lease Term.* The Lease Term shall be the period of five (5) years (a) commencing on the earlier of the date of this Lease Agreement as set forth above or the date on which Lessor issued its general obligation notes (the "Notes") for the specific purpose of acquiring the funds used to purchase the Demised Premises, and (b) terminating five (5) years after the commencement date.

2.02. *Lease Hold-Over Provisions.* If Lessee remains in possession of the Demised Premises after the expiration of the Lease Term, Lessee shall be deemed to be a tenant from month-to-month only, subject to all of the terms and provisions of this Lease Agreement except as to the duration of the Lease Term, until Lessee or Lessor shall have given to the other thirty (30) days' notice of termination of such tenancy from month-to-month.

2.03. *Separate Lease Agreements.* Upon written request from Lessee to Lessor, Lessor shall from time to time and at any time during the Lease Term demise and let to Lessee under a separate lease agreement any portion of the Demised Premises to be designated by Lessee, which portion shall thereafter cease to be a part of the Demised Premises under this Lease Agreement. The relevant rights and obligations of Lessor and Lessee under any such separate lease agreement shall be substantially identical to those contained in this Lease Agreement. The purchase price of the purchase option in any such separate lease agreement shall be an appropriate portion of the purchase price of the purchase option established in Section 6.01 of this Lease Agreement; and the purchase price of the purchase option established in Section 6.01 of this Lease Agreement shall be reduced by an amount equal to the purchase price of the purchase option in any such separate lease agreement.

2.04. *Termination of Lease Term.* Lessee may terminate the Lease Term in respect of all or any portion of the Demised Premises, from time to time and at any time by giving sixty (60) days' notice to that effect to Lessor, if either (a) Lessor terminates the Financial Agreement entered into between Lessor and Lessee on _____, _____, (the "Financial Agreement") at a time when Lessee is in full compliance with the provisions of the Financial Agreement, or (b) Lessee terminates the Financial Agreement in accordance with the provisions of Section 32 (thirty-two) of the Financial Agreement as a result of Lessor's violation of the provisions of the Financial Agreement.

ARTICLE THREE
Consideration for Demised Premises

3.01. *Rent.* As a part of the consideration for the Demised Premises during the Lease Term, Lessee shall pay to Lessor annual rent in an amount calculated by multiplying the annual interest rate on the Notes times the purchase price of the purchase option provided in Section 6.01 of this Lease Agreement. Payment of said rent shall be made in appropriate installments due and payable by Lessee not later than ten (10) days before the interest on the Notes shall become due and payable to the holders of the Notes.

3.02. *Service Charges in Lieu of Taxes.* As additional consideration for the Demised Premises during the Lease Term, Lessee shall pay all semi-annual service charges in lieu of taxes on the Leased Premises payable in accordance with the provisions of Section 7 (seven) of the Financial Agreement.

3.03. *Taxes and Assessments.* As additional consideration for the Demised Premises for the Lease Term, Lessee shall pay all intangible, personal and real estate taxes and installments of assessments, both general and special, and all other charges of any and every kind heretofore or hereafter lawfully levied, assessed, charged, taxed or imposed during the Lease Term upon the Demised Premises and upon any improvements now or hereafter placed thereon, except (a) that any monies so payable by Lessee which are levied, due or payable, or which are a lien upon the Demised Premises at the commencement of the Lease Term shall be pro-rated at the commencement of the Lease Term and (b) that any monies so payable by Lessee which are a lien upon the Demised Premises in the collection period during which the Lease Term expires, shall be pro-rated to such termination date. Lessor shall make all necessary arrangements to have the collecting authorities send all pertinent statements and bills in respect of such monies to be paid by Lessee directly to Lessee, and Lessee shall not be liable for any penalties or interest resulting from Lessor's failure to cause any such statement or bill to be given to Lessee at least twenty (20) days prior to the date when the same is due for payment.

3.04. *Maintenance of Buildings.* During the Lease Term, Lessor shall have no obligation whatsoever to maintain any buildings or other improvements (a) existing on the Demised Premises at the commencement of the Lease Term or (b) added to the Demised Premises thereafter. All such maintenance shall be provided by Lessee to such extent, if any, as Lessee shall consider appropriate.

3.05. *Taxes Personal to Lessor.* Nothing herein contained shall require Lessee to pay any franchise or corporate tax (or tax of a similar nature) payable on account of the ownership by Lessor of all or any interest in the Demised Premises, or any income tax (or tax of a similar nature) that may be payable by Lessor under any existing or future tax law of the United States or of the State of Ohio or any other governmental authority on account of the transfer of the interest of Lessor in the premises to any transferee or transferees or on account of the receipt by Lessor of the rent herein reserved.

3.06. *Right to Contest Taxes.* Lessee shall have the right in Lessee's own name (or in Lessor's name where appropriate), but at Lessee's own cost and expense, to contest the amount or legality of any real property taxes, personal property taxes, assessments, impositions or all other claims and charges which it is obligated to pay hereunder and make application for the reduction thereof, or any assessment upon which the same may be based; and Lessor agrees at the request of Lessee to execute or join in the execution of any documents necessary in connection with such contest or application.

ARTICLE FOUR
Use of Demised Premises

4.01. *Use of Demised Premises.* Lessee may use and occupy the Demised Premises during the Lease Term for the purpose of performing its obligations under the Financial Agreement and for any other lawful purpose.

ARTICLE FIVE
Improvements and Encumbrances

5.01. *Removal of Buildings.* Lessee shall have the right, without the consent of Lessor, from time to time and at any time during the Lease Term, to remove or demolish, at its sole cost and expense, any buildings, other improvements and other property existing or located on the Demised Premises.

5.02. *Construction of Buildings.* To the extent permitted by law and by the Financial Agreement, Lessee shall have the right, without the consent of Lessor, from time to time and at any time during the Lease Term, to construct such buildings and to make such other alterations, improvements and additions to the Demised Premises as Lessee may deem necessary or desirable.

5.03. *Securing of Variances and Approvals.* Lessor shall cooperate with and, where possible, join with Lessee in executing and prosecuting to completion, at Lessee's cost and expense, such applications for such orders, zoning variances, regulations and approvals of or by any governmental or regulatory authorities as may, in the opinion of Lessee be necessary or desirable in connection with the exercise by Lessee of its rights under this Lease Agreement.

5.04. *Vacation of Secondary Streets.* Upon receipt of a written request from Lessee, Lessor shall, to the extent permitted by law, take such actions as are necessary and appropriate to vacate and transfer to Lessee (at no cost to Lessee) any part of Pearl Street, Chapel Street, Walnut Street or Cherry Street (or any other secondary street or alley) which borders or passes through the Demised Premises and which divides land owned or leased by Lessee; provided, however, that such vacation shall neither impair the public health, peace and safety, nor cause the normal activities necessary to service such lands to be conducted from major thoroughfares bordering on or crossing through the Demised Premises.

5.05. *Encumbrances.* Lessee shall have the right, from time to time and at any time during the Lease Term, to subject all or any part of its leasehold interest in the Demised Premises (without further act by Lessor) to the lien of one or more mortgages or other encumbrances in order to obtain debt financing in connection with the exercise of its rights under Sections 5.01 and 5.02 of this Lease Agreement.

ARTICLE SIX
Purchase Option

6.01. *Purchase Option.* Lessor hereby grants to Lessee the right and option to purchase the Demised Premises from the Lessor for a purchase price of _____ Dollars ($ _____) cash. This option shall be exercisable upon written notice by Lessee to Lessor given at any time during the Lease Term, but not later than sixty (60) days prior to the expiration of the Lease Term. The closing shall be held within sixty (60) days after Lessor's receipt of notice of Lessee's exercise of its option to purchase or on such later date as the parties shall mutually agree in writing. Ten (10) days prior to the closing, Lessor shall furnish to Lessee, at Lessee's expense, a title insurance commitment and thereafter a policy issued by a title insurance company authorized to do business in the State of Ohio in the amount of the total purchase price, said commitment showing in Lessor and said policy insuring in Lessee a good and marketable title in fee simple to the Demised Premises free and clear of all defects, liens, mortgages, encumbrances, easements, restrictions, reservations, conditions, agreements and encroachments except (a) taxes and assessments due and payable after the date of such purchase, (b) zoning laws and regulations and other laws and ordinances affecting the use of the Demised Premises, (c) utility easements, (d) public streets, roads and highways, and (e) such exceptions to title as Lessee may be willing to waive in writing. Within thirty (30) days after the original closing date, Lessor shall, at Lessee's expense, remedy any unacceptable defects in the title as may be found to exist by Lessee. Lessor shall convey said premises to Lessee by good, sufficient and recordable deed of general warranty upon payment of the purchase price. Upon delivery of said deed and on payment of said purchase price by Lessee to Lessor, this Lease Agreement and everything contained herein shall terminate, and the parties hereto shall be fully released from all of the obligations hereunder.

ARTICLE SEVEN
Zoning, Restrictions and Variances

7.01. *Zoning, Restrictions and Variances.* In the event that the Demised Premises shall, from time to time or at any time during the Lease Term, be subject to any zoning law, regulation, restrictive covenant or other restriction which prohibits or in any material way intereferes with the performance by Lessee of its obligations under the Financial Agreement or with the reasonable redevelopment by Lessee of the Demised Premises in accordance with the uses outlined in the Financial Agreement, Lessee shall at its expense and in the normal manner first seek whatever variance is required in order to eliminate such prohibition or material interference; but if such variance shall not be granted to Lessee in a timely manner, and if Lessee shall subsequently give notice to Lessor of Lessee's request for the elimination of such zoning law, regulation, restrictive covenant or other restriction, then if Lessor fails to eliminate the same within ninety (90) days after Lessee's giving of such notice, Lessee shall have the right to terminate this Lease Agreement by giving sixty (60) days' notice to that effect to Lessor and, in that event, Lessor shall (in addition to complying with Lessor's obligations described in Section 15.01 of this Lease Agreement) promptly pay to Lessee (a) the then fair market value of all buildings and improvements (minus the aggregate amount of Lessee's indebtedness not evidenced by the Notes but secured by mortgages and other liens granted by Lessee and encumbering the Demised Premises) located on the Demised Premises which, upon such termination, become the property of Lessor under the provisions of this Lease Agreement, plus (c) the value (as shown on Lessee's books) of all fixtures and personal property affixed thereto or used in connection therewith (minus the aggregate amount of Lessee's indebtedness secured only by liens granted by Lessee and encumbering such fixtures and personal property), which fixtures and personal property shall thereupon become the property of Lessor.

ARTICLE EIGHT
Inspection, Damages and Insurance

8.01. *Inspection of Premises by Lessor.* Lessor and its duly authorized representatives may enter the Demised Premises at all reasonable times on twenty-four (24) hours' prior written notice to Lessee, to view and inspect the same, and to inspect all repairs, additions and alterations, and to perform any work therein which may be necessary by reason of Lessee's default under the terms of this Lease.

8.02. *Damage by Casualty.* Damage to or destruction of the Demised Premises or any building or other improvement located thereon, from time to time and at any time during the Lease Term, by fire or other casualty shall not terminate, abate, reduce or otherwise affect the Lease Term, and this Lease Agreement shall continue in full force and effect; and Lessee shall have the right to repair or restore any such damage or destruction.

8.03. *Liability Insurance.* At all times during the Lease Term, Lessee shall carry and maintain for the mutual benefit of Lessor and Lessee general public liability insurance against claims for personal injury, wrongful death and property damage occurring on or about the Demised Premises, with responsible insurers and with minimum amounts of $1,000,000 on account of bodily injury to or death of one or more persons, and $1,000,000 in the case of damage to property. Lessor and Lessee shall be named as insureds under these required liability insurance policies.

ARTICLE NINE
Indemnification

9.01. *Indemnification.* Lessee shall indemnify and save Lessor harmless from and against all loss, liability or damage for injury to or death of persons or damages to property sustained in, on or about the Demised Premises (other than such injury, death or damage resulting from an act of Lessor or Lessor's employees, agents, servants or representatives) resulting from the occupancy or use of the Demised Premises by Lessee or Lessee's agents, employees, customers, licensees or invitees.

ARTICLE TEN
Utility Charges

10.01. *Utility Charges.* Lessee shall pay all charges for gas, water, electricity, sewer or other utility services furnished to the Demised Premises during the Lease Term at the request of Lessee and those claiming through Lessee.

ARTICLE ELEVEN
Waiver of Subrogation

11.01. *Waiver by Lessor.* Lessor hereby waives any and all rights that it may have to recover from Lessee damages for any loss occurring to the Demised Premises by reason of any act or omission of Lessee; provided, however, that this waiver is limited to those losses for which Lessor is actually compensated by its insurers.

11.02. *Waiver by Lessee.* Lessee hereby waives any and all right that it may have to recover from Lessor damages for any loss occurring to property of Lessee by reason of any act or omission of Lessor; provided, however, that this waiver is limited to those losses for which Lessee is actually compensated by its insurers.

ARTICLE TWELVE
Assignment and Subletting

12.01. *Assignment.* Lessee may not assign this Lease Agreement or any interest therein without the prior written consent of Lessor, which consent shall not be unreasonably withheld by Lessor.

12.02. *Subletting.* Lessee may sublet the Demised Premises or any portion thereof from time to time and at any time during the Lease Term, without the consent of Lessor; provided, however, that no such subletting shall relieve Lessee from any of its obligations under this Lease Agreement and under the Financial Agreement. In consideration of any sublessees' agreement to enter into subleases of the Demised Premises or any portion thereof, Lessor approves of all of the terms and conditions of such subleases which are consistent with the provisions of this Lease Agreement. If after any such sublease is executed this Lease Agreement is terminated for any reason, such sublease shall continue in full force and effect (a) with Lessor succeeding to the rights and obligations of Lessee, (b) without any disturbance of the sublessee's right to occupy the subleased premises in accordance with the provisions of such sublease, and (c) with the sublessee attorning to Lessor under the same terms and provisions set forth in this Lease Agreement.

ARTICLE THIRTEEN
Quiet Enjoyment and Title

13.01. *Quiet Enjoyment.* Lessor covenants with and warrants and represents to Lessee that Lessee shall at all times during the Lease Term peaceably and quietly have, hold and occupy the Demised Premises and the appurtenances thereunto belonging without hindrance or molestation by Lessor or by any person claiming rights to the Demised Premises superior to those of Lessee.

13.02. *Lessor's Right to Effect Lease Agreement.* Lessor covenants with and warrants and represents to Lessee that Lessor has the lawful right to effect this Lease Agreement for the Lease Term and to perform the obligations of Lessor provided under this Lease Agreement, and that all necessary action has been taken to authorize Lessor lawfully to enter into this Lease Agreement.

13.03. *Warranty of Ownership.* Lessor covenants with and warrants and represents to Lessee that Lessor owns good and merchantable fee simple title to the Demised Premises free and clear from all defects, liens, mortgages, encumbrances, easements, restrictions, reservations, conditions, agreements and encroachments except (a) taxes and assessments due and payable after the commencement of the Lease Term, (b) zoning laws and regulations and other laws and ordinances affecting the use of the Demised Premises, (c) public streets, roads and highways, and (d) such exceptions to title as Lessee has waived in writing. Lessor covenants with and warrants and represents to Lessee that it has not granted any mortgage or created any liens encumbering the Demised Premises since Lessor acquired title thereto and that it will not commit or suffer the commission of any act (other than acts taken or requested by Lessee) during the Lease Term which will diminish in any way the quality of Lessor's title to the Demised Premises.

ARTICLE FOURTEEN
Condemnation

14.01. *Appropriation by Lessor.* If all or any portion of the Demised Premises is appropriated by Lessor under its power of eminent domain, Lessee may elect either to terminate the Lease Term or to take the appropriation award.

14.02. *Election by Lessee.* Lessee shall exercise the election provided by Section 14.01 of this Lease Agreement by giving notice of the election to Lessor, but if Lessee shall not give such notice within sixty (60) days after the final determination and payment of the appropriation award, it shall be conclusively presumed that Lessee elected to take the appropriation award.

14.03. *Appropriation by Other Condemning Authority.* If all or any portion of the Demised Premises is appropriated by any condemning authority other than Lessor under the power of eminent domain or by purchase or other acquisition under threat of appropriation, (a) Lessor shall directly take that portion of the appropriation award or consideration which is directly attributable to the value of land and use such funds to pay off all or a portion of the Notes, (b) the purchase price of the purchase option established in Section 6.01 of this Lease Agreement shall be reduced by an amount equal to such portion of the appropriation award or consideration, and (c) Lessee shall take all of the remainder of the appropriation award or consideration.

ARTICLE FIFTEEN
Termination by Lessee

15.01. *Termination by Lessee.* If Lessee shall terminate the Lease Term as provided in Sections 2.04, 7.01 or 14.01 of this Lease Agreement following (a) Lessor's actions resulting in the termination of the Financial Agreement, (b) Lessor's interference with contemplated land uses, or (c) Lessor's condemnation of the Demised Premises (which three circumstances are more fully described in said sections of this Lease Agreement) then Lessee shall be released from all of its obligations (except for obligations in respect of that portion of the Demised Premises as to which Lessee has not terminated the Lease Term) under this Lease Agreement, and Lessor (and any appropriate agency, corporation or organization designated by Lessor), to the extent permitted by law, shall:

(A) Automatically (without further act by Lessor, Lessee or any other party) assume and perform all of Lessee's obligations (except for obligations in respect of that portion of the Demised Premises as to which Lessee has not terminated the Lease Term) under:

(i) all contracts and agreements existing at the date of such termination and relating to the construction of buildings and other improvements on the Demised Premises and those relating to the purchase and installation of fixtures and other personal property to be affixed thereto and used in connection therewith; and

(ii) all construction and other loan and financing agreements existing at the date of such termination and relating to the financing of the construction of buildings and improvements existing or to be constructed on the Demised Premises and to the financing of the purchase and installation of fixtures and other personal property then or thereafter to be affixed thereto or used in connection therewith; and

(iii) all promissory notes entered into and made in connection with financing the construction of buildings and other improvements existing or to be constructed on the Demised Premises and to the financing of the purchase and installation of fixtures and other personal property then or thereafter affixed thereto or used in connection therewith; and

(iv) all mortgages and other liens encumbering the Demised Premises to secure performance of any obligation of Lessee assumed and to be performed by Lessor as contemplated by this Section 15.01 of this Lease Agreement; and

(v) each sublease, assignment and other agreement under which one or more persons succeed to all or any part of Lessee's interest in the Demised Premises; and

(B) Indemnify Lessee and save it harmless from and against any and all loss, liability, damage or claims of whatever nature to any person, property or business interests caused by or resulting from the failure of Lessor to perform any obligation assumed by it as contemplated by this Section 15.01 of this Lease Agreement, and from and against any and all costs, expenses and liabilities incurred by Lessee in connection with any claim, action or proceeding in respect thereof (including without limitation the fees of attorneys, investigators and experts). In the event that any claim, action or proceeding is brought against Lessee by reason of any such failure on the part of Lessor, Lessor shall, if requested by Lessee, cause the same to be resisted or defended at Lessor's sole cost and expense.

ARTICLE SIXTEEN
Default

16.01. *Lessor's Rights upon Default.* If Lessee fails to pay any money obligation to be paid by Lessee under the terms of this Lease Agreement, and if such money obligation remains unpaid for a period of thirty (30) days after notice of such default has been given to Lessee by Lessor; or if Lessee shall fail to perform or observe any of the other obligations of Lessee under the terms of this Lease Agreement and shall fail to commence the correction of such default within sixty (60) days after written notice to Lessee by Lessor of such time thereafter; or if Lessee abandons or vacates the Demised Premises during the Lease Term; or if Lessee is adjudicated a bankrupt or makes an assignment for the benefit of creditors or suffers a receiver to be appointed in any action or proceeding by or against it; or if any proceeding under the Bankruptcy Act is filed by Lessee; or if Lessee's interest in the Demised Premises is sold upon execution or other legal process, Lessor shall have the sole option to give Lessee written notice of Lessor's intention to terminate the right of Lessee to occupy the Demised Premises and Lessor shall have the right to re-enter the Demised Premises on the date stated in said notice, and in that event, all of the rights and obligations of Lessor and of Lessee under this Lease Agreement shall terminate as of the date of such termination and re-entry.

16.02. *Rights of Assignees, Sublessees and Lienholders.* Anything contained in Section 16.01 of this Lease Agreement or elsewhere to the contrary notwithstanding, if Lessee shall have given notice to Lessor that Lessee has assigned this Lease Agreement, subleased all or any portion of the Demised Premises or caused or suffered its leasehold interest in the Demised Premises to be subjected to the lien of any mortgage or other encumbrance (which notice shall have specified the name and address of such assignee, sublessee and the holder of any such mortgage or other encumbrance), or if a memorandum, notice or copy of such assignment, sublease, mortgage or other encumbrance shall be of record in the office of the Recorder of Franklin County, Ohio, then:

(A) Lessor shall not have the right to terminate this Lease Agreement and to re-enter the Demised Premises for any reason prior to the expiration of the Lease Term unless any of the covenants, agreements or obligations herein made or assumed by Lessee are not performed or observed and if correction thereof is not commenced within one hundred twenty (120) days after written notice is given by Lessor to each such assignee, sublessee and the holder of each such mortgage and other encumbrance and to Lessee of such failure and if correction thereof is not completed within a reasonable time thereafter; and

(B) Any such default may be cured or corrected by Lessee or by any such assignee, sublessee or the holder of any such mortgage or other encumbrance.

ARTICLE SEVENTEEN
Notices and Payments

17.01. *Initial Addresses.* All notices and other communications required or permitted to be given or delivered under this Lease Agreement by Lessor or Lessee, which notices or communications shall be in writing, and all payment or money required to be made by Lessor or Lessee to the other under the provisions of this Lease Agreement, shall be mailed, postage prepaid, addressed as follows:

(A) If to Lessor, to:
Mayor of the City of Columbus
City Hall
Columbus, Ohio 43215
with a copy to:
City Attorney of Columbus
City Hall
Columbus, Ohio 43215
(B) If to Lessee, to:
Capitol South Community Urban
Redevelopment Corporation
101 East Town Street
Columbus, Ohio 43215
with a copy to:
Vorys, Sater, Seymour and Pease
52 East Gay Street
Columbus, Ohio 43215.

17.02. *Change of Address.* Lessor or Lessee may, by notice received by the other, from time to time and at any time designate a different address for the making of payments required to be made to the party designating such new address and for the giving of notices or other communications to the party designating such new address.

17.03. *Completion upon Mailing.* Any notice, communication or payment required or permitted to be given in accordance with this Lease Agreement shall be deemed to have been given when the same shall have been placed in the mail, postage prepaid, addressed in accordance with this Article Seventeen of this Lease Agreement.

ARTICLE EIGHTEEN
Miscellaneous Provisions

18.01. *Memorandum of Lease.* From time to time and at any time during the Lease Term, Lessor shall, upon request by Lessee, execute and deliver to Lessee a Memorandum of Lease reflecting such of the terms of this Lease Agreement as Lessee may designate, each of which shall be in a form recordable under the laws of the State of Ohio and which Lessee may record in public offices.

18.02. *Successors and Assigns.* This Lease Agreement shall inure to the benefit of and be binding upon the respective successors and assigns (including successive, as well as immediate, successors and assignees) of Lessor and of Lessee.

18.03. *Governing Law and Forum.* This Lease Agreement shall be governed by and construed in accordance with the laws of the State of Ohio.

18.04. *Remedies Cumulative.* All rights and remedies of Lessor and of Lessee enumerated in this Lease Agreement shall be cumulative and, except as specifically contemplated otherwise by this Lease Agreement, none shall exclude any other right or remedy allowed at law or in equity, and said rights or remedies may be exercised and enforced concurrently. No waiver by Lessor or by Lessee of any covenant or condition of this Lease Agreement to be kept or performed by the other party shall constitute a waiver by the waiving party of any subsequent breach of such covenant or condition or authorize the breach or non-observance on any other occasion of the same or any other covenant or condition of this Lease Agreement.

18.05. *Duplicate Originals.* This Lease Agreement may be executed in one or more counterparts, each of which shall be deemed to be a duplicate original, but all of which, taken together, shall constitute a single instrument.

18.06. *Article and Section Headings.* The article and section headings contained in this Lease Agreement are included only for convenience of reference and do not define, limit, explain or modify this Lease Agreement or its interpretation, construction or meaning and are in no way to be construed as part of this Lease Agreement.

18.07. *Provisions Separable.* If any provision of this Lease Agreement or the application of any such provision to any person or any circumstance shall be determined to be invalid or unenforceable, then such determination shall not affect any other provisions of this Lease Agreement or the application of such provision to any other person or circumstance, all of which other provisions shall remain in full force and effect; and if any provision of this Lease Agreement is capable of two constructions, one of which would render the provision void and the other of which would render the provision valid, then such provision shall have the meaning which renders it valid.

18.08. *Entire Agreement.* This Lease Agreement constitutes the entire agreement between Lessor and Lessee in respect of the subject matter hereof, and this Lease Agreement supersedes all prior and contemporaneous agreements between Lessor and Lessee in connection with the subject matter of this Lease Agreement. No officer, employee or other servant or agent of Lessor or of Lessee is authorized to make any representation, warranty or other promise not contained in this Lease Agreement. No change, termination or attempted waiver of any of the provisions of this Lease Agreement shall be binding upon Lessor or Lessee unless in writing and signed by the party affected.

CITY OF COLUMBUS, OHIO

By _____
    Mayor

CAPITOL SOUTH COMMUNITY URBAN REDEVELOPMENT CORPORATION

By _____
    Executive Director

EXHIBIT D

Fiscal Plan for Financing the Project

The fiscal plan for financing the Project is based upon the concept that most of the redevelopment will be undertaken by other private or public developers utilizing their own financial resources. The Company[1] plans to derive income from these redevelopments primarily by negotiating appropriate leases or subleases with the developers. The particular rental schedules and terms of such leases or subleases will obviously vary due to the fact that they

---
[1] As a non-profit corporation, the Company itself has no stock or paid-in capital. Investment of private capital in the Company can (except for outright grants and donations) consist only of loans for which the usual evidences of indebtedness can be issued. The sources, method and amounts of such investments, if any, cannot now be determined by the Company.

---

must be tailored to meet the circumstances necessary to attract the investment by developers in the specific redevelopments desired by the Company.

Although the total cost of the Project has been estimated at $200,000,000, this expenditure will be phased over a period of years. Initially using grants from federal, state and local sources as well as loans from organizations and individuals, the Company plans from time to time to lease from the City those portions of the Property for which redevelopment in accordance with the provisions of the Financial Agreement seems most appropriate and timely.

It is anticipated by the Company that the leases or subleases under which most of the development will occur will provide that the developer will bear all of the redevelopment expenses including (a) operations and maintenance, (b) construction, financing and other interest, and (c) amortization of debts, reserves and mortgages. These items will not directly affect the Company and are not now known by the Company.

Since most of the improvements will have a useful life greatly in excess of five years, most of the redevelopment will occur following the exercise by the Company of its option to purchase real estate which it will lease from the City. The option price will, in most instances, be paid from funds obtained directly from the developer or from funds borrowed by the Company to be repaid out of the lease rent. In either event, the schedule of rents for the particular phase of the Project (supplemented in some instances by other sources) will be such as to service any funds borrowed by the Company for the development of the phase, including payments of principal and interest, amortization of debts and reserves, and payments to the City required under the Financial Agreement.

APPENDIX H(2)

First Amendment to Financial Agreement

THIS AGREEMENT, made this _____ day of _____, _____, by and between the CITY OF COLUMBUS, OHIO (the "City"), an Ohio municipal corporation, and CAPITOL SOUTH COMMUNITY URBAN REDEVELOPMENT CORPORATION (the "Company"), an Ohio non-profit public purpose corporation with its principal place of business located at 101 East Town Street, Columbus, Ohio 43215;

WITNESSETH:

WHEREAS, the Company submitted its application for a Financial Agreement to the City and this application was approved by the City (the "Application"); and

WHEREAS, Columbus City Council authorized the Mayor to execute a Financial Agreement with the Company in Ordinance No. 1855–76 on December 13, 1976; and

WHEREAS, the City and Company entered into Financial Agreement, on the 21st day of January, 1977; and

WHEREAS, the City and Company wish to modify this Financial Agreement;

NOW, THEREFORE, in consideration of the premises and the mutual covenants and agreements contained in the Financial Agreement and this First Amendment to Financial Agreement, it is mutually agreed between the City and the Company as follows:

1. The City and Company mutually acknowledge that an unintended omission exists in Section 7 of the Financial Agreement and agree that the words "one half of" should be inserted and hereby are inserted in the fifteenth (15) line on page 7 of the Financial Agreement following the words "equal to."

2. Section 4 of the Financial Agreement should be amended and read as follows:

"4. **Use of Notes and Bonds.** For the purpose of obtaining the funds needed to purchase the parcels of the Property to be acquired by the City hereunder, the City Council shall cause the City to issue general obligations notes having a term of not more than five (5) years and paying the lowest rate of interest then obtainable. The City shall convert its short-term notes to long-term bonds, which bonds shall be for a period not to exceed thirty (30) years, and on the terms and conditions contained in Exhibit E."

3. Section 41 should be added to the Financial Agreement and read as follows:

"41. **Long-Term Lease.** When the City acquires a parcel or parcels of the Property in accordance with the provisions of this Financial Agreement, or after it has acquired a parcel or parcels of the Property and is leasing them to the Company pursuant to Exhibit C hereto, the City hereby agrees to lease such parcel or parcels of the Property to the Company upon written request by the Company for a period of years which shall in no event exceed thirty (30) years in accordance with the terms and conditions of the Long-Term Lease Agreement attached hereto as Exhibit E and incorporated herein. This Long-Term Lease Agreement shall be in substantially the same form as Exhibit E. The City shall convert its short-term notes to long-term bonds which bonds will be for a period not to exceed thirty (30) years and on the terms and conditions contained in Exhibit E."

4. Section 42 should be added to the Financial Agreement and read as follows:

"42. **Adding Additional Parties to the Financial Agreement.**

A. Any community urban redevelopment corporation which is (1) a lessee hereunder, (2) a sublessee hereunder, (3) a mortgagee of a lessee or sublessee, or (4) a wholly-owned subsidiary of a lessee, sublessee or mortgagee, shall automatically become an additional party ("Additional Party") to this Financial Agreement if it gives notice of its intent to become a party to the City and Company, including its name, address and status under this Financial Agreement, in accordance with Section 33 of this Financial Agreement.

B. Thereafter, no notice given by the City or the Company, pursuant to Section 33 of the Financial Agreement, shall be effective unless a copy of such notice is given both (1) to each Additional Party and (2) to the holder of any mortgage on the Company's or any Additional Party's interest in the Property if the City and Company have been notified in writing of holder's name, address and status hereunder.

C. In the event that the Company fails to remedy a default claimed by the City within the sixty (60) day period provided in Section 32 of the Financial Agreement, each Additional Party or each holder of any mortgage who has notified the City and Company of its interests herein as provided above shall have an additional period of sixty (60) days thereafter within which to remedy the alleged default to the satisfaction of the City or to submit the matter to arbitration as provided in this Financial Agreement.

D. Any act required by this Financial Agreement on the part of the Company, may be performed by any Additional Party or any other person and the City shall accept such performance as the performance of the Company.

E. In the event any of the following should occur:

1. The Company shall lose its qualification pursuant to Chapter 1728 of the Ohio Revised Code, or

2. The Company shall no longer be obligated under or be a party to the Financial Agreement, or

3. The Company breaches and fails to cure any default under the Financial Agreement, the City shall nonetheless continue to honor the Financial Agreement as an agreement with each Additional Party in the place and stead of the Company to the extent of such Additional Party's interests in the Property if such Additional Party shall attorn to the City and perform all of the obligations of the Company under the Financial Agreement with respect to such Additional Party's interests in the Property."

5. The City and Company hereby agree that each and every term and provision of the Financial Agreement shall be and remain unchanged, except as specifically modified herein, and the City and Company hereby ratify and confirm the Financial Agreement as modified hereby.

6. The City and Company agree that this First Amendment to Financial Agreement shall be attached to and be made a part of the Financial Agreement.

7. This First Amendment to Financial Agreement shall be binding upon and inure to the benefit of the parties hereto, their successors and assigns, as if originally a part of the Financial Agreement.

IN WITNESS WHEREOF, the parties have hereunto set their hands or caused these presents to be executed by their duly authorized officials as of the day and year first above written.

CITY OF COLUMBUS, OHIO

By _____
    Mayor

CAPITOL SOUTH COMMUNITY
URBAN REDEVELOPMENT CORPORATION

By _____
    Executive Director

APPROVED AS TO FORM BY:

_____
    City Attorney

EXHIBIT E

Long-Term Lease Agreement

This Lease Agreement made and entered into at Columbus, Ohio, this _____ day of _____, _____, by and between the City of Columbus, Ohio, a municipal corporation duly organized and existing under and by virtue of the Constitution of the State of Ohio (the "Lessor"), and Capitol South Community Urban Redevelopment Corporation, a non-profit public purpose corporation organized and existing under the laws of the State of Ohio (the "Lessee");

WITNESSETH:

That for and in consideration of the premises and of the covenants herein contained, the parties hereto make the following agreement, intending to be legally bound thereby:

ARTICLE ONE
Demised Premises

1.01 *Leasing of Premises.* Lessor does hereby demise and let unto Lessee, and Lessee does hereby lease and hire from Lessor, all of the real property situated in the City of Columbus, Franklin County, Ohio, described in the Legal Description Annex which is included herewith and incorporated herein, together with any and all improvements which are now situated on said real property and the appurtenances thereunto belonging (the "Demised Premises").

1.02 *Ownership of Buildings and Improvements.* The Demised Premises shall not include any buildings or other improvements which may hereafter be placed thereon by Lessee, a lessee of Lessee, a parallel lessee or other person claiming through Lessee (the "Lessee or its Sublessees") which buildings and improvements shall be the sole property of Lessee or its Sublessees during the Lease Term.

1.03 *Ownership of Fixtures and Personal Property.* The Demised Premises shall not include any fixtures, trade fixtures, furniture, furnishings, equipment or other property installed or maintained on the Demised Premises by Lessee or its Sublessees.

ARTICLE TWO
Lease Term and Form

2.01 *Lease Term.* The Lease Term shall be the period of thirty (30) years or a shorter period mutually established by the parties commencing on the later of the date of this Lease Agreement as set forth above or the date on which Lessor issued its general obligation bonds (the "Bonds") for the specific purpose of acquiring the funds used to purchase the Demised Premises or refinance the purchase of the Demised Premises and terminating thirty (30) years after the commencement date or a shorter period mutually established by the parties. This term may commence when the Lessor initially acquires the Demised Premises, during the term of the five year lease permitted by the Financial Agreement (the "Short-Term Lease") or at the end of the term of the Short-Term Lease.

2.02 *Lease Hold-Over Provisions.* If Lessee remains in possession of the Demised Premises after the expiration of the Lease Term, Lessee shall be deemed to be a tenant from month-to-month only, subject to all of the terms and provisions of this Lease Agreement except as to the duration of the Lease Term, until Lessee or Lessor shall have given to the other thirty (30) days' notice of termination of such tenancy from month-to-month.

2.03 *Separate Lease Agreements.* Upon written request from Lessee to Lessor, Lessor shall from time to time and at any time during the Lease Term demise and let to Lessee under a separate lease agreement any portion of the Demised Premises to be designated by Lessee, which portion shall thereafter cease to be a part of the Demised Premises under this Lease Agreement. The relevant rights and obligations of Lessor and Lessee under any such separate lease agreement shall be substantially identical to those contained in this Lease Agreement with appropriate adjustments for rent.

2.04 *Termination of Lease Term.* Lessee may terminate the Lease Term in respect of all or any portion of the Demised Premises, from time to time and at any time by giving sixty (60) days' written notice to that effect to Lessor, if either (a) Lessor terminates the Financial Agreement entered into between Lessor and Lessee on January 21, 1977 (the "Financial Agreement"), at a time when Lessee is in full compliance with the provisions of the Financial Agreement, or (b) Lessee terminates the Financial Agreement in accordance with provisions of Section 32 (thirty-two) of the Financial Agreement as a result of Lessor's violation of the provisions of the Financial Agreement. This termination shall not affect the rights of any sublessee or parallel lessee unless they consent in writing to the termination of their sublease or lease.

ARTICLE THREE
Consideration for Demised Premises

3.01 *Rent.* As a part of the consideration for the Demised Premises during the Lease term, Lessee shall pay to Lessor rent in an amount which will allow the Lessor to pay principal and interest on its Bonds in a timely manner. The payment schedule of these Bonds shall be established by the Director of Finance of Lessor after consultation with Lessee; provided, however, payment of said rent shall be made in appropriate installments due and payable by Lessee not later than ten (10) days before the principal and/or interest on the Bonds shall become due and payable to the holders of the Bonds and the term shall not exceed thirty (30) years.

3.02 *Administrative Fee to Lessor.* As additional consideration for the Demised Premises during the lease term, Lessee shall pay Lessor one half of one percent (.5%) of the average amount of the principal of the Bonds (the "Administrative Fee") outstanding during the year preceding each anniversary date and issued to acquire the Demised Premises or refinance the Demised Premises on each anniversary of the rent commencement date and the final payment when the Bonds are paid in full. If any payment of this Administrative Fee is made other than on an anniversary date, it shall be pro-rated to the date of payment by multiplying the annual Administrative Fee times a fraction whose numerator is the number of days since the last Administrative Fee payment and whose denominator is 365.

3.03 *Service Charges in Lieu of Taxes.* As additional consideration for the Demised Premises during the Lease Term, Lessee or its Sublessees shall pay all semi-annual service charges in lieu of taxes on the Demised Premises payable in accordance with the provisions of Section 7 (seven) of the Financial Agreement.

3.04 *Taxes and Assessments.* As additional consideration for the Demised Premises for the Lease Term, Lessee or its Sublessees shall pay all real estate taxes and installments of assessments, both general and special, and all other charges of any and every kind heretofore or hereafter lawfully levied, assessed, charged, taxed or imposed during the Lease Term upon the Demised Premises and upon any improvements now or hereafter placed thereon, except (a) that any monies so payable by Lessee or its Sublessees which are levied, due or payable, or which are a lien upon the Demised Premises at the commencement of the Lease Term and are not the responsibility of Lessee or its Sublessees under any other agreement shall be pro-rated at the commencement of the Lease Term and (b) that any monies so payable by Lessee which are a lien upon the Demised Premises in the collection period during which the Lease Term expires, shall be pro-rated to such termination date. Lessor shall make all necessary arrangements to have the collecting authorities send all pertinent statements and bills in respect of such monies to be paid by Lessee directly to Lessee, and Lessee shall not be liable for any penalties or interest resulting from Lessor's failure to cause any such statement or bill to be given to Lessee at least twenty (20) days prior to the date when the same is due for payment.

3.05 *Maintenance of Buildings.* During the Lease Term, Lessor shall have no obligation whatsoever to maintain any buildings or other improvements (a) existing on the Demised Premises at the commencement of the Lease Term or (b) added to the Demised Premises thereafter. All such maintenance shall be provided by Lessee or its Sub-

lessees to such extent, if any, as Lessee or its Sublessees shall consider appropriate.

3.06 *Taxes Personal to Lessor.* Nothing herein contained shall require Lessee or its Sublessees to pay any franchise or corporate tax (or tax of a similar nature) payable on account of the ownership by Lessor of all or any interest in the Demised Premises, or any income tax (or tax of a similar nature) that may be payable by Lessor under any existing or future tax law of the United States or of the State of Ohio or any other governmental authority on account of the transfer of the interest of Lessor in the premises to any transferee or transferees or on account of the receipt by Lessor of the rent herein reserved.

3.07 *Right to Contest Taxes.* Lessee or its Sublessees shall have the right in Lessee's own name (or in Lessor's name where appropriate) but at Lessee's or its Sublessees' own cost and expense, to contest the amount or legality of any real property taxes, personal property taxes, assessments, impositions or all other claims and charges which it is obligated to pay hereunder and make application for the reduction thereof, or any assessment upon which the same may be based; and Lessor agrees at the request of Lessee or its Sublessees to execute or join in the execution of any documents necessary in connection with such contest or application.

ARTICLE FOUR
Use of Demised Premises

4.01 *Right to Sublease.* Lessee shall have the right to sublease the Demised Premises to third persons or an entity composed of Lessee and third persons who are willing to develop the Demised Premises in accordance with the terms and conditions of this Long-Term Lease Agreement and the Financial Agreement.

4.02 *Use of Demised Premises.* Lessee or its Sublessees may use and occupy the Demised Premises during the Lease Term for the purpose of performing Lessee's obligations under the Financial Agreement and for any other lawful purpose.

ARTICLE FIVE
Improvements and Encumbrances

5.01 *Removal of Buildings.* Lessee or its Sublessees shall have the right, without the consent of Lessor, from time to time and at any time during the Lease Term, to remove or demolish, at its sole cost and expense, any buildings, other improvements and other property existing or located on the Demised Premises.

5.02 *Construction of Buildings.* To the extent permitted by law and by the Financial Agreement, Lessee or its Sublessees shall have the right, without the consent of Lessor, from time to time and at any time during the Lease Term, to construct such buildings and to make such other alterations, improvements and additions to the Demised Premises as Lessee or its Sublessees may deem necessary or desirable.

5.03 *Securing of Variances and Approvals.* Lessor shall cooperate with and, where possible, join with Lessee or its Sublessees in executing and prosecuting to completion, at Lessee's or its Sublessees' cost and expense, such applications for such orders, zoning variances, regulations and approvals of or by any governmental or regulatory authorities as may, in the opinion of Lessee or its Sublessees be necessary or desirable in connection with the exercise by Lessee of its rights under this Lease Agreement.

5.04 *Vacation of Secondary Streets.* Upon receipt of a written request from Lessee, Lessor shall, to the extent permitted by law, take such actions as are necessary and appropriate to vacate, transfer and/or lease to Lessee (at no cost to Lessee) any part of Pearl Street, Chapel Street, Walnut Street or Cherry Street (or any other secondary street or alley) which borders or passes through the Demised Premises; provided, however, that such vacation shall neither impair the public health, peace and safety, nor cause the normal activities necessary to service such lands to be conducted from major thoroughfares bordering on or crossing through the Demised Premises.

5.05 *Encumbrances.* Lessee or its Sublessees shall have the right, from time to time and at any time during the Lease Term, to subject all or any part of their leasehold interest in the Demised Premises (without further act by Lessor) to the lien of one or more mortgages or other encumbrances in order to obtain debt financing in connection with the exercise of their rights under Sections 5.01 and 5.02 of this Long-Term Lease Agreement.

ARTICLE SIX
Conveyance at End of Lease Term

6.01 *Conveyance at End of Lease Term.* Once the principal and interest on the Bonds have been paid in full, all

Administrative Fees have been paid, and all other obligations of Lessee hereunder have been performed, Lessor agrees to transfer to Lessee good and marketable title in fee simple to the Demised Premises free and clear of all defects, liens, mortgages, encumbrances, easements, restrictions, reservations, conditions, agreements and encroachments, except (a) taxes and assessments due and payable after the date of such conveyance, (b) zoning laws and regulations and other laws and ordinances affecting the use of the Demised Premises, (c) utility easements existing at the date of this Lease Agreement or consented to in writing by Lessee, (d) public streets, roads and highways, and (e) such exceptions to title as Lessee may be willing to waive in writing.

6.02 *Purchase Option.* Lessor hereby grants to Lessee the right and option to purchase the Demised Premises from the Lessor by paying the total unpaid principal and cumulative interest on the Bonds issued to acquire or refinance the acquisition of the Demised Premises in full plus the cumulative Administrative Fee due through the end of the term or such other amount as shall be mutually established by Lessor and Lessee. The original principal on the Bonds is _____ Dollars. This option shall be exercisable upon written notice by Lessee to Lessor given at any time during the Lease Term, but not later than sixty (60) days prior to the expiration of the Lease Term. The closing shall be held within sixty (60) days after Lessor's receipt of notice of Lessee's exercise of its option to purchase or on such later date as the parties shall mutually agree in writing. Ten (10) days prior to the closing, Lessor shall furnish to Lessee, at Lessee's expense, a title insurance commitment and thereafter a policy issued by a title insurance company authorized to do business in the State of Ohio in the amount of the total purchase price, said commitment showing in Lessor and said policy insuring in Lessee a good and marketable title in fee simple to the Demised Premises free and clear of all defects, liens, mortgages, encumbrances, easements, restrictions, reservations, conditions, agreements and encroachments except (a) taxes and assessments due and payable after the date of such purchase, (b) zoning laws and regulations and other laws and ordinances affecting the use of the Demised Premises, (c) utility easements existing at the date of this Lease Agreement or consented to in writing by Lessee, (d) public streets, roads and highways, and (e) such exceptions to title as Lessee may be willing to waive in writing. Within thirty (30) days after the original closing date, Lessor shall, at Lessee's expense, remedy any unacceptable defects in the title as may be found to exist by Lessee. Lessor shall convey the Demised Premises to Lessee by good, sufficient and recordable general warranty deed upon payment of the purchase price. Upon delivery of said deed and on payment of said purchase price by Lessee to Lessor, this Lease Agreement and everything contained herein shall terminate, and the parties hereto shall be fully released from all of the obligations hereunder.

ARTICLE SEVEN
Zoning, Restrictions and Variances

7.01 *Zoning, Restrictions and Variances.* In the event that the Demised Premises shall, from time to time or at any time during the Lease Term, be subject to any zoning law, regulation, restrictive covenant or other restriction which prohibits or in any material way interferes with the performance by Lessee of its obligations under the Financial Agreement or with the reasonable redevelopment by Lessee or its Sublessees of the Demised Premises in accordance with the uses outlined in the Financial Agreement, Lessee or its Sublessees shall at their expense and in the normal manner first seek whatever variance is required in order to eliminate such prohibition or material interference; but if such variance shall not be granted to Lessee or its Sublessees in a timely manner, and if Lessee or its Sublessees shall subsequently give notice to Lessor of Lessee's or its Sublessees' request for the elimination of such zoning law, regulation, restrictive covenant or other restriction, then if Lessor fails to eliminate the same within ninety (90) days after Lessee's or its Sublessees' giving of such notice, Lessee shall have the right to terminate this Lease Agreement by giving sixty (60) days' notice to that effect to Lessor and, in that event, Lessor shall (in addition to complying with Lessor's obligations described in Section 15.01 of this Lease Agreement) promptly pay to Lessee or its Sublessees (a) the then fair market value of all buildings and improvements (minus the aggregate amount of Lessee's indebtedness not evidenced by the Bonds but secured by mortgages and other liens granted by Lessee or its Sublessees and encumbering the building and improvements) located on the Demised Premises which, upon such termination, become the property of

Lessor under the provisions of this Lease Agreement, plus (b) the value (as shown on Lessee's or its Sublessees' books) of all fixtures and personal property affixed thereto or used in connection therewith (minus the aggregate amount of Lessee's or its Sublessees' indebtedness secured only by liens granted by Lessee or its Sublessees and encumbering such fixtures and personal property), which fixtures and personal property shall thereupon become the property of Lessor and Lessor shall release Lessee from all obligations under this Lease Agreement and the Bonds.

ARTICLE EIGHT
Inspections, Damages and Insurance

8.01 *Inspections of Demised Premises by Lessor.* Lessor and its duly authorized representatives may enter the Demised Premises at all reasonable times on twenty-four (24) hours' prior written notice to Lessee or its Sublessees, to view and inspect the same, and to inspect all repairs, additions and alterations, and to perform any work therein which may be necessary by reason of Lessee's default under the terms of this Lease.

8.02 *Damage by Casualty.* Damage to or destruction of the Demised Premises or any building or other improvement located thereon, from time to time and at any time during the Lease Term, by fire or other casualty shall not terminate, abate, reduce or otherwise affect the Lease Term, and this Lease Agreement shall continue in full force and effect; and Lessee or its Sublessees shall have the right to repair or restore any such damage or destruction.

8.03 *Liability Insurance.* At all times during the Lease Term, Lessee or its Sublessees shall carry and maintain for the mutual benefit of Lessor, Lessee and its Sublessees general public liability insurance against claims for personal injury, wrongful death and property damage occurring on or about the Demised Premises, with responsible insurers and with minimum amounts of $1,000,000 on account of bodily injury to or death of one or more persons, and $1,000,000 in the case of damage to property. Lessor and Lessee shall be named as insureds under these required liability insurance policies.

ARTICLE NINE
Indemnification

9.01 *Indemnification.* Lessee or its Sublessees shall indemnify and save Lessor harmless from and against all loss, liability or damage for injury to or death of persons or damages to property sustained in, on or about the Demised Premises (other than such injury, death or damage resulting from an act of Lessor or Lessor's employees, agents, servants or representatives) resulting from the occupancy or use of the Demised Premises by Lessee, its Sublessees or Lessee's or its Sublessees' agents, employees, customers, licensees or invitees.

ARTICLE TEN
Utility Charges

10.01 *Utility Charges.* Lessee or its Sublessees shall pay all charges for gas, water, electricity, sewer or other utility services furnished to the Demised Premises during the Lease Term at the request of Lessee or its Sublessees.

ARTICLE ELEVEN
Waiver of Subrogation

11.01 *Waiver by Lessor.* Lessor hereby waives any and all rights that it may have to recover from Lessee or its Sublessees damages for any loss occurring to the Demised Premises by reason of any act or omission of Lessee or its Sublessees; provided, however, that this waiver is limited to those losses for which Lessor is actually compensated by its insurers.

11.02 *Waiver by Lessee.* Lessee hereby waives any and all right that it may have to recover from Lessor damages for any loss occurring to property of Lessee by reason of any act or omission of Lessor; provided, however, that this waiver is limited to those losses for which Lessee is actually compensated by its insurers.

ARTICLE TWELVE
Assignment and Subletting

12.01 *Assignment.* Lessee may not assign this Lease Agreement or any interest therein without the prior written consent of Lessor, which consent shall not be unreasonably withheld by Lessor.

12.02 *Subletting.* Lessee may sublet the Demised Premises or any portion thereof from time to time and at any time during the Lease Term, without the consent of Lessor; provided, however, that no such subletting shall relieve Lessee from any of its obligations under this Lease Agreement and the Financial Agreement without the prior written consent of Lessor. In consideration of any sublessee's agreement to enter into subleases of the Demised Premises or any portion thereof, Lessor hereby approves all of the terms and conditions of such subleases

which are not in conflict with the provisions of this Long-Term Lease Agreement. If any of the provisions of any sublease are in conflict with the provisions of this Long-Term Lease Agreement, these conflicting provisions shall be submitted to Lessor in writing for its approval. Lessee may submit these subleases to the City Attorney to determine whether any conflict exists and the sublessee may rely on the City Attorney's determination that no conflict exists and a no conflict determination by the City Attorney shall be final and binding on the Lessor. If after any such sublease is executed this Long-Term Lease Agreement is terminated for any reason, such sublease shall continue in full force and effect (a) with Lessor succeeding to the rights and obligations of Lessee, (b) without any disturbance of the sublessee's right to occupy the subleased premises in accordance with the provisions of such sublease, and (c) with the sublessee attorning to Lessor under the same terms and provisions set forth in this Long-Term Lease Agreement. Upon the written request of Lessee, Lessor shall join with Lessee in executing any such sublease in a form which will provide that the sublessee has a direct leasehold interest from Lessor in the event that this Lease Agreement shall fail for any reason.

ARTICLE THIRTEEN
Quiet Enjoyment and Title

13.01 *Quiet Enjoyment.* Lessor covenants with and warrants and represents to Lessee that Lessee shall at all times during the Lease Term peaceably and quietly have, hold and occupy the Demised Premises and the appurtenances thereunto belonging without hindrance or molestation by Lessor or by any person claiming rights to the Demised Premises superior to those of Lessee.

13.02 *Lessor's Right to Effect Lease Agreement.* Lessor covenants with and warrants and represents to Lessee that Lessor has the lawful right to effect this Long-Term Lease Agreement for the Lease Term and to perform the obligations of Lessor provided under this Lease Agreement, and that all necessary action has been taken to authorize Lessor lawfully to enter into this Lease Agreement.

13.03 *Warranty of Ownership.* Lessor covenants with and warrants and represents to Lessee that Lessor owns good and merchantable fee simple title to the Demised Premises free and clear from all defects, liens, mortgages, encumbrances, easements, restrictions, reservations, conditions, agreements and encroachments except (a) taxes and assessments due and payable after the commencement of the Lease Term, (b) zoning laws and regulations and other laws and ordinances affecting the use of the Demised Premises, (c) public streets, roads and highways, and (d) such exceptions to title as Lessee has waived in writing. Lessor covenants with and warrants and represents to Lessee that it has not granted any mortgage or created any liens encumbering the Demised Premises since Lessor acquired title thereto and that it will not commit or suffer the commission of any act (other than acts taken or requested by Lessee or its Sublessees) during the Lease Term which will diminish in any way the quality of Lessor's title to the Demised Premises.

ARTICLE FOURTEEN
Condemnation

14.01 *Appropriation by Lessor.* If all or any portion of the Demised Premises or the leasehold estate created by this Lease Agreement is appropriated by Lessor under its power of eminent domain, Lessee may elect either to terminate the Lease Term or to take the appropriation award.

14.02 *Election by Lessee.* Lessee shall exercise the election provided by Section 14.01 of this Long-Term Lease Agreement by giving written notice of the election to Lessor, but if Lessee shall not give such notice within sixty (60) days after the final determination and payment of the appropriation award, it shall be conclusively presumed that Lessee elected to take the appropriation award.

14.03 *Appropriation by Other Condemning Authority.* If all or any portion of the Demised Premises is appropriated by any condemning authority other than Lessor under the power of eminent domain or by purchase or other acquisition under threat of appropriation, (a) Lessor shall directly take that portion of the appropriation award or consideration which is directly attributable to the value of land and use such funds to pay off all or a portion of the Bonds plus any Administrative Fees due on the date of payment, (b) the purchase price of the purchase option established in Section 6.02 of this Long-Term Lease Agreement shall be reduced by an amount equal to such portion of the appropriation award or consideration, and (c) Lessee shall take all of the remainder of the appropriation award or consideration. If the purchase option price and Administrative Fees are paid in full, the Lessor shall

convey fee simple title to the Demised Premises to Lessee as provided in Section 6.02 of this Long-Term Lease Agreement.

ARTICLE FIFTEEN
Termination by Lessee

15.01 *Termination by Lessee.* If Lessee shall terminate the Lease Term as provided in Sections 2.04, 7.01 or 14.01 of this Long-Term Lease Agreement following (a) Lessor's actions resulting in the termination of the Financial Agreement, (b) Lessor's interference with contemplated land uses, or (c) Lessor's condemnation of the Demised Premises (which three circumstances are more fully described in said sections of this Long-Term Lease Agreement), then Lessee shall be released from all of its obligations (except for obligations in respect of that portion of the Demised Premises as to which Lessee has not terminated the Lease Term) under this Long-Term Lease Agreement, and Lessor (and any appropriate agency, corporation or organization designated by Lessor), shall:

(A) Automatically (without further act by Lessor, Lessee or any other party) assume and perform all of Lessee's or its Sublessees' obligations (except for obligations in respect of that portion of the Demised Premises as to which Lessee has not terminated the Lease Term) under:

(i) all contracts and agreements existing at the date of such termination and relating to the construction of buildings and other improvements on the Demised Premises and those relating to the purchase and installation of fixtures and other personal property to be affixed thereto and used in connection therewith; and

(ii) all construction and other loan and financing agreements existing at the date of such termination and relating to the financing of the construction of buildings and improvements existing or to be constructed on the Demised Premises and to the financing of the purchase and installation of fixtures and other personal property then or thereafter to be affixed thereto or used in connection therewith; and

(iii) all promissory notes entered into and made in connection with financing the construction of buildings and other improvements existing or to be constructed on the Demised Premises and to the financing of the purchase and installation of fixtures and other personal property then or thereafter affixed thereto or used in connection therewith; and

(iv) all mortgages and other liens encumbering the Demised Premises to secure performance of any obligation of Lessee assumed and to be performed by Lessor as contemplated by this Section 15.01 of this Lease Agreement; and

(v) each sublease, assignment and other agreement under which one or more persons succeed to all or any part of Lessee's interest in the Demised Premises; and

(B) To the extent permitted by law, indemnify Lessee and save it harmless from and against any and all loss, liability, damage or claims of whatever nature to any person, property or business interests caused by or resulting from the failure of Lessor to perform any obligation assumed by it as contemplated by this Section 15.01 of this Lease Agreement, and from and against any and all costs, expenses and liabilities incurred by Lessee in connection with any claim, action or proceeding in respect thereof (including without limitation the fees of attorneys, investigators and experts). In the event that any claim, action or proceeding is brought against Lessee by reason of any such failure on the part of Lessor, Lessor shall, if requested by Lessee, cause the same to be resisted or defended at Lessor's sole cost and expense.

ARTICLE SIXTEEN
Default

16.01 *Lessor's Rights upon Default.* If Lessee fails to pay any money obligation to be paid by Lessee under the terms of this Long-Term Lease Agreement, and if such money obligation remains unpaid for a period of thirty (30) days after notice of such default has been given to Lessee by Lessor; or if Lessee shall fail to perform or observe any of the other obligations of Lessee under the terms of this Long-Term Lease Agreement and shall fail to commence the correction of such default within sixty (60) days after written notice to Lessee by Lessor of such default; or if Lessee is adjudicated a bankrupt or makes an assignment for the benefit of creditors or suffers a receiver to be appointed in any action or proceeding by or against it; or if Lessee's interest in the Demised Premises is sold upon execution or other legal process, Lessor shall have the sole option to give Lessee written notice of Lessor's intention to terminate the right of Lessee to occupy the Demised Premises and Lessor shall have the right to re-enter the Demised Premises on the date stated in said notice, and in that event, all of the rights and obligations of Lessor and of Lessee under this Lease Agreement shall terminate as of the date of such termination and re-entry, except the obligations of the Lessor to any sublessee, parallel lessee or mortgagee.

16.02 *Rights of Assignees, Sublessees and Lienholders.* Anything contained in Section 16.01 of this Long-Term Lease Agreement or elsewhere to the contrary notwithstanding, if Lessee shall have given notice to Lessor that Lessee has assigned this Lease Agreement, subleased all or any portion of the Demised Premises or caused or suffered its and/or its Sublessees' leasehold interest in the Demised Premises to be subjected to the lien of any mortgage or other encumbrance (which notice shall have specified the name and address of such assignee, sublessee and the holder of any such mortgage or other encumbrance), or if a memorandum, notice or copy of such assignment, sublease, mortgage or other encumbrance shall be of record in the office of the Recorder of Franklin County, Ohio, then:

(A) Lessor shall not have the right to terminate this Lease Agreement and to re-enter the Demised Premises for any reason prior to the expiration of the Lease Term unless any of the covenants, agreements or obligations herein made or assumed by Lessee are not performed or observed and if correction thereof is not commenced within one hundred twenty (120) days after written notice is given by Lessor to each such assignee, sublessee and the holder of each such mortgage and other encumbrance and to Lessee of such failure and if correction thereof is not completed within a reasonable time thereafter; and

(B) Any such default may be cured or corrected by Lessee or by any such assignee, sublessee or the holder of any such mortgage or other encumbrance.

ARTICLE SEVENTEEN
Development of the Demised Premises

17.01 *Development of the Demised Premises.* As provided elsewhere in this Long-Term Lease Agreement, Lessee shall have the right to develop the Demised Premises itself or in conjunction with another person or persons by subleasing the Demised Premises to third persons, leasing the Demised Premises in conjunction with Lessor to third persons, subleasing to an entity composed of Lessee and another person or persons, or other arrangement permitted by this Long-Term Lease Agreement and the Financial Agreement. In conjunction with such development, Lessee and/or its Sublessees, including parallel lessees, shall have the right at any time to mortgage, encumber or pledge their right, title and interest in and to the leasehold estate created hereby, or any buildings or improvements on the Demised Premises. Lessee and the other developers shall have the absolute right to refinance any debt subject to the terms and conditions of this Lease Agreement.

17.02 *Lessee's and Its Sublessees' Right to Transfer Their Interests in the Demised Premises.* Notwithstanding any other provisions contained herein, any person who develops the Demised Premises or any mortgagee which provides construction or permanent financing for tbe development of the Demised Premises shall have the unqualified right, without any approval or consent of the Lessor, to sell, convey, assign or otherwise transfer or dispose of any or all of its rights, title and interest in and to the Demised Premises or its mortgage, including any and all claims arising thereunder or arising out of the mortgage transaction, but subject to all the terms and conditions and restrictions hereof.

17.03 *Copy of Notice of Breach of Covenant or Default.* Whenever Lessor shall deliver any notice or demand to the Lessee with respect to any breach of covenant or default by Lessee in the obligations of Lessee under this Long-Term Lease Agreement, Lessor shall at the same time, furnish a copy of such written notice or demand to any Sublessee or any mortgagee of whom Lessor has been notified at the last address of such sublessee or mortgagee as shown in the records of Lessor. No such notice to the Lessee shall be effective unless a copy thereof is given to all sublessees and mortgagees.

17.04 *Sublessee's and Mortgagee's Right to Cure Default by Lessee.* If the Lessee shall not cure or remedy any breach of covenant or default by the Lessee under this Long-Term Lease Agreement within the period provided therefor, Lessor shall give notice to that effect to all sublessees and mortgagees, who shall thereupon have a period equal to that provided Lessee hereunder to cure, or cause to be cured, such default. Any such sublessee, parallel lessee or mortgagee shall have the right but not the obligation, to cure or remedy, or cause to be cured or remedied, such default or breach, and Lessor shall accept such cure or remedy by a sublessee, parallel lessee or mortgagee as though the same had been cured or remedied by the Lessee.

17.05 *Sublessee's, Parallel Lessee's or Mortgagee's Rights if Unable to Cure Default.* If the sublessee, parallel lessee or mortgagee determines that it will be unable to cure any default or breach of covenant of the Lessee within the period provided under this Lease, the sublessee, parallel lessee or mortgagee shall, within 20 days after receiving written notice of such default, notify Lessor in writing of such determination and within 30 days thereafter the sublessee, parallel lessee or mortgagee may, but shall not be required to, exercise one of the following rights:

(A) The sublessee, parallel lessee or mortgagee or, at the option of the sublessee, parallel lessee or mortgagee, a redevelopment corporation established by the sublessee, parallel lessee or mortgagee for such purpose, may, by foreclosure or otherwise, acquire the interest of the Lessee under this Lease subject to the mortgage and assume the obligations of the Lessee under this Lease with respect thereto, including those in default and, in such event, Lessor shall not exercise the right of termination under this Lease with respect to such default. Upon subsequent transfer by such sublessee, parallel lessee or mortgagee or redevelopment corporation of the interest so acquired, upon request therefor and assumption by the assignee of the assignor's obligations, Lessor shall release such sublessee, parallel lessee, or mortgagee, or redevelopment corporation from all obligations arising under this Lease after such transfer. The instruments of assignment, assumption and release shall be in recordable form and shall be promptly recorded by the sublessee, parallel lessee or mortgagee and duplicate originals or certified copies thereof furnished to Lessor; or

(B) The sublessee, parallel lessee or mortgagee may enter into a new Lease with Lessor with respect to the interest of the Lessee subject to the mortgage. Such new Lease shall be for the balance of the Lease Term, shall be at the same rental (or, if the interest subject to the mortgage is less than the entire Demised Premises, at the appropriate proportional rental), and upon the same terms, covenants and conditions as contained in this Lease and shall require the sublessee or mortgagee to perform all unfulfilled obligations of the Lessee under this Lease with respect to interest of the Lessee subject to the mortgage. Lessor, shall, upon request of the sublessee or mortgagee, enter into such new Lease and shall not terminate this Lease until such new Lease has been executed and delivered. At the option of the sublessee or mortgagee, the lessee under such new Lease may be a redevelopment corporation established by the sublessee or mortgagee for such purpose or may be such other nominee as the sublessee or mortgagee may designate.

17.06 *Lessor, Lessee and Its Sublessees Including Parallel Lessees Shall Furnish Certificates.* At any time and from time to time upon written request of another party, Lessee's sublessees, parallel lessees or any mortgagee, Lessor or Lessee, as the case may be, shall execute, acknowledge and deliver to the party, Lessee's sublessees, parallel lessees or to the mortgagee requesting the same, a certificate in recordable form evidencing whether or not (a) this Lease is in full force and effect; (b) this Lease has been modified or amended in any respect and attaching a conformed copy of such modifications or amendments, if any, or identifying the official record in which such modifications or amendments are recorded; and (c) there are any existing defaults under this Lease to the knowledge of the party executing the certificate, and specifying the nature of such defaults, if any.

17.07 *Obligations of Persons Other Than Mortgagee Acquiring Leasehold.* Any person, corporation or other legal entity (other than a mortgagee) acquiring any or all of the rights, title and interest of the Lessee in and to the leasehold estate in the Demised Premises (a) under any judicial sale made under a mortgage permitted by this Lease or as the result of any action or remedy provided therein, (b) by foreclosure proceeding or action in lieu thereof, in connection with any such mortgage, or (c) as a result of any legal process or proceedings (other than eminent domain proceedings by public authority), shall thereby become liable under and be fully bound by all of the provisions of this Long-Term Lease Agreement.

ARTICLE EIGHTEEN
Nondiscrimination

18.01 *Nondiscrimination.* Lessee agrees it will not discriminate upon the basis of race, color, creed, national origin, age or sex in the construction, subleasing, use, occupancy or operation of the Demised Premises or the Improvements to be erected thereon, and that each contract, sublease or agreement with respect thereto shall specifically contain this provision:

18.02 *Equal Opportunity Provision.*

(A) In the construction and operation of the Improvements neither Lessee nor any contractor or manager employed by Lessee shall discriminate against any employee or applicant for employment because of race, color, religion, age, sex or national origin, and they shall take affirmative action to ensure that applicants are employed, and that employees are treated during employment without regard to their race, color, religion, age, sex or national origin. Such action shall include, but not be limited to the following: Employment, upgrading, demotion or transfer; recruitment or recruitment advertising; layoff or termination; rates of pay or other forms of compensation; and selection for training including apprenticeship. The Lessee agrees to post in conspicuous places, available to employees and applicants for employment, notices to be provided by Lessor setting forth the provisions of this Equal Opportunity Clause, and to cause any contractor, subcontractor or manager to do likewise.

(B) The Lessee, its Sublessees and any contractor or manager shall, in all solicitations or advertisements for employees placed by them or on their behalf, state that all qualified applicants will receive consideration for employment without regard to race, color, religion, age, sex or national origin. They shall send to each labor union or representative of workers with which they, or any of them, have a collective bargaining agreement or other contract or understanding, a notice, to be provided by Lessor, advising the labor union or workers' representative of their commitments under this Equal Opportunity Clause, and shall post copies of the notice in conspicuous places available to employees and applicants for employment. Any sublessee, contractor or subcontractor shall comply with all provisions of Executive Order No. 11246 of September 24, 1965, and of the rules, regulations and relevant orders of the Secretary of Labor and shall furnish all information and reports required by Executive Order No. 11246 of September 24, 1965, and by the rules, regulations and orders of the Secretary of Labor, or pursuant thereto, and will permit access to its books, records and accounts by Lessor and the Secretary of Labor for purposes of investigation to ascertain compliance with such rules, regulations and orders.

18.03 *Certification of Nonsegregated Facilities.* Lessee certifies that it does not maintain or provide for its employees any segregated facilities at any of its establishments, and that it does not permit its employees to perform their services at any location, under its control, where segregated facilities are maintained. Lessee certifies further that it will not maintain or provide for its employees any segregated facilities at any of its establishments, and that it will not permit its employees to perform their services at any location, under its control, where segregated facilities are maintained. As used in this Certification, the term "segregated facilities" means any waiting rooms, work areas, rest rooms and wash rooms, restaurants and other eating areas, time clocks, locker rooms and other storage or dressing areas, parking lots, drinking fountains, recreation or entertainment areas, transportation and housing facilities provided for employees which are segregated by explicit directive or are in fact segregated on the basis of race, color, religion or national origin, because of habit, local custom or otherwise. Lessee further agrees that it will obtain identical certifications from proposed sublessees, contractors, subcontractors and managers prior to the award of any contracts and that it will retain such certifications in its files.

ARTICLE NINETEEN
City Income Taxes

19.01 *City Income Taxes.* Lessee hereby agrees to withhold and to require all of its Sublessees, including parallel lessees, contractors or managers to withhold all city income taxes due or payable under the provisions of Chapter 361, Columbus City Codes, 1959, for wages, salaries and commissions paid to their employees.

ARTICLE TWENTY
Prevailing Wages

20.01 *Prevailing Wages.* All persons working on construction contracts awarded by Lessee, its Sublessees, including parallel lessees or contractors employed by them, shall be paid the prevailing wage rate for the particular classification which describes their work in accordance with Sections 4115.03 through 4115.10, inclusive, of the Revised Code of Ohio.

ARTICLE TWENTY-ONE
Arbitration

21.01 *Arbitration.* In the event of any dispute between the parties, the matters in controversy shall be resolved by arbitration to the extent permitted by law. Such dispute shall be submitted to arbitration by a panel of three disinterested arbitrators. The panel shall be composed of one arbitrator appointed by the Lessor, one appointed by the Lessee, and the third, who shall be an attorney admitted to practice in the State of Ohio, shall be appointed by the mutual agreement of the two arbitrators chosen by the Lessor and the Lessee. If the two arbitrators chosen by the Lessor and the Lessee are unable to agree upon the choice of the third arbitrator, the third arbitrator shall be appointed by the presiding Judge of the Court of Common Pleas of Franklin County, Ohio. The panel shall sit in Columbus, Ohio, and its procedures shall be governed by the Ohio Arbitration Act contained in Chapter 2711 of the Revised Code of Ohio. Any decision made by a majority of the arbitrators shall be final, binding and conclusive on the parties for all purposes, and judgment may be entered thereon by any court having jurisdiction thereof. The cost of arbitration shall be borne equally by the parties.

ARTICLE TWENTY-TWO
Provisions of Law Deemed Included

22.01 *Provisions of Law Deemed Included.* Each and every provision of law and clause required by law to be included in this Long-Term Lease Agreement shall be deemed to be included herein, and this lease shall be read, construed and enforced as though the same were included herein. If, through mistake, inadvertent or otherwise, any such provision or clause is not included herein or is incorrectly included herein, then, upon application of either party hereto, this lease shall forthwith be amended to include the same or to correct the inclusions of same.

ARTICLE TWENTY-THREE
Amendments to the Long-Term Lease Agreement

23.01 *Amendments to the Long-Term Lease Agreement.* Lessor and Lessee are hereby authorized to amend this Long-Term Lease Agreement at any time by written amendment executed by Lessor and Lessee and approved as to form and compliance with all applicable laws by the City Attorney; provided, however, no amendment shall reduce or eliminate the rights of any sublessee, parallel lessee or mortgagee having a sublease, parallel lease or mortgage, notice of which is of record in the Franklin County Recorder's Office when the amendment is executed, without their written consent.

ARTICLE TWENTY-FOUR
Notices and Payments

24.01 *Initial Addresses.* All notices and other communications required or permitted to be given or delivered under this Long-Term Lease Agreement by Lessor or Lessee, which notices or communications shall be in writing, and all payment or money required to be made by Lessor or Lessee to the other under the provisions of this Lease Agreement, shall be mailed, postage prepaid, addressed as follows:

(A) If to Lessor, to:
Mayor of the City of Columbus
City Hall
Columbus, Ohio 43215

with a copy to:
City Attorney of Columbus
City Hall
Columbus, Ohio 43215

(B) If to Lessee, to:
Capitol South Community Urban
Redevelopment Corporation
101 East Town Street
Columbus, Ohio 43215

with a copy to:
Attention: Statutory Agent Corporation
Vorys, Sater, Seymour and Pease
52 East Gay Street
Columbus, Ohio 43215

24.02 *Change of Address.* Lessor or Lessee may, by notice received by the other, from time to time and at any time designate a different address for the making of payments required to be made to the party designating such new address and for the giving of notices or other communications to the party designating such new address.

24.03 *Completion upon Mailing.* Any notice, communication or payment required or permitted to be given in accordance with this Lease Agreement shall be deemed to have been given when the same shall be delivered in accordance with this Article Twenty-Four of this Long-Term Lease Agreement.

ARTICLE TWENTY-FIVE
Miscellaneous Provisions

25.01 *Memorandum of Lease.* From time to time and at any time during the Lease Term, Lessor shall, upon request by Lessee, execute and deliver to Lessee a Memorandum of Lease reflecting such of the terms of this Long-Term Lease Agreement as Lessee may designate, each of which shall be in a form recordable under the laws of the State of Ohio and which Lessee may record in public offices.

25.02 *Successors and Assigns.* This Long-Term Lease Agreement shall inure to the benefit of and be binding upon the respective successors and assigns (including successive, as well as immediate, successors and assignees) of Lessor and of Lessee.

25.03 *Governing Law and Forum.* This Lease Agreement shall be governed by and construed in accordance with the laws of the State of Ohio.

25.04 *Remedies Cumulative.* All rights and remedies of Lessor and of Lessee enumerated in this Long-Term Lease Agreement shall be cumulative and, except as specifically contemplated otherwise by this Lease Agreement, none shall exclude any other right or remedy allowed at law or in equity, and said rights or remedies may be exercised and enforced concurrently. No waiver by Lessor or by Lessee of any covenant or condition of this Long-Term Lease Agreement to be kept or performed by the other party shall constitute a waiver by the waiving party of any subsequent breach of such covenant or condition or authorize the breach or non-observance on any other occasion of the same or any other covenant or condition of this Long-Term Lease Agreement.

25.05 *Duplicate Originals.* This Long-Term Lease Agreement may be executed in one or more counterparts, each of which shall be deemed to be a duplicate original, but all of which, taken together, shall constitute a single instrument.

25.06 *Article and Section Headings.* The article and section headings contained in this Long-Term Lease Agreement are included only for convenience of reference and do not define, limit, explain or modify this Long-Term Lease Agreement or its interpretation, construction or meaning and are in no way to be construed as part of this Long-Term Lease Agreement.

25.07 *Provisions Separable.* If any provision of this Long-Term Lease Agreement or the application of any such provision to any person or any circumstance shall be determined to be invalid or unenforceable, then such determination shall not affect any other provisions of this Long-Term Lease Agreement or the application of such provision to any other person or circumstance, all of which other provisions shall remain in full force and effect; and if any provision of this Long-Term Lease Agreement is capable of two constructions, one of which would render the provision void and the other of which would render the provision valid, then such provision shall have the meaning which renders it valid.

25.08 *Entire Agreement.* This Long-Term Lease Agreement constitutes the entire agreement between Lessor and Lessee in respect of the subject matter hereof, and this Long-Term Lease Agreement supersedes all prior and contemporaneous agreements between Lessor and Lessee in connection with this Long-Term Lease Agreement. No officer, employee or other servant or agent of Lessor or of Lessee is authorized to make any representation, warranty or other promise not contained in this Long-Term Lease Agreement. No change, termination or attempted waiver of any of the provisions of this Long-Term Lease Agreement shall be binding upon Lessor or Lessee unless in writing and signed by the party affected.

25.09 *Definitions.* For purposes of this Lease Agreement, the following terms shall mean:

(A) *Mortgagee.* Any person who has been granted a mortgage by the Lessee, any sublessee or parallel lessee on the leasehold estate created by this Lease Agreement, the leasehold estate created by any sublease or parallel lease and/or any buildings or improvements located on the Demised Premises.

(B) *Parallel Lessee.* A parallel lessee is any person having a lease on all or part of the Demised Premises created jointly by the Lessor and Lessee.

(C) *Person.* A person is any individual, partnership, corporation, firm, joint venture or other entity, or any combination thereof.

(D) *Sublessee.* Sublessee is a person having a lease on all or part of the Demised Premises created by Lessee.

CITY OF COLUMBUS, OHIO

By _____
Mayor

CAPITOL SOUTH COMMUNITY URBAN
REDEVELOPMENT CORPORATION

By _____
Executive Director

Approved as to form by

_____
City Attorney

APPENDIX H(3)

Memorandum of Intent
with a Sub-developer

This Memorandum of Intent, made this _____ day of _____, _____, between CAPITOL SOUTH COMMUNITY URBAN REDEVELOPMENT CORPORATION, 101 East Town Street, Columbus, Ohio 43215 (hereinafter called "Capitol South") and _____ (hereinafter called the "Developer");

WITNESSETH:

WHEREAS, Capitol South wants to redevelop the three square block area bound on the north by State Street, on the east by Third Street, on the south by Main Street and on the west by High Street, in accordance with the Land Use Plan and Urban Design concept to be prepared by Capitol South;

WHEREAS, Developer wants to participate in the redevelopment of this three square block area by developing and leasing a multistory office building containing approximately _____ square feet, which building will comply with the Land Use Plan and Urban Design concept to be prepared by Capitol South;

WHEREAS, Developer wants to participate in the Land Use Plan and Urban Design concept by assisting to prepare the site design concept including the proposed Urban Park facilities, parking requirements and building locations, in cooperation with Capitol South, for the specific real estate to be selected by Capitol South and the Developer for the Building;

WHEREAS, Capitol South will cooperate, to the extent possible, in seeking governmental assistance for the Developer to pay for the site design concept of the Building;

NOW, THEREFORE, in consideration of the sum of Twenty-Five Dollars ($25.00), other good and valuable consideration, and the mutual agreements and covenants contained herein, Capitol South and the Developer hereby agree as follows:

1. Capitol South agrees to grant Developer the exclusive option to develop an approximately _____ square foot multistory office building (hereinafter called "Building") and Developer agrees to use its best efforts to develop this Building.

2. Capitol South and Developer hereby represent and agree that they will take the following action and use their

best efforts to develop this Building during the life of this Memorandum of Intent.

3. Capitol South and the Developer agree that the obligations and responsibility of the parties will be undertaken in three Stages. During Stage I, the following action will be taken:

A. Between _____, _____, and _____, _____, Capitol South will complete its Land Use Plan and Marketability Study. Capitol South agrees to allow Developer to review the Land Use Plan and Marketability Study prepared by it and to allow Developer to offer suggestions to the Study.

B. Between _____, _____, and _____, _____, Capitol South agrees to explore and develop various methods of financing the acquisition of the real estate located in the three square block area, including the real estate to be selected by Capitol South and the Developer for the construction of the Building.

C. Between _____, _____, and _____, _____, Capitol South agrees to use its best efforts to obtain the right to acquire title to all of the real estate located in the three square block area and particularly, to acquire the right to acquire the real estate where the Building will be constructed. Capitol South agrees to negotiate with the property owners to obtain the right to acquire this real estate in fee simple, a long term lease or other appropriate manner so this real estate can be made available to the Developer for the development of the Building. Capitol South agrees to consult with Developer on a regular basis concerning its approach to obtaining the right to acquire the real estate where the Building will be constructed and the terms of this acquisition.

D. Capitol South and Developer agree to mutually select the real estate to be used for the construction of the Building and agree that this selection must be consistent with the Land Use Plan and Marketability Study prepared by Capitol South.

E. Between _____, _____, and _____, _____, Capitol South agrees to determine the type of parking needed to develop this three square block area and the appropriate method of financing the development of the parking. This parking may include underground, aboveground or both types of parking.

(1) Developer will be consulted on a regular basis concerning the type of parking and the appropriate method of financing the parking by Capitol South.

(2) Capitol South will determine the construction and development schedule for the construction of the parking, particularly as it relates to the development of the Building and will advise Developer on a regular basis of its progress, and Developer and Capitol South agree that in the event permanent parking facilities adequate to meet the needs of the Building's tenants will not be completed by the time that the Building is ready for occupancy, then in such event temporary parking facilities to service the Building's tenants are to be made available by Capitol South.

F. Between _____, _____, and _____, _____, Capitol South will prepare the general development schedule for the entire three square block area, including the Building and will consult with Developer on a regular basis concerning the development of the Building and its schedule.

4. On or before _____, _____, Capitol South and the Developer will have the right to determine whether they wish to proceed with the development of the Building, and either party may withdraw by giving notice to the other party in writing by _____.

5. If Capitol South and Developer agree to proceed, the parties will assume the following obligations in Stage II:

A. Between _____, _____, and _____, _____, Capitol South shall attempt to obtain all of the necessary permits, authorizations, financing and other approvals needed to develop the three square block area, including the development of the Building by Capitol South and the Developer. Developer agrees to use its best efforts to assist Capitol South in obtaining all of the items discussed in this paragraph A of paragraph 5. Within the framework of the Financial Agreement to be executed between Capitol South and the City of Columbus, Capitol South will make reasonable efforts to obtain the maximum tax abatement on the Building as may be permitted by Chapter 1728 of the Ohio Revised Code and by the Financial Agreement.

B. Between _____, _____, and _____, _____, or sooner at the Developer's option, Developer would prepare a preliminary design and schematics for the Building and submit these documents to Capitol South for review and approval and Capitol South would complete said review within thirty (30) days from date it receives the same.

C. Between _____, _____, and _____, _____, or sooner at the Developer's option, Developer would determine the type of tenants which will lease the space in the Building and attempt to prelease this space to tenants. Capitol South agrees to use its best efforts to assist Developer in this effort.

D. Between _____, _____, and _____, _____, Developer agrees to use its best efforts to obtain financing for the development and construction of the Building, and Capitol South agrees to use its best efforts to assist Developer in these efforts.

E. By _____, _____, Developer agrees to determine what legal structure he will use to develop the Building and to advise Capitol South in writing of the legal structure.

6. On or before _____, _____, Capitol South will give Developer thirty (30) days written notice to decide whether to exercise the exclusive option to develop the Building. Developer will have thirty (30) days to determine whether to exercise the option to develop the Building and to give Capitol South written notice of its decision; provided that this Memorandum of Intent may be extended for a period of ninety (90) days by mutual consent of the parties hereto, which consent shall not be unreasonably withheld by either of said parties.

7. If Developer agrees to exercise the option to develop the Building, Developer agrees to proceed with the development of the Building as quickly as practicable, including the design, construction, leasing and operation of the Building.

8. If Developer proceeds, Developer and Capitol South agree to enter into all the necessary legal documents and agreements to develop the Building, and take all other action necessary to develop the Building.

9. Among other obligations related to the final development of the Building, Developer agrees to submit the final design of the Building, the plans and specifications and other architectural and engineering documents to Capitol South for review and approval.

10. In addition to the other rights to terminate discussed in earlier sections of this Memorandum of Intent, Developer may terminate this Memorandum of Intent and shall be relieved of any obligations under it if any of the following occur:

A. Developer cannot obtain financing for the development of the Building on commercially reasonable terms.

B. Developer cannot obtain all the necessary governmental licenses, approvals, permits or other authorizations necessary to develop, construct and operate the Building.

C. Developer cannot obtain all the other necessary approvals, documents and authorizations necessary to develop, construct and operate the Building.

D. Developer is not satisfied with the final land acquisition cost offered to it by Capitol South for the fee purchase of the site for the Building or in the event the transfer of the site to the Developer is to be effected pursuant to a lease, the Developer is not satisfied with the final lease terms offered to it by Capitol South.

11. In addition to all the other rights to terminate discussed in earlier sections of this Memorandum of Intent, Capitol South may terminate this Memorandum of Intent and shall be relieved of any obligations under it if any of the following occur:

A. Developer's preliminary design and plans or final design and plans for the Building are not in accordance with the Land Use Plan and Urban Design concept to be prepared by Capitol South, except that Developer will have sixty (60) days within which to revise its preliminary design and plans or final design and plans for the Building in accordance with said Land Use Plan and Urban Design concept, from the date that it receives notification from Capitol South that the same are not in accordance with the Land Use Plan and Urban Design concept prepared by Capitol South.

B. Capitol South is unable to obtain fee simple title or a long term lease for the acquisition of the real estate selected by the parties for the development of the Building.

C. Capitol South is unable to obtain financing or the approvals, licenses, materials and authorizations necessary to redevelop the three square block area.

D. Capitol South is unable to redevelop the three square block area because of failure to obtain authorization from the City of Columbus or other governmental agency.

12. This Memorandum of Intent shall be governed by the laws of the State of Ohio.

13. This Memorandum of Intent shall bind the heirs, successors and assigns of the parties and inure to the benefit of their heirs, successors and assigns.

IN WITNESS WHEREOF, Capitol South and Developer have caused this Memorandum of Intent to be duly executed as of the date first above written.

CAPITOL SOUTH COMMUNITY URBAN REDEVELOPMENT CORPORATION

By _____

DEVELOPER

By _____

APPENDIX H(4)

Ohio Revised Code

Chapter 1728: Community Redevelopment Corporations

§ 1728.01 Definitions.

As used in sections 1728.01 to 1728.13 of the Revised Code:

(A) "Governing body" means, in the case of a municipal corporation, the city council or legislative authority.

(B) "Community urban redevelopment corporation" means a corporation qualified under Chapter 1728. of the Revised Code, to acquire, construct, operate, and maintain a project hereunder, or to acquire, operate, and maintain a project constructed by a corporation so qualified under Chapter 1728. of the Revised Code, and the term "corporation" when used within Chapter 1728. of the Revised Code, shall be understood to be a contraction of the term "community urban redevelopment corporation" except when the context indicates otherwise.

(C) "Impacted city" means a municipal corporation that meets the requirements of either division (C)(1) or (C)(2) of this section:

(1) In attempting to cope with the problems of urbanization, to create or preserve jobs and employment opportunities, and to improve the economic welfare of the people of the municipal corporation, the municipal corporation has at some time:

(a) Taken affirmative action by its legislative body to permit the construction of housing by a metropolitan housing authority organized pursuant to sections 3735.27 to 3735.39 of the Revised Code within its corporate boundaries or to permit such a metropolitan housing authority to lease dwelling units within its corporate boundaries; and

(b) Been certified by the director of the department of economic and community development that a workable program for community improvement (which shall include an official plan of action for effectively dealing with the problem of urban slums and blight within the community and for the establishment and preservation of a well-planned community with well-organized residential neighborhoods of decent homes and suitable living environment for adequate family life) for utilizing appropriate private and public resources to eliminate, and to prevent the development or spread of, slums and urban blight, to encourage needed urban rehabilitation, to provide for the redevelopment of blighted, deteriorated, or slum areas, to undertake such activities or other feasible community activities as may be suitably employed to achieve the objectives of such a program has been adopted. A determination by the United States that the impacted city's workable program meets the federal workable program requirements shall be sufficient for the director's certification.

(2) Been declared a major disaster area, or part of a major disaster area, pursuant to the "Disaster Relief Act of 1970," 84 Stat. 1744, 42 U.S.C. 4401, as now or hereafter amended, and has been extensively damaged or destroyed by a major disaster, provided that impacted city status obtained pursuant to division (C)(2) of this section lasts for only a limited period from the date of the declaration, as determined by the rules promulgated pursuant to division (G) of section 122.06 of the Revised Code, but in the event that an impacted city, while qualified under such division, enters into a financial agreement with a community urban redevelopment corporation pursuant to section 1728.07 of the Revised Code, a loss of certification under such rules shall not affect that agreement or the project to which it relates.

(D) "Community development plan" means a plan, as it exists from time to time, for the redevelopment and renewal of a blighted area, which plan shall conform to the general plan for the municipality, and shall be sufficiently complete to indicate such land acquisition, demolition, and removal of structures, redevelopment, improvements, and rehabilitation as may be proposed to be carried out in such blighted area, zoning, and any planning changes, land uses, maximum densities, and building requirements.

(E) "Blighted area" means an area within a municipality containing a majority of structures that have been extensively damaged or destroyed by a major disaster, or that, by reason of dilapidation, deterioration, age or obsolescence, inadequate provision for ventilation, light, air, sanitation, or open spaces, unsafe and unsanitary conditions or the existence of conditions which endanger lives or properties by fire or other hazards and causes, or that, by reason of location in an area with inadequate street layout, incompatible land uses or land use relationships, overcrowding of buildings on the land, excessive dwelling unit density, or other identified hazards to health and safety, are conducive to ill health, transmission of disease, juvenile delinquency and crime and are detrimental to the public health, safety, morals and general welfare.

(F) "Project" means:

(1) As to blighted areas within all municipal corporations, the undertaking and execution of the redevelopment of a blighted area by a community urban redevelopment corporation, in whole or in part, pursuant to a community development plan approved by the governing body of the municipal corporation in which such blighted area is situated and in accordance with an agreement for the sale or lease of all or a portion of the land concerned in such redevelopment to the corporation by a municipal corporation, or agency, or authority, including the work to be done in reference thereto, the designation of the particular proposed buildings to be constructed and their uses and purposes, the landscaping of the premises, the streets and access roads, recreational facilities, if any, the furnishing of the public utilities, the financial arrangements, and the terms and conditions of the proposed municipal corporation and approval; and

(2) In addition as to blighted areas within impacted cities, the undertaking and activities of a community urban redevelopment corporation in a blighted area for the elimination and for the prevention of the development or spread of blight pursuant to a community development plan approved by the governing body of the impacted city and to the extent agreed to by the governing body of the impacted city in the financial agreement provided for in section 1728.07 of the Revised Code and may involve clearance and redevelopment, or rehabilitation or conservation or any combination or part thereof, in accordance with such community development plan, and such aforesaid undertakings and activities may include acquisition of a blighted area or portion by purchase or otherwise, and demolition and removal of buildings and improvements.

(G) "Total project unit cost" or "total project cost" means the aggregate of the following items as related to any unit of a project if the project is to be undertaken in units or to the total project if the project is not to be undertaken in units:

(1) Cost of the land to the community urban redevelopment corporation;

(2) Architects', engineers', and attorneys' fees paid or payable by the corporation in connection with the planning, construction, and financing of the project;

(3) Surveying and testing charges in connection therewith;

(4) Actual construction cost as certified by the architect, including the cost of any preparation of the site undertaken at the corporation's expense;

(5) Insurance, interest, and finance costs during construction;

(6) Cost of obtaining initial permanent financing;

(7) Commissions and other expenses paid or payable in connection with initial leasing;

(8) Real estate taxes and assessments during the construction period;

(9) Developer's overhead based on a percentage of division (G)(4) of this section, to be computed in accordance with the following schedule:

$500,000 or less— 10 percent

$500,001 through $1,000,000—$50,000 plus 8 percent on excess above $500,000

$1,000,001 through $2,000,000—$90,000 plus 7 percent on excess above $1,000,000

$2,000,001 through $3,500,000—$160,000 plus 5.6667 percent on excess above $2,000,000

$3,500,001 through $5,500,000—$245,000 plus 4.25 percent on excess above $3,500,000

$5,500,001 through $10,000,000—$330,000 plus 3.7778 percent on excess above $5,500,000

Over $10,000,000—5 percent

(H) "Annual gross revenue" means the total annual gross rental and other income of a community urban redevelopment corporation from the project. If in any leasing, any real estate taxes or assessments on property included in the project, any premiums for fire or other insurance on or concerning property included in the project, or any operating or maintenance expenses ordinarily paid by a landlord are to be paid by the tenant, such payments shall be computed and deemed to be part of the rent and shall be included in the annual gross revenue. The financial agreement provided for in section 1728.07 of the Revised Code shall establish the method of computing such additional revenue, and may establish a method of arbitration where either the landlord or the tenant disputes the amount of such payments so included in the annual gross revenue.

(I) "Major disaster" means any tornado, storm, flood, high water, wind-driven water, tidal wave, earthquake, fire, or other catastrophe.

§ 1728.02 Incorporation; requirements.

(A) Any corporation formed, or which shall be formed, under Chapter 1701. or 1702. of the Revised Code may qualify to operate under Chapter 1728. of the Revised Code, if its articles of incorporation, originally or by amendment thereof, contain the following provisions:

(1) The name of the corporation shall include the words "community urban redevelopment."

(2) The object for which it is formed shall be to operate under Chapter 1728. of the Revised Code, and to initiate and conduct projects for the clearance, replanning, development, and redevelopment of blighted areas within municipal corporations and, when so authorized by financial agreement with a municipal corporation pursuant to section 1728.07 of the Revised Code, to acquire, plan, develop, construct, alter, maintain, or operate one or more projects, under such conditions of use, ownership, management, and control as are regulated pursuant to Chapter 1728. of the Revised Code.

(3) A declaration that the corporation has been organized to serve a public purpose, that its operation shall be directed towards providing for and making possible the original acquisition, to the extent agreed to by the governing body of a city, clearance, replanning, development, or redevelopment of blighted areas or the acquisition, management, and operation of a project; and that it is subject to regulation by the municipal corporation in which its project is situated for as long as it remains obligated under a financial agreement as provided in section 1728.07 of the Revised Code.

(B) Any community urban redevelopment corporation qualifying under Chapter 1728. of the Revised Code, may undertake a project, and when so authorized by a financial agreement with a municipal corporation pursuant to section 1728.07 of the Revised Code, may acquire, plan, develop, construct, alter, maintain, or operate one or more projects. The conditions of use, ownership, management, and control of the improvements in any such project shall be regulated as provided in Chapter 1728. of the Revised Code.

§ 1728.03 Municipal corporation may sell land.

When any municipal corporation or agency or authority thereof has acquired land constituting or being a part of a blighted area, the governing body of the municipal corporation, or the agency or authority, by resolution, may make such land available for use for a project by a community urban redevelopment corporation, qualified under Chapter 1728. of the Revised Code, by private sale or lease, upon such terms and conditions as are agreed upon by the governing body or agency or authority and the corporation. Any such resolution shall include a determination of the use value of the land, and the price or rental to be paid therefor by the corporation shall not be less than the amount so determined if made available by sale, and shall not be less than a fair return thereon if made available by lease.

§ 1728.04 Restrictions on business.

(A) So long as a community urban redevelopment corporation is obligated under a financial agreement with a municipal corporation made pursuant to section 1728.07 of the Revised Code, it shall engage in no business other than the acquisition, ownership, construction, operation, and management of such project or projects.

(B) The corporation shall not voluntarily transfer the project undertaken by it under Chapter 1728. of the Revised Code, until it has first removed both itself and the project from all restrictions under such chapter in the manner set forth.

The foregoing restriction shall not be applied to prevent the transfer of a project to another community urban redevelopment corporation which, with the consent of the municipal corporation in which the project is located, assumes all the contractual obligations of the transferor corporation under its financial agreement with the municipal corporation, nor to prevent the transfer of a portion of the project as to which the tax exemption has terminated pursuant to section 1728.12 of the Revised Code, nor to prevent the operation and management of all or a portion of a project by the lease thereof to a lessee approved by the governing body of the municipal corporation, which lessee need not be a community urban redevelopment corporation, under terms and conditions approved by the governing body of the municipal corporation, which terms and conditions may include an option or agreement to purchase at a minimal price at not earlier than the termination of the financial agreement.

(C) If a corporation frees itself and its project from the restrictions of Chapter 1728. of the Revised Code, and its financial agreement with the municipal corporation, in the manner provided in such chapter, it shall no longer exercise any of the powers, or be subject to any of the restrictions contained in Chapter 1728. of the Revised Code with respect to that project.

(D) When a corporation, with the consent of the municipal corporation in which its project is located, has transferred its project to another such corporation which has assumed the contractual obligations of the transferor corporation with the municipal corporation, the transferor corporation shall be discharged from any further obligation under the said financial agreement.

§ 1728.05 Federal loans and guarantees.

A community urban redevelopment corporation in carrying out projects may:

(A) Accept loans from the federal government or an agency thereof in aid of a project owned or to be acquired or undertaken by the corporation.

(B) Obtain, or aid in obtaining, from the federal government any insurance or guarantee, or commitment therefor, as to, or for the payment or repayment of interest or principal, or both, or any part thereof, of any loan or other extension of credit, or any instrument evidencing or securing the same, obtained or to be obtained or entered into by it, and to enter into any agreement or contract, or execute any instrument whatsoever with respect to any such insurance or guarantee.

(C) Acquire public or private lands by purchase or otherwise, on such terms and in such manner as it deems proper which lands are necessary for the undertaking and carrying out of a community development plan approved by the governing body of the impacted city and to the extent agreed to by the governing body of an impacted city in a financial agreement provided for in section 1728.07 of the Revised Code.

§ 1728.06 Application for financial agreement.

Every community urban redevelopment corporation qualifying under Chapter 1728. of the Revised Code, before proceeding with any project authorized in such chapter, shall make written application to the municipal corporation for approval thereof. Said application shall be in such form and shall certify to such facts and data as shall be required by the municipal corporation, and may include but not be limited to:

(A) A general statement of the nature of the proposed project, that the undertaking conforms to all applicable municipal ordinances, that its completion will meet an existing need, and that the project accords with the master plan or official map, if any, of the municipality;

(B) A description of the proposed project outlining the area included and a description of each unit thereof if the project is to be undertaken in units and setting out such architectural and site plans as may be required;

(C) A statement of the estimated cost of the proposed project in such detail as may be required, including the estimated cost of each unit if it is to be so undertaken;

(D) The source, method, and amount of money to be subscribed through the investment of private capital, setting forth the amount of stock or other securities to be issued therefor;

(E) A fiscal plan for the project outlining a schedule of rents, the estimated expenditures for operation and maintenance, payments for interest, amortization of debt and reserves, and payments to the municipal corporation to be made pursuant to a financial agreement to be entered into with said municipal corporation;

(F) A relocation plan providing for the relocation of persons, including families, business concerns and others, displaced by the project, which relocation plan shall include, but not be limited to, the proposed method for the relocation of residents who will be displaced from their dwelling accommodations in decent, safe and sanitary dwelling accommodations within their means, or with provision for adjustment payments to bring such accommodations within their means, and without undue hardship, and reasonable moving costs;

(G) The names and tax mailing addresses, as determined from the records of the county auditor not more than five days prior to the submission of the application to the mayor of the municipality, of the owners of all property which the corporation proposes in its application to acquire.

Such application shall be addressed and submitted to the mayor of the municipality, who shall, within sixty days after receipt thereof, submit it with his recommendations to the governing body. The application shall be a matter of public record upon receipt by the mayor. The governing body shall by notice published once a week for two consecutive weeks in a newspaper of general circulation in the municipal corporation, by written notice, by certified mail or personal service, to the owners of property which the corporation proposes in its application to purchase at the tax mailing address as set forth in the corporation's application, by the putting up of signs in at least five places within the area covered by the application, and by giving written notice, by certified mail or personal service, to community organizations known by the clerk of the governing body to represent a substantial number of the residents of the area covered by the application, advise that the application is on file in the office of the clerk of the governing body of the municipal corporation and is available for inspection by the general public during business hours and advise that a public hearing shall be held thereon, stating the place and time of the public hearing, which time shall be not less than fourteen days after the first publication, or after sending the mailed notice, or after the putting up of said signs, whichever is later. Following the public hearing, the governing body, taking into consideration the financial impact on the community, shall by resolution approve or disapprove the application, approval to be by an affirmative vote of not less than three-fifths of the governing body, but in the event of disapproval, changes may be suggested to secure its approval. An application may be revised or resubmitted in the same manner and subject to the same procedures as an original application. The clerk of the governing body shall diligently discharge the duties imposed on the clerk by this division, provided failure of the clerk to send written notices to all community organizations, in a good faith effort by the clerk to give the required notice, shall not invalidate any proceedings under Chapter 1728. of the Revised Code. The failure of delivery of notice given by certified mail under this division shall not invalidate any proceedings under Chapter 1728. of the Revised Code.

§ 1728.07 Financial agreement; form; requisite provisions.

Every approved project shall be evidenced by a financial agreement between the municipal corporation and the community urban redevelopment corporation. Such agreement shall be prepared by the community urban redevelopment corporation and submitted as a separate part of its application for project approval.

The financial agreement shall be in the form of a contract requiring full performance within twenty years from the date of completion of the project and shall, as a minimum, include the following:

(A) That all improvements in the project to be constructed or acquired by the corporation shall be exempt from taxation as provided by section 1728.10 of the Revised Code;

(B) That the corporation shall make payments in lieu of real estate taxes not less than the amount as provided by section 1728.11 of the Revised Code; or, if the municipal corporation is an impacted city, not less than the amount as provided by section 1728.111 [1728.11.1] of the Revised Code;

(C) That the corporation, its successors and assigns, shall use, develop, and redevelop the real property of the project in accordance with, and for the period of, the community development plan approved by the governing body of the municipal corporation for the blighted area in which the project is situated and shall so bind its successors and assigns by appropriate agreements and covenants running with the land enforceable by the municipal corporation;

(D) If the municipal corporation is an impacted city, the extent of the undertakings and activities of the corporation for the elimination and for the prevention of the development or spread of blight;

(E) That the corporation or the municipal corporation, or both, shall provide for carrying out relocation of persons, families, business concerns, and others displaced by the project, pursuant to a relocation plan, including the method for the relocation of residents in decent, safe and sanitary dwelling accommodations, and reasonable moving costs, determined to be feasible by the governing body of the municipal corporation. Where the relocation plan is carried out by the corporation, its officers, employees, agents, or lessees, the municipal corporation shall enforce and supervise the corporation's compliance with the relocation plan. If the corporation refuses or fails to comply with the relocation plan and the municipal corporation fails or refuses to enforce compliance with such plan, the director of the department of economic and community development may request the attorney general to commence a civil action against the municipality and the corporation to require compliance with such relocation plan. Prior to requesting action by the attorney general the director shall give notice of the proposed action to the municipality and the corporation, provide an opportunity to such municipality and corporation for discussions on the matter, and allow a reasonable time in which the corporation may begin compliance with the relocation plan, or the municipality may commence enforcement of the relocation plan;

(F) That the corporation shall submit annually, within ninety days after the close of its fiscal year, its auditor's reports to the mayor and governing body of the municipal corporation;

(G) That the corporation shall, upon request, permit inspection of property, equipment, buildings, and other facilities of the corporation, and also permit examination and audit of its books, contracts, records, documents, and papers by authorized representatives of the municipal corporation;

(H) That in the event of any dispute between the parties the matters in controversy shall be resolved by arbitration in the manner provided therein;

(I) That operation under the financial agreement is terminable by the corporation in the manner provided by Chapter 1728. of the Revised Code;

(J) That the corporation shall, at all times prior to the expiration or other termination of the financial agreement, remain bound by Chapter 1728. of the Revised Code.

(K) That all wages paid to laborers and mechanics employed for work on such projects, other than for residential structures containing seven or less family units, shall be paid at the prevailing rates of wages of laborers and mechanics for the class of work called for by the project, which wages shall be determined in accordance with the requirements of Chapter 4115. of the Revised Code for determination of prevailing wage rates, provided that the requirements of this division do not apply where the federal government or any of its agencies furnishes by law or grant all or any part of the funds used in connection with such project and prescribes predetermined minimum wages to be paid to such laborers and mechanics.

Modifications of the financial agreement may from time to time be made by agreement between the governing body of the municipal corporation and the community urban redevelopment corporation.

§ 1728.08 Consent to sale; bond; municipal work.

(A) The financial agreement provided for in section 1728.07 of the Revised Code may provide that the municipal corporation will consent to a sale of the project by the community urban redevelopment corporation to another such corporation and that, upon assumption by the transferee corporation of the transferor's obligations under the financial agreement the tax exemption of the improvement as provided by section 1728.10 of the Revised Code shall continue and inure to the transferee corporation.

(B) The financial agreement shall provide that the corporation furnish bond with good and sufficient sureties approved by the governing body of the impacted city or other security for the completion of the project and for the disposition of the project property including the buildings in the event of a default in construction or abandonment of the work. The municipal corporation shall within the limits of its legal powers complete or cause the completion of a project undertaken pursuant to this chapter in the event of the termination of the financial agreement by reason of default by the corporation under the terms of the financial agreement.

(C) The financial agreement may further provide that the municipal corporation for its part will undertake and carry out any work, which a municipal corporation may legally undertake, in order to assist in the completion of the project.

§ 1728.09 Plans for management; financing.

The financial agreement provided for in section 1728.07 of the Revised Code shall contain detailed representations and covenants by the community urban redevelopment corporation as to the manner in which it proposes to manage or operate the project. The financial agreement shall further set forth the plans for financing the project, including the estimated total project cost, the amortization rate on the total project cost, the source of funds, the interest rates to be paid on the construction financing, the source and amount of paid-in capital, the terms of mortgage amortization or payment of principal on any mortgage, and the rental schedules and lease terms to be used in the project.

§ 1728.10 Exempt from taxes.

The improvements made in the development or redevelopment of a blighted area, pursuant to Chapter 1728. of the Revised Code, are hereby declared to be a public purpose and shall be exempt from taxation for a period of not more than thirty years for one, two, or three family residential dwelling units and twenty years for all other uses of the improvements from the date of the execution of a financial agreement for the development or redevelopment of the property upon which the improvements are to be made pursuant to a financial agreement entered into with the municipal corporation in which said area is situated. Any such exemption shall be claimed and allowed in the same or a similar manner as in the case of other real property exemptions and no such claim shall be allowed unless the municipal corporation wherein said property is situated certifies that a financial agreement with a community urban redevelopment corporation for the development or the redevelopment of the property has been entered into and is in effect as required by Chapter 1728. of the Revised Code. In event that an exemption status changes during a tax year, the procedure for the apportionment of the taxes for said year shall be the same as in the case of other changes in tax exemption status during the tax year.

§ 1728.11 Payment in lieu of taxes.

The community urban redevelopment corporation entering into a financial agreement with a municipal corporation other than an impacted city shall make payment to the county treasurer on or before the final date for payment of real estate taxes in the county for each half year of a semi-annual service charge in lieu of taxes on the real property of the corporation in the project, whether acquired by purchase or lease, in a semi-annual amount of not less than seven and one-half percent of the annual gross revenues from each unit of the project, if the project is undertaken in units, or from the total project if the project is not to be undertaken in units, for each of the years of operation commencing with the date of the completion of such unit or of the project, as the case may be. Where, because of the nature of the development, ownership, use, or occupancy of the project or any unit thereof if the project is to be undertaken in units, the total annual gross rental cannot be reasonably ascertained, the governing body shall provide in the financial agreement that the annual service charge shall be a sum of not less than two percent of the total project cost or total project unit cost, calculated from the first day of the month following the substantial completion of the project or any unit thereof if the project is undertaken in units. In no event shall such payment together with the taxes on the land, in any year after first occupancy of the project, be less than the total taxes assessed on all real property in the area covered by the project in the calendar year immediately preceding the acquisition of the said area by the municipality or its agency.

Against such annual charge the corporation is entitled to credit for the amount, without interest, of the real estate taxes on land paid by it in the last two preceding semi-annual installments. On or before the fifteenth of January in each year each taxing district shall report to the county auditor, in such form as is approved by the tax commissioner, the amount of the service charge in excess of the taxes on the land chargeable for the preceding calendar year for each project or unit thereof subject to Chapter 1728. of the Revised Code. Such payments shall be distributed by the county auditor to the taxing subdivision levying taxes in the subdivisions in which the property is located, in the same proportions in which the current general property tax is distributed.

At the end of thirty years for one, two, or three family residential dwelling units and twenty years for all other uses of the improvements from the date of the execution of a financial agreement or earlier by agreement of the parties thereto, the tax exemption upon any unit, if the project is undertaken in units, or upon the entire project, if the project is not undertaken in units, ceases and the improvements and any other property of the corporation as well as the land shall be assessed and taxed, according to general law, like other property within the municipal corporation.

At the same date all restrictions and limitations upon the corporation shall terminate and be at an end upon the corporation's rendering its final account with the municipal corporation.

[§ 1728.11.1] § 1728.111 [Agreement with impacted city.]

The community urban redevelopment corporation entering into a financial agreement with an impacted city shall make payment to the county treasurer, on or before the final date for payment of real estate taxes in the county for each half year, of a semi-annual service charge in lieu of taxes on the real property of the corporation in the project, whether acquired by purchase or lease, which, together with the taxes on the land, in any year after first occupancy of the project, shall be not less than one-half of the total taxes assessed on all real property in the area covered by the project in the calendar year immediately preceding the initial acquisition of the area or any part thereof by the municipality or the corporation, whichever shall have occurred first.

Such payments shall be distributed by the county auditor to the taxing subdivision levying taxes in the subdivisions in which the property is located, in the same proportions in which the current general property tax is distributed.

At the end of thirty years for one, two, or three family residential dwelling units and twenty years for all other uses of the improvements from the date of the execution of a financial agreement, or earlier by agreement of the parties thereto, the taxing exemption upon any unit, if the project is undertaken in units, or upon the entire project, if the project is not undertaken in units, ceases and the improvements and any other property of the corporation as well as the land shall be assessed and taxed, according to general law, like other property within the municipal corporation.

At the same date all restrictions and limitation upon the corporation shall terminate and be at an end upon the corporation's rendering its final account with the municipal corporation.

§ 1728.12 Termination of exemption, agreement.

The tax exemption provided by section 1728.10 of the Revised Code applies only so long as the community urban redevelopment corporation and its project remain subject to Chapter 1728. of the Revised Code, but in no event longer than thirty years for one, two, or three family residential dwelling units and twenty years for all other uses of the improvements from the date of the execution of the financial agreement. Any corporation organized under Chapter 1728. may, at any time after the expiration of one year from the completion date of a project, notify the governing body of the municipal corporation with which it has entered into a financial agreement that, as of a certain date designated in the notice, it relinquishes its status under Chapter 1728. of the Revised Code as to all or any of the real property included in the project. As of the date so set, the tax exemption and the payments in lieu of taxes shall terminate as to the real property specified in the notice.

§ 1728.13 Relationship to public utilities.

(A) A community urban redevelopment corporation does not have the power, nor shall any financial agreement made pursuant to Chapter 1728. of the Revised Code, provide that the municipal corporation for its part will undertake, to construct, install, acquire, maintain, or operate any property, plant, equipment, or facilities which would be competitive with any public utility as the same is defined in section 4905.02 of the Revised Code or used by any public utility subject to regulation, supervision, or control by any federal regulatory body.

(B) A municipal corporation may not acquire by the exercise of the right of eminent domain, for any of the purposes of Chapter 1728. of the Revised Code, any property used by any public utility as the same is defined in section 4905.02 of the Revised Code or used by any public utility subject to regulation, supervision, or control by any federal regulatory body, in furnishing any commodity or service which, by law, it is authorized to furnish.

(C) If any municipal corporation, or its duly authorized agency, as part of or in connection with any plan, plan of a project or projects initiated or undertaken in accordance with Chapter 1728. of the Revised Code, vacates any street, avenue, highway, road, or other public place or way, referred to in this section as "street," on, in, or under which is located any property owned or used by any public utility as defined in section 4905.02 of the Revised Code, or owned or used by any public utility subject to regulation, supervision, or control by any federal regulatory body in furnishing any commodity or service which, by law, it is authorized to furnish, such municipal corporation shall determine, upon the completion of the vacation proceedings, whether the retention of such property in the existing location will interfere with the consummation of the project.

(D) If such municipal corporation, or its duly authorized agency, determines that the retention of such property in such location will interfere with the consummation of the project, it shall make an order requiring the public utility using such property to remove, relocate, rearrange, or change such property in accordance with such order, and the cost and expense of such removal, rearrangement, or change, including the cost of installing such property in a new location or locations or changed condition, and the cost of any lands or any rights or interest in lands and any other rights acquired to accomplish such removal, relocation, rearrangement, or change shall be paid by the municipal corporation or its duly authorized agency as part of the cost of making land available for use by a community urban redevelopment corporation. In case of the relocation of any such property, the public utility using the same, its successors and assigns, may maintain and operate such property with the necessary appurtenances, in the new locations for as long a period and upon the same terms and conditions and with the same franchise rights as it had the right to maintain and operate such property in its former location.

(E) If such municipal corporation, or its duly authorized agency, determines that the retention of such property in its existing location will not interfere with the consummation of the project, it shall express such determination in a writing which shall be delivered to such public utility, and such public utility, its successors and assigns, may enter upon the lands which comprised such street prior to its vacation, for the purpose of maintaining, repairing, renewing, or removing any such property.

(F) If any municipal corporation, or its duly authorized agency, as a part of or in connection with any plan, plan of a project or projects initiated or undertaken in accordance with Chapter 1728. of the Revised Code, determines that any property owned or used by any public utility as defined in section 4905.02 of the Revised Code, or owned or used by any public utility subject to regulation, supervision, or control by a federal regulatory body, in furnishing any commodity or service which it is authorized by law to furnish, which is located in, on, along, over, or under any street, shall be removed, relocated, rearranged, changed, reconstructed, or abandoned, the cost and expense of the removal, relocation, rearrangement, change, reconstruction, or abandonment of such property, including the cost of installing, reconstructing, and replacing such property in a new location or locations and the cost of any lands or any rights or interest in lands and any other rights acquired to accomplish such removal, relocation, rearrangement, change, reconstruction, or replacement of such property shall be paid by the municipal corporation or its duly authorized agency as a part of the cost of making land available for use by a community urban redevelopment corporation. In case of the relocation of any such property the public utility using the same, its successors and assigns, may maintain and operate such property, with the necessary appurtenances, in the new locations for as long a period and upon the same terms and conditions as it had a right to maintain and operate such property in its former location.

APPENDIX I
Sample Lease Agreement

THE STATE OF _____
COUNTY OF _____
THIS LEASE AGREEMENT made and entered into on this the _____ day of _____, between _____ (hereinafter called "Lessor"), whose address for purposes hereof is _____
and _____
(hereinafter called "Leseee").

Lessee's address for purposes hereof until commencement of the term of this lease being _____ _____ and thereafter being that of the "Building" (hereinafter defined),

WITNESSETH:
I.
Leased Premises
1. Subject to and upon the terms, provisions and conditions hereinafter set forth, and each in consideration of the duties, covenants and obligations of the other hereunder Lessor does hereby lease, demise and let to Lessee and Lessee does hereby lease from Lessor those certain premisee (hereinafter sometimes called the "leased premises") in the building known as _____ (herein called the "Building") located on _____ . . . .
The term "net rentable area," as used herein, shall refer to _____
_____
_____

The net rentable area in the leased premises . . . is hereby stipulated for all purposes hereof to be _____ square feet, whether the same should be more or less as a result of minor variations resulting from actual construction and completion of the leased premises for occupancy so long as such work is done in accordance with the terms and provisions hereof.
II.
Term
1. Subject to and upon the terms and conditions set forth herein, or in any exhibit or addendum hereto, this lease shall continue in force for a term of _____(_____) months, beginning on the _____ day of _____, 19_____, and ending on the _____ day of _____, 19_____. In the event the leased premises should not be ready for occupancy by said commencement date for any reason, Lessor shall not be liable or responsible for any claims, damages or liabilities in connection therewith or by reason thereof. This Lease Agreement shall be effective only from the time that the leased premises are ready for occupancy by Lessee which date shall be the date of commencement of the term of this lease. Should the term of this lease commence on a date other than that specified in this Paragraph 1 of Article II, Lessor and Lessee will, at the request of either, execute a declaration specifying the beginning date of the term of this Lease Agreement. In such event, rental under this Lease Agreement shall not commence until said revised commencement date, and the stated term in this Lease Agreement shall thereupon commence and the expiration date shall be extended so as to give effect to the full stated term. Also, in such event, Lessor shall give Lessee written notice of such revised commencement date at least fifteen days in advance thereof.

Use
2. The lease premises are to be used and occupied by Lessee solely for the purpose of office space.

Base Rental
3. Lessee hereby agrees to pay a base annual rental (herein called "Base Rental") in the sum of _____ _____ per year. Such Base Rental, together with any adjustments of rent provided for herein then in effect, shall be due and payable in twelve (12) equal installments on the first day of each calendar month during the initial term or any extensions or renewals thereof, and Lessee hereby agrees to so pay such rent to Lessor at Lessor's address as provided herein monthly in advance without demand. If the term of this Lease Agreement as heretofore established commences on other than the first day of a month or terminates on other than the last day of a month, then the installment of Base Rental of such month or months shall be prorated and the installment or installments so prorated shall be paid in advance. All past

due installments of rent shall bear interest at the rate of 10% per annum from date due until paid.

Base Rental Adjustment Prior to End of Base Year
4. The Base Rental Adjustment shall be calculated in accordance with the following factors:
(a) Ad Valorem Tax Factor—the ad valorem tax factor for the building is stipulated to be $.50/square foot of net rentable area.
(b) Operating Expense Factor—the minimum allowable wage payable to janitorial personnel in _____ _____ after _____, 19___, and prior to the end of the Base Year. The minimum allowable wage, as of _____, 19___, is hereby stipulated to be $2.10 per hour.
(c) Utilities Cost Factor—the cost of utilities, such as gas, electricity and water necessary for the operation of the Building. The Utility Cost Factor has been determined by published schedules and Fuel Adjustments applicable to the Building as of _____, 19___.
The "Base Year," as used herein, means the calendar year _____. Prior to the end of the Base Year, the Base Rental shall be adjusted upward or downward as provided below, except that in no case shall the Base Rental be reduced below the initial Base Rental previously specified in Paragraph 3 of this Article II:
(a) On account of the Ad Valorem Tax Factor, if the actual Ad Valorem Tax Factor is greater than the above projected Ad Valorem Tax Factor, the Base Rental will be adjusted by the amount of the difference between the actual and projected Ad Valorem Tax Factors times the number of square feet of net rentable area contained in the leased premises.
(b) On account of the Operating Expense Factor, by an amount equal to $0.01 per year per square foot of the net rentable area contained in the leased premises for each 1% increase or decrease in the Operating Expense Factor; and
(c) On account of the Utilities Cost Factor, by adjusting the Base Rate $.0054/square foot of net rentable area contained in the premises for each 1% change in the Utilities Cost Factor.
An adjustment of the Base Rental, if required pursuant to the terms hereof, shall be made effective as of the commencement date of this lease stated above (which date shall be the commencement date stated above or the revised commencement date, whichever is applicable), and subsequent adjustments of the Base Rental, if required, shall be made as of the effective date of change of the various base rental adjustment factors through the end of the Base Year.

Base Rental Adjustment Following Base Year
5. In the event that the Basic Cost (as hereinafter defined) of Lessor's operation of the Building during the first calendar year of occupancy after the Base Year, or any subsequent year, shall differ from the Basic Cost of Lessor therefor during the prior year, Lessee shall pay the year's increases or share in decreases in the proportion its net rentable area bears to the total net rentable area in the Building. Any increase due under this provision shall be deemed additional rent. Lessor shall, within the period of one hundred fifty days after the close of each calendar year, give Lessee a statement of the year's Basic Cost and a comparison with the prior year's Basic Cost. The statement will be prepared by a certified public accountant. If the more recent year's Basic Costs are greater than the previous year's Basic Cost, Lessee will pay Lessor, within thirty days of statement receipt, his proportionate share of such increase. If the more recent year's Basic Costs are less than the previous year's Basic Cost, Lessor will pay Lessee, within thirty days of statement issuance, Lessee's proportionate share of Lessor's cost savings.
Whenever the provisions of the foregoing paragraph operate to cause a rental reconciliation, Lessee shall thereafter pay an Adjusted Base Rental which reflects the most recent year's Basic Cost. Concurrent with delivery of the Basic Cost statement, Lessor will deliver to Lessee a Rental Adjustment Notice. Annual rental for the then current year will be adjusted to include the per square foot increase or decrease in the prior year's Basic Cost. If rental is to be increased, Lessee will pay to Lessor within thirty days of receipt of the notice the total of monthly increases due for the previous months in the then current year and thereafter will pay the Adjusted Base Rental. If rental is to

be reduced, Lessor will pay to Lessee the total of monthly decreases due for the previous months in the then current year and Lessee will thereafter pay the Adjusted Base Rental.
In no case will an Adjusted Base Rental be lower than the Base Rental stated in Article II, Paragraph 3 of this Lease.
"Basic Cost" as said term is used herein shall consist of the operating expenses of the Building, which shall be computed on the accrual basis and shall consist of all expenditures by Lessor to maintain all facilities in operation during the Base Year and such additional facilities in subsequent years as may be determined by Lessor to be necessary. All operating expenses shall be determined in accordance with generally accepted accounting principles which shall be consistently applied. The term "operating expenses" as used herein shall mean all expenses, costs and disbursements (but not general office expense nor specific costs especially billed to and paid by specific tenants) of every kind and nature which Lessor shall pay or become obligated to pay because of or in connection with the ownership and operation of the Building, including but not limited to, the following:
(a) Wages and salaries of all employees engaged in operation and maintenance of the Building, including taxes, insurance and benefits relating thereto.
(b) All supplies and materials used in operation and maintenance of the Building.
(c) Cost of water and power, heating, lighting, air conditioning and ventilating the Building.
(d) Cost of all maintenance and service agreements on equipment, including alarm service, window cleaning and elevator maintenance.
(e) Cost of casualty and liability insurance applicable to the Building and Lessor's personal property used in connection therewith.
(f) All taxes and assessments and governmental charges whether federal, state, county or municipal, and whether they be by taxing districts or authorities presently taxing the leased premises or by others, subsequently created or otherwise, and any other taxes and assessments attributable to the Building or its operation excluding, however, federal and state taxes on income. It is agreed that Lessee will be responsible for ad valorem taxes on its personal property and on the value of leasehold improvements to the extent that same exceed standard building allowances.
(g) Cost of repairs and general maintenance.
Notwithstanding any other provision herein to the contrary, it is agreed that in the event the Building is not fully occupied during the Base Year or any subsequent year, an adjustment shall be made in computing the ad valorem taxes and the operating expenses for such year so that the ad valorem taxes and the cost of water and power, heating, lighting, air conditioning and ventilating the Building and the cost of furnishing the janitorial services to the Building shall be computed for such year as though the Building has been fully occupied during such year.
Lessee at its expense shall have the right at all reasonable times to audit Lessor's books and records relating to this Lease for the Base Year and any year or years for which additional rental payments become due; or at Lessor's sole discretion Lessor will provide such audit prepared by a certified public accountant.
III.
Services to Be Furnished by Lessor
Lessor covenants and agrees with Lessee:
1. To furnish the electricity, gas and water utilized in operating any and all facilities serving the leased premises, except as otherwise provided herein.
2. To furnish Lessee while occupying the premises:
(a) Hot and cold water at those points of supply provided for general use of other tenants in the Building; central heat and air conditioning in season, at such times as Lessor normally furnishes these services to other tenants in the Building, and at such temperatures and in such amounts as are considered by Lessor to be standard, but such service on Saturday afternoons, Sundays and holidays to be furnished only upon the request of Lessee, who shall bear the entire cost thereof; routine maintenance, and electric lighting service for all public areas and special service areas of the Building in the manner and to the extent deemed by Lessor to be standard. Lessor will fur-

nish janitor service on a five (5) day week basis at no extra charge; provided, however, if Lessee's floor covering or other improvements are other than building standard as provided in the Schedule 1 hereto Lessee shall pay the additional cleaning cost attributable thereto as additional rent. Failure by Lessor to any extent to furnish these defined services, or any cessation thereof, resulting from causes beyond the control of Lessor, shall not render Lessor liable in any respect for damages to either person or property, nor be construed as an eviction of Lessee, nor work an abatement of rent, nor relieve Lessee from fulfillment of any covenant or agreement hereof. Should any of the equipment or machinery break down, or for any cause cease to function properly, Lessor shall use reasonable diligence to repair same promptly, but Lessee shall have no claim for rebate of rent or damages on account of any interruptions in service occasioned thereby or resulting therefrom.

(b) Proper electrical facilities to furnish sufficient power for typewriters, voice writers, calculating machines and other machines of similar low electrical consumption; but not including electricity required for electronic data processing equipment, special lighting in excess of building standard, and any other item of electrical equipment which (singly) consumes more than .5 kilowatts per hour at rated capacity or requires a voltage other than 120 volts single phase. Lessor, at its expense, shall furnish and pay for all fluorescent bulb replacement in all areas and all incandescent bulb replacement in public areas, toilet and restroom areas and stairwells.

3. To use Lessor's best efforts to control access to the truck loading area and provide security to the Building during the weekends and after normal working hours during the week. Lessor shall not be liable to Lessee for losses due to theft or burglary, or for damages done by unauthorized persons on the premises.

4. To furnish Lessee, free of charge, with two keys for each corridor door entering the leased premises, and additional keys will be furnished at a charge by Lessor equal to its cost plus 15% on an order signed by Lessee or Lessee's authorized representative. All such keys shall remain the property of Lessor. No additional locks shall be allowed on any door of leased premises without Lessor's permission, and Lessee shall not make, or permit to be made any duplicate keys, except those furnished by Lessor. Upon termination of this lease Lessee shall surrender to Lessor all keys of the leased premises, and give to Lessor the explanation of the combination of all locks for safes, safe cabinets and vault doors, if any, in the leased premises.

5. To provide and install, at Lessee's cost, all letters or numerals on doors in the leased premises; all such letters and numerals shall be in the Building's standard graphics, and no others shall be used or permitted on the premises.

Improvements to Be Made by Lessor

6. In preparing the leased premises for occupancy by Lessee, Lessor shall be required to bear the expense of installing the items listed in Schedule 1, attached hereto and made a part hereof, only to the extent that they do not exceed the respective allowances indicated in said Schedule 1. All installations in excess thereof shall be for Lessee's account and at Lessee's cost (and Lessee shall pay ad valorem taxes thereon), which cost shall be payable by Lessee to Lessor as additional rent hereunder promptly upon being invoiced therefor, and failure by Lessee to pay same in full within 30 days shall constitute failure to pay rent when due and an event of default by Lessee hereunder giving rise to all remedies available to Lessor under this lease and at law for nonpayment of rent.

Peaceful Enjoyment

7. That Lessee shall, and may peacefully have, hold and enjoy the leased premises, subject to the other terms hereof, provided that Lessee pays the rental herein recited and performs all of Lessee's covenants and agreements herein contained. It is understood and agreed that this covenant and any and all other covenants of Lessor contained in this lease shall be binding upon Lessor and its successors only with respect to breaches occurring during its and their respective ownerships of the Lessor's interest hereunder. In addition, Lessee specifically agrees to look solely to Lessor's interest in the Building for the recovery of any judgment from Lessor; it being agreed that Lessor shall never be personally liable for any such judgment. The provision contained in the foregoing sentence is not intended to, and shall not, limit any right that Lessee might otherwise have to obtain injunctive relief against Lessor or Lessor's successors in interest, or any other action not involving the personal liability of Lessor to respond in monetary damages from assets other than Lessor's interest in the Building, or any suit or action in connection with enforcement or collection of amounts which may become owing or payable under or on account of insurance maintained by Lessor.

Parking

8. Lessee shall at all times during the term of this lease park ______________ cars . . . in the parking garage located adjacent to the Building. No specific spaces in the parking garage are to be assigned to Lessee, but Lessor will issue to Lessee the aforesaid number of parking stickers or tags, each of which will authorize parking in the parking garage of a car on which the sticker or tag is displayed, or Lessor will provide a reasonable alternative means of identifying and controlling cars authorized to be parked in the parking garage. Lessor may designate the area within which each such car may be parked, and Lessor may change such designations from time to time. Lessor may make, modify and enforce rules and regulations relating to the parking of automobiles in the parking garage, and Lessee will abide by such rules and regulations.

IV.

Payments by Lessee

Lessee covenants and agrees with Lessor:

1. To pay all rent and sums provided to be paid to Lessor hereunder at the times and in the manner herein provided.

Obligation of Lessee to Furnish Floor Plans

2. Lessee agrees to deliver to Lessor no later than ______________________, 19____, a detailed floor plan layout, together with working drawings and written instructions sufficiently detailed to enable Lessor to let firm contracts (herein called "Lessee's Plans"), reflecting the partitions and improvements desired by Lessee in said leased premises. After receipt thereof, Lessor will partition and prepare said leased premises in accordance therewith; however, Lessor shall not be required to install any partitions or improvements which are not in conformity with the plans and specifications for the Building or which are not approved by Lessor or Lessor's architect, and Lessor shall be required to bear the expense of installing the items listed in Schedule 1 hereto only to the extent that they do not exceed the respective allowances indicated in said Schedule 1. All installation in excess thereof shall be for Lessee's account, and Lessee shall pay, as additional rent hereunder, to Lessor therefor an amount equal to Lessor's actual cost plus an additional charge of 15% to cover overhead, promptly upon being invoiced therefor. Failure by Lessee to pay such sum in full within 30 days after its receipt of the invoice will constitute failure to pay rent when due and an event of default by Lessee hereunder, giving rise to all remedies, available to Lessor under this lease and at law for nonpayment of rent. It is stipulated that time is of the essence in connection with delivery of Lessee's Plans by Lessee to Lessor. Should Lessee fail to deliver Lessee's Plans as scheduled, Lessee shall pay to Lessor, as rent and for the purpose of reimbursing Lessor for additional expenses which will be incurred by Lessor because of inability to proceed with the work as scheduled, one day's rent on the leased premises for each day beyond the scheduled delivery date specified above that delivery of Lessee's Plans is delayed. Such additional rent shall be paid by Lessee to Lessor within thirty days after receipt by Lessee of Lessor's invoice therefor.

Lessor agrees to install partitions and improvements in the quantity allowed in Schedule 1 within the period of time between the dates shown in this Agreement for (1) Commencement Date in Article II, paragraph 1, and (2) the date of delivery of Lessee's Plans by Lessee in Article IV, paragraph 2. It shall be recognized that Lessee may indicate on his plans quantities in excess of those shown in Schedule 1 or he may indicate on those Plans improvements that are not Building Standards and the sum of all such work shall be defined as "Tenant Extra Work" and the cost to perform that work shall be defined as "Tenant Extra Cost." As provided herein, Lessee shall pay Tenant Extra Cost but it shall be recognized that the time required to perform the Tenant Extra Work may be longer than the time stipulated to perform the work allowed in Schedule 1. Any such additional time shall be treated in the same manner as described for delays by Lessee in delivering his Plans to Lessor.

Repairs by Lessor

3. Unless otherwise expressly stipulated herein, Lessor shall not be required to make any improvements or repairs of any kind or character on the leased premises during the term of this lease, except such repairs as may be required for normal maintenance operations, which shall include the painting of and repairs to walls, floors, corridors, windows and other structures and equipment within and serving the leased premises, and such additional maintenance as may be necessary because of damages by persons other than Lessee, its agents, employees, invitees or visitors. The obligation of Lessor to maintain and repair the leased premises shall be limited to building standard items. Special leasehold improvements will, at Lessee's written request, be maintained by Lessor at Lessee's cost, plus an additional charge of 15% of such cost to cover overhead.

Repairs by Lessee

4. At its own cost and expense, to repair or replace any damage or injury done to the Building, or any part thereof, caused by Lessee or Lessee's agents, employees, invitees or visitors; provided, however, if Lessee fails to make such repairs or replacement promptly Lessor may, at its option, make such repairs or replacements, and Lessee shall repay the cost thereof to the Lessor on demand.

Care of the Leased Premises

5. Lessee agrees not to commit or allow any waste or damage to be committed on any portion of the leased premises, and at the termination of this lease, by lapse of time or otherwise, to deliver up said leased premises to Lessor in as good condition as at date of possession by Lessee, ordinary wear and tear excepted, and upon such termination of this lease, Lessor shall have the right to reenter and resume possession of the leased premises.

Assignment or Sublease

6. In the event Lessee should desire to assign this Agreement or sublet the leased premises or any part thereof, Lessee shall give Lessor written notice of such desire at least sixty (60) days in advance of the date on which Lessee desires to make such assignment or sublease. Lessor shall then have a period of thirty (30) days following receipt of such notice within which to notify Lessee in writing that Lessor elects either (1) to terminate this Agreement as to the space so affected as of the date so specified by Lessee in which event Lessee will be relieved of all further obligation hereunder as to such space, or (2) to permit Lessee to assign or sublet such space, subject, however, to subsequent written approval of the proposed assignee or sublessee by Lessor. If Lessor should fail to notify Lessee in writing of such election within said thirty (30) day period, Lessor shall be deemed to have elected option (2) above, but subsequent written approval by Lessor of the proposed assignee or sublessee shall be required. If Lessor elects to exercise option (2) above, Lessee agrees to provide, at its expense, direct access from the assignment or sublease space to a public corridor of the Building. No assignment or subletting by Lessee shall relieve Lessee of any obligation under this lease.

Alterations, Additions, Improvements

7. Not to permit the leased premises to be used for any purpose other than that stated in the use clause hereof, or make or allow to be made any alterations or physical additions in or to the leased premises without first obtaining the written consent of Lessor. Any and all such alterations, physical additions, or improvements, when made to the leased premises by Lessee, shall at once become the property of Lessor and shall be surrendered to Lessor upon the termination of this lease by lapse of time or otherwise; provided, however, this clause shall not apply to movable equipment or furniture owned by Lessee. Lessee agrees specifically that no food, soft drink or other vending machine will be installed within the leased premises.

Legal Use and Violations of Insurance Coverage

8. Not to occupy or use, or permit any portion of the leased premises to be occupied or used for any business or purpose which is unlawful, disreputable or deemed to be extra-hazardous on account of fire, or permit anything to be done which would in any way increase the rate of fire insurance coverage on said Building and/or its contents.

Laws and Regulations; Rules of Building

9. To comply with all laws, ordinances, orders, rules and regulations (state, federal, municipal and other agencies or bodies having any jurisdiction thereof) relating to the use, condition or occupancy of the leased premises. Lessee will comply with the rules of the Building adopted by Lessor from time to time for the safety, care and cleanliness of the leased premises and for preservation of good order therein, all of which will be sent by Lessor to Lessee in writing and shall be thereafter carried out and observed by Lessee.

Entry for Repairs and Inspection

10. To permit Lessor or its agents or representatives to enter into and upon any part of the leased premises at all reasonable hours to inspect same, clean or make repairs, alterations or additions thereto, as Lessor may deem necessary or desirable, and Lessee shall not be entitled to any abatement or reduction of rent by reason thereof.

Nuisance

11. To conduct its business and control its agents, employees, invitees and visitors in such manner as not to create any nuisance, or interfere with, annoy or disturb any other tenant or Lessor in his operation of the Building.

Subordination to Mortgage

12. This lease is subject and subordinate to any first lien mortgage or deed of trust which may now or hereafter encumber the Building of which the leased premises form a part and to all renewals, modifications, consolidations, replacements and extensions thereof. This clause shall be self-operative and no further instrument of subordination need be required by any mortgagee. In confirmation of such subordination, however, Lessee shall at Lessor's request execute promptly any appropriate certificate or instrument that Lessor may request. Lessee hereby constitutes and appoints Lessor the Lessee's attorney-in-fact to execute any such certificate or instrument for and on behalf of Lessee. In the event of the enforcement by the trustee or the beneficiary under any such mortgage or deed of trust of the remedies provided for by law or by such mortgage or deed of trust, Lessee will, upon request of any person or party succeeding to the interest of Lessor as a result of such enforcement, automatically become the Lessee of such successor in interest without change in the terms or other provisions of such lease; provided, however, that such successor in interest shall not be bound by (i) any payment of rent or additional rent for more than one month in advance except prepayments in the nature of security for the performance by Lessee of its obligations under this lease or (ii) any amendment or modification of this lease made without the written consent of such trustee or such beneficiary or such successor in interest. Upon request by such successor in interest, Lessee shall execute and deliver an instrument or instruments confirming the attornment herein provided for.

Estoppel Certificate or Three-Party Agreement

13. At Lessor's request Lessee will execute either an estoppel certificate addressed to Lessor's mortgagee or a three-party agreement among Lessor, Lessee and said mortgagee certifying as to such facts (if true) and agreeing to such notice provisions and other matters as such Mortgagee may reasonably require in connection with Lessor's financing.

V.

Condemnation and Loss or Damage

Lessor and Lessee mutually covenant and agree as follows:

1. If the leased premises shall be taken or condemned for any public purpose to such an extent as to render the leased premises untenantable this lease shall, at the option of either party, forthwith cease and terminate. Lessor shall not be liable or responsible to Lessee for any loss or damage to any property or person occasioned by theft, fire, act of God, public enemy, injunction, riot, strike, insurrection, war, court order, requisition or order of governmental body or authority; or for any damage or inconvenience which may arise through repair or alteration of any part of the Building, or failure to make any such repairs.

Lien for Rent

2. In consideration of the mutual benefits arising under this agreement, Lessee hereby grants to Lessor a lien and security interest on all property of Lessee now or hereafter placed in or upon the leased premises, and such property shall be and remain subject to such lien and security interest of Lessor for payment of all rent and other sums agreed to be paid by Lessee herein. Said lien and security interest shall be in addition to and cumulative of the landlord's liens provided by law. This lease shall constitute a security agreement under the Uniform Commercial Code so that Lessor shall have and may enforce a security interest on all property of Lessee now or hereafter placed in or on the leased premises, including but not limited to all fixtures, machinery, equipment, furnishings and other articles of personal property now or hereafter placed in or upon the leased premises by Lessee. Lessee and each of them agree to execute as debtor such financing statement or statements as Lessor may now or hereafter reasonably request in order that such security interest or interests may be protected pursuant to said Code. Lessor may at its election at any time file a copy of this lease as a financing statement. Lessor, as secured party, shall be entitled to all of the rights and remedies afforded a secured party under said Uniform Commercial Code, which rights and remedies shall be in addition to and cumulative of the landlord's liens and rights provided by law or by the other terms and provisions of this lease.

Lessor's Right to Relet

3. In the event the leased premises are abandoned by Lessee, Lessor shall have the right, but not the obligation, to relet same for the remainder of the term provided for herein; and if the rent received through such reletting does not at least equal the rent provided for herein, Lessee shall pay and satisfy any deficiency between the amount of the rent so provided for and that received through reletting, and, in addition thereto, shall pay all reasonable expenses incurred in connection with any such reletting, including, but not limited to, the cost of renovating, altering and decorating for a new occupant. Nothing herein shall be construed as in any way denying Lessor the right in the event of abandonment of said premises or other breach of this agreement by Lessee, to treat the same as an entire breach and at Lessor's option to immediately sue for the entire breach of this agreement and any and all damages which Lessor suffers thereby.

Holding Over

4. In the event of holding over by Lessee after expiration or termination of this lease without the written consent of Lessor, Lessee shall pay as liquidated damages double rent for the entire holdover period. No holding over by Lessee after the term of this lease shall operate to extend the lease; in the event of any unauthorized holding over, Lessee shall indemnify Lessor against all claims for damages by any other lessee to whom Lessor may have leased all or any part of the premises covered hereby effective upon the termination of this lease. Any holding over with the consent of Lessor in writing shall thereafter constitute this lease a lease from month to month.

Fire Clause

5. In the event of a fire in the leased premises, Lessee shall immediately give notice thereof to Lessor. If the leased premises, through no fault or neglect of Lessee, its agents, employees, invitees or visitors, shall be partially destroyed by fire or other casualty so as to render the premises untenantable, the rental herein shall abate thereafter until such time as the leased premises are made tenantable by Lessor. In the event of the total destruction of the leased premises without fault or neglect of Lessee, its agents, employees, invitees or visitors, or if from such cause the same shall be so damaged that Lessor shall decide not to rebuild, then all rent owed up to the time of such destruction or termination shall be paid by Lessee and thenceforth this lease shall cease and come to an end.

Attorney's Fees

6. In the event Lessee makes default in the performance of any of the terms, covenants, agreements or conditions contained in this lease and Lessor places the enforcement of this lease, or any part thereof, or the collection of any rent due, or to become due hereunder, or recovery of the possession of the leased premises in the hands of an attorney, or files suit upon the same, Lessee agrees to pay Lessor a reasonable attorney's fees incurred by Lessor.

Alteration

7. This agreement may not be altered, changed or amended, except by an instrument in writing, signed by both parties hereto.

Assignment

8. Lessor shall have the right to transfer and assign, in whole or in part, all its rights and obligation hereunder and in the Building and property referred to herein, and in such event and upon its transferee's assuming Lessor's obligations hereunder (any such transferee to have the benefit of, and be subject to, the provisions of Paragraph 7 of Article III hereof) no further liability or obligation shall thereafter accrue against Lessor hereunder.

Default by Lessee

9. Default on the part of the Lessee in paying rent or any installment thereof, as herein provided, or default on Lessee's part in keeping or performing any other term, covenant or condition of this lease, shall authorize Lessor, at its option, at any time after such default has continued for a period of ten (10) days and without prior notice to Lessee, to declare this lease terminated, and upon the occurrence of any one or more of such defaults, Lessor immediately, or at any time thereafter, may re-enter said premises and remove all persons therefrom with or without legal process, and without prejudice to any of its other legal rights, and all claims for damages by reason of such re-entry are expressly waived, as also are all claims for damages by reason of any eviction proceedings or proceedings by way of sequestration or any other legal proceeding which Lessor may employ to recover said rents or possession of said premises.

Waiver

10. Failure of Lessor to declare any default immediately upon occurrence thereof, or delay in taking action in connection therewith, shall not waive such default, but Lessor shall have the right to declare any such default at any time and take such action as might be lawful or authorized hereunder, either in law or in equity.

Bankruptcy by Lessee

11. If voluntary bankruptcy proceedings are instituted by Lessee, or if Lessee is adjudged a bankrupt, or if Lessee makes an assignment for the benefit of its creditors, or if execution is issued against it, or if the interest of Lessee hereunder passes by operation of law to any person other than Lessee, this lease may, at the option of Lessor, be terminated by notice mailed by registered mail and addressed to Lessee.

Casualty Insurance

12. Lessor shall, at all times during the term of this lease, at its expense, maintain a policy or policies of insurance with the premiums thereon fully paid in advance, issued by and binding upon some solvent insurance company, insuring the Building against loss or damage by fire, explosion, or other hazards and contingencies for the full insurable value thereof; provided that Lessor shall not be obligated to insure any furniture, equipment, machinery, goods or supplies not covered by this lease which Lessee may bring or obtain upon the leased premises, or any additional improvement which Lessee may construct thereon. If the annual premiums charged Lessor for such casualty insurance exceed the standard premium rates because the nature of Lessee's operations results in extrahazardous exposure, then Lessee shall upon receipt of appropriate premium invoices reimburse Lessor for such increases in such premiums.

Liability Insurance

13. Lessor shall likewise, at its expense, maintain a policy or policies of comprehensive general liability insurance with the premiums thereon fully paid in advance, issued by and binding upon some solvent insurance company, such insurance to afford minimum protection of not less than One Hundred Thousand Dollars ($100,000.00) in respect of personal injury or death to any one person, and of not less than Three Hundred Thousand Dollars ($300,000.00) in respect to any one occurrence, and of not less than One Hundred Thousand Dollars ($100,000.00) for property damage in any one occurrence.

Hold Harmless

14. Lessor shall not be liable to Lessee, or to Lessee's agents, servants, employees, customers or invitees for any damage to person or property caused by any act, omission or neglect of Lessee, and Lessee agrees to hold Lessor harmless from all claims for any such damage. Lessee shall not be liable to Lessor, or to Lessor's agents, servants, employees, customers or invitees for any damage to person or property caused by any act, omission or neglect of Lessor, and Lessor agrees to hold Lessee harmless from all claims for such damage.

Waiver of Subrogation Rights

15. Anything in this lease to the contrary notwithstanding, Lessor and Lessee each hereby waive any and all rights of recovery, claim, action or cause of action, against the other, its agents, officers or employees, for any loss or damage that may occur to the premises hereby demised, or any improvements thereto, or said Building of which the demised premises are a part, or any improvements thereto, or any personal property of such party therein, by reason of fire, the elements, or any other cause which could be insured against under the terms of standard fire and extended coverage insurance policies, regardless of cause or origin, including negligence of the other party hereto, its agents, officers or employees, and covenants that no insurer shall hold any right of subrogation against such other party.

This lease shall be binding upon and inure to the benefit of the successors and assigns of Lessor, and shall be binding upon and inure to the benefit of Lessee, its successors, and, to the extent assignment may be approved by Lessor hereunder, Lessee's assigns. The pronouns of any gender shall include the other genders, and either the singular or the plural shall include the other.

All rights and remedies of Lessor under this lease shall be cumulative and none shall exclude any other rights or remedies allowed by law, and . . . all of the terms thereof shall be construed according to the laws of the State of ________________.

IN TESTIMONY WHEREOF, the parties hereto have executed this lease as of the date aforesaid.

By ____________________
LESSOR

By ____________________
LESSEE

Schedule 1 to Lease Agreement between

____

("Lessor") and

____

("Lessee")

Allowances

1. ________ Linear feet of partitioning. 1 linear foot/12 sq.ft. NRA.
2. ________ Doors. 1 door/300 sq.ft. NRA.

3. _____ Telephone wall outlets. 1 outlet/210 sq.ft. NRA.
4. _____ Electrical wall outlets. 1 outlet/120 sq.ft. NRA.
5. _____ Light fixtures. 1 fixture/75 sq.ft. NRA.
6. _____ Wall toggle switches. 1 switch per door.
7. Building standard carpet throughout office premises.

Addendum 1 to Lease Agreement between

_____

("Lessor") and

_____

("Lessee")

As the Basic Parking Charge, Lessee covenants and agrees to pay Lessor during the term of this Lease, as additional rental hereunder, the sum of $ _____ per car per month for each of the stickers to be issued by Lessor as herein provided, such sum to be payable monthly in advance on the first day of each and every calendar month during the lease term, and a pro rata portion of such sum shall be payable for the first partial calendar month in the event the lease term commences on a date other than the first day of a calendar month. The Basic Parking Charge shall be adjusted from time to time at any time that the Base Rental hereunder is adjusted, and each such adjustment in the Basic Parking Charge shall be at the same ratio as the current adjustment in the Base Rental hereunder bears to the Base Rental immediately prior to such adjustment. Lessee's obligation to pay the Parking Charge shall be considered an obligation to pay rent for all purposes hereunder and shall be secured in like manner as is Lessee's obligation to pay rent. Default in payment of such Parking Charge (after notice as hereinafter provided) shall be deemed to be a default in payment of rent.

IN TESTIMONY WHEREOF, the parties hereto have executed this addendum as of the date aforesaid.

By _____
   LESSOR

By _____
   LESSEE

APPENDIX J

Request for Qualifications
Kentucky Center for the Arts

INTRODUCTION

With state and local jurisdictional approval, a study committee of the Louisville Development Committee was formulated in February of 1977, to determine need and consensus for a Performing Arts Center located in downtown Louisville. More specifically, the group considered its charge to "explore the feasibility of constructing a state performing arts center in Louisville based on the assumption that a facility (if need and consensus were established) would be constructed as a state facility and at the capital expense of state and local governments, and would receive an annual operating subsidy from the appropriate governmental units so that operating costs would not burden or restrict the art groups' limited operating budgets."

The study group effort enhanced two previous attempts to seek a feasible method to construct a Performing Arts Center in downtown Louisville. The initial effort was in 1967, when the future use of the Macauley (former Brown Theater) was questionable. At that time, the President of the University of Louisville instigated a study that concluded that such a center was vital and should be constructed on a site now known as Shipping Port Square, on the north side of Main Street between Fourth and Third Streets. Architect Harry Weese of Chicago was engaged to provide schematic plans. However, subsequent priorities caused the abandonment of these efforts as other community development absorbed available public funding and commitment. In mid-1975, the Center City Commission, perceiving that higher priority projects were approaching completion or commitment, initiated another study; however, it was never fully completed nor agreed upon by participating governmental entities before dissolution of the Commission.

The latest study group was able to satisfactorily reach consensus and forwarded its recommendations to the Commonwealth on May 26, 1977. . . .

Upon submission of the study group's report to the Governor and an examination of the merits of its recommendations, Governor Julian Carroll on October 4, 1977, announced his administration's support for the construction of the Cultural Arts Complex, including the construction of a Performing Arts Center. The Governor's comments included: ". . . The appointment of a small, dedicated and highly qualified group of people to serve as an executive committee to spearhead the project planning."

The Committee, subsequently named the Kentucky Cultural Complex Committee (KCCC), and its advisory group, Cultural Complex Task Force, are responsible for "directing the initial Part I, predevelopment programming, including recommendation of an Architect and approval of the contract for construction."

On December 6, 1977, KCCC, acting upon authorities and procedures of the study group report, announced the selection of Gerald D. Hines Interests of Houston, Texas, as the responsible party to assist the Committee in defining the size and scope of the project and obtaining specialized consultation, as required. The contractual designation resulted from the Committee's belief that the "designated" site area offers the opportunity to develop a combination of public and private buildings and uses: namely, a "mixed-use" development project consisting in part of a performing and visual arts center, art studios, galleries, eating and entertainment complex, major office facilities, and a variety of public site improvements, parking garage(s), plaza extensions, malls, etc.

Commitments between KCCC and Hines, contained in a Memorandum of Understanding executed on December 6, 1977, included a series of interrelated commitments, as described below:

PUBLIC SECTOR COMMITMENTS

A. The Commonwealth intends to develop as a component of the Complex a multi-arts center containing at least a 2,500-seat facility, as well as other auditoria and ancillary facilities in support of the performing and visual arts groups. The sizes and arrangements of these and other facilities within the Center will be determined pursuant to an analysis to be prepared by Hines under contract to the Committee and in cooperation with the Task Force and advisory groups appointed to represent Commonwealth interests, the art and business community, and local pub-

lic interests. It is intended, upon completion, that the components of the complex will be owned by the Commonwealth and operated by the University of Louisville.

B. The Commonwealth intends to develop sufficient parking garage(s) or spaces as an integral part of the entire complex, underneath, adjacent, or contiguous to the proposed Performing Arts Center. Subject to the architectural programming by the Committee's designated developer, the parking facility will have direct access to other structures contained in the area by means of steps, elevators or escalators for the parking level.

C. The Commonwealth intends or will cause the development of a suitable open space system, with the view to linking all surrounding and adjoining commercial and public centers to the complex.

PRIVATE SECTOR COMMITMENTS

A. Gerald D. Hines Interests intends to cause the purchase or ground lease of designated land from the Commonwealth or its agent in a manner consistent with applicable law on which to construct a number of buildings, as permitted in the Committee's Adopted Development Plan, which Hines intends to own and manage. The privately owned buildings to be constructed by Hines will include, but not be limited to, the provision of several large-scale offices (employing up to 3,000 daytime persons), retail and entertainment outlets (movie theater, commercial or retail shops, small boutiques, art shops, galleries, and outlets compatible with the philosophy of the Complex).

B. Hines will rehabilitate or cause to be rehabilitated several older buildings as offices for the art groups, rehearsal rooms, shops, or other uses for artists, performers, and others.

C. Hines agrees that the design of the private-sector components of the Complex are of paramount importance to the City of Louisville and Commonwealth, and for that reason will allow the appropriate public agencies to exercise the approval rights (including Hines' selection of an architect) over the subsequent detailed design plans of the private-sector components. It is understood and agreed to by all parties that such approvals shall not be unreasonably withheld.

COOPERATIVE COMMITMENT

The parties to this Memorandum intend to develop a project in which the public and private components complement each other as well as present a continuity of design. For this reason, the Committee intends to utilize the Development Management procedure to accomplish the planning, design, and construction of the public improvements subsequent to the completion of the Predevelopment Work Program (a nine-month predevelopment work program directed by Hines and scheduled for completion on October 1, 1978), including the parking facilities and pedestrian system, the Performing and Visual Arts Center and supporting public facilities deemed appropriate and approved by the Committee. Employing this procedure, the Committee shall execute a contract with Hines directing Hines to engage a Committee-selected architect or architects to prepare the appropriate documents for subsequent construction of the aforementioned public facilities. Upon award of each respective construction contract, Hines shall act as the Committee's Development and Construction Manager under a mutually acceptable fee arrangement. This contract shall include appropriate safeguards and approval points to ensure the protection of public interests. Upon award of the state service contract to Hines, the firm, with KCCC approval, has retained the following organization to render assistance in predevelopment programming:

Zuchelli, Hunter & Associates, Inc., Annapolis, Maryland—Managing Subcontractor for Development Programming with specialists acting as consultants for:

- Urban Design, Engineering and Traffic Planning—Sasaki Associates, Inc., Watertown, Massachusetts;
- Architectural Programming (for Performing Arts Center)—Caudill Rowlett Scott, Houston, Texas;
- Arts Facilities Consultation—Mr. Ralph Burgard, Scarsdale, New York;
- Audio-Visual Presentation—Design Communication Collaborative, Washington, D.C.

The Part I Predevelopment Programming activities are directed to preparing an acceptable development plan during a nine-month period extending through October 1978, with a report of pertinent findings to be submitted to the Commonwealth in the latter part of 1978. Upon acceptance by the state of the findings, or modifications as appropriate, and upon authorization to proceed, the designated developer (Hines) shall initiate contract negotiations with the KCCC's designated architect (for publicly funded facilities).

Should the negotiations fail for any reason, the Committee (KCCC) will be fully informed of the substance of the disagreement. If no mutually agreeable basis for reopening the negotiations can be found, the Hines organization will begin negotiations with the next-ranked architect, upon concurrence of KCCC.

The option, at the sole discretion of Hines subject to KCCC concurrence, is available to utilize KCCC's architect for the private components to ensure a unity of design. No implied obligation, direct or indirect, is encumbent upon Hines to utilize a single architect for all use components.

At the commencement of the programming activities (Part I), the announced intentions of the Commonwealth and the Committee was to sponsor an "AIA-sanctioned" design competition to select the architect, utilizing a professional jury in accordance with the Guidelines for Architectural Design Competitions of the American Institute of Architects. Subsequent evaluation by KCCC as to the cost, duration, and other relevant factors has led to the decision to use the Comparative Selection Process in lieu of the Design Competition for designation of a preferred architect.

Accordingly, KCCC instructed the Hines Team (more particularly, Zuchelli, Hunter & Associates) to prepare a Request for Qualifications statement (RFQ) and the appropriate criteria for the selection of the architect. This selection procedure was documented and adopted by KCCC and herein is being carried out. The process, then, is for a competition in terms of (1) the firms' background and qualifications, and (2) the firms' philosophies and approaches to several unique aspects inherent in the design of the Cultural Complex.

KCCC has selected five architectural firms for further consideration for the design contract on the Performing Arts Center. Each organization shall receive two weighted evaluation scores. The initial scoring will be upon the offering(s) of the RFQ which requests fifteen (15) copies of a written statement of capabilities, personnel, projects, references, and design approach. Also included with the offering(s) will be a single submission of a portfolio of the architects' relevant design work, including any pertinent photographs and brochures.

The second scoring will be upon a subsequent interview presentation and questions. It is intended that all firms responsive to this RFQ will be interviewed by the Cultural Complex Architect Selection Panel. That Panel will present their recommendations to the KCCC for adoption.

PROJECT SCOPE

The *Kentucky Cultural Complex* is defined as the total proposed development: integrating public and private, cultural and commercial components. The *Performing Arts Center* is the major state-sponsored component within the Complex. It should be noted that what is referred to as the Performing Arts Center is not limited to serving the performing arts, but also includes visual arts facilities.

This RFQ relates specifically to the architectural services for the Performing Arts Center only. The future designated developer for the related private development has the separate responsibility for architect selection for that work. Likewise, design services for related public improvements which are distinct from the Performing Arts Center are not the subject of this RFQ. This is not intended, however, to preclude any eventual combination of any or all of these components under a single contract.

ARCHITECTURAL PROGRAM

One of the initial efforts in the nine-month predevelopment planning process was the preparation of a schematic architectural program for the Performing Arts Center. Extensive interviews and work sessions were conducted with all major identified user groups. The resulting program was adopted by the KCCC and incorporated into the urban design concept. (This formal adoption of a program statement supersedes the earlier statements contained in the Recommendation(s) section of the Committee's report to the Commonwealth dated May 26, 1977.) The program will provide the base information for the subsequent design effort by the Center's architect.

The figures below represent space requirements and preliminary budget estimates for the publicly funded Performing Arts Center. In all likelihood, certain commercial facilities will logically fall within the design responsibility of the architect of the Center. Likewise, land acquisition and parking facility costs have been excluded from this program. An analysis of parking requirements for the total complex is currently being conducted as a part of the urban design work. Parking requirements which are reasonably integral with the Center may be added to the above program.

USER GROUPS

The Performing Arts Center is programmed to meet the expressed needs of Louisville's performing and visual arts communities, as well as to provide for anticipated, but not specifically identified, miscellaneous productions and events.

The major identified user groups are as follows:

Performance/Production
   Louisville Orchestra
   Louisville Opera Association
   Louisville Ballet
   Louisville Bach Society
   Children's Theater

Administrative
   Arts Center Administration
   Fund for the Arts
   Children's Theater
   Louisville Orchestra
   Louisville Opera Association
   Louisville Ballet
   Louisville Bach Society
   Actors Theater

Visual Arts
   Louisville School of Art
   Junior Art Gallery

SITE

The site area for the Kentucky Cultural Complex has been generally defined as including: (1) Five Riverfront Plaza; (2) the block immediately south, bounded by Main, Market, Fifth, and Sixth Streets; and (3) a possible extension to the west to include the south side of Main Street between Sixth and Seventh Streets. . . . This site area overlaps, in part, the West Main Street Preservation District. A specific site, or sites, for the Performing Arts Center components of the Complex will be defined within the framework of the urban design plan which is currently under preparation.

Five Riverfront Plaza is a cleared site of approximately 2.75 acres abutting the recently constructed Riverfront Plaza (also referred to as the Belvedere) on the north, Place Montpelier on the east, Main Street on the south, and Sixth Streets on the west. The line of abutment to the Riverfront Plaza is a floodwall rising to the underside of the main level of the Plaza. The Plaza covers a three-level, 1,600-space public parking facility. (The lower levels of that facility are subject to flooding from the Ohio River.)

The block to the south, bounded by Main, Market, Fifth and Sixth Streets, contains approximately 4.0 acres, nearly half of which is occupied by existing small structures ranging in height from one to five stories. Those structures fronting Main Street are included within the West Main Street Preservation District.

The site area lies at an important interface point between new Louisville to the north and east, and historic Louisville to the west. Likewise, the site area represents the sole remaining opportunity to strongly reconnect downtown Louisville to the Ohio River. The Belvedere was the initial step, but it remains a somewhat isolated island. The Cultural Complex can provide the bridge back into the life of the downtown.

The Historic Landmark and Preservation Districts Commission is keenly interested in the proposed Cultural Complex and has prepared a report entitled *West Main Street Survey, 500-600 Blocks, South Side*. . . . Following is an excerpt from the report:

. . . The information gathered stresses the architectural and historical importance of the existing buildings on West Main Street as well as their economic value. We contend further that adaptive use of these multi-faceted buildings would appropriately bring the art of architecture to the variety of arts available in the Cultural Arts Center to educate and entertain visitors. One need only look at the Junior League's building, Stairways, at 627 West Main Street, the Derby Festival building at 621 West Main Street, and the Museum of Natural History and Science at 727 West Main Street—as outstanding examples of adaption—to realize the possibilities at hand for integrating the existing buildings in the program and design of the Cultural Arts Center.

This survey is by no means complete: Coordination with the programming and subsequent design phases of the Cultural Arts Center is intended to be an ongoing process. A survey of structural conditions, both interior and exterior, location of existing plans and layouts, and a listing of those buildings which have had inappropriate alterations to their original design (and proposed remedies) will follow this examination.

. . . The structures are all masonry bearing structures with a bearing thickness of 20 in. or 16 in. at the base (depending on the height of the structure) and tapering to a top floor thickness of 12 in. Since these structures were historically warehouses, most offer a clear span of their building width. However, the former Romar-Gleeson building (600-606) and the Bernheim

Building (626) have interior columns to interrupt the span. The front curtain-wall facades are predominately cast-iron elements, with some limestone, brick, or terra-cotta elements. The cast-iron facades on West Main Street are judged by national experts to be second only to those in New York City in quality and quantity. Therefore, every attempt should be made to preserve these structures intact as a swiftly vanishing national resource which will be appreciated by Louisvillians and visitors alike.

SCOPE OF SERVICES

The selected architect will be instructed by the KCCC to associate himself with an architectural firm having home offices within the Commonwealth of Kentucky and acceptable to the KCCC (by that Committee's concurrence). Likewise, any or all required consulting engineering services (except acoustical and theatrical) which are not included within the prime architect's firm shall be performed by one or more consulting engineering firms having home offices within the Commonwealth. These firms shall be selected by the prime architect, subject to the concurrence of the KCCC.

The KCCC will provide the prime architect with the names of three acoustical consultants and three theater consultants which are acceptable to the Committee, and from which the prime architect may select.

Consistent with the Commonwealth's desire to use a Development and Construction Management approach to the implementation of the Cultural Complex, Gerald D. Hines Interests, if designated, has reserved the right to contract individually with any or all associates and consultants selected by the prime architect, with concurrence by the KCCC. Should negotiations between Hines and any consultant or associate fail for any reason, the KCCC and the prime architect will be fully informed of the substance of the disagreement. If no mutually agreeable basis can be found for reopening the negotiations, the Hines organization will begin negotiations with the prime architect's next preference, subject to the concurrence of the KCCC.

Because of the variety of options open for architectural and engineering design implementation, it is not possible at this time to specify the exact scope of services of the prime architect. It is expected, however, that those services will, at the very least, include the following items in conjunction with the associated local architect (ALA):

Part I: Schematic Design

This work shall consist of investigating the site and earlier design "inputs" from Part One: Predevelopment Programming and advising the client, through the designated developer, as to possible design concept alterations, if warranted. The client's stated needs and requirements shall be carefully confirmed. All applicable regulations and codes affecting the work shall be analyzed. Sketches and statement of probable construction costs shall be confirmed for client review.

Part II: Design Development

Upon approval of the Schematic Design, the architect will proceed with the development of the plans and elevations of the building. Type of construction, mechanical systems, and material shall be described and recommendations discussed with the client and developer. Drawings establishing all major elements and outline specifications shall be prepared. A revised statement of probable construction costs shall be made. All this material shall be submitted to the designated developer for his review and subsequent submission to the client for approval.

Part III: Construction Documents

Design development drawings and specifications shall be finalized by the architect and provided to the associated local architect and consulting engineers for completion of contract documents. Materials and color schedules shall be determined with the developer and concurred with the client. Bidding documents and forms shall be prepared by the associated local architect and discussed with the developer, with assistance, if required by ALA, provided by the designated (prime) architect. Cost statements shall be finalized and approved.

Part IV:

The architect and ALA, as required, shall assist the developer in qualifying bidders and obtaining proposals. During the construction period, the ALA shall review and approve shop drawings, and prepare such supplementary drawings as may be required. The architect shall direct the ALA to make periodic visits to the site to determine if the work is in compliance with the design and, as requested by the developer, shall comment on the relative progress and quality of construction, issue contract change orders, and make final inspection.

SUBMISSION REQUIREMENTS

The architects' offering to this RFQ must be in two (2)

Following is a summary of the Performing Arts Center program.

Facility	Programmed Gross Sq. Ft.	Preliminary Construction
2,100-Seat Multi-Purpose Hall	152,708	$15,632,410
Including public spaces, performance and performance support, production and related storage, dressing facilities, administration, and miscellaneous support.		
700-Seat Multi-Purpose Hall	27,430	2,320,578
Including support space for publicity, performance, and production.		
Miscellaneous Performing Arts Support	23,743	660,053
Arts Organizations' Offices	22,727	761,351
Including offices for eight organizations, plus common support space.		
Art School	73,330	3,167,852
Art Gallery	13,178	474,407
Subtotal, New Construction	180,138	$17,952,988
Subtotal, Adaptive Reuse	132,978	$ 5,063,663
Total	313,116	$23,016,651
Options		
Amphitheater	17,218	$ 672,625
Storage	57,300	637,176
Subtotal, New Construction	197,356	$18,625,613
Subtotal, Adaptive Reuse	190,278	5,700,839
Architectural Art		300,000
Pipe Organ		350,000
Total	387,634	$24,976,452

parts: (A) a written response in fifteen (15) copies to items (1) through (7) below; and (B) a single portfolio of the firm's relevant design work and background information.

A. WRITTEN RESPONSE
1. a summary of the firm's background and capabilities, including information on the firm's history, areas of specialization or particular expertise, awards and other special recognition, and current staffing
2. a statement of the firm's philosophy of design and approach to design problem-solving, as evidenced by past projects and as applicable to the Kentucky Center for the Arts
3. a statement of the firm's proven techniques for managing architectural and engineering design and production, including interdisciplinary coordination, client involvement, and project cost control
4. the proposed organizational chart for the project with the names and responsibilities of key individuals
5. resumes of those key individuals
6. a list of at least five projects (completed or under construction) for which the firm had primary design responsibilities, including year of completion, project cost, consultants, client, client contact for reference, and a brief written description of the project
7. a list of all the firm's projects currently being designed or having construction documents prepared, including estimated construction cost, percent completion of services (through construction documents), and client.

B. PORTFOLIO
The content of the portfolio is at the architect's discretion. Photographs and other representations of design work should be clearly identified by project title, location, construction cost, year of completion, and consultants and associates. Previously prepared brochures and other background information may be included; however, it will be helpful to the Committee if your portfolio is kept compact and relevant.

SUBMISSION FORMAT
1. Written Response (15 copies)
For simplicity and fairness, it is requested that the written response (items A(1) through A(7) of the Submission Requirements) be 8½ in. × 11 in., typewritten, and not illustrated (other than single line drawing as may be required for any charts or diagrams). Simple edge binding is recommended. Covers may be graphically illustrated and the firm's name should be included on the cover.

2. Portfolio
Portfolio information may be bound or loose or any combination thereof, provided an appropriate folder or container is included. It is recommended that the portfolio size not exceed 11 in. × 17 in. and that large folded exhibits be avoided.

PROJECT BRIEFING
To facilitate the fullest understanding of the project objectives and the imparting of technical data and information, the Architect Selection Panel will convene a briefing on project status in Louisville on April 17, 1978, at 2:00 p.m. at _____

Attendance at this session is strongly urged to ensure the completeness of each architect's offering, though not mandatory. Attendance at the briefing shall be at the expense of the participating firms without reimbursement by KCCC.

For those organizations choosing not to attend the briefing, the briefing package of materials intended to amplify this RFQ shall be mailed on the day immediately preceding the Briefing. It is requested that Zuchelli, Hunter & Associates, Inc., 160 South Street, Annapolis, Maryland 21401, be notified in writing prior to April 10, 1978, as to the intention of each firm to participate in the briefing.

INTERVIEWS
Upon receipt of the architects' offering(s) to this RFQ, the Architect Selection Panel, consisting of seven voting persons and two professional, non-voting advisors, shall evaluate the offering(s) and record scores on an evaluation form. Initial scoring shall be considered preliminary, subject to finalization during the interview process and the value of the offering(s) and a reference check shall account for approximately sixty (60) percent of the available scoring.

Upon completion of the initial scoring and subsequent to the briefing, the Panel shall announce an interview schedule. This schedule will be verified by telephone with the competitors and adjusted to ensure the fullest degree of convenience to all affected parties. A letter of confirmation of the time and place of the interview shall be sent including a description of the format of the interview. The interview proceedings shall be closed to observers and shall last two (2) hours—approximately one hour for presentation and one hour for questions and answers. All interviews shall be scheduled within two consecutive days with the results announced upon concurrence by KCCC on the third day, scheduling permitting.

ISSUES
The Performing Arts Center is envisioned as a tightly integrated component of the larger Kentucky Cultural Complex, which will include public and private, cultural and commercial uses internally interrelated and externally knitted into the fabric of downtown Louisville, including adaptive reuse of selected existing buildings within the West Main Street Preservation District, and possible adaptation and design integration of portions of the existing Riverfront Plaza (Belvedere). This conception presents the architect(s) with a particularly complex problem statement.

The competitors will be instructed to focus their interview presentations on four of those problems which have been identified by the Committee as especially important. These four problems are:
1. How can a natural and functional integration of cultural and commercial uses best be achieved within the Complex?
2. What can be done to ensure successful "fit" between the Cultural Complex/Performing Arts Center and the existing and evolving surrounding environment?
3. What are the possibilities for achieving visually and functionally harmonious relationships between new construction and adaptive reuse components of the Center?
4. What problems are inherent in a situation which requires separate designers to work on components of a single integrated concept? And how can those problems be overcome?

If any point necessitates further clarification, please address your questions, prior to the scheduled briefing, to:
Mr. Donald R. Zuchelli, President
Zuchelli, Hunter & Associates, Inc.
160 South Street
Annapolis, Maryland 21401
(301) 269-6565

Any questions arising subsequent to the briefing shall be handled independently, with the pertinent questions and directions given also to the other four involved firms.

APPENDIX K

Agreement to Lease and to Construct Improvements Fountain Square South

THIS AGREEMENT made and entered into this ________ day of ________________, __________, by and between the City of Cincinnati, an Ohio municipal corporation (the "City") and John W. Galbreath of Columbus, Ohio, d.b.a. John W. Galbreath & Co. ("Galbreath").

WITNESSETH:

WHEREAS, the City, by Ordinance No. 252–1962 adopted an Urban Renewal Plan for its downtown project known as the Central Business District Core Urban Renewal Project, and amended said Plan by Ordinance No. ________–1976 in order to include property located South of Fifth Street between Vine and Walnut Streets now designated as the Fountain Square South Project; and

WHEREAS, in carrying out the purposes of the Urban Renewal Plan the City proposes to acquire the Fountain Square South property for the purpose of developing a multi-level underground parking garage and building service level together with support structures for surface building improvements which service plaza and support structures the City intends to make available for private development; and

WHEREAS, the City pursuant to Resolution No. 211–1975 has designated Galbreath as the preferred developer for Fountain Square South (the "Project") pursuant to proposals heretofore presented to the City by Galbreath and pursuant to recommendations of the City Manager and the City Evaluation Team, subject to the negotiating of a mutually acceptable development agreement; and

WHEREAS, the parties intend, by this instrument, to set forth their mutual agreement for the total development of the Project which shall include, in addition to the aforesaid underground improvements, the development by Galbreath, or his designee, of office, hotel, retail, and related facilities which will complement and be compatible with the existing Fountain Square development all as more fully hereinafter described;

NOW, THEREFORE, in consideration of the Premises, and of the covenants and agreements hereinafter set forth, the parties do hereby agree as follows:

1. **Super Structure Schematic Designs.** Galbreath has engaged architects to prepare, and will cause to be completed, Schematic Designs for an office building, and also for a hotel, with related retail and public area facilities to be constructed in the Project. The office building design shall provide for an approximately 29-story structure. The hotel design shall provide for a luxury hotel of approximately 450 rooms with restaurants, meeting rooms, recreational, and health facilities. The design of both buildings (the "Buildings") shall be developed concurrently, shall include approximately 80,000 square feet of gross retail space within the Project boundaries, shall ultimately include the treatment and finish completion of the total surface area, and shall provide public atrium space within the Project boundaries. The design shall further include such additional ground level plaza and second level pedestrian concourse development in addition to the buildings, as the parties may mutually agree upon. All such Galbreath improvements listed in this clause shall hereinafter be called the "Super Structure Development."

2. **Sub Structure Schematic Designs.** The City has engaged architects to prepare, and will cause to be completed, Schematic Designs for a three-level Sub Structure development. The same shall be built to grade level and so designed as to permit the erection thereof of the Super Structure Development. Such Sub Structure shall incorporate all necessary structural support for the Super Structure Development, including all necessary framing extensions to tie in properly to the Super Structure, all framed openings and all slabs including the top or plaza level, all elevator shafts, pits, and crash pads, and such variations in slab elevation at plaza level as are reasonably necessary to accommodate the Super Structure and permit access by automobile and truck to appropriate levels of the Sub Structure. The same shall also include and the City shall cause to be provided passenger elevators servicing the two garage levels to the plaza level and to the second floor of the Super Structure and any tunnels or connectors between the existing Fountain Square Garage and the new garage levels, transformer vaults for the total project, metering of all utilities serving the garage spaces to be occupied by the City, utilities to the site for connection to the Super Structure Development at taps to be provided on the service level. The Designs shall include and the City will provide all mechanical and operating equipment for the garage and housing for the same on one of the two garage levels, and a completed truck dock area, including, but not limited to, electrical, mechanical, plumbing, and sprinkler system, dock appurtenances such as levelers and bumpers, wall, and doors (all such City improvements herein called the "Sub Structure Development").

3. **Scope of Design.**

(a) The scope of design for the Sub Structure Development shall include the following items:

1. Excavation and Sheeting
   - a) Relocation as required of all utilities.
   - b) Complete excavation and backfill including necessary protection.
   - c) Sheeting and underpinning.
2. Foundations
   - a) Complete including footings, mats, foundation wall and dampproofing, electrical grounds, elevator pits.
   - b) Slab on grade (lowest parking level).
3. Structural Frame
   - a) Columns, beams, girders, etc., 3 slabs (parking, service, and plaza).
   - b) Fireproofing as required.
   - c) Framed openings for Super Structure services including elevators.
   - d) Penetrations of framing members necessary to accommodate Super Structure services.
   - e) Slab depressions.
   - f) Framing extensions and provisions for Super Structure tie-in to Sub Structure.
   - g) Ramps, truck dock, elevator crash pads, transfer girders.
   - h) Design live loads per Super Structure requirements.
4. Interior Finishes
   - a) Garage, ramps, loading dock complete, including dock appurtenances such as levelers and dock bumpers; and walls, doors, etc., to provide dock security.
   - b) Stairs to the Plaza level complete.
   - c) Garage and truck dock area signs.
5. Elevators
   - a) Garage elevators complete including shafts and service to the Plaza level and the Hotel Lobby level.
   - b) Elevator pits, openings, and shafts to the Plaza level for all elevators.
   - c) Escalator pits.
6. Electric, Heating, Ventilating, Plumbing, and Sprinklers
   - a) Complete in Garage, Ramps, and Truck Dock Area.
   - b) Utilities brought to locations acceptable to Galbreath at service level. Utilities include electric, telephone, domestic water, fire protection, water, sanitary sewer, storm sewer, and gas.
   - c) Transformer vaults for the entire project.
   - d) Openings and/or sleeves through the slabs for Super Structure services.
   - e) Garage and truck dock area fire alarm system tied into Super Structure annunciator.

City work shall include Finishes in the truck dock area and in common areas providing pedestrian and automobile access from the streets and from the plaza level, exclusive, however, of the Finishes on the service level, waterproofing of the plaza level and for surface finish of the plaza level inside the property lines which will be provided by Galbreath.

4. **Architect Cooperation.** The respective architects of the parties hereto (including the Urban Development Design Section on behalf of the City) shall be required at all times to coordinate their total effort and provide full and mutual cooperation in order to achieve harmonious planning and design, adequate structurally and esthetically for the total development contemplated by this Agreement and consistent with the cost limitations of the respective developments as directed by each of the parties hereto.

5. **Schematic Design Approvals.** The Schematic Designs of each of the parties hereto shall be subject to the approval of the other parties.

The Schematic Designs of the City shall be submitted to Galbreath within 2 months from the date of this Agreement, and those of Galbreath shall be submitted to the City within 2 months from the date of this Agreement. Within thirty (30) days after submission, the party to whom submitted shall advise the other in writing of its approval, or of its disapproval and the reasons therefor. If the Schematic Designs of a party are disapproved, revised Schematic Designs shall be submitted promptly and, again, approved or disapproved in the manner aforesaid within thirty (30) days after such submission. If the written approvals of both parties to the Schematic Designs of both are not given within 6 months from the date of this Agreement, either party, at its option, may terminate this Agreement in the manner provided in clause 31 or 32 hereof.

6. **Preliminary Design Phase.** Subject to the full approvals provided for in the preceding paragraph, the parties shall cause their respective architects to proceed with the preliminary design phase of their respective developments. The Preliminary Plans so prepared shall be consistent with the Schematic Designs previously approved by the parties and shall include the following:

(a) A site plan (minimum scale $\frac{1}{16}'' = 1'0''$) showing all features of proposed development including:

1. Property lines and dimensions.
2. Building floor plans at principal pedestrian levels.
3. Landscape development including extent and type of paving; extent and type of planting; and other features such as seating, walls, pools, sculpture.
4. Night lighting.

(b) Building plans at all other levels (minimum scale $\frac{1}{16}'' = 1'0''$), except that a typical plan shall suffice where multi-story plans are essentially repetitive; and roof plan.

(c) All building elevations (minimum scale $\frac{1}{16}'' = 1'0''$) including location and approximate design of all signs and showing all exterior features of mechanical systems.

(d) An outline specification of building and site development materials.

(e) Samples of exposed exterior materials in colors proposed.

(f) A more detailed scale model (minimum scale $\frac{1}{16}'' = 1'0''$) showing development in relationship to surroundings described in Schematic Designs if changes have been made since approval of Schematic Designs.

(g) Illustrations of facade treatment and site development features such as lighting fixtures, seating, sculpture, and other works of art.

(h) Preliminary drawings and exposed interior drawings and materials for the atrium and public easements through the retail areas on the first and second levels of the Super Structure Development, all of which, at the option of either party hereto, may be deferred to the Working Drawing Phase.

7. **Preliminary Plan Approvals.** The Preliminary Plans of each of the parties shall similarly be submitted for the approval of the other party within 6 months from the date of approval of the submitting party's Schematic Designs. The Preliminary Plans of Galbreath shall also include design parameters which will be followed by the City in its design of second level pedestrian concourses across Vine and Walnut Streets, and such Plans shall also indicate the tie-in of such concourse with and through the Super Structure Development. The approval and resubmission procedure set forth in clause 5 hereof shall be followed, and if the written approval of a party's Preliminary Plan is not given within 9 months from the date of approval of submitting party's Schematic Designs, either party, at its option, may terminate this Agreement in the manner provided in clause 31 or 32 hereof. Neither party shall refuse to approve Preliminary Plans of the other for reasons which are inconsistent with the approvals previously given with respect to Schematic Designs.

8. **Certification of City Progress.** If full approvals of the Preliminary Plans are given as provided in the preceding paragraph, the City shall promptly submit to Galbreath written evidence reasonably satisfactory to Galbreath of

the following:

(a) The fact that the City has acquired or is in the process of acquiring good record and marketable title to all of the real property comprising the Project, and that the City will be able to furnish to Galbreath, within the time hereinafter limited for approval of complete Working Drawings, title evidence in respect to the real property interest to be acquired by Galbreath in the form of a written commitment to issue owner's title insurance by a major and responsible title insurer authorized to do business in the State of Ohio, insuring, in the amount of $3,000,000, that status and quality of title to the leasehold and easement estates to be conveyed to Galbreath, described in clause 14(d) hereof.

(b) That the City will be legally authorized and otherwise able to lease to Galbreath, the leasehold estates and to convey any necessary easements as described in clauses 14 and 20 hereof within the time period contemplated hereby.

(c) That the City will be able to finance and to complete the Sub Structure Development within the time period contemplated hereby, and that the fiscal officer of the City anticipates with reasonable certainty being able to certify to the availability of funds set aside for such purpose.

(d) That the Project will be zoned to a classification suitable for the contemplated improvements, and the absence of any local, state, or federal law, regulation, or court or governmental agency order which would preclude the construction thereof or the furnishing of necessary services or utilities thereto, subject however to applicable state and local building code regulations.

9. Working Drawing Phase. Subject to satisfaction of all the conditions set forth in clause 8 above, the parties shall cause their respective architects to proceed with the preparation of complete working plans and specifications for the Sub Structure and Super Structure Developments (the "Working Drawings"). The Working Drawings shall be consistent with the Preliminary Plans previously approved by the parties and shall, similarly, be submitted for the approval of each of the parties. Working Drawings for the Sub Structure Development shall be submitted to Galbreath within 6 months from the approval of Preliminary Plans therefor, and those for the Super Structure Development shall be submitted to the City within 6 months from the approval of Preliminary Plans therefor. The approval and resubmission procedure set forth in clause 5 hereof shall be followed. If either party shall not approve the Working Drawings of the other within thirty (30) days of their submission or resubmission (if resubmitted) to such party, the submitting party at its option, may terminate this Agreement. Neither party shall refuse to approve the Working Drawings of the other for reasons which are inconsistent with the approvals previously given with respect to Preliminary Plans, or with respect to partially completed Working Drawings previously approved pursuant to clause 14(b).

10. Changes in Drawings. Either party may submit proposed material changes in Schematic Designs, Preliminary Plans, and Working Drawings after approvals have been previously given. Within thirty (30) days after submission, the party to whom submitted shall advise the other in writing of its approval, or of its disapproval and the reasons therefor. Resubmissions may be made in like manner. No approval given by either party shall relieve the other or any assignee from compliance with state and local laws in the construction of improvements.

11. Certifying to Third Parties. If at any time the Preliminary Plans, Working Drawings, or modifications of either have been approved, the approving party shall, upon request of the other party, furnish certificates, upon which any third party, including a mortgagee, may rely, evidencing such approval and acknowledging that such Plans, Drawings, or modifications meet the requirements of the City's Urban Renewal Plan and this Agreement.

12. Development of Sub Structure. Subject to Galbreath's full approval of the City's Working Drawings, the City shall promptly take bids and otherwise negotiate the construction cost of the Sub Structure Development and, if satisfactory to the City in its sole and unlimited discretion, shall contract for and cause commencement of construction thereon. The City shall cause Substantial Completion thereof no later than 10 months following execution of the Leases as provided in clause 14 hereof (subject, however, to the excusable delay provision in clause 30 infra). "Substantial Completion" shall be that degree of completion which will permit Galbreath's commencement and uninterrupted progress of construction of the Super Structure Development without material additional cost or expense accruing by reason of the absence of full completion of the Sub Structure, as deter-

mined by the architects of the parties, or, in the event of disagreement by an architect wholly independent of the parties but selected by them. If the parties are unable to select the independent architect, either party may request the presiding Judge of the Common Pleas Court of Hamilton County to select the independent architect. If the City determines that it cannot achieve Substantial Completion by such date, the City may terminate this Agreement by giving written notice to Galbreath prior to the date for executing such Leases.

13. Additional City Action. In addition to or as a part of the full completion of the Sub Structure Development, the City agrees to cause to be constructed and to be made available to the Project, or cause to be effected, done, or performed, the following:

(a) The demolition of all buildings and structures in the Project area, the removal of all utility lines and facilities, and the removal of all debris resulting therefrom.

(b) The vacation of all alleys or streets within the boundaries of the Project and the rezoning, if necessary, of such area in accordance with the Urban Renewal Plan and the building objectives of this Agreement.

(c) The installation of all utility services necessary to reasonably serve the buildings in the Super Structure Development in a manner suitable for, and to a point within the service level of the Project area where the same can be connected to the Super Structure Development as provided in the Working Drawings therefor.

(d) The extension of the City's existing second level pedestrian concourse walkway across Vine and Walnut Streets to the Buildings in the Super Structure Development in a manner suitable to tie into the Super Structure Development as indicated in the Working Drawings therefor. The design of the City's concourse shall be subject to the prior and reasonable approval of Galbreath, shall follow the design parameters referred to in clause 7 hereof, and shall be prepared and approved at a time adequate to permit construction and completion concurrently with that of the Super Structure Development.

(e) The construction of all ramps, sidewalks, curbs, and other improvements located adjacent to the Project Area necessary to full and finished pedestrian and vehicular access to the Sub and Super Structure Developments and to complete all planned public improvements between the Project Area boundaries and the curb line of the public streets surrounding the same. This shall include sidewalks with special finish, waterproofing under sidewalk above service level, street and alley restoration, and any and all other associated work outside the property lines of the Project including landscaping.

(f) All governmental action necessary to permit the leasing of the real estate and the construction by Galbreath of the Super Structure Development.

The foregoing obligations shall be undertaken and effected at times appropriate to the objective contemplated and otherwise in a manner and time that will not delay the progress and completion of the Super Structure Development and, in any event, final completion of all such City obligations shall not be later than the time of full completion of the Super Structure Development. The City shall have the right to open its garage for business prior to Super Structure completion if in the reasonable opinion of the construction contractor for the Super Structure, such opening shall not interfere with work progress.

14. Development of Super Structure. Prior to the estimated time for commencement of construction of the Sub Structure Development, Galbreath shall proceed to negotiate for construction contract prices and for temporary and permanent mortgage financing adequate, together with committed equity, to finance completion of the Super Structure Development. Prior to actual commencement of Sub Structure construction, and subject to the satisfaction of the prior conditions set forth in this Agreement, the City and Galbreath agree to execute a ground lease for the office building parcel ("Parcel A"). . . . Concurrently therewith, the City and Galbreath shall similarly execute a ground lease for the hotel building parcel ("Parcel B"). . . . The execution and delivery of the Leases shall be subject to the satisfaction of the following conditions:

(a) The City shall enter into a construction contract for the Sub Structure Development, prior to or concurrently with execution of the Leases, which contract contemplates Substantial Completion by the time limited in clause 12 hereof, with such assurances, guarantees, or penalties in connection therewith as may be reasonably satisfactory to assure Galbreath of the meeting of such Substantial Completion objective.

(b) The City shall have fully approved Galbreath's Working Drawings to the extent necessary to permit the

taking of construction bids and obtaining any required lender approval.

(c) Temporary and permanent financing commitments shall have been obtained to finance the construction and permanent financing of the complete Super Structure Development upon terms and condition acceptable and satisfactory to Galbreath in his sole and unlimited discretion, it being understood that under no circumstances will Galbreath proceed with Improvements upon only one as opposed to both Parcels.

(d) The City shall have acquired good and marketable record title to the Project and shall have furnished to the Lessee of the respective Parcel the title insurance commitment of a major and responsible title insurance company, authorized to do business in the State of Ohio, to issue a Leasehold Title Insurance Policy insuring in the Lessee, at the cost of the City, good record and marketable title to the leasehold estate created by the Lease and to the easements described in clause 23 hereof, in the sum of $2,100,000 as to Parcel A and $900,000 as to Parcel B, in ALTA form, and showing no exceptions other than the following:

1. The terms and provisions of the Leases and deeds of easements for the subject Parcel.
2. Such easements within the Project Area as it shall have been necessary for the City to grant or reserve for utility lines and related facilities, provided that such lines and facilities shall be located below or within the surface slab of Sub Structure Development and that no such easement shall give rise to any right in the owner thereof to require the removal or relocation of any improvements to be made by the Lessee pursuant to this Agreement.
3. The terms and provisions of the Central Business District Core Urban Renewal Plan.
4. Real Estate taxes and assessments not due and payable as of the date of executing the Lease.
5. Applicable zoning ordinances.

(e) Galbreath shall have determined that the aforesaid commitment of the title insurer can also be obtained in connection with mortgagee policies in amounts equal to the approximate cost of improvements and as required by any proposed financing commitments.

(f) There shall not be in existence any pending or threatened local, state, or federal law, regulation, or court or governmental agency order which would preclude the construction of the Sub or Super Structure Developments or the furnishing of necessary services or utilities thereto.

(g) Galbreath shall have determined that utility services necessary to the intended use and occupancy of the Buildings will be available upon completion of the Buildings.

(h) The applicable zoning ordinances and Central Business District Core Urban Renewal Plan provisions are consistent with and do not prohibit the improvements contemplated by the Working Drawings.

15. Legal Description and Lease Modifications. Prior to the execution of each Lease, the City shall cause a survey of the respective Parcel to be made by a registered surveyor or engineer together with a description and plat thereof. If such survey discloses that, due to the location of surface or Sub Structure improvements, the Buildings and related improvements will not be within the respective descriptions therefor . . ., such [descriptions] will be revised to conform to descriptions which will wholly contain the respective improvements, which descriptions shall be appropriately substituted in the form of Lease for the respective Parcel. Also, the Leases . . . shall be subject to such modifications and changes in form as do not materially alter the transaction contemplated . . . and as the parties may mutually agree upon, the City hereby approving such modifications and changes as may be acceptable to the City Manager as evidenced by his executing the Leases.

16. Proposal of Assignment. At any time prior to execution of the Leases, Galbreath shall have the right to propose a firm, corporation, partnership, or other development venture or entity (the "Designee") to whom Galbreath desires to assign the Lease for Parcel A (together with the rights and benefits accruing under this Agreement relating to such Parcel), or the Lease for Parcel B (together with such rights and benefits), or both. A separate Designee in respect to each Parcel may be proposed. Such proposal shall include the following information:

(a) A description identifying the Designee, including the names and address of all partners, joint venturers, or in the case of corporations, the shareholders and directors comprising the Designee. It is agreed that John W. Galbreath or members of his family or corporations owned or controlled by such persons shall be the owner of a material interest in such Designee (this information to be furnished at least 30 days prior to formally submitting the aforesaid proposal of Designee).

(b) A true copy of all temporary and permanent financing commitments accepted or which will be accepted by the Designee at the time of executing the Leases in connection with the financing of the improvements on the respective parcel.

(c) Reasonable evidence that the Designee has met, or is able to meet, all of the conditions to the lenders' performance as set forth in the financing commitments.

(d) Written statements of major office building tenants acknowledging their agreement to lease space in such building upon completion thereof on Parcel A.

(e) The written statement of a major hotel operator acknowledging its agreement to manage and operate the Hotel building upon completion thereof on Parcel B.

(f) A true copy of the construction contract accepted, or which will be accepted at the time of execution of the Leases, for the construction of the improvements on the respective parcel.

(g) The form of the proposed assignment instrument which will be executed at the time of execution of the Leases and which shall obligate the Designee to the performance of all of the Lessee obligations in the respective Lease, together with those in this Agreement so far as the same affects the respective Parcel.

(h) The financial statement of the Designee disclosing assets and liabilities as of a current date.

Promptly upon receipt of such information, the City shall review the same and within thirty (30) days following such receipt shall either approve or disapprove in its sole and unlimited discretion and in writing, the proposed assignment of leasehold. Subject to such approval, and upon such assignment (and assumption of obligations by the Designee), Galbreath shall be wholly released and relieved of obligation or liability with respect to the Lease for the respective parcel and this Agreement to the extent that the obligations hereunder relate to such parcel. The release of Galbreath shall be self-operative subject only to such approval of assignment by the City and assumption by such Designee. If the City fails to approve the proposed assignment to Designee, Galbreath may elect to terminate this Agreement as provided in clause 27(d) hereof.

17. Term. The basic term of both Leases for Parcels A and B shall be sixty-five years and shall commence on the first day of the month following the date when the Sub Structure improvements to be constructed by City are substantially completed in accordance with the provisions of Section 12 of the Agreement to Lease and shall terminate sixty-five years thereafter, subject to renewal as hereinafter provided. The date of such Substantial Completion shall be evidenced by a certificate of Substantial Completion to be executed by KZF Environmental Design Consultants, Inc., Architects, and by Harrison and Abramovitz, Architects, or otherwise as provided in such Section 12. City shall be entitled to possession of Parcel A and B until the commencement of the Term of the Leases.

18. Renewal. Lessees shall have three (3) successive options to renew the term of the Lease for Parcel A or Parcel B, or both, for separate additional terms of ten (10) years each; provided that Lessees shall not have such options from and after the date when the City, at least sixteen months prior to the expiration of the basic or any renewal term, gives written notice to either Lessee, or both, in good faith, that City intends to discontinue the use of the Building as an office building or hotel. All of the provisions of each Lease other than rental provisions shall apply to each respective renewal term.

If either Lessee desires to exercise its option to renew its Lease, it shall, at least 16 months prior to the expiration of the basic term give City written preliminary notice thereof (the "Preliminary Notice"). City and such Lessee shall promptly thereafter negotiate in good faith to establish the fair market rental (including both Basic and Additional Rentals) of either Parcels A or B, or both (including the Improvements) for the first renewal term. If the parties have not agreed in writing with respect to such rental by the end of the sixty-fourth Lease Year, such rental shall be determined by a board of arbitrators in accordance with the following provisions of this Section.

Each party shall, not later than 11 months prior to the expiration of the basic term, select an arbitrator qualified to appraise commercial real estate within the City of Cincinnati and notify the other party of the arbitrator so selected. Within 30 days thereafter, the two arbitrators so selected shall select a third arbitrator, similarly qualified. If the two arbitrators are unable to so select the third arbitrator, either Lessor or Lessee may request the presiding Judge of the Common Pleas Court of Hamilton County to select a third arbitrator. If no such Common Pleas Court then exists, either party may make such request to the senior judge of the state trial court having general jurisdiction within the City of Cincinnati. The parties shall use their best efforts to cause the board of arbitrators to render a prompt written decision as to the fair market rental (including both Basic and Additional Rentals) of either Parcel A or B, or both, for the renewal term and deliver copies thereof to both parties. The decision of a majority of the arbitrators shall constitute the decision of the board of arbitrators and shall be incontestably binding upon and enforceable against each party thereto.

Such rental, so determined, shall also apply to the first renewal term. Each subsequent renewal term shall be renewed upon either Lessee's giving City at least twelve (12) months notice prior to expiration of the then present term of said Lessee's election, subject to City's right to discontinue use as hereinabove provided. The rental for each subsequent renewal term shall be determined in the same manner as for the first renewal term as hereinabove provided with respect for the first renewal term.

Each party shall bear the costs of the arbitrator appointed by it under this Section, and the costs of the third arbitrator and all other costs of the arbitration shall be borne by the parties equally.

As used herein, the word "Term" shall mean the term of either the Lease for Parcel A or Parcel B including, where appropriate, any renewal term or terms.

19. Basic Lease Rental. The annual basic rental for the initial term for each Parcel shall be $140,000 with respect to Parcel A and $60,000 with respect to Parcel B, payable quarterly and in advance, together with such addition rental as is set forth in the Lease for each Parcel. The rental in respect to each Parcel shall commence upon the first day of the month next following the date of Substantial Completion as determined in accordance with clause 12 hereof. The parties shall execute and deliver a memorandum of lease, suitable for recording purposes, establishing the dates of commencement and expiration of lease term and the date of commencement of the first quarter's rent. Concurrently with the execution of the Leases, Galbreath has deposited $140,000 with respect to Parcel A and $60,000 with respect to Parcel B as prepaid rent, which together with $200,000 Good Faith Deposit made hereunder shall be applied in payment of the first two years Basic Rental due hereunder.

20. Additional Rental Office and Hotel.

(a) *Additional Rental Office.* In addition to the Basic Rental of $140,000 for Parcel A, Lessee shall pay to City annually in respect to each fiscal year of Lessee, during the initial Term and any renewal Term, following issuance of the Certificate of Completion, Additional Rental in an amount equal to twelve percent (12%) of Participation Income, but subject to the provisions in respect to net cash flow deficits as hereinafter defined and provided. "Participation Income" shall mean Gross Income derived from Parcel A which is in excess of 22% of Cost of Improvements as hereinafter defined. The term "Gross Income" shall mean the total dollar value of all rentals, service charges, fees, income, and revenues of every kind and character received by Lessee and derived from, arising out of, or paid on account of the Improvements, less and except proceeds from any loans or financing, condemnation awards, or insurance recovery claims, and except any "pass through" charges paid by a subtenant of Lessee or paid by other parties to Lessee, including but not limited to reimbursements for operating expenses, utilities, taxes, and insurance, and any other payments received by Lessee for transmittal to others on a basis whereby no economic benefits accrue to Lessee.

Following issuance of the Certificate of Completion, Lessee shall certify to City the calendar dates of Lessee's fiscal year in which such Certificate shall issue. Such fiscal year dates shall, for purposes of this subparagraph 20(a) not be changed without Lessor's written consent. Within six (6) months following such fiscal year, and following each fiscal year thereafter, Lessee shall cause its certified public accountants to certify to City the aggregate Cost of Improvements as at the end of any such fiscal year. The term "Cost of Improvements" shall mean all project costs incurred by Lessee in connection with the construction of the Improvements and preparation thereof for initial tenant occupancy of each rental unit, including but not limited to building material costs, construction rental and equipment, materials and other testing, license fees, contractors' charges, financing fees, interest and taxes during construction, architects', attorneys', and engineers' fees, legal fees, title insurance and other insurance premiums, developer's overhead, developer's fees, rental paid under this Lease for Parcel A during the first two years of the Term hereof, commissions, advertising and leasing fees, reimbursable management property expenses, preopening and opening expenses, preopening sales, tenant improvement costs not reimbursed by the tenant directly or indirectly, and all items of Lessee's overhead reasonably attributable to the planning and construction of the Improvements as charged and reflected on the books and records of Lessee and its successors in interest.

Notwithstanding anything in this subparagraph 20(a) to the contrary, no Additional Rent shall be due or payable on any Participation Income in respect to which there exists any unrecovered net cash flow deficit determined as hereinafter provided. The term "net cash flow deficit" for any fiscal year as used in this subparagraph 20(a) shall be defined as the total of any net deficiency between Gross Income and the sum of all operating expense ("Operating Expense") for such year, including but not limited to the field costs of management, all debt service whether principal, interest, or contingent interest, all ad valorem taxes, leasing expenses, and maintenance and repair costs, but specifically not including depreciation, or any Federal, state, or local taxes on gross or net income. Calculation and accumulation of net cash flow deficit shall not include those expenses which are a part of the foregoing determination of Cost of Improvements. During the first fiscal year in respect to which Participation Income is realized, there shall be subtracted therefrom the aggregate of all net cash flow deficit in respect to prior fiscal years before application of the twelve percent Additional Rental factor. If aggregate net cash flow deficit exceeds Participation Income, such excess shall be similarly applied and subtracted (i.e., recovered) in subsequent fiscal years in which Participation Income is realized, along with any further net cash flow deficit for such subsequent fiscal years, it being the intention of the parties, that any net cash flow deficit not previously so applied shall be accumulated and offset against future Participation Income so long as there remains or is experienced any such net cash flow deficit.

Within six (6) months after the expiration of each Fiscal Year the City shall be furnished an audit of the operation of Parcel A showing in detail the total income received and total expenses, together with a computation of the Additional Rental payable to City in accordance with this Lease, prepared and certified by a certified public accountant duly licensed in the State of Ohio. Such statement shall be accompanied by the Additional Rental payment due in respect to such Fiscal Year. The City shall have the right to examine the books, records, and accounts of the Lessee insofar as they relate to the Demised Premises, Parcel A, and to make copies thereof, and Lessee shall exhibit such books, accounts, and records to the City or to any person designated by the City for that purpose, and if such examination shall disclose that the actual Gross Income for any Fiscal Year exceeded that reported to the City by more than three percent (3%), the Lessee shall pay the cost of such examination.

All rentals shall be payable at City Hall, Cincinnati, Ohio, 45202 or at such other address as City may designate in writing.

(b) *Additional Rental Hotel.* In addition to Basic Rental of $60,000 for Parcel B, Lessee shall pay to City annually during the initial Term and any renewal Term, Additional Rental commencing upon the expiration of the fifth fiscal year of Lessee following the fiscal year in which the Certificate of Completion issues. Such Additional Rental shall be in an amount equal to twelve percent (12%) of Participation Income, but subject to the provisions in respect to net cash flow deficits as hereinafter defined and provided. "Participation Income" shall mean Gross Profit derived from the Premises which is in excess of 20% of Cost of Improvements as hereinafter defined. The term "Gross Profit" as used in this subparagraph 20(b) shall be defined as the sum of the following for any given fiscal year of Lessee:

(i) gross operating profits, as said term is customarily defined in standard hotel accounting practices, received by Lessee, including specifically the net income or loss from operating Parcel B before deductions of any undistributed operating expenses, as such term is customarily defined in standard hotel accounting practices, including but not limited to property and liability insurance, ad valorem taxes, interest, depreciation, federal, state, or local income taxes, the Basic Rental hereunder, and capital reserves for furniture, fixtures, and equipment replacement;

(ii) less that amount by which the undistributed operating expenses, as defined above, for the subject fiscal year exceed the undistributed operating expenses of that certain fiscal year immediately subsequent to the fiscal year in which the Improvements are first opened for occupancy or operation;

(iii) any additional rentals, service charge, fees, income, and revenue of every kind and nature received by Lessee, and derived from, arising out of, or paid on account of the Improvements, over and above those already included in item (i) above of this subparagraph 20(b);

(iv) less any "pass through" charges paid by a subtenant of Lessee or paid by other parties to Lessee, including but not limited to reimbursements for operating expenses, utilities, taxes, and insurance, and any other payments received by Lessee for transmittal to others on a basis whereby no economic benefits accrue to Lessee; and

(v) specifically excepting proceeds from any loan or financing condemnation awards or insurance claim recoveries.

Following issuance of the Certificate of Completion, Lessee shall certify to City the calendar dates of Lessee's fiscal year in which such Certificate shall issue. Such fiscal year dates shall, for purposes of this subparagraph 20(b) not be changed without City's written consent. Within six (6) months following such fiscal year, and following each fiscal year thereafter, Lessee shall cause its certified public accountants to certify to City the aggregate Cost of Improvements as at the end of any such fiscal year. The term "Cost of Improvements" shall mean all project costs incurred by Lessee in connection with the construction of the Improvements and preparation thereof for tenant occupancy, including but not limited to building material costs, construction rental and equipment costs, material testing and other testing fees, furniture, fixtures, and equipment costs, license fees, contractors' charges, financing fees, interest and taxes during construction, architects', attorneys', and engineers' fees, legal fees, title insurance and other insurance premiums, developer's overhead, developer's fees, rental paid under this Lease for Parcel B during the first two years of the Term hereof, commissions, advertising and leasing fees, reimbursable management property expenses, preopening and opening expenses, preopening sales, tenant improvement costs not reimbursed by the tenant directly or indirectly, and all items of Lessee's overhead reasonably attributable to the planning and construction of the Improvements as charged and reflected on the books and records of Lessee and its successors in interest.

Notwithstanding anything in this subparagraph 20(b) to the contrary, no Additional Rental shall be due or payable on any Participation Income in respect to which net cash flow deficit accumulated during the first five (5) full fiscal years of Lessee following issuance of the Certificate of Completion, shall not have first been set off in the manner herein provided. The term "net cash flow deficit" shall mean the aggregate total of any net deficiency between Gross Income and Operating Expense (as hereafter defined) for the aforesaid five (5) fiscal years following issuance of the Certificate of Completion. "Operating Expense" shall mean all costs of operation including, but not limited to, field costs of management, all debt service whether principal, interest, or contingent interest, all ad valorem taxes, leasing expenses, and maintenance and repair costs, but specifically not including depreciation, amortization, or any federal, state, or local taxes on gross or net income. Calculation and accumulation of net cash flow deficit shall not include those expenses which are a part of the foregoing determination of Cost of Improvements. During the first fiscal year following said five (5) year period in respect to which Participation Income is realized, there shall be subtracted and set off from Participation Income the accumulated net cash flow deficit to the extent of such Participation Income. If such deficit exceeds Participation Income for such year, such excess shall similarly be applied and subtracted in subsequent fiscal years in which Participation Income is realized until such net cash flow deficit has been fully eliminated (i.e., set off) by such application. The twelve percent (12%) Additional Rental shall be calculated and applied to Participation Income adjusted as hereinabove provided.

Within six (6) months after the expiration of each Fiscal Year the City shall be furnished an audit of the operation of the Premises showing in detail the total income received and total expenses, together with a computation of the Additional Rental payable to City in accordance with this Lease, prepared and certified by a certified public accountant duly licensed in the State of Ohio. Such statement shall be accompanied by the Additional Rental payment due in respect to such Fiscal Year. The City shall have the right to examine the books, records, and accounts of the Lessee insofar as they relate to the Demised Premises, Parcel B, and to make copies thereof, and Lessee shall exhibit such books, accounts, and records to the City or to any person designated by the City for that purpose, and if such examination shall disclose that the actual Gross Income for any Fiscal Year exceeded that reported to the City by more than three percent (3%), the Lessee shall pay the cost of such examination.

All rentals shall be payable at City's City Hall, Cincinnati, Ohio, 45202 or at such other address as City may designate in writing.

21. Equal Employment Opportunity. During the performance of this Agreement, Galbreath agrees as follows:

(a) Galbreath will not discriminate against any employee or applicant for employment because of race, color, religion, sex, or national origin. Galbreath will take affirmative action to ensure that applicants are employed and that employees are treated during employment without regard to their race, color, religion, sex, or national origin. Such action shall include, but not be limited to, the following: employment, upgrading, demotion, or transfer; recruitment or recruitment advertising; layoff or termination; rates of pay or other forms of compensation; and selection for training, including apprenticeship.

Galbreath agrees to post in conspicuous places, available to employees and applicants for employment, notices to be provided by the City setting forth the provisions of this nondiscrimination clause.

(b) Galbreath will, in all solicitations or advertisements for employees placed by or on behalf of Galbreath, state that all qualified applicants will receive consideration for employment without regard to race, color, religion, sex, or national origin.

(c) Galbreath will cause the foregoing provisions to be inserted in all subcontracts for any work covered by this Contract so that such provisions will be binding upon each subcontractor, provided that the foregoing provisions shall not apply to contracts or subcontracts for standard commercial supplies or raw materials.

(d) Galbreath will cause all prime contractors and subcontractors participating in the construction of the project to adhere to the United States Department of Labor Bid Conditions for the Cincinnati Home Town Plan.

22. Rights of Mortgagees. In the event any institutional mortgage lender or investor loaning or agreeing to loan money to finance or refinance the construction of the Buildings in the Super Structure Development, or the furnishing or equipping thereof, requests any modification in the Lease for either Parcel, the City shall, within twenty (20) days of receiving such request, consent thereto and execute such requested modification or state in writing its reasons for refusal of such request. The City shall not withhold its consent to any such request which complies with all of the following conditions, to wit: a) the modification relates to the giving of notice of default or opportunities to cure such default, b) the same does not modify Lease rental (includingnboth basic Leases and Additional Rentals) or the payment thereof, and c) does not substantially modify the rights or benefits which accrue to the City or Landlord under the Lease.

23. Easements. Concurrently with the execution and delivery of the Lease for each Parcel, the City shall execute and deliver to the Lessee as to such Parcel, deeds conveying to the Lessee for the use and benefit of each Parcel a deed or deeds of easement in form and content reasonably satisfactory to the Lessee and adequate to provide the following:

(a) Support for each Super Structure Building in, through, and under the Sub Structure Development including footers, columns, pilings, foundations, and other structures.

(b) Utility lines and services in and through the Sub Structure necessary to service each Parcel development, its use, and occupancy.

(c) Vehicular and pedestrian access throughout the top level (first of three underground levels) of the Sub Structure Development and the use of such top level for truck loading and unloading and other uses as Galbreath or the Lessee deems necessary or desirable in connection with the construction, use, and operation of the Building improvements, including the maintenance, repair, and restoration of the plaza surface slab or any Building improvements.

(d) Temporary easements for access to and use of the Sub Structure Development to the extent necessary to accommodate construction of the Super Structure Development.

The easements (except temporary easements) shall be for terms coextensive with that of the Lease for each Parcel and any renewal thereof, including any lease which replaces or supersedes either such Lease, and shall terminate upon expiration of the Lease term or any renewal thereof. An assignment of Lease shall operate as an assignment of the easements relating to or benefiting the Parcel assigned. Galbreath shall specify the easements required and their location prior to execution of each Lease at a time adequate to permit the City to review the same and determine that such easements will not unreasonably interfere with the City's use of the Sub Structure Development as a public parking facility or other public use, provided that such use shall not interfere with truck loading or unloading or truck access or egress for such purposes. Further, such deed or deeds of easement shall obligate the City to maintain the Sub Structure Development (excluding portions exclusively occupied by Galbreath or his assignee) and all fixtures, machinery, and equipment therein, of any kind or nature, provided, purchased, or installed by the City, in a good and neat state of maintenance and repair, properly lighted and free from accumulation of dirt, snow, rubbish, or ice.

24. Parking. Throughout the term of the Leases and any renewals thereof, priority in the use of parking spaces in the Sub Structure Development shall be reserved for the benefit of occupants of the Building on Parcel A and for the exclusive use of Parcel B patrons, guests, and invitees. Such reserved parking may be achieved through Valet service to be provided by the operator of the hotel facility thereon or otherwise as the parties may mutually agree upon, it being the intention of the parties that hotel guests shall have normal and customary parking convenience comparable to that provided in modern metropolitan hotel facilities in major cities. Such parking shall be made available at rates not greater than that charged in the Fountain Square underground garage immediately to the North. Upon request of the owner or operator of the Parcel B improvements the City shall execute a separate written agreement establishing the availability of such parking, the rates and other conditions regulating the use thereof which are not inconsistent with the terms of and with the convenient hotel parking objectives contemplated by this paragraph. Such agreement shall not be in conflict with the existing Parking System Facilities Indenture and shall otherwise be subject to the approval of the City's duly designated Parking Consultant and the Trustees under the Parking Indenture.

25. Taxes. Upon and after execution of the Lease for each Parcel, the City shall pay any taxes attributable to the land and Sub Structure Development only, provided that the Lessee of the Parcel shall pay all taxes or service payments in the nature of or in lieu of taxes applicable to Lessee's improvements during the term of the Lease as provided in the lease instrument.

26. Good Faith Deposit. Prior to the execution of this Agreement, Galbreath has delivered to the City a good faith deposit in the form of a certificate of deposit in the amount of $200,000 as security for the performance of those obligations to be performed by Galbreath and his assigns under this Agreement prior to the return or retention of such deposit amount in accordance herewith. The good faith deposit provided for herein is hereinafter referred to as "Deposit Amount."

The certificate of deposit with a Cincinnati bank provided for herein shall be in a depository and accompanied by a disbursement agreement to the order of the City, satisfactory to the City. The City shall be under no obligation to pay or earn interest on the Deposit Amount, but any interest paid on the certificate of deposit shall be the sole property of Galbreath absent any default by Galbreath or his assigns. If this Agreement shall not have been terminated pursuant to either clause 31 or 32 hereof, the City shall apply the principal amount of such deposit to the first year's basic rent due pursuant to the Leases at the time for commencement of basic rental as herein and in such Leases provided.

27. Antiassignment Clause. Subject to the provisions of clause 16 hereof, prior to completion of the contemplated improvements with respect to either Parcel A or Parcel B, the Lessee thereof may not assign its rights under this Agreement or under the Lease for such Parcel without the prior written consent of the City. Such Lessee shall have the right, however, to mortgage all or any part of its interest in such Parcel or any of the improvements to be constructed thereon to one or more mortgagees or otherwise assign, pledge, or hypothecate the same as security for any bona fide loan given to finance the construction, furnishing, or equipping of such improvements or any portion thereof, or to enter into any other financing arrangement or arrangements therefor using such security or to refinance any such loan or other financing arrangement. Such mortgagees shall have such rights as are provided in the Lease for each Parcel; provided that the City's interest in either Parcel shall in no event be subordinated to any mortgage, assignment, pledge, or hypothecation.

28. Commencement and Completion. The Lessees shall promptly begin construction of the Improvements on both Parcels A and B at the same time, and shall thereafter diligently prosecute such construction to completion in accordance with the Working Drawings and modifications thereto approved as provided herein. Such construction shall begin within two months after commencement of the Term of each Lease, and subject to the provisions of clause 34 hereof, the Improvements on Parcels A and B shall be completed within 30 months after the commencement of the Term for the respective Lease.

29. Certificate of Completion. Promptly after completion of the improvements (the "Improvements") in accordance with the Working Drawings for the Improvements on either Parcel in the Super Structure Development, the City shall furnish the Lessee with a Certificate of Completion which shall constitute (and shall so state) a conclusive determination by the City that the Lessee has fully complied with its obligations under this Agreement to construct the Improvements and to pay rentals then due on such Parcel, that such Improvements were constructed in compliance with the Urban Renewal Plan and this Agreement, and that the Lessee's obligations under this Agreement with respect to the construction of Improvements on such Parcel are fulfilled and terminated. No such Certificate of Completion shall constitute evidence of compliance with or satisfaction of any obligation of any party to the holder of any mortgage or the insurer of any mortgage securing money loaned to finance such Improvements or any part thereof. Each Certificate of Completion shall be in such form as will enable it to be recorded in the office of the Recorder of Hamilton County, Ohio. If the City shall refuse or fail to provide any Certificate of Completion in accordance with the provisions of this paragraph, it shall, within 30 days after written request therefor by the Lessee, provide the Lessee with a written statement, indicating in adequate detail in what respect the Lessee has failed to complete the Improvements in accordance with the provisions of this Agreement, or is otherwise in default and what measures or acts must, in the opinion of the City, be taken or performed by the Lessee in order to obtain such Certificate of Completion.

30. Urban Renewal Amendments. Area C of the Urban Renewal Plan shall not hereafter be amended, modified, or terminated without the prior written consent of: (i) Galbreath prior to the execution and delivery of the Leases provided for in clause 14 hereof and (ii) thereafter, the Lessee and its assignees and sublessees of all of each Parcel.

31. Termination. This Agreement may be terminated by written notice given by either party to the other (unless hereinafter and otherwise provided) on account of the occurrence of any of the following conditions, in which event the Deposit Amount given pursuant to clause 26 hereof shall be and become the sole property of the City and neither Party shall have any further rights against or liability to the other under this Agreement, to wit:

(a) Failure of Galbreath to furnish Schematic Designs, Preliminary Plans, or Working Drawings when and as required by this Agreement.

(b) If Galbreath alone, or Galbreath and the City both, fail to approve designs, plans, or drawings of the submitting Party and written notice of termination is given by either Party pursuant to clauses 5, 7, or 9 hereof.

(c) Failure of Galbreath to obtain, prior to execution of the Leases, either temporary or permanent mortgage commitments to finance the construction and permanent financing of the complete Super Structure Development upon terms and conditions acceptable and satisfactory, to Galbreath in his sole and unlimited discretion.

(d) The City shall refuse to approve the Designees proposed in accordance with clause 16 hereof, and Galbreath shall determine not to execute the Leases.

(e) Substantial Completion of the Sub Structure is delayed beyond ninety (90) days due to causes beyond the City's control and Galbreath or the Lessee shall terminate this Agreement and both Leases. . . .

32. Additional Termination. This agreement may be terminated by written notice given by Galbreath to the City (unless hereinafter and otherwise provided) on account of the occurrence of any of the following conditions, in which event the Good Faith Deposit Amount given pursuant to clause 26 hereof shall be refunded to Galbreath and neither Party shall have any further rights against or liability to the other, to wit:

(a) Failure of the City to furnish Schematic Designs, Preliminary Plans, or Working Drawings when and as required by this Agreement.

(b) If the City alone fails to approve designs, plans, or drawings of Galbreath and written notice of termination is given by either Party pursuant to clause 5, 7, or 9 hereof.

(c) Failure of the City to satisfy the conditions of clause 8 hereof to the reasonable satisfaction of Galbreath.

(d) Failure of the City to proceed with Sub Structure construction or notice of termination given by the City pursuant to clause 12 hereof.

(e) Failure of the City to satisfy, or the lack of satisfaction of, the conditions described in clause 14 hereof other than subsection (c) thereof.

(f) Failure of the City to tender the Leases and deeds of easement for both Parcels duly executed by the City.

33. Default.

A. Generally. Except in the event of termination of this Agreement pursuant to clauses 31 or 32 hereof, and except as otherwise provided in this Agreement, in the event of any default in any of the terms or conditions of this Agreement by either party or any successor to such party prior to the execution of the Leases, such party or successor, shall, upon written notice from the other, proceed promptly, and in any event within sixty (60) days after receipt of such notice, to cure or remedy such default. In case such action is not commenced within such time or thereafter diligently pursued, or if the default shall not be cured or remedied within a reasonable time, the aggrieved party may institute such proceedings as may be necessary or desirable in its opinion to recover damages suffered as the result of such default or to cure and remedy such default, including, but not limited to, proceedings against the party in default to compel specific performance of its obligations.

B. *Default by Lessee.* In the event that subsequent to the execution of the Leases:

(a) Galbreath, or in the event of an assignment by Galbreath to a Designee then such Designee (Galbreath or such Designee hereinafter called the "Lessee") shall be in material default in its obligations under this Agreement or under the Leases with respect to the construction of the Improvements thereon, and the dates for the beginning and completion thereof, or shall abandon or substantially suspend construction work, and any such default, abandonment, or suspension shall not be cured, ended, or remedied within sixty (60) days (six months if the default is with respect to the date for completion of such Improvements) after written demand by the City so to do; or

(b) The Lessee shall fail to pay the taxes, assessments, and other charges as and when required by Section 6A of the lease for a Parcel and, subject to the rights granted to the Lessee in Section 6C thereof, such payments shall not be made within thirty (30) days after written demand by the City so to do; or

(c) The Lessee shall suffer any materialman's or mechanic's lien to be filed against a Parcel, and such lien shall not have been removed or discharged within ninety (90) days after written demand by the City so to do, unless the Lessee is in good faith contesting the validity or amount of such lien; the City shall retain the Deposit Amount and any prepaid rent made pursuant to the Lease with respect to which such default has occurred, as liquidated damages, Lessee shall cause to be transferred to City all plans and specifications for Improvements on Parcel involved in the default, and the City shall have the right to terminate the Lease for the Parcel leased to such Lessee with respect to which any such default has occurred, provided, however, that prior to the termination of the Lease, the City shall first provide to the holder of any mortgage, securing money loaned to finance or refinance the construction, furnishing, or equipping of any Improvements on such Parcel or any portion thereof, the rights provided to such mortgage holder in the Lease for such Parcel. No default by the Lessee with respect to either Parcel shall affect or subject to any liability, encumbrance, lien, or remedy the other Parcel with respect to which no default has occurred or with respect to which a Certificate of Completion shall have been given.

C. *Default by Lessor.* Except as provided for in clause 34 hereof (with respect to excusable delay in the City's Substantial Completion of Sub Structure or other City Improvements), if subsequent to the execution of the Leases and prior to City's Substantial Completion of Sub Structure, the City shall be in material default in its obligations under this Agreement or the Leases with respect to the construction of the Sub Structure, or shall abandon or substantially suspend construction works, and any such default, abandonment, or suspension shall not be cured, ended, or remedied within sixty (60) days, the Lessee shall be entitled to recover the Deposit Amount and any prepaid rent made pursuant to the Leases as liquidated damages, and the Lessee shall have the right to terminate the Leases.

34. Excusable Delay. Neither the City nor Galbreath, his Designee or Lessee, as the case may be, shall be considered in default in the obligations to be performed by it hereunder if delay in the performance of such obligations is due to unforeseeable causes beyond its control and without its fault or negligence, including, but not limited to, acts of God or of the public enemy, acts of the Federal Government or of the Government of the State of Ohio, acts or delays of the other party, litigation which has or could have the effect of divesting either Party of the rights or benefits created hereby or by the Lease or Leases, fires, floods, unusually severe weather, epidemics, quarantine restrictions, freight embargoes, unavailability of materials, strikes or delays of contractors, subcontractors, or materialmen due to any of such causes; it being the purpose and intent of this clause that in the event of the occurrence of any such enforced delay, the time or times for performance of the obligations of the City with respect to the Sub Structure or other City Improvements, or of the Lessee with respect to construction of the Super Structure, shall be extended for the period of the enforced delay; provided that the party seeking the benefit of the provisions of this clause shall, (i) within thirty (30) days after the beginning of any such enforced delay, have in writing notified the other party thereof and of the cause or causes thereof and of the duration thereof or, if continuing, the estimated duration thereof, and (ii) if the delay is continuing on the date of notification, shall, within thirty (30) days after the end of the delay, have notified the other party or its successor in writing of the duration of the delay.

Notwithstanding the foregoing, however, if there occurs any actual or clearly evident delay in Substantial Completion of three (3) months or more, or if there occurs any event which, pursuant to the preceding paragraph, extends the time for Substantial Completion, three (3) months or more, then the Lessee or Lessees (including Galbreath) shall have the right and option to cause termination of his or its Lease or Leases, and of all obligation under this Agreement with respect to the development which is the subject of such Lease or Leases, subject, further, to the following:

(a) Such three (3) months period to e extended by a period of time equal to that which may be given by all temporary and permanent lenders for the Parcel improvements:

(1) Extending the time for commencement and completion of the Building improvements on sucn Parcel, or Parcels, and

(2) Extending for a period of time equal to that in (1) above, the maturity of the temporary or construction financing and the expiration date of the permanent financing commitment or commitments for such Parcel or Parcels.

(b) If extensions in (a) (1) and (2) above are not given, then Lessee shall have option to terminate and the Lessee, upon exercise of such right and option, to terminate, shall cause to be transferred and assigned to the City, all plans and specifications prepared in respect to the improvements for the Parcel involved in such termination.

(c) So much of the Deposit Amount as has or would be applied as basic rental for the Parcel involved, shall be forfeited to and retained as the sole property of the City.

35. Separability. Anything in this Agreement to the contrary notwithstanding, following execution and delivery of the Leases, neither Parcel nor the leasehold or other rights of anyone having any interest therein shall be affected by or subjected to any liability, encumbrance, lien, or remedy by reason of the default of any term, provision, obligation, or duty in or imposed by this Agreement if such default relates only to the other Parcel. This clause shall not apply to the provisions of this Agreement relating to the Deposit Amount.

36. Delegation of Authority. The City Manager, or such other person as he may from time to time designate, shall be the person authorized and designated to act for the City in giving approvals, issuing Certificates of Completion, and taking other appropriate action under this Agreement. No designation of any successor shall be effective as to Galbreath or his assigns until written notice thereof has been given to Galbreath or such assigns.

37. Notice. Any notice or communication required or permitted to be given under this Agreement by either party to the other, or its successor, as the case may be, shall be deemed sufficiently given if mailed by U.S. registered or certified mail, postage prepaid, return receipt requested, and

(a) If to the City, addressed as follows:
City Manager
The City of Cincinnati
City Hall
Cincinnati, Ohio 45202

(b) If to Galbreath, addressed as follows:
John W. Galbreath & Co.
Room 900
180 East Broad Street
Columbus, Ohio 43215

Either party may, from time to time, change its mailing address by giving notice to the other party as provided in this clause.

38. Non Merger of Covenants. Subject to the provisions of clause 29 regarding termination of covenants upon the issuance by the City of a Certificate of Completion, the terms and provisions of this Agreement shall not otherwise be merged into but shall survive the Lease for each Parcel.

39. Successors and Assigns. All rights and obligations under this Agreement and the Leases and deeds of easement to be executed and delivered pursuant hereto shall be binding upon and shall inure to the benefit of the parties hereto and their respective heirs, administrators, executors, successors, and assigns.

40. No Delay. No consent, approval, certificate, or other documents provided herein to be given by either party shall be unreasonably withheld or delayed.

IN WITNESS WHEREOF, the City and Galbreath have caused this Agreement to be executed as of the day and year first above written by their representatives thereunto duly authorized.

JOHN W. GALBREATH & CO.

By: _____

THE CITY OF CINCINNATI, OHIO

By: _____
    City Manager

Approved by Council of the City on

_____, _____.

_____
Clerk of Council

APPROVED AS TO FORM:

_____
City Attorney

APPENDIX L

Example Agreement for Sublease, Operation and Maintenance of Parking Facilities

THIS AGREEMENT made as of ________________, by and between the CITY OF ________________________ (the "City"), a municipal corporation duly organized and existing under the laws of the State of ____________ ____________, and ________________________________ (the "Operator").

WITNESSETH:

WHEREAS, the Community Redevelopment Agency of the City of ________________ (the "Agency") is implementing a Redevelopment Plan (the "Redevelopment Plan") in the City of ________________________, adopted by the City by Ordinance No. ______________ on ____________, ________, pursuant to the ______________ Community Redevelopment Law (Health and Safety Code Sections 33000 et seq.) for a redevelopment project designated the ________________________________ Project (the "Project"); and

WHEREAS, the Agency has entered into a Disposition and Development Agreement dated ________________, ____________, as supplemented by First Implementation Agreement, dated even date herewith (collectively, the "Disposition and Development Agreement" or "DDA"), with the Operator (as Developer) for the sale of certain land to the Operator and other parties for development thereon of a regional shopping center and related office and commercial buildings and facilities (including surface parking not part of Authority's Parking Facilities); and

WHEREAS, the Agency has also entered into an agreement with the Parking Authority of the City of ________________________ (the "Authority") providing for the sale and disposition by the Agency to the Authority of certain land and air rights parcels for ownership and development by the Authority thereon and therein of offstreet parking facilities of approximately 3,600 spaces to serve the Project (said parcels and facilities being hereinafter collectively referred to as the "Parking Facilities"), which Parking Facilities are to be leased to the City pursuant to the Parking Facilities Lease (. . . said Lease being hereinafter referred to as the "Master Lease"); and

WHEREAS, at the end of the term of the Master Lease, fee title to the Parking Facilities shall vest in the City; and

WHEREAS, pursuant to and in order to implement the Redevelopment Plan and the Disposition and Development Agreement, the City and the Operator desire to enter into this Agreement for the purpose of providing for the sublease to, and the operation and maintenance by the Operator of, the Parking Facilities; and

WHEREAS, the Operator, Authority and Agency have entered into a Construction, Operation and Reciprocal Easement Agreement (hereinafter referred to as the "REA") with major department stores providing for the construction, operation and maintenance of the regional shopping center and related office and commercial buildings and facilities (including surface parking not part of the Parking Facilities) and the Parking Facilities as described and shown therein.

NOW, THEREFORE, in consideration of the mutual promises and agreements herein contained, the parties hereto agree as follows:

Section 1. Sublease of Parking Facilities. Subject to the Master Lease, the Operator subleases from the City and the City demises and leases unto the Operator, the Parking Facilities . . . on the terms and conditions hereinafter set forth. In the event that the Master Lease terminates prior to the term hereof, and fee title to the Parking Facilities vests in the City, the City and the Operator hereby covenant that the terms, provisions, covenants and agreements contained in this Sublease shall continue in full force and effect.

Section 2. Term.

a. *Initial Term.* The initial term of this Sublease shall commence on the date of commencement of the term of the Master Lease (as said date shall be designated in written notice given by the City to the Operator at least 15 days prior to said date of commencement) and shall terminate on midnight of the last day of the 600th month thereafter (hereinafter referred to as the "Initial Term"), unless extended or sooner terminated as provided herein. Upon the determination of the commencement date of the term of the Sublease hereunder, the parties shall execute an appropriate document, in recordable form, setting forth the commencement and termination date of the Sublease term.

b. *City's Option to Enter into New Lease or Management Agreement.* At the end of the Initial Term hereof, the City may, at its sole option:

(1) Enter into a new lease with Operator, on the same terms and conditions as contained in this Sublease, for a term not to exceed forty-nine (49) years, with the Operator having the option to terminate such lease at the end of each ten (10) year period thereof by giving notice in writing at least 180 days before the end of such ten (10) year period; or

(2) Enter into a management agreement with the Operator obligating the Operator to manage the Parking Facilities in accordance with the REA standards of operation and maintenance, for such term or terms as the City may specify but not exceeding the remaining term of the REA, with the Operator having the option to terminate such management agreement at the end of each ten (10) year period thereof by giving notice in writing at least 180 days before the end of such ten (10) year period.

c. *Conditions of Entering into New Lease or Management Agreement.* City's right to renew this Sublease or enter into such management agreement is subject to:

(1) The following conditions precedent:

(a) This Sublease shall be in effect at the time that the City delivers its notice of exercise of option to the Overator and on the last day of the Initial Term.

(b) The City shall not be in default under any provision of this Sublease at the time that the City delivers its notice of exercise of option to the Operator and on the last day of the Initial Term.

(2) At least one hundred eighty (180) days before the last day of the Initial Term, the City shall give to the Operator notice irrevocably exercising the option to enter into a new lease or management agreement.

(3) The REA shall be in full force and effect at the time that the option is exercised and shall have an unexpired term remaining of not less than the term of the new lease or management agreement.

In the case of a new lease, each party shall, at the request of the other, execute a new lease on the same terms and conditions as contained herein. Alternatively, each party shall, at the request of the other, execute a memorandum, in recordable form, acknowledging the fact that the option has been exercised and otherwise complying with the requirements of law for an effective memorandum or abstract of lease. In the case of a management agreement, the terms of said agreement (including payments to City and Operator's obligations to operate without compensation from the City) shall be consistent with this Sublease and the REA. Each party shall, at the request of the other, execute the management agreement.

d. *Operator's Option to Purchase Parking Facilities.* City grants to Operator an option to purchase the Parking Facilities on the terms and conditions hereinafter set forth.

(1) The option to purchase the Parking Facilities shall be exercisable only in the event that all of the following conditions exist:

(a) this Sublease expires at the end of the Initial Term or during any new lease term, other than by termination by the City, its successors or assigns, by reason of breach or default hereunder by Operator, its successors or assigns; and

(b) the City, or its successors or assigns, at any time after said termination, shall abandon the use of the Parking Facilities, that is, shall permanently cease to operate and maintain the Parking Facilities on a non-exclusive basis for members of the general public patronizing the shopping center and other office and commercial buildings and facilities in the Project; and

(c) the REA shall be in full force and effect and the shopping center shall be in operation at the time the option to purchase is exercised; and

(d) any Lease Revenue Bonds issued by the Parking Authority shall have been repaid or will be repaid from the purchase price, as determined below, so that title to the Parking Facilities vests in the City.

Operator may exercise the option to purchase the Parking Facilities in their entirety and not in part.

(2) The purchase price (hereinafter referred to as the "Purchase Price") for the Parking Facilities shall be the fair market value of the Parking Facilities as of the date the option to purchase is exercised (excluding, however, the value of any air rights and improvements therein to the extent that a right of reentry or reverter has been exercised in accordance with grant deed provisions so that title thereto will not remain in the Parking Authority or the City, as the case may be), but in no event less than the principal amount, plus interest and other charges and costs, required to pay off and fully retire any indebtedness of the Authority, Agency or City or any agency thereof, incurred to acquire and construct or repair or rebuild the Parking Facilities. Said Purchase Price shall be determined by the parties hereto, if possible, but if they cannot agree within thirty (30) days then by a real estate appraiser promptly selected by the City and a real estate appraiser promptly selected by the Operator. If the appointed real estate appraisers cannot agree as to the Purchase Price within thirty (30) days, the two appraisers shall promptly appoint a third appraiser of their joint choosing. If the two appraisers are unable to select such a third appraiser, such appraiser shall be appointed by a Presiding Judge of a competent Court in the County of ________________, State of ____, at the request of either appraiser or party to this agreement. All appraisers appointed pursuant to the provisions hereof shall be impartial and unrelated, directly or indirectly, so far as employment of services is concerned, to any of the parties hereto. Within ten (10) days from such appointment, all appraisers shall meet and determine the purchase price within twenty (20) days from the date of selection of the third appraiser. If the three appraisers are unable to agree within such time, the Purchase Price shall then be determined by a majority of the three appraisers, but if a majority cannot agree, then the arithmetic average of the two closest of the three final appraisals shall be deemed to be the Purchase Price. In arriving at the Purchase Price, the appraisers shall not take into consideration the fact that the Operator owns property adjoining the Parking Facilities or that said Parking Facilities would be more valuable to the Operator than they would be to some third party not owning adjacent property. Each party shall bear its own expense except that relating to the selection and services of the third appraiser, which shall be borne equally by the Operator and the City.

(3) This option to purchase shall survive the expiration of this Sublease, but it shall be exercised by written notice given by the Operator to the City within one hundred twenty (120) days from the date of occurrence of the later of the two events set forth in paragraphs (1)(a) and (1)(b) of this subsection d. If not so exercised by the Operator, this Option shall lapse and Operator shall have no further rights hereunder.

Section 3. Use; Covenant of Parking Availability.

a. *Use.* The Parking Facilities shall be used, managed and operated by the Operator hereunder to provide parking on a non-exclusive basis for members of the general public patronizing the shopping center and other office and commercial buildings and facilities in the Project, and for no other purpose.

b. *Covenant of Parking Availability.* The City covenants, for itself and its successors and assigns, that so long as (i) the Parking Facilities are in existence, (ii) this Sublease is in effect, (iii) the Operator's rental payments are paid as herein provided, and (iv) no default under this Sublease shall exist, the Parking Facilities shall be available to the Operator hereunder on a non-exclusive basis for members of the general public patronizing the shopping center and other office and commercial buildings and facilities in the Project. This covenant is subject to any laws, regulations or rules of any governmental authority which may hereafter restrict or impose conditions upon the use and operation of the Parking Facilities.

Section 4. Rental.

a. *Base Rental.* The Operator agrees to pay to the City as annual rental (hereinafter called the "Base Rental") for the use of the Parking Facilities, the sum of Three Hundred Thousand Dollars ($300,000.00), subject to adjustment as hereinafter provided. The Base Rental shall be paid to the City on the basis of the City's fiscal year, which commences July 1st and ends on June 30th. The Base Rental, as it may be adjusted hereunder, shall be paid without offset or deduction except as hereinafter expressly allowed under subsection d. of this Section 4 and under subsection b. of Section 9 of this Sublease. The Base Rental for any partial fiscal year (or fiscal quarter) shall be prorated on a daily basis. The first payment of Base Rental shall be paid within thirty (30) days from the date that the shopping center or any portion thereof (comprising either mall stores or at least one major department store) is opened for business, or _____, _____, whichever date first occurs, and shall be in an amount computed from such date of completion or opening, or _____, _____, as the case may be, to the end of the then current fiscal quarter of the City. Thereafter, said payments of Base Rental shall be due and payable, for each fiscal year that this Sublease is in effect, in equal quarterly installments in advance on the first day of July, October, January and April of each fiscal year of the City.

b. *Period of Payment.* In reliance upon the Operator's agreement to enter into this Sublease, the City has created the Authority which has issued bonds for the purpose of providing the funds to acquire and construct the Parking Facilities, and the City has entered into the Master Lease for the purpose of securing the payments by the Authority of principal and interest on said bonds. In consideration for said actions by the City, the Operator agrees that, subject to the availability of the Parking Facilities under this Sublease as set forth in Subsection b. of Section 3, it shall not terminate this Sublease prior to the termination date set forth in Section 2 hereof and shall make payments of Base Rental and Additional Rental to the City and discharge its obligations hereunder until said termination date and for so long thereafter as this Sublease shall remain in force and effect.

c. *Adjustment of Base Rental.* Upon the commencement of the eleventh full fiscal year of the City following the commencement of payments of Base Rental hereunder, and thereafter at 10-year intervals for so long as this Sublease shall remain in effect, the amount of Base Rental shall be increased or decreased, as the case may be, to adjust the amount of Base Rental for each of the next ten fiscal years of the City or portion thereof to an amount which shall equal twenty percent (20%) of the amount of the ad valorem taxes assessed and levied against the land and improvements of the shopping center (including land and improvements leased or owned by department stores) for the fiscal year of the City immediately preceding the year of adjustment; provided, however, that in no event shall the amount of Base Rental be reduced below $300,000.00 annually for so long as the bonds and indebtedness of the Authority or of the Agency with respect to the Project or to the Parking Facilities remain outstanding and unpaid. If the parties are unable to agree upon the amount of ad valorem taxes assessed and levied against such land and improvements, then they shall be bound by the written joint determination of said amount by the Assessor and Tax Collector (or other appropriate County officials exercising said functions) of the County of _____. If at the time of said determination by the Assessor and Tax Collector the amount of the assessed valuation of the shopping center or any part thereof is being regularly challenged in assessment appeal procedures or in judicial action, said determination shall be adjusted, and the parties shall similarly revise the adjustment of base rental hereunder, based on the final outcome of the assessment appeal or judicial action. The foregoing sentence does not confer upon the Operator or any Party to the REA any separate or independent right to challenge the determination made hereunder, but is intended only to assure that such determination will, in fact, be based on the actual assessed value of any taxes levied on the shopping center. For purposes of this subsection c., the term "shopping center" shall mean and include all taxable parcels of land, property interests (including leaseholds), buildings, structures and improvements (including leasehold improvements) in the Project from time to time, but excluding store fixtures and inventories assessed as personal property and excluding the Parking Facilities, any taxable interest in the Parking Facilities by reason of this Sublease or other right to parking therein, and other non-taxable publicly owned property.

d. *Credit against Base Rental.* The Operator shall receive a credit against the amount of Base Rental due in each fiscal year of the City by the amount of any ad valorem taxes, or any tax in lieu of ad valorem tax which results in general fund revenues to the City, assessed against the Operator as lessee of the Parking Facilities and solely by reason of its interests as lessee or on a possessory interest basis by reason of any interest of the Operator or any of the other Parties to the REA (hereinafter "REA Parties") in the Parking Facilities (excluding the interest or ownership of the Operator or REA Parties in or to interests in property which may be located in the Parking Facilities but which are not part of the Parking Facilities such as private utilities, foundations, supports, ramps, bridges and easements) and paid by the Operator or REA Parties during the preceding fiscal year; provided, however, that in no event shall the amount of the credit exceed the amount of the Base Rental. If the Operator and City are unable to agree upon the amount of said ad valorem taxes or in lieu ad valorem taxes assessed against the Operator or REA Parties on a possessory interest basis by reason of any interest of the Operator or such other party in the Parking Facilities (excluding the interest or ownership of the Operator or any such REA Parties in or to interests in property which may be located in the Parking Facilities but which are not part of the Parking Facilities such as private utilities, foundations, supports, ramps, bridges and easements), then they shall be bound by the written joint determination of said amount by the Assessor and Tax Collector (or other appropriate County officials exercising said functions) of the County of _____.

e. *Additional Rental.* During the term of this Sublease, including any extension thereof, as additional rental hereunder, the Operator agrees to promptly pay and discharge:

(1) Subject to the credit of ad valorem or in lieu ad valorem tax payments against Base Rental provided in subsection d. above, all charges and levies for utilities, taxes and assessments of any nature whatsoever for state, federal and other governmental parking regulation fees, excises, taxes, ad valorem and specific lien special assessments and gross receipts taxes, if any, levied upon or assessed against the Parking Facilities or upon or against the Authority's or the City's interest therein or upon the Authority's or City's rental income derived therefrom.

(2) Insurance premiums, if any, on insurance purchased by and maintained by the Operator as required by the provisions of Section 9 of this Sublease.

(3) All costs and expenses which the City may incur in consequence of or because of any default by the Operator under this Sublease, including reasonable attorneys' fees and costs of suit or action at law to enforce the terms and conditions of this Sublease.

Each portion of the foregoing shall be paid on or before the payment date to which the same applies or relates.

Section 5. Repair, Maintenance and Operation.

Except for repair or restoration of the Parking Facilities to be made by the Authority pursuant to Subsection 1 of Section 8 and Section 11 of the Master Lease, or by the City pursuant to the terms hereof, the Operator shall at its own expense repair and maintain, during the term of this Sublease, the Parking Facilities (including railroad grade crossing safety devices for vehicle and pedestrian access between the Parking Facilities and between the Parking Facilities and the shopping center) in good order, condition and repair and shall pay all costs and expenses of operating the same as non-exclusive public parking facilities for members of the public patronizing the shopping center, office and commercial buildings and other facilities of the Project (including the costs of all utilities, and all public charges, taxes and assessments of any nature whatsoever for which the Operator is liable), it being understood and agreed that the City shall be under no obligation to pay any cost or expense of any kind or character in connection with or related to the repair, management, operation or maintenance of the Parking Facilities during the term of this Sublease. The standards of maintenance required under this Sublease are set forth in Section X-B of the REA. Operator's obligations hereunder shall include, without limitation, the repair and maintenance of all Common Building Components (as defined and designated in the REA) according to the requirements of the REA as same relate to the Parking Facilities and/or the obligations of the Authority or City with respect thereto. Operator shall at all times comply with and maintain the parking ratios required under Section IV-A of the REA and shall at all times comply with all other provisions of the REA relating to the operation and maintenance of the Parking Facilities. In the event the Operator fails to perform the maintenance, repair and operation of the Parking Facilities as provided herein, the City shall notify the Operator and the REA Parties in writing of such failure to perform, specifying the respects in which it considers the Operator's performance to be unsatisfactory. Upon the failure of the Operator to improve or to commence and diligently proceed to improve such performance within thirty (30) days after such notice, the City shall give the Operator and the REA Parties a second written notice of such failure to perform. Upon the failure of the Operator to improve or to commence and diligently proceed to improve such performance within fifteen (15) days after such second written notice, the REA Parties, on written notice to the City, shall collectively or individually have the right to enter the Parking Facilities and undertake or cause to be undertaken such maintenance, repair and operational activities in the manner provided in the REA. Upon the failure of the REA Parties to collectively or individually take over such maintenance, repair or operational activities, the City shall have the right to enter the Parking Facilities and undertake or cause to be undertaken such maintenance, repair and operational activities and, in such event, the Operator shall promptly upon demand reimburse the City for all reasonable costs and expenses incurred by the City for such maintenance, repair and operational activities. The City agrees to keep the Parking Facilities free and clear of all liens and encumbrances, except for those caused or consented to by the Authority and by the Operator and except that the City may pledge revenues to be derived therefrom.

Section 6. No Charge for Parking.

The Operator shall not impose or permit the imposition of any charge for the use of the Parking Facilities without the City's consent, unless such charge is specifically provided for in the REA approved by the Agency; provided, however, that the provisions of this Section shall not apply to charges of any kind whatsoever imposed by any governmental authority on the Authority, the City, the Operator, or the users of the Parking Facilities as part of a parking management program, transportation control plan, or other governmental regulation of parking: and provided, further, that the Operator may charge and collect the payments and expenses incurred under this Sublease from tenants of the shopping center and from the REA Parties to the extent provided in the respective tenant leases or the REA.

Section 7. Additions and Improvements.

a. *By the City.* With the consent of the parties to the REA (which consent shall not be unreasonably withheld), the City shall have the right during the term of this Sublease, at its own expense, to make or permit to be made, any addition to or improvements to the Parking Facilities which are consistent with the REA and do not impair the utility thereof for use as parking facilities and for other purposes which are now or may hereafter be permitted by law, to attach fixtures, structures or signs thereto, and to place any personal property on or in the Parking Facilities, provided the utility and use of the Parking Facilities as parking facilities is not unreasonably interfered with and provided that no such work by the City shall be inconsistent with the operation of the shopping center according to normal rules of operation therefor. Title to all such personal property or to fixtures which may be removed without damage to the Parking Facilities shall remain in the City or in such person as may be legally entitled thereto.

b. *By the Operator.* With the approval of the City, the Operator during the term of this Sublease, may, at its own cost and expense, make or permit to be made, any addition to or improvements to the Parking Facilities which are consistent with the REA and do not impair the utility thereof for use as parking facilities, to attach fixtures, structures or signs thereto, and place any personal property on or in the Parking Facilities, provided the utility and use of the Parking Facilities as parking facilities is not unreasonably interfered with. Title to all such personal property or to fixtures which may be removed without damage to the Parking Facilities shall remain in the Operator or in such person as may be legally entitled thereto.

Section 8. Policies and Rules.

The Operator shall establish and maintain such general policies, rules and regulations for the repair, management, maintenance and operation, and use of the Parking Facilities consistent with the provisions of this Sublease, the Master Lease, the Redevelopment Plan and the REA as may be necessary. Such policies, rules and regulations shall be submitted to the City prior to their effective date and shall become effective thirty (30) days after the date of such delivery unless they are suspended or disapproved by action of the City Council. The initial general policies, rules and regulations of the Operator, as contained in Exhibit E of the REA, are hereby approved by the City.

Section 9. Insurance.

a. *Obligations of Operator.* During the term of this Lease, the Operator at its own cost and expense shall:

(1) Maintain or cause to be maintained in full force and effect, the following insurance covering the Parking Facilities: comprehensive public liability insurance, in-

cluding coverage for any accident resulting in personal injury or death any person and consequential damages arising therefrom, including comprehensive property damage insurance, in the amount of $2,000,000 with respect to bodily injury or death to any one or more persons and $100,000 with respect to damage to property. Operator shall furnish to the City, on or before the effective date of any such policy, evidence that the insurance referred to in this subsection a. of Section 9 is in force and effect and that the premiums therefor have been paid;

(2) Maintain or cause to be maintained, fire and extended coverage insurance in an amount at least equal to 90% of the replacement cost (as defined below in subsection c. of this Section 9) of the Parking Facilities to insure against loss or damage to the Parking Facilities resulting from risks ordinarily within the classification of fire and extended coverage and especially against the following perils: fire, wind storm, cyclone, tornado, hail, explosion, riot, riot attending a strike, civil commotion, malicious mischief, vandalism, aircraft, vehicle, smoke damage and sprinkler leakage. Such insurance shall be carried with financially responsible insurance companies and may be carried under a policy or policies covering other property owned by the Operator; provided, that such policy or policies shall allocate to the Parking Facilities an amount not less than 90% of the replacement cost of the Parking Facilities.

Operator shall furnish to the City prior to the effective date of any such policy, evidence that the insurance required by this subsection is in force and effect and that premiums therefor have been paid.

(3) Maintain or cause to be maintained workmen's compensation insurance issued by a responsible carrier authorized under the laws of the State of California to insure employers against liability for compensation under the Workmen's Compensation Insurance and Safety Act now in force in California, or any act hereafter enacted as an amendment or supplement thereto or in lieu thereof, such workmen's compensation insurance to cover all persons employed by Operator or the REA Parties in connection with the Parking Facilities and to cover full liability for compensation under any such act aforesaid, based upon death or bodily injury claims made by, for or on behalf of any person incurring or suffering injury or death during or in connection with the Parking Facilities or the operation thereof by the Authority, Citv or Operator.

(4) Maintain or cause to be maintained such additional earthquake insurance coverage, not provided by City pursuant to Section 9.b.(1) below, as Operator shall desire.

b. *Obligations of City.* To the extent required under the provisions of the Master Lease or the REA, the City without cost or expense to the Operator shall:

(1) Keep or cause to be kept the Parking Facilities insured by earthquake insurance (if such insurance is obtainable on the open market from reputable insurance companies) against loss or damage by earthquake in an amount not less than the full replacement cost of the Parking Facilities (as defined below in subsection c. of this Section 9) or the amount of the outstanding bonds of the Authority, whichever amount is greater, with deductible conditions of not to exceed 10% for any one loss; and

(2) Maintain or cause to be maintained use and occupancy or business interruption or rental income insurance against the perils of earthquake and/or fire, lightning, vandalism and malicious mischief and such other perils ordinarily included in "extended coverage" fire insurance policies, in an amount equal to not less than twelve (12) months' rental under the Master Lease. Provided, however, that the City, at its option, may elect that the insurance under this subsection b. shall be maintained by the Operator, in which event the Operator may deduct the amount of premiums paid by the Operator and allocable to said insurance from the Base Rental due under this Sublease. In the event that the cost of such insurance exceeds the amount of Base Rental, after adjustment, payable to the City, the City shall reimburse the Operator for the amount of such excess. At any time during the term of this Sublease the City may rescind its election and maintain said insurance itself.

c. *Definition of Term "Replacement Cost."* The term "replacement cost" as used in this Section 9 shall mean the actual cost of replacing the Parking Facilities (including amounts for construction, architectural, engineering, legal and administrative fees, and inspection and supervision during construction, and the cost of restoring surface grounds owned or leased by the Authority or the City, but excluding (i) the cost of restoring trees, plants and shrubs, (ii) the cost of Common Building Components and structural elements and support paid for or contributed to by the REA Parties, (iii) as to fire and extended coverage insurance, the cost of excavation, foundation and footings below the lowest floor and without deduction for depreciation, and (iv) as to earthquake insurance, the cost of excavation) using the items of value set forth parenthetically above. Said replacement cost shall be determined from time to time but not less frequently than once in every 36 months.

d. *General Provisions.* All insurance provided under subsection a. of this Section 9 shall be for the benefit of the Operator, Authority, Agency and City, as named insureds, during the term of the Master Lease and thereafter for the benefit of the Agdncy, City and Operator, as named insureds.

All insurance provided under subsection a. of this Section 9 shall be periodically reviewed by the parties for the purpose of mutually increasing the minimum limits of such insurance, from time to time, to amounts which may be reasonable and customary for similar facilities of like size and operation.

All insurance provided under subsection b. of this Section 9 shall be for the benefit of the Authority and the City, as named insureds, during the term of the Master Lease and thereafter for the benefit of the City and the Operator, as named insureds, and the insurance provided under subsection b.(1) shall also be for the benefit of the Operator and the REA Parties as their interests may appear under the REA, as named insureds. Adjustment of any losses shall be made by Authority or City in consultation with Operator.

All insurance herein provided for under this Section 9 shall be effected under policies issued by insurers of recognized responsibility, licensed or permitted to do business in the State of ______________________.

All policies or certificates issued by the respective insurers for insurance shall provide that such policies or certificates shall not be cancelled or materially changed without at least thirty (30) days' prior written notice to the Operator, the City, the Treasurer of the Authority, and the Trustee under the Authority's bonds. Copies of such policies shall be deposited with the City, the Treasurer of the Authority, and the Trustee under the Authority's bonds, together with appropriate evidence of payment of the premiums therefor; and, at least thirty (30) days prior to expiration dates of expiring policies or contracts held by said Treasurer and said Trustee, copies of renewal or new policies or contracts or certificates shall be deposited with said Treasurer and said Trustee.

All proceeds of insurance with respect to loss or damage to the Parking Facilities during the term of the Master Lease shall be paid to the Authority to be applied as provided in Section 10 hereof. All proceeds of insurance with respect to loss or damage to the Parking Facilities after the expiration of the term of the Master Lease shall be paid to the City.

Section 10. Damage to the Parking Facilities. Damage to or destruction of the Parking Facilities by fire or other casualty or event so that the Parking Facilities become wholly or partially unusable shall be governed by Paragraph 1 of Section 8 of the Master Lease, and Sections XIII, F and G, of the REA, and the term "Project" as used in the Master Lease shall be understood to refer to the Parking Facilities under this Agreement. In implementation of Section 8 of the Master Lease, and Section XIII, F and G, of the REA, insofar as they may pertain to this Sublease, the City and Operator agree as follows:

a. *City's Obligation.* Whenever under the terms of the REA the Parking Facilities or any part thereof are required to be repaired or rebuilt, the City will cause the Authority to repair or rebuild the Parking Facilities or will undertake itself to repair or rebuild the Parking Facilities, and will give such consents as may be required under Section 8 of the Master Lease for such action, subject to the following conditions:

(1) This Sublease is in effect;

(2) Either the Authority or the City have the legal capacity to so repair or rebuild the Parking Facilities;

(3) There is a lawful and sufficient source of funds, including the proceeds of any insurance (other than use or occupancy insurance) maintained upon the Parking Facilities, and including contributions from any REA Party available to either the Authority, the City, or the Agency, so to repair, rebuild or reconstruct the Parking Facilities, or, if bonds must be issued by either the Authority or City or Agency, said bonds may be lawfully issued and sold in accordance with generally accepted standards of feasibility based upon similar terms as those applicable to the Authority's initial lease revenue bonds issued in connection with the Master Lease to provide funds to acquire and construct the Parking Facilities. Following the first thirty (30) years of the term of the REA, such bonds need not be issued and sold, or any other indebtedness need not be incurred, unless and until (i) at least two (2) of the Majors to the REA, in a written agreement in recordable form, agree to Operate for a ten (10) year period commencing on the earlier of the date of completion of such repair, rebuilding or reconstruction or eighteen (18) months after the date of such damage or destruction, and (ii) Operator offers to extend the term of this Sublease for a similar ten (10) year period.

(4) Cn addition to the provisions of Section XIII-J of the REA, if all or part of the shopping center (excluding the office building), other than the Parking Facilities, is damaged or destroyed, the obligation of the Authority, or the City, as the case may be, shall be to restore only so much of the Parking Facilities as shall be required to maintain the parking ratio specified in Section IV-A of the REA within four hundred feet (400') of each Store (as defined in the REA) after the repair, rebuilding or reconstruction of such damaged portions, in such manner that the Parking Facilities so restored shall constitute an operational unit.

b. *Operator Reconstruction.* In the event that the City is not required under subsection a. of this Section 10 to repair or rebuild the Parking Facilities or any portion thereof so damaged or destroyed, the Operator, with the consent of the City, may undertake to repair or rebuild the Parking Facilities or portion thereof damaged or destroyed under such terms and conditions, including the abatement of Base Rental, as the City shall have consented to. If it undertakes to repair or rebuild the Parking Facilities pursuant to this subsection b., the Operator shall be entitled to use insurance proceeds for that purpose, to the extent that said proceeds may lawfully be paid to the Operator for such purpose.

c. *Operator Options If City Does Not Reconstruct.* In the event that the City is not required under subsection a. of this Section 10 to repair or rebuild the Parking Facilities or any portion thereof so damaged or destroyed, the Operator shall have the option, exercisable upon ninety (90) days written notice following the date that it is deemed that the City is not required so to repair or rebuild the Parking Facilities, to: (i) terminate this Sublease as to the portion of the Parking Facilities not repaired or rebuilt; or (ii) purchase the Parking Facilities (in their entirety and in their damaged or destroyed condition) for a purchase price equal to the greater of the principal amount, plus interest and other charges and costs, required to pay off and fully retire any indebtedness of the Authority, Agency or City or any agency thereof incurred to acquire and construct or repair or rebuild the Parking Facilities or the fair market value of the Parking Facilities and underlying land or air rights, as the case may be, in their damaged condition, which market value shall be determined by the appraisal procedure set forth in subsection 2.d. of this Sublease, provided, however, that the value of air rights and improvements therein shall not be included in such fair market value to the extent that a right of re-entry or reverter has been exercised in accordance with grant deed provisions so that title thereto will not remain in the Parking Authority or City, as the case may be.

d. *Abatement of Base Rental.* During such time as the Parking Facilities are unusable, Base Rental shall cease. No further Base Rental payments shall accrue until the Parking Facilities are again ready for occupancy, and Base Rental payments already made, if any, shall be equitably abated and adjusted accordingly. In the event of partial damage to, or destruction of, the Parking Facilities, so as to render a portion thereof unusable by the Operator, such Base Rental payments (including those already made, if any) shall, during the period of the partial unusability of the Parking Facilities, be prorated to correspond with the proportion that the number of usable parking spaces bears to the total original number of parking spaces in the Parking Facilities.

Section 11. Assignment and Sublease.

a. *Prohibited.* Neither this Sublease nor any interest of the Operator herein shall, at any time after the date hereof, without the prior written consent of the City, be mortgaged, pledged, assigned or transferred by the Operator by voluntary act or by operation of law, or otherwise, except as provided herein, in Section 5 hereof, and in Section X-H of the REA. Notwithstanding the foregoing, Operator may make any mortgage, pledge, assignment or transfer of the Operator's interest under this Sublease (but not of this Sublease itself or any interest of the Authority or City herein or in the Parking Facilities) required for any reasonable and customary method of construction or permanent financing of the Operator's shopping center land and improvements without the City's consent, provided that no additional obligation or burden is imposed on the Authority or the City as a result thereof; and provided, further, that all rights acquired under any such mortgage, pledge, assignment or transfer shall be subject to each and all of the covenants, conditions and restrictions set forth in this Sublease, and to all rights and interests of the Authority and the City herein, none of which covenants, conditions or restrictions is or shall be waived by the City by reason of giving its consent hereunder. Operator shall give Authority and City written notice of any such mortgage, pledge, assignment or transfer together with a written representation by the Operator that the provisions of this Section 11.a. are not violated. The Operator shall at all times remain liable for the performance of the covenants and conditions on its part to be performed, notwithstanding any assigning, transferring or subletting which may be made.

b. *Designation of Operator.* The City recognizes that the REA provides therein for the management, maintenance and operation of the Parking Facilities by the "Operator" (as said term is defined in the REA, the initial "Operator" under the REA is the lessee under this Sublease). The REA further provides that upon the occurrence of certain events a successor to the Operator may be appointed to undertake such management, maintenance and operation of the Parking Facilities. In the event such successor is so appointed in accordance with the terms of the REA, the City hereby agrees to accept performance by such successor of such management, maintenance and operation without relieving the Operator hereunder of its liability unless the City shall have expressly approved in writing the financial capability and responsibility of the successor Operator.

Section 12. Eminent Domain.

a. *Complete Taking.* If the whole of the Parking Facilities shall be taken under the power of eminent domain or sold to any governmental agency threatening to exercise the power of eminent domain, the provisions of Section 11 of the Master Lease and Section XVI of the REA shall govern, and the term "Project" as used in the Master Lease shall be understood to refer to the Parking Facilities under this Sublease. In implementation of Section 11 of the Master Lease and Section XVI of the REA, insofar as they may pertain under this Sublease, the City and Operator agree that if the whole of the Parking Facilities, or so much thereof as to render the remainder unusable for parking purposes so that the REA is terminated pursuant to Section XVI-D thereof, shall be taken under the power of eminent domain or sold to any governmental agency threatening to exercise the power of eminent domain, then this Sublease shall terminate.

b. *Partial Taking.* If less than the whole of the Parking Facilities shall be taken under the power of eminent domain or sold to any governmental agency threatening to exercise the power of eminent domain, and the remainder is usable for parking purposes so that the REA is not terminated pursuant to Section XVI-D thereof, the provisions of paragraph 1 of Section 8 of the Master Lease and Section XVI of the REA shall govern, and the term "Project" as used in the Master Lease shall be understood to refer to the Parking Facilities under this Sublease. In the event of any taking by eminent domain Base Rental hereunder shall proportionately abate for any period during which all or any portion of Parking Facilities are unusable by Operator. In implementation of paragraph 1 of Section 8 of the Master Lease and Section XVI of the REA, insofar as they may pertain to this Sublease, the City and Operator agree that whenever under the terms of the REA the Parking Facilities are required to be restored or rebuilt, the City will cause the Authority to restore or rebuild the Parking Facilities or will undertake itself to restore or rebuild the Parking Facilities, and will give such consents as may be required under paragraph 1 of Section 8 of the Master Lease for such action, subject to the same conditions to such restoration or rebuilding as are set forth in subsection 10.a. of this Sublease for repair or rebuilding of the Parking Facilities.

c. In the event that the City is not required under subsections a. or b. of this Section 12 to restore or rebuild the Parking Facilities or any portion thereof so taken by eminent domain, the Operator, with the consent of the City, may undertake to restore or rebuild the Parking Facilities or portion thereof so taken by eminent domain under such terms and conditions, including the abatement of Base Rental, as the City shall have consented to. If it undertakes to restore or rebuild the Parking Facilities pursuant to this subsection c., the Operator shall be entitled to use proceeds from any eminent domain award, to the extent that such proceeds may lawfully be paid to Operator for such purpose.

d. Any award made in eminent domain proceedings for the taking or damaging of the Parking Facilities in whole or in part, or any proceeds received from the sale thereof, shall be applied to the restoration of the Parking Facilities to the extent that such restoration is required pursuant to this Sublease. To the extent that restoration is not required pursuant to this Sublease, any award made to the Authority or the City shall be paid to the Authority or, if the term of the Master Lease has expired, such proceeds shall be paid to the City. The Operator shall have no interest in or thereto and shall not be entitled to any part of such award; provided, however, that nothing herein shall prevent the Operator and those claiming under or through the Operator from separately claiming any damages against the condemning agency which may be lawfully claimed by the Operator or such persons by reason of damage to or taking of property of the Operator or such persons, including their interests under this Sublease as the same may appear.

Section 13. Voluntary Termination. Surrender.

a. *Voluntary Termination.* Subject to the consent of the Agency and with the prior consent of the Majors (as the term "Majors" is defined in the REA), the City and the Operator may mutually terminate this Sublease or may modify the terms and provisions hereof. Notwithstanding the provisions of Section 4.b. hereof, after the term of the Master Lease expires and provided there are no outstanding and unpaid bonds or other indebtedness of the Agency, Authority or City issued or incurred with respect to the Parking Facilities, and subject to the provisions of Sections 10 and 11 hereof, the City or the Operator, at the election of either, by one hundred twenty (120) days prior written notice to the other, may terminate this Sublease if the REA shall be terminated for any reason as provided therein. In the event of such termination pursuant to the provisions of the foregoing sentence, the provisions of Section 2.d. of this Sublease shall not apply.

b. *Surrender upon Termination.* Upon the termination of this Sublease, the Operator agrees that it shall surrender to the City the Parking Facilities in good order and condition and in a state of repair that is consistent with prudent use and conscientious maintenance except for reasonable wear and tear, and except for any damage to the Parking Facilities caused by casualty or by a taking as a result of eminent domain proceedings which result in termination of the Sublease.

Section 14. Liens. The Operator agrees to pay, when due, all sums of money that may become due for, or purporting to be due for, any labor, services, materials, supplies or equipment alleged to have been furnished or to be furnished to or for the Operator in, upon or about the Parking Facilities and which may be secured by mechanics', materialmen's or other liens against the Parking Facilities, and/or the interests of the City or Authority therein, and will cause each such lien to be fully discharged and released at the time the performance of any obligation secured by such lien matures and/or becomes due; provided, however, that if Operator desires to contest any such lien, it may do so upon providing City with a bond or other lawful security such as a guarantee, in form and amount satisfactory to City, to guarantee payment of such lien and provided, further, that notwithstanding any such contest, if any such lien shall be reduced to final judgment and such judgment or such process as may be issued for the enforcement thereof is not promptly stayed, or if so stayed and said stay thereafter expires, then and in such event the Operator shall forthwith pay and discharge said judgment.

Section 15. Quiet Enjoyment. The parties hereto mutually covenant and agree that the Operator, by keeping and performing the covenants and agreements herein contained, shall at all times during the term hereof, peaceably and quietly, have, hold and enjoy the Parking Facilities, without suit, trouble or hindrance from the City.

Section 16. Vesting. Anything to the contrary in this Sublease notwithstanding, the interest provided for in this Sublease shall vest, and the term thereof begin, if at all, not later than the number of years specified and set forth in Sections ________ and ________ of the Civil Code of the State of ____________________, said specific period of years to be measured from the date of this Sublease.

Section 17. Law Governing. This Sublease shall be governed by the laws of the State of ____________________ ____________, subject to the waivers, exclusions and provisions herein contained.

Section 18. Notices. All notices, statements, demands, requests, consents, approvals, authorizations, offers, agreements, appointments or designations hereunder by either party to the other shall be in writing and shall be sufficiently given and served upon the other party, if sent by United States registered mail, return receipt requested, postage prepaid and addressed as follows:

City—______________________________
____
____

Operator—______________________________
____
____

or at such other address as either party shall later designate for such purpose by written notice to the other party.

Section 19. Waiver. The waiver by the City of any breach by the Operator of any term, covenant or condition hereof shall not operate as a waiver of any subsequent breach of the same or any other term, covenant or condition hereof.

Section 20. Default by Operator. If (a) the Operator shall fail to pay any rental payable hereunder within 30 days from the date such rental is payable, or (b) the Operator shall fail to observe or perform any such other terms, covenants or conditions contained herein for a period of 60 days after written notice thereof from the City to the Operator, or (c) the Operator shall abandon or vacate the Parking Facilities, or (d) the Operator's interest in this Sublease or any part hereof shall be assigned or transferred without the written consent of the City, either voluntarily or by operation of law, except as permitted hereunder, or (e) the Operator shall file any petition or institute any proceedings wherein or whereby the Operator asks or seeks or prays to be adjudicated a bankrupt, or to be discharged from any or all of its debts or obligations, or offers to the Operator's creditors to effect a composition or extension of time to pay the Operator's debts, or asks, seeks or prays for a reorganization or to effect a plan or reorganization, or for a readjustment of the Operator's debts, or for any other similar relief, then and in any of such events, the Operator shall be deemed to be in default hereunder.

If the Operator should, after notice of such default, fail to remedy any default or commence the correction thereof with all reasonable dispatch, in not exceeding 30 days, (with respect to failure to pay any rent) or in not exceeding 60 days (with respect to the failure to observe or perform any other term, covenant or condition contained herein; provided, that if such default cannot be cured within 60 days, Operator does not commence the correction thereof with all reasonable dispatch within said 60 days), then the City shall have the right, at its option, without any further demand or notice:

(i) to terminate this Sublease and to re-enter the Parking Facilities and eject all parties in possession therefrom, in which case this Sublease shall terminate, and the Operator shall have no further claim hereunder; or

(ii) to continue this Sublease in effect for so long as it does not terminate the Operator's right to possession, in which case it may enforce all of its rights and remedies hereunder, including the right to recover rent and other charges required to be paid by the Operator as they become due.

In the event the City terminates this Sublease as hereinabove provided, the City shall be entitled to recover as damages all of the following:

(a) The worth at the time of the award of any unpaid rent or other charges which had been earned at the time of termination;

(b) The worth at the time of the award of the amount by which the unpaid rent and other charges which would have been earned after termination until the time of the award exceeds the amount of the loss of such rental or other charges that the Operator proves could have been reasonably avoided;

(c) The worth at the time of the award of the amount by which the unpaid rent and other charges for the balance of the term after the time of the award exceeds the amount of the loss of such rental and other charges that the Operator proves could have been reasonably avoided;

(d) Any other amount necessary to compensate the City for the detriment proximately caused by the Operator's failure to perform its obligations under this Sublease or which in the ordinary course of things would be likely to result therefrom.

The foregoing remedies of the City are in addition to and not exclusive of any other remedy of the City. Any such re-entry shall be allowed by the Operator without hindrance and the City shall not be liable in damages for such re-entry or be guilty of trespass.

Section 21. Rights of Others to Cure Default by Operator.

a. *By Parties to the REA.*

(1) The City shall, upon serving the Operator with any notice of default under this Sublease, simultaneously serve a copy of said notice upon each of the other parties to the REA at the last address designated by said party pursuant to the REA. Each of said parties shall thereupon have fifteen (15) days more time than is given to the Operator to cure any such default or commence the correction thereof in accordance with the terms of this Sublease, and the City shall accept such performance by or at the instigation of the other parties to the REA, or any of them, as if the same had been done by the Operator.

(2) Anything herein contained notwithstanding, while the REA remains in effect, if any event or events of default shall occur which, under the provisions of this Sublease shall entitle City to terminate this Sublease, City shall give Operator and each of the other parties to the REA written notice of City's election to terminate this

Sublease and if before the expiration of twenty (20) days from the date of service of said termination notice the other parties to the REA, or any of them, shall have paid to City all rent and additional rent due, plus interest thereon at seven percent (7%) from the due date, shall have paid to the proper governmental authorities all taxes and assessments that may then be due, including any and all delinquency payments, late charges and interest, shall have made all payments of insurance premiums on policies required under this Sublease, and shall have made such other payments of money as required in this Sublease which are then in default and shall have fully complied within the time period specified in this Sublease as extended hereby for such compliance, or shall have taken or proceeded to take all reasonably practicable steps to the satisfaction of City in order to remedy such event or events of default and has diligently proceeded to perform all the other requirements of this Sublease, if any, which are then in default, then in such event City shall not be entitled to terminate this Sublease and any notice of termination therefor given shall not result in a cancellation of this Sublease and shall be of no further force and effect.

b. *By Operator's Mortgagee.*

(1) The City shall, upon serving the Operator with any notice of default under this Sublease, simultaneously serve a copy of said Notice upon any mortgagee or secured lender of Operator (as referred to in Section 11 of this Sublease) requesting said notice at the last address designated by said mortgagee or lender. Unless the other parties to the REA, or any of them, shall first have cured any such default or shall have commenced the correction thereof as provided in subsection a. of this Section 21, said mortgagee or secured lender shall thereupon have fifteen (15) more days time than is given to the other parties to the REA under subsection a. of this Section 21 to cure any such default or commence the correction thereof in accordance with the terms of this Sublease, and the City shall accept such performance by or at the instigation of said mortgagee or secured lender as if the same had been done by the Operator.

(2) Anything herein contained notwithstanding, while such mortgagee or secured lender (as referred to in Section 11 of this Sublease) remains unsatisfied of record, if an event or events of default shall occur, which under any provision of this Sublease shall entitle City to terminate this Sublease, and if before the expiration of thirty (30) days of the date of service of said notice, such mortgagee or secured lender shall have paid to City all rental and additional rental and other payments herein provided for, and then in default, and shall have complied or shall have engaged in the work of complying with all of the other requirements of this Sublease within the time limits prescribed herein, if any are then in default, then in such event City shall not be entitled to terminate this Sublease and any notice of termination theretofore given shall be void and of no effect.

(3) If the City shall elect to terminate this Sublease by reason of any default of the Operator, such mortgagee or secured lender shall not only have and be subrogated to any and all rights of the Operator with respect to curing such default, but shall also have the right to postpone and extend the specified date for the termination of this Sublease as fixed by the City in its notice of termination, for a period of not more than six (6) months, provided such mortgagee or secured lender shall cure or cause to be cured any then existing money defaults and meanwhile pay the rent, additional rent and comply with and perform all of the other terms, conditions and provisions of this Sublease on the Operator's part to be complied with and performed, and if no further defaults shall occur hereunder during such extended period, and mortgagee or secured lender shall forthwith take steps to acquire the Operator's interest herein, the time of said mortgagee or secured lender to comply with the provisions of this Section shall be extended for such period as shall be necessary to complete such steps with due diligence and continuity, provided that during any such extensions no further default by the Operator or mortgagee or secured lender shall be permitted to continue hereunder.

(4) City agrees within ten (10) days after the request in writing by the Operator or such mortgagee or secured lender, to furnish the party requesting same with a written statement duly acknowledged of the fact that this Sublease is in full force and effect and that there are no defaults hereunder by the Operator, if such is the fact. If any defaults then exist, City agrees that in such statement it will specify the particular default or defaults which City claims to exist.

(5) City agrees that in the event of termination of this Sublease by reason of any default by Operator other than for nonpayment of rent or additional rent and other payments herein provided for, that the City will acknowledge the holder of any mortgage or trust deed permitted under Section 21 of this Sublease or its nominee (the mortgagee or trustee) shall be entitled to enter into a new Sublease of the Parking Facilities as the new Operator with all of the rights and obligations of the Operator hereunder for the remainder of the term, which new Sublease shall be effective as of the date of such termination, and shall be at the rent and upon the terms, provisions, covenants and agreements as herein contained and subject only to the same conditions of title as this Sublease is subject on the date of the execution hereof, and to the rights, if any, of any parties then in possession of any part of the leased premises, provided:

(a) Said mortgagee shall make written request upon City for such new Sublease within thirty (30) days after the date of such termination and such written request is accompanied by payment to the City of sums then due to the City under this Sublease.

(b) Said mortgagee shall pay to the City at such time of execution of the new Sublease any and all sums which would at such time be due under this Sublease but for such termination and in addition thereto any expenses including legal and attorneys' fees which the City necessarily shall have paid by reason of such default.

(c) Said mortgagee or its nominee shall perform and observe all covenants herein contained on the Operator's part to be performed and shall further remedy any other conditions which the prior Operator was obligated to perform under the terms of this Sublease.

The Operator under such substitution shall have the same right, title and interest in and to the buildings and improvements on the leased premises as the Operator had under this Sublease.

(6) As used in this Section, all reference to a "mortgage" shall be deemed to include a Deed of Trust, and all reference to the "holder" of a mortgage or to a "mortgagee" shall be deemed to include the beneficiary and/or trustee under a Deed of Trust.

Section 22. Right of Agency to Cure Default by City under Master Lease. Notwithstanding anything herein to the contrary, the Agency shall have the right to cure any default of the City under the Master Lease or under this Sublease and thereby prevent the Master Lease or this Sublease from terminating and, in such event, the Agency at its option shall be recognized under this Sublease as the successor to the City and this Sublease shall remain in full force and effect and binding upon the Operator.

Section 23. Net Lease. This Sublease shall be deemed and construed to be a "net lease" and the Operator hereby agrees that the rental provided for herein shall be an absolute net return to the City free and clear of any expenses, charges or setoffs whatsoever except as provided in subsection a. of Section 4 hereof.

Section 24. Nondiscrimination. The Operator covenants by and for itself, administrators and assigns, and all persons claiming under or through it, and this Sublease is made and accepted upon and subject to the following conditions:

That there shall be no discrimination against or segregation of any person or group of persons, on account of sex, race, color, creed, national origin or ancestry, in the leasing, subleasing, transferring, use or enjoyment of the premises herein leased nor shall the Operator itself, or any person claiming under or through it, establish or permit any such practice or practices of discrimination or segregation with reference to the selection, location, number, use or occupancy, of tenants, lessees, sublessees, subtenants or vendees in the premises herein leased.

Section 25. Indemnification. The City and the Authority shall not be liable at any time for any loss, damage or injury to the property or person of any person whomsoever at any time occasioned by or arising out of any act or omission of the Operator, or of anyone holding under the Operator or the occupancy or use of the Parking Facilities or any part thereof by or under the Operator, or directly or indirectly from any state or condition of the Parking Facilities or any part thereof during the term of this Sublease except for the intentional acts or omissions of the City or the Authority.

Notwithstanding anything to the contrary under this Sublease, and irrespective of any insurance carried by the Operator for the benefit of the City and the Authority, the Operator agrees to protect, defend, indemnify and hold the City and the Authority and the Parking Facilities harmless from any and all damages or liabilities of whatsoever nature arising under the terms of this Sublease or arising out of or in connection with the operation carried on by Operator on, or the use and occupancy of, the Parking Facilities.

Section 26. Attorneys' Fees and Court Costs. In the event that either the City or the Operator shall bring or commence an action to enforce the terms and conditions of this Sublease or to obtain damages against the other party arising from any default under or violation of this Sublease, then the prevailing party shall be entitled to and shall be paid reasonable attorneys' fees and court costs therefor.

Section 27. Execution. This Sublease may be simultaneously executed in any number of counterparts, each of which when so executed shall be deemed to be an original, but all together shall constitute but one and the same Sublease, and it is also understood and agreed that separate counterparts of this Sublease may be separately executed by the City and the Operator, all with the same full force and effect as though the same counterpart had been executed simultaneously by both the City and the Operator.

Section 28. Validity. If any one or more of the terms, provisions, promises, covenants, conditions or option provisions of this Sublease shall to any extent be adjudged invalid, unenforceable, void or voidable for any reason whatsoever by a court of competent jurisdiction, each and all of the remainingnterms, provisions, promises, covenants, conditions, and option provisions of this Sublease shall not be affected thereby and shall be valid and enforceable to the fullest extent permitted by law.

If for any reason this Sublease shall be held by a court of competent jurisdiction, void, voidable or unenforceable by the City or by the Operator, or if for any reason it is held by such court that the covenants and conditions of the Operator hereunder, including the covenant to pay rent hereunder, is unenforceable for the full term hereunder, then and in such event for and in consideration of the right of the Operator to possess, occupy and use the Parking Facilities, which right in such event is hereby granted, this Sublease shall thereupon become, and shall be deemed to be, a lease from year to year under which the annual rentals herein specified will be paid by the Operator.

Section 29. Binding Effect. This Sublease, and the terms, provisions, promises, covenants, conditions and option provisions hereof, shall be binding upon and shall inure to the benefit of the parties hereto and their respective heirs, legal representatives, successors and assigns.

IN WITNESS WHEREOF, the parties hereto have caused this Sublease to be executed and attested by their proper officers thereunto duly authorized, and their official seals to be hereto affixed, as of the day and year first above written.

CITY OF

By _____

Mayor

ATTEST:

_____

City Clerk

APPENDIX M

The Gallery at Market East
Mall Maintenance Contribution Agreement

THIS AGREEMENT is made as of the _______ day of _________________, __________, by and between ____, a duly organized body under the laws of the Commonwealth of Pennsylvania ("Philadelphia"), THE REDEVELOPMENT AUTHORITY OF THE CITY OF PHILADELPHIA (the "Authority"), a public body and a body corporate and politic, duly created and organized pursuant to and in accordance with the provisions of the Urban Redevelopment Law of May 24, 1945, of the Commonwealth of Pennsylvania as the same may have been supplemented to date, GIMBEL BROTHERS, INC. ("Gimbels"), a New York corporation, STRAWBRIDGE & CLOTHIER ("S&C"), a Pennsylvania corporation, ROUSE PHILADELPHIA, INC. ("Rouse"), a Maryland corporation, and MALL MAINTENANCE CORPORATION ("MMC"), a Pennsylvania corporation.

WITNESSETH:

WHEREAS, the Authority and Rouse entered into a lease concerning the project generally known as The Gallery at Market East, which lease is dated as of December 16, 1975 (the "Lease"); and

WHEREAS, pursuant to the Gimbel Agreement (as defined below) and the Lease, the Authority desires to assign certain of its rights and obligations under the Lease and the Gimbel Agreement to a separate maintenance corporation; and

WHEREAS, Gimbels has entered into an agreement with the Authority dated June 25, 1974, concerning, inter alia, the maintenance of the lands comprising aforesaid project (the "Gimbel Agreement"); and

WHEREAS, S&C has agreed herein to make a contribution toward the maintenance of the land and improvements of the aforesaid project; and

WHEREAS, having leased to the Authority certain premises above and below Ninth Street within the above project area pursuant to two leases both dated January 30, 1976 (the "City Leases"), the City of Philadelphia (the "City") desires to provide for part of the maintenance of the public's access through the Public Areas under the Lease and under the Gimbel Agreement, and therefore the City has agreed by separate instrument dated _____________________________, 1977, to provide the necessary funds to Philadelphia for Philadelphia to carry out its obligations under this Agreement; and

WHEREAS, Philadelphia, the Authority, Gimbels, S&C and Rouse have approved the formation of MMC in accordance with the by-laws. . . .

NOW, THEREFORE, in consideration of the above agreements and for other valuable consideration, receipt of which is hereby acknowledged by each party to the other, the parties hereby agree as follows:

ARTICLE I
Definitions

Section 1.1.

(A) For the purposes of this Agreement, the term "Maintenance Obligation" shall mean the totality of: (i) all maintenance and related obligations of the Authority and MMC and all maintenance obligations of Gimbels to be performed pursuant to the terms of Sections 3A.14 through 3A.17 and the obligation to provide liability insurance as provided for in Section 3A.13 of the Gimbel Agreement and (ii) all maintenance and related obligations of the Authority and MMC under Sections 8.2, 8.3 and 8.4 of the Lease; all as the same may be expanded by the Mall Maintenance Corporation Policies. . . . Said obligations are also referred to in Section 2 of the MMC By-Laws.

(B) For the purposes of this Agreement the term "Total Cost" shall mean the total expense incurred by MMC to perform or cause to be performed the Maintenance Obligation including without limitation: (i) to police and provide security, operate and maintain the Public Area as defined under the Lease which shall include but shall not be limited to the cleaning, window-washing, landscaping, lighting, ventilating, heating, air-cooling and repair including any necessary replacement of the enclosed pedestrian mall areas (exclusive of any windows forming part of the premises leased by Rouse as landlord to any tenant), keeping the sidewalks and other Public Area paving repaired and properly drained and free of ice, surface water, snow, litter and rubbish, and planting, replanting and replacing flowers and landscaping and installing and maintaining such directional signs, markers and painted lines as from time to time may be necessary or proper for the control and safety of traffic, loading and unloading within the truck and tunnel and dock facilities, (ii) to clean and keep in good order and repair (including any necesssary replacement), all fixtures and other installations in the Public Area including, but not limited to pools, fountains, telephone booths, vending machines, benches and the like, and (iii) to clean the stairways and walkways of the retail area pursuant to Section 8.3 of the Lease between the Redevelopment Authority and Rouse.

(C) For the purposes of this Agreement the term "Fiscal Year" shall mean the twelve calendar month period beginning on _______________ and ending _______________ during the term of this Agreement.

ARTICLE II
Department Store Contributions

Section 2.1.

(A) During Term "B" of the Lease, Gimbels hereby agrees to contribute to MMC an annual sum set forth in Section 2.1(B) towards performance by or on behalf of MMC of the Maintenance Obligation as herein defined in full payment of all obligations of Gimbels including without limitation the obligations of Gimbels under the Gimbel Agreement to maintain the Mall or parts thereof and to contribute to the cost of such maintenance all as provided in Sections 3A.14, to and including 3A.17 of the Gimbel Agreement. Gimbels, the Authority and MMC specifically agree that such contribution shall be used solely to cover or pay part of the Total Costs including the costs of maintenance, repair and replacement, insurance, and other expenses provided for in the Gimbel Agreement. Gimbels and the Authority further agree that it shall not be deemed thereby that Gimbels has waived with respect to the Authority any provision of Section 3A.17 of the Gimbel Agreement.

(B) The "Gimbels Contribution" shall be the greater of the following: (i) One Hundred Thousand Dollars ($100,000.00) or (ii) a proportionate share of the Total Cost to perform the Maintenance Obligation, equal to the present proposed share of Gimbels in the estimated budget for the Total Cost which share is $100,000/$625,000 or 16.0%. . . . The amount of Gimbels Contribution shall be estimated by MMC each Fiscal Year based on MMC's approved budget for that year, and on the first day of each calendar month during the Fiscal Year Gimbels shall pay to MMC one-twelfth (1/12) of the estimated Gimbels Contribution. Within thirty (30) days after the end of the Fiscal Year MMC shall (i) inform Gimbels of any overpayment by Gimbels of the Gimbels Contribution and credit such amount to the earliest unpaid installment of the Gimbels Contribution for the then current Fiscal Year, or (ii) request the adjustment and payment to MMC by Gimbels of any underpayment of the Gimbels Contribution by Gimbels paying such amount to MMC within thirty (30) days of such notice of underpayment; if no such information under clause (i) is given by MMC and no protest is made by Gimbels within one hundred fifty (150) days after the end of said preceding Fiscal Year or, if no such request under clause (ii) is made by MMC within such time period, the obligations of Gimbels to make the Gimbel Contribution for such preceding Fiscal Year shall be deemed paid correctly and in full.

Section 2.2.

Each year Gimbels shall only be obligated to make the Gimbels Contribution if and so long as: (i) Rouse or any other subsidiary or affiliate of The Rouse Company is (a) the Lessee of the Retail Area in the Property of the Authority extending from approximately the store of S&C through the recently constructed Gimbel Building and to the north side of Tenth Street in Philadelphia, Pennsylvania (as more particularly set forth in the Gimbel Agreement and the Lease), and (b) principally involved in the supervision and management of the Maintenance Obligation including the maintenance of the public improvements, public areas and related space of said Mall; (ii) Philadelphia (or the Authority), S&C and Rouse shall each have made or be legally obligated to make their Contributions as required in this Agreement and if requested by Gimbels, such condition shall be certified to by an executive officer of MMC; (iii) the Authority shall have assigned to MMC all Contributions related to the Maintenance Obligation which are payable to or may have been paid to the Authority or, if such Contributions are not assigned to MMC hereunder, the Authority shall have segregated such Contributions for the payment of the Total Costs herein; and (iv) MMC shall not have defaulted as provided in Section 6.1 hereunder in the performance of the Maintenance Obligation. In addition, a condition of Gimbels making any contribution in excess of One Hundred Thousand Dollars ($100,000) in the first Fiscal Year or, in any year thereafter, in excess of the Gimbels Contribution payable for the previous Fiscal Year shall be that no material increase shall be made in the scope of services or other obligations being provided by MMC as part of the Maintenance Obligation unless such change shall have been approved by Gimbels. Such increase in scope shall include, without limitation, a material increase in the hours of operation of the aforesaid Mall.

Section 2.3.

(A) During Term "B" of the Lease, S&C hereby agrees to contribute to MMC an annual sum set forth in Section 2.3(B) towards the performance by or on behalf of MMC of the Maintenance Obligation. S&C, the Authority and MMC specifically agree that such contribution shall be used solely to cover or pay part of the Total Costs to perform the Maintenance Obligation.

(B) The "S&C Contribution" shall be equal to the greater of the following: (i) One Hundred Thousand Dollars ($100,000.00) or (ii) a proportionate share of the Total Cost to perform the Maintenance Obligation, equal to the present proposed share of S&C in the estimated budget for the Total Cost which share is $100,000/$625,000 or 16.0% . . . . The amount of the S&C Contribution shall be estimated by MMC each Fiscal Year based on MMC's approved budget for that year, and on the first day of each calendar month during the Fiscal Year S&C shall pay to MMC one-twelfth (1/12) of the estimated S&C Contribution. Within thirty (30) days after the end of the Fiscal Year MMC shall (i) inform S&C of any overpayment by S&C of the S&C Contribution and credit such amount to the earliest unpaid installment of the S&C Contribution for the then current Fiscal Year, or (ii) request the adjustment and payment to MMC by S&C of any underpayment of the S&C Contribution within thirty (30) days of such notice of underpayment; if no such information under clause (i) is given by MMC and no protest is made by S&C within one hundred fifty (150) days after the end of said preceding Fiscal Year or, if no such request under clause (ii) is made by MMC within such time period, the obligations of S&C to make the S&C Contribution for such preceding Fiscal Year shall be deemed paid correctly and in full.

Section 2.4.

Each year S&C shall only be obligated to make the S&C Contribution if and so long as: (i) Rouse or any other subsidiary or affiliate of The Rouse Company is (a) the Lessee of the Retail Area in the Property of the Authority (as defined above), and (b) principally involved in the supervision and management of the Maintenance Obligation; (ii) Philadelphia (or the Authority), Gimbels and Rouse shall each have made or be legally obligated to make their contributions as required in this Agreement, and if requested by S&C, such condition shall be certified to by an executive officer of MMC; (iii) the Authority shall have assigned to MMC all Contributions related to the Maintenance Obligation which are payable to or may have been paid to the Authority or if such Contributions are not assigned to MMC hereunder, the Authority shall have segregated such Contributions for the payment of the Total Costs herein; and (iv) MMC shall not have defaulted in the performance of the Maintenance Obligation as provided in Section 6.1 hereunder. In addition, a condition of S&C's making any contribution in excess of One Hundred Thousand Dollars ($100,000) in the first Fiscal Year or, in any year thereafter, in excess of the S&C Contribution payable for the previous Fiscal Year shall be that no material increase shall be made in the scope of services or other obligations being provided by MMC as part of the Maintenance Obligation unless such increase shall have been approved by S&C. Such increase in scope shall include, without limitation, a material increase in the hours of operation of the aforesaid Mall.

ARTICLE III
Rouse's Contribution

Section 3.1.

(A) Pursuant to Sections 8.2, 8.3 and 8.4 of the Lease, Rouse has agreed to pay the Authority the following amounts during Term "B" of the Lease ("Rouse's Contribution"): (i) Forty cents (40¢) per square foot of the Leasable Area (as said term is defined in the Lease) within the Retail Area for maintenance and operation of the Public Area including the provision of heated and/or cooled air; (ii) An annual amount of three cents (03¢) per square foot of the aforesaid Leasable Area for maintenance and operation of the service corridors, service and passenger elevators and truck dock facilities; and (iii) Commencing with the thirty-first (31st) year of Term "B," the annual amount of fifty cents (50¢) per square foot of said Leasable Area as part of a reserve fund for replacements; all of which annual amounts above are to be paid in accordance with and subject to the adjustments as more particularly provided in the Lease.

(B) Rouse hereby agrees to pay the Rouse Contribution, and Rouse and the Authority hereby agree that such Contribution and rental payments under the Lease shall be assigned to MMC provided such sums are used to cover or pay for the Total Costs hereunder.

(C) The amount of Rouse's Additional Contribution shall be estimated by MMC each Fiscal Year based upon MMC's approved budget for that year, and on the first day of each calendar month during the Fiscal Year Rouse shall pay to MMC one-twelfth of the estimated amount of Rouse's Additional Contribution as defined in clause (ii) of Section 3.2 below. Within thirty (30) days after the end of the Fiscal Year, MMC shall (i) inform Rouse of any overpayment by Rouse in the payment of the Rouse Contribution or Rouse's Additional Contribution under said clause (ii) and credit such amount to the earliest unpaid installment of the said Contributions for the then current Fiscal Year, or (ii) request the adjustment and payment to MMC by Rouse of any underpayment of the said Contribution by means of Rouse paying such amount to MMC within thirty (30) days of such notice of underpayment; moreover, in the same manner as provided in Section 2.1(B) as to Gimbels and Section 2.3(B) as to S&C, if no such information by MMC, or protest by Rouse, or request by MMC above is made within the same period of one hundred fifty (150) days as is provided in said Sections, the obligations of Rouse to make the Rouse Contribution and Rouse's Additional Contribution shall be deemed paid correctly and in full.

Section 3.2.

In addition to Rouse's Contribution, Rouse hereby agrees to make the following contributions to MMC as "Rouse's Additional Contribution": (i) the use of such mall office space (in the Retail Area), office equipment, mall manager services, assistant manager services or other related services or equipment as may in Rouse's reasonable opinion be necessary or desirable for the proper performance by Rouse of such portion of the Maintenance Obligation as Rouse may be responsible as the General Manager/Treasurer of MMC and (ii) a sum which, in addition to the sums paid as Rouse's Contribution in Section 3.1 above will bring Rouse's said Contribution to a total amount which equals 13.0% of the Total Cost (i.e. an amount which bears the same ratio to the Total Cost of the Maintenance Obligation as $81,000 bears to $625,000).

Section 3.3.

(A) In each year Rouse's Additional Contribution is hereby specifically made subject to the fulfillment of the following conditions: (i) Rouse or any other subsidiary or affiliate of The Rouse Company shall be (a) the Lessee of the Authority with respect to the Retail Area of the Property (as defined above) under the Lease, and (b) principally involved in the supervision of the Maintenance Obligation including, without limitation, the performance by Rouse of such duties as it may have as General Manager/Treasurer of MMC as set forth above unless this condition of clause (b) is not met by reason of default by Rouse in any applicable provision of the Lease or any related applicable contractual obligation; (ii) Philadelphia (or the Authority), Gimbels and S&C shall each have made or be legally obligated to make their respective Contributions as required in this Agreement and, if requested by Rouse, such condition shall be certified to by an executive officer of MMC; (iii) the Authority shall have assigned to MMC all Contributions related to the Maintenance Obligation which are payable to or may have been paid to the Authority or, if such Contributions are not assigned to MMC hereunder the Authority shall have segregated such Contributions for the payment of the Total Costs herein; and (iv) MMC shall not have defaulted as provided in Section 6.1 hereunder in the performance of the Maintenance Obligation.

(B) In addition, Rouse's making any contribution above in excess of Eighty-One Thousand Dollars ($81,000) in the first Fiscal Year or, in any year thereafter, in excess of said amount plus Rouse's Additional Contribution set forth in clause (ii) of Section 3.2 shall be conditioned on there being no material increase in the scope of services or other obligations being provided by MMC as part of the Maintenance Obligation unless such increase shall have been approved by Rouse. Such increase in scope shall include, without limitation, a material increase in the hours of operation of the aforesaid Mall.

Section 3.4.

Pursuant to the provisions of Section 8.2 of the Lease, Rouse hereby agrees to the assignment by the Authority to MMC of the Maintenance Obligation conditioned upon the following:

(A) MMC hereby agrees to assume and be bound by all the obligations of the Authority with respect to the Maintenance Obligation. MMC and the Authority agree that Rouse may (without it being deemed a waiver of its rights with respect to the Authority) exercise the same rights in relation to MMC concerning such Maintenance Obligation and the Contributions as Rouse might otherwise exercise with respect to the Authority under the Lease, and that performance by MMC of any such obligation shall be deemed to be performance by the Authority (for the purposes of the Lease). In addition, payment by Rouse to MMC or performance for MMC by Rouse of any other obligation (related to Maintenance Obligation) which would otherwise be paid by Rouse to or performed by Rouse for the Authority under the Lease (including but not limited to payment of Rouse's Contribution) shall be deemed acceptable performance and discharge by Rouse of Rouse's such payment or performance obligation.

(B) Notwithstanding the assignment of obligations by the Authority to MMC pursuant to this Agreement, the Authority shall remain liable for the performance of the Maintenance Obligation or any other obligations assigned to MMC by the Authority.

(C) The above consent by Rouse of the assignment to MMC by the Authority of the Maintenance Obligation shall not be deemed to be a consent by Rouse to any further assignment by the Authority or MMC of its or their rights or obligations (including the Maintenance Obligation) under the Lease or any part thereof.

ARTICLE IV
Philadelphia and the Authority's Contribution

Section 4.1.

Philadelphia hereby agrees to make an annual contribution to MMC (or any successor entity) towards the performance by or on behalf of MMC of the Maintenance Obligation. Philadelphia's Contribution shall be that portion of the Total Cost not paid for by Gimbels, S&C and Rouse as provided herein. It is presently estimated that Philadelphia shall pay 55.0% of the Total Cost under the present estimated budget (i.e. $344,000/$625,000 or 55.0%).

Section 4.2.

Philadelphia's Contribution shall be subject to the conditions that: (i) MMC shall not have defaulted as provided in Section 6.1 hereunder in the performance of the Maintenance Obligation for the preceding Fiscal Year, and (ii) Gimbels, S&C and Rouse shall have made or be legally obligated to make their Contributions as required in this Agreement.

Section 4.3.

Philadelphia and the Authority hereby warrant that MMC may purchase from the City at the City's cost, supplies (including, without limitation, energy), materials, equipment and other items as may be related to the performance by MMC of the Maintenance Obligation or the operation of the aforesaid Mall of the Authority. MMC will not be required in any way to purchase items from the City but may do so whenever MMC believes such purchases will be advantageous to it.

Section 4.4.

The Authority hereby agrees that the provisions of this Agreement will not release the Authority from its basic obligation to perform or cause the performance of the Maintenance Obligation. In such regard the Authority hereby unconditionally guarantees as surety, the payment by Philadelphia of Philadelphia's Contribution as provided in this Article without any such conditions on such payment as are hereinabove provided.

Section 4.5.

The Authority further agrees that, in order to defray and as a credit against the amounts being contributed by Philadelphia as Philadelphia's Contribution, the Authority will: (i) pay for the public liability, casualty and pressure vessel insurance to be carried by MMC with respect to the Property, and (ii) will assign and directly pay over to MMC the balance of all funds (including all rental payments under the Lease) received from whatever source by the Authority with respect to the Maintenance Obligation or any other maintenance obligation related to the Property.

ARTICLE V
Mortgages

Section 5.1.

The provisions of this Agreement shall inure to the benefit of and, subject to the provisions of Section 5.2., shall be binding on the parties and their successors and permitted assigns.

Section 5.2.

Nothing in this Agreement shall in any way restrict Gimbels', S&C's or Rouse's right to sell, assign or otherwise convey or encumber ("transfer") their respective premises, namely the Gimbel Building and land (on the north side of Market Street between Ninth and Tenth Streets), the S&C Building and land (on the north side of Market Street between Eighth and Ninth Streets) and the area leased by Rouse (between the S&C Building and Tenth Street on the north side of Market Street), provided that such transfer shall be subject to the provisions of this Agreement and provided further that no party making any such transfer shall be released from its obligations under this Agreement until the transferring party shall provide the other parties herein with a copy of the assumption in writing by the transferee of the obligations of the transferring party hereunder. Nothing in this Agreement shall prevent any such party from making a mortgage, deed of trust, sale and leaseback (or lease and subleaseback), pledge of stock or other financing transfer ("conveyance"), subject and subordinate to this Agreement, provided that (i) no person to whom a financing conveyance is made hereunder ("mortgagee") shall be obligated to perform the conveying party's obligations hereunder until the mortgagee shall have foreclosed or otherwise realized its security under the conveyance for such financing, and even then nothing shall require any such mortgagee to perform part or all of the Maintenance Obligation or any personal services hereunder other than payment of the applicable Contribution. With respect to Rouse "mortgagee" shall include any Leasehold Mortgagee or any other Institutional Lender (as such terms are defined under the Lease) holding a Mortgage or Mortgages or other security instruments on or with respect to Rouse's Leasehold in the Retail Area including such Mortgage or Mortgages as may also include a Mortgage of the Authority's fee simple interest in the Retail Area, and in addition, nothing in this Agreement shall alter or affect the terms of an Agreement made by and between the Authority and First Pennsylvania Bank N.A., a national banking association (and said Bank's successors or transferees including the Philadelphia Savings Fund Society), dated as of November 10, 1976, which Agreement concerns the aforesaid project and Retail Area and the First Mortgage or Second Mortgage held by such banking association (as said Mortgages are defined in such Agreement).

ARTICLE VI
Default and General

Section 6.1.

If MMC shall not keep or perform the Maintenance Obligation or any portion thereof or any other obligation or covenant hereunder and (i) such failure to perform shall continue for a period of thirty (30) days after written notice to MMC from any other party hereunder, or (ii) in case of a default which cannot with due diligence be cured within such thirty (30) day period, if MMC shall not commence to cure such failure to perform within said thirty (30) day period and continue with due diligence and continuity to cure such failure, then, for the purposes of this Agreement, MMC shall be deemed to be in default hereunder.

Section 6.2.

Except as supplemented above, the parties agree that the provisions of the Lease and the Gimbel Agreement are unmodified or amended and remain in full force and effect.

Section 6.3.

MMC hereby agrees that in its performance of the Maintenance Obligation it will not discriminate in the conduct of its business against any person or group of persons because of race, creed, color, sex, age, national origin or ancestry.

By _____
THE REDEVELOPMENT AUTHORITY OF THE CITY OF
PHILADELPHIA

By _____
Executive Director

GIMBEL BROTHERS, INC.
By _____
STRAWBRIDGE & CLOTHIER
By _____
ROUSE PHILADELPHIA, INC.
By _____
    President

MALL MAINTENANCE CORPORATION
By _____
    Vice-President

Redevelopment Authority/Rouse Philadelphia, Inc., Lease
December 16, 1975

ARTICLE VIII
Maintenance, Ownership and
Alteration of Improvements

Section 8.1. *Maintenance of Retail Area.* Subject to the provisions of ARTICLE VII, and Section 8.3 hereof, Tenant shall, at all times and at its expense, keep and maintain the Retail Area in good and safe condition and repair and appearance, except for ordinary wear and tear, and will make with reasonable promptness all non-structural, foreseen and unforeseen and ordinary and extraordinary changes and repairs of every kind and nature which may be required to be made upon or in connection with the Retail Area or any part thereof in order to keep and maintain the Retail Area in good and safe condition and appearance. Landlord shall be responsible for keeping the structural portions of the Retail Area in good and safe condition and repair.

Section 8.2. *Maintenance of Public Area.* In accordance with the standards that obtain in good quality regional shopping centers having enclosed malls, at no cost to Tenant except as provided in this Section 8.2, Landlord shall (i) police and provide security, operate and maintain the Public Area (which shall include but shall not be limited to the cleaning, window-washing, landscaping, lighting, ventilating, heating, air-cooling and repair—including any necessary replacement—of the enclosed pedestrian mall areas, exclusive of any windows forming part of a Subtenant's premises, and keeping the sidewalks and other Public Area paving repaired and properly drained and free of ice, surface water, snow, litter and rubbish, and planting, replanting and replacing flowers and landscaping and installing and maintaining such directional signs, markers and painted lines as from time to time may be necessary or proper for the control and safety of traffic, loading and unloading within the truck tunnel and dock facilities) and (ii) clean and keep in good order and repair (including any necessary replacement), all

fixtures and other installations in the Public Area including, but not limited to, pools, fountains, telephone booths, vending machines, benches and the like. The Public Area shall be open and operated, and all public entrances thereto shall be open, during the hours when the Retail Area or any part thereof is open for business, and also for one-half hour prior to the opening and one-half hour after the close of business of the Retail Area. The Public Area allowing ingress and egress to and from all transportation facilities shall remain open at all times except when closing may be required for security purposes.

Landlord shall utilize a system of engineering controls (whether by varying pressures or otherwise) which will ensure that the heating and/or air cooling of the pedestrian mall areas shall not draw heated and/or cooled air from the Retail Area and, similarly, Tenant shall utilize a system of engineering controls (whether by varying pressure or otherwise) which shall ensure that the heating and/or air cooling of the Retail Area shall not draw heated and/or cooled air from the pedestrian mall areas.

It is agreed that the obligations to be performed by Landlord under this Section 8.2 may be assigned by Landlord to a separate maintenance corporation or other appropriate body, provided that Landlord shall in such event remain liable for such performance unless (i) Tenant shall have approved such assignee on the basis of its qualifications and financial responsibility, as determined by Tenant, being adequate to fulfill the obligations undertaken in this Section 8.2 by Landlord, and (ii) such assignee, by instrument in writing satisfactory to Tenant and in form recordable among the land records, shall for the benefit of Tenant have expressly assumed all of the obligations of the Landlord under this Section 8.2.

During Term B hereof, in respect of Landlord's maintenance and operation of the Public Area including the providing of heated and/or cooled air, the Tenant shall pay, on an equal monthly basis at the time of payment of Basic Rent, an annual amount equal to forty cents ($.40)

multiplied by the number of square feet of Leasable Area in the Retail Area; provided, however, that said amount of forty cents ($.40) shall be adjusted at three-year intervals dating from the Commencement Date in accordance with changes as of the date of adjustment in the Consumer Price Index (U. S. City Average) of the U. S. Bureau of Labor Statistics as compared to such Index as of the Commencement Date.

If the compilation and/or publication of such Consumer Price Index shall be transferred to any other governmental department or agency or shall be discontinued, Landlord and Tenant shall fix, by agreement, an alternate index or method to adjust the Public Area charge payable by Tenant, but if they cannot agree, the matter will be submitted to arbitration under the provisions of ARTICLE XIV.

If Landlord fails to satisfactorily perform its obligations under Section 8.2 with respect to the Public Area and/or under Section 8.3 with respect to the service corridors, service and passenger elevators, and truck dock facilities located within the Retail Area, Tenant shall have the right and option, in addition to any other remedies provided in this Lease, upon thirty (30) days' notice to Landlord (unless within said thirty (30) day period, Landlord commences the necessary action and thereafter continues the same with due diligence) to terminate Landlord's obligations under Section 8.2 and/or Section 8.3, as the case may be, with the exception of Landlord's obligation to police and provide security, and to takeover the maintenance and operation of the area in question in accordance with the standards set forth in Section 8.2. In the event of any such termination and takeover of maintenance and operation responsibilities, Tenant shall have the right to deduct the cost of such maintenance and operation from the charges otherwise payable by Tenant under Sections 8.2 and 8.3 and, if such deduction does not cover Tenant's maintenance and operation costs, then from Rent and additional rent otherwise payable pursuant to Article IV hereof.

Redevelopment Authority/Gimbel Agreement
June 25, 1974

3A.14. *Maintenance of the Public Improvements.* Until the creation of a mall maintenance and management corporation under paragraph 3A.17 of this Agreement, the REDEVELOPER agrees to maintain at its sole expense and solely to the extent provided in subparagraphs (1) through (15) of this paragraph, the portion and only the portion of the Public Improvements within the area of the Development Block which are adjacent to the premises, . . . and only to the extent the same constitutes or would have constituted an open, unenclosed, unheated, unventilated and unair-conditioned mall. REDEVELOPER shall have no obligation to maintain the roof, space frame and glass panels for space frame, or such other facilities as may be constructed for the purpose of enclosing the mall or to maintain or operate any heating, ventilating and/or air-

conditioning equipment for such enclosed mall, all of which shall be the responsibility of the AUTHORITY unless otherwise agreed. The AUTHORITY agrees to obtain from SEPTA, Strawbridge and Clothier, Lit Brothers and all persons who hereafter become redevelopers of property within the Mall Phase One similar agreements to maintain the Public Improvements adjacent to their respective properties. The AUTHORITY agrees similarly to maintain the Public Improvements not maintained by others within the Mall Phase One including but not limited to Public Improvements which are adjacent to properties which have not been redeveloped. . . . The AUTHORITY further agrees to obtain from the City its agreement to provide adequate police protection within the Mall Phase One. The AUTHORITY also agrees to make

similar provision for the maintenance and security of those public improvements constructed in the later phases of Market Street East for the protection of the public, the City, the AUTHORITY and the REDEVELOPER and other participants in the Mall Phase One.

The AUTHORITY and the REDEVELOPER agree that the Public Improvement in the Mall Phase One shall be maintained, both before and after the creation of the mall maintenance and management corporation, in accordance with the standards, terms and conditions set forth below:

(1) The mall and plaza area of the Mall Phase One shall at all times be kept free and clear of debris, ice and snow and shall be swept and washed with sufficient frequency to maintain the same in a clean and neat condition;

(2) all exterior lighting fixtures and lighting fixtures in

249

the shopping mall and the mall and plaza areas shall be operated and kept in good operating condition, and bulbs and fluorescent tubes therein shall be replaced promptly as necessary. The surface of the mall shall be kept adequately illuminated at the AUTHORITY'S expense at all times during which the REDEVELOPER's store premises shall be open for business and for one hour before and for one hour thereafter in order to permit safe ingress to and egress from the REDEVELOPER's store premises by public and shall also be illuminated at the AUTHORITY'S expense during other hours to such extent as will afford reasonable security for the Mall Phase One;

(3) landscaping services shall be provided so as to keep the planting in the mall and plaza areas and in adjoining outdoor areas in attractive condition;

(4) all trash and rubbish containers in the shopping mall and plaza areas shall be emptied regularly and shall be maintained in a clean condition;

(5) all drains serving the common areas and the REDEVELOPER's premises shall be cleaned regularly;

(6) all paved and terrazzo surfaces in the shopping mall and the mall and plaza areas shall be inspected at regular intervals;

(7) all stairways in the mall and plaza areas shall be swept and washed at regular intervals sufficient to maintain the same in a clean, safe condition and, inspected at regular intervals;

(8) all glass, plate glass and glass enclosures, not including space frame panels or roof, in the mall and plaza areas shall be cleaned at frequent, regular intervals;

(9) all benches and institutional, directional, traffic and other signs shall be inspected at regular intervals, maintained in a clean and attractive surface condition;

(10) all escalators, including the stairs, sidewalls and adjacent areas, shall be maintained in a clean and orderly condition and shall be regularly inspected, adjusted and maintained with an escalator equipment lubrication schedule;

(11) no sound amplification system audible in the mall and plaza areas shall be used except one providing soft background music;

(12) the mall and plaza areas shall be used only for public uses and no vendors shall be permitted in the mall and plaza area except as indicated on Exhibit L;

(13) adequate equipment and personnel will be provided to supervise and perform the foregoing;

(14) the AUTHORITY will obtain from the City an agreement to provide adequate security forces with respect to the Mall Phase One. Such security forces shall patrol the mall and plaza areas at regular intervals, and shall also be responsible for maintaining good public order and discipline within the Public Improvements at all times and shall take reasonable, proper and legally allowable steps to eject or remove from the Mall Phase One persons disturbing such good order and discipline; and

(15) the truck tunnel shall be kept clean, free of ice, snow and debris and adequately ventilated and in good repair so that it can properly serve its intended function.

3A.15. *Repair and Replacement of Public Improvements.* In the event that any Public Improvement constituting a portion of the Mall Phase One or any extension or expansion thereof shall become worn out, in disrepair, damaged or destroyed, the AUTHORITY shall repair,

restore and reconstruct the same in such a manner that, upon the completion of such repairs, restoration and reconstruction, such improvement shall conform to the plans, specifications and controls established by the Plan and this Agreement; provided, however, that when a mall maintenance and management corporation is created as provided in paragraph 3A.17, the duties or any part of the duties of the AUTHORITY under this paragraph may, subject to the provisions of paragraph 3A.17, be assumed by and become the duties and obligations of the mall maintenance and management corporation, in which case the AUTHORITY shall have no further responsibilities for the duties so assigned so long as the mall maintenance and management corporation continues to carry out these responsibilities.

3A.16. *Insurance of Public Improvements and Adjacent Buildings.* In order to assure the continuance of the Mall Phase One as a first class shopping mall, the AUTHORITY at its own expense shall keep or cause the mall maintenance and management corporation to keep the Public Improvements owned or constructed by or for the AUTHORITY at the time constituting a part of the Mall Phase One and any similar public improvements hereafter constructed in any extension or expansion of the Mall Phase One whether completed or in the course of construction, insured in responsible insurance companies licensed to do business in the Commonwealth of Pennsylvania against loss or damage:

(1) by fire and such other casualties as are included in coverage of the type now known as the broad form of extended coverage in an amount which will prevent the insured from being a co-insured and in any event in an amount not less than eighty (80%) percent of the full insurable value thereof (excluding foundation and excavation costs) and

(2) by other insurable hazards against which insurance is then commonly carried on other buildings in the City of Philadelphia, of a character and occupancy similar to the building constituting a part of the Property, in an amount which will prevent the insured from being a co-insurer, first deductions excepted.

The full insurable value shall be the amount agreed upon by the REDEVELOPER and the AUTHORITY or the mall maintenance and management corporation as appropriate (hereinafter "the insured") and in case they shall be unable to agree upon the amount thereof then such amount shall be determined by arbitration at the request of either the REDEVELOPER or the insured from time to time (but not more frequently than once in every three (3) years).

All insurance policies evidencing such insurance shall be issued in the name of the insured and shall at the option of the insured include any other insurable interests, as such other interests may appear. The insured shall furnish the REDEVELOPER, upon request, with duplicate originals or certificates of all such policies. At least fifteen (15) days prior to the expiration of each such policy the insured shall furnish the REDEVELOPER with appropriate proof of the issuance of a policy continuing in force the insurance covered by the policy so expiring. Binders binding the issuance of such policies shall be accepted by the REDEVELOPER in the event the definitive policies or certificates thereof are not obtainable at the time in

question due to any building or improvements being in the course of construction, or other cause of temporary duration.

The AUTHORITY shall further require all redevelopers in the Mall Phase One and any extension or expansion thereof, by the inclusion in all redevelopment agreements of language substantially identical with paragraphs 3.15, 3.16 and 3.17 of this Agreement, to maintain, restore and insure all buildings adjacent to the public improvements in the mall, and shall use all reasonable means to enforce such portions of the said redevelopment agreements. The AUTHORITY also agrees to use all reasonable means to obtain and enforce similar agreements from the City, the Parking Authority, SEPTA, Strawbridge and Clothier and Lit Brothers with respect to their property adjacent to the Mall Phase One and any extension or expansion thereof.

3A.17. *Mall Maintenance and Management Agreements.* The AUTHORITY intends that a quasi-public independent corporation shall be created during the course of or at the conclusion of the redevelopment program for the Mall Phase One and that the obligations and duties for maintenance of the public improvements, restoration thereof in the event of damage or destruction by casualty, the maintenance of insurance against risks of loss and liability all as required of the AUTHORITY or the REDEVELOPER, respectively, as provided in paragraphs 3A.13, 3A.14, 3A.15 and 3A.16 of this Agreement, together with other duties and obligations respecting the repair, maintenance, keeping order and preserving the mall as dealt with in this Agreement shall be assumed by such corporation. Accordingly, REDEVELOPER and AUTHORITY agree to negotiate in good faith with each other and other appropriate parties and their successors and assigns concerning the formation of such independent mall maintenance and management corporation and the assumption by it of the obligations respecting the mall recited above, provided that it shall be demonstrated at the time that the mall maintenance and management corporation has or can reasonably obtain funds adequate for the purpose and the agreement by all others having obligations respecting these matters can reasonably be obtained. REDEVELOPER shall have no obligation to make any contributions of funds to the mall maintenance and management corporation without its express written consent, and in no event shall its obligation to contribute extend beyond the cost of its obligations as set forth in paragraph 3A.14 hereof. If the mall maintenance and management corporation assumes the obligations of the various parties provided for in paragraphs 3A.14, 3A.15 and 3A.16 and any obligations similar thereto provided for in this Agreement, the obligation of REDEVELOPER and of the AUTHORITY respectively, as set forth in the said paragraphs and portions of this Agreement, shall cease and end, and neither shall thereafter have any such obligations except as may be provided in the Agreement with the mall maintenance and management corporation so long as the mall maintenance and management corporation continues to carry out these obligations.

The AUTHORITY shall cause provisions substantially identical with the provisions of this Paragraph to be included in each agreement entered into by the AUTHORITY with a redeveloper for any portion of the Market Street East Urban Renewal Area.

APPENDIX N

UDAG Case Studies

Seventh Place Town Square Project
St. Paul, Minnesota

St. Paul is in the midst of a 2-decade-long revitalization of its central business district. Begun in the 1960s with the help of the Urban Renewal Program, the city's far-reaching effort is transforming the downtown area into a 24-hour activity center. Phase 1 of the effort concentrated on promoting office development. Phase 2, now underway, seeks to add office space and promote major retail development. And phase 3 will emphasize the development of both subsidized and unsubsidized housing.

The Seventh Place Town Square project is the capstone to phase 2. It is a major mixed use project covering two square blocks and containing 600,000 square feet of office space in two highrise towers, 300,000 square feet of retail space, a 550-car garage, a 250-room hotel, and a public mall. The mall, which is three stories high, serves as a center for retail businesses and connects the office buildings and the hotel. The mall is built over 7th Street. The city is using a UDAG of $4.8 million and approximately $4 million of local public funds to finance the public portion of the project.

The project is significant for a number of reasons. First, it points out the importance of a redevelopment plan, conceived over the course of a decade, that ultimately gathers sufficient public support and private interest required for the success of the project. Second, it shows the value of public action, in this case for land acquisition and street improvements, that anticipates private development. Third, it demonstrates the necessity of bringing together the right mix of events and people necessary for the completion of a major redevelopment project. Between 1976 and 1978, these events and people included strong and aggressive city officials, interested and capable developers, the right economic climate, and a federal subsidy program flexible enough to provide gap financing for a complex project.

The project will cost over $100 million, $10 million of which is public money. Many of the deals between the city and two developers were worked out before approval of the UDAG application. Had the federal money not been available, the project as presently conceived would probably not have been built. Most certainly, there would have been a cutback in the size and configuration of public space. Commitments made to the developers, however, would have been met. The project was and is deemed so vitally important to the interests of the city that other public financing would have been sought and probably found if HUD had not approved the grant. The use of local financing tools would, however, have placed a great burden on the city.

Background

The 7th Street area had long been thought of as the focal point for downtown revitalization. Concerned about the loss of major retail businesses to the suburban malls, St. Paul was the first major city to develop enclosed, heated skyways connecting downtown buildings. The 7th Street corridor is an important link in the skywalk system, primarily because the two major department stores—Donaldson's and Dayton's—front on the street a block away from each other. By connecting them with a mall and by adding other activity centers, many believed that the central business district could be effectively revitalized.

Up to the time the project was initiated in 1978, the downtown area of St. Paul had been steadily declining over a 20-year period. The loss of population and businesses in the CBD contributed to tax base deterioration, job loss, and reduced retail sales, which occurred even in the face of over $20 million in public investment, including a major renewal project begun in 1964 and improvements to a convention center. The city needed a retail environment appealing to shoppers and hotel rooms adequate to serve events such as conventions.

Early in the 1970s, local business interests in the downtown area formed an organization called Operation '85, whose mission was to identify a plan of action for revitalizing the CBD. Their first goal was to devise a strategy to promote office development. The effort took much of their energy in the early part of the decade. Their second goal was to improve the retail climate. Over the past 5 years, they have helped to formulate the Town Square idea, and as it came closer to reality, acted as a major advocate. Assuming that Town Square achieves the success anticipated and assuming other retail activity springs up around it, Operation '85 will refocus its efforts on a third major objective—the development of housing.

One very important preliminary step to the development of the project was the preparation of a transportation plan for the downtown district. The plan was completed in 1970; it recommended a street plan that would allow for a "vehicle-free" zone on 7th Street. The street was closed in July 1978 to facilitate construction activities and remains free of vehicular traffic.

The concept of a major retail mall on 7th Street had been around since the 1920s. Plans were drawn up in the 1960s in conjunction with the skyway plans that envisioned a pedestrian environment free of vehicular traffic.

Though plans and ideas abounded for years, it was not until the mid-1970s that a real project came into view. In 1975, the Housing and Redevelopment Authority and Operation '85 prepared a Seventh Place concept plan that gained general public approval and that also produced developer interest. Radisson Hotel Corporation, headquartered in Minneapolis, and owners and managers of a 400-room hotel in downtown St. Paul, became enthusiastic about Block A—an old urban renewal site. The corporation was interested in building a new facility that could be linked via the skyway system to its old hotel. The Oxford Development Group (located in Edmonton, Alberta, Canada, but increasingly active in U.S. cities) was intrigued by the possibility of combining office and retail space, especially in an enclosed mall with two department stores serving as anchors.

The two developers with their architects designed a project that called for a three-level enclosed shopping arcade, including a new store for Donaldson's department store, an office tower, a convention hotel, and a parking facility. The design appealed to the city and to the mayor, George Latimer, who took upon himself the task of putting the pieces together. The energy of the mayor coupled with strong support from the chief operating people of both Oxford and Radisson enabled the project to overcome many difficulties associated with the complicated structure of the development deal.

Both private developers were able to arrange conventional financing for their portions of the project. The city turned to three sources to finance its portion. The St. Paul Port Authority raised funds through an interim bond sale for construction of the parking facility (since sold to Oxford); second, UDAG covered the major portion of the cost of the public mall; and third, tax increment bonds were used to cover the balance of the public expenditures. The UDAG source was the last to close in 1978 (the grant was only 70 percent of the amount requested in the application), and within 2 weeks ground was broken on the project.

Project Formulation
Major Participants

The major participants in the formulation of the project were city officials, especially the mayor, George Latimer; Donald Love, President of Oxford Development; Kurt Carlson, President of Carlson Companies, the parent of Radisson Hotel Company; and leaders of Operation '85. Their interest and dedication over 3 to 5 years made the project possible.

Mayor Latimer's role was probably the most unique, though not necessarily the most important, in ensuring the venture's success. The Town Square, like many major redevelopment projects in older cities, required direct public involvement. Writing down the cost of land or even building a parking facility was not sufficient to create an economic environment suitable for large-scale development. The mayor, when he came into office in 1976, seized the initiative on the Seventh

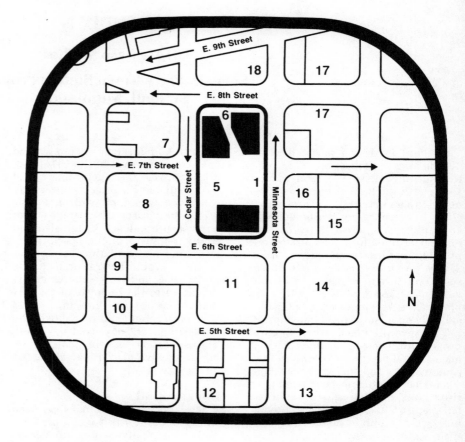

1. Town Square
2. North Central Life Tower
3. Office Tower II
4. Radisson Plaza Hotel
5. St. Paul's Park
6. Donaldsons Department Store
7. Future Oxford Development
8. Dayton's Department Store
9. Northern Federal Building
10. Osborn Building
11. Northwestern National Bank and Skyway Buildings
12. St. Paul Athletic Club
13. 1st National Bank Building
14. American National Bank Building
15. Twin City Federal Building
16. Bremer Building
17. Donaldsons Building & Ramp
18. Planned Parking Ramp

Place project by defining the public role and by serving as a broker to the private developers. He was so convinced of the project's importance to the city that he committed public resources to build the mall even before the availability of UDAG was assured. This commitment was double-edged, for it required the city to come up with all funds for the public spaces even if a UDAG could not be negotiated. The developers believed the mayor would deliver, and they thus made deals before securing public financing.

Donald Love, President of Oxford Development Company, was also an important catalyst in pulling the project together. He felt strongly that central city projects could be profitable, and he had thus undertaken a number of projects in new markets. His company had entered the U.S. market in a number of cities, taking on projects

that U.S. developers found unattractive. The Town Square was one such project; there were others in Denver and Minneapolis. Love knew how the pieces fit together, and he was certain that the market existed.

Kurt Carlson, President of the Radisson Hotel's parent company, had become interested in a new hotel in St. Paul even before Oxford committed to building the retail and office component. Radisson had an existing hotel in the city near the project site, and Carlson wanted to upgrade some of its facilities and add more rooms. The new site was a logical choice for this addition, for it could be connected to the older hotel by a skyway. Carlson worked directly with the other key participants to ensure that the complicated deals proved workable.

Operation '85 had been involved in the formulation of the project over a 10-year period. Bob Van Hoef, a vice president of 1st National Bank in the city, was the driving force for the organization over the years. The commitment of the private business interests to the downtown area, as represented by his organization, was invaluable to both the city officials and the developers, as they worked their way through the difficulties of putting the deal into final form. Without the interest of local business, it is unlikely that an out-of-town developer would have been bold enough to undertake such a large retail and office complex.

Key Considerations

The location and scope of the project and the complexity of the deals imposed some important constraints on the decision-makers. The three most important considerations were in the areas of design, economics, and financing. Few political hurdles had to be overcome. Most of the major public and private interests were enthusiastic about the venture, and they supported it. The Town Square was accepted by a broad spectrum of citizens as an appropriate and desirable project for the site.

The key design requirements for the project centered on the location—the hub of downtown. The planned, though presently shelved, downtown people mover (DPM) system was to have its major station in the project. The skywalk system was to tie all the surrounding buildings into the project, which would serve as the center of the pedestrian network. The design of the project had to take account of all these factors and blend them together in a way that would create an attractive, functional, and appealing environment.

The major economic problem of the project was the obvious need for a public component. Neither the retail mall nor the hotel was economically viable without a parking structure, yet neither could afford the cost. The city's role in the financing of the structure was essential. Similarly, the public mall space, conceived as the hub of the project and the surrounding area, offered no direct economic return and therefore could not be absorbed by the private sector as a project cost. The city or one of its agencies had to be the developer of this public space and to bear its costs. Fortunately, the political consensus in support of the project realized the importance of the public expense and neither criticized nor objected to it.

The financing of the project presented some problems, but unlike many other central city developments, the major obstacle was the funding of the public portion, not the private portion. Both Oxford and Radisson turned to their conventional lenders for financing, and they received firm commitments without much difficulty. The city, on the other hand, had to scramble to find adequate monies to pay for all the public improvements. It turned to the Port Authority to finance the parking structure, to the CDBG program to finance property acquisition, to tax increment bonds (redeemed by assessments against prop-

erty in the development district) to cover part of the cost of the mall, and finally to UDAG to supply the balance. The entire public financing package was not completed until April 1978, when the action grant agreement was approved.

The Deals

The Town Square project saw three distinct types of complex deals. The first had to do with the disposition of land and air rights. The second was concerned with construction relationships. The third dealt with the management of completed facilities.

Disposition of Land and Air Rights

The two square blocks of property that contain the project were acquired through Title I urban renewal funds and Community Development Block Grant funds. Block A, which holds the parking structure, the Radisson Hotel, and part of the retail mall, was assembled between 1964 and 1974. Block 27, which comprises the office towers, was assembled in early 1978. The city, which owned the title to both, disposed of them differently. The fee title to Block 27 was sold outright to Oxford Development. Within the air space of the building, easements were obtained for both the proposed Capital Shuttle line of the DPM and for the skywalk system. In addition, on the top of the retail portion of the site, the city retained an easement for use as a park.

Block A was handled differently. The city transferred title to the St. Paul Port Authority, which built a parking structure that was then leased back to the city. The air rights over the structure were sold to Radisson. Radisson leased to Oxford that portion of the site that was incorporated into the mall and retained easements through the structures on the second floor for the skywalk system and on the roof of the retail area for a park.

The city also maintained the air rights over 7th Street, which will contain the public mall area and the east-west DPM line if it is built. The mall area begins at street level, which is closed to vehicular traffic, and it uses up to four floors on either side of the mall. Second story connectors tie the two halves of the retail mall together and also provide the links for the skywalk system.

Construction Relationships

Under Minnesota law, construction undertaken for government agencies must be put out to public bid. This requirement dictated that all public spaces in the project be bid separately. To avoid friction and potential overlap from four separate general contractors, the city chose to appoint Poole, Oxford's general contractor, as construction manager. Poole entered into 17 subcontracts on the public space and also coordinated activity with Oxford's and Radisson's general contractors. This system has proved satisfactory to date, partly because the contract for the parking structure was awarded to the same contractor who was acting as Radisson's general contractor. This arrangement allowed the necessary coordination in design and engineering and in the construction of the footings and the support structure, which serves both the hotel and the parking garage.

Construction agreements also had to be written between the city and Oxford. Because it owns all the space between the store fronts on the opposite sides of the mall, the city was required to build it. Unfortunately, the physical structure did not lend itself well to this division of ownership. To accommodate necessary overlap in construction, the city put out to bid and managed some of the work that was for Oxford's benefit. The private developer, under the terms of the agreement, paid the city for this work. In total, almost $3 million of construction was handled this way.

Management of Completed Facilities

Oxford Development will manage its two office towers, the parking facility, and the retail area of the mall. Radisson will manage the hotel. The city will maintain the skywalk areas and the parks on the roof through maintenance contracts.

Project Payoffs

In its UDAG application the city identified four major benefits to be realized by the project: (1) to revitalize the deteriorating central business district; (2) to recapture taxable property; (3) to provide a competitive retail and employment center; and (4) to reduce population outmigration. The numbers they tied to these projections include an increase in property taxes estimated to be $2,282,595 per year, an increase in sales taxes of from $600,000 to $1,200,000 per year, and $15 million to $30 million of new retail sales per year within 3 years of project completion. In addition, it was estimated that 430 construction jobs will be created for 2 years, that 2,873 permanent jobs will result from the project, and that approximately 160 permanent jobs will be retained.

The nonmonetary payoffs include an increased pride in the downtown on the part of many citizens as well as potential new investment by private businesses and individuals interested in providing commercial and residential opportunities near the project site.

General Comments

The Town Square points up the importance, perhaps even the necessity, of public action in anticipation of private development. Had the city not acquired land, undertaken a transportation plan, and won general approval for a pedestrian mall, it would have been impossible for even the most dedicated of developers to achieve all the approvals that would have been necessary within an acceptable time frame. Having much of the dirty work done in advance, both Oxford and Radisson could concentrate on the most important factors to them: determining market demand and then designing and constructing a project that was accepted and returned a profit.

The project was quite complex. Retail developments, especially in older cities in the northeast and midwest, are very difficult to put together. Most require perfect timing, the right actors, and the availability of some extraordinary financing tools such as UDAG. Without this mix, developers become weary, their lenders lose interest, and economic conditions change. A good retail or mixed use project in the downtown requires good leadership from the public sector and some creative and optimistic supporters who can find solutions to a seemingly endless array of problems. The cities that can plan these projects and make them work have, like St. Paul, done a great amount of preliminary work, and they are the beneficiaries of strong officials who have a will to succeed.

Greenville Commons
Greenville, South Carolina

The $5.5 million HUD Urban Development Action Grant to the city of Greenville, South Carolina, will pay for the major portion of public costs involved in the development of a hotel–convention center–office complex in downtown Greenville. The project illustrates how federal grant funds, in this case the UDAG and $1.9 million from EDA, can be combined with local investment funds to attract the large amounts of outside private capital required to develop a major project in a very weak market. Moreover, it demonstrates that public and private components can be successfully integrated even though it may require fairly complicated agreements regarding property rights, responsibilities, and design and construction management. Indeed, the Greenville project is at the limit to which one can go in maintaining a separation of public and private ownership but still integrating the separate components so that they will operate as a single unit. In other words, the project will look like it was the product of a single developer/owner, yet the components will be owned separately. In fact, the public and private entities involved instructed the architect serving both parties to design the project without regard to property boundaries. After the project was designed, the lawyers were then asked to delineate the necessary boundaries. Beyond dem-

onstrating the way in which a high degree of public and private property integration can be achieved, the project demonstrates that local investors can play a key role in initiating and formulating a project and in providing the key equity funds required for the project.

The project is located at the northern end of downtown, facing onto Main Street, the major shopping strip of the area in years past. An important component of the project is the reduction of traffic lanes on Main Street from four to two and the improvement of the street through new, wider sidewalks, plantings, street furniture, midblock pedestrian crosswalks, and the like. Thus, the project will have an attractive pedestrian link to the stores along Main Street and to other major activity centers such as City Hall, the SCN office building, the Bankers Trust building, and the Daniel building. The components of the multiple-use complex will be a 100,000–square foot office building, a 350-room hotel, a 45,000–square foot convention center, 16,000 square feet of retail space, an enclosed atrium, and parking for approximately 540 cars. The parking, convention center, atrium, and some open landscaped areas will be owned by the city. The hotel, office, and retail space will be owned by Hyatt Greenville Corporation, a private company. The office space has been preleased to

the IBM Corporation. The Hyatt Corporation will operate the hotel and convention center under lease agreements with Hyatt Greenville and the city. The parking garage will be operated by the city although arrangements have been made to reserve 280 of the spaces for use by IBM. The project is under construction; ground was broken in January 1979.

Background

The history of efforts to revitalize downtown Greenville goes back to the mid and late 1960s, when the typical signs of downtown decline were beginning to show. Suburbanization of the population and the development of suburban retail malls weakened the market for downtown shopping; sales declined and investment slowed. The city responded with a series of broad planning studies and the development of a specific plan and program for downtown in 1968. The plan called for a partnership between the private and public sectors and included recommendations for a government complex as a southern anchor for the downtown, landscaped sidewalks, additional parking facilities, improved vehicular circulation, a new motel, a department store, and a mall facility. The philosophy behind these recommendations was that they would create various coordinated centers of activity and at the same time diversify

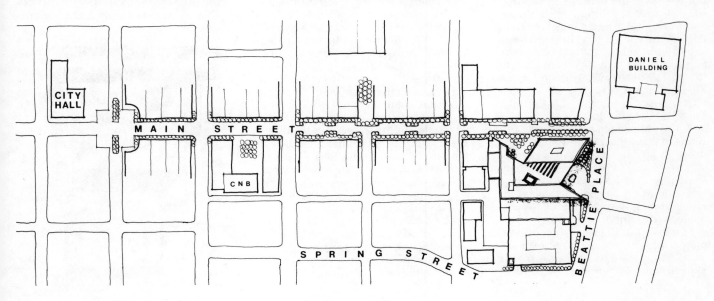

and strengthen the downtown's economic base.

Some of these recommendations have been realized and some have not. For example, many local financial institutions constructed or renovated facilities in the downtown. They include Fidelity Federal and First Federal Savings and Loan, South Carolina National Bank, Banker's Trust, First Citizens Bank, First National Bank, and Community Bank.

Coffee Street Mall was constructed using both urban renewal funds and a private grant from Banker's Trust. The People's Market has been opened in a vacant department store as a downtown center for the sale of local crafts and artifacts. Spring-Falls and River-Richardson Streets have been improved to alleviate much of the congested vehicular traffic from Main Street. Likewise, the downtown has seen the development of a new City Hall as well as the Senior Action Center and McBee Avenue Apartments for the elderly and physically handicapped. Moreover, Greenville's cultural environment has been enhanced through the construction of Heritage Green, just three blocks from Main Street. Included in this complex are a new library, art museum, and fine arts theater, the latter being built solely with private funds. Finally, the downtown's natural environment was enhanced not only through the planting of trees on Main Street, but also through the development of Reedy River Park, Greenville's founding site, located at the southern end of the downtown. Through the joint efforts of the city and the Carolina Foothills Garden Club, the park has been landscaped and developed with picnic areas, walkways, and a new bike trail. An historic cottage has also been renovated with public and private funds and serves not only as an entrance to the park, but also as a home for the Metropolitan Arts Council, the Greenville Artist Guild, and the Carolina Foothills Garden Club.

A downtown loan pool, using CDBG funds to subsidize rehabilitation loans down to an interest rate of 3 percent was organized in conjunction with all the Greenville financial institutions, which jointly pledged $2,150,000 for rehabilitation, property purchase, and business development loans.

The amount of these other investments, which have occurred over approximately the past 10 years, exceeds $90 million. Furthermore, as a result of these efforts, more than 6,000 jobs have been created in the central business district. However, the downtown has not been revitalized. It is still confronted by many of the same problems that it faced 10 years ago. As shown on the following table, prior to and concurrent with this new development, the downtown was plagued by declining retail sales, tax assessments, and business license fees. Along with the general inflationary trends of the times, these factors significantly retarded the ability of the public and private sectors to maximize the potential benefits of the capital investments.

Downtown Investments

	1965–1969	1969–1977	TOTAL
Public	N/A	$22,025,400	$22,025,400
Private	$14,971,366	$54,000,000	$68,971,366
	$14,971,366	$76,025,400	$90,996,766

Downtown Disinvestments

Decline retail sales 1970–1974:
  $31,171,965 – $20,866,307
  = $10,305,658 = – 33%
Decline ad valorem tax Main Street 1970–1974: 52%
Number of vacancies on Main Street:
  80 buildings – 20 vacant = 25%

Source: Community Development Division, City of Greenville, 1977.

One problem has been that none of the various projects are physically or aesthetically coordinated. They were not only designed by different people, but they were also designed in and of themselves with no relation to their surrounding uses. Hence, it is difficult for the pedestrian or motorist to get from one area of activity to another. They have not created the anticipated spin-off of private development. Because of weak market conditions, the private sector has not provided the amenities that entice people to the downtown and help create a strong central city. Thus, the downtown lacks adequate quality restaurants, hotel space, and entertainment facilities. Finally, no one strong focal point of activity exists in the downtown. Several diffuse centers offer a limited variety of 9-to-5 activities with no incentive for extended use.

The Greenville Commons project seeks to address these problems by providing the facilities in the right location and of the right design to create an attractive focal point for downtown and to create an activity center that will bring people back into downtown. The project also seeks to improve the links between the activity centers and thereby enhance the cohesiveness of the various elements of downtown.

The seeds of the current project were sown in 1975 when the Mayor, Max Heller, initiated a major effort to combine public and private investment to undertake a series of projects downtown. The city hired a consultant to assist in the development of alternatives for revitalizing the downtown. At that time, a hotel–convention center–public commons complex was decided on as the key ingredient in a larger program of additional downtown improvements. Alternative sites were considered and the current site was chosen, although the original site of 6 acres was later reduced to 4.5 acres. Preliminary designs were developed by architectural firms and feasibility studies were undertaken. Initial financial analyses indicated that approximately $4.5 million in private equity funds would be required in addition to $7 to $8 million in public investment. Given that there was very little hope of interesting conventional equity investors because of the probable low rates of return projected, the political and civic leaders decided that the $4.5 million would have to be raised locally. With major commitments from a few large locally based corporations and individuals, the business leaders established two vehicles for raising funds: The Greenville Community Corporation, a for-profit corporation offering preferred stock to investors, and Greenville County Foundation, a philanthropic organization that is eligible to receive tax-deductible dona-

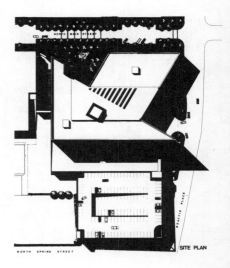

NORTH SPRING STREET   SITE PLAN

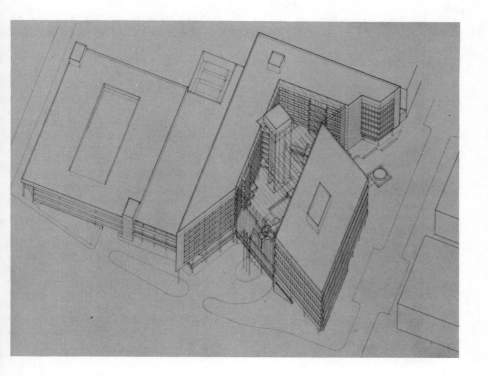

tions. From 1975 to 1977, the two organizations raised the bulk of the equity funds required for the project. Most of the funds were raised before a professional developer was obtained for the project.

Another key element in the formulative stages of the project was the use of a consulting firm with strong expertise in development and development financing to assist the city in developing a design and financial package that would attract the necessary developer. The firm of Zuchelli, Hunter and Associates, Inc., and Don Zuchelli in particular performed this function and negotiated with potential developers on behalf of the city and local investors. Zuchelli's role was particularly important given the situation in Greenville because the weak market made it impossible to elicit developer interest and involvement early in the design phases. Therefore, Zuchelli's involvement ensured that the early work without a developer would result in a project that would ultimately be attractive to a developer. That Greenville was in the end able to attract one of the top hotel developers and top hotel chains in the country is testimony to the success of the Greenville approach in at least getting the project under construction.

It should be noted also, to provide a complete background, that the city

had originally planned to finance the $7 million to $8 million worth of public improvements involved in the project through a combination of local public bond proceeds, federal Community Development Block Grant funds, and other sources. The establishment of the HUD UDAG program offered an alternative funding source to the city for a major portion of the public funding required. The availability of UDAG funds was fortunate in that the feasibility of raising funds through a bond issuance was questionable and in that the project would have otherwise diverted CDBG funds from other critical needs. In addition, the UDAG enabled city and developer to expand the hotel/convention center complex to a more efficient scale.

Structure of the Deal

Real estate development projects often involve complex deals between land owners, equity investors, permanent and construction lenders, the developer, and lessees or buyers. This project is unusually complex because of the public involvement and the mix of uses in the project. The major elements are as follows.

- The City acquired the land for the development and completed the basic design and planning required to define the project. Under a master project agreement, the city agreed to de-

velop the convention center parking garage and atrium, to sell the land required for the hotel and office buildings to Greenville Community Corporation, and to turn operation of the convention center over to Hyatt Greenville Corporation under subordinated lease arrangement.

- Greenville Community Corporation obtained title to the land for the hotel and office and entered into a partnership with Camel Corporation, an allied corporation of Hyatt Corporation. The partnership agreement established the amounts of equity to be contributed by each party and how the net proceeds or losses from the operation of the hotel and office operation would be shared. The details of this agreement and the distribution of earned income have not been made public, but it is known that the income, the tax consequences of depreciation allowances, will be distributed disproportionately among the equity contributors in favor of the outside investors. A disproportionate formula was required to attract the outside developer/investor, who was key to bringing Hyatt Corporation into the project as the hotel operator.

- The Hyatt Greenville Corporation was established by the GCC-Camel partnership to serve as the developer/owner. Hyatt Greenville entered into a prelease agreement with the IBM Corporation for the office space to be constructed and an agreement with Hyatt Corporation for the operation of the hotel. Hyatt Greenville leased the land from the GCC-Camel partnership and also obtained approximately $5.5 million in equity capital from the partnership. Hyatt Greenville, with its equity capital and agreements with IBM and Hyatt, was then able to obtain a $16 million permanent loan commitment from New England Mutual Life and a construction loan from Continental Illinois Bank.

- The city and Hyatt Corporation also agreed to a common construction manager (Daniel Construction Company, a large national firm) to supervise construction of the public and private components of the project.

- The city will build and operate the parking garage with 280 spaces reserved for use by the IBM Corporation. The city will obtain the revenues from the parking garage.

- The Hyatt Greenville Corporation will pay the city a fixed fee of $35,000 per year for 20 years for the use of the convention center plus 50 percent of the net cash flow after debt service from project operations up to $55,000 annually for 20 years. If net cash flow in any year is under $110,000 so that the annual payment is under $55,000, the difference will accumulate and be payable at the end of 20 years.

Benefits to the City

The major benefits to the city expected from the projects are indirect in that the project is expected support expanded office activity downtown, improve the retail function, and create a more attractive environment for various types of activities. More directly, the city expects the project to generate 215 construction jobs and 544 permanent jobs as well as to increase property taxes from $17,000 to approximately $162,000 annually.

General Comments

The project demonstrates well the requirements necessary to launch an ambitious project in a situation where the market support for such a project is demonstrably weak. In this case, the city basically had to pay for the construction of parking, banquet, and meeting facilities, which are often provided by the private developer in a convention hotel, and local investors had to provide the major share of equity funds required for the hotel and office buildings with reduced expectation for initial return yet favorable long-term appreciation benefits. Availability of federal funds to pay the bulk of the city's share eased the burden on the city considerably, ensured the development of a quality project, and enabled the city to continue to provide funds for other projects.

Because of the heavy public investment in the project, the leveraging ratio of public to private funds is relatively low compared to HUD leveraging standards (roughly $1 to $3 versus an average of $1 to $6 on action grant projects). However, direct leveraging ratios are not the only criteria for evaluating the desirability or effectiveness of public investments of this type. Since the city, local business leaders, and downtown planners were convinced that a project of the nature of Greenville Commons was needed to stimulate activity and support other investment in downtown, the indirect leveraging associated with the project will be the payoff to the city.

It is also to the credit of the city and local business leaders that they recognized that the major portion of equity investment in the project would have to be local money that could be put in the project and that a consulting firm with strong development expertise should be brought into the project early to ensure that the project was designed and formulated in a manner that would attract a competent developer.

Index

260